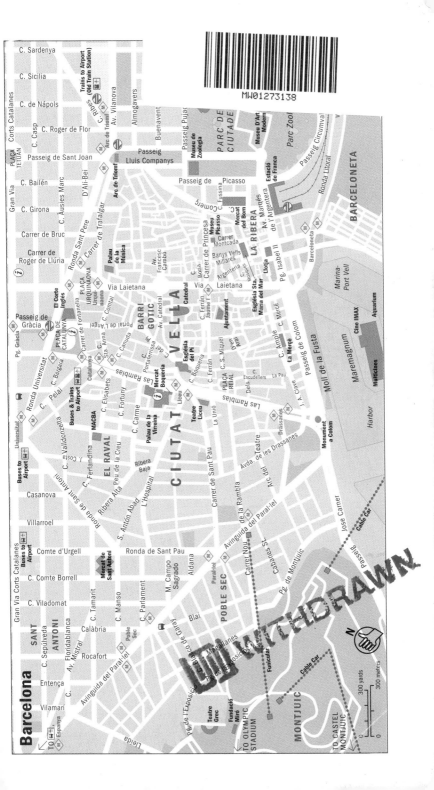

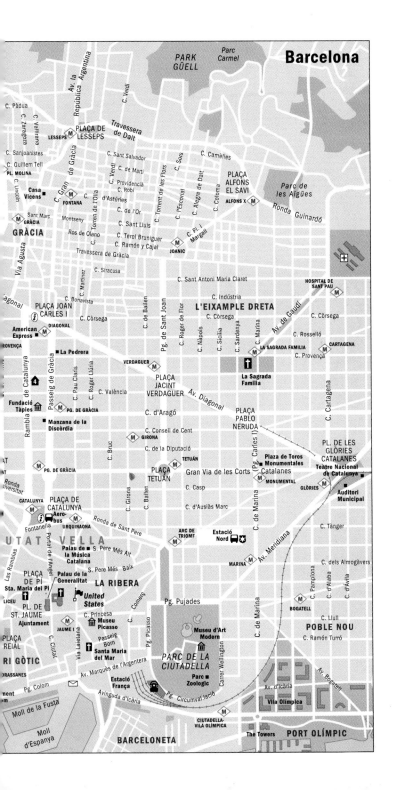

Barcelona Metro

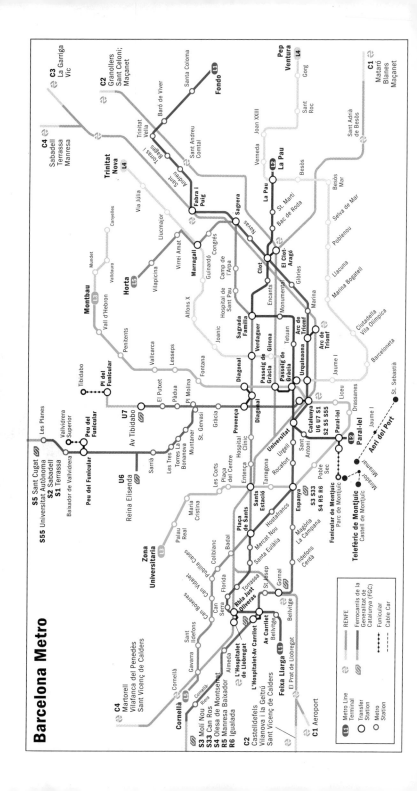

🖾 Let's Go writers travel on your budget.

"Guides that penetrate the veneer of the holiday brochures and mine the grit of real life."

—*The Economist*

"The writers seem to have experienced every rooster-packed bus and lunar-surfaced mattress about which they write."

—*The New York Times*

"All the dirt, dirt cheap."

—*People*

🖾 Great for independent travelers.

"The guides are aimed not only at young budget travelers but at the independent traveler; a sort of streetwise cookbook for traveling alone."

—*The New York Times*

"A guide should tell you what to expect from a destination. Here *Let's Go* shines."

—*The Chicago Tribune*

"An indispensible resource, *Let's Go*'s practical information can be used by every traveler."

—*The Chattanooga Free Press*

🖾 Let's Go is completely revised each year.

"A publishing phenomenon...the only major guidebook series updated annually. *Let's Go* is the big kahuna."

—*The Boston Globe*

"Unbeatable: good sight-seeing advice; up-to-date info on restaurants, hotels, and inns; a commitment to money-saving travel; and a wry style that brightens nearly every page."

—*The Washington Post*

🖾 All the important information you need.

"*Let's Go* authors provide a comedic element while still providing concise information and thorough coverage of the country. Anything you need to know about budget traveling is detailed in this book."

—*The Chicago Sun-Times*

"*Let's Go* guidebooks take night life seriously."

—*The Chicago Tribune*

Let's Go Publications

Let's Go: Alaska & the Pacific Northwest 2002
Let's Go: Amsterdam 2002 **New Title!**
Let's Go: Australia 2002
Let's Go: Austria & Switzerland 2002
Let's Go: Barcelona 2002 **New Title!**
Let's Go: Boston 2002
Let's Go: Britain & Ireland 2002
Let's Go: California 2002
Let's Go: Central America 2002
Let's Go: China 2002
Let's Go: Eastern Europe 2002
Let's Go: Egypt 2002 **New Title!**
Let's Go: Europe 2002
Let's Go: France 2002
Let's Go: Germany 2002
Let's Go: Greece 2002
Let's Go: India & Nepal 2002
Let's Go: Ireland 2002
Let's Go: Israel 2002
Let's Go: Italy 2002
Let's Go: London 2002
Let's Go: Mexico 2002
Let's Go: Middle East 2002
Let's Go: New York City 2002
Let's Go: New Zealand 2002
Let's Go: Paris 2002
Let's Go: Peru, Ecuador & Bolivia 2002
Let's Go: Rome 2002
Let's Go: San Francisco 2002
Let's Go: South Africa with Southern Africa 2002
Let's Go: Southeast Asia 2002
Let's Go: Southwest USA 2002 **New Title!**
Let's Go: Spain & Portugal 2002
Let's Go: Turkey 2002
Let's Go: USA 2002
Let's Go: Washington, D.C. 2002
Let's Go: Western Europe 2002

Let's Go *Map Guides*

Amsterdam	New Orleans
Berlin	New York City
Boston	Paris
Chicago	Prague
Dublin	Rome
Florence	San Francisco
Hong Kong	Seattle
London	Sydney
Los Angeles	Venice
Madrid	Washington, D.C.

Let's Go

Barcelona
2002

Sarah Thérèse Kenney editor
Monica Noelle Sullivan associate editor

researcher-writers
Emily Gann
Tom Malone
Meredith Petrin

Ankur Ghosh managing editor
Andrea R. Quintana map editor
Vanessa Bertozzi photographer

St. Martin's Press ≈ New York

DEC -- 2001

ᴍᵀ(ᵒ⁵)

Maps by David Lindroth copyright © 2002, 2001, 2000, 1999, 1998, 1997, 1996, 1995, 1994, 1993, 1992, 1991, 1990, 1989, 1988 by St. Martin's Press.

Distributed outside the USA and Canada by Macmillan.

Let's Go: Barcelona Copyright © 2002 by Let's Go, Inc. All rights reserved. Printed in the United States of America. No part of this book may be used or reproduced in any manner whatsoever without written permission except in the case of brief quotations embodied in critical articles or reviews. Let's Go is available for purchase in bulk by institutions and authorized resellers. For information, address St. Martin's Press, 175 Fifth Avenue, New York, NY 10010, USA.

ISBN: 0-312-28459-4

First edition
10 9 8 7 6 5 4 3 2 1

Let's Go: Barcelona is written by Let's Go Publications, 67 Mount Auburn Street, Cambridge, MA 02138, USA.

Let's Go® and the thumb logo are trademarks of Let's Go, Inc.
Printed in the USA on recycled paper with biodegradable soy ink.

Contents

HOW TO USE THIS BOOK

Welcome to *Let's Go: Barcelona 2002*. After many months of planning, studying, researching, writing, editing, correcting, and bonding, this brand-spanking new guide is finally ready to be read and loved by you.

BEFORE YOU GO. Plan your jaunt to Barcelona with **Discover Barcelona,** which lists the city's top 20 sights, with suggested itineraries, themed tours, Let's Go Picks (the best and quirkiest of Barcelona), and **walking tours** (complete with maps). Peruse **Life and Times** for a quick survey of Barcelona's history and culture, from the hairiest monarch ever to a one-eyed ride through the heart of Modernisme. For the details of planning your urban sojourn, flip to the end, where you'll find **Planning Your Trip** (with advice about passports, plane tickets, insurance, and more), the **Accommodations** section for booking a room from home, and even a chapter on **Living in Barcelona,** which details everything from obtaining a visa to finding housing for those planning to spend months (or years) in Barcelona.

ONCE THERE. When you reach Spain, **Once in Barcelona** will be your best friend, dishing the dirt on neighborhoods and offering tips on acting like a true Barcelonan. For navigating, the neighborhood breakdown here is the same as the other chapters: working its way from the historic old city, to l'Eixample, waterfront neighborhoods, mountainous Montjuïc, and ending with the outlying Zona Alta. You'll spend most of your time in the city flipping through the chapters that follow: **Sights, Museums, Food & Drink, Nightlife, Entertainment,** and **Shopping.** Listings in these sections are organized in the order of our preference within each neighborhood; the restaurant we think is the best is at the top of the list. The Let's Go thumbs-up (🖐) next to a listing lets you know it's one of our favorites—those places, things, or gorillas that are either super cheap, super hip, or just plain super.

MAPS AND MORE. All neighborhoods—complete with hotels, museums, monuments, and Metro stops—are plotted in the **map appendix** at the back of this book, marked off with a black strip down the side. Right before the maps comes the **Index,** an **Appendix** (including a phrase book), and a useful **Service Directory,** listing all the different services you might require during your trip, from taxis to pharmacies. Should you want to leave the city, **Daytripping** will help you strike out on your own into Catalunya, including skiing in the Pyrenees, wandering through Dalí's various and abundant hometowns, and beach-hopping along the Costa Dorada.

THE INSIDE SCOOP. Tips on how best to explore Barcelona are found in the nifty **black sidebars** found on various pages scattered throughout the guide. Aside from the untitled sidebars that give the low-down on all that is quirky, interesting, and fab about the city, there are **Big Splurge** and **On The Cheap** to advise you on how to spend your money, **LGB Barcelona** and **Kids in the City** boxes for recommendations for special interests, and **Get SmArt** boxes for art insight. The absolute essentials are highlighted in white **Essential Information** boxes.

Just a final note: remember that this guide is great, but it's just that—a *guide*, not the be-all-end-all of travel in Barcelona. Put this thing down once in a while and strike out on your own; you'll be glad you did.

A NOTE TO OUR READERS The information for this book was gathered by *Let's Go* researchers from May through August of 2001. Each listing is based on one researcher's opinion, formed during his or her visit at a particular time. Those traveling at other times may have different experiences since prices, dates, hours, and conditions are always subject to change. You are urged to check the facts presented in this book beforehand to avoid inconvenience and surprises.

RESEARCHER-WRITERS

Emily Gann *La Ribera, Montjuïc, Gràcia, l'Eixample Esquerra, Sarrià, Tossa de Mar, Cadaqués, Figueres, Púbol, L'Escala, Puigcerdà*

The only newcomer to this team of RWs, Emily didn't need any time to catch up—this girl can turn even an airport into a thing of beauty. Armed with a love for art, an appetite for *tapas*, and good working relationship with Floquet, Emily ripped through Modernisme and Surrealism with a sharp eye, thoughtful insight, and a healthy dose of sass. How fortunate are the generations of tourists who have her copy to direct them to the coolest *tapas* bars, to help them desipher Dalí, to lead them to the best artisan stores! How blessed are those that have the wisdom of this smart cookie to help them navigate the impenetrable parks Ciutadella, Montjuïc, and Güell! How miserable are those heart-broken, Barcelonan waiters when she answers that yes, this delicate flower must take even her eyes back to America with her!

Tom Malone *Las Ramblas, El Raval, Port Vell, Pedralbes, Les Corts, Barceloneta, Sitges, Tarragona, Mataró, Ripoll, Palafrugell*

A veteran of *Let's Go: Mexico 2001* and an award-winning essayist, Tom returned to Let's Go to work his magic on Barcelona (and vice versa). While a weaker person may have been distracted by the tempting calls of absinthe, soccer, and Swedes, our own personal James Bond never let the crazy world he was assigned to investigate interfere with his mission to incorporate every aspect of his eclectic experiences into constructive and educational advice for tourists. This international man of mystery adapted with chameleon-like agility to every situation we put him in: from fighting the crowds of drunken Americans in Maremagnum to fighting the crowds of drunken Spaniards in Camp Nou, Tom never blew his sleuth-like cover. His expertise in Classical history and his capacity to retain Catalan historical anecdotes laced his copy with a class and a perspective that lesser researchers can only dream of.

Meredith Petrin *Barri Gòtic, Pg. de Gràcia, l'Eixample Dreta, Tibidabo, Horta, Sants, Aigüestortes, Girona, Montserrat, Val d'Aran*

A former editor of *Let's Go: Spain & Portugal*, Meredith was fueled in her researching exploits by the same determination that made her push for a new guide to Barcelona in the first place. Like Mary Poppins, Meredith was practically perfect in every way: over the course of six weeks, she covered everything from grungy pubs to slick Euroslut clubs, from sewer museums to hearse collections, from the biggest Modernist sights to the most impenetrable national parks—all without ever staying home for a night. Meredith went to any and every length to get her scoop, whether it meant camping out on strange mattresses with French couples or charming knowledgeable (sketchy?) taxi drivers. Yet even with all this responsibility, she still found time to protect the virtue and artistic integrity of Vanessa, our beloved photog.

Vanessa Bertozzi	*Photo Researcher*
George de Brigard	*Editor, Spain & Portugal 2002*
Sofia Velez, Sarah Jessop	*Associate Editors, Spain & Portugal 2002*
Floquet de Neu, Ankur Ghosh	*Handsome Mascots*

ACKNOWLEDGMENTS

The Let's Go 2002 series is dedicated to the memory of Haley Surti

Sarah thanks: From L.G, my special and unique snowflakes, Monica and Floquet, my basement-dwelling compatriots (even Karen), my RWs (without whom I would have been lost, hurt, and alone), the incomparable Ankur (sorry I took you to Maremagnum), Big V, Sarah KenneDy, Andrea, and the poor souls in production who tolerated my incompetence. I also thank my Harvard consultants, the ever-dynamic Catalan goddess Anna Maria Llaurado, and the world's foremost specialist on all thing things Catalan (and a great guy), Brad Epps. Other people who I like and thank: la Mayita (claro), special anthropological advisor Dr. M. B. Stern, wise John Reuland, dirty left-hand Kampff, Ali, Fizzy, and the wedding party, Josh for eating dog while I was at work, Clara and Javier for taking me and my entourage about, las con quienes estuve la primera vez (de puta madre, todas), Mum (don't let it go to your head), and Mr. Brian Thos. Costello. Again, to my bookteam, thank you for your long days, thorough research, letting me yell at you, and being wicked good.

Monica thanks: Sarah, for her gentle voice, long trendy sweaters (yours will always be longer, thus trendier), new words, and munchkins—someday I'll have as much flabor as you. Karen, for coming to my defense in the Kenney Wars (thankfully!), giving me a reason to decorate my desk, and pancake cruises—I'll miss you. Ankur, for being sooo funny, our great RWs, Andrea, Vanessa, Jen for fixing my computer so cheerfully (everyday), and the Basement for keeping things fun and lively, even after the flies were gone. Jim for early morning baseball talks, Ken for lunch breaks, Rich for good times and Camp David Accords, Brian, and Theresa for Floquet and 13—next time we bring boys and win Curious George! To Mookie for teacups, picnics on the Quad, Notting Hill benches, and the eternal dilemma: Rambo or Muffin. Annette, thanks for late night Life games; thirteen years and counting, and I couldn't have wished for a better best friend. To John, thanks for everything; I'll always save you the swing beside me. Ms. Meyer for her advice and hugs, Meyer for coffee and laughs, and Amy, my little sister. But most of all, my family, especially Mommy, Daddy, and Dave for being there when it mattered and even when it didn't—I love you.

Editor
Sarah Thérèse Kenney
Associate Editor
Monica Noelle Sullivan
Managing Editor
Ankur Ghosh
Map Editor
Andrea R. Quintana

Discover Barcelona

If you make it until 6am, you'll see the quietest side of Barcelona, for about an hour. While the city is still dark, the occasional street worker battles Catalan separatist graffiti, the empty streets are silently scrubbed by hulking machines, and pigeons, parrots, and doves share the same branch, cooing with their heads under their wings. Enjoy the calm—it won't last.

When the sun finally comes up, you'll see quite a different city. Street vendors tug produce and popsicles onto every corner; cash boxes ring with the sounds of commerce and style; tourists marvel at medieval monsters that residents mistake for buildings; museums fill with tomorrow's avant-garde; pedestrians salivate at plates of exotic delicacies; beaches overflow with bronzed nudity; a white gorilla terrifies and delights children of all ages; street protesters demand independence. On this side of 6am, Barcelona is sensory overload: only the attentive will notice that the Modernist masterpieces change colors slightly at every moment, and that no two *tapas* bars waft quite the same scent through the air. After you spend a day immersed in Barcelona's schizophrenic personalities and a night rubbing elbows with her even more schizophrenic nightlife, Barcelona will have exhausted herself—and you. When 6am rolls around again, you'll be glad for the quiet.

Barcelona is a gateway city: the gateway to Catalunya, to Spain, to the Mediterranean, to the Pyrenees. Pack your swimsuit and your skis, your art history book and your clubbing shoes, an extra bag to fill up with souvenirs (everything from fake poop to emus), and don't worry about the fact that you don't speak Spanish: neither does Barcelona.

1

BARCELONA BY THE NUMBERS

City population: 1.5 million.

Metropolitan area: 4.2 million.

White geese in residence: 13 (visit the cathedral; see p. 64).

White gorillas in residence: 1 (see p. 73).

Average annual rainfall: 23.2 in. (590mm).

Pork consumed per person annually: 55.78kg.

Percentage of population that chain smokes: 25%.

Percentage population that is Roman Catholic: 90%.

Number of statues in the Barri Gòtic: 37.

Percentage of those that are living: 65%.

Density of mimes on Las Ramblas: 4 every 2½ ft.

Number of words the English language drawn from Catalan: 1 (it's yacht).

Military strongholds turned into parks: 2.

Bars with Roman walls running through them: 7.

Absinthes required to knock you out: 3.

TOP 20 SIGHTS

If you want to catch as many of the sights as possible, try our walking tours (see p. 13), or our quirky themed tours (see p. 12).

20. Poble Espanyol, a recreation of all of Spain's greatest hotspots. Hey, if you can't hit the real thing, go for the tacky imitation (see p. 91).

19. The Aquarium, the largest in Europe, complete with an underwater tunnel that guides visitors through the briney deep (see p. 88).

18. The Sardana, the traditional Catalan dance, performed impromtu in front of the Cathedral on Sunday mornings (see p. 64).

17. Fonts Luminoses, a night-time show of lights, music, water, and magic! (see p. 90).

18. Museu d'Art Modern, showcasing the best and the brightest of Catalunya's painters from the past century (see p. 110).

15. Museu Nacional d'Art de Catalunya (Palau Nacional), a religious experience in and of itself (see p. 118).

14. The Mediterranean, a fool-proof pleaser. Enjoy swimming, fishing, boating, waterskiing, parasailing, jetskiing, diving...(see p. 165).

13. El Barça, Barcelona's world-class soccer team and the stars of some killer matches (p. 168).

12. Floquet de Neu, the world's only white gorilla. And isn't he dashing! (see p. 73).

11. Els Quatre Gats, the Barri Gòtic hangout of such giants as Pablo Picasso and Ramon Casas still serves the best coffee in the city (see p. 128).

10. Park Güell, Gaudí's unfinished housing project, now the wackiest park in the world. Hikes lead to spectacular views: buns of steel not included (see p. 92).

9. The Cathedral, the religious center of Barcelona. A cloister, geese, Roman ruins, and mimes out front add to your average Gothic cathedral-going experience (see p. 64).

8. Fundació Miró, Miró's artistic legacy to his homeland, showcasing his own work and the work of up-and-coming Catalan artists (see p. 116).

7. Museu Picasso, one of the best collections of Picasso's works anywhere, from his earliest painting to his late engravings (see p. 109).

6. Palau de la Música Catalana, Domènech i Montaner's amazing architectural tribute to good music (see p. 70).

5. La Mazana de la Discòrdia, the city block with a Modernist identity crisis, where Modernisme's three most famous sons—Puig i Cadafalch, Domènech i Montaner, and Gaudí—duke it out to be the tourists' favorite (see p. 79).

4. Passeig de Gràcia, the Fifth Avenue of Barcelona: home to several Modernist landmarks (see p. 79 and p. 82), outdoor dining (see p. 133), and designer stores labels (see p. 181).

3. Casa Milà (La Pedrera), Gaudí's finished masterpiece and the best look inside his work and his head (see p. 77).

2. Las Ramblas, the central and most colorful street in Barcelona's oldest district, complete with mimes, flowers, and baby emus (see p. 60).

1. La Sagrada Família, Gaudí's unfinished masterpiece, and his tomb (see p. 75).

SUGGESTED ITINERARIES

THREE DAYS

DAY 1: MODERNISME 101

Head out to the **Sagrada Família** (see p. 75) early in the morning to avoid fighting past the high-season crowds; snatch some *churros y chocolate* at one of the nearby cafés. From there, make your way to the Pl. de Catalunya (M: Catalunya) and take the half-day walking tour through **l'Eixample** (which you have now started in reverse; see p. 5), Barcelona's gridded upper neighborhood that is jam-packed with Modernist sights (including Casa Milà and La Manzana de la Discòrdia, where you can pick up the Ruta del Modernisme pass that offers discounts on sights all over the city). After pondering the chimneys of Casa Milà, catch the #24 bus from the Pg . de Gràcia up to your last Modernist stop of the day: **Park Güell** in Gràcia (see p. 92). Wander through the colonnades, park it on the longest and most crooked bench in the world, and snap a photo with the drooling lizard. Damn, you must be tired! Head down to Gràcia's **Plaça Sol** for *tapas* and drinks, some low-key nightlife (see p. 140), or even a little dancing, if you have the energy (see p. 161).

DAY 2: OLD TOWN SUPER-TOURIST

Start out at the Pl. de Catalunya (M: Catalunya), but this time, head down **Las Ramblas** (see p. 60) to see the traditional **Boqueria** market, where you can buy pastries or fruit for breakfast (see p. 63). Check out the various offerings of the different sections of Las Ramblas (who on earth buys those baby emus they sell there?), then head into the **Barri Gòtic** via C. Portaferrissa, which will turn into C. dels Boters and drop you at the **cathedral** (see p. 64). After you've seen the resident geese, mimes, and Roman walls, head to Modernist hangout **Els Quatre Gats** for a quick bite (see p. 128). Get your Ruta de Modernisme pass ready for your next stop just off the Via Laietana, the **Palau de la Música Catalana** in La Ribera (see p. 70). Make your way through La

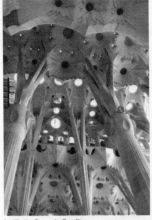

Inside La Sagrada Família

Balcony at Park Güell

Ducklings for Sale on Las Ramblas

BEST OF BARCELONA

🔹 Most aesthetically pleasing bathroom experience: **Els Quatre Gats** (see p. 128).

🔹 Best place to get high: **La Sagrada Família** (see p. 75).

🔹 Best (and only) white gorilla in the whole wide world: **Floquet de Neu** (see p. 73).

🔹 Best place to get an emu, sunflower, or prostitute: **Las Ramblas** (see p. 60).

🔹 Most obscene photo op: the giant phallus in the **Museu de l'Eròtica** (see p. 106).

Best place to take a date: **Mirador de Vila Paula** (see p. 101).

Best Catalan pork product: **Jamón País** (see p. 123).

Best place to see the sun set: **Palau Nacional** (see p. 118).

Best place to see eggs: it's a tie! The **dancing eggs** during the Corpus Cristi Festival (see p. 14) are pretty cool, but so are the eggs on top of the **Dalí Museum** (see p. 190).

Ribera's twisting alleys to the **Museu Picasso** (see p. 109). Check out the galleries in the labyrinth of streets (see p. 121) and stay in the area for *tapas* or dinner at the restaurants around **Santa Maria del Mar** (see p. 71). Finish up the night by heading back into the Barri Gòtic for the clubs and bars around the **Plaça Reial** (see p. 150).

DAY 3: ATHLETIC ART

Eat breakfast before heading up to **Montjuïc,** as culinary pickings are slim on the mountain. Take a quick ride up to the mountain from the waterfront on the **Transbordador Aeri cable car** (see p. 88), and then head over to the **Fundació Miró** to explore your inner child (see p. 116). Bring your swimsuit and take a dive in the **Olympic pool** (see p. 168). Wander around the other Olympic edifices and then satiate your desire to visit the rest of Spain in the artificial and nostalgic **Poble Espanyol** (see p. 91). Poble Espanyol is also a reasonable place to grab lunch before you trek onwards to the **Museu Nacional d'Art de Catalunya** (see p. 118). On your way out of the museum, try to catch one of the shows of the **Fonts Luminoses** (see p. 90). If you still have energy and you're ready to party, you can return to Poble Espanyol, which gets much cooler after dark, and party until 6am at **Las Torres de Ávila** (see p. 160).

FIVE DAYS

If three days just isn't enough, read on....

DAY 4: THE WATERFRONT

Start out your day in the **Parc de la Ciutadella** with the most important stop on your trip: a visit to the Barcelona **zoo** and its lovable mascot, **Floquet de Neu** (Snowflake), the world's only albino gorilla (see p. 73). If you can tear yourself away from Floquet (and we understand if you can't), stop by the **Museu d'Art Modern** (see p. 110), a good collection of Catalan artists. Get lunch at the café in the modernist **Hivernacle** (see p. 72) before heading out of the park and down to the **Moll d'Espanya** to Barcelona's **aquarium,** the biggest (and some say best) in Europe (see p. 60). If all this family fun is too much for you, swing up **Las Ramblas** to the nearby, ever-raunchy **Museu de l'Eròtica** (see p. 106). The S&M display will clearly whet your appetite; good thing **Les Quinze Nit's** tasty and affordable paella is so nearby in the **Plaça Reial** (see p. 125). After dinner, grab a Guinness at one of the nearby Irish pubs (see p. 148) before you get your funk on in one of the Pl. Reial's resident hip-hop clubs (see p. 150).

DAY 5: DALILAND

Get up early: you've got a train to catch, to nearby **Figueres** (see p. 188). Spend the morning at the surreal **Teatro-Museu Dalí,** the second-most popular museum in Spain, where you can stand on Dalí's tomb (see p. 190), listen to rain inside a Cadillac, or watch a room turn into Mae West. After lunch, stop by the toy museum to see a good collection of *caganers* ("shitters;" see **Holy Shit!**, p. 192). You can make it back to Barcelona before sundown, and after some rest (or getting tattooed and pierced; see p. 185), lose yourself in **Poble Nou's** alternative music and bar scene (see p. 157).

SEVEN DAYS

Still want more? We don't blame you.

DAY 6: EL BARÇA & EL RAVAL

By now you've had plenty of time to get tickets to a **soccer game** (see p. 170), featuring the city's beloved team, **El Barça**. Before you head over to Camp Nou, do some thrift shopping in El Raval's **Mercat Alternatiu** (see p. 182) and stop by Gaudí's spooky **Palau Güell** (see p. 74). Grab lunch in blue-collar El Raval (see p. 131), then head to the **Museu FCB** (see p. 119), *fútbol*-lover's personal version of heaven. Follow the crowds into the game at **Camp Nou** (see p. 170), and then follow them to the nightlife on the way out.

Foosball!

DAY 7: DAYTRIPPING

What you'll want to do on your last day depends on the weather. If you're traveling in the summer, a daytrip to beachy **Sitges** (see p. 214) is a great way to enjoy your last day in Catalunya, with its own wild (and very gay-friendly) nightlife. If it's too cold for the beach, the nearby mountains and monastery at **Montserrat** (see p. 223) are one of the wonders of Catalunya. If you're looking for something to do after dark, don't tell the monks you're headed to **l'Eixample's** racy clubs and bars (see p. 153).

Flamenco Dancer at the Museu de Cera

WALKING TOURS

L'EIXAMPLE

⏱ Suggested Time: *5hr.* **Distance:** *about 21 blocks (2mi.).* **When to go:** *A weekday afternoon, on a clear day.* **Public Transportation:** *begin at M: Catalunya and end at M: Sagrada Família.*

This tour takes you through l'Eixample (the Enlargement), the newest neighborhood in Barcelona, and perhaps the most fashionable. The walk will guide you past all of the shopping and all of the big sights of Modernisme, the intensely visual architectural movement that swept through Barcelona in the late 19th century. Start at Pl. de Catalunya, and begin by stopping by **El Corte Inglés** (see p. 183) for a free map of the city and anything else you might need (like a pair of

Fundació Miró

View of Sagrada Família from Roof of Casa Milà

Courtyard in the Barri Gòtic

Entry of the Liceu Opera House

shoes—you'll be walking a lot); make sure to visit the gourmet food shop to pick up a bottle of *cava* to bring home. Exit onto Pg. de Gràcia, and walk up several blocks to number 39, the oh-so-economical (that's free!) **Museu del Perfum** (see p. 115). When you come out of the museum, continue up Pg. de Gràcia, but don't rush, as this street has the best designer **shopping** (see p. 180) in Barcelona. Window shop to your heart's content until you reach **La Manzana de la Discòrdia** (just before C. Aragó; see p. 79); enter Casa Amatller to buy a **Ruta del Modernisme** (see p. 59) pass. This pass is good for discounts at Modernist sight all over the city, including a free tour of the façades of the three houses that make up La Manzana de la Discòrdia: Casa Amatller, Casa Lleó Morera, and Casa Batlló. By now you must be hungry; turn onto **C. Aragó** (see p. 134) for a leisurely Catalan lunch at one of the street's reasonably priced and quality restaurants. For those who can handle modern abstract art, the **Fundació Tàpies** (see p. 113) is also on C. Aragó. Return to Pg. de Gràcia and cross the street to Gaudí's **Casa Milà** (see p. 77), a Modernist masterpiece with an unusual rooftop and an even more unforgettable rooftop view (don't miss the preview of coming attractions, La Sagrada Família). Exit on to C. Provença and follow it (without crossing the Pg. de Gràcia again; with your back to the Pl. de Catalunya, follow C. Provença to the right) for 11 blocks to **La Sagrada Família** (see p. 75), another Gaudí jewel (this one unfinished—117 years and counting) with infinitely complex views and façades.

LA RIBERA

⛏ Suggested Time: *5hr.* **Distance:** *about 1½mi.* **When to go:** *Any weekday without rain (check the hours of each of the sights and plan accordingly).* **Public Transportation:** *begin at M: Arc de Triomf and end at M: Parc de la Vila Olímpica.*

This walking tour is a trip through La Ribera, one of the oldest sections of the city, with great public spaces and museums. Begin your day early with a light breakfast at a restaurant near your hostel (see p. 123) and stop by your local grocery store for picnic fixings. Take the Metro to Arc de Triomf; in front of you will be the **Arc de Triomf** (see p. 72), a Modernist work inspired by the 1888 Exposition. Follow Pg. Lluís Companys towards Parc de la Ciutadella (about four blocks), one of Barcelona's most beautiful public spaces. To your left will be the **Cascade Fountains** (see p. 73), where you can unpack your lunch and relax by the water as couples pass you hand-in-hand, children chase pigeons, and orange trees sway in the wind. Rent a **boat** (see p. 73) or stroll towards the **Museu de Zoologia** (see p. 111), directly across from the Fountains. Marvel at Domènech i Montaner's creation, originally called **Castell dels Tres Dragons,** one of the first creations that spawned Barcelona's famous architectural movement, Modernisme (see **Life & Times,** p. 51). Now head on over to the **Museu d'Art Modern** (see p. 110), where you can gaze at one of the finest collections of Noucentiste (see p. 110) sculptures in the world or study some of Dalí's early paintings, the only works by Dalí in Barcelona. After you've purchased prints and postcards of your favorite pieces of art, visit Barcelona's favorite celebrity: **Floquet de Nou,** the world's only albino gorilla, who resides in the **Parc Zoològic** (see p. 73). Exit the zoo onto Av. Marquès de l'Argentera and take a right onto C. Vidreira. On your left you'll pass the **Església Santa Maria del Mar** (see p. 71); take a moment to enjoy the plaça and then take a right onto Pg. del Born to try some **tapas** at one of the fabulous *tapas* bars in La Ribera (see p. 129). From here you can also start our On the Waterfront tour for a night on the town.

Girl with Birdcage on Las Ramblas

ON THE WATERFRONT

◤ *Suggested Time:* until you drop. *Distance:* about 1½ mi. *When to Go:* from dusk to dawn, preferably on a weekend. *Public Transportation:* begin at M: Jaume I and end with a taxi or a Nitbus to Pl. de Catalunya.

Don your best threads, take a breath mint, find that perfect combination of walking/dancing shoe, and for the love of God, put on some deodorant. This walking tour is a night on the town, so hooch it up and step out for a night of revelry and booty-bumpin'. Begin in La Ribera, an old neighborhood in the Ciutat Vella with some of the coolest dinner spots in the city. From M: Jaume I, cross Via Laietana and take a right on to C. de l'Argentera. Follow C. de l'Argentera until you hit **Pl. Santa Maria del Mar** (see p. 71) and its beautiful, low-rise church. The area is home to a few street musicians and is lined with great **tapas** bars (see p. 129). Fill up on these delicacies for an hour or two, then wander the streets of the old city for a pre-party drink (see p. 129 for some suggestions). Walk back to the Via Laietana and take a left; follow it to the end, and then turn right on to Ronda del Litoral, which runs along the water. Continue along that road until you see the **Monument a Colom** (Columbus monument; see p. 63), where you'll bear right onto Las Ramblas. Elbow your way through throngs of tourists, streets musicians, post-opera-going Barceloneses, and prostitutes to your second right, onto a small alley where the wax museum is to grab a drink at **El Bosq de les Fades** (see p. 148). Hopefully you haven't had any absinthe yet (see **Absinthe Minded,** p. 152), or this trippy, fairy-tale themed bar will be more than you bargained for. By about midnight, the clubs at **Maremagnum** (see p. 159), the world's only mall-disco, should have a few confused

Barceloneta Boats

La Boqueria

Flex your Ruta muscles in the **Fundació Tàpies**, where you can see abstract Catalan postmodern angst at its finest (p. 113).

Dizzy your way up to the top of **La Sagrada Familia** If you endure the vertigo-inducing towers, you'll enjoy one of the other best views in the city (p. 75).

From **Casa Milà**'s roof, take in one of the best views of the city; pay special attention to your next stop! (p. 77).

Chow down on a *menú del día* at one of **C. Aragó**'s tasty restaurants (p. 134).

Strut your stuff down designer **Passeig de Gràcia**; a stop in the free Museu del Perfum will compensate for any extravagant purchases you make along the way (p. 115).

Introduce yourself to the wonderful world of Modernisme with the **Manzana de la Discòrdia** where you can buy your Ruta del Modernisme pass to help you through the rest of the day (p. 79).

Check out the commercial wonder that is the **El Corte Inglés** department store (p. 183).

L'EIXAMPLE
From El Corte Inglés to La Sagrada Familia

Walking Tour 1

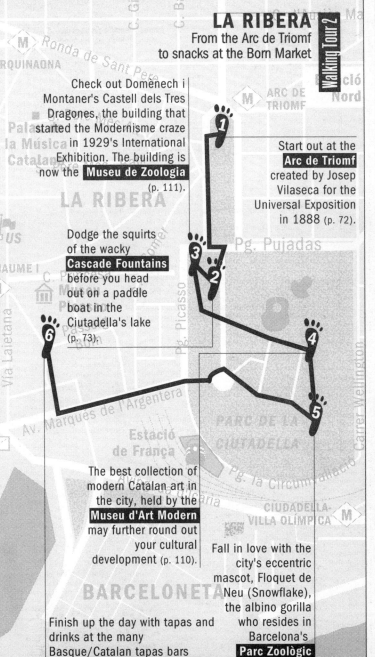

LA RIBERA

From the Arc de Triomf
to snacks at the Born Market

Walking Tour 2

Check out Domènech i Montaner's Castell dels Tres Dragones, the building that started the Modernisme craze in 1929's International Exhibition. The building is now the **Museu de Zoologia** (p. 111).

Start out at the **Arc de Triomf** created by Josep Vilaseca for the Universal Exposition in 1888 (p. 72).

Dodge the squirts of the wacky **Cascade Fountains** before you head out on a paddle boat in the Ciutadella's lake (p. 73).

The best collection of modern Catalan art in the city, held by the **Museu d'Art Modern** may further round out your cultural development (p. 110).

Fall in love with the city's eccentric mascot, Floquet de Neu (Snowflake), the albino gorilla who resides in Barcelona's **Parc Zoològic** (p. 73).

Finish up the day with tapas and drinks at the many Basque/Catalan tapas bars around **Santa Maria del Mar** and the **Born Market** (p. 71, 129).

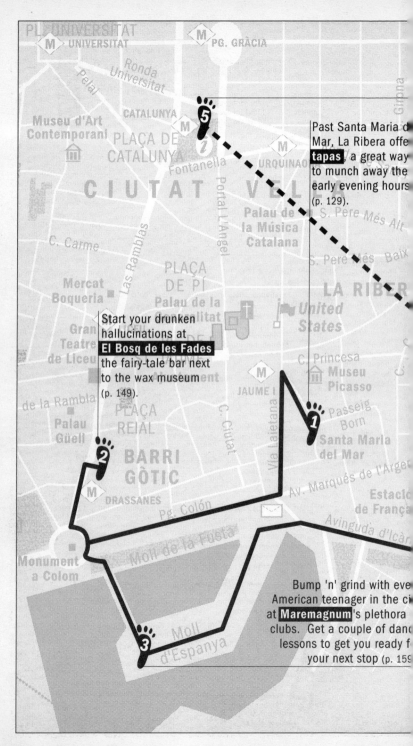

Past Santa Maria d
Mar, La Ribera offe
tapas, a great way
to munch away the
early evening hours
(p. 129).

Start your drunken
hallucinations at
El Bosq de les Fades
the fairy-tale bar next
to the wax museum
(p. 149).

Bump 'n' grind with eve
American teenager in the ci
at **Maremagnum**'s plethora
clubs. Get a couple of danc
lessons to get you ready f
your next stop (p. 159

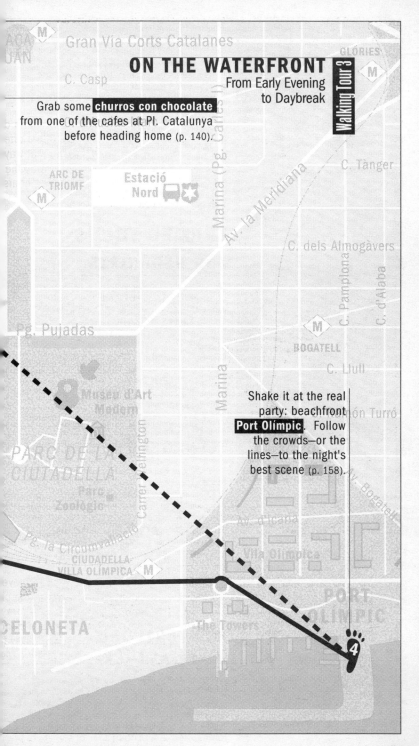

ON THE WATERFRONT

From Early Evening
to Daybreak

Grab some **churros con chocolate** from one of the cafes at Pl. Catalunya before heading home (p. 140).

Shake it at the real party: beachfront **Port Olímpic**. Follow the crowds—or the lines—to the night's best scene (p. 158).

Gran Via Corts Catalanes

C. Casp

GLÒRIES

C. Tànger

ARC DE TRIOMF

Estació Nord

Av. la Meridiana

Marina (Pg. Calles)

C. dels Almogàvers

C. Pamplona

C. d'Àlaba

Pg. Pujadas

BOGATELL

C. Llull

Marina

Museu d'Art Modern

ón Turró

PARC DE LA CIUTADELLA

Carrer Wellington

Parc Zoològic

Av. d'Icaria

Av. Bogatell

Pg. la Circumval·lació

Vila Olímpica

CIUDADELLA VILLA OLÍMPICA

PORT OLÍMPIC

ELONETA

The Towers

4

On the Barceloneta Beach

Lingerie Ponyride

Bull

Americans in them. After dance lessons and *mojitos* in one of the dozen clubs there, head back down Las Ramblas to the ocean and walk over to the **Moll d'Espanya** (see p. 21); hopefully you're still sober enough to appreciate the view of Montjuïc. By 2am, the real clubs should be hopping; stumble back down to Ronda del Litoral and veer right, past Barceloneta, until you reach the **Port Olímpic** (see p. 158). Take your pick of the many beachfront clubs and bars, and boogy until 6am. If you catch the Nitbus (see p. 29) back up to the Pl. de Catalunya before returning to your hostel, grab some *churros con chocolate* (see p. 140) from one of the surrounding cafés for breakfast—no night/morning in Barcelona is complete without them.

THEMED TOURS

FOR HEDONISTS

Marvel at the artistic insight of 1920s pornographers at the **Museu de l'Eròtica** (see p. 106), then enjoy the good weather at Barceloneta's nude beach, **Platja San Sebastià** (see p. 166). Head up Las Ramblas; don't get sidetracked by the prostitutes, because you're on your way to El Raval for some absinthe at **Marsella Bar** (see p. 153). Hallucinate your way back to the beach, this time around **Port Olímpic** (see p. 158), for some of the wildest nightlife around, best enjoyed with easy Americans.

FOR ANGST-RIDDEN TEENAGERS

You say you want a revolution? Catalunya is the place to be. Get some anti-establishment threads at El Raval's **Mercat Alternatiu** (see p. 182) before you head off to the Barri Gòtic and stick it to the Man with a **tattoo** (see p. 185). Plot with native anarchists over a cigarette and mid-day beer at a grungy bar (see p. 147), then ponder the postmodern artistic brotherhood at the **Fundació Tàpies** (see p. 112) before you grab some oh-so-anti-establishment dinner—**vegetarian,** of course (see p. 125). Spend the night fighting the Man some more at **Poble Nou's** raging alternative music scene (see p. 157).

FOR TORTURED INTELLECTUALS

Savor an early-morning smoke and an espresso (*café con leche* just isn't strong enough to overcome your malaise) at Picasso's old hangout, **Els Quatre Gats** (see p. 128) before you head off to his very own **Museu Picasso** (see p. 109). After three or four hours, tourists here will interfere with your metaphysical insights into the Blue Period, so head off to the **Museu d'Art Modern** (see p. 110) to lose yourself in Ramon Casas' sordid reinterpretation of the crowd. Dine in Gràcia's **Plaça Sol** (see p. 140) and bemoan how touristed even the bohemian, netheregions of the city have become.

FOR EUROSLUTS

Armed with daddy's credit card, strut your designer-clad stuff at one of the hottest hotspots in Europe. As you stroll along **Pg. de Gràcia,** stop to misinterpret **Casa Milà** (see p. 77), but yikes, don't stop long, as those boutiques (see p. 180) you were looking for are just around the corner. Take a break from all that shopping and grab a burger at the **Hard Rock Café** (see p. 145)—it's totally international. Slap on some lotion and work on that perfect tan (and this one doesn't come out of a bottle!) at the **Platja Nova Icària** (see p. 165). Anyone who's anyone starts the night at **Port Olímpic,** for dinner with glitzy tourists. Don't eat too much: you're going clubbing at **Maremagnum** (see p. 159) tonight, and you just have to fit into those new **Mango** (see p. 181) clothes you just bought.

WHEN TO GO

The tourist season officially runs from mid-June through late August, when the city is filled to capacity with travelers and the weather is at its most beachy; be aware that July and especially August are also the months when the natives of Barcelona take advantage of their month off from work and vacate the city. Cheaper tickets and comparably good weather prevail throughout the spring and early fall. Travel to Barcelona around Christmas can get expensive, as travel companies know that Christian Europeans will scramble and pay exorbitant amounts of money to celebrate the holidays with their families.

SEASONAL HIGHLIGHTS

Rest up, because it's time to party Barcelona-style. While Barcelona is quite different from the rest of Spain, the city shares at least one thing in common with the rest of the country—it knows how to have fun. Festivals abound in this happening city; the trick is to know what will be going on during your visit. For information on all festivals, call 93 301 77 75 (open M-F 10am-2pm and 4-8pm). Below is a summary of the major festivals in and around Barcelona.

SPRING

With the warm breezes and chirping birds, love is in the air every spring in Barcelona. **Día de Sant**

Lesbian Tango

Young Woman with Pet

Public Parks Designed with Style

Girl Running in Park by Sant Pau

Jordi, celebrated on April 24th, is a favorite day for the love birds out there. A festival in honor of one of Barcelona's favorite saints, the festivities involve men purchasing roses for their girlfriends, while women purchase books for their boyfriends. Check out the flower district on Las Ramblas during this time, as it will be selling both books and flowers just for this special occasion (see p. 61). **Setmana Santa** (Catholic Holy week, the week leading up to Easter) is a huge festival complete with huge processions; Barcelona natives pour into the streets to celebrate. On May 11th, **Fira de Sant Ponç,** a festival dedicated to the patron saint of beekeepers, is celebrated on C. Hospital near Las Ramblas (see p. 60). To satisfy your inner child, head over to Estació de França for the **International Comics Fair,** held every May.

SUMMER

Festivals dubbed **"Festa Major"** are known for their size and popularity. Both Gràcia (see p. 23) and Sitges (see p. 218) host these huge summer festivals. **Focs de Sant Joan** is held in Girona on June 24 (see p. 199). For those on the life-long quest to find a dancing egg, your journey stops in Barcelona. The **Corpus Cristi** festival occurs in June and includes huge parades, huge carnival figures, and of course, the traditional *ou com balla*—the dancing egg.

AUTUMN

Bring your Catalan flag and other favorite Catalan pride paraphernelia to the **Catalan National Day Festival,** held September 11. You'll find people dressed in traditional costumes and homes and balconies decorated with the flag and shield pattern. Wine makers pile into Barcelona from the surrounding areas along with *butifarra* (sausage) makers to present their goods during the **Feria de Cuina i Vins de Catalunya;** for one entire fall week, you can taste food and wine for only a small price. September 24th brings fireworks and devils to town for the **Festa de la Verge de la Mercè,** when *correfocs* (devils) run through the streets, flashing their pitchforks at the nearby residents. To retaliate, people throw buckets of water at the devils. Human towers (see **I've Got the Tower,** p. 216) are also a common occurrence in the streets around this time of year. Come October, Barceloneses trade their pitchforks and buckets for saxophones as the **Festival Internacional de Jazz** comes to town. Be prepared to hear lots of jazz in the streets and clubs, as some of the finest musicians perform for this event. **The Festival del Sant Çito** begins in November, and all in all, becomes one of the best city-wide parties. Make your way to Las Ramblas and let the Barceloneses teach you how to party like you never have before.

Women at a Catholic Festival

Port Vell

WINTER

Christmastime proves to be a major time for festivities, but people do tend to spend more time with their families than on the streets. Rather than a huge celebration occurring on Christmas Eve or Day, Spaniards tend to have a family dinner on *Nochebuena* (Christmas Eve), the most important holiday of the year. While the exact kind of food varies from family to family depending on family tradition, some of the typical foods include: *entremeses de jamón serrano, lomo, chorizo y queso* (appetizers of serrano ham, red hard sausage, and cheese), *ensalda de escarola y aceitunas y vinagre* (salad with olives and oil and vinegar), *langostinos* and *gambas* (shrimp), *cordero asado* (roasted lamb with garlic) and *pavo* (turkey). There are also many sweets associated with *Nochebuena*, like *turrón* (a chocolate-like treat that can be plain or include goodies like almonds or coconut), *mazapán* (marzipan), and *polvorones* (made from crushed almonds and sugar).

Pl. Espanya at Night

Spaniards hold off on exchanging presents until January 5, the **Epiphany,** the day the Three Kings ride their camels into Spain. The night of January 4th, children put their shoes outside to be filled with gifts and candy by the visiting Kings. That night, people gather to devour *roscón,* an oval-shaped sweet bread with a small toy baked into it. The race begins to escape finding the special toy, as the unlucky individual who finds the toy is supposed to pay for it (but is also dubbed King or Queen for the year). Speaking of special prizes, the **caganer** ("shitter") become even more popular during this season; just be careful where you step (see p. 136). As residents prepare for the new year, the price for grapes will suddenly sky rocket. Why? For good luck, Spaniards gather all of their friends together on **New Year's Eve,** and when the clock strikes midnight, people begin to pop a grape into their mouth for each chime, twelve in all.

Headstand

Come February, join other natives in celebrating **Festes de Santa Eulàlia,** dedicated to Barcelona's first patron saint. The Mayor's office organizes events for the city and arranges the special guest appearances by *mulasses* (dragons) in parades. Concerts abound during this time as well. **Festa de San Medir,** held in Tibidabo, is a time when Barcelona's young and old race to the mountain to be showered with candy by men galloping on horses down the mountain. From February 7th to the 13th, residents celebrate the end of winter with **Carnaval.** For the more daring, head over to Sitges (see p. 214) or Vilanova i la Geltrù (see p. 219) for some especially rowdy partying.

Barceloneta Church

Rambles

Once in Barcelona

ORIENTATION

Barcelona's layout is quite simple. Imagine yourself perched atop Columbus' head at the **Monument a Colom** (on **Passeig de Colom,** parallel to the shore), viewing the city with the sea at your back. From the harbor, the city slopes upward toward the mountains. Keep this in mind if you need to re-orient yourself. From the Columbus monument, **Las Ramblas** (see p. 18), the main thoroughfare, runs from the harbor up to **Plaça de Catalunya** (M: Catalunya; see p. 20), the city's center. The **Ciutat Vella** (Old City; see p. 18) is the heavily-touristed historical neighborhood, which centers around Las Ramblas and includes the Barri Gòtic, La Ribera, and El Raval. The **Barri Gòtic** (see p. 18) is east of Las Ramblas (to the right, with your back to the sea; see p. 18), enclosed on the other side by **Via Laietana.** East of Via Laietana lies the maze-like neighborhood of **La Ribera** (see p. 18), which borders Parc de la Ciutadella and the Estació de França train station. On the west side of Las Ramblas (to the left, with your back to the sea) is **El Raval** (see p. 19).

Beyond Parc de la Ciutadella (farther east, outside the Ciutat Vella) is the **Poble Nou** neighborhood and the **Vila Olímpica** (see p. 21), with its twin towers (the tallest buildings in Barcelona; see p. 21) and a shiny assortment of malls, discos, and restaurants (see p. 21). Beyond El Raval (to the west) rises **Montjuïc** (see p. 22), crammed with gardens, museums, the 1992 Olympic grounds, the Montjuïc castle, and other tourist attractions.

Directly behind you as you sit atop the Monument a Colom is the **Port Vell** (Old Port; see p. 21) development, where a wavy bridge leads across to the ultra-modern shopping and entertainment complexes **Moll d'Espanya** and **Maremagnum** (see p. 177).

In front of you, beyond the Ciutat Vella, is **l'Eixample** (see p. 20), the gridded neighborhood created during the urban expansion of the 1860s, which runs from Pl. de Catalunya toward the mountains. **Gran Via de les Corts Catalanes** defines its lower edge and **Passeig**

BIG TROU-BLE IN LIT-TLE CHINA

El Raval has long been considered Barcelona's dirty little secret, the side of the city the hyper image-conscious urban planners don't want visitors to see. In the 19th century, industrialization hit the neighborhood hard. Workers and their families crammed into the low-rent housing, making it one of the most densely populated urban areas in Europe. Pollution, crime, and prostitution soon followed, making this a rough port-side slum, a startling contrast to the glamor of Las Ramblas, just to the east.

In the time between the two world wars, the southern half of the neighborhood was given the nickname "El Barri Xino," or Chinatown. Though there were never any Chinese immigrants living there, it reminded some of the red-light districts of Chinatowns in American cities, with its many brothels and generally debaucherous atmosphere. The nickname has begun to fall out of use in recent years, largely because the neighborhood has improved so much. The brothels have closed, and crime has dropped (though prostitution and petty crime still thrive). Now the most ethnically diverse of the city's neighborhoods, "Barri Xino" is home to a large immigrant population from Pakistan and northern Africa—but still few Chinese.

de Gràcia, l'Eixample's main commercial street, bisects the neighborhood. **Avinguda Diagonal** marks the upper limit of the grid-planned neighborhoods, separating l'Eixample from the **Zona Alta** ("Uptown;" see p. 23), which includes Pedralbes, Sarrià, Gràcia, and Horta, some of the older neighborhoods in the foothills. The peak of Tibidabo, the northwest border of the city and its highest point in Barcelona, offers the most comprehensive view of the city.

NEIGHBORHOODS

CIUTAT VELLA

see map pp. 316-317

BARRI GÒTIC AND LAS RAMBLAS

🚩 *Orientation: Between Las Ramblas in the west and Via Laietana in the east. The ocean borders the neighborhood to the south and C. Fontanella borders it to the north.* **Sights:** *see p. 60.* **Museums:** *see p. 104.* **Food & Drink:** *see p. 123.* **Nightlife:** *see p. 147.* **Accommodations:** *see p. 264, p. 265, and p. 267.* **Public Transportation:** *M: Catalunya, Liceu, Drassanes, and Jaume I. Because of the narrow streets, no buses run through the Barri Gòtic, but down the bordering streets. Bus #14, 38, 59, and 91 traverse Las Ramblas, while bus #17 and 19 drive down Via Laietana.*

As the oldest section of Barcelona, the Barri Gòtic and Las Ramblas are the tourist centers of the city. Originally settled by the Romans in the third century BC, the Barri Gòtic is built on top of the original Roman city, Barcino, which at times pokes above the surface. Subsequent layers of medieval Catholic rule cover Barcino in a labyrinth of narrow, cobbled streets and dense spread of historic and artistic landmarks. The modern tourist industry has added shops, hostels, and bars to the churches and other monuments left over from the Middle Ages. Amid the museums and tacky tourist shops are some truly unique cultural phenomena, such as religious parades of towering plaster dolls and spontaneous performances of the *sardana*. The Barri Gòtic is a neighborhood with an identity crisis; while many complain that it is overridden by tourists drawn to its diversity and maze-like charm, it remains a symbolic center of Catalan culture and life.

LA RIBERA

🚩 *Orientation: La Ribera is separated from the Barri Gòtic by Via Laietana and is bordered on the east by C. Wellington, past the Parc de la Ciutadella. Often lumped together with its northwestern neighbor, Sant Pere, the district extends to Ronda de Sant Pere and southeast to*

Av. Marqués de l'Argentera and the Estació de França.
Sights: *see p. 70.* **Museums:** *see p. 108.* **Food & Drink:** *see p. 129.* **Nightlife:** *see p. 151.* **Accommodations:** *see p. 269.* **Public Transportation:** *The most convenient Metro stops are M: Urquinaona and Jaume I. La Ribera is a fifteen minute walk from Pl. de Catalunya. Buses #17 and 19 drive down Via Laietana.*

As the stomping ground of Barcelona's many fishermen and local merchants, La Ribera has always had a very plebeian feel. In the 18th century, Felipe V demolished much of La Ribera, then the city's commercial hub, to make space for the impressive Ciutadella, the seat of Madrid's oppressive control, now a park (see **Life & Times,** p. 42). In recent years, the neighborhood has evolved into Barcelona's bohemian nucleus, attracting a young, artsy crowd of locals and a few expats and tourists in the know. Art galleries, offbeat shops, chic eateries, and exclusive bars line the major thoroughfares C. Montcada and the Pg. del Born, while you'll find others nearly hidden on smaller side streets. After dark, La Ribera makes for a relaxing evening of delicious *tapas*, extensive wine and *cava* menus, and fashionable but reasonably unpretentious bars.

Walking Over the Miró Mosaic

EL RAVAL

⁊ Orientation: *El Raval is the neighborhood to the west of Las Ramblas. It is bordered on its far sides by Av. Paral.lel and the Rondas St. Pau, St. Antoni, and Universitat. C. Hospital is the main street which divides the neighborhood into two halves: the quainter northern area and the more run-down southern side, the Barri Xino.* **Sights:** *see p. 74.* **Museums:** *see p. 111.* **Food & Drink:** *see p. 131.* **Nightlife:** *see p. 151.* **Public Transportation:** *M: Liceu, Drassanes, Universitat, and Sant Antoni. Buses #14, 38, 59, and 91 traverse Las Ramblas.*

The ancient neighborhood just next to Las Ramblas and the Barri Gòtic can feel astonishingly different from its touristy and more glamorous neighbors. This working-class neighborhood has a charm of its own, with small, quirky shops and eateries, welcoming bars, and hidden historical attractions. Beginning as a small rural area outside of the city walls, El Raval was enveloped by the new city boundaries in the 14th century, and has been squeezing people in ever since. The situation became critical in the late 19th and early 20th centuries, when over-crowding led to an urban nightmare of rampant crime, prostitution, and drug use (see **Big Trouble in Little China,** p. 18). Revitalization efforts have worked wonders, however; new museums and cultural centers have paved the way for some of the city's trendiest new restaurants and bars. A delicate balance of working-class ethnic neighborhood and up-and-coming hotspots make El Raval an intriguing place to explore.

Bike Tricks at Miró Park

View of Port

PL. DE CATALUNYA

see map p. 314-315

🛈 Orientation: *The most important streets in the city emanate from Pl. de Catalunya. The Aerobus airport shuttle drops off newcomers on the El Corte Inglés side of the plaça. The city's main* **tourist information office** *is directly across the street from the store, underground. On this side of the plaça one can also catch the* **Bus Turístic** *red route (see p. 59), which visits the city's northern areas of interest. Looking out onto the plaça from El Corte Inglés, you'll see the Hard Rock Café side of the plaça on the left. The legendary avenue Las Ramblas begins next to this popular restaurant. Directly across the plaça from El Corte Inglés is the Triangle shopping center, featuring a FNAC store and the crowded* **Café Zurich.** *The line for the Bus Turístic blue route, which hits the southern sights, form on this side. To the right is the Banco Español de Credito. Across the street from here is the plaça's underground police station.* **Ronda Universitat** *runs in front of the Banco Español.* **Passeig de Gràcia,** *the city's showcase of modernist architecture and upscale shopping, begins between the Banco Español and El Corte Inglés. The* **Avinguda Portal de l'Angel,** *a wide pedestrian way, and* **Carrer Fontanella,** *with a few accommodations, start from between El Corte Inglés and the Hard Rock Café block.*

Chances are, visitors to Barcelona will eventually find themselves in Pl. de Catalunya, the gateway between the Ciutat Vella (Old City) and the more carefully laid out l'Eixample. Nearly every city bus, the airport shuttle, and a fleet of tourist buses pass through here, creating snarling traffic jams several times a day. The *plaça* itself contains little greenery but plenty of fountains and statues, over 20 in all. Of these, the most visible is the **Monument a Macia** (1991) by Josep Subirachs (see p. 75). The Subirachs monument, on the Ramblas corner of the *plaça*, looks like two sets of steps piled precariously on top of one another; the bust of Macia, president of the Generalitat in the 1930s, isn't all that attractive either. For over a century, the city has wanted to develop the *plaça* into a space worthy of Barcelona's center, but somehow plans have never taken shape. Today, the *plaça* is known for its commercial shopping centers, busy traffic, and amazingly docile, over-fed pigeons.

L'EIXAMPLE

see map pp. 314-315

🛈 Orientation: *Bound by C. Ausiàs Marc and Pl. de Catalunya in the south, C. Còrsega in the north, C. Tarragona in the west, and C. del Dos de Maig in the east. L'Eixample is bisected vertically by the Pg. de Gràcia into l'Eixample Esquerra (Left Enlargement) to the west and l'Eixample Dreta (Right Enlargement) to the east.* **Sights:** *see p. 75.* **Museums:** *see p. 112.* **Food & Drink:** *see p. 133.* **Nightlife:** *see p. 153.* **Public Transportation:** *Metro lines 3, 4, 5, and the FCG trains run through l'Eixample; about half the city buses pass through this neighborhood, and all Nitbuses originate at Pl. de Catalunya.*

Barcelona's l'Eixample (the Enlargement) is remarkable for the unusual circumstances leading to its development. Right around the time when the oppressive Bourbon walls around the old city were finally demolished, the Catalan cultural Renaixença was picking up. As the number of wealthy benefactors of industrialization grew, utopian socialist theories circulated like wildfire through philosophical circles, including that of l'Eixample designer **Ildefons Cerdà.** Cerdà's plan for Barcelona's enlargement was to impose an equal social community through uniformity of space and building design; however, once l'Eixample was built, rich industrialists harassed rising young architects to turn the new houses into overt displays of privilege. Land-developers ignored Cerdà's garden designs and maximum height proposals in the interest of greater profits, and the result is what you see today: largely gardenless avenues jam-packed with cars on every corner, but boasting hundreds of interesting building facades.

Despite the fact that today's l'Eixample is not an accurate incarnation of Cerdà's original plan, the neighborhood is still a pleasant and worthwhile place to visit, particularly for those claustrophobes who feel cramped by the tight spaces of the older neighborhoods. L'Eixample's gridded streets are filled with relatively wealthy residents, designer shops, corporate buildings, and plenty more. Most tourists only see the Pg. de Gràcia and Sagrada Família areas, but if you have the energy to explore the whole neighborhood, you'll get a great lesson in Modernisme, and a better feel for the Barcelona beyond the tourists.

POBLE NOU & PORT OLÍMPIC

🚩 Orientation: *Bound by C. de Marina, Av. Diagonal, the Vila Olímpica, and the ocean.* **Sights:** *see p. 88.* **Museums:** *see p. 115.* **Food & Drink:** *see p. 138.* **Nightlife:** *see p. 157.* **Public Transportation:** *M: Marina, Bogatell, Llacuna, Ciutadella/Vila Olímpic, and Poble Nou are most central; Glories and Selva de Mar lie at the outskirts of the neighborhood. Bus lines include #6, 7, 36, 41, 71, and 92.*

see map p. 321

While industrial Poble Nou fueled Barcelona's economic growth in the nineteenth century, it enjoyed little of that era's wealth. Until the last few decades, Poble Nou consisted mainly of factories, warehouses, and low-income housing. Auto shops and commercial supply stores still abound, but the major factories were all removed in time for the **1992 Olympics.** When Barcelona was granted its Olympic bid in 1986, this privilege presented a two-sided problem: comfortably housing 15,000 athletes while beautifying the city's long-ignored coastline. Oriol Bohigas, Josep Martorell, David Mackay, and Albert Puig Domènech designed the solution: the **Vila Olímpica,** a residential area with wide streets, symmetrical apartment buildings, pristine parks, and open-air art pieces. The Vila Olímpica includes one shiny Americanized mall, a municipal sports center, and some restaurants, but most social activity in the area takes place in the L-shaped **Port Olímpic,** home to docked sailboats, more than 20 restaurants, a large casino, and a long strip of brash nightclubs.

   In the wake of this development, old industrial buildings are slowly being converted into more apartments and nightclubs. With the exception of the Olympic areas, the atmosphere in Poble Nou is village-like compared to most of Barcelona: nondescript corner bars abound, and the tree-lined Rambla de Poble Nou is more likely to be filled with chatting grandmothers, small children, and gossiping teens than street artists and tourists. Besides its Olympic structures, Poble Nou's claims to fame are its sparkling city beaches and raging alternative/hard rock music scene.

BARCELONETA

🚩 Orientation: *Barceloneta lies between Port Vell and Port Olímpic on the waterfront. Pg. Joan de Borbo, running along the port, is the neighborhood's main street, while the Pg. Marítim borders the beach area.* **Sights:** *see p. 88.* **Museums:** *see p. 115.* **Food & Drink:** *see p. 139.* **Public Transportation:** *M: Barceloneta. Buses #59 and 14 both run down Las Ramblas to the waterfront area. Also accessible by buses #17, 36, 40, 45, 51, 57, and N8.*

see map p. 322

Barceloneta, or "Little Barcelona," was born out of necessity. In 1718, La Ribera was butchered to make room for the enormous Ciutadella fortress (see p. 42); the destruction of this historic neighborhood left thousands homeless, and it was only after over 30 years that the city created Barceloneta to house the displaced refugees. This area, a triangle jutting into Port Vell, follows a carefully planned grid pattern, which would later influence the design of l'Eixample. Because of its seaside location, Barceloneta became home to the city's sailors, fishermen, and their families.

   It is hard to believe that only twenty years ago Barceloneta was a neglected industrial area. Despite rapid development of the port area for the 1992 Summer Olympics, Barceloneta retains its working-class residential flavor; while not the most touristed area of the city, it is popular with urban beach-bums and seafood lovers.

PORT VELL

🚩 Orientation: *At the end of Las Ramblas by the water. Extends from Av. Paral.lel in the west to Via Laietana in the east. Facing the water near the Columbus monument (Monument a Colom), the brand-new World Trade Center and Trasmediterránea ferries are on the right, at the Moll (wharf) de Barcelona. Pg. de Colom and Moll de la Fusta run along the entire port, from the Columbus statue to the post office and Barceloneta. To get to Moll d'Espanya, the pedestrian dock that holds Maremagnum and other attractions, cross the port at La Rambla del Mar wooden footbridge, the wavy seaside extension of Las Ramblas.* **Sights:** *see p. 88.* **Museums:** *see p. 116.* **Food & Drink:** *p. 139.* **Nightlife:** *see p. 159.*

see map p. 322

Teleferic Cablecar

Funicular

Outdoor Escalator at Park Güell

Public Transportation: *M: Drassanes or Barceloneta. Buses #14, 38, and 59 run from Pl. de Catalunya to the waterfront via Las Ramblas.*

In the frenzy of renovation and development surrounding the '92 Olympic Games (see **Life & Times,** p. 46), the city's ports, overlooked for centuries and marred by heavy industry and pollution, emerged as the biggest winners. Barcelona's drive to refurbish its seafront resulted in the expansion of Port Vell, the waterfront area near **Monument a Colom** (see p. 63). After moving the congested coastal road underground, the city opened Moll de la Fusta, a wide pedestrian zone that leads down to the neighborhood and beaches of Barceloneta (see **Entertainment,** p. 166), and connects to the bright **Maremagnum** (p. 183) mall and the **Moll d'Espanya** (p. 183). The port is picturesque day or night, and clamors with the bustle of seaside eateries, loud discos, and overpriced shops. Today, the rejuvenated Port Vell—the "Old Port"—is as shiny, happy, and new as Barcelona gets.

MONTJUÏC

see map p. 320

🛈 Orientation: *Montjuïc lies in the southwest corner of the city, bordering the Poble Sec neighborhood.* **Sights:** *see p. 89.* **Museums:** *see p. 116.* **Food & Drink:** *see p. 140.* **Nightlife:** *see p. 160.* **Accommodations:** *see p. 275.* **Public Transportation:** *M: Espanya or Paral.lel. The underground* **funicular** *to Montjuïc is a convenient way to reach the Fundació Miró, Miramar, and the Castell de Montjuïc; it lets off on Av. Miramar. The funicular runs from inside the M: Paral.lel station at Av. Paral.lel and Nou de la Rambla (Apr.-June daily 10:45am-8pm, June-Oct. daily 11am-10pm, Nov.-Apr. Sa-Su 10:45am-8pm. One-way trip 275ptas/€1,65; round-trip 400ptas/€2,40). Wheelchair accessible. To reach the more distant Montjuïc sights like the Olympic area, catch* **bus #50** *either at Av. Reina Maria Cristina (flanked by 2 large brick towers) or as it heads uphill (every 10min.).*

Montjuïc (mon-joo-EEK), the hill at the southwest end of the city, is one of the oldest sections of Barcelona; throughout Barcelona's history, whoever controlled Montjuïc's peak controlled the city. The Laietani collected oysters on Montjuïc before they were subdued by the Romans (see **Life & Times,** p. 38), who erected a temple to Jupiter on its slopes. Since then, dozens of despotic rulers have constructed and modified the **Castell de Montjuïc,** built atop the ancient Jewish cemetery (hence the name "Montjuïc," which means "Jew Hill"). In the 20th century, Franco made the Castell de Montjuïc one of his "interrogation" headquarters; somewhere deep in the recesses of the structure, his *beneméritos* ("honorable ones," a.k.a. the militia) shot Catalunya's former president, Lluís Companys, in 1941. The fort was not available for recreational use until Franco rededicated it to the city in 1960.

Since re-acquiring the mountain, Barcelona has given Montjuïc a new identity, transforming it from a military stronghold into a vast park that hoards tourist attractions. Montjuïc served as the site of the 1992 Olympics (see **Life & Times,** p. 46), and today the park is one of the city's most visited attractions, with a little bit of something for everyone—museums and theater, Olympic history and facilities, walking and biking trails, and a healthy dose of nightlife.

Visitors should be forewarned; as it is a park rather than a neighborhood, Montjuïc is not the easiest area to navigate. Street signs are scant and the park is immense. In times of need, a simple map marking particular locations and the curves of major roads is most helpful—the Barcelona tourist office map (see **Service Directory,** p. 294) or El Corte Inglés map (see **Shopping,** p. 183) works well, as does the map in the map index at the back of this book.

Metro

ZONA ALTA

see maps p. 318 & 319

Zona Alta ("Uptown") is the section of Barcelona that lies at the top of most maps: past l'Eixample, in and around the Collserola mountains, and away from the low-lying waterfront districts. The Zona Alta is made of several formerly independent towns. Although all of these have now been incorporated into Barcelona's city limits as residential areas, each neighborhood retains its own character and attractions.

GRÀCIA

🚩 *Orientation: Gràcia lies past l'Eixample, above Av. Diagonal and C. de Còrsega, and stretches up to the Park Güell.* **Sights:** *see p. 23.* **Food & Drink:** *see p. 140.* **Nightlife:** *see p. 161.* **Public Transportation:** *M: Lesseps, Fontana, and Joanic, or FGC: Gràcia. Bus #24, 25, 28, and N4 service the area.*

Woody the Woodpecker at Sants Estaciò

Originally an independent, largely working-class village, Gràcia was incorporated into Barcelona in 1897, to the protest of its residents. Calls for Gràcian independence continue even today, albeit with less frequency. The area has always had a political streak—a theme that appears in the names of Mercat de Llibertat, Pl. de la Revolució, and others. After incorporation, the area continued to be a center of left-wing activism and resistance, even throughout the oppressive Franco regime. Gràcia still retains plenty of its independent, activist spirit—political graffiti and rallies are common sights.

Gràcia packs a surprising number of Modernist buildings and parks (like Park Güell, see p. 92), off-beat restaurants, and chic shops into its relatively small area, making it very walkable. The people here come from diverse back-

Estació França

grounds, fitting nicely into a neighborhood that charms and confuses with its narrow alleys and numerous *plaças*. It is both a solidly middle-class residential area and an up-and-coming young bohemia. If you're in town in August, be sure to check out the *Festa Major* (see p. 14), a weeklong party that draws in Barcelonenses from all corners of the city.

HORTA & VALL D'HEBRON

⚐ Orientation: *Horta and Vall d'Hebron lie past l'Eixample Dreta, in the upper northeastern corner of the city.* **Sights:** *see p. 96.* **Food & Drink:** *see p. 141.* **Public Transportation:** *M: Horta and Vall d'Hebron.*

Horta did not lose its status as an independent village until 1904, and its abundance of narrow pedestrian streets and old apartment buildings attest to that small town history. It boasts a few farmhouses and fortresses from the Middle Ages, as well as aristocratic estates dating from the 19th century, when the base of the Collserola mountains were a popular place for wealthy country homes. In contrast, the neighboring **Vall d'Hebron** was built up specifically to serve as one of 1992's four main Olympic venues, serving as the center of the cycling, tennis, and archery competitions.

PEDRALBES & LES CORTS

⚐ Orientation: *Pedralbes and Les Corts lie above Sants, below the mountains, and west of C. Numància.* **Sights:** *see p. 98.* **Food & Drink:** *see p. 142.* **Public Transportation:** *M: Palau Reial or Collblanc. Bus #22, 63, 64, 75, and 114 run through the neighborhood as well.*

Welcome to Pedralbes 90210, home to Barcelona's rich and famous. Sights here consist mostly of upscale apartment buildings and carefully landscaped lawns. In the 1950s, the growing University of Barcelona moved most of its academic buildings to the area, but the neighborhood is hardly a "college town," as it remains one of the city's most exclusive residential areas. Of course, the most beloved residents are the *fútbol* superstars, **El Barça** (see p. 170), whose stadium Camp Nou is here.

SANTS

⚐ Orientation: *Sants occupies the western end of the city, between Gran Via de Carles III and C. Tarragona, the area's border with l'Eixample. Montjuïc borders on the ocean side and Les Corts toward the mountains.* **Food & Drink:** *see p. 142.* **Accommodations:** *see p. 276.* **Public Transportation:** *M: Sants-Estació and Pl. de Sants. Bus lines include #32, 44, 78, and 109, coming mostly from the outskirts of the city.*

The Sants neighborhood has two histories: an older one as a resting post for travelers headed into historic walled Barcelona (the city gates closed shortly after dark), and a more recent one as a textile manufacturing zone. The mix has left narrow streets with low-level apartment buildings, plazas, a park where factories once stood, and a population with fervent political beliefs manifested on walls and buildings throughout the area. The Parc de l'Espanya Industrial might warrant a short stay, but the biggest tourist destination here is the international train station, **Estació Barcelona-Sants** (see p. 26).

SARRIÀ

⚐ Orientation: *Sarrià lies at the base of the Collserola mountains and is loosely bordered by Av. Pedralbes and Av. Tibidabo on either side. Its eastern boundary, closest to the center of Barcelona, divides Sarrià from l'Eixample and Les Corts by Av. Diagonal, while Via Augusta separates it from Gràcia.* **Sights:** *see p. 99.* **Food & Drink:** *see p. 143.* **Public Transportation:** *FGC: Bonanova, Tres Torres, Sarrià, and Reina Elisenda. Bus lines include #66, 30, and 34.*

Sarrià enjoys both meanings of the name Zona Alta ("Uptown")—economic prosperity and an elevated altitude. The last neighborhood to be incorporated into the city (1921), Sarrià often falls off the edge of Barcelona maps. Its geographical fringe status, however, holds many un-touristed sights and residential splendor. Sarrià is home to some of the city's most coveted apartments, mansions, and chic boutiques, yet the neighborhood's center, marked by Pl. Sarrià, still retains its Old World village feel.

COLLSEROLAS & TIBIDABO

◪ Orientation: *The Collserola mountain range, 17km long and 6km wide, marks the western limit of Barcelona, and incorporates the neighborhoods of Tibidabo and Vallvidrera. **Sights:** see p. 100. **Food and Drink:** see p. 143. **Public Transportation:** the **Tibibus** runs from Pl. de Catalunya to Pl. Tibidabo (the very top of the mountain) stopping only once en route (every 30-40min., only when the Parc d'Attracions is open; 285ptas/€1,71). The first bus from Pl. de Catalunya leaves 1hr. before park opening and the last usually leaves Pl. Tibidabo at 10pm, but schedules change frequently; for current details, call 010. Wheelchair accessible. An **FGC train** (U7 line) runs from Pl. de Catalunya to the Tibidabo stop (160ptas/€0,96); it stops at the foot of the peak in Pl. JFK, where C. Balmes turns into the Av. Tibidabo. **Bus #58** also runs from Pl. de Catalunya to Pl. JFK. The **neighborhood bus** (every 20 min.; M-F 7:45am-10:50pm, Sa-Su and holidays 8:10am-10:50pm; 160ptas/€0,96) and the 100 year-old **Tram Via Blue** (every 20 min. Sa, Su, and holidays 10am-7:45pm, every 15min. 11am-6:45pm; one-way 300ptas/€1,80, round-trip 425ptas/€2,55) ascend the steep Av. Tibidabo from Pl. JFK. Both the bus and tram take about 5min. to get to tiny Pl. Dr. Andreu, where the **funicular** continues to Pl. Tibidabo (6min. every 30min.; departure schedules change to match the park's hours; one-way 300ptas/€1,80, round-trip 500ptas/€3; over 60 one-way 200ptas/€1,20, round-trip 300ptas/€1,80; under 3 free). Not wheelchair accessible. A Metro pass covers the FGC train and funicular on a single ticket; this combination is the cheapest way up the mountain and the only way to reach the church when the amusement park is closed.*

The Collserola mountains hovered between wilderness and civilization for centuries. With the fall of the Roman Empire (see **Life & Times,** p. 38), peasants from Barcelona retreated into the hills to defend themselves against invasions from the north and south. For most of the last 1000 years, the area has been home to agricultural people who built the area's historic chapels and *masias* (traditional Catalan farmhouses). In 1860, with the Industrial Revolution, the people of Barcelona began to notice the area's potential for leisure and summer housing; in the last century, the installation of railtracks, trams, and funiculars has made the mountains easily accessible to urban residents wanting to take advantage of the mountains' offerings.

The **Parc de Collserola** (see **Sights,** p. 101) encompasses essentially the entire chain of mountains; the landscape ranges from almost entirely wild to well-populated. Tibidabo, the highest peak (512m), hosts a century-old amusement park and the popular Sagrat Cor church, while the hilltop town of Vallvidrera and the communications tower **Torre de Collserola** occupy a slightly lower peak nearby (see **Sights,** p. 101).

The man most responsible for the development of Tibidabo and surrounding slopes was Dr. Salvador Andreu, who in 1899 founded the Tibidabo Society and invested heavily in the land, installing transportation and building hotels, the amusement park, and an extravagant casino, now in ruins. Soon after, the Barcelona bourgeoisie rushed to outdo one another in country-home construction, and the hillsides are now dotted with outstanding examples of early 20th-century Modernist and Noucentist architecture (see **Life & Times,** p. 51). Many of these former homes now house offices and schools.

GETTING TO & FROM BARCELONA

BY PLANE (EL PRAT DE LLOBREGAT)

All flights land at **El Prat de Llobregat** airport (☎93 298 38 38; www.aena.es/ae/bcn/homepage), 12km (8 mi.) southwest of Barcelona. From the airport, there are several options for transport into the city. The **Aerobus** links the airport to Pl. de Espanya and Pl. de Catalunya, the center of town (approx. 40min.; every 15min.; to Pl. de Catalunya M-F 6am-midnight and Sa-Su 6:30am-midnight, to the airport M-F 5:30am-11:15pm and Sa-Su 6am-11:20pm; 525ptas/€3,16).

RENFE (24hr. info ☎93 491 31 83; www.renfe.es) trains provide slightly cheaper transportation to and from the airport (20-25min.; every 30min.; 6:13am-11:15pm from airport, 5:43am-11:24pm from Sants; 350ptas/€2,10). The most useful stops are **Estació Barcelona-Sants** and **Plaça de Catalunya**. Tickets are sold at the red automatic machines. In Sants, buy tickets at the "Aeroport" window (open 5am-11pm). After 11pm, get them from the ticket machines or the Recorridos Cercanías window.

GET sm**art**

Artsy Airport

When you arrive in Barcelona, cranky and travel-weary, pause for a moment to appreciate the architectural and artistic feat that is El Prat de Llobregat Airport. Designed just in time for the 1992 Olympics, the international terminal is a graceful, minimalist structure composed of floor-to-ceiling glass walls and slim concrete columns. The terminal's architect, Ricardo Bofill, explains: "I wanted to design a different airport, pleasant, closer to an architectural work than a gloomy waiting room." As you move past the ticket counters on your way out to the buses and trains, take a minute to enjoy the artwork that lurks around every corner, daring harrowed travelers to rush by; from a *bona fide* Botero fat horse sculpture to a Miró mural, the airport is practically a gallery in itself. Don't enjoy the aesthetics too much, though; Barcelona's got more where that came from....

The city **bus** offers the only inexpensive late-night service. Take bus EN (called EA during the day) from the airport to Pl. de Espanya (every hr.; airport to Pl. de Espanya 6:20am-2:40am, Pl. de Espanya to airport 7:10am-3:15am; 160ptas/€0,96). The stop in Pl. de Espanya is on the corner of Gran Via de les Corts Catalanes and Av. Reina Maria Cristina. A **taxi** ride between Barcelona and the airport costs 3000-4500ptas/€18,03-27,05.

Three **national airlines** serve all domestic and major international destinations. **Iberia/Aviaco,** Pg. de Gràcia 30 (☎93 401 32 82; 24hr. reservation and info ☎902 40 05 00), has the most extensive coverage. Iberia/Aviaco usually offers student discounts (except on already reduced fares). **Air Europa** (24hr. reservation and info ☎902 40 15 01; www.air-europa.com) and **Spanair,** Pg. de Gràcia 57 (☎93 216 4626; 24hr. reservation and info ☎902 13 14 15) offer fares that are often cheaper.

All major **international airlines** serve Barcelona, including **British Airways,** airport office ☎93 298 34 55, 24hr. reservation and info ☎ 02 11 13 33; open 6am-7pm) and **Delta** (24hr. reservation and info ☎901 11 69 46; www.delta-air.com). **Easy Jet** (24hr. reservation and info ☎902 29 99 92; www.easyjet.com) also offers flights from Barcelona to Amsterdam, Geneva, Liverpool, and London. For more information on international reservations, visit a travel agency in Barcelona (see **Service Directory,** p. 295).

BY TRAIN

Spain prides itself on having prompt, cheap, and fast trains; trains are an easy and affordable way to travel within Catalunya and Spain. Barcelona has two main stations which serve different destinations. When in doubt, go to Estació Barcelona-Sants; while all domestic trains leaving Estació França pass through here, not all trains leaving Barcelona-Sants necessarily pass through Estació França. A taxi between either station and the Pl. de Catalunya will cost approximately 1000ptas/€6. For general information about trains and train stations in Barcelona, call RENFE, Spain's main train company (☎902 244 02 02).

Estació Barcelona-Sants, in Pl. Països Catalans. M: Sants-Estació. Buses to the station include #30 from Pl. de Espanya, 44 through L'Eixample (stops at La Sagrada Família), and N2. Barcelona-Sants is the main terminal for domestic and international traffic. For late arrivals, the N14 Nitbus shuttles to Pl. de Catalunya (every 30min. 10:30pm-4:30am, 160ptas). Currency exchange (open 8am-9:30pm), ATMs, pharmacy, tourist office, restaurants, phone center, and tourist-oriented shopping. Large lockers 700ptas for

24hr., small 500ptas (storage open daily 5:30am-11:00pm). Station open M-F 4:30am-midnight, Sa-Su 5am-midnight.

Estació França, Av. Marqués de l'Argentera (☎902 24 02 02). M: Barceloneta. Buses include #17 from Pl. de Catalunya and N6. Open daily 7am-10pm. This recently restored 19th-century station on the edge of the Ciutat Vella serves regional destinations on RENFE, including Girona, Tarragona, and Zaragoza, as well as some international arrivals.

BY BUS

Buses are often cheaper and more direct than trains, if you don't mind the lengthy travel times. Most—but not all—buses arrive at the **Barcelona Nord Estació d'Autobuses,** C. Ali-bei 80. The small Nord station features a sandwich shop, restaurant, candy shop, and even a butcher, with money exchange and luggage storage services. The building also houses an office of the **Guardia Urbana,** the local police. (☎93 265 61 32. M: Arc de Triomf, exit to Nàpols. Info office open daily 7am-9pm.) Buses that go there include #54 along Gran Via (a block from Pl. de Catalunya) and N11. A taxi from the Pl. de Catalunya to the station will cost approximately 700ptas/€4. Other buses, particularly **international buses,** arrive at the **Estació d'Autobuses de Sants** station, next to the train station in Pl. Països Catalans (see above). The following companies operate out of Estació Nord:

Enatcar (☎902 422 242; www.enatcar.es). To: **Alicante** (9hr., 5 per day, 4650ptas/€27,95); **Madrid** (8hr., 18 per day, 2690ptas/€16,17); **Valencia** (4hr., 16 per day, 2690ptas/€16,27). Open daily 7am-1am.

Sarfa (☎902 30 20 25; www.sarfa.com). Sarfa buses stop at many beach towns along the Costa Brava, north of Barcelona. To: **Cadaqués** (2½hr., 10:45am and 7:45pm, 2250ptas/€13,52); **Palafrugell** (2hr., 13 per day); **Tossa de Mar** (1½hr., 9 per day 8:15am-8:15pm, 1070ptas/€6,43). Open daily 8am-8:30pm.

Linebús (☎93 265 07 00). Discounts for travelers under 26 and over 60. To **London** (25hr., 3 per week, 14,650ptas/€88,05) and **Paris** (15hr., 8pm M-Sa 12,800-23,600ptas/€76,93-141,84). Also has daily service to southern France and Morocco. Open M-F 8am-2pm and 3-8pm, Sa 8:30am-1:30pm and 4:30-8pm.

Alsa (☎902 422 242; www.alsa.es). Division of Enatcar. To: **Gijon** (12hr., 1 per day, 4850ptas). **Lisbon** (17hr., F 2:30pm, 12,000ptas/€72,12); **Naples** (24hr., 5:15pm, 18700ptas/€112,39); **Zaragoza** (4½hr., 2 per day, 1655ptas/€9,95); **Zurich** (17hr., F 12:45am, 13250ptas/€79,63).

BY FERRY

Barcelona's prime Mediterranean location makes the city an ideal gateway to the **Balearic Islands,** three islands renowned for their beaches, raging clubs, and resorts. The main ferry station is **Estació Marítima,** in the Port Vell.

Trasmediterránea, Estació Marítima-Moll Barcelona, Moll de Sant Bertran (☎902 45 46 45; fax 93 295 91 34; www.transmediterranea.es). M: Drassanes. Head down Las Ramblas to the **Monument a Colom** (see p. 63). Columbus points straight toward the Estació Marítima. Cross the street and walk right, along the waterfront, until you see the large Trasmediterránea building on your left. In the summer only to: **Ibiza** (9hr.; 1 per day, 2 per day M, F, Sa); **Mallorca** (3hr., 3 per day); **Menorca** (1 per day starting mid-June). One way trips start at 8000ptas/€48,08 and quickly rise to over 10,000ptas/€60,10. Tickets are available at any travel agency, but the station office is open daily 10am-4pm.

GETTING AROUND BARCELONA
BY METRO AND FGC

Barcelona's public transportation system (info ☎010, claims ☎93 318 70 74) is quick and inexpensive. The *Guia d'Autobuses Urbans de Barcelona,* free at tourist offices and in Metro stations, maps out the city's bus routes and the five Metro lines; the small book *Guia Facil del Bus per Mour't per Barcelona,* also free, describes the routes in even more detail.

If you plan to use public transportation extensively, consider buying one of the several *abonos* (passes) available, all of which work interchangeably for the Metro, bus, urban lines of the FGC commuter trains, and the Nitbus. The **T-1 pass** (885ptas/€5,32) is valid for 10 rides and saves you nearly 50% off the cost of single tickets. The **T-Dia** pass (670ptas/€4,03) is good for a full day of unlimited travel, while the **T-Mes** (5825ptas/€35,04) offers the same for a month. The **T-50/30** (3700ptas/€22,24) buys 50 trips in a 30-day period. Finally, for short stays, the **3 Dies** pass (1700ptas/€10,22) gets you three days of unlimited travel; the **5 Dies** (2600ptas/€15.63) is good for five days. Both save you money if you use the Metro more than three times per day.

Metro (☎ 93 486 07 52; www.tmb.net). Automatic vending machines and ticket windows sell Metro passes. Stations indicated by red diamonds with the letter "M" inside of them. Hold on to your ticket until you leave the Metro—an official with a white-and-red pinstriped shirt may ask to see it. Riding without a ticket carries a hefty fine of 5000ptas/€30,05. Trains run M-Th 5am-11pm, F-Sa 5am-2am, Su 6am-midnight. 160ptas for a *sencillo* (single ride).

Ferrocarrils de la Generalitat de Catalunya (FGC): ☎ 93 205 15 15; www.fgc.catalunya.net. Commuter trains with main stations at Pl. de Catalunya and Pl. de Espanya. Service to **Montserrat** (from Pl. de Espanya). Symbols resembling two interlocking "V"s mark connections with the Metro. The commuter line charges the same as the Metro (160ptas/€0,96) until Tibidabo. After that, rates go up by zone: zone 2 destinations cost 240ptas/€1,44 and zone 3 destinations cost 340ptas/€2,04. Metro passes are valid on FGC trains. Information office at the Pl. de Catalunya station, open M-F 7am-9pm.

BY BUS

Barcelona has a comprehensive bus system, with more than 80 lines connecting different parts of the city. Bus stops have red signs and brown benches under a small roof; bus lines that use the stop will be posted there. Always respect the line at the bus stop. Try to buy a ticket before you get on the bus, as the drivers tend to be cranky about cash and may even refuse to make change. When you get on the bus, you'll see two machines at the front; if you have a Metro pass, insert your ticket into it, printed side facing you, arrow pointing down, and the machine will stamp your ticket. To ring the bell and get off, press the strips on the walls. Most major lines are partially wheelchair-adapted, meaning that at least some, though not all, of the buses on the line have lifts for wheelchairs (see Travelers with Disabilities in **Planning Your Trip,** p. 258). Buses keep the same hours and charge the same fees as the metro trains (see above). Some of the most useful lines include the following; see the *Guia de 'Autobuses Urbans* or *Guia Facil del Bus*, free at tourist offices or Metro stations, for more detail.

#10: Bisects the city from top to bottom, passing by the Parc de la Vall d'Hebron, La Sagrada Família, Teatre Nacional, Parc de la Ciutadella, Museu d'Art Modern, and Parc de las Cascades on the way to its final stop on Pg. Marítim, right in front of Platja Barceloneta. Partially wheelchair accessible.

#14: Begins above l'Eixample Dreta and runs down Las Ramblas, stopping near the Mercat de la Boqueria, Palau de la Música Catalana, Catedral, and Gran Teatre de Liceu. Continues from there to the Museu Marítim and Port Vell and then takes Pg. Colom past the Estació de França, Parc de la Ciutadella, Estació de Autobuses Barcelona Nord, and finally Vila Olímpica. Partially wheelchair accessible.

#19: Starts in Port Vell and passes near the Museu Picasso, Palau de la Música Catalana, the Arc de Triomf, and La Sagrada Família. Partially wheelchair accessible.

#24: Runs from Pl. de Catalunya up Pg. de Gràcia to Park Güell, along the way passing by La Manzana de la Discòrdia, Casa Milà, and the Palau Robert. Partially wheelchair accessible.

#50: The most useful part of this line connects Montjuïc to the Sagrada Família, passing by the Palau Nacional, Estadi Olímpic, and Poble Espanyol. Partially wheelchair accessible

Bus Turístic: Departing from the Pl. de Catalunya, this bus is one of the easiest way to get between all the tourist attractions in the city (see **Sights,** p. 59).

BY NITBUS

When the regular bus system and Metro close, the Nitbus begins. Sixteen different lines run 10:30pm-4:30am, usually every 20-30 min., depending on the line; a few run until 5:30am as well. All of the buses depart from the Pl. de Catalunya; a Metro pass is valid on the Nitbus. The buses stop in front of most of the club complexes and work their way through the Ciutat Vella and the Zona Alta. Maps are available at *estancos* (tobacco shops) and marked by signs in Metro stations. (☎901 511 151; *sencillo* (single ride) 60ptas/€0,96.)

BY TAXI

Taxis are everywhere in Barcelona. On weekend nights, you may wait up to 30min. in some locations; long lines form at popular club spots like the Port Olímpic. A *lliure* or *libre* sign in the windshield or a lit green light on the roof means they are vacant; yellow means they are occupied. To summon a cab by phone, try the companies listed in the **Service Directory**, p. 293. Disabled travelers should call 93 420 80 88. Taxi prices are set: Monday through Friday the first six minutes or 1.9km cost 300ptas/€1,80; each additional km is 110ptas/€0,66. After 10pm on Saturday, Sunday, and fiesta days, the first six minutes or 1.9km cost 325ptas/€1,95, and each additional km 140ptas/€0,84.

BY BICYCLE AND MOPED

Bicycles are not very visible in Barcelona, as most prefer a *moto* (motorcycle). It seems as though everyone in Barcelona owns a moto. As you make your way through the streets of the city, be wary of speeding businessmen and grandmas on *motos*. To change your status from the hunted to the hunter, visit one of Barcelona's many rental shops.

Vanguard Rent a Car, C. Londres 31 (☎93 439 38 80). Mopeds start at Tu-Th 4760ptas/28,61 per day, F-M 7280ptas/€43,75 per day. 2-person motos start at 6200ptas per weekday. Insurance, helmet, and IVA included. Min. age 19 to rent (ID required).

Over-Rent S.A., Av. Josep Terradellas 42 (☎93 405 26 60). Call at least a week ahead to reserve a vehicle. Motorcycles for rent 2500-8200ptas/€15,03-49,28 per day. Min. age 23 to rent (ID required).

BY CAR

Public transportation is by far the easiest way to get around the city; cars are more of a hassle than they are useful. Spanish drivers are notoriously aggressive, gas is expensive, and parking in Barcelona is an adventure every day. If you plan to drive in the hazardously tight Ciutat Vella, you had better have nerves of steel and above average dexterity. To drive a car while in Spain, you must be over 18; an International Driving Permit (IDP; see **Planning Your Trip,** p. 256), is highly recommended.

FINDING YOUR PIMPMOBILE

Depending on how old you are, what you like to drive, and how much you're willing to spend on gas, renting a car may deflate your bank account. Traveling in Spain and living in Barcelona do not necessitate the use of a car. For those who desire that get-up-and-go convenience, you can generally make reservations before you leave by calling major international offices in your home country. However, occasionally the price and availability information they give doesn't jive with what the local offices in your country will tell you. Check with both offices and make sure you get the correct price and information. For a listing of the car rental agencies in Barcelona, check the **Service Directory,** p. 290.

To rent a car from most of these establishments, you need to be at least 21 years old. Some agencies require renters to be 25, and most charge those aged 21-24 an additional insurance fee (around US $5-6 per day). Policies and prices vary from agency to agency. Small local operations occasionally rent to people under 21, but be sure to ask about the insurance coverage and deductible, and always check the fine print. Try to get a policy that includes **roadside assistance.**

COSTS AND INSURANCE

Including basic insurance and taxes, rental car prices start at around US $125 a day from national companies. Expect to pay more for larger cars and for 4WD. Cars with **automatic transmission** can cost twice as much as standard manuals (stick shift), and in some places, automatic transmission is hard to find in the first place. It is virtually impossible, no matter where you are, to find an automatic 4WD.

Many rental packages offer unlimited km, while others offer a set number of km per day with a per-km surcharge after that. Be sure to ask whether the price includes **insurance** against theft and collision. Remember that if you are driving a conventional vehicle on an **unpaved road** in a rental car, you are almost never covered by insurance; ask about this before leaving the rental agency. Beware that cars rented on an **American Express** or **Visa/Mastercard Gold or Platinum** credit cards in Spain might *not* carry the automatic insurance that they would in some other countries; check with your credit card company. Insurance plans almost always come with an **excess** (or **deductible**) for conventional vehicles; this means you pay for all damage up to that sum, unless they are the fault of another vehicle. The excess you will be quoted applies to collisions with other vehicles; collisions with non-vehicles, such as trees, ("single-vehicle collisions") will cost you even more. The excess can often be reduced or waived entirely if you pay an additional charge.

MEDITERRANEAN MANNERS

CHURCH ETIQUETTE. Catalunya's religious buildings are open to the public at various hours; while these landmarks are on every tourist's itinerary, be aware that a visit to these edifices requires a certain dress code and respectful attitude. Shorts and tank tops are considered disrespectful; keep your arms and legs covered if you don't want to be ushered out by a clergy member. There are often chapels that are reserved for devotional purposes only; please respect these restrictions and only enter if you are worshiping. Camera regulations vary from site to site, but flash is almost never permitted. Noise above a whisper is inappropriate, unless you are participating in a mass.

EUROPEANS WHO DISAPPEAR IN AUGUST. The European summer schedule is quite pleasant for those who work in Europe and quite bizarre for those who come to visit. Generally, employees have a month off in the summer, which they usually take in August. Barcelona's native residents clear out of the city in August and head for the beach towns that line the coast. The city is noticeably deflated at his time of year, although the tourists keep coming; be prepared for some small businesses, such as hostels and restaurants, to close down for a few weeks in the summer.

HOURS. Spaniards observe the *siesta*, which can be a nap, but also serves to describe an even grander tradition. Save larger companies and needed services, all of Spain shuts down for a period of three hours in the afternoon so the family can eat their midday meal—also their largest—together. Businesses generally open around 9 or 10 am, close from 2pm until 5, and open again at 5pm until after 9.

SMOKING. Spaniards smoke a lot. They also smoke virtually everywhere, even where it is clearly prohibited, such as the Metro platforms. Restaurants, bars, and clubs accommodate a smoking clientele.

TIPPING & BARGAINING. They don't exist. Businesses in Spain expect you to pay no more and no less than the posted price, and may even be offended if you leave more than you owe.

KEEPING IN TOUCH

BY TELEPHONE

How much a given phone call will cost is dependent upon what sort of a call it is; this edition of *Let's Go* has formatted telephone numbers to reflect those price differences. The city code for Barcelona is 93; a number that begins with 93 is a call within the city. Other areas in Catalunya use the code 97. You must dial this city code, even within the city; it is not charged as a long distance call.

Spain is currently ensnared in a phone number format dilemma. Regional phone numbers can be listed either in the 2-3-2-2 format or the 3-3-3 format; that is, a number in Barcelona may appear either as 93 555 55 55 or 935 555 555. *Let's Go* uses the 2-3-2-2 format to visually separate local or regional calls from other sorts of calls, which begin with a three-digit prefix. A number that begins with the three-digit prefix 900 is a toll-free number; other three digit prefixes are toll numbers or mobile phone numbers that will cost copious amounts of money.

CALLING CARDS

Pay phones in Spain always accept coins, but coins are not the best way to make a local or international call in Spain. Opt for prepaid **calling cards,** issued in denominations of 1000ptas/€6 and 2000ptas/€12, and sold at *estancos* (tobacco shops, identifiable by brown signs with yellow lettering and tobacco leaf icons) and most post offices. Some *kioscos* (newsstands) and many tourists shops along Las Ramblas also sell calling cards. You'll want to buy a certain kind of phone card, depending on who you want to call. For **local calls** or calls from **payphones,** the cards that you insert into the payphone are best; for **international calls** or calls made from **private phones,** the telephone cards with a Personal Identification Number (PIN) and a toll-free access number are best. Instead of inserting this card into the phone, call the access number and follow the directions on the card. These cards can be used to make international as well as domestic calls, and may offer discount rates on calls to certain countries.

ESSENTIAL INFORMATION

EMERGENCY PHONE INFO

Police: ☎091.

Ambulance: ☎061.

Medical Emergency: ☎061.

Directory Assistance: ☎1003 for numbers within in Spain, ☎1008 for numbers within in Europe, ☎1005 for numbers outside Europe.

PHONE FACTS

To call home from Barcelona:

1. The **international dialing prefix:** 00.

2. The **country code** of the country you want to call. To call **Australia,** dial 61; **Canada** or the **US,** 1; the **Republic of Ireland,** 353; **New Zealand,** 64; **South Africa,** 27; the **UK,** 44.

3. The **city/area code.** If the first digit is a zero (e.g., 020 for London), omit the zero when calling from abroad (e.g., dial 20 from Barcelona to reach London).

4. The **local number.**

LOCAL CALLS

The one-and-only Spanish phone company is **Telefónica.** Phone booths are marked by signs that say *Teléfono público,* and most bars have pay phones, though they are coin-operated only and tend to cost more than public pay phones. Local calls cost 25ptas/€0,15 to dial and then 8ptas/€0,05 per min. (8am-6pm) and 4ptas/€0,02 per min. (6pm-8am). Be aware that it is almost five times as expensive to call mobile phones (around 40ptas/€0,24 per min. 8am-6pm and 20ptas/€0,12 per min. 6pm-8am, with a minimum charge of 110ptas/€0,66). Phone numbers in Barcelona begin with the area code 93; if a phone number does not begin with 93 or does not have nine digits, it is probably to a mobile phone (see **By Telephone,** above).

Private phone and fax service are available at Estació Barcelona-Sants (☎/fax 93 490 76 50. M: Sants-Estació; 1st page 250ptas/€1,50, each additional page 100ptas/€0,60; open M-Sa 8am-9:15pm). For directory assistance or information, dial 003.

INTERNATIONAL CALLS

There are two different sets of rates for international calls: *normal* and *reducida.* *Normal* rates apply 8am-8pm, and *reducida* rates apply 8pm-8am. The minimum charge for making an international call is 300ptas/€1,80. The following are the *normal-reducida* rates. for calls from Barcelona, using change or a Telefónica phone card. To the US and Canada, 90-85ptas/€0,54-0,50 per min.; to England or Ireland 80-70ptas/€0,48-0,44 per min.; to Australia or New Zealand 235-200ptas/€1,41-1,20 per min.; to South Africa 275-255ptas/€1,65-1,50 per min. You can also buy competing phone company cards, which vary wildly in per-minute charges. (For instance, a 1000ptas/€60,10 card can by you anywhere between 35 and 100 min. of call time to the US or Europe, or 40-90min. to Australia and New Zealand). If you want to save money, tell the shop owner where you are calling and ask which card gives the best rates to that particular location (he will have detailed rate lists behind the counter). Beware also that with some cards, calling mobile phones at home will be significantly more expensive than with others.

The best option, for most people, is to bring an international calling card from home issued by your phone company. Calls are billed collect or to your account. You can frequently call collect without even possessing a company's calling card just by calling their access number and following the instructions. **To obtain a calling card** from your national telecommunications service before leaving home, contact the appropriate company listed below. To **call home with a calling card,** contact the operator for your service provider in Spain by dialing the appropriate toll-free access number below:

COMPANY	TO OBTAIN A CARD, DIAL:	TO CALL ABROAD, DIAL:
AT&T (US)	888-288-4685	900 990 011
British Telecom Direct	800 34 51 44	900 964 495
Canada Direct	800-668-6878	900 990 015
MCI (US)	800 444-3333	900 990 014
New Zealand Direct	0800 00 00 00	900 991 836

Call 025 for an international Telefónica operator (600ptas/€3,61). Placing a **collect call** through an international operator is more expensive, but may be necessary in case of emergency.

MOBILE PHONES

For a longer stay in the city, a mobile phone might be a good investment and a great convenience, but be sure to do comparative shopping between the major companies (Telefónica, Movistar, and Airtel offer the best service) before purchasing. For shorter stays, you can rent a Nokia phone from **Rent-A-Phone,** C. Numància 212. Pay the up-front deposit of 25,000ptas/€150,25 with a credit card (AmEx/MC/V); the company will charge the same credit card about 250ptas/€1,50 per min. for calls in Spain, and 300-450ptas/€1,80-2,70 per min. for international calls (minimum charge of 1080ptas/€6,49 per day). You can also rent phones that work from other countries, for 350ptas/€2,10 per min. (minimum charge 1750ptas/€10,52 per day); Rent-A-Phone will retrieve these phones for free from any European country. (☎93 280 21 31. M: Maria Christina. Walk down Diagonal with El Corte Inglés on your right, then go left on C. Numància. Open M-F 9:30am-2pm and 4-7:30pm. Branch: Maremagnum, 2nd fl., open daily 11am-11pm.)

TIME DIFFERENCES

Barcelona is one hour ahead of Greenwich Mean Time (GMT), and 2 hours ahead during daylight savings time. Barcelona is 6 hours ahead of New York, 9 hours ahead of Vancouver and San Francisco. Spain observes daylight savings time, and fall and spring switchover times vary between countries. Because of this factor, in Spain's winter, Spain is 1 hour behind Johannesburg, 10 hours behind Sydney, and 12 hours behind Auckland; in Spain's summer, Spain is on the same time as Johannesburg, 8 hours behind Sydney, and 10 hours behind Auckland.

BY MAIL

SENDING MAIL HOME FROM BARCELONA

Air mail (*por avión*) takes five to eight business days to reach the US or Canada; service is faster to the UK and Ireland and slower to Australia and New Zealand. Standard postage is 115ptas/€0,70 to North America. Surface mail (*por barco*), while onsiderably less expensive than air mail, can take over a month, and packages will ake two to three months. Registered or express mail (*registrado* or *certificado*) is ne most reliable way to send a letter or parcel home, and takes four to seven busi-ess days. Spain's overnight mail is not worth the added expense, since it is not xactly "overnight." For better service, try private companies such as DHL, UPS, or ne Spanish company SEUR; look under *mensajerías* in the yellow pages. Their reli-bility does, however, come at a high cost. Stamps (*sellos*) are sold at post offices nd tobacconists (*estancos* or *tabacos*). Mail letters and postcards from the yellow nailboxes scattered throughout the city, or from the post office in small towns.

RECEIVING MAIL IN BARCELONA

There are several ways to arrange pick-up of letters sent to you by friends and rela-ives while you are abroad. Mail can be sent via **Poste Restante** (General Delivery) to lmost any city or town in Spain with a post office. This is not the quickest way to get nail. Address *Poste Restante* letters like so:

> Brian Thos. <u>COSTELLO</u>
> Poste Restante
> Lista de Correos
> 08070, Barcelona
> SPAIN

The mail will go to a special desk in the central post office, unless you specify a post office by street address or postal code. It's best to use the largest post office, since nail may be sent there regardless. Bring your passport (or other photo ID) for pick-up; there may be a small fee. If the clerks insist that there is nothing for you, have hem check under your first name as well (i.e. if your name is John Luna, have them check under "John" and "Luna," and even "Mr."). *Let's Go* lists post offices in the **Service Directory** for Barcelona and the **Practical Information** section for other towns.

BY EMAIL & INTERNET

Internet addicts won't have to worry about withdrawal symptoms, thanks to Barce-lona's plethora of Internet cafés. You can surf the Web in almost any electronics store, or try more posh locales where you can surf with a drink and *bocadillo* at your side. Although it will usually be possible to connect to your home server, it may be faster (and thus less expensive) to take advantage of free **web-based email accounts** (e.g., www.hotmail.com and http://mail.yahoo.com). In general, connec-tions in Spain tend to be more sluggish than those in the US or Canada. Travelers with laptops can call an Internet service provider via a **modem.** Long-distance phone cards specifically intended for such calls can defray normally high phone charges; check with your long-distance phone provider to see if it offers this option.

Internet access costs about 600-1000ptas/€3,60-6 per hour; if you'll be going to the same establishment for email for a while, buying an *abono*, that is, a voucher for a certain number of access hours paid up front, is the most economical. The website www.tangaworld.com lists nearly 200 cybercafés across Spain by location and name. **Internet cafes** are available all over the city and listed in the **Service Directory**, p. 292. The largest and most popular are also listed below.

▨ **Easy Everything,** Las Ramblas 31 (www.easyeverything.com). M: Liceu, on **Las Ramblas.** This new branch of Europe's Internet chain offers high speed Internet access in an ideal loca-tion. Tourists flock to its 450 computers, equipped with telnet and messaging services like Yahoo, AOL, and ICQ. 200ptas/€1,20 for about 40min. Price fluctuates according to the number of computers in use. Early risers or late-night party-goers might want to come in at 5am, where 200ptas/€1,20 will buy 3hr. of time. The cafe serves snacks and drinks for about 200ptas/€1,20 each. Open 24hr. Branch: Ronda Universitat 35, right next to Pl. de Catalunya, with 300 computers at the same prices.

▨ **Café Interlight,** Av. Pau Claris 106 (☎93 301 11 80; interlight@bcn.servicom.es). M: Urquinaona. Jarring aqua seat compartments and silver piping make this cafe feel like a scene out of 2050. 100ptas/€0,96 per 15min., 250ptas per hr. Coffee and 1hr. Internet 300ptas/€1,80 9am-3pm. Live music F.

Internet Exchange, Las Ramblas 130 (☎93 317 73 27). From its prime location at the t
of Las Ramblas, this few-frills cybercafé has close to fifty computers with a decent connecti
speed. 10ptas/€0,06 per min., cheaper in bulk: 5hr. for 2000ptas/€12; 20 hr. f
4500ptas/€27,05. Students get 10hr. for 2500ptas/€15,03; 30hr. for 5000ptas/€30,0

TOURIST OFFICES

Tourist office representatives dot the Barri Gòtic in the summer. (July-Sept. 10ar
8pm.) Look for officials wearing red vests.

Informació Turística Plaça Catalunya, Pl. de Catalunya 17S, below Pl. de Catalunya.
Catalunya. The big kahuna on the tourist info scene. Provides multilingual advice, map
pamphlets, transportation passes, hotel information and reservations, currency exchang
telephone cards, email kiosks, and souvenirs for purchase. Open daily 9am-9pm.

Informació Turística Plaça Sant Jaume, Pl. Sant Jaume 1, off C. Ciutat. M: Jaume I. Few
services and more personal attention than its big sister in Pl. de Catalunya. Open M-S
10am-8pm, Su 10am-2pm.

Aeroport El Prat de Llobregat (☎93 478 05 65), in the international terminal at the airpor
Open daily 9am to 9pm. English-speaking agents offer information on Catalunya and Barc
lona, maps, and hotel reservations.

Oficina de Turisme de Catalunya, Palau Robert, Pg. de Gràcia 107 (☎93 238 40 00; fax 9
292 12 70; www.gencat.es/probert). M: Diagonal. The place to come for info all about Cata
lunya as a whole, including camping, national parks, and driving routes. Also a student offic
that can help with youth accommodations, a tourist book shop, and computers for searchin
their website. Open M-Sa 10am-7pm, Su 10am-2pm.

LOCAL MEDIA
TELEVISION

Sadly, for English-language viewing, the small screen is not your best option. Mos
Spanish television consists of poorly dubbed American programming—*The Sim
psons* are all the rage—and some original Spanish fare including a hefty dose of *tele
novelas* (soap operas). Check the *Guía del Ocio* for weekly listings and T
highlights. Daily newspapers (see below) also carry the goods.

TVE1: Features dubbed American series and a good selection of late-night movies.

TVE2: News and some documentaries along with made-for-TV movies, Spanish style.

TV3 and Canal 33: All Catalan programming, all the time.

Tele 5: Dubbed American programming from *Club Disney* to *The Simpsons* to *Melrose Place*
Don't miss the Spanish version of *Who Wants to be a Millionaire?* minus Regis; it's *¿Quiere
Ser Millonario?*.

Antena 3: Regional news, and dubbed and original series. Heavy on family programming.

BTV: City station with local news and some off-beat programming.

Canal Plus: A special paid channel, much like the US's HBO, with special television pro
grams, music specials, and movies. Programming is almost entirely in Spanish.

RADIO

When you turn on the radio in Barcelona, expect to hear lots of Catalan—nearly all
the DJs prefer to speak in the mother tongue rather than Castilian. Many also have
the irritating habit of jabbering over at least half of the song being played. Categoriz
ing stations is a challenge, since most change genre according to the time of day.

95.5 The dependable "Radio Club 25" can always be counted on not to stray too far from
top-40 pop. The station where you'll hear the song of the moment at least hourly.

96.6 Independent radio, can shift from house to jazz to metal in a matter of moments.

100.8 Dance, you fool, dance! Con el ritmo latino.

101.5 Catalunya Música, soothing classical and opera sounds.

102.0 Catalunya Radio, all the latest news—in Catalan, but they'll throw some Spanish in there, too.

105.0 Soft rock, except for when it's rocking out with dance pop.

105.7 The most popular choice of the young set—all house music, all the time. Afternoon dance party, anyone?

106.6 Oldies ranging from the 50s to the 80s, depending on their mood.

NEWSPAPERS & MAGAZINES

Barceloneans read more than their fellow Spaniards, but the newspapers they choose to buy vary widely by postal code. Two Catalunya-published papers dominate shelf space in the bourgeois l'Eixample: **El Periódico,** a left-leaning publication available in Catalan and Spanish, and **La VanGuardia,** a more conservative paper published in Spanish. For the more radical Catalanists, there's the **Abui,** a nationalist paper produced in Catalan only, and for the far left there's **El País,** based in Madrid but popular among Barcelona's immigrant and working class population. Also from Madrid are the arch-conservative **ABC** and the more mildly rightist **La Razón.** Not surprisingly, none of the Madrid papers make it into Catalunya without a special section dedicated to affairs of the fair northeastern province.

Of course, Spain would not be Spain (and Barcelona has to count itself in here) without a thriving *prensa rosa,* or tabloid press. By far the most popular magazines are **Hola!,** a sensationalist gossip magazine splashed with up-close pictures and details on the lives of the rich and famous, and **Lecturas,** an equally sensationalist but less picture-heavy review that's ever-so-slightly more in touch with the non-jetset crowd. For movie buffs there's **Fotogramas,** and for science, ecology, and technology nerds, **Muy Interesante** keeps up to date on all of the latest breakthroughs. **Quo,** meanwhile, has a better-rounded selection of writing on health, nature, news, and more.

For **English-speaking** expats, the English monthly **Barcelona Metropolitan** is full of personal experience stories, advice, and news about the city, while the **Broadsheet** covers Spain as a whole with more long feature articles on history, culture, and news. For all of you burgeoning young Hemingways, the semi-literature magazine **Outsider** just might give you a chance to be featured in print.

And of course, last but far from least, there's the indispensable **Guía del Ocio,** Barcelona's comprehensive guide to how to have fun every single weekend; it includes restaurant, nightlife and theater listings, as well as info on the week's cultural events and performances. The guide is in Spanish , but listings are easy enough to understand even for the non-speaker (what about *Harry Potter* 9pm isn't clear?). Directions to venues are often lacking, but may be available in the **Entertainment** chapter (see p. 165) of this guide. Do not miss your copy, available at the kiosk nearest you.

Life & Times

The city of Barcelona lies within the country of Spain, but to equate Barcelona with Spain is not entirely accurate. Barcelona is shaped by politics and events that influence all of Spain, and so the history of the city often converges with the history of the modern nation. Spain, however, is a recent creation, and a combination of many formerly independent cultures and nations. Consequently, when Barcelona expresses patriotism, it is often to an alternate homeland: **Catalunya** (Catalonia or *Cataluña* in Spanish).

Barceloneses have long been the privileged class of Spain. During the Middle Ages, the city was the commercial center of a vast Mediterranean empire. Barcelona suffered financial decline in the 15th century as both the "discovery" of America and Sevilla's trade monopoly shifted commercial routes away from the Mediterranean. The Industrial Revolution's textile mills, however, propelled a turn-of-the-century economic boom, and the aristocracy grew in status and power. As the twentieth century approached, Josep Batlló, Antoni Amatller, and their compatriots commissioned architects like Domènech i Montaner, Puig i Cadafalch, and the legendary Antoni Gaudí to build private residences in l'Eixample, a spacious, gridded "upper" Barcelona district, higher in elevation and status than the tangled, lower-class Barri Gòtic. The result of these architectural pursuits was Modernisme, an artistic movement drawing its inspiration from nature. Even the suffocating years of Franco's Fascist regime could not dampen Barcelona's stature as the world's premier showcase of avant-garde architecture. Today, brilliantly daring buildings and parks stud the cityscape, battling for attention; only the people themselves, with their trend-setting fashion sense and dynamic lifestyle, offer any real competition.

Today Catalunya is a region in Spain; in medieval times it was its own nation, and Barcelona was its capital. Catalunya has its own distinct history and language, and as a result, modern Barcelona has a strong sense of identity, a distinctive political sensibility, a living language, a novel approach to art, and a healthy secession movement. To appreciate the

WILLY THE WOOLY

Guifré el Pilós, a.k.a. Wilfred the Hairy, is one of the most beloved figures of Catalan history, in spite of (because of?) his massive quantities of hair. According to legend, he was sent away as a young boy of two, and when he returned home sixteen years later, his mother was able to recognize him instantly because he had hair on parts of his body where it's just plain wrong to have hair. After being installed as count of the region by his convenient counterpart **Charles the Bald** in 874, Guifré wreaked hirsute havoc as he unified the region and expanded his territory.

Legend also attributes the origin of the Catalan flag to Guifré. According to tradition, the four red stripes on the gold background are the mark of Louis the Pious, a Frankish favorite, who dipped his four fingers in Guifré's blood and dragged them down Guifré's gold shield. Since the men were not contemporaries, the story has no historical basis.

diversity of Spain, one has to visit Barcelona; to appreciate Barcelona, one has to consider it separately from Spain.

HISTORY

ANCIENTY HISTORY

A smattering of archaeological evidence indicates a stable Bronze age population in Catalunya and Barcelona, known by the name **Laietani;** the modern Via Laietana, the street which divides the Barri Gòtic from La Ribera, is named for them. The Laietani were an agricultural society that inhabited Montjuïc and collected oysters. While it is certain that they predate the Romans, archaeologists have yet to discover anything particularly tantalizing about these oyster-loving folk.

ROMAN TIMES

In an effort to subdue the North African powers in Carthage, the Romans ripped through Spain with a vengeance in the third century BC. They subjugated the resident Laietani and settled next to Montjuïc in 210 BC. In honor of Augustine's rule in 15 BC, the Romans gave the small town the unwieldy name of Colonia Julia Augusta Faventia Paterna Barcino. **Barcino**—Roman Barcelona—lies mostly underneath the modern day Barri Gòtic, although Roman walls and columns occasionally poke above the ground.

Modern Barcelona is a swinging metropolis, but Barcino, like her oyster-crazed neighbors, was anything but interesting. She served as an unimportant provincial town, dwarfed in importance by her southern neighbor, **Tarragona,** the Roman provincial capital, now home to better beaches and ruins (see p. 219).

In close to seven centuries, the Romans drastically altered the face and character of Spain, introducing Rome's language, architecture, roads, orgies, irrigation techniques, grapes, olives, and wheat. Constantine declared **Christianity** the official religion of the region in AD 312. As in the rest of the Roman Empire, Roman power in Catalunya declined after Constantine's rule.

VANDALS, VISIGOTHS, MOORS, & FRANKS

A slew of Germanic tribes, including Swabians and Vandals, swept over Iberia in the early fifth century, but the **Visigoths,** under newly converted Christian Ataülf, emerged above the rest. The Visigoths established their court at Barcelona in 415 and laid the foundations of the Catalan feudal society of later centuries. The

Visigoths effectively ruled Spain for the next 300 years, although more as a collection of politically disorganized and rather fragmented tribes than as a unified whole.

The Visigoths' disorganization paved the way for the next wave of invaders, this time from the south. Following Muslim unification and their victory tour through the Middle East and North Africa, a small force of Arabs, Berbers, and Syrians invaded Spain in 711. Practically welcomed by the divided Visigoths, the **Moors** encountered little resistance, and the peninsula soon fell under the control of the caliphate of Damascus.

While the Moors had a ruling presence in some parts of Spain for as long as 750 years, their presence in Catalunya was short lived. Christian resistance was never completely crushed anywhere in Iberia, and when the Christian **Franks** entered Catalunya in the later part of the 8th century, they were warmly received. Charlemagne undermined Moorish power in the late 700s, and his son, Louis the Pious, defeated the Moors in Catalunya in 801. The government Louis the Pious left behind dominated the Catalan Middle Ages.

Because the Franks swept into the Iberian peninsula so quickly, the Moorish influence in Barcelona is nonexistent, compared to other regions of Spain. The relative brevity of the Moorish presence in this part of Iberia is one aspect of Catalan history that distinguishes Catalunya from the rest of Iberia. While most of Spain spent centuries under Islamic rule, the Franks reinstated Christian power so promptly that Catalunya enjoyed almost continuous Christian rule since Constantine.

Barri Gòtic

THE MIDDLE & GOLDEN AGES

The common Christianity of the Frankish counts and the Catalans they ruled made the Catalan Middle Ages a relatively cooperative time, with a couple of notable characters. The popular favorite is **Guifré el Pilós,** or Wilfred the Hairy (d. 898); according to legend, he was born hairy as a mountain troll, with hair on the soles of his feet (see p. 38). The Frankish king, **Charles the Bald** (oh, the irony), installed Wilfred the Hairy as count of the region in 874. Guifré spent his life defending his monarch, endowing religious institutions, moving power and importance from Tarragona to Barcelona, unifying various parts of Catalunya, and growing more hair every day. His house held power in Catalunya until 1410.

The Moorish return to Barcelona in 985 marked the beginning of Catalan independence. Guifré's descendant **Count Borrell,** a man with unknown quantities of bodily hair, asked the Frankish king for aid in the form of military

Outdoor Mass

Restoration Work

Barcelona's Center of Government

Columbus Comes Down From His Tower

Pl. Reial

defense from Moorish invasion. When the king ignored this request, Barcelona ceased to acknowledge his sovereignty. Catalunya became independent of Frankish control, and after defeating the Moors on their own, Catalunya was totally independent.

Barcelona grew wealthy at the start of the new millennium under the successive power of four counts by the same name of **Ramon Berenguer,** all of whom expanded the geographical boundaries of Catalunya. Ramon Berenguer III married Princess Dolça of Provence and so extended Catalan power into modern-day France. **Ramon Berenguer IV** is of particular historical relevance because of his 1137 marriage to the distastefully underage **Petronella of Aragón,** the daughter of the king of Aragón (a neighboring province). As the toddler bride enjoyed her terrible twos, Catalunya grew even more powerful through solidarity with Aragón. In the long term, the union of these two regions doomed Catalunya to Madrid's dominance, but in the short term, this cooperation with Aragón meant that Catalunya could comfortably look toward the Mediterranean and focus on more commercial affairs.

Catalunya's most lucrative exports at this time were iron and wool. As **Jaume I** (1213-76) expanded the waterfront under Catalan control by conquering Valencia and the Balearic Islands, Barcelona surfed the maritime wave of commercial success into the Catalan **Golden Age** of painting and literature that accompanied such prosperity. Oceanfront expansion aside, Jaume I also gave the city the government infrastructures of **Les Corts** and the **Generalitat**—the modern regional government—and finally renounced Catalan power over the Pyrenees in France.

The fourteenth century saw the success of Catalunya's brief-yet-glorious designs at an empire. With so much seafront property under their control, Barcelona was one of the wealthiest ports in the Mediterranean; it was also very desirable to the rest of Spain. A series of events left Barcelona open to a takeover. As in the rest of Europe, the **Black Death** killed a substantial portion of the population in the 1340s, leaving the city noticeably weakened. When the last of Guifré's ruling descendants, Martí I, died childless in 1410, power in Catalunya was again up for grabs.

THE DECADÈNCIA

The Decadència is a misnomer that refers to the period of time when Catalunya's history began to unite with Spain's. During this time, Catalunya's development was subject to a centralized, non-Catalan authority, all because of a very consequential wedding between Fernando and Isabel (see below). It is unclear to us here at Let's Go precisely why this period has this name, as it was not a period of decadence, but of oppression.

CATHOLIC MONARCHS

In 1469, the marriage of **Los Reyes Católicos** (the Catholic Monarchs), **Fernando de Aragón** and **Isabel de Castilla,** joined Iberia's two mightiest Christian kingdoms, Castilla and Aragón. Since Aragón was already loosely united with Catalunya, Fernando inherited Catalunya in 1479. By 1492, the dynamic duo had captured Granada (the last Moorish stronghold) and shuttled off **Columbus** to explore the New World. The Catholic Monarchs introduced the **Inquisition** in 1478, executing and then burning heretics, principally Jews (even those who had converted earlier). The Inquisition had two aims: to strengthen the authority of the Church and to unify Spain; since Barcelona and other cities in Catalunya had a continuous Jewish population, the Inquisition hit Catalunya with the same destructive force as it did the rest of Spain.

On the Steps to Palau d'Art Catalana

Barcelona now took orders from the court at Segovia, in the distant region of Castilla y Leon. With the world's attention on the New World, the Mediterranean was no longer a fashionable place for trade, and Catalunya was officially banned from trade in the New World by the Catholic Monarchs. In approximately 50 years of rule, the Catholic Monarchs heightened Spain's position as a world economic, political, and cultural power (made all the more enduring by lucrative conquests in the Americas). Prosperity for a newly united Spain did not mean prosperity for Catalunya, which lost its autonomy and faced a crippling economic recession.

THE HABSBURG DYNASTY

The daughter of Fernando and Isabel, **Juana la Loca** (the Mad), married **Felipe el Hermoso** (the Fair) of the powerful Hapsburg dynasty. Mr. Handsome (who died playing *cesta punta*, or "jai alai," best described as a fun-yet-apparently-lethal combination of lacrosse and racquetball) and Mrs. Crazy (who refused to believe that he had died and dragged his corpse through the streets) produced **Carlos I** (1516-1556), who reigned as the last Roman Emperor over an immense empire comprising modern-day Holland, Belgium, Austria, Spain, parts of Germany and Italy, and the massive American colonies. Spain was arguably the most powerful empire in the world under the Habsburgs, even as subsequent Habsburg monarchs began to lose some of their territory; this period of virtual world domination led to Spain's own **Golden Age** of painting and literature.

Graffiti

However, as most of Spain enjoyed the Golden Age, Catalunya found herself more and more marginalized, economically and culturally. While central Spain mass produced revolutionary painters like Velázquez and El Greco, the main product of Catalunya at this time was rebellion.

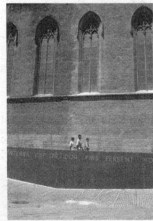
El Fossar de les Moreres

Barcelona had lost her importance as a trade city, and Catalunya was inconveniently in the midst of numerous battles between the French and Spanish, beginning in 1635. The result of these constraints was the **Guerra dels Segadors** (Reapers' War) in 1640.

The Guerra dels Segadors—a title which later became the Catalan national anthem—was a Catalan attempt at independence originating from within the oppressed masses. The 12 years of war began with civil disobedience, not a plan; disgruntled Catalan workers happened across a Spanish viceroy and worked out their tensions on him until there were only pieces left. In the confusion following this trouble, Catalunya used the tense Franco-Iberian relations to her advantage by siding with France, hoping that France would support the Catalan cry for independence. France did: **Louis XIII** of France even went so far as to send troops into Barcelona to help the Catalans defend themselves. However, the war was administrated badly on the Catalan side, and the French eventually betrayed Catalunya and created an alliance with Spain. When the war ended in 1652, these two nations divided the spoils. A treaty returned Catalunya to Habsburg control, with the exception of the northeastern corner, which was ceded to France.

WAR OF SPANISH SUCCESSION

The War of Spanish Succession, a.k.a. the Next Big Disaster, came about when Habsburg king **Carlos II** died before producing an heir. Europe was generally very excited at Carlos' oversight, as it presented the opportunity for some lucky European nation X to install an X-friendly ruler on the Spanish throne. There were two main candidates for the position of Spanish monarch: the Austrian **Archduke Carlos**, and **Felipe V**, a Bourbon from France and grandson of Louis XIV. Catalunya had a vested interest in this succession that was distinct from the interests of the rest of Spain. Still bitter with France about their betrayal in the Guerra dels Segadors, Catalunya backed the Austrian candidate. While Spain and France supported the French contender, in 1713, it was clear Catalunya had made the wrong choice. The **Treaty of Utrecht** made Felipe V the new monarch; his rule started a legacy of Catalan oppression that would continue through Franco.

GROWING PAINS

BOURBON ON THE ROCKS

Felipe V (1713-1746) built showy palaces and cultivated a flamboyant, debauched court. If his own life was undisciplined, his leadership was not. He came down with an iron fist on Catalunya, punishing the region for her ill-fated political preferences. Felipe had a flare for attacking Catalunya where it would hurt the most: under Felipe, the Catalan language was attacked and restricted. In the school room and in the press, Catalan was now illegal. Felipe also built the infamous **Ciutadella** (citadel), now a park, in 1718 (see p. 70); this oppressive new addition to the city boundaries left a visible military presence, a reminder to Barcelona not to cross Felipe again.

The Bourbons who followed Felipe ably administered the Empire and lightened the restrictions on Catalunya. They constructed scores of new canals and roads, organized settlements, and instituted agricultural reform and industrial expansion, all of which benefited Barcelona's natural inclination to trade. **Carlos III** (1759-1788) lifted the ban on Catalan trade with the Americas in 1778, and this final development in the commercial sphere led Barcelona to another economic boom.

These good times didn't last. **Napoleon** rained on Catalunya's parade when he invaded Spain in 1808 as part of his world domination kick, which kicked Catalan economic growth to the ground and then kicked it some more. This incident is one of the rare times that Catalunya showed total solidarity with Spain, cooperating with Madrid in an effort to push out the French. The cooperation worked: the French were expelled in 1814, at which point industry and trade started up again. However, at this point, under **Fernando VII** (1814-1833), Spain started to lose control of her empire. Galvanized by Fernando's ineptitude and inspired by liberal ideas in the brand-spanking new Spanish **constitution,** most of Spain's Latin American empire soon attained independence. Domestically, parliamentary liberalism was restored in 1833 upon Fernando VII's death and survived the conservative challenge of the **Carl-**

ist Wars (1833-1840); it would dominate Spanish politics until **Primo de Rivera's** comparatively mild and brief dictatorship in the 1920s.

EXPANSION, THE RENAIXENÇA, & ANARCHY

Rapid industrialization and prosperity marked 19th-century Spain. A messy yet productive series of riots, demonstrations, and revolts made steady progress in the deplorable living circumstances of the working classes, even as a bourgeois class grew. As walled Barcelona grew too fast, too much, and way too unsanitary for the two classes to live so close together, the **old walls** were finally torn down in 1854; this monumental bit of urban planning led to the expansion of Barcelona, in the form of **l'Eixample** (the Enlargement).

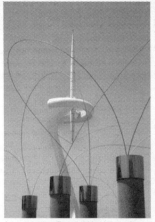
Communications Tower on Montjuïc

When the news broke that Barcelona was to be expanded, several strapping young lads offered plans for this neighborhood to the government administration; **Antoni Rovira i Trias** won Barcelona's municipal support for his plan, which maintained the original city's position as central to the new city. However, authorities in Madrid did not much care to hear the opinions of the citizens that would be affected by the expansion of Barcelona, and in 1860—after considerable intrigue and scandal—the powers that were chose another plan for l'Eixample. The chosen plan was designed by one **Idlefons Cerdà i Sunyer,** whose vision for l'Eixample is only nominally realized in the grid of wide avenues that currently dominates Barcelona. Critics often note that Cerdà's plan, while not the popular choice, has a certain potential for crowd control that was lacking in Rovira's. For more on the planning of l'Eixample see p. 75.

The late nineteenth and early twentieth centuries yielded Catalunya's industrial-inspired **Renaixença** (Renaissance), one of the most creative artistic periods of Catalan and Spanish history. The gridded blocks of l'Eixample were slowly filled in with bourgeois and buildings from Barcelona's **Modernisme** movement in architecture and design (see p. 51); artists like Picasso and Ramon Casas swapped techniques at the swanky underground café Els Quatre Gats. The Renaixença also saw the rise of Catalan nationalism: the Catalan language was standardized and reaffirmed, and literature in Catalan boomed.

The Joy of a Chihuahua

The liberal mayor **Francesc de Paula Rius i Taulet** was a defining force in Barcelona at this time, fundamental to her economic, cultural, and physical growth. In 1888, Rius i Taulet hosted the **Universal Exposition** in Barcelona, an event which introduced Catalan Modernisme to the world and transformed the face of the city. In a master stroke of symbolism, Rius i Taulet held

Chucky Says Drink Cava

the exposition in a formerly hated location: the site of Felipe V's oppressive Ciutadella, now transformed into a park. The event was an excuse to revamp and develop
the city, as well as an opportunity to showcase Barcelona's artistic developments to
the world. Despite the debt it left on the city, the Universal Exposition was an important moment for the rejuvenation Barcelona, as the Olympics would be years later.

The last half of the 19th century also saw the rise of **anarchy** in Barcelona, mostly
popular among the overworked working class. In the 1890s, a series of bombings
announced Barcelona's unlikely status as anarchy world headquarters. The most
notable of these disasters was the 1891 bombing of the Liceu opera house (now
restored, see p. 64), designed to attack the wealthy and make a statement against
centralized authority.

True anarchy hit the city in 1909 with the **Setmana Trágica (Tragic Week).** Protests
against an unpopular imperialist war with Morocco drew support from Socialists
and Anarchists; as the central government tried to stamp out the protests, they only
drew more popular support. Protests turned into organized strikes, which in turn
morphed into unorganized revolts, mob riots, and violence. The week ended in the
destruction of almost one hundred buildings, most of them religious, and over one
hundred dead citizens.

DICTATORSHIPS & DRAMA

THE FIRST DICTATOR & THE SECOND REPUBLIC

Spain was deeply affected by **World War I,** although she did not participate. Europe's
wartime economy brought waves of rural Catalans and impoverished Andalucian
southerners to Barcelona. The influx of people looking for work rocked labor standards, invited chaos, and led Barcelona's Castillian Captain General **Miguel Primo de
Rivera** to shut down Parliament and ascend to dictatorship in 1923, with the permission of **King Alfonso XIII** (1902-1931).

Primo de Rivera's years in power are often quickly passed over in history books
because they pale in comparison to the dictatorship that would follow; however, the
dictatorship was no treat for Catalunya. Once again, Catalunya's language and culture were repressed, although this dictatorship was not as stifling as Franco's. In
1929, Primo de Rivera put on Barcelona's **International Exhibition** in an attempt to
demonstrate that Barcelona was still blossom, although the resulting tourist-trap
monstrosity **Poble Espanyol** may or may not have achieved this goal (see p. 91).

In the 1920s, Spain had both a dictator and a monarch; by 1931, it had neither.
Primo de Rivera retired at the turn of the decade, and King Alfonso XIII, disgraced
by his support for Primo de Rivera's dictatorship, fled Spain in April of 1931. His
flight gave rise to the **Second Republic** (1931-1936), beloved by liberals and intellectuals everywhere. During this short time, Republican liberals and Socialists established safeguards for farmers and industrial workers, granted women's suffrage,
assured religious tolerance, and chipped away at traditional military dominance.

National euphoria faded fast. The 1933 elections split the Republican-Socialist
coalition, in the process increasing the power of right wing and Catholic parties. Military dissatisfaction led to a heightened profile of the Fascist **Falange** (founded by
Primo de Rivera's son José), which further polarized national politics. By 1936, radi-
cals, anarchists, Socialists, and Republicans had formed a loose, federated alliance
to win the next elections; since the republic was weak, victory was short-lived. Once
Generalísimo Francisco Franco snatched control of the Spanish army, militarist upris-
ings ensued, and the nation plunged into war.

THE CIVIL WAR

The three-year **Civil War** (1936-1939) ignited worldwide ideological passions; the
causes and effects of the Civil War touch every aspect of 20th century Spain. Germany and Italy dropped troops, supplies, and munitions into Franco's lap, while the
stubbornly isolationist US and the liberal European states were slow to aid the
Republicans. Although Franco and the Nationalists enjoyed popular support in
Andalucia, Galicia, Navarra, and parts of Castilla, the Republicans controlled population and industrial centers. Barcelona was actually the Republican capital from

1937 until Franco finally won the Civil War in 1939. The Soviet Union, somewhat indirectly, called for a **Popular Front** of Communists, Socialists, and other leftist sympathizers to battle Franco's Fascism. But soon after, the West abandoned the coalition, and aid from the Soviet Union waned as Stalin began to see the benefits of an alliance with Hitler. Without international aid, Republican forces found themselves cut off from supplies and food, and began to surrender to the Nationalists. All told, bombings, executions, combat, starvation, and disease took nearly 600,000 lives nationwide, and in 1939 Franco's forces marched into Madrid and ended the war.

FRANCO

By the time the Civil War ended, **World War II** was already in full swing; with so many dead and such extensive poverty in the wake of their own war, it was impossible for Spain to participate. Franco is generally regarded as a Bad Guy by the outside world and Catalunya, but he did make one positive contribution to World War II, helping Jews out of France as the situation there declined.

Brain-drain (as leading intellectuals emigrated or were assassinated), worker dissatisfaction, student unrest, regional discontent, and international isolation characterized the first decades of Franco's dictatorship. Barcelona lost virtually all of her innovative painters, artists, and writers to intimidation and exile (with the exception of Dalí, who suddenly became very controversial without producing any art of consequence). With intellectual and artistic growth thus stunted, Franco moved on to old-fashioned oppression: the Catalan language was again outlawed and dubbed an inferior dialect. Although Barcelona was, as usual, one of the wealthiest places in Spain, money was constantly drained out of Catalunya and redistributed where Franco saw fit; as a result, Barcelona was a constant source of protest. In 1960, **Jordi Pujol,** the future leader of Catalunya, even went so far as to sing the decidedly illegal Catalan national anthem in front of Franco at a concert on one of the dictator's visits. He spent three years in jail for his alternative patriotism, but was still able to help out his homeland during the Franco years when he founded a Catalan bank in 1959.

In his old age, Franco tried to smooth international relations by joining NATO and encouraging tourism, but the "national tragedy" (as the war and dictatorship were later called) did not officially end until Franco's death in 1975. Shortly before his own death, Franco reinstated **King Juan Carlos I** (1975-), grandson of Alfonso XIII. Juan Carlos I carefully set out to undo Franco's damage; he is idolized in all of Spain for reinstituting democracy when he could have conceivably continued the cycle of political oppression. In 1978, under premier **Adolfo Suárez,** Spain adopted a new constitution in a national referendum that led to the restoration of parliamentary government, which assured a comfortable degree of regional autonomy for Catalunya.

(POST)MODERNITY

TRANSITION TO DEMOCRACY

The post-Franco years have been marked by progressive social change. Divorce was legalized; women regained suffrage and educational opportunities. After being imprisoned for sauciness by the Generalísimo, **Jordi Pujol** became president of the Catalan Generalitat, the regional government, in 1980, and continues to lead the region today. Catalunya still has a secession movement, but it is not violent. The region is generally comfortable with the degree of autonomy it has, which celebrates the Catalan language in public schools and allows Catalan control over all major Catalan resources.

Charismatic **Felipe González** led the PSOE (Spanish Socialist Worker's Party) to victory in the 1982 elections. In 1986, González opened the Spanish economy and championed consensus policies, overseeing Spain's integration into what was then the European Community (EC) and is now known by the dramatically different title of **European Union (EU).** Despite unpopular economic stands, González was reelected in 1986 and continued a program of massive public investment. The years 1986 to 1990 were outstanding for Spain's economy; by the end of 1993, recession set in. In 1993, González and the PSOE only barely maintained a majority in Parliament over the increasingly popular conservative **Partido Popular (PP). José Maria Aznar** led the PP

HUH?

into power after González's support eroded and has maintained a delicately balanced coalition with the support of the Catalan regional party.

THE OLYMPICS

From 1982 to 1997, the industrious Socialist **Pasqual Maragall** was the mayor of Barcelona; through his efforts, the **1992 Summer Olympics** were held in Barcelona. Maragall used the pressure of the international spotlight as an opportunity to completely revamp the city. New athletic arenas and apartment complexes were built; the beaches were cleaned up, and the waterfront was remodeled into party central; the prostitutes were (very temporarily) shuffled into less visible neighborhoods of the city and were generally disgruntled. The **Poble Nou** neighborhood (see p. 21) and **Montjuïc** (see p. 22) were visibly transformed in this process. Cleaned up and built up, Barcelona greeted the athletes, hospitably hosted the games, and remains cleaner and spiffier for the experience.

CURRENT EVENTS

The last decade has seen mixed progress in one of Spain's most pressing areas of concern—Basque nationalism and terrorism, carried out by the Basque separatist group, **ETA.** This issue concerns the whole country; while Basque hostility is not traditionally directed at Catalunya, there has been increasing hostility toward Catalunya and the east coast in recent times. Basque violence generally occurs in the form of assassinations of political figures and terrorist bombings. Between September and December 2000, two politicians and one police officer were shot within Barcelona's city limits; two bomb attacks during the same months injured others. More recently, in March 2001, there was an attack in Catalunya, in Rosas, north of Barcelona, which killed a police officer; in that same month, a car bomb was successfully diffused in Valencia.

On a brighter national note, the Spanish economy is currently in good and improving shape, and Barcelona is one of the wealthiest cities in Spain. Aznar describes visions of "a new Spain" and plans to reduce unemployment even further, draw more women into the workforce, and improve the faltering birthrate by restructuring family and work arrangements.

Despite some odd scenarios during election times, Catalan regional politics is also in good shape. In a sticky race that mimics the American Bush/Gore presidential fiasco, former mayor Joan Maragall ran against Catalan hero Jordi Pujol for control of the regional government, the **Generalitat;** the immense popularity of both men made the race a close one, but in the end, Pujol remains in power. Maragall has vacated the mayor's office, the **Ajuntament;** the current mayor of Barcelona is the Socialist **Joan Clos**, who does justice to Maragall's legacy by continuing to look ahead to improve the city.

LANGUAGE

Catalunya, like many other regions of Spain, is bilingual. **Castellano** *(*Castillian or *Castellà* in Catalan*)*, a.k.a. **Spanish,** spoken by almost everyone with varying degrees of ease, is Spain's official language. **Català (Catalan)** is spoken in all of Catalunya and has given rise through permutations to *Valencià*, the language of Valencia in the east, *Mallorquín* of Mallorca, *Menorquín* of Menorca, and *Evissinc* of Ibiza.

Despite politically fueled rumors to the contrary, Catalan is not a dialect of Spanish or a combination of French and Spanish, but a full-fledged Romance language. Catalans will rightfully get insulted if a tourist—or a Spaniard—casually refers to their language as a dialect. Catalan and Castillian both have standardized grammars and rich literary traditions, both oral and written. Regional television broadcasts, strong political associations, the use of Catalan as vernacular and in church, and extensive schooling have saved Catalan from extinction.

Street Performers Taking a Break

City and provincial names in this book are usually listed in Catalan, followed by the English in parentheses, and Castillian where appropriate. Since towns in Catalunya are almost exclusively referred to by their Catalan names, we have written them as such. Information within cities (i.e. street or plaza names) are also listed in Catalan. Generally, when traveling throughout Spain, Castillian names are understood; however, it is wise to exercise politeness and respect towards Catalan; particularly in restaurants, the use of Catalan may get you better service. For more on the many layers of language in Catalunya, see p. 46.

Paintings for Sale in Pl. Pi

ART & ARCHITECTURE

PAINTING & SCULPTURE

Over its long history, Catalan painting has seen a series of luminaries separated by several lulls. Flemish, French, and Italian techniques influenced the Middle Ages and the Renaissance; in recent history, the Surrealists have forged a dazzling, distinctive, and hugely influential body of work.

EARLY, GOTHIC, & RENAISSANCE

As Catalunya's economy was separate from Spain's for so many centuries, the **Spanish Golden Age** and the **Catalan Golden Age** occurred at two

Tàpies Foundation

GET sm**art**

I Dream of Dalí

As an adult, Dalí always appeared to be confident in his talents, but he was not always so confident in every aspect of his life. From an early age, Salvador Dalí was plagued by nightmares and insecurities. Sexually inexperienced until a late age, Dalí was sexually ambiguous and had a fear of sexual contact and impotence.

The defining moment in Dalí's artistic and personal development came when he moved to Madrid in the 1920s. Dalí arrived a terrified, inexperienced boy who could not cross the street on his own; the friendships he made in Madrid—with such artistic giants as Federico García Lorca, Pablo Neruda, and Luís Buñuel—dragged him out of his shell.

Even as he grew into the extroverted spectacle the world came to know, Dalí's fears were one of the two central subjects of his work; the other was landscapes—themes which he often combined. Dalí, influenced by Sigmund Freud, created his own brand of Surrealism. With it, he sought to connect the unconscious with the conscious by exploring the dreams of the unconscious in his paintings of the conscious, waking world.

different times. The 16th century produced such giants as El Greco and Velázquez in central Spain, but the most productive time for Catalan painting came much earlier, when Catalunya was independent. In the 11th and 12th centuries through the Renaissance (not to be confused with the 19th century Catalan Renaixença, see p. 43), the most significant paintings were frescoes that decorated churches and their libraries. Fourteenth century **Ferrer Bassa** is the most renowned painter of this sort; his frescoes can be seen in the Monestir de Pedralbes (see p. 98). The works of some of the most famous painters from this period, such as 15th century **Jaume Huguet** and Flemish-influenced **Bartolomé Bermejo,** are on display in the MNAC (see p. 118); Huguet also has an important work in the Museu d'Història de Catalunya (see p. 105).

BIRTH OF MODERNISM

Catalan painting experienced a lull under the Habsburgs until the 1800s, when Impressionist-inspired **Marià Fortuny** started to gain recognition; his paintings can be seen in the Museu d'Art Modern (see p. 110). His appearance reenergized art in Catalunya and began a long line of talented painters that would emerge in the nineteenth and twentieth centuries. This renewed interest in art spawned several distinct movements.

MODERNISME

Although Catalan Modernist painting, which mostly just followed the latest trends in Paris, is not as internationally recognized as Catalan Modernist architecture (see p. 51), it still produced some memorable characters and admirable works. One such fellow is **Ramon Casas** (1866-1932), a patron of the ever-famous **Els Quatre Gats** café (see p. 128), illustrator of the popular literary magazine **Pel i Plom,** owner of the first car in Barcelona, hot commodity in the advertising industry, and painter extraordinaire. His contemporary, **Santiago Rusinyol** (1861-1931), was another significant chap on the Modernist scene; despite his addiction to morphine and his literary aspirations, his novel use of color in his representations of nature produced a number of memorable works. Both artists are represented in the Museu d'Art Modern (see p. 110).

SURREALISM

Surrealism explores the experience of the subconscious through various approaches: the world of childhood, the world of dreams, the world of madness. While this movement was started in France by **André Breton** with his avant-garde literary homage to a madwoman, *Nadja,* Catalunya produced three of the most innovative painters and sculptors of this movement. Painter and sculptor **Joan Miró** (1893-1983) approached the subconscious from the perspective of childhood (see p. 116). His cryptic and symbolic squiggles became a statement against the authoritarian society of the post-Civil War years; indeed, his works are so closely tied to the events of the 20th century in Spain that one can date his works simply by observing the colors and images Miró uses. By contrast, fellow Catalan **Salvador Dalí** (1904-1989) scandalized high society and leftist intellectuals in France and Spain by reportedly supporting the Fascists; in reality, Dalí knew nothing about politics and he probably only encouraged such rumors to keep the spotlight on himself. The wildly mustached painter tapped into dreams and the unconscious for odd images like soft faces, bureau-women, and rotting donkeys, as well as repetitive images like melting clocks, his wife Gala, and praying peasants. A self-congratulatory fellow, Dalí founded the Teatro-Museu Dalí in Figueres, the second-most visited museum in Spain after the Prado (see p. 190). **Picasso** also dabbled in Surrealism with a degree of skill, but his main contribution to the artistic world came in quite another form.

CUBISM

It is hard to imagine an artist who has had as profound an effect upon 20th-century painting as Andalucian-born **Pablo Ruíz Picasso** (1881-1973). A child prodigy, Picasso headed for Barcelona, hothouse for Modernist architecture and political activism. Bouncing back and forth between Barcelona and Paris, Picasso in 1900 inaugurated his Blue Period, characterized by somber depictions of society's outcasts. His permanent move to Paris in 1904 initiated his Rose Period, during which he probed into the curiously engrossing lives of clowns and acrobats. This thematic and stylistic evolution led Picasso to his own revolutionary style.

With his French colleague Georges Braque, Picasso founded Cubism, a method of painting objects simultaneously from multiple perspectives. Cubism evolved slowly, but the first Cubist painting is commonly recognized as **Les Demoiselles d'Avignon (the Ladies of Avignon**) in 1907. Most well-known of cubist works is his gigantic 1937 mural *Guernica*, portraying the bombing of that Basque city by Nazi planes in cahoots with Fascist forces during the Spanish Civil War. A vehement protest against violence and fascism, *Guernica* now resides in the Centro de Arte Reina Sofía in Madrid. Barcelona's Museu Picasso has a commendable chronological spread of Picasso's work, from his earliest paintings to his Cubist engravings (see p. 109).

ABSTRACT

Since Franco's death in 1975, a new generation of artists has thrived. With new museums in Madrid, Barcelona, Valencia, Sevilla, and Bilbao, Spanish painters and sculptors once again have a national forum for their work. Catalan **Antoni Tàpies** constructs definition-defying works (painting? sculptures? collages?) out of unusual and unorthodox materials most would refer to as trash. Tàpies is a founding member of the self-proclaimed "Abstract Generation," which sponsored the magazine **Dau al Set.** Tàpies work is commonly interpreted as an expression of urban alienation and decay in the wake of Franco's oppression. The Fundació Tàpies showcases his postmodern angst (see p. 112).

ARCHITECTURE

Barcelona's architecture logically reflects her political and social developments. While Barcelona went through distinct architectural periods with the rest of Spain, it also had its own individualized style distinct from other regions of Iberia. This individualization peaked in Barcelona's departure from Spanish influence in the creation of the **Modernisme** movement. It is important to note that Barcelona and Catalunya lack many styles that are considered "typically" Spanish, particularly the Arab-influenced style that is so prevalent in southern Spain.

ENTER THE ROMANS: UP WITH THE ARCH

From the third century BC until the fourth century AD, Roman power was the be-all, end-all in Spain. The numerous **Roman ruins** that sprinkle the Spanish countryside

GET sm**art**

Gaudí

Revered by many as the "father of Barcelona," architect **Antoni Gaudí** was an eccentric who spent most of his life alone and far from the limelight. Born in Reus, Spain in 1852, he read incessantly as a student, soaking up the theories which would influence his work. Religion and nature were his main inspirations, and he was known to sit in front of the sea for hours at a time, proclaiming that each wave was telling him something. He never married (though it is said he did have one great love) and agreed to pose for a photograph only once.

The last 11 years of his life, he lived in a makeshift house in **La Sagrada Família's** basement, hardly interacting with anyone; in 1926, he was killed by a streetcar while leaving the church. Taken to a pauper's morgue because of his shabby clothing, he remained unidentified for weeks. Despite controversy, the city allows different architects and private benefactors to continue building Gaudí's final masterpiece.

Barcelona recently petitioned the Vatican to honor Gaudí as a saint. Besides his devout and almost supernatural buildings (**Casa Milà** was conceived as a monument of the Immaculate Conception), Gaudí's miracles include persuading unlikely converts to get funky with Catholicism, and generally reenergizing Spain's spirituality. The Pope is investigating the beatification.

testify to six centuries of colonization. While the Barcelona city borders hold a few remnants of the Romans' inhabitation (in the form of columns, walls, and sewers), the ruins just beyond the city in **Tarragona** and **Empúries** are much more extensive, including an aqueduct, an amphitheater, and a forum (see p. 219). Arguably the most important contribution of the Romans is their use of the invincible **arch** as a central element to the structure of their buildings. Just as with other Roman creations, these ruins are in surprisingly good shape. The Romans felt their empire was here to stay, and built things to last.

ROMANESQUE: BABY (AIN'T) GOT BUTTRESS

Few remnants remain of architecture under Catalunya's temporary rulers, the Visigoths, who inhabited the area from 415 AD until the eighth century. These centuries, and on to the 12th century, were when the **Romanesque** style prevailed in Iberia. The Romanesque style is characterized by extreme simplicity. The **Monestir Sant Pau del Camp** is one example of Romanesque architecture inside Barcelona that probably wouldn't stand out if there were other examples to choose from (see p. 74). North of the city in Ripoll, **Santa Maria de Ripoll** is a better example (see p. 227).

GOTHIC STYLE: ADD SOME LOW-RISE CATALAN FLAVAH

The **Spanish Gothic** style, like Gothic elsewhere in Europe, brought experimentation with pointed arches, flying buttresses, slender walls, airy spaces, and stained-glass windows. In keeping with their patriotic love of deviation, the Catalan developed their own style by employing internal wall supports rather than external buttresses. The **Catalan Gothic** movement, dominating from the 13th to the 15th century, differs in that it is not as ornate and flamboyant as the rest of the world's take on the Gothic style, but more plain and simple in decoration, in the tradition of the Romanesque style. Rather than high pointy towers, the Catalan created hexagonal towers. Instead of trying to surpass other buildings in vertical height, the Barcelona architects tested the use of horizontal planes in their surprisingly flat Gothic buildings. Using materials such as iron and stone, they created huge facades protecting beautiful gardens inside. Other Spanish riffs on the French original include centrally placed *coros* (choirs) and oversized *retablos* (brightly colored carved pieces placed above the high altar). **Santa Mar del Mar** and **Santa Maria del Pi** are two churches which exemplify this style (see p. 69). The Gothic period also inspired many of Catalunya's countryside castles.

RENAISSANCE & BAROQUE: ISN'T IT PLATERESQUE

New World riches inspired the **Plateresque** ("in the manner of a silversmith") style, a flashy extreme of Gothic that transformed wealthier parts of Spain, such as southern Andalucia. Intricate stonework and extravagant use of gold and silver splashed 15th- and 16th-century buildings. In the late 16th century, **Italian Renaissance** innovations in perspective and symmetry arrived in Spain to sober up the Plateresque style.

Opulence seized center stage once again in 17th- and 18th-century **Baroque** Spain, which came in the form of renovations to Gothic structures. The Baroque movement is responsible for the **Església de la Mercè** (see p. 70) church and the **Palau Dalmases** (see p. 121).

MODERNISME: FUNKY FRESH OR SUPER FLY?

The Modernisme movement was born out of a growing sense of Catalan pride and nationalism, establishing a symbolic and creative outlet for the province's increasing political autonomy. While Modernisme was not limited to Barcelona (known as *art nouveau* in France and *Jugendstil* in Germany, and even spread to the New World through Group of Seven in Canada), **Catalan Modernisme** has a unique flavor of its own. While the Modernisme movement included literature, visual arts, and other artistic forms, Catalan Modernisme is best known for its innovative and intriguing architecture. It exploded onto the European architecture scene at the **1888 Universal Exposition** and remained at its height through the first decade or so of the 20th century.

Modernisme rebelled against the 19th century's realism. Where realism employed such conventional techniques as straight lines, rigidity, and order in form, Modernisme instead combined Nordic Gothic architecture with natural influences and imaginative materials, shapes, and designs. While this highly daring style looked to the past to influence its new structures, a significant Arab influence is lacking on the whole, although present in the works of some individuals. While some critics have dismissed the Modernisme movement as pretentious, the popularity of Barcelona's **Ruta del Modernisme** and support from the Surrealist movement is evidence for its overwhelming intrigue (see p. 59).

Antoni Gaudí i Comet, the most famous of the Modernisme architects, constructed the two most touristed sites in Barcelona:, **La Casa Milà** (Milà House) and **La Sagrada Família** (The Sacred Family) are both by Gaudí and are prime examples of his varied style (see sidebar p. 50).

Barceloneta

Gaudí's Deathmask

Palau Güell

GETTIN' JIGGY WIT IT

Those expecting to see flowing dresses and castanets will be disappointed: Catalunya does not have a tradition of flamenco dance. Instead, Catalans hold the **sardana** dear to their heart. The *sardana* is dance done in the round where young and old, male and female dance together. The dancers perform a variety of complicated skips and jumps. The dance is dependent on the cooperation of the entire group, symbolizing the unity of the village.

Unlike the flamenco, the *sardana* is a somber dance and is taken seriously by both the dancers and the viewers; while the rest of Spain, and most foreign viewers, mock the *sardana* for its nearly comatose pace, the Catalan take pride in their traditional dance and consider it an integral part of their culture. A good place to catch the *sardana* is in front of the cathedral after mass on Sunday morning (see p. 64).

Gaudí's genius comes in his understanding of space and his personal vision of the finished project. He became interested in Gothic architecture during his youth, and the Gothic style became the foundation of his later work. Combining Gothic influences with inspiration from nature and innovative materials, Gaudí created such marvels as **Casa Batlló** and **Park Güell** (see p. 81 and p. 92). His infusion of history and nature in his structures are his defining characteristics. In particular, Gaudí's chimneys are known for their bold departure from the standard and for their intricate design. He frequently included reptiles and amphibians in his works, such as the tortoises found on the columns for the Nativity façade on La Sagrada Família, and the Park Güell's salamander fountain. Gaudí's works were so innovative that he actually work alongside the craftsmen to implement his vision. His work is typically separated into four stages, each building on the previous stage and culminating in his work on La Sagrada Família, a building he spent over forty years creating and which remains unfinished today.

While **Antoni Gaudí i Comet** is the most famous of the Modernisme architects, it is the creations of two other architects, Lluís Domènech i Montaner and Josep Puig i Cadafalch that exemplify the Modernisme style. As the director of Barcelona's School of Architecture, **Lluís Domènech i Montaner** definitely was in the position to not only influence Barcelona's architecture, but also its future architects. At the Universal Exposition of 1888 he presented his **Castell de Tres Dragones** (Castle of Three Dragons), designed as a restaurant for the Exposition. It was a huge success and marked the official beginning of the Modernisme movement. Domènech was especially innovative in his choice of building materials. He used stucco to imitate stone and also departed from the then-current disdain for the use of brick. While bricks were considered unattractive by most Spaniards and Europeans at the end of the 19th century, he was drawn to its organic quality and felt that its connection to the earth made it a legitimate and worthy building material. Like other architects of the Modernisme movement, he combined history with the Catalan culture to create his works; he also used some Moorish influences in his work. A Catalan through and through, he never built anything outside of Barcelona; his most renowned works are the **Hospital de la Santa Creu i Sant Pau** and the **Palau de la Música Catalana** (see p. 82 and p. 70).

Josep Puig i Cadafalch is the youngest of the main Modernisme architects of Barcelona. He resented his works being labeled as Modernisme, as he felt that his and his peers' works exhibited more local flare than the beginnings of an international architectural movement. His use of spatial effects are especially notable, as is his attention to surfaces and materials. Puig was more of a planner than Gaudí or Domènech, and his works are clearly influenced by 15th century Gothic architecture; his most well-known building is **Casa Amatller** (see p. 80).

NOUCENTISME: UP WITH THE ARCH, YET AGAIN

Noucentisme—a movement which covered all spheres of visual arts—is often overshadowed by other movements; indeed the movement pales in comparison to her Modernist architectural counterpart. A reaction to the disorder that Modernisme and World War I brought, Noucentisme is a Neoclassical revival that focused on order and simplicity. Puig i Cadafalch, reborn as a Noucentisme architect, was responsible for the redesign of Pl. de Catalunya. For examples of this minimally influential movement, check out the area surrounding the plaça, the **Estació França,** and the **Museu Arqueològic,** both built for the 1929 International Exhibition (see p. 44).

Park Güell Structures

FROM FASCISM TO THE PRESENT: CLEANING UP THE CITY

For the 1929 International Exposition, dictator Primo de Rivera commissioned **Poble Espanyol** to illustrate different types of Spanish architecture through the work of respected architects and designers **Ramon Reventós, Francesc Folguera,** and **Miquel Utrillo** (see p. 91). While arguably lame, this Disney Landish mini-town offers a compact walking tour of the different kinds of architecture found throughout Spain. So while the Arab influence never reached Barcelona, those visiting Spain will be comforted by the watered down grandeur of Andalucia right in Barcelona.

Bike-riding Fish-monger

After the Civil War destroyed Spain's economy and Franco entered the Spanish scene, growth and development of Barcelona's once prospering architectural innovations came to a stop. Few noteworthy architectural developments occurred during this era. What Franco did do was sponsor the building of the university, although construction stopped a few years later due to a lack of funding. The building of **Camp Nou,** the soccer stadium, was funded by the people of Barcelona and allowed its patriotic citizens to watch their *fútbol* team play soccer against Franco's Real Madrid.

Today, while a significant style is not currently noticeable, the city is going through rapid urban development. After Franco's death, there has been a movement toward eliminating the changes he had made to Barcelona as well as a focus on beautifying the city. Mayor **Pasqual Maragall** was the key player in this endeavor; after managing to secure the **1992 Summer Olym-**

Pl. del Sol

53

AND THE WINNER IS...

The **Jocs Florals** (Floral Games), a Catalan poetry competition started in the 14th century by **Joan I** and was temporarily reinstituted in the 19th, is a phenomenon that necessitates some explanation. The competition has enormous cultural importance because it represents the validity of Catalan as a language and the productivity of the culture as a whole; it's also remarkably anti-climatic. Although the *Jocs* received boatloads of entries by all accounts, the competition produced remarkably little poetry of acclaim; **Jacint Verdaguer** (d. 1902) is the exception. The nature of the first prize can perhaps account, in part, for the unremarkable nature of most of the entries. Third prize and second prize were silver and gold flowers respectively, but first prize winners were expected to be content with a nice-yet-worthless real flower; the honor of winning being supposedly prize enough. Contrary to the intentions of the contest, even the first prize poems were rarely of a quality to be memorable.

pics for the city, he brought modern high-rises to Barcelona's beachfront property, and turned the waterfront into Nightlife Central.

LET'S GET LITERARY

Since Catalunya has its own language, its literary tradition is decidedly distinct from Spain's; while Spain boasts such giants as Cervantes and Lorca, Catalunya has its own prodigies. Although various Spanish governments have tried to repress and depreciate the language, and although Catalunya has certainly experienced dry spells, the Catalan tradition is full of masterpieces that can be read in the original Catalan. Almost all Catalan works are translated into Spanish, and many are translated into English.

THE CATALAN GOLDEN AGE

The centuries Catalunya spent as an independent mercantile nation produced her own Golden Age, in a distinct language and moment in time from the Golden Age of Spain. In the late 1300s, the *Jocs Florals* (Floral Games) literary competition was introduced; the coveted grand prize, a golden rose, drew a number of poetry submissions from the gentry (see sidebar p. 54). Literary activity thus revitalized, the 1400s saw the development of some consequential authors. Valencian **Ausiàs March** (d. 1459) developed a body of poetic work in Catalan that is still considered fundamental to the Catalan tradition. On the prose front, **Joanot Martorell** (d. 1465) is famous for his novel *Tirant lo blanc,* the first prose novel on the continent, beloved by Cervantes, confronts the admirable morals of chivalry with the reality of sexuality.

THE RENAIXENÇA

When the Catalan culture and language was oppressed, Catalan literature naturally went through a dry spell. These centuries of writers' block ended only in the 1800s, when renewed Catalan nationalism encouraged productivity on all creative fronts. However, the realm of literature did not benefit so much from the Renaixença as art and architecture did. The medieval **Jocs Florals**, which had ended centuries ago, were temporarily reinstituted at this time; while this second round of contests drew a slew of poetry submissions, again from the gentry, the vast majority of them were painfully mediocre. Still, the Renaixença boasts Catalunya's most beloved poet: **Jacint Verdaguer** (1845-1902), a priest from the countryside who competed and won recognition in the *Jocs Florals*. His epic poem *L'Atlantida* won first prize in the 1879 competition and is as important to the Catalans as *The Iliad* is to the Greeks. Although he died amidst scandal with the Church authorities in

1902, he remains a national hero. The *Renaix-ença* also saw some great prose from a skilled female writer, although the public didn't know it at the time. The writer **Caterina Albert** wrote her 1905 crowning achievement, the realist novel *Solitut* (*Solitude*) under a masculine pseud-onym, **Víctor Català.**

PRODUCTS OF OPPRESSION

Relatively little happened under our favorite Fascist dictator, Generalísimo Francisco Franco. While writers in other parts of Spain managed to sneak several novels of importance past the conservative censors, Catalunya only produced one work of lasting consequence in the first decade of the dictatorship. With harsh repression of intellectual life and Catalan lan-guage and culture, it is amazing that Catalunya produced anything at all, but when 23-year-old Barcelona native **Carmen Laforet** exploded onto the scene in 1944, her riveting novel *Nada* (*Nothing*) won the *Premio Nadal*, the highest literary honor Iberia has to offer. The sheer quality of this book, which details a young girl's coming of age in an eccentric family and is a vir-tual tour of Barcelona, makes up for the scarcity of Catalan publications in this first decade or so of the dictatorship.

On the Beach

In subsequent Franco years, other writers started to grab attention. Along with Laforet's *Nada*, **Manuel Pedrolo i Molina's** plays, poems, and novels are the Catalan contribution to exis-tentialism. **Mercè Rodoreda's** short stories and novels span the decades before, during, and after Franco; her best known work is her 1962 novel *La Plaça del Diamante*, named for the Barcelona plaça where the story takes place. This novel addresses the quality of life in Barce-lona during and after the Civil War; no familiar-ity with Spanish history is necessary to appreciate the dramatic banality of the narra-tor's life. **Joan Marsé's** 1964 novel *Últimas tar-des con Teresa* (*Last Afternoons with Teresa*) also confronts life in Barcelona under the dictatorship; although sharply critical, this novel's racy edge and flare for biting satire makes it a popular favorite.

Gay Pride Parade

ROCKING OUT WITH DEMOCRACY

The excitement and productivity of the Renaix-ença was interrupted by the politics and oppres-sion of the Civil War and Franco; when he finally went gentle into that good night, Catalan litera-ture made a roaring comeback. Beginning in the late seventies and continuing through today, Catalunya, like the rest of Spain, has spewed forth a host of female writers ready to redefine femininity and sexuality in the wake of Franco's patriarchal society. **Carme Riera's** gender-bend-

Bull Fighting Arena

MORE THAN A RIVALRY

When Franco came to power in 1936, he tried to destroy regionalism by creating a centralized Spain, controlled by Madrid, and dominated by Castillian culture. The Catalan flag and language were banned; the **Fútbol Club Barcelona,** which had already established a following, became the only outlet for Catalan nationalism. The team's logo bears the Catalan coat of arms, with a red cross and red and gold stripes above the blue and burgundy stripes of Barça.

Because Catalan nationalism was so oppressed, **Real Madrid,** Franco's team, became a hated rival, both for its excellence on the field and the fascism it represented. In 1941, the FCB was told they had to lose a cup match against Madrid. The disgusted team protested the fix by allowing Madrid to win 11-1; Barça's goalie was suspended for life for his flagrant nonchalance. When Barça became a powerhouse in the 1950s, the government forced the team to give up one of its star players, Di Stefano, to Madrid. Soon after, the entire Barça board of directors resigned to protest the ridiculous situation.

Today the rivalry no longer holds the same political implications as it did, but it remains every bit as intense. The two teams, both with enormous financial resources and fiercely loyal fans, regularly battle for the championship of the Spanish First Division. Each time the teams meet, the match feels more like a war than a game: Barça versus Real Madrid, Catalunya versus Castilla.

ing compilation of short stories, *Te deix, amor, la mar com a penyora* (*I Leave You, My Love, the Sea as a Keepsake*) ripped through Franco's archaic concepts of femininity and love in 1975. The ever-present Catalan literary force, **Esther Tusquets,** quickly followed suit with her 1978 novel, *El mismo mar de todos los veranos* (*The Same Sea of Every Summer*); her subsequent works continue to question patriarchal norms with her heavy-handed narrative style. **Ana María Moix** is another feminist Barcelona native whose collection of short stories, *Las virtudes peligrosas* (*Dangerous Virtues*) won several important prizes.

SO YOU WANNA BE IN PICTURES? (CINEMA)

While Barcelona is not necessarily known for producing world-famous movies, it is home to the University of Barcelona, which serves as a training ground for aspiring film directors and actors and offers international film seminars. It also sponsors a surprising number of film festivals like the **Barcelona Film Festival** held every summer, the **International Festival of Fantasy and Horror Films** held in nearby Sitges in October, and the **Erotic International Film Festival.** The Generalitat is also known for its willingness to sponsor movies in Catalan, thus providing the groundwork for a thriving movie industry based around the Catalan culture. In fact, Internet rumors spread a few years ago, that the first ever Catalan-language pornography film was shot in Catalunya using actors from around the world. For movies set in Barcelona try:

Barcelona (1994). An uptight American working in the Barcelona office of a US corporation is paid a sudden visit by his free-spirited brother. Follow their one-eyed ride through Barcelona and see how the unexpected visit changes their lives.

All About my Mother (1999). **Pedro Almodovar's** Oscar-winning hit movie about a single mother and the transvestite father of her son took the world by storm. This story of love, friendship, and grief is set in Barcelona.

¡Dispara! (1993). This film featuring **Antonio Banderas** will take you through Barcelona, Madrid, and Hell. Ana, an equestrian sharpshooter for a circus, and Marcos, a reporter, fall in love—then tragedy strikes.

Amic/Amat (1998). **Ventura Pons'** Catalan-language interpretation of just how racy the life of a terminally ill, medieval literature professor can be.

SPORTS

Barcelona's proximity to the ocean and to the mountains lends itself to outdoor activities; while windsurfing, swimming, and boating prevail in seaside towns, hiking, biking, and winter sports dominate the mountains. Skiing is popular in the Pyrenees; everyone from the Spanish crown prince to the French cover the slopes in the winter time.

In terms of organized competitive sports, the most popular is, of course, **fútbol** (soccer or football, as you prefer). *Fútbol* is a uniting passion for Spaniards; championship wins send fans into the streets for hours, even days, with painted faces, flags waving from cars, special horn-honks, and extended disco hours. Their pride is well-warranted: despite a shocking early knock out in the first round of the 1998 World Cup, the Spanish national team ranks with the finest in Europe.

Barcelona's blue- and red-clad team, affectionately called **el Barça**, more formally known as **Fútbol Club Barcelona**, is among the best in the Europe; hardcore fans follow the soccer team with an almost cultish fervor. The stadium, **Camp Nou,** is a nonstop party when an important game is in town (see p. 170). The more die-hard among this group consider loyalty to their team more of a way of life than a hobby. El Barça has participated in every European cup tournament since the first, beginning in 1955. They won in the 1991-1992 season, and the team is very proud of their numerous trophies from various competitions. **Vítor Borba Ferreira Rivaldo,** a Brazilian forward, is a popular favorite, having been chosen as third world player in 2000 by **FIFA**, the organization that does that sort of thing.

Visitors to Spain are often eager to see a **bullfight,** or *corrida de toros.* Bullfighting is not native to Catalunya, but it has crept its way up to this corner of the peninsula, although it enjoys only modest popularity among the locals (see p. 171).

Sights

TOURS

RUTA DEL MODERNISME

For those with a few days in the city and an interest in seeing all the biggest sights, the Ruta del Modernisme is the cheapest and most flexible option. The Ruta del Modernisme isn't a tour precisely, in the sense that it doesn't offer a guide or organized transportation; it's a ticket which gives discounted entrance to Modernist sites, to be used at the owner's discretion. Passes (600ptas/€3,80; students and over 65 400ptas/€2,20; groups over 10 people 500ptas/€3 per person) are good for a month and give holders a 50% discount on entrance to Palau Güell (see p. 74), La Sagrada Família (see p. 75), Casa Milà (La Pedrera; see p. 77), Palau de la Música Catalana (see p. 70), Casa-Museu Gaudí (see p. 95), Fundació Antoni Tàpies (see p. 112), the Museu d'Art Modern (see p. 110), the Museu de Zoologia (see p. 111), a tour of El Hospital de la Santa Creu i Sant Pau (see p. 82), tours of the façades of La Manzana de la Discòrdia (Casas Amatller, Lleó Morera, and Batlló; see p. 79), and other attractions. The pass also comes with a map and a booklet which give a history of the movement and prioritize the sites. Purchase passes at **Casa Amatller,** Pg. Gràcia 41 (☎93 488 01 39. M: Pg. de Gràcia; see p. 80) near the intersection with C. Consedel. As many of these sights have mandatory hour-long tours or tours that only leave on the half-hour or hour, visiting all of them on the same day is impossible.

BUS TURÍSTIC

The clearly marked Bus Turístic stops at 26 points of interest along 2 different routes (red for the north-bound buses, blue for the south-bound); a ticket comes with a comprehen-

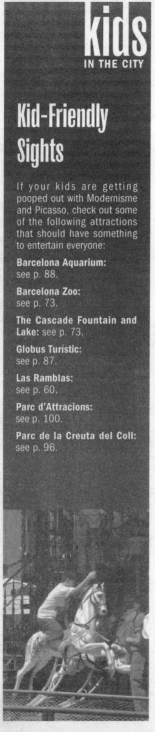

kids
IN THE CITY

Kid-Friendly Sights

If your kids are getting pooped out with Modernisme and Picasso, check out some of the following attractions that should have something to entertain everyone:

Barcelona Aquarium: see p. 88.

Barcelona Zoo: see p. 73.

The Cascade Fountain and Lake: see p. 73.

Globus Turístic: see p. 87.

Las Ramblas: see p. 60.

Parc d'Attracions: see p. 100.

Parc de la Creuta del Coll: see p. 96.

sive info guide in 6 languages about each important sight. A full ride on both routes takes about 3½ hours, but you can get on and off as often as you wish. The easiest place to hop on the Bus Turístic is **Pl. de Catalunya,** in front of El Corte Inglés (see **Shopping,** p. 183). Many of the museums and sights covered by the tour bus are closed on Mondays. Purchase tickets on the bus, the Pl. de Catalunya tourist office, or at Estació Barcelona-Sants. (Daily except Dec. 25 and Jan. 1; every 10-30min., 9am-9:30pm; 1-day pass 2200ptas/€13,22, children aged 4-12 1300ptas/€7,81, 2-day pass 2800ptas/€16,83.)

LAS RAMBLAS

🚇 M: *Catalunya, Liceu,* or *Drassanes. Addresses with low numbers lie towards the port, while higher numbers head towards the Pl. de Catalunya.*

Las Ramblas' pedestrian-only median strip is a veritable urban carnival, where street performers dance, fortune-tellers survey palms, human statues shift poses, vendors vend birds, and artists sell caricatures—all for the benefit of droves of tourists and all, of course, for a small fee. A stroll along this bustling avenue can be an adventure at any hour, day or night. The wide, tree-lined thoroughfare dubbed Las Ramblas is actually composed of five distinct *ramblas* (promenades) that together form one long boulevard, about 1km long. What follows below is a description of the different segments of Las Ramblas and the sights along the way, beginning with Pl. de Catalunya in the north and heading towards the port in the south. Although Las Ramblas is officially five different streets, and although we divide up Las Ramblas according to that format for organization's sake, the streets are generally just referred to as one, Las Ramblas, and not by individual names.

La Rambla de les Canaletes and La Rambla dels Estudis are both accessible from M: Catalunya; La Rambla de Sant Josep and La Rambla dels Caputxins are accessible from M: Liceu; La Rambla de Santa ⬛Monica is accessible from M: Drassanes. All of the different segments are, of course, and easy walk from one to the other.

LA RAMBLA DE LES CANALETES

The port-ward journey begins at the **Font de les Canaletes,** more of a pump than a fountain, recognizable by it four faucets and the Catalan crests (red crosses next to red and yellow stripes) that adorn it; this section of Las Ramblas is named for the fountain. Legend has it that visitors who sample the water will fall in love with the city (if they haven't already) and are bound to return to Barcelona someday. Stationed around here are the first of many **living statues** (see **Stand in the Place Where You Are,** p. 62) that line the walkway during the day. Because of its symbolic position on the Pl. de Catalunya and its central location in the city, La Rambla de les Canaletes also sees a fair deal of political demonstrations.

LA RAMBLA DELS ESTUDIS

You'll hear the squawking of the residents of the next section of Las Ramblas before you see them. The next stretch of Las Ramblas, which extends to C. Carme and C. Portaferrissa, is often referred to as La Rambla dels Ocells—the **Rambla of the Birds.** A number of stalls here sell birds of nearly every kind: roosters, parrots, doves, and even baby emus (good luck trying to sneak these cute and fuzzy souvenirs through customs). Rabbits, fish, gerbils, turtles, and other caged critters are also available. The official name of this stretch of *rambla* comes from the university that used to be located here; "*estudis*" is Catalan for "studies."

LA RAMBLA DE SANT JOSEP

While still in earshot of the birds, you'll start to smell the roses. A block later, the screeching bird stalls give way to the sunflowers, roses, and irises of *La Rambla de les Flors* (the Rambla of the Flowers). Vendors here have offered a good variety of bouquets since the mid 1800s. In April, the flower stands are joined by book vendors in preparation for the **Día de Sant Jordi,** a Catalan variety of Valentine's Day. On April 24, couples exchange gifts: women and girls receive flowers and men and boys receive books. The hulking stone building at the corner of C. Carme is the Església de Betlem, a baroque church whose interior never recovered from an anarchist torching during the Civil War. A bit farther down is the famous traditional Catalan market, **Mercat de la Boqueria** (see p. 63), the oldest of the city's 40 markets, and the infamous **Museu de l'Eròtica** (see **Museums,** p. 106). The Boqueria market is officially name **El Mercat de Sant Josep;** the market and the *rambla* are named for the same saint. At Pl. Boqueria, just before the Metro station, you'll walk across Joan Miró's circular pavement mosaic, created for the city in 1976 and now a popular meeting point.

LA BOQUERIA (MERCAT DE SANT JOSEP)

🛈 *Las Ramblas 95. M: Liceu, outside the station (Mercat exit). Open M-Sa 8am-8pm.*

Besides being one of the cheapest ways to get food in the city, la Boqueria is a sight in itself: a traditional Catalan market located right on Las Ramblas. Specialized vendors sell their goods—produce, dairy, meat, etc.—from independent stands inside the market complex, which is an an all-steel Modernist structure. The wonderland of fresh foods offers wholesale prices for fruit, cheese, meat, bread, wine, and more. The butcher displays are not for the faint of heart.

PALAU DE LA VIRREINA

🛈 *Las Ramblas 99, on the corner of C. Carme. M: Liceu.☎ 93 316 10 00. Open Tu-Sa 11am-8:30pm and Su 11am-3pm. Free.*

Once the residence of a Peruvian viceroy, this 18th-century palace houses temporary photography, music, and graphics exhibits. Also on display are the latest incarnations of the 10-15ft. tall giant dolls who have taken part in the city's Carnival celebrations since as far back as 1320. The imposing couple Jaume and Violant, dressed in long, regal robes, are the undisputed king and queen of the Carnival parade. The cultural institute here, **ICUB** (see p. 294), serves as information headquarters for Barcelona's cultural festivals. Be sure to also check out the famous rainbow stained-glass façade of the Casa Beethoven next-door at no.97, now a well-stocked music store (see **Shopping,** p. 184).

STAND IN THE PLACE WHERE YOU LIVE

In a city as rich in artistic heritage as Barcelona, it is not surprising to find a series of sculptures lining Las Ramblas. What's surprising is when one of these suspiciously life-like statues begins to shimmy and shake. Hopefully you would have figured this out on your own, but these "statues" are in fact real people, putting in a hard day's work for tourist *pesetas*. Living statues are Las Ramblas' signature tourist attraction, drawing daily crowds of fascinated gawkers. Men and women dress in costumes and paint themselves head to toe in a solid color, then stand dead still on a platform for hours at a time. The best ones shift positions only when a coin is dropped into their jar, at which point they come alive in jerky motions, posing for pictures or thanking the donor. During a typical day, one might find silver mermaids, marble nuns, bronze Roman soldiers, and golden sax players. Toss them a 100- *peseta* piece and watch them stand and deliver.

LA RAMBLA DELS CAPUTXINS

Miró's street mosaic marks the beginning of La Rambla dels Caputxins, the most user-friendly of the five Rambla sisters and the first of Las Ramblas to be converted into a promenade. The pedestrian area widens, and the majestic trees provide a constant blanket of shade. Across from the recently renovated opera house (the **Liceu**; see below), a strip of restaurants with outdoor seating vie for tourist *pesetas*, offering decent but unremarkable and fairly expensive food and of course prime people-watching perches. When you're in the area, go to the Miró mosaic plaça (intersection of La Rambla dels Caputxins and C. Boqueria) and look up: if you see umbrellas sticking out of one of the buildings, that's no accident, but a former umbrella store of some acclaim.

GRAN TEATRE DEL LICEU

🚩 *Las Ramblas 51-59, on the corner of C. Sant Pau. Information office open M-F 2-8:30pm and 1hr. before performances.* ☎ *93 485 99 13. Guided tours 9:30-11am, reservation only (call 93 485 99 00). 800ptas/€4,81, students 600ptas/€3,61.*

The Gran Teatre del Liceu has been Barcelona's opera house for over a century. It was once one of Europe's leading stages, playing host to the likes of José Carreras in his early years. Ravaged by a fire in January 1994, it reopened for performances in 1999 (see **Smooth Opera-ater**, p. 64). It is adorned with palatial ornamentation, gold façades, sculptures, and grand circular side rooms—a Spanish hall of mirrors.

LA RAMBLA DE SANTA MONICA

Following the tradition of nicknaming the parts of Las Ramblas after the goods sold there, this stretch would most likely be nicknamed *La Rambla de las Prostitutas*. After nightfall, women of the night patrol this wide area leading up to the port, beckoning passers-by with loud kissing noises. During the day, however, the street distinguishes itself with some of the city's most skilled practitioners of a different fine art. These wizards can whip up dead-on caricatures in just five minutes, or invest hours on startlingly life-like portraits of their paying customers. Roving galleries sell landscapes and colorful psychedelic pieces worthy of a Pink Floyd album cover. La Rambla de Santa Monica is also home to the **Centre d'Art de Santa Monica** and the **Museu de Cera** (see p. 104). Although the area's nighttime reputation is notorious, La Rambla de Santa Monica is not particularly unsafe, although

oup travel is always a good idea. Las Ramblas
ds at the seafront-end of La Rambla de Santa
onica with one very visible statue.

ONUMENT A COLOM

*Portal de la Pau. M: Drassanes. Elevator open June-
pt. 9am-8:30pm; Oct.-Mar. M-F 10am-1:30pm and
30-6:30pm, Sa-Su 10am-6:30pm; Apr.-May 10am-
30pm and 3:30-7:30pm, Sa-Su 10am-7:30pm.
00ptas/€1,80, children and over 65200ptas/€1,20.*

the port end of Las Ramblas, Ruis i Taulet's
onument a Colom towers 80m above the city.
hen Renaixença enthusiasts (see **Life & Times,**
43) "rediscovered" Spain's role in the discov-
y of the Americas, they convinced themselves
at Christopher Columbus was really Catalan,
om a northern town near Girona. The fact that
e statue points proudly toward Libya, not the
mericas, doesn't help their claim; historians
w agree that Columbus was actually from
enoa, Italy. At night, spotlights turn the statue,
rst erected in 1888 and renovated in 1982, into a
rebrand. Take the **elevator** up to the top and get
stunning view of Barcelona.

Chicks for Sale on Las Ramblas

ee map pp. 310-311

BARRI GÒTIC

*For walking tours, call 906 301
282. Sa-Su at 10am in English and
noon in Catalan and Spanish. Tour
group size is limited; buy tickets in
dvance. 1100ptas/€6,60, children aged 4-12
00ptas/€3.*

he Barri Gòtic offers everything that Barce-
na's Modernist architecture and l'Eixample do
ot. Its narrow, winding streets are not the prod-
cts of careful planning and rapid execution, but
ave developed out of centuries of architectural
nd cultural mixing, from early Roman through
Romanesque, medieval, and Gothic times. This
rea is best enjoyed wandering slowly and pay-
ng close attention to your surroundings; nearly
very street has at least a few interesting histori-
al sights and endless array of shops, eateries,
nd cafés. The Barcelona Tourism Office also
eads professional **walking tours** of the Barri
Gòtic, leaving from the information office in Pl.
le Catalunya; you can buy tickets there or at the
juntament (see p. 68) in Pl. St. Jaume.

Portrait Painter on Las Ramblas

PLAÇA DE L'ANGEL

M: Jaume I.

he Jaume I Metro stop lets out into the Plaça
le l'Angel, where the main gate into Roman
Barcino was once located. The plaça gets its
name from the legend surrounding the moving
of Sta. Eulalia's remains from Santa Maria del
Mar to the cathedral: supposedly the martyred

Miró Mosaic

SMOOTH OPERA- ATOR

The grand old dame of Barcelona high culture, the **Gran Teatre de Liceu** has been a leading European opera house since its founding in 1847. But beneath this spectacularly restored theater is a tumultuous history. Not long after its opening as Europe's largest theater, an 1861 fire ravaged the Liceu, destroying its interior. The theater was rebuilt practically from scratch, but soon reopened. In 1868, an angry mob of commoners stormed the Liceu, a favorite bourgeoisie bastion. They snatched the marble bust of Queen Isabel II from the lobby, paraded it down Las Ramblas, and tossed it into the sea.

The social unrest became more dangerous in 1893; on the opening night, a packed house of Barcelona bourgeoisie was enjoying Rossini's "William Tell." During the second act, an anarchist named Santiago Salvador threw a bomb into the crowd from an upper balcony, killing twenty and wounding many others. Salvador was executed, and the theater reopened the following season, but for years tickets were not sold for the seats of the tragedy's victims. 100 years later, in 1994, disaster struck again, when fire consumed the ill-fated interior for a second time. A multi-billion *peseta* restoration project, has returned the Liceu to its former grandeur while allowing modernization of the facilities.

saint's body suddenly became too heavy carry, and an angel appeared in the plaça poin ing a finger at one of the church officials, wh it turned out, had secretly stolen one of Eul lia's toes. The angel statue placed in the plaça the 17th century to commemorate the event now kept in the **Museu d'Història de la Ciut** (see **Museums,** p. 104).

ROMAN WALLS

M: Jaume I.

Several sections of the northeastern walls Roman Barcino are still standing near the cath dral. C. Tapineria runs from Pl. de l'Angel (on th right, facing away from Via Laietana) to **P Ramon Berenguer,** where you can see a larg stretch of fourth-century defense wall, under th Palau Reial Major. Continuing along C. Tapiner to the right lands you in Pl. Seu, where you ca see the only intact octagonal corner tower le today, a part of the **Museu Diocesà** (see **Museum** p. 107). To the right of the cathedral are sever more Roman towers and a reconstruction of or of the two aqueducts which ran through here t supply water to Barcino.

CATHEDRAL & ENVIRONS

M: Jaume I.

The cathedral's plaça boasts a notable publi work by Joan Brossa: a giant, stylized letter spell ou the word "Barcino" to commemorat the site of the original Roman city (see **Life Times,** p. 38).

ESGLÉSIA CATEDRAL DE LA SANTA CREU

In Pl. Seu, up C. Bisbe from Pl. St. Jaume. Cathedra open daily 8am-1:30pm and 4-7:30pm. Cloister ope 9am-1:15pm and 4-7pm. Elevator to the roof open M- 10:30am-12:30pm and 4:30-6pm, Sa-Su 10:30am 12:30pm, 225ptas/€1,40. Choir area open M-F 9am 1pm and 4-7pm, Sa-Su 9am-1pm. 150ptas/€0,90. Sal capitular 100ptas/€0,60. History recording (in English 200ptas/€1,20.

La Catedral de la Santa Creu (the Cathedral o the Holy Cross) is one of Barcelona's most popu lar historical monuments. More than 3 million people visit it every year, and it still serves as the active center of the archbishopry of Barcelona Three separate buildings have actually existed on the site: a fourth-century basilica, an 11th century Romanesque church, and finally the present Gothic cathedral, begun in 1298. The much-photographed main façade comes from yet another era (1882), when it was tacked on to the main structure by architect Josep Mestres Adding to the architectural mix, it appears tha

Mestres worked from a plan drawn up by a Frenchman, Carles Galtés de Ruán, in 1408.

The first thing you will see upon entering through the main door is the cathedral **choir.** The backs of the stalls are painted with 46 coats of arms commemorating the Chapter of the Order of the Golden Fleece, an early United Nations meeting of sorts held in Barcelona nearly 500 years ago, in 1519. The area below the choir seats is decorated with detailed sculptures of hunting and game-playing scenes. Beyond the choir await the most important liturgical elements of the cathedral, including the marble **cathedra** (bishop's throne; the origin of the word "cathedral"), the altar with the bronze **cross** designed by Frederic Marès in 1976, and most famous of all, the sunken **Crypt of Santa Eulalia,** one of Barcelona's patron saints. Completed in 1334, the crypt holds a white marble sarcophagus which depicts scenes from the saint's martyrdom at age 13. Discovered in the Santa Maria del Mar in 877, her remains were not transported here until 1339. Also at rest in the cathedral is **Saint Olegario,** who died in 1137 after serving as archbishop of Tarragona (see p. 219). His perfectly preserved body, in full regalia, is visible through glass on either side of the **Chapel of El Santo Cristo de Lepanto,** directly to your right at the front of the church after entering through the main door. (This chapel is often reserved for those in prayer and closed to the public.)

La Rambla del Mar

Almost directly behind the altar you will find the Chapel of St. Joan Baptista i St. Josep, which features one of the most famous pieces of artwork in the cathedral, the *Transfiguration of the Lord* altarpiece created by Bernat Martorell in 1450. The **elevator** to the roof is to the left of the altar, and the cathedral **treasury** to the right, behind the sacristy door. The treasury is not always open, but when it is, it is worth going inside to see the famous **monstrance** (the receptacle used for holding the Host, the holy bread of the Catholic religion), made of gold and silver and dripping with precious jewels. Once used for Corpus Christi processions, legend has it that the monstrance was given to the cathedral by the last Catalan king, Martí, during his reign (1396-1410; see p. 40). Right outside of the sacristy you will see on the wall the **tombs** of Ramon Berenguer I and his wife, founders of the Romanesque cathedral, the second building on this site.

Cheese at La Boqueria

Just to the right of the tombs is the exit into the peaceful **cloister,** home to the **Fountain of St. Jordi** and 13 white geese which serve as reminders of Sta. Eulalia's age at the time of her death. The chapels in the cloister were once dedicated to the various guilds of Barcelona, and a few of them are still maintained today (including the shoe-makers' and electricians'; see **Godfather Part Zero,** p. 66). The coats of arms of private families as well as the guilds adorn the cloister

Entertainer on Las Ramblas

GODFA-THER, PART ZERO

One of the most defining features of medieval Barcelona was its workers' guilds; but these were not the quaint, mildly cooperative operations that history sometimes paints them to be. Rather, they were like families– in the New York Italian sense of the word. One was not allowed to practice a trade without guild approval, and once you were a member your economic and social survival was utterly dependent upon your obeying all price fixings, quality controls, and production rules. The guilds had close connections to both the government and the Church (most maintained their own chapels, many of which are still visible in the Cathedral cloister), and when war broke out, they were often the first source of organized fighters. Naturally, the guilds tended to set up shop near one another for the purpose of sharing resources, and it is from their geographic concentrations that many of the streets in the Barri Gòtic get their names: needle-makers worked in C. Agullers, rope-weavers in C. Corders, cotton-sewers in C. Cotoners, shield-makers in C. Escudellers, glass-makers in C. Vidre, knife-molders in C. Dagueria, and so on and so forth.

walkways, and if you look back toward th cathedral interior, you can see the only remai ing piece of the Romanesque structure, the lar arched doorway leading back inside. The earli fourth-century building was almost entire destroyed by Muslim invaders in 985; what litt is left is visible underground in the Muse d'Història de la Ciutat (see **Museums,** p. 104). the near right corner of the cloister, coming fro the cathedral, you will find the **cathedral museu** whose most notable holding is Bartolomé Be mejo's renowned oil painting of a *pietà*, th image of Christ dying in the arms of his moth (in the Sala Capitular, to the left up on entrance

The front of the cathedral is also the place catch an impromtu performance of the **sardan** the traditional Catalan dance (see **Gettin' Jig with it,** p. 52). Performances generally occur Su day mornings and afternoons after mass (noon and 6:30 pm).

CARRER DEL BISBE

🚇 M: Jaume I. From Pl. de l'Angel, walk down C. Llibret ria; C. del Bisbe will be the fifth right.

In Roman times, C. del Bisbe served as the ma north-south thoroughfare of the city. Today it lined with various official buildings. Immediate to your left upon leaving the cathedral area is th medieval **Casa de l'Ardiaca,** once home to th archdeacon and now the location of Barcelona newspaper archives. Stop and check out th mailslot designed by Domènech i Montaner i 1902, when the house served as a school for law yers. He juxtaposed a sculpted swallow and to toise—according to one theory, an expression his opinion of the postal service (supposedl quick as a bird but actually slow as a turtle) Walking down C. Bisbe takes you between th Palau de la Generalitat on the right (see p. 67 and the **Casa de los Canónigos** on the left, onc home to the religious canons and now the Cata lan president Jordi Pujol's official residence. Th two are connected by a neo-Gothic bridge built i 1929 as part of the restoration of the Barri Gòtic.

The **Capela de Santa Llúcia,** located just off C Bisbe next the cathedral, was built in 1268 an is one of only a few remaining Romanesqu churches in the entire city (see **Life & Times,** p 50). Every December 13, on the Day of Sant Llúcia, locals pay their respects to the saint an the Fair of Sant Llúcia begins around the Cathe dral, with craftsmen and sellers of Nativity scene figures setting up temporary shops for th holiday season.

ROMAN TOMBS

🚇 From Las Ramblas, turn onto C. Portaferrissa and take the first left; it will lead directly to the Pl. de la Vila de Madrid.

In the Upper Barri Gòtic, between C. Portaferrissa and C. Canuda, the **Plaça de la Vila de Madrid** contains one final Roman site worth visiting: a row of 2nd- to 4th-century Roman tombs, lined up just as they originally were along a road leading out of Barcino (Roman law forbade burial within the city walls). The tombs are significantly lower than the rest of the plaça, proof of how much the physical terrain of Barcelona has changed over the past 2000 years.

PLAÇA DE SANT JAUME & AROUND

▶ M: Jaume I. From the Metro, walk to the Pl. de l'Angel, on the Via Laietana, and then down either C. Jaume I or C. Llibreteria to the plaça.

When Roman colonizers constructed new outpost towns, they always followed the same basic plan, laying down two main streets that intersected in the shape of a short cross (in Barcino, the longer C. Bisbe ran north-south and the shorter C. Llibreteria east-west). At the central intersection they would build their forum, the center of civic and political life. (Under Augustus' rule, the forum also had to include a temple to the emperor.) The site of Barcino's original forum has never ceased serving as the seat of power in Barcelona, and today the city government and provincial government face off across the broad square, the Ajuntament on the C. Jaume I side, and the Generalitat on the C. Llibreteria side. *Sardanas* are frequently danced here (see **Gettin' jiggy with it**, p. 52), and the plaça always fills with merrymaking crowds on Catalan holidays. Just off the plaça, the Gothic **Església de Sants Just i Pastor** (1342) occupies a small square just off C. Ciutat. This is the only remaining church in the city which honors living wills: someone about to die can make a will to a friend, who can then repeat his last words at this altar, whereupon they become legally binding. The Pl. de Sant Jaume also houses the **Museu d'Història de la Ciutat** (see p. 104).

PALAU DE LA GENERALITAT

▶ Pl. St. Jaume. ☎ 93 402 46 16. Enter to the right on C. Bisbe. M: Jaume I. Open the 2nd and 4th Su of every month 10:30am-1:30pm. Closed Aug. Mandatory tours in Catalan, Spanish, or English every 30min. starting at 10:30am (in English usually 11:00 and 11:30, but call to be sure). Tours are limited, so come early, and bring ID. Free. Limited wheelchair accessibility. The first Su of every month the Palace also hosts a free bell concert at noon.

Located in the same place as the original Roman forum, the Palace of the Generalitat is the head of Catalunya's regional government. It has served as the seat of power for 115 presidents of Catalunya, from Berenguer de Cruïlles in 1359 to the current president Jordi Pujol. The oldest

Barri Gòtic

Holding Hands at the Pier

Palau Güell Façade

67

CATALAN JEWS

The history of Jews in Spain has been nothing short of contradictory; they have been the most persecuted people in the land but also make up a substantial percentage of the country's most culturally accomplished, financially successful, and intellectually renowned historical figures. The paradox inherent in this situation loomed particularly large during Christopher Columbus's voyages to the New World. The sailor's first trip was financed mainly by King Fernando's treasurer Lluís Santagel, a converted Jew from Valencia, and the news of Columbus's shocking discoveries was spread throughout Europe by another converted Jew, publisher Leandre de Coscó. Meanwhile, Fernando and Isabel were busy recapturing Granada from the Muslims, and Santagel ended up financing Columbus's second trip predominantly with confiscated goods...from all of the Jews expelled from Spain in 1492. Even as the centralized Spanish government tried to oppress Catalanism, displaced Catalan Jews kept it alive. Today, there are still Jews in parts of the Middle East who speak a form of Catalan and cook decidedly Catalan food, descendants of the Jews expelled from Barcelona in the 1400s.

part of the building is the Gothic façade in C. Bisbe, where the original entrance was; the government officials who commissioned it in 1416 were so happy with the St. Jordi medallion that Marc Safont designed that they paid him double what they had originally promised. Most of the center of the palace was added in the 16th and 17th centuries, including the beautiful **Pati dels Tarongers** (Patio of Oranges) and the **Salón Dorado** (Gold Room), a meeting room with an ornate gold ceiling and Petrarch-inspired tapestries depicting the triumph of honor over death, and of time over honor. Also notable is the **Salón de Sant Jordi,** whose cupola is visible from the Pl. St. Jaume. Part of the 17th-century additions which included the plaça façade, this extravagant room features a St. Jordi statue by Frederic Marès and is covered in allegorical paintings referring to the history of Catalunya.

AJUNTAMENT

🖪 Open Su 10am-1:45pm. Tours at 10:30, 11:30am, and 12:30pm or as needed by large groups, usually in Catalan or Spanish. For English or French call 93 268 24 44. Self-guided tours also allowed; pamphlet guides are available in Catalan, Spanish, English, and French. Free. Not wheelchair accessible.

The Ajuntament is Barcelona's city hall and office of Socialist Mayor Joan Clos. In the late 14th century, Barcelona's elite Consell de Cent (Council of One Hundred) decided to build their meeting house on the site of the original Roman forum. The most impressive room in the building, the **Saló de Cent,** was completed in 1369, and King Pere III had his first meeting with the Consell de Cent there in 1373. With red-and-gold-brocaded walls, high arches, and a profusion of crystal chandeliers, it practically glows with Catalan pride. Smaller but equally stunning is the **Saló de la Reina Regente,** designed in 1860 for plenary meetings and boasting a half-dome stained glass skylight. The **Saló de las Crónicas** is lined with wall decorations by Josep Marià Sert, depicting episodes from Roger de Flor's expedition to the Far East in the 14th century. The entrance **courtyard,** meanwhile, serves as a display space for sculptures by some of Barcelona's most famous artists, including Josep Llimona, Josep Subirachs, and Joan Miró.

TEMPLE OF AUGUSTUS

🖪 Inside the Centre Excursionista de Catalunya building. The protective gate opens Tu-Su 10am-2pm, but the remains are visible through the gate as well.

Upon entering Pl. St. Jaume from C. Bisbe, make an immediate sharp left (basically a U-turn) into tiny C. Paradís. At the end of this street is mounted a plaque marking **Mont Tàber,** the highest point of Roman Barcino: all of 16.9m above sea level. Right behind the plaque, inside the protective walls of the **Centre Excursionista Catalu-**

nya, a local outdoors club, you will find four columns from the original Roman **Temple of Augustus.** Built on the formerly towering summit of Mont Tàber over 2000 years ago, the now eye-level columns have not moved from their original position.

SOUTHERN ROMAN WALLS

🛈 *C. Regomir 3. From Pl. St. Jaume, take C. Ciutat; just as the street turns into C. Regomir, the Centre Pati Llimona will be on your left. ☎93 268 21 70. M: Jaume I. Centre Pati Llimona open M-F 9am-10pm and Sa-Su 10am-2pm.*

The second concentrated stretch of Roman wall remains in the Barri Gòtic are located in what was the southeastern corner of the original city, near present-day Pl. Regomir and Pl. Traginers. This civic center hosts free art exhibitions in its front room (usually photography) and also showcases a substantial piece of first-century Roman wall. The wall is visible from the street through a glass window but is also accessible for free via a ramp inside the building.

Soon after passing the civic center, turn left on C. Correu Vell. A tiny alley, C. de Groch, branches off to the left into a space where you can see a stretch of 4th-century wall and two square towers. If you then go back and take C. Correu Vell to its end, you will find yourself in small, quiet **Plaça Traginers,** which hosts yet another substantial segment of fourth-century walls.

EL CALL (JEWISH QUARTER)

🛈 *M: Jaume I.*

Records indicate that Jewish families started moving to Roman Barcino as early as the 2nd century; they tended to congregate near one another and intermarry, and soon El Call, or the Jewish quarter, sprang to life near the center of town, between present-day Pl. St. Jaume, C. Ferran, C. Banys Nous, and the Església Santa Maria del Pi. For centuries, El Call was the most vibrant center of intellectual and financial activity in all of Barcelona; Jews even received a certain amount of governmental support and protection in return for their substantial financial and cultural contributions to the city. In 1243, however, Jaume I ordered the complete isolation of the Jewish quarter from the rest of the city, and he forced all Jews to wear identifying red-and-yellow buttons. Anti-Semitism spread as citizens looked for scapegoats for the growing plagues and poverty of the 14th century, and in 1348, hundreds of Jews were blamed for the Black Death and tortured mercilessly until they "confessed" to their crime. In 1391, as harassment of Jews spread throughout Spain, an anti-Semitic riot ended in the murder of nearly 1000 Jews in Barcelona's Call. By 1401, every single synagogue and Jewish cemetery was abolished, making the forced conversion law of 1492 an easy next step (see **Catalan Jews,** p. 68).

One Jewish synagogue was turned into a church which is still in use today, the **Església de Sant Jaume** (C. Ferran 28). The only tangible evidence of Jewish inhabitants in El Call that remains intact today, however, is the ancient **Hebrew plaque** in tiny C. Marlet. To see it, take C. Call from Pl. St. Jaume, turn right onto C. Sant Domènech de Call and then left onto C. Marlet; it will be at the end on the right.

One of the best-known alleys in El Call actually has nothing to do with the Jews: to the left off the end of C. Sant Domènech de Call (coming from C. Call) is the **Baixada de Sta. Eulalia,** said be the place where the city's patron saint was tortured to death and turned into a Christian martyr. On the wall at the start of the street a plaque written by Catalan poet Jacint Verdaguer commemorates the legend.

SANTA MARIA DEL PI

🛈 *M: Liceu. Be sure to observe proper church etiquette (see **Once in Barcelona,** p. 30). Take C. Cardenal Casañas from Las Ramblas. Open M-F 8:30am-1pm and 4:30-8:30pm, Sa 8:30am-1pm and 4-9pm, Su 9am-2pm and 5-9pm.*

As far as religious buildings go, the Catedral de la Santa Creu tends to usurp tourist attention in the Barri Gòtic. However, he most popular among locals is the Església de Santa Maria del Pi, a small 14th-century church with Gothic stained glass windows. The three plaças surrounding the church (Pl. del Pi, Placeta del Pi, and Pl. de St. Oriol) are some of the most pleasant places for relaxing in the entire Barri Gòtic.

BORN AGAIN

The old Born market which sits at the head of Pg. del Born has a long and sordid past. In the 14th century, jousting tournaments were held in the Pl. del Born underneath the current market site. In fact, the word "born" originates from the name of the tips of the jousting spears used in these tournaments, which continued through the 17th century. Carrying on its violent tradition, the plaça was briefly used as a site for the *autos-da-fé* during the Inquisition later that century. From the late 19th century, however, the plaça's bloody legacy was present only in the meat stalls in the Mercat del Born.

Josep Fontseré was commissioned to design the market along with his work in the nearby Parc de la Ciutadella (see p. 72). His creation, a marvel of steel and glass that allowed for plenty of natural light, served as the city's major wholesale market for almost 100 years. When the market was moved out of the city in 1976, the building stood unused for many years. Finally, a joint project between the Ajuntament, the Ministry of Education and Culture, and the Generalitat was launched to convert the old market into a provincial library for Barcelona, slated to be open in 2005 with as much of Fontseré's original design preserved as possible. Meanwhile, a team of archaeologists from the Museu d'Història de la Ciutat (see p. 104) is working hard to uncover any medieval relics.

PLAÇA REIAL

🚩 *M: Liceu or Drassanes. Be careful at night.*

The most crowded, happening plaça in the entire Barri Gòtic is the **Pl. Reial**, where tourists and locals alike congregate to eat and drink at night, and to sell stamps and coins at the Sunday morning flea market. Francesc Daniel Milona designed the plaça in one of Barcelona's first spurts of constructive (rather than oppressive) urban planning, replacing decrepit Barri Gòtic streets with a large, architecturally cohesive plaça in the 1850s. Near the fountain in the center of the square are two street lamps designed by Antoni Gaudí at the very beginning of his architectural career. The plaça is a great place to grab a drink, whether it's a midday coffee or an early evening pint.

OTHER PLAÇAS IN THE BARRI GÒTIC

🚩 *M: Liceu or Jaume I.*

Farther toward the water, off C. Ample, the much newer **Pl. Mercé** is a popular spot for weddings, as well as for Barcelona's soccer team: the **Església de la Mercé** (see **Life & Times,** p. 51) on one side holds the image of the mother of God to which FCB players dedicate all of their successful games. One last plaça worth seeing is the **Pl. de Sant Felip Neri,** a right off C. Bisbe coming from the cathedral. It is peaceful and pretty today, but has a rather morbid past: it was once the site of a Jewish cemetery, and in January 1938 a Civil War bomb exploded here, killing 20 children; the shrapnel marks are still visible on the façade of the Església de Sant Felip Neri.

LA RIBERA
🏛 PALAU DE LA MÚSICA CATALANA

see map pp. 310-311

🚩 *C. Sant Francesc de Paula 2. ☎93 295 72 00; www.palaumusica.org. M: Jaume I. Off Via Laietana near Pl. Urquinaona. Head up Via Laietana to the intersection of C. Ionqueres. Entrance only with a tour; in English on the hr., in Spanish on the half-hr. It is wise to reserve 1 day in advance. Buy tickets for a tour at the gift shop next to the Palau. Palau open daily 10am-3:30pm, Aug. 10am-6pm. Box office open M-Sa 10am-9pm, Su from 1hr. prior to the concert. No concerts in Aug.; check the Guía del Ocio for listings. 800ptas/€4,80, students and seniors 600ptas/€3,60; with Ruta del Modernisme pass 400ptas/€2,40. Concert tickets 1300-26,000ptas/€7,80-125. MC/V.*

In 1891, the growing Orfeó Catalan choir society commissioned Modernist architect Luis Domènech i Montaner to design this must-see concert venue. The music hall glows with tall, stained-glass windows, an ornate chandelier, marble reliefs, intricate woodwork, and ceramic mosaics. A major renovation in the 80s improved the music hall's notoriously poor acoustics and a team of architects added a tasteful modern wing. In 1997, UNESCO declared this magical palace a World Heritage Site. Three years later, the church next door to the palace was demolished, letting in more light and enhancing the color and sparkle of Montaner's creation. Debate continues over the political message of the inverted dome (weighing in, incidentally, at one ton of glass and iron), which is painted with 40 women dressed as angels. Some believe that Montaner was implying that women sing like angels and should have been allowed in the choir (at that time it was exclusively male). Others argue he was depicting women's fickleness by painting them with 40 different faces. The 2073-seat concert hall is also home to a 3000-pipe-tubed organ, currently undergoing restoration. Concerts given at the Palau include all varieties of symphonic and choral music in addition to more modern forms of pop, rock, and jazz.

SANTA MARIA DEL MAR

🚶 ☎ 93 310 23 90. Open M-Sa 9am-1:30pm and 4:30-8pm, Su 9am-2pm and 5-8:30pm. Free. For concert information, call Dispacho Parrochial 93 319 05 16.

La Ribera's streets converge at the foot of the Església Santa Maria del Mar's octagonal towers. Built in the 14th century in a quick 55 years, Santa Maria del Mar (Mary of the Sea) was especially important to the growing population of sailors living in La Ribera at the time. The church was constructed from stone taken from Montjuïc and boasts an impressive doorway, which radiates out to either side and is punctuated by statues of Saint Peter and Saint Paul. Inside, it is a surprisingly low, wide, open space. At a distance of 13m apart, the supporting columns span a width greater than any other medieval building in the world. This church is also a fascinating example of the limits of Gothic architecture—were it 2 ft.higher it would collapse from structural instability. The Santa Maria del Mar occasionally holds classical, gospel, and folk concerts; call for information.

EL FOSSAR DE LES MORERES

🚶 Off C. de Santa Maria and next to the church's back entrance.

Though today it is nothing more than a brick-covered depression in the ground, the Fossar de les Moreres carries great significance as a reminder of Barcelona's past and of the Catalan struggle for cultural autonomy. The Catalans who resisted Felipe V's conquering troops in 1714 (see p. 41) were buried here in a mass grave, commemorated by mulberry trees (*les moreres*) and a plaque with a verse by the poet Sefari Pitarra: *In the Mulberry Cemetery no traitors are buried. Even though we lose our flags, this will be the urn of honor.* The monument is sunken to recall the sinking of the grave as the bodies decomposed. Demonstrators and patriots converge on the fossar on Catalan National Day, Sept. 11th, to commemorate the siege of Barcelona and the ensuing banishment of outward displays of Catalan nationalism.

MERCAT DE SANTA CATERINE

🚶 M: Arc de Triomf. Open July-Sept. Sa-Th 7:30am-3pm and 5-8pm, F 7:30am-8pm; Sept.-July Tu and Th 7:30am-3pm and 5-8pm.

Located in the wide middle section of Pg. Lluís Companys and across from the elaborate Palacio de Justicia, the Mercat de Santa Caterine is another traditional market. It is also a great, cheap place to pick up food before entering the park. Dozens of vendors sell produce, flowers, meats, and fish.

OTHER SIGHTS IN LA RIBERA

Carrer de Montcada, beginning behind the church, validates Barcelona's reputation as "*la ciudad del diseño*" (the city of design). Museums, art galleries, workshops, and baroque palaces that once housed Barcelona's 16th-century bureaucrats are packed into just two blocks. The **Museu Picasso** (see p. 109) inhabits several such mansions, and the **Galería Maeght** (C. de Montcada 26; see p. 121), a prestigious art gallery on the block, was once a medieval aristocrat's manor (see p. 121). Off the Placeta de Montcada at the Pg. del Born end is the city's narrowest street, C. de les Mosques (Street of Flies), which was finally closed off in 1991 after residents complained that the narrow alley was being used far too frequently as a public urinal. Also worth a look is Antoni Tàpies' **Homenatge a Picasso,** a glass-enclosed sculpture on Pg. Picasso in front of the Museu Geologia. Installed in 1983, the sculptural jumble of wood furniture and steel beams was inspired by Picasso's comment that "A picture is not something to decorate a sitting room, but a weapon of attack and of defense against the enemy."

PARC DE LA CIUTADELLA

⚐ Orientation and Transportation: *The park is bordered by Pg. Pujades to the west, Pg. Cicumval.lació to the east, C. Wellington to the north, and Pg. Picasso to the south. The **Museu de Zoologia** (see **Museums,** p. 111), **Hivernacle, Museu de Geologia** (see **Museums,** p. 110), and **Umbracle** all line the Pg. Picasso side, while the **Museu d'Art Modern** (see **Museums,** p. 110) and the **Pl. D'Armes** are on the side of the park closer to C. Wellington. The **Cascada fountain** (see p. 73) is at the corner of C. Wellington and Pg. Pujades and faces the small lake. The **zoo** (see p. 73) has an entrance on C. Wellington. M: Arc de Triomf is the best way to enter the park. Exit the Metro past the arch and walk down Pg. Lluís Companys, which leads directly to the main entrance by the Museu de Zoologia. In addition, Bus #14 runs from Pl. de Catalunya and stops at the Pg.Picasso/Avda. Marqués de l'Argentera entrance. Pick up a free map of the park from the info booth located behind the Museu Zoologia, open until 2:30pm. **Bike rental** is available from Los Paticletos (☎93 319 78 85) at Pg. Picasso 44 (rentals from 400ptas/€2,40 per hr). Park gates open daily from 7:30am-10pm.*

Sandwiched between La Ribera and Poble Nou, and a quick walk from Barceloneta and Barri Gòtic, Parc de la Ciutadella is a convenient break from the steady beat of urban Barcelona. The park includes an impressive collection of well-labeled horticulture. Birds flock in by the dozens to nibble at the fruit dropped from the park's orange trees. The well manicured grounds also attract a good number of couples nibbling at each other, as well as picnickers, jugglers, musicians, and frolicking children.

Barcelona's military resistance to the Bourbon monarchy in the early 18th century convinced Felipe V to quarantine Barcelona's influential citizens in the Ciutadella, a large citadel on what is now Pg. Picasso. An entire neighborhood was razed and its citizens evacuated to make room for the citadel, which lorded threateningly over Barcelona. The city demolished the fortress in 1868, under the direction of General Joan Prim (honored with a statue at the end of Pg. Til.les), and replaced it with the peaceful promenades of Parc de la Ciutadella. Architect Josep Fontseré won the competition to design the new park, and brought with him newcomers Domènech i Montaner (of Palau de la Música Catalana fame, see p. 70) and Antoni Gaudí. Several Modernist buildings went up years later when Ciutadella hosted the Universal Exposition in 1888 (see **Life & Times,** p. 43), including Montaner's stately **Castell dels Tres Dragons** (now **Museu de Zoologia**). Expo '88 also inspired the **Arc de Triomf,** just across Pg. Pujades from the park.

ARC DE TRIOMF

⚐ *M: Arc de Triomf.*

Rather than commemorating a military triumph, Barcelona's own **Arc de Triomf** was designed as the entrance to the 1888 Universal Exposition along with several sites in the Parc de la Ciutadella. The spectacular red brick structure, which sits at the head of Pg. Lluís Companys, is adorned with green ceramic tiles and the sculpted forms of bats, angels, and lions.

▧ HIVERNACLE

⚐ *On Pg. Picasso, behind the Museu de Zoologia. M: Arc de Triomf. café (☎93 295 40 17) menú del día 1950ptas/€12, salads and bocadillos 465-940ptas/€3-5,50. Open M-Sa 10am-midnight, Su 10am-4pm. MC/V.*

Josep Amergós' Hivernacle is a spectacular iron and glass greenhouse which houses some of the park's most delicate vegetation. The Hivernacle's café is a lovely place for a meal or drink, and also houses the park's public restrooms. On Wednesday evenings from May through July (10:30pm), the Hivernacle holds jazz concerts (400ptas/€2,40), and Thursday nights in July free classical music concerts begin at 10:15pm. Further down the Pg. Picasso on the other side of the Museu Geologia, the Fontseré's **Umbracle** has an iron slatted roof which acts as a mock-canopy to shade the inhabitants of the park's other greenhouse.

CASCADA FOUNTAIN & LAKE

🚻 *In the northeast corner of the park, directly accessible by Pg. Pujades/C. Wellington entrance. Open M-F noon-7pm, Sa-Su 11am-8:30pm. Boat rental 300ptas/€1,80 per hr.*

The grandiose, often excessive details of Ciutadella's Cascada fountain are, not surprisingly, the work of Fontseré's young assistant Antoni Gaudí. The palatial fountain is eye-catching even from the other side of the park. Grecian statues, dragons, and a Venus on the half shell adorn the top of the structure, with double staircases leading to its upper levels. The front of the fountain faces a snack bar and a full-scale statue of a Mammoth, a representation of the large beasts whose fossil remains have been discovered near Les Corts. Behind the bar, the park's small lake rents paddle boats—a favorite of young visitors.

Palau Güell Roof Terrace

🖼 PARC ZOOLÒGIC

🚻 *M: Ciutadella. If you are going straight to the zoo, go to M: Ciutadella and follow C. Wellington out of the Metro. The zoo is accessible from a separate entrance on C. Wellington. From inside the park, the zoo entrance is next to the Museu d'Art Modern/Parliament building.* ☎ *93 225 67 80. Open Nov.-Feb. 10am-5pm, Mar and Oct 10am-6pm, Apr. and Sept. 10am-7pm, May-Aug. 9:30am-7:30pm. Entrance 1600ptas/€9,62; children ages 3-12 1025ptas/€6,16; seniors over 65 925ptas/€5,50. After 5pm May-Sept., entrance 1050ptas/€6,31, children 625ptas/€3,76, and seniors 575ptas/€3,46. AmEx/D/MC/V. The zoo has its own restaurants and snack bars.*

Animal rights activists be prepared: standards for zoos and animal treatment in Spain may be different than those in other countries. Though the quarters are cramped for the zoo's residents (there are plans to relocate the institution out of the park), the zoo still draws park-goers young and old. Charismatic 🖼**Floquet de Neu** (Snowflake), the world's only albino gorilla, is the zoo's main attraction, although the elephants, hippos, seals, and other residents also draw crowds. The zoo also features an aquarium, petting zoo, and the famous **Senyoreta del Paraigua** sculpture.

Sta. Maria del Mar

An enduring symbol from the 1888 Exposition, the sculpture and fountain has become an emblem of Barcelona. *Senyoreta del Paraigua* (Lady with the Umbrella; 1885) was designed by the sculptor Joan Roig i Solé, who was a founder of the Sitges school, painting seascapes in an impressionistic style. The *senyoreta*, who shoots water from the top of her umbrella, was modeled after the Catalan painter Pepita Teixidor and is known informally to many Barcelonenses simply as "Pepita."

Sant Pau in El Raval

MATING GAME

You've seen him in your dreams for months now. Walking around the city, you can feel his presence. Finally, it's time for a private audience. Though some call him Snowflake, in his native Catalan he's Floquet de Neu (Floquet to his friends), the world's only white gorilla, who bears more than a passing resemblance to Willie Nelson. Taken from the forest in west Africa in the 60s, Floquet has been the toast of Barcelona ever since.

Spend some time with him at the zoo (see p. 73), and you may be lucky enough to observe a behavior common to both captive and wild gorillas—coprophagy, or eating one's own excrement. Vitamin D is not available in the gorillas' natural habitat, but is produced by bacteria in their hind gut; eating everything twice helps satisfy their nutritional needs. Floquet has made an art form of the practice, and sometimes spends minutes on end smearing and sampling, strange expressions passing over his countenance all the while.

PLAÇA D'ARMES

Situated in front of the Museu d'Art Modern and the Parliament of Catalunya. Enter through the gate at Pg. Picasso/Av. Marqués de L'Argentera and continue straight past the statue of General Prim.

Formal, square hedged gardens surround a quiet pond. At its center, a copy (the only non-original work in the park) of Josep Llimona's sculpture *Desconsol* (1907) collapses in melancholy. Surrounding the plaça are the only remaining buildings of the former citadel including the arsenal, Governor's Palace (now used as a school), and a striking church.

EL RAVAL

see map pp. 316-317

PALAU GÜELL

C. Nou de La Rambla 3-5. ☎93 317 39 74; fax 93 317 37 79. M: Liceu, two blocks from the Opera Liceu, off Las Ramblas. Visits by guided tour only, departing every 15min. Open M-Sa 10am-1pm and 4:15-7pm. 400ptas/€2,40; students 200ptas/€1,20.

Antoni Gaudí's Palau Güell (1886)—a dark, haunting Modernist residence built for patron Eusebi Güell (of Park Güell fame)—has one of Barcelona's most spectacular interiors. Güell and Gaudí spared no expense in the construction of this sumptuous home, with which some say Gaudí truly came into his own as a premier architect. The 20 unique rooftop chimneys display Gaudí's first use of the *trencadís*—the covering of surfaces with irregular shards of ceramic or glass, a technique often seen in his later work.

ESGLÉSIA DE SANT PAU DEL CAMP

M: Paral.lel, at the intersection of C. Sant Pau and C. Carretes, 2 blocks off Av. Paral.lel. Open W-M 5-8pm, closed Tu.

When this church was first founded in the year 912, it stood in the country, well outside the city walls. The current church building, built in the 12th century and now very much a part of the city, is the most important example of Romanesque architecture (see **Life & Times,** p. 50) in the city of Barcelona. Guifré Borrell, the church's founder and the son of Wilfred the Hairy (see **Life & Times,** p. 38), is buried here.

UNIVERSITAT DE BARCELONA

Pl. Universitat. M: Universitat. Open M-F 9am-10pm.

This palatial 19th-century building housed the University of Barcelona until much of its campus moved north to Pedralbes in the 1950s.

Today, the religion, mathematics, and language departments remain, along with regal hallways, columns, and high arches, and several green, shady courtyards.

L'EIXAMPLE

see map pp. 314-315

As Barcelona's bourgeoisie have increasingly moved uptown, the earliest residential districts in l'Eixample, around Pg. de Gràcia, have been filling with offices, services, and shops. The Modernist original architecture that draws visitors to this vast part of Barcelona remains intact. The buildings on Pg. de Gràcia (such as Casa Milà, p. 77, and La Manzana de la Discòrdia, p. 79), Gaudí's Sagrada Família, and Domènech i Montaner's Hospital de la Santa Creu i Sant Pau are the landmark attractions, while more dedicated architecture lovers wander the streets of the so-called *Quadrant d'Or*, the area bounded by Av. Diagonal, C. Aribau, Pg. St. Joan, and the lower Rondas (Ronda Universitat and Rda. St. Pere). In this neighborhood you will find the majority of expensive homes first built when the walls of the old city were torn down. If you plan on seeing a lot of the sights in l'Eixample, be sure to get a **Ruta del Modernisme** pass; see p. 59.

⬛ LA SAGRADA FAMÍLIA

🚩 *C. Mallorca 401; main entrance on C. Sardenya between C. Provença and C. Mallorca. M: Sagrada Família. ☎ 93 207 30 31. Open Nov.-Feb. 9am-6pm, elevator 9:30am-5:45pm; Mar., Sept., and Oct. 9am-7pm, elevator 9:30am-6:45pm; April-Aug. 9am-8pm, elevator 9:30am-7:45pm. Guided tours Apr.-Oct. daily 11:30am, 1pm, 4pm, and 5:30pm; Nov.-Mar. F-M 11:30am and 1pm; 500ptas/€3 (buy tickets right inside the Sardenya entrance). Combined ticket for the Sagrada Família and Casa-Museu Gaudí (in the Park Güell, see p. 92) 1000ptas/€6. Just La Sagrada Família and its museum 850ptas/€5, students 650ptas/€4,50, with the Ruta pass 425ptas/€2,50. Cash only.*

Although Gaudí's unfinished masterpiece is barely even a shell of the intended finished product, La Sagrada Família is without a doubt the world's most-visited construction site. Despite the facts that only eight of the church's 18 planned towers have been completed (and those the shortest, at that) and the church still doesn't have an "inside," millions of people flock to see it every year. Ticket profits subsidize private donations for the continued construction of the church. Unfinished or not, La Sagrada Família has become tightly intertwined with the image of Barcelona.

La Sagrada Família was commissioned not by the Roman Catholic Church, but by an extremely pious right-wing organization called

Stay with him a little longer, and you may see a behavior not common in the wild—incest. With gorillas and the other apes in endangered species status (in danger of extinction in the wild in the next 20 years), zoos all over the world are making concerted efforts to aid these species in breeding. Because of Floquet's dashing good looks, special measures are being taken in his case. In an effort to breed another white gorilla (Floquet's blue eyes mean he is not, in fact, an albino, but lucistic, an even rarer genetic abnormality), he has been encouraged to breed with his daughters. With over a dozen offspring to date, there is still no Floquet Jr.; Floquet de Neu may be the last of his kind (although a gorilla with white fingertips was once found in the forest where Floquet is from). Floquet's uniqueness is all the more reason for a pilgrimage to Barcelona.

Gaze deep into Floquet's blue eyes. Does he know the extent of his fame? Does he recognize the god-like reverence he commands, the important duty he performs by being a spokesman for his wild cousins? Probably. He's a pretty cool ape.

GET sm**art**

Far-out Façade

Gaudí was a religious man, and his plans for La Sagrada Família called for elaborate and deliberate symbolism in almost every single decorative element of the church. On the left of the **Passion Façade,** a snake lurks behind Judas, symbolizing the disciple's betrayal of Jesus. The 4x4 box of numbers next to Him contains 310 possible combinations of four numbers, each of which adds up to 33, Christ's age when He died. The faceless woman in the center of the façade, **Veronica,** represents the Biblical woman with the same name and the miraculous appearance of Christ's face on the cloth she compassionately wiped Him with. The cypress tree on the **Nativity Façade,** according to one theory, symbolizes the stairway to heaven (cypress trees do not put down deeper roots with time but only grow increasingly taller); the tree is crowned with the word "Tau," Greek for the name of God. Similarly, the top of each of the eight finished towers carries the first letter of one of the names of the apostles (and the words "Hosanna" and "Excelsis" are written in a spiral up the sides of the towers). Inside, on the **Portal of the Rosary,** overt references to modern life lurk amongst more traditional religious imagery: the Temptation of Man is represented in one carving by the devil handing a bomb to a terrorist and in another by his waving a purse at a prostitute.

the Spiritual Association for Devotion to St. Joseph, or the Josephines. Founded in 1866 in reaction to the liberal ideas spreading throughout Europe, the group was determined to build for Barcelona an Expiatory Temple, where the city could reaffirm its faith to the Holy Family of Jesus, Mary, and Joseph, hence the building's full name, **Templo Expiatori de la Sagrada Família.** The first architect they chose quit almost immediately, and they replaced him with Gaudí in 1884, when he was only 32 years old. For the first 15 or 20 years, private contributions kept the building process going, but as the mood and culture of the city changed with the onset of the modern age, construction slowed drastically, and the Civil War (see p. 44) brought it to a complete halt. Gaudí died in an accident in 1926 having completed only one façade, the **Nativity Façade,** and in 1936, arsonists broke into the crypt, opened Gaudí's tomb, smashed his plaster models, and burned every single document in the workshop.

Today, the building remains under the auspices of the Josephines; architect Jordi Bonet, whose father worked directly with Gaudí, is heading up the project with sculptor Josep Marià Subirachs, who finished the Passion Façade in 1998. Hampered by the lack of Gaudí's exact calculations, they are working from ongoing reconstructions of Gaudí's original plaster models; and the computer models which engineers are using to recreate his underlying mathematical logic are so complicated that only three people in the world know how to use them. As today's workers slowly put into form what they think Gaudí had in mind, they are doing things, architecturally, that have literally never been done before. For this reason (in addition to the project's reliance on private donations), no one can even set a projected date for the completion of the church, although it is generally assumed that it will be completed before 2100.

The continuation of Gaudí's greatest obsession has been fraught with fierce controversy. Some, like Salvador Dalí, have argued that the church should have been left uncompleted as a monument to the architect. Others believe that La Sagrada Família should be finished, but in a more "authentic" manner. Critics usually attack most vehemently Subirachs' abstract, Cubist Passion Façade, which contrasts starkly with the more traditional Nativity Façade, which depicts Christ's birth and faces the Pl. de Gaudí. The controversial Passion Façade, which faces the Pl. de la Sagrada Família, depicts Christ's Passion—Catholic lingo for his crucifixion, death, and resurrection. When completed, the front of the temple—the Glory Façade—will feature four more bell towers like those that already exist; together the 12 towers will represent the 12 apostles. Above the center of the church will rise a massive 170m Tower of Jesus, with a shorter spire just behind dedicated to Mary. The Jesus tower will in turn be surrounded by four more towers symbolizing the four Evangelists, (the authors of the four holy gospels). As finishing touches, Gaudí envisioned an extravagant spouting fountain in front of the main Glory Façade and a tall purifying flame at the back. Gaudí's dedication to religious themes in his work on La Sagrada Família (see Far-Out façade, p. p. 76) has even earned the attention of the Vatican (see **Gaudí**, p. 50).

Visitors today can see detailed paintings of the projected church in the museum in the crypt. Also on display are numerous pictures from the early years of the project, sketches by Gaudí, the glass-walled workshop where his models are still being restored, and various sculptures and decorative pieces from the temple. The elevator ride up to the top allows a closer look at the building's stonework, as does the breathtaking, if slightly treacherous, trip up the labyrinthine stairs that climb up the insides of the towers.

Parc de la Ciutadella

◼ CASA MILÀ (LA PEDRERA)

🔲 *Pg. de Gràcia 92; enter around the corner on C. Provença. ☎93 484 59 95. Open daily 10am-8pm, last entry 7:30pm. 1000ptas/€6; students, over 65 and with the Ruta del Modernisme pass 500ptas/€3. Free guided tours M-F at 5:30pm (English and Catalan) and 6pm (Spanish), Sa-Su at 11am (English and Catalan) and 11:30pm (Spanish); you can also reserve a private group tour for 4000ptas/€24 total. Audio-guides for the Espai Gaudí and apartment 500ptas/€3, available in English. Wheelchair-accessible. MC/V.*

Built between 1906 and 1912, the Casa Milà apartment building, commonly called "La Pedrera" for its resemblance to a stone quarry, was Gaudí's last civic work. It is also one of his most famous, surpassed only by La Sagrada Família. Some admirers liken the curving stone façade and tangled iron balconies to ocean waves and seaweed, while others argue that Gaudí must have gotten his inspiration from nearby mountains like Montserrat. The building does not have a single straight line, and the billowing, sinuous chimneys on the roof are so unusual they have been described as delirious or hallucinatory. It is even said that the "face" of one of the smaller chimneys served as the model for the mask of *Star Wars'* Darth Vader.

Penguin at the Zoo

Few visitors, though, are aware of the important role *functionality* played in Gaudí's work. The six largest rooftop structures, for instance, have the most efficient shape possible for their triple role as stairwells, air ventilation passages, and water tank holders, and the so-called "Prussian helmets" of the soldier-like chimneys

Cascada Fountain

GET sm**art**

It Takes Two to Tango

The name of Antoni Gaudí has gained such international fame that he tends to be unilaterally associated with his greatest works. In reality, though, Gaudí usually operated more as a loose coordinator of a host of extremely skilled sculptors, iron-workers, and painters, some of whom he gave huge creative leeway. This was particularly true of his collaborative relationship with a man named **Josep Marià Jujol.** Some critics actually consider Jujol to be directly responsible for Gaudí's shift, between 1904 and 1908, from his earlier heavier designs to the much more fluid, almost magical ones of his later years. Jujol designed the furniture for Casa Batlló, had complete control over the construction of the La Pedrera roof while Gaudí was away on other projects, and even created the famous ceramic-clad, winding bench at the Park Güell. There are those who believe, in fact, that not passing the Sagrada Família to Jujol's control after Gaudí's death was an extremely regrettable mistake.

serve the very specific purpose of preventing smoke from re-entering the building. The windows in the attic were placed specifically to create a strong air flow for drying laundry, and even the façade itself owes its distinctive appearance in part to the pillar-and-column internal structure which Gaudí chose in order to achieve maximum natural lighting. Unlike most traditional façades, this one does not bear much of the building's weight but rather decorates it like a curtain.

These unusual designs were not all well-accepted 100 years ago. The building's namesake, wealthy businessman Pere Milà, hired Gaudí because he liked his work on neighboring Casa Batlló, but as the project progressed his wife Roser Segimon became increasingly unhappy with both the aesthetics and excessive cost of the building. Gaudí eventually filed a lawsuit against the couple over his fees, and the Casa Milà ended up being the only residence he designed for which he did not also craft the furniture; instead, Roser Segimon had the interior done competely in artificial Louis XV style. (Gaudí won the lawsuit, incidentally, and promptly gave all of the money to the poor.) Gaudí also originally intended to place a massive sculpture of the Virgin and Child in the most prominent corner of the rooftop. Either the Milàs just didn't like it, or they were afraid to boast such a display of faith after the horrific violence of the *Setmana Santa* (Tragic Week; see **Life and Times,** p. 44) and Gaudí was denied his cherished final touch.

Cartoons of the day mocked the Casa Milà with comparisons to a layer cake, airplane hanger, or multi-leveled gunwall, and the municipal authorities declared it in violation of building codes. Gaudí responded that if he was forced to alter his building, he would place a prominent plaque on the front naming every person responsible for the mutilation; soon after it was decided that an exception to the rules could be made just this once.

Gaudí himself predicted that his creation would one day cease to be a private residence and would serve the public instead. In 1986, the Fundació Caixa Catalunya fulfilled his prophecy by buying the grimy, decaying building, restoring it to pristine perfection, and turning it partially into a museum. Today, you can visit the entrance foyer, wander the rooftop, and tour an apartment decorated as it might have been in Gaudí's time. The second floor hosts temporary art exhibitions, and the attic has been turned into the **Espai Gaudí,** a fabulous multimedia presentation on the development of the architect's distinctive style. It's a good way to see, on video, the buildings of his which are closed to the public.

■ LA MANZANA DE LA DISCÒRDIA

🛪 Pg. de Gràcia 35 (Casa Lleó Morera), 41 (Casa Amatller), and 43 (Casa Batlló). M: Pg. de Gràcia. 1st fl. of Casa Amatller, where Ruta del Modernisme passes are sold (see p. 59), open M-Sa 10am-7pm, Su and holidays 10am-2pm. ☎ 93 488 01 39. With the Ruta pass, free tours of all 3 façades available daily 10am-6pm on the hr. (10am, noon, 1, 3, 4, and 6pm in English); bring your Ruta pass to the desk at Casa Amatller. Interiors of the houses only open for special educational years: Casa Amatller is open in 2001 for the Year of Puig i Cadafalch. Limited tours of Casa Batlló may be available in 2002 for the Year of Gaudí; inquire at the Ruta del Modernisme desk in Casa Amatller.

According to Greek myth, a piece of fruit was responsible for the Trojan War: the goddess of Discord created a golden apple as a prize for the most beautiful goddess, and divine disharmony ensued (See **The Battle of the Apple**, p. 80). Barcelona has its own competition for the golden apple going on, on the block of Pg. de Gràcia between C. Consell de Cent and C.'Aragó, where trademark houses by the three most important architects of Modernism tower side by side in proud disharmony: the **Casa Lleó Morera** by Domènech i Montaner, the **Casa Amatller** by Puig i Cadafalch, and the **Casa Batlló** by Gaudí. Even the strongest Catalanists haven't wanted to give up the pun in the old name *"la manzana,"* which in Castilian means both "block" and "apple." All of these creations are renovations of older, pre-existing edifices. To see the architectural contrast most clearly, take a look from the other side of Pg. de Gràcia. For more on the Modernist movement, see **Life & Times**, p. 51.

CASA LLEÓ MORERA

In 1902, textile tycoon Albert Lleó Morera hired Domènech i Montaner to add some pizazz to his boring 1864 home on the corner of Pg. de Gràcia and C. Consell de Cent. Montaner responded by creating one of the most lavish examples of decorative architecture Barcelona. The house's interior ceramic, glass, and wood decorations, its window designs, and its exterior sculptures are an exceptional example of Modernism's application of numerous art forms toward one harmonious whole. Much of the street-level exterior was destroyed by the Loewe leather shop which now occupies the entry, but if you look up at the second-floor balconies on either side of the corner tribune, you can see two nymphs on each balcony, holding (from left to right) a gramophone, an electric lightbulb, a telephone, and a camera, symbols of the new leisure technology available to the bourgeoisie of the early 1900s. On the wall of the balcony above the tribune itself you can see carved lions; mulberry leaves lace around the tops of

Façade of Sagrada Família

Spiral Staircase at Sagrada Família

Looking Down from Sagrada Família

BATTLE OF THE APPLE

Note to self: *invite the Goddess of Discord to your wedding*. Last time she was passed over, she interrupted the VIP-filled celebration by flinging a golden apple through the window labeled "for the most beautiful goddess of all." Hera, Athena, and Aphrodite immediately began claiming it as their own, and Zeus was faced with the impossible task of making peace between his own wife and daughters. Like most head honchos, he decided to pass the buck and chose the young Trojan prince Paris to make the choice for him. Hera bribed the boy with all of the riches in the land, Athena offered him supreme wisdom, and Aphrodite promised him Helen, the most beautiful woman in the world. Apparently Paris let his second brain do the thinking, and Helen's husband (yup, she was taken) responded by sending battleships to Troy.

For Barcelona's own version of this mythical battle, see **La Manzana de la Discòrdia**, p. 79.

the tribune's vertical columns. Together these refer to the family name: *lleó* in Catalan means "lion," and *morera* means "mulberry tree".

The mezzanine level of the interior, unfortunately closed to the public, boasts a stunning dining room with glimmering stained-glass windows and detailed ceramic mosaics of the Lleó Morera family picnicking outdoors. The famous furniture which Gaspar Homar originally designed for this room is now on display at the Museu d'Art Modern (see **Museums,** p. 110), and the Ruta del Modernisme booklet guide has a decent picture of the gorgeous stained-glass wall (as do most coffee-table books on Barcelona architecture).

CASA AMATLLER

Chocolate mogul Antoni Amatller laid the first seed for La Manzana de la Discòrdia in 1898, when he commissioned Puig i Cadafalch to redo the façade of his prominent home. Cadafalch turned out a mix of neo-Gothic, Islamic, and Dutch architecture best known for its stylized, geometric, pink, blue, and cream upper façade. The lower exterior of the house is also noteworthy; look carefully and you can see various facets of the owner's personality inscribed in sculpture. Above the main door, the prominent carving of Catalan hero St. Jordi battling the dragon demonstrates Amatller's Catalan nationalism; the four figures engaged in painting, sculpture, architecture, and music represent Amatller's broad cultural interests. On either side of the main second-floor windows, there are caricatures of Amatller's favorite pastimes. On the left, small monkeys and rabbits busily mold iron (the main Catalan industry of Amatller's time), and a donkey with glasses reads a book while another plays with a camera; on the right side, frogs and pigs hold glass vases and pottery, a reference to Amatller's passion for vase-collecting. A huge "A" for Amatller adorns the outside of the entrance, intertwined with almond leaves (*amatller* means "almond" in Catalan).

The building's façade resembles Flanders, a former Spanish colony, which some argue is a reference to the fact that Amatller traded chocolate there. Others suggest that the resemblance to Flanders was a political statement by Puig i Cadafalch, a protest against Catalunya's own near-colonial relationship with the central government in Madrid. Still others believe that it was simply the best shape to cover the photography studio on the top floor.

Inside, the entrance foyer still has fascinating iron and glass lamps, bright decorative tiles, and a stained glass skylight just to the right off the main hallway. When the Ruta del Modernisme office on the first floor is open, you can wander the small temporary art exhibit in the back room and buy some Amatller chocolate to see for yourself whether he deserved his fortune. The apartment where the millionaire lived with his daughter is now home to the **Institut Amatller d'Art Hispànic,** open to students of the institute.

The **Joieria Bagués,** which holds a well-known collection of Modernist pieces from the Masriera tradition, occupies the right side of the entrance level. Descendants of founder Lluís Masriera still use his original molds and firing techniques from a century ago; a tour of his sparkling dragonflies, nymphs, and flowers are worth a walk through the store (allowed with the Ruta pass).

La Pedrera's Roof Terrace

CASA BATLLÓ

Eager to sow his wild oats with fair-faced Helen, young Paris could not help but give the golden apple to Aphrodite, Goddess of Beauty. Today, even without his vigorous sexual appetite, most visitors choose to bestow the same honor upon the most fantastical member of the Block of Discord, Gaudí's Casa Batlló. Shimmering and curving in shades of blue and green, the house looks slightly different at every hour of the day. Every visitor has their favorite time of day to see Casa Batlló; perhaps the evening light best flatters its creepy lines and squiggles. Most see the building as a depiction of the legend of St. Jordi and the dragon. This interpretation incorporates all the major facets of the building: the tall pinnacle on the left symbolizes the knight's lance after it has pierced the dragon's scaly back, represented by the warped, multi-colored, ceramic roof. The stairwell inside has been interpreted as the winding of the dragon's tail or the curves of his vertebrae, the outside balconies as skulls, and the molded columns as the bones of his unfortunate victims.

Façade of La Pedrera

Like the other houses on the block, Casa Batlló was a remodeling job on an older, ordinary building, this one requested in 1904 by Josep Batlló, yet another wealthy beneficiary of the Industrial Revolution's textile boom. Gaudí hardly left a single wall intact when he renovated Batlló's private apartment; as with the Casa Milà, he did away with straight lines altogether, even in the furniture. Particularly interesting is the way he tiled the central inner patio, dark blue on the top and lighter on the bottom in order to distribute the light from above as evenly as possible.

Apparently candy manufacturers have a sweet-tooth for Modernism: the ChupaChups lollipop company now owns the Casa Batlló; it is usually closed to the public unless you want to rent it for a cool 1,000,000ptas/€6,025 per night. Fortunately, the Espai Gaudí in Casa Milà has a good video presentation which allows you to see the tiled walls, colorful mosaics, and sensuous curves of the inside of the house as well as interesting details on the exterior. Casa Batlló may also be open for limited tours in 2002; see p. 79.

Courtyard of Casa Milà

81

MORE MODERNISM ON PG. DE GRÀCIA

🚩 *M: Catalunya, or bus #24.*

If the Casa Milà and Manzana de la Discòrdia have not satiated your appetite fo. Modernist architecture in l'Eixample, there are plenty of other buildings to keep ar eye out for as you walk along the Pg. de Gràcia. Start at M: Catalunya and make you way up the Pg. de Gràcia. Coming up from the Pl. de Catalunya, you will see on the right at no. 18 the **Joieria Roca**; this glass-block, curving building was way ahead of it: time in 1934, when architect Josep Lluís Sert sparked a serious conservative back lash with his unconventional design for the façade. **Casa Olano**, at no. 60, was used a: headquarters for the Basque government during the Spanish Civil War; a plaque to this effect still hangs above the doorway. The building earned its nickname "Pirate House" from the rendition of sailor Juan Sebastian Elcano on the front wall. Up a lit tle further at no.66 is one of the most attractive corner façades on the Pg. de Gràcia, part of the **Casa Vidua Marfà**, built by Manual Comas Thos in 1905. Today it houses Barcelona's School of Tourism, but you can walk into the entrance foyer and look up at the multi-colored skylight.

A few blocks further at no. 96, the **Casa Casas** shares the limelight with Casa Milà. Notable mainly for its previous inhabitant, the Catalan painter Ramon Casas, the first two floors are now occupied by the Vinçon furniture and knick-knack store (see **Shopping**, p. 184). Walk inside to see the house's original stone entry, stairwell, and an imposing carved fireplace, or outside to the back patio, where you can see the reddish-colored back side of La Pedrera.

One block over at the intersection of Diagonal and Rambla de Catalunya (no. 126), the literally two-faced **Can Serra** is worth a look as well. The original turreted pink-and-peach stone building, in French Gothic style, was built by Puig i Cadafalch in 1908 and is adorned with a sculpture by Eusebi Arnau of St. Jordi, the dragon, the princess, and some strangely entangled centaurs. The bulk of the house was razed in 1981, and now the old Gothic façade wraps around a smooth, black, glossy structure home to the Disputació of Barcelona.

& EVEN MORE WITHIN A FEW BLOCKS...

Still want more? Then go back to Pl. de Catalunya and walk up the Pg. de Gràcia only one block to C. Casp, where you will turn right and continue for a few blocks to no. 48, **Casa Calvet**. This house was Gaudí's first apartment building. It was also, in fact, the only thing he ever won an award for during his lifetime: the Ajuntament's first annual prize for Best Building of the Year, given out in 1900. From Casa Calvet, back-track half a block to C. Roger de Llúria, turn right, and walk up 2½ blocks. On your right, at no. 56, will be a small passageway leading to the **Torre de les Aigües**, the water tower built by Josep Oriol Mestres in 1879 to supply water to the first houses of l'Eixample. Today it overlooks a small summertime pool for neighborhood children. A half-block further up, at the intersection of C. Roger de Llúria with C. Consell de Cent, you will see the pink-and-peach painted exterior of the oldest house in l'Eixample, built in 1864. Four houses at once were actually built here, one on each corner, for landowner Josep Cerdà, but only this one remains today.

HOSPITAL DE LA SANTA CREU I SANT PAU

🚩 *Entrance at corner of C. Cartagena and C. St. Antonia Maria Claret (9 blocks in area). M: Hospital de St. Pau, C. Cartagena exit. ☎ 93 488 20 78; www.santpau.es. 50min. guided tours Sa-Su 10am-2pm every 30min., in Catalan, Spanish, or English as needed. Last tour leaves at 1:30pm. 700ptas/€4,20, students and over 65 500ptas/€3. Cash only. Hospital grounds open 24hr.*

Designated a UNESCO monument in 1997, the brilliant Modernist Hospital de la Santa Creu i Sant Pau was Domènech i Montaner's (of Palau fame) lifetime master-piece. The entire complex covers nine full L'Eixample blocks, or 320 acres, and the pavilions designed by Domènech i Montaner are so colorful and whimsically decorated they almost resemble gingerbread houses. The outdoor spaces, meanwhile, are often compared to an oasis or garden city in a sea of monotonous city gridding; they once included a small forest for walking and still boast more than 300 different types of plants, as well as plenty of wide, shaded paths.

Begun in 1905, this unusual hospital owes its existence to a wealthy Catalan banker named Pau Gil who spent his entire adult life in Paris. While there, he was influenced by new French theories on proper hygiene and therapeutic hospital designs, and he endowed Barcelona with three million *pesetas* to build a new type of city hospital: not only sanitary, but also aesthetically pleasing, a more complete healing experience. A design by architect Domènech i Estapa was originally chosen for the building, but he was soon dropped in favor of Domènech i Montaner, who did a better job of incorporating medical and sanitary concerns. Domènech i Montaner designed a set of 12 pavilions, each of which would be no more than one or two stories and would serve only 28 patients. The interior of each pavilion was painted various shades of green, and each room had plenty of natural light. Domènech i Montaner took note of wind patterns and put the most infectious wards at the back of the hospital, at the "end" of the current. In a bold, new step for his time, he also built a complex network of underground service tunnels for hospital staff, in order to keep the ground level feeling as unlike a hospital as possible.

Gaudí's Casa Batlló

The money for Domènech i Montaner's design ran out just as he finished up in 1910, and construction on the hospital was not continued until 1915, when it gained further financial backing by merging with the city's ancient Hospital de la Santa Creu (founded 1401). Domènech i Montaner's son undertook the expansion of his father's work, though in a completely different style (Modernism fell out of fashion as soon as he began working), and the completed joint complex, with a total of 48 pavilions, was officially opened in 1930 by King Alfonso XIII. Even with the vast additions to Montaner's pavilions, the Hospital de la Santa Creu i Sant Pau still has one of the highest space-to-patient ratios in all of Europe, with 140 sq. m. for each of the 600 patients.

Girl at Casa Batlló

The hospital grounds are meant for pleasant walking, and the exterior of the Montaner pavilions are worth at least a quick glance. The most interesting attraction for most tourists, though, is the main administrative building, which is steeped in decorative symbolism. The letters P and G, a tribute to Pau Gil, recur over and over in various surprising motifs. The four sculptured figures on the front façade represent faith, hope, charity, and work, and the multi-domed ceiling of the entrance foyer is covered with the symbols of Catalunya, Barcelona, St. Jordi (the patron saint of Barcelona), and even the city of Paris and the bankers' association (a nod to Pau Gil again), as well as the years in which the Modernist portion was begun and finished.

Casa Amatller, Sant Jordi detail

The hospital is actually slated to close in 2004, when the medical services will be relocated to more modern facilities nearby. The future fate of the complex has not yet been set in stone, but rumor has it that it may become a particularly stunning university.

PLAÇA GLÒRIES

🖪 *M: Glòries.*

The two most prominent plaças on the right side of l'Eixample (east of the Pg. de Gràcia) are **Pl. Glòries** and **Pl. Tetuán,** both of which are home to weighty city monuments. The Pl. Glòries is by far the biggest in l'Eixample; at the intersection of Av. Meridiana and Av. Diagonal, its small central park is entirely circled by a wide roadway packed with fast-moving cars. The bizarre **Monument to the Metre** crosses the length of the park; donated by the Dunkirk (Ireland) City Council in 1992, it commemorates the 200th anniversary of the measuring of the Prime Meridian between Barcelona and Dunkirk. The twelve black plaques around the plaça use famous quotations or excerpts to memorialize 12 "glorious" elements of Catalan history, including Romanesque art, Gothic architecture, industrialization, science and technology contributions, Catalan law, self-government, and more.

PLAÇA TETUÁN

🖪 *M: Tetuán*

The centerpiece of the Pl. Tetuán is a hefty **monument to Bartomeu Robert,** a piece done by Josep Llimona in 1910 in honor of the former city mayor. It was torn down under Franco because of its excessive nationalistic symbolism, but was finally replaced and recognized by King Juan Carlos and Queen Sofia in 1985.

MONUMENTS IN L'EIXAMPLE DRETA

🖪 *M: Verdaguer, which is at the intersection of Av. Diagonal and Pg. de St. Joan*

A good number of Barcelona's more than 400 monuments adorn l'Eixample, where wide streets and open corners lend them plenty of visibility. Some of the better known include the submarine sculpture in honor of inventor **Narcís Monturiol** (C. Girona and Av. Diagonal, M: Verdaguer), the monument to **Anton Clavé,** founder of the popular choral societies (Pg. de St. Joan and Trav. de Gràcia; also accessible from M: Joanic), and the monument to Catalan poet **Jacint Verdaguer** (Pg. St. Joan and Av. Diagonal).

Casa Lleó Morera

Detail on Palau de la Música Catalana

Modernist and Modern

OTHER SIGHTS IN L'EIXAMPLE DRETA

🚇 *M: Diagonal.*

One of the most famous Modernist houses in the city sits near the intersection of Av. Diagonal and C. Roger de Llúria, at Av. Diagonal 416; also accessible from M: Joanic. Designed by Puig i Cadafalch in 1905, it is called the **Casa de las Punxes (House of Spikes)** for its distinctively pointy medieval turrets. On the same block, Salvador Valeri's **Casa Comalet** (Av. Diagonal 422) has two façades, the one facing Av. Diagonal well-decorated with colorful ceramics. Nearby, Puig i Cadafalch's **Palau del Baló de Quadras** (Av. Diagonal 373), has an even more ornate façade, almost entirely covered with varied sculptures.

Casa de les Punxes

L'EIXAMPLE ESQUERRA

❧ THE *LET'S GO* BULL

🚇 *M: Catalunya. From Pl. de Catalunya, walk up La Rambla de Catalunya one block to Gran Via; look at the cover of your book, and look around for the real life version. Open all day, every day.*

At the bottom of Rambla de Catalunya near Gran Via sits our beloved mascot, lost in deep contemplation. You may recognize this thoughtful bull from the cover of such hits as: *Let's Go: Barcelona 2002.* Officially titled *Meditation*, his pose mimics that of Rodin's *The Thinker.* Easy to miss, but impossible to forget, his brooding countenance will be forever emblazoned on your memory—if only for having seen him every time you pick up this darn handy guide. At the opposite end of the avenue, his cousin *Coquette*, a flirtatious giraffe of questionable virtue, seduces passers-by on the Av. Diagonal.

Aquarium

ESGLÉSIA DE LES SALESES

🚇 *Pg. de St. Joan, M: Verdaguer.*

The Església de le Saleses stands out as one of the prettiest churches in the entire city of Barcelona. Built in 1885 by Joan Martorell i Montells, one of Gaudí's mentors, it originally served as a nun's convent and was severely damaged during the 1909 *Setmana Trágicas* (Tragic Week; see **Life & Times,** p. 42). It became a school and finally a Catholic parish in 1945, after it was repaired. It is generally considered a direct precursor to the Modernist movement, with its detailed, almost coquettish brick, stone, and glass exterior decorations.

ManMagnum

UTOPIA, LTD.

Nearly two centuries ago, a Frenchman named Etienne Cabot developed a vision of a perfect, egalitarian worker's utopia which he named Icària, after the high-aiming figure Icarus in Greek myth. Cabot and 70 followers sailed to America to test his theory on open land, but before he left he passed his dream to Catalunya via a man named Narcis Monturiol (who, incidentally, designed the world's first submarine to ease the labor of Poble Nou fishermen and has a statue to him in l'Eixample; see p. 84). Monturiol's supporters called their neighborhood Icària, in hope of a better future. The Ajuntament, however, changed the name to Poble Nou, and it was not until 1986 that the original was revived in the government's name for the building project that created Vila Olímpica: "Nova Icària Ltd." The athlete housing was originally intended to serve as low-income housing after the Olympics, but exactly the opposite has occurred, and the city seems to have moved on to its next stab at utopia: the promotion of world peace through the Universal Forum of Cultures slated to be hosted by Barcelona in 2004.

OTHER SIGHTS IN L'EIXAMPLE ESQUERRA

🚇 M: Urgell and other stops.

L'Eixample Esquerra is home to several Modernist masterpieces. **Casa Golferichs** at Gran Via 491 (M: Urgell), a brown brick structure with Moorish influences, was designed by one of Gaudí's collaborators, Joan Rubió in 1901. Concerts are often held in the courtyard during the summer, and the interior hosts art exhibitions. (☎ 93 323 77 90. Open M-F 5-9pm and Sa 10am-2pm. Wheelchair accessible. Free.) Further down the Gran Via at number 475, Pere Falqués and Antoni de Flaguerra's **Casa de Lactància** (M: Urgell) is now a nursing home. Its stone carvings by Eusebi Arnau and mosaic flag of Barcelona can be viewed from outside, but step inside the foyer to see the equally impressive wrought iron interior balcony and delicate stained glass windows. At the other end of l'Eixample, **Casa Company** at C. Buenos Aires 56-58 (M: Hospital Clinic) was constructed in 1911 by Puig i Cadafalch for a local family. The creamy white Art Deco building with painted decorations was converted into Dr. Melcior Colet's gynecological practice in 1940, and later donated to the government of Catalunya. Today, it houses the Museu de l'Esport Dr. Melcior Colet (see p. 114).

POBLE NOU & PORT OLÍMPIC

see map p. 321

WALKING TOUR

The **Vila Olímpica** and **Port Olímpic** are best viewed in an easy loop beginning and ending at M: Ciutadella/Vila Olímpica. Come out of the Metro with the twin skyscrapers to your right and cross C. Ramon Trias Fargos to get to the intersection of C. de Marina and **Avinguda d'Icària.** Follow Av. Icària for three blocks or so. As you walk, the **Parc de Carles I** will be on your left, with its tall, infamous **Culo de Urculo** statue (Urculo's, um, posterior). The huge metal sculptures down the center of the street, something like a mix of thatched roofs and telephone poles, were named **Pergolas** by architect Enric Miralles; they are certainly an ultramodern take on the original meaning of the word (latticed rooftop gardens with climbing plants, common in ancient Egypt). To the right on the second block of Av. Icària is the **Centre de la Vila,** a three-story shopping mall, complete with a 15-screen cinema complex.

At the intersection with Av. Bogatell and C. Frederic Mompau, take the ramp to the right leading upward into a red brick apartment complex. At the end of this ramp you will find yourself in the Pl. Tirant lo Blanc, the center of the athlete housing, and the perfect place to sit and imagine what it must have been like to live in the Vila Olímpica in 1992. In classic Barcelona style, even the curbs of the sidewalks curve in long wavy lines. From here, facing the sea, cross one of the four wooden bridges over the highway and waterway, into the Parc dels Ponts, then turn right onto the sandy path. This path leads to the Pl. dels Champions, site of the tiered concrete platform used to honor gold, silver, and bronze medal-winners. Continuing onward brings you to the Parc del Port Olímpic, a long, triumphant sand walkway lined by tall white spires and culminating in Robert Llimos' Marc statue, an apt symbol for this city, known for muscling past both physical boundaries and architectural norms. Across the fountain from here lies the Parc de Cascades, home to Antoni Llena's stick-figure-like David and Goliath. Finally, to get from here to Frank Gehry's copper Peix (Fish) and the Port Olímpic, return to the fountain, turn right toward the water, and go left at the beach.

Festival Time in Barceloneta

Poble Nou's own small Rambla makes for a pleasant afternoon walk free of the hordes of people in the city center, and it offers a glimpse of real Catalan life, unaffected by tourism. Otherwise, Poble Nou offers **beaches,** a small **hearse museum** (see p. 115), and some other novel attractions.

OTHER SIGHTS

CEMENTIRI DE L'EST

At the dead-end of Av. Icària. M: Llacuna. From the Metro, walk down C. Ciutat de Granada toward the waterfront towers; at the T-intersection with C. Taulat, turn right and follow the white walls of the cemetery to the gated opening. Open daily 8am-6pm.

Pre-l'Eixample Barcelona desperately needed every inch inside city walls for living space, so in 1773 this cemetery was built outside the walls to safely house some of Barcelona's most important dead. Crumbling monuments and miniature churches crowd the back of the plot, behind stacked graves emblazoned with flowers. The cemetery also is home to the famous **Kiss of Death** statue.

Barceloneta Clocktower

GLOBUS TURÍSTIC

At the intersection of Pg. Circumval.lació and C. Wellington. From M: Ciutadella/Vila Olímpica, turn left and walk about 1 block on Pg. Circumval.lació. ☎93 597 11 40. 1900ptas/€11,42 1100ptas/€6,61 over 65 and ages 4-12. Children up to 3yrs old free). Open daily June-Aug. 11am-9pm, Sept.-May 10am-7pm, weather permitting. MC/V.

A huge hot air balloon with Gaudí-esque decorations departs every 15min. for a phenomenal view of the harbor and city.

Circular Shark tank at the Aquarium

SANT JORDI

English speakers usually know the legend of Saint George and the Dragon from the British religious and folkloric tradition; Saint George is, after all, the patron saint of Britain, renowned for battling a dragon and saving the Christians. However, the English are not the only people with a claim to Saint George, known in Barcelona by his Catalan name, Sant Jordi. In the 13th century, King Jaume I had a vision of Sant Jordi aiding him in battle against Mallorca, and this historic hallucination started Catalunya's long-founded obsession with the saint. Names and images of him are everywhere: the Olympic Palau d'Esports Sant Jordi, April 24th's romantic Día de Sant Jordi, the Casa Batlló's scaly, dragonesque rooftoop. Jordi is also one of the most popular Catalan first names, as it symbolizes heroism and high moral caliber.

BARCELONETA

If you're in Barceloneta to see any of these sights, it will also be worth your while to check out the nearby **Museu d'Història de Catalunya** (see **Museums**, p. 115)

☙ TORRE SAN SEBASTIÀ

🚩 *Pg. Joan de Borbo. M: Drassanes. ☎93 441 48 20. In the Port Vell, as you walk down Joan de Borbo and see the beaches to the left, stay right and look for the obvious high tower. To Colom: 1200ptas, to Montjuïc: one way 1200ptas/€7,71; roundtrip 1400ptas/€8,41. Also accessible from Montjuïc (see the **Jardins Verdaguer**, p. 91). Open daily 11am-8pm.*

One of the easiest and best ways to view the city is on these cable cars, which span the entire Port Vell, connecting beachy Barceloneta with mountainous Montjuïc. The full ride, which takes about 10min. each way and offers an intermediate stop, gives an aerial perspective of the entire city. Bring your camera and it will thank you.

PORT VELL

☙ L'AQUÀRIUM DE BARCELONA

🚩 *On the Moll d'Espanya, next to Maremagnum and the cinema. M: Drassanes or Barceloneta. ☎93 221 74 74. Open daily July-Aug. 9:30am-11pm; Sept.-June 9:30am-9pm. 1550ptas/€9,30; children under 12 and seniors 950ptas/€5,70, students 10% off. Last entrance 1hr. before closing. Wheelchair accessible.*

Barcelona's new aquarium—the largest in Europe—is a state-of-the-art aquatic wonder. The museum features over twenty tanks that focus on the sealife of the Mediterranean, with nods to the Great Barrier Reef and other climates, copious amounts of octopi, and a plethora of penguins. The museum's layout is as fascinating as the very best snorkeling dives, minus the wetness and jellyfish stings. For those not still terrified by the *Jaws* movies, the visit's highlight is an 80m-long glass tunnel (with moving walkway) through an ocean tank of sharks, sting rays, and one two-dimensional fish with no fins. Just four inches of glass separate the crowds from the water, filled with thousands of fish and over a million gallons of Mediterranean water. The tour ends with a series of over 50 interactive exhibits about the ocean and its inhabitants, which kids (and playful adults) will adore.

OTHER SIGHTS AROUND PORT VELL

🚇 M: Drassanes or Barceloneta.

Ever-ambitious Barcelona wishes to become known as the greatest port on the Mediterranean, and has made amazing progress toward that goal in just over a decade. The newest addition to the waterfront is the brand-new **World Trade Center,** designed by the renowned architect I. M. Pei (who built the glass pyramid in front of Paris' Louvre Museum, among others). The design reminds many of a cruise ship, only fitting considering its proximity to the cruise-ship docks of the port, which have room for eight full-size liners in all. Still under development and somewhat lifeless, plans are in the works for a luxury hotel, office space, and a convention center at the World Trade Center complex. At the other end of Pg. Colom in front of the post office (a sight in and of itself—a postal palace created for the 1929 International Exhibition; see p. 44) is **Cap de Barcelona,** also known as Barcelona Head. This 60 foot-plus sculpture, a bright, cartoonish woman's face, was created by the late American pop artist Roy Lichtenstein for the 1992 Olympics.

View of Industrial Area from Montjuïc Castle

MONTJUÏC

CASTELL DE MONTJUÏC

see map p. 320

🚇 From M: Paral.lel, take the funicular to Av. Miramar and then the Teleféric de Montjuïc cable car, which runs up to the castle via the site of the former Parc d'Attracions. The funicular runs from inside the M: Paral.lel station at Av. Paral.lel and Nou de la Rambla. Teleféric open M-Sa 11:15am-9pm. One-way 500ptas/€3, round-trip 700ptas/€4,20. Alternatively, walk up the steep slope on C. Foc, next to the funicular station. Open Mar. 15-Nov. 15 Tu-Su 9:30am-8pm, Nov. 16-Mar. 14 Tu-Su 9:30am-5pm. Mirador only, 100ptas/€0,60.

Cannon Café at Montjuïc Castle

A visit to this historic fortress and its **Museum Militar** (see **Museums,** p. 117) is a great way to get an overview of the city—both of its layout and its history. From the castle's exterior *mirador*, gaze over the bay and the city. Enjoy a sandwich and coffee at the outdoor café while 19th-century cannons stare you down.

FONTS LUMINOSES

🚇 Shows June-Sept. Th-Su every 30min., 9:30pm-12:30am; Oct.-May F-Sa 7-8:30pm. Free.

The Fonts Luminoses (Illuminated Fountains) run alongside Av. Reina Maria Cristina and are dominated by the huge central **Font Mágica** (Magic Fountain). The fountains are visible from

Montjuïc Steps

Pl. d'Espanya, in front of the **Palau Nacional** (see **Museums,** p. 118). During the weekends, colored lights and cheesy music bring the fountains to life in a spectacular display not to be missed.

PAVELLÓ BARCELONA

🛱 *From M: Espanya, follow Av. Reina Maria Cristina and take escalators to the Font Mágica. Face the Palau Nacional and the Font Mágica; the Pavelló is to the right. ☎ 93 423 40 16; www.mies-bcn.com. Open daily 10am-8pm. 500ptas/€3; students 250ptas/€1,50; under 18 free.*

Not only does German architect Mies van der Rohe have the world's best name, he's also a fine designer of pavilions. This one—also known as the **Pavelló Mies van der Rohe**—is small, lovely, and architecturally significant. Van der Rohe built a pavilion for the 1929 International Exhibition, but his contribution—a minimalist marvel of glass, stone, marble, and steel—was demolished in 1930 when no one bought it. The pavilion standing in its place today is a replica commissioned by the Barcelona city government. The clean lines of the pavilion and open-air courtyard spaces are also home to Georg Kolbe's graceful statue *Morning* and several copies of van der Rohe's famous work known as the *Barcelona chair*.

ANELLA OLÍMPICA

🛱 *The easiest route to the Olympic Area is from M: Paral.lel, followed by the funicular. Funicular runs from inside the M: Paral.lel station at Av. Paral.lel and Nou de la Rambla. (Apr.-June daily 10:45am-8pm, June-Oct. daily 11am-10pm, Nov.-Apr. Sa-Su 10:45am-8pm; 275ptas/€1,65, round-trip 400ptas/€2,40.) Wheelchair accessible. Turn left out of the funicular station on to Av. Miramar and follow it past the Fundació Miró. The road turns into Av. de l'Estadi; the stadium is on your left. For athletic opportunities at the Olympic stadium, see **Entertainment,** p. 167.*

In 1929, Barcelona inaugurated the Estadi Olímpic de Montjuïc (Olympic Stadium) in its bid for the 1932 Olympic games. Over 50 years later, Catalan architects Federic Correa and Alfons Milà, designers of the *Anella Olímpica* (Olympic Ring) esplanade, completed the facilities in time for the '92 Games, with the help of Italian architect Vittorio Gregotti. The **Torre de Telefónica,** designed by Valencian Santiago Calatrava, commands the Olympic skyline at 394 ft. Ten years later, Montjuïc's Olympic area is still a major tourist draw. In addition to commemorating Barcelona's role as host in '92, the *Anella Olímpica* lives on as a well-equipped arena serving the sporting needs of professionals, amateurs, and tourists alike. Today, you can catch a soccer game at the **Estadi Olímpic** (see **Entertainment,** p. 175) or swim in the Piscines Bernat Picorne II (see p. 168).

PALAU D'ESPORTS SANT JORDI

🛱 *☎ 93 426 20 89. Call in advance to visit. For concert information, check www.agendabcn.com or the Guía del Ocio, available at any newsstand.*

Designed by Japanese architect Arata Isozaki, the Palau Sant Jordi is the most technologically sophisticated of the Olympic structures. The roof was built on the ground and was lifted and secured into its present position over the course of 10 days. Standing in front of the palace are *utsuroshi* (change), concrete and metal tree-like structures designed by Isozaki's wife, Aiko Miyawaki. Palau Sant Jordi currently serves as one of the city's biggest concert venues, playing host to big name superstars like Madonna, who kicked off her 2001 world tour here.

GALERÍA OLÍMPICA

🛱 *At the far end of the Estadi Olímpic, toward Palau Sant Jordi. ☎ 93 426 06 60. Open Oct.-Mar. M-F 10am-1pm and 4-6pm; Apr.-May M-F 10am-2pm and 4-7pm; June M-Sa 10am-2pm and 4-7pm, Su 10am-2pm; July-Sept. M-Sa 10am-2pm and 4-8pm, Su 10am-2pm. 400ptas/€2,40; students 350ptas/€2; seniors 170ptas/€1. Combined visit with Poble Espanyol (see below) 1200ptas/€7.*

This permanent exhibition showcases Barcelona's 25th Olympic Games, with a small section detailing the history of the Olympics since 1896. Check out the vast, colorful array of medals, sports equipment, costumes, and merchandise as well as plenty of photos and a video segment commemorating the 1992 Games.

POBLE ESPANYOL

On Av. Marqués de Comillas, to the right when facing the Palau Nacional. M: Espanya, up the outdoor escalators.☎ 93 508 63 00; www.poble-espanyol.com. Open Su 9am-midnight, M 9am-8pm, Tu-Th 9am-2am, F-Sa 9am-4am. 975ptas/€5,80; students 775ptas/€4,66; seniors 600ptas/€3,60; children 7-12 550ptas/€3,30; guided tour 500ptas/€3,30 extra. MC/V.

Built for the International Exhibition in 1929 (see **Life & Times,** p. 44), this tourist-oriented "town" features replicas of famous buildings and sights from every region of Spain. Shops and artists' workshops sell everything from tacky souvenirs to gallery pieces, and the large open-air courtyard occasionally serves as a concert or theater venue. During daylight hours, Poble Espanyol is not much more than an artificial souvenir bazaar with several mediocre restaurants, but at night the disco scene here brings new meaning to the word "party."

Olympic Structures

JARDINS VERDAGUER

Av. Miramar. Located between the Fundació Miró and the Castell de Montjuïc. From M: Paral.lel, take a funicular to Av. Miramar. Turn right out of the funicular and walk along Av. Miramar, then uphill on C. Montjuïc. Alternatively, take the teleféric and ask to get off at the 1st of 2 stops, Jardins Verdaguer.

Named after the Catalan poet Mossén Jacint Verdaguer (see **Life & Times,** p. 54), these gardens have suffered from the barren scars left from the departure of the old Parc d'Attracions. The old fairgrounds are slated for renovation by 2004, but until then, the Mirador de L'Alcalde on the other side of C. Montjuïc—with a splendid view of the sea, a cascading fountain, and mosaic work in the ground—is an attraction in itself. In a small island in the middle of C. Montjuïc, the **Sardana** statue (see **Life & Times,** p. 52), crafted by Josep Cañas in 1966, commemorates this traditional Catalan dance. Farther downhill, where C. Montjuïc meets Av. Miramar, the Miramar lookout hosts a restaurant and bar with fine views of the city and sea. The *teleféric* cable car to Barceloneta leaves from here (see p. 88).

Palau Sant Jordi

PARC JOAN MIRÓ

C. Tarragona. M: Espanya or Tarragona. A 5min. walk down C. Tarragona from Pl. de Espanya.

Miró's giant *Dona i ocell* (*Woman and Bird*, 1982) holds court in the center of a park dedicated to the artist. This colorful, phallic sculpture is a mosaic of greens, yellows, reds, and blues in homage to Gaudí. Miró changed the name from *Le Coq* after city planners objected.

Architecture at Poble Espanyol

GET sm art

Wet n' Wild

If you take a break from a hectic tour of Park Güell, don't be surprised to find that your seat on the concrete **serpentine bench** is actually quite comfortable. Legend has it that Gaudí's assistant Josep Maria Jujol, who was primarily responsible for this bench (the world's longest) created its seats by having one of the workers sit bare-assed in the wet cement.

CEMENTIRI DEL SUD-OEST

⊼ *Bus #38 from Pl. de Catalunya. Or, from inside Montjuïc, follow Av. del Castell to the left with your back to the Castell de Montjuïc. The cemetery is about a 10min. walk downhill and will be on your left. To get to Fossar de la Pedrera, turn left on Via Santa Eulalia by the cemetery entrance, and then take the 2nd right onto Sant Josep. Follow this paved path and look for signs directing you to Fossar. A helpful cemetery map is available from the administration offices at the main entrance, across from the bus stop. Open daily 8am-6pm. Free.*

Some of the finest architecture, sculpture, and stained glass in all of Barcelona can be found in this Modernist cemetery dating from 1883. Watch out for the flocks of black Mercedes that speed through on weekends. Of special note are the Amatller family tomb designed by Puig i Cadafalch (who also designed their house in l'Eixample; see p. 80) and the statuary-topped Batlló family resting place (of Casa Batlló fame; see p. 81). Winding paths lead uphill from the main entrance, curving along the terraced cliff and providing lovely views of the sea.

In the cemetery's northeast corner, the **Fossar de la Pedrera** commemorates the Republican heroes of the Civil War (see **Life & Times,** p. 44), marking the site where many of them were rounded up and shot immediately following the war. Stone pillars are engraved with the names of the victims, and an arched statue set in a small pond honors Catalan President Lluís Companys who was assassinated by Franco on this very spot in 1940.

ZONA ALTA
GRÀCIA

see maps p. 318 & 319

▣ PARK GÜELL

⊼ Orientation and Transportation: *Park Güell is located in the upper limits of Gràcia, several blocks west of the major thoroughfare Trav. de Dalt. The park's main entrance faces C. Olot, though there are other entrances on Av. Sant Josep de la Muntanya, Carretera del Carmel, and Av. del Coll del Portell. The easiest way to reach the park is by bus #24 from Pl. de Catalunya, which runs up Pg. de Gràcia and stops at the upper park entrance towards the end of its route. Bus #25 connects the park to the Sagrada Família. If a 5-10min. uphill hike does not disturb you, the most scenic way to enter the park is to take the Metro to Vallarca, walk straight out of the Metro down Av. l'Hospital Militar for 4 blocks, turn left onto Baixada de la Gloria, and take the outdoor escalators uphill to the park's back entrance. There are 2 cafés in the park, though prices are relatively high and during busy times it can be difficult to find an open table. For cheaper eating, a small grocery store on C. Laddard 57 is open daily 10am-8pm and offers the classic picnic staples. Park ☎ 93 219 38 11. Free. Open daily May-Sept. 10am-9pm; Mar.-Apr and Oct. 10am-7pm; Nov.-Feb. 10am-6pm.*

On a hill at the northern edge of Gràcia lies one of Barcelona's greatest treasures and the world's most enchanting public park. The park was designed entirely by Gaudí, and—in typical Gaudí fashion—was not completed until after his death. Eusebi Güell, a Catalan industrialist and arts patron, commissioned the renowned Gaudí to fashion a garden city in the tradition of Hampstead Heath and other parks in England, where Güell had spent many years. The English spelling of "park" is a nod to the Anglo gardens Güell wished to imitate. Intended by Güell as a housing development to isolate the city's elite from the lower classes, the park was to have 60 houses. However, due to Güell's death in 1918 and the postponement of construction during World War I only three houses went up before Gaudí passed away. Barceloneses at the turn of the century tended to be put off by Gaudí's shockingly bold designs and disparaged the park's then great distance from the city, and as a result, only two aristocrats signed on. As a housing development, it was a failure.

Park Güell Structures

As a park, it is fantastic. In 1922, the Barcelona city council bought Park Güell and opened up its multicolored dwarfish buildings and sparkling ceramic-mosaic stairways to the public. The park has since been honored by being named a UNESCO World Heritage Site. Combining natural influences, Catalan themes, and religious symbolism, Gaudí's Park Güell is a symphony of color and form. It is at once dreamy and whimsical, organic and tactile. The most eye-catching elements of the park—the surreal mosaics and fairy tale fountains—are clustered around the main entrance on C. Olot. The entrance's **Palmetto Gate,** a replica of the iron work on Gaudí's Casa Vicens, is flanked by two dwarfish buildings originally meant to house the community's administration offices and the porter. Visitors

Lizard at Park Güell

today can stop by the **LAIE** book and gift shop in the house on the left as you face the park (☎93 284 62 00, open during park hours). These otherworldly houses were inspired by a Catalan production of *Hansel and Gretel*, the spire-topped construction belonging to the children and the other, crowned with a bright red poisonous mushroom, belonging to the witch. Lavishly decorated with fan-shaped mosaics, the roofs almost resemble edible gingerbread and cream frosting. Behind Hansel and Gretel's house, you will find the park's restrooms and a popular café. (Coffee 300ptas/€1,50; *tapas* 200-450ptas/€1,20-2,70; *bocadillos* 400-600ptas/€2,40-3,60. Open during park hours.)

Facing the majestic double staircase, a cavernous stone area to the right was originally meant to house the carriages of park residents, and now serves as a shaded rest area for visitors. Some say if you look at it the right way, it resembles an elephant. The staircase itself is divided

Fishmonger

IT'S AMAZING!

According to Greek legend, the king of Crete left seven young men and women a year to their death in the Palace of Knossos, an impossible labyrinth of rooms and courtyards in which roamed the half-man, half-bull Minotaur. The yearly tradition did not end until the king's daughter Ariadne fell in love with Theseus, one of the doomed, and offered him a thread to find his way out after fighting the beast. In this case, the labyrinth was power, and (not-so-shockingly) love conquered all. Mazes have taken on a variety of meanings over time, however: The knotted confusion of Egyptian tombs symbolized the path from life to death, and the painted labyrinths in some Gothic churches represent the path of sinners, wandering and often wrong, but eventually reaching God. Fortunately for the average hapless traveler, the *Jardins del Laberint d'Horta* have nothing to do with power, death or sin; the only thing waiting at the end is the goddess Eros, looking to make somebody fall in love.

into three sections, each with its own mosaic attraction. Walking up, the first is a jumble of roots and plants overseen by a snake which peers out from the shield of Catalunya. Up the stairs, tourists jostle to take pictures of their loved ones with Gaudí's gaping, multicolored **lizard** fountain as it drools into the basin below. A popular symbol of the park, the lizard's sleek body is covered with a tightly woven mosaic of green, orange, and blue. Some believe that the animal is a reference to the shield of the French city of Nîmes, the northern boundary of Old Catalunya. At the next level, a curvaceous red mosaic fountain sits in front of a mouth-like bench which is supposedly entirely protected from the wind.

The stairs lead up to the **Hall of One Hundred Columns (Teatro Griego),** a Modernist masterpiece of 86 Doric columns. A spectacular open space meant for the community's market, the hall's columns support a ceiling constructed of white-tiled domes. Towards the center, where musicians often play classical music, multicolored medallions are interspersed among the ceiling domes. Josep Maria Jujol, Gaudí's right-hand man, created each medallions, using bits of mirror, plates, glasses, and even porcelain dolls.

Stairs on either side of the hall lead up to the **Pl. de la Naturalesa,** a barren open area partly supported by the columned hall below, and surrounded by the **Serpentine bench,** the longest park bench in the world. The shape of the bench is not only aesthetic, but is also architecturally necessary given the position of the columns below. It is also designed to cradle visitor's buttocks and is consequently damn comfy (see **Wet & Wild,** opposite). Pieced together from broken ceramic remnants from local pottery workshops, Gaudí and Jujol's multicolored bench is covered with brightly colored flowers, geometric patterns, and the odd religious image or two. During the park's restoration in 1995, workers discovered that 21 distinct tones of white—all cast-offs from the Casa Milà (see p. 77)—had been cemented in the bench. The bench's abstract collage later became a great inspiration for Joan Miró's Surrealist work. Overlooking the plaça, a self-service café offers outdoor tables. (Juice and water 350ptas/€1,80; beer and *sangría* 350-600ptas/€1,80-3,60; *bocadillos* 500-600ptas/€3-3,60. Open during park hours.)

From here, sweeping paths supported by columns (meant to resemble palm trees) swerve through hedges and ascend to the park's summit, which commands tremendous views of the city. A pleasant, less crowded walk through the grounds begins at the path directly to right of the lizard fountain when walking up the stairs. Follow the wide path past the sunny flower beds and open grassy area and continue to the right as smaller paths branch off into semi-enclosed shaded areas with benches and ping-pong tables. As the path twists uphill it skirts the turreted, pink **Casa-Museu Gaudí** (see **Museums**, p. 118). Continue on the now-elevated path, supported by organic stone pillars, as it curves towards the Carretera. del Carmel entrance. Farther ahead, the **Pont dels Enamorats** offers views of the city all the way to the sea. Along the left-hand side, Gaudí's **stone trees**—tall columns topped with agave plants—are interspersed with curved benches which seem to hang in midair. Around the next curve is **Casa Trias** (1905), the park's third house, which was purchased by the lawyer Trías Domènech and is still owned by his family. Less scenic walking paths split off to the right a few hundred yards ahead, and loop around to the left along Av. del Coll del Portell.

Continuing on the main path, a staircase on the left leads back down to the Pl. de la Naturalesa. Farther along the wide path, to the left of the Av. del Coll del Portell entrance, a grassy area hosts a small playground and plenty of benches. Making its way around to the other side of the park, the path slopes uphill again and spirals around and up to **El Turo de Les Tres Creus.** Originally destined to be the park residents' church, the small tower is topped only with three crosses which appear to form one when you look toward the east. This peak is the park's highest point, and it offers a dazzling 360° view. To head back down, follow the twisty path that slopes downwards toward the sea. The walk downhill offers some good top-angle views of the Hansel and Gretel houses and other park structures. At the Av. Sant Josep de la Muntanya entrance, follow a narrow path to the right which becomes **El Viaducte de la Bugadera** as it passes Güell's house (now a school) on the right. The irregularly shaped stone columns that support the covered passageway are each composed of fascinating, unusual shapes and configurations. You'll find the statue of **La Bugadera** (the washerwoman) herself, one of the last columns in the passageway. Stairs ahead lead back to the Pl. de la Naturalesa.

CASAS IN GRÀCIA

Aside from the Park Güell, Gràcia is home to several of Modernisme's hidden architectural gems. Since these buildings truly are *casas* (private houses), their interiors are unfortunately closed to the public; however, the captivating external designs and details are worth a look.

CASA VICENS

🚩 *C. Carolines 24-26. M: Fontana, walk uphill Gran de Gràcia and turn left onto C. Carolines.*

One of Gaudí's earliest projects, Casa Vicens was designed for a local tile manufacturer, and as such, is fittingly decorated with blocks of cheerful red, green, and yellow ceramic tiles. The *casa* illustrates the colorful influence of Arabic architecture and a rigidness of angles that is uncharacteristic of Gaudí's later works. The hard lines are contrasted with Gaudí's trademark—graceful, fluid ironwork that spills out of the windows as balconies and creeps up the façade as a palm-fronted gate.

OTHER CASAS

🚩 *Throughout Gràcia. M: Lesseps for Casa Ramos and Diagonal for Casa Cama and Casa Fuster.*

Several blocks up the Gran de Gràcia at Pl. Lesseps, **Casa Ramos** was completed by Jaume Torres in 1906 and is in fact three separate buildings which share a façade. Although the building is partially blocked by a tangle of telephone poles and store fronts, its Modernist floral motif and insect-patterned grilles still manage to stand out. **Casa Ferrer**, at Pg. de Gràcia 113 was completed in 1905 by Pere Falqués. Though its stone façade has been somewhat neglected, it nevertheless remains a remarkable construction. On the Gran de Gràcia, **Casa Cama** (no.15) is one of Berenguer's designs, with delicate stained-glass windows. Across the street, at Pg. de Gràcia 132, **Casa Fuster** marks the transition between Gran de Gràcia and the Pg. de Gràcia. Lluís Domènech i Montaner fashioned this impressive neo-Gothic marble building from 1908 to 1911, putting heavy emphasis on the cylindrical corner windows. Get up close to see the nesting birds sculpted at the top of each column.

PLAÇAS IN GRÀCIA

🚩 *M: Diagonal or Fontana.*

Gràcia has several notable plaças where locals gather over long meals at outdoor tables, day and night; a quick stroll through them is a great way to get acquainted with the neighborhood. **Pl. Ruis i Taulet,** two blocks below Trav. de Gràcia near the Gran de Gràcia, is home to the **Torre del Reloj** (Clock tower), an emblem of the Revolution of 1868. Facing the plaça is Gràcia's sky-blue town hall, a Modernist work designed by local architect Francesc Berenguer and adorned with Gràcia's town shield. Several blocks down C. Puigmartí at the intersection of C. Girona, is **Pl. de John Lennon,** which honors the rock legend with a record-shaped plaque engraved with "Give Peace a Chance" in Catalan, and is a favorite playground spot for local children and their parents. While the **Pl. del Poble Romaní,** one block down C. Siracusa, is not the loveliest of the group, it is the former site of the Puigmartí textile factory and now commemorates the local Gypsy community as well as Gràcia's working-class roots. **Pl. del Diamante,** farther uphill on C. Astúries, was made famous by Catalan author Mercè Rodoreda's novel of the same title. The novel is commemorated with *La Colometa*, a dramatic bronze statue of Rodoreda's heroine. **Pl. Virreina,** farther along C. Astúries, is bordered by *tapas* bars, pastel painted houses, and the grand Church of Sant Joan de Gràcia. Across C. L'Or, the pink and cream **Casa Rubina** at no.44 is one of Berenguer's most festive works. **Pl. del Sol,** one block above Trav. de Gràcia off C. Cano, is skirted by a fantastic selection of cafés and bars and is crowded with young locals at night.

MARKETS IN GRÀCIA

🚇 *FCG: Gràcia.*

Gràcia's markets are some of the best places to get a feel for this eclectic community, as older residents shop alongside hip young things. Two major markets offer inexpensive food options and are interesting places to wander through. The meat and fish stands are not for the faint of heart. **Mercat de la Llibertat,** in the Pl. de la Llibertat, one block off Via Augusta from the Gràcia FGC stop, was originally designed as an open-air market by Berenguer in 1875 but was covered years later. The wrought iron gates and floral details are particularly impressive, as is the drinking fountain, which bears Gràcia's shield, at the front of the market. Vendors offer everything from fresh eggs to dried fruit. (☎93 415 90 93; open M 5-8pm, Tu-Th 8am-2pm and 5-8pm, F 8am-8pm, Sa 7am-3pm). **Mercat de L'Adaceria Central** is conveniently located in the heart of Gràcia at the intersection of Trav. de Gràcia and C. Torrijos. Hundreds of produce stalls on the inside of the building, while outside vendors sell flowers, clothing, and trinkets. (From FCG: Gràcia, walk down via Augusta and take a left on Trav. de Gràcia; continue on several blocks until you reach C. Torrijos. Open M-Th 6am-2:30pm and 5:30-8:30pm, F-Sa 6am-3pm and 5-8:30pm.)

HORTA & VALL D'HEBRON

The most interesting sights in the Horta area are far apart from one another. Be prepared to spend some time walking, and pay attention to your surroundings; some of the most interesting aspects of the neighborhood are its street sculptures.

PARC DE LA CREUTA DEL COLL

🚇 *Pg. Mare de Déu del Coll 93. M: Penitents or bus #25, 28, or 87. From the Anna Piferrer exit of the Metro, face Av. L'Hospital Militar and go right. Turn left from there onto C. de Gustavo Bécquer, which makes a sharp right turn without changing name. At the bridge, go uphill and take a left onto Pg. Mare de Déu del Coll, which you will follow for about 15min., mostly uphill; the park entrance lies above an obvious set of sandstone steps. ☎93 459 24 27. Beach chairs 400ptas/€2,50. Swimming 450ptas/€3 M-F and 500ptas/€3 Sa, Su, and holidays. Pool open M-F 10am-4pm and weekends 10am-8pm. Park gates open daily Nov.-Feb. 10am-6pm; Mar. and Oct. 10am-7pm; Apr. and Sept. 10am-8pm; May-Aug. 10am-9pm.*

This park is like a small, arid, man-made valley basin, carved out of a steep hillside and complete with a long, shallow pool. The pool for the kids and the beach chairs for the parents make this a great place to bring young children on a hot day.

JARDINS DEL LABERINT D'HORTA

C. dels Germans Desvalts, directly behind the Velo-dróm, up the steep concrete steps. M: Montbau. From the Montbau exit, facing the Jardins Pedro Muñez Seca, turn right and follow Pg. de Vall d'Hebron for about 20min., turning right at the Velodróm cycling facility. ☎ 93 428 39 34. Guided tours leave at 11am on the first Su of some months, particularly in summer (225ptas/€1,35). To arrange a private group tour call 93 413 24 22. Open Nov.-Feb. 10am-6pm; Mar. and Oct. 10am-7pm; Apr. and Sept. 10am-8pm; May-Aug. 10am-9pm. Entrance fee M-Tu and Th-Sa 275ptas/€1,65 or 175ptas/€1,05 with a carnet joven, under 5 free. Su and W free. Not wheelchair accessible.

Once the private grounds of a wealthy marquis, this pristine 17-acre garden—complete with manicured walkways, a love canal, a romantic garden, a cascade and, of course, the labyrinth—warrants the trip from town. For more on labyrinths, see **The Power of the Maze,** p. 94.

Gràcia Markets

STREET SCULPTURES

Joan Brossa's *Visual Poem* marks the entrance to the Velodróm; look for the oversized concrete "A" and punctuation marks in the grass on the hillside. A little bit further off the Ronda, Claes Oldenberg's *Matches* light up Av. Cardenal Vidal i Barraguer (go down the street right after the tennis center, coming from the sports center). The gargantuan concrete match replicas are painted with bright red and yellow, the exact tones of the Catalan flag—an interesting touch, given the city's history of anarchist arson.

PAVILION OF THE SPANISH REPUBLIC

At the corner of Av. Cardenal Vidal i Barraquer and C. Jorge Manrique. Walk toward the Velódrom from M: Montbau and turn right down Jorge Manrique. Closed indefinitely at the time of writing.

Josep Lluís Sert built the original Pavilion of the Spanish Republic for the 1937 Paris Exposition Universal, when it held Picasso's *Guernica* and Alexander Calder's *Mercury Fountain*, among other Spanish works. This reconstruction was built for the 1992 Olympics but is closed for the time being, as no one seems to be quite sure what actual functional purpose it should serve.

Monastery of Pedralbes

PEDRALBES & LES CORTS

MONESTIR DE PEDRALBES

Baixada del Monestir 9. FGC: Reina Elisenda. A 10min. walk down Pg. Reina Elisenda. Also accessible by bus #22, 63, 64, and 78. ☎ 93 203 92 82. 600ptas/€3,60; students 300ptas/€1,80; under 16 free. Combined ticket with art collection 800ptas/€4,80; students 500ptas/€3; under 16 free. Open Oct.-Apr. Tu-Su, 10am-2pm. June-Sept. 10am-3pm.

Tomb at Monastery of Pedralbes

The devout Queen Elisenda founded this monastery in 1327 to atone for her earthly sins, and it has housed the Poor Clares order ever since. Today, visitors can peek into the lives these women led centuries ago: their courtyard, infirmary, kitchen, and dining hall are all open to the public. The tiny cells where the nuns spent their days in prayer will make visitors appreciate their own cramped hostels. The artistic highlight of the cloister is the Capella St. Miguel, where a set of frescoes by the Italian artist Ferrer Bassa depict the seven joys of the Blessed Virgin on the bottom level, and scenes from the Passion of Christ on the top level. The monastery also received part of the Thyssen Bornemisza collection; see **Museums**, p. 118.

PALAU REIAL DE PEDRALBES

🚾 *Av. Diagonal 686, recognizable by its distinctive pale orange entrance. M: Palau Reial. For an audio tour of the park and its points of interest, cell phone users can call 629 003 998 to hear descriptions in English, Spanish, or Catalan; simply press the number corresponding to the area to hear a short history and explanation. At the far end of the park is the Palau Real de Pedralbes.*

Chirping birds almost manage to drown out the blaring traffic of Av. Diagonal in this green and shady park laid out in classical style with greenery from the royal palace originally on the site. Gaudí enthusiasts will want to check out the drinking fountain, designed by the young Gaudí and promptly ignored by the city. The fountain lies off the main path, to the left as you approach the palace, in a small forest of bamboo shoots; the simple design is a twisting iron dragon that spouts water over a Catalan shield. Above, a bust of Hercules surveys the proceedings. "Rediscovered" in 1983 after decades of neglect, the fountain was restored, and now provides perfectly drinkable water to visitors of the park.

When the Güell family wanted to thank the King of Spain for making their father **Eusebi Güell** a count, they didn't say it with flowers—they said it with a royal palace, given to Spain on the occasion of the International Exposition of 1929. The pale orange mansion, with its uninspiring design and painted-on façade, borders on tacky, but conceals an elegant interior. The palace also houses the **Museu de les Arts Decoratives** and the **Museu de Cerámica**; see p. 119.

FINCA GÜELL

🚾 *Av. Pedralbes 7. M: Palau Reial, a 5min. walk from Av. Diagonal, on the left. Private residence, closed to the public.*

Those disappointed with the relatively unimposing Gaudí iron dragon in the Parc del Palau Reial should head up Av. Pedralbes to see the beast Gaudí created for this estate's gate—now *that's* a dragon. The ferocious 15 ft. dragon guards the front fence of the *finca* (farm), flashing fearsome fangs. Visitors can only see as far as the twisted wrought-iron dragon, but it's worth the short walk up from the park.

SARRIÀ

🚾 *FGC: Sarrià. Follow C. Canet to the end and turn onto C. Major Sarrià. Most of the sights will be off this main road. (Jardins Vil.la Cecilia park hours Dec.-Feb. 10am-6pm, Mar. and Oct. 10am-7pm, Apr. and Sept. 10am-8pm, May-Aug. 10am-9pm).*

In the sea of tourist literature on Gaudí and his frenetic genius, the architect's two works in Sarrià are often completely ignored. Lest you follow the Sarrià-hating ways of tourist dogma, a visit to Casa Bellesguard and the Col.legi de les Teresianes is in order.

While Sarrià is not crowded with tourists or tourist attractions, a visit to the neighborhood is a pleasant way to see residential Barcelona and the traditional home of the Catalan bourgeois. The upper part of Sarrià, closer to the Collserola hills, is the place to stroll and gawk at gated mansions and private schools; **C. Iradier** and **C. Escoles Pies** are particularly well-endowed. The lower, older area of Sarrià is concentrated around the **Pl. Sarrià**, notable for the neoclassical **Sant Vicenç de Sarrià** church (1816). The front entrance of the church faces **C. Major de Sarrià**, the area's main street.

In the middle of Sarrià's car-width streets, the low-traffic **Pl. Sant Vicenç** serves as a shady stop for locals meandering off C. Major de Sarrià. The plaça is bordered by a mix of classic, older homes and brightly colored new ones. In the plaça's center, **Sant Vicenç** himself stands guard, despite the gradual loss of his nose due to statuary wear and tear. Once a year, on May 11th, plaça Sant Vicenç hosts La Fira de Sant Ponç, a festival honoring the patron saint of herbalists and beekeepers, during which various herbs, medicinal plants, honey products, and cheeses are put out for the occasion.

Sarrià also boasts some of the most relaxing and well-manicured public spaces in the city. More like a park than a formal garden, **Jardins de la Vil.la Amelia** attract dog-walkers and mid-afternoon loungers to its orderly, well-kept grounds. Palm tree and eucalyptus lined paths radiate out from a central fountain, and there is plenty of bench space to go around. A pleasant yet unobtrusive café lies in between the park's restrooms and playground area. Across C. Sant Amelia, the **Jardins Vil.la Cecilia** are not quite as lush, but they do boast an impressive hedge maze.

Stone Fox Architectural Detail

CASA BELLESGUARD

🚶 *C. Bellesguard 16-20. FCG: Sarrià or Av. Tibidabo. Take buses #14, 30, 66, 70, 72 to Pg. Bonanova, take C. Escoles Pies up the steep hill to where it dead-ends at C. Immaculada, and make a right. Walk for several long blocks until C. Immaculada dead ends at C. Bellesguard and make a left up the hill; Casa Bellesguard is on your right.*

Casa Bellesguard's striking design merits a look, even if your thighs burn all the way up the steep incline. The building, now a private home, is closed to the public, but for true Gaudí fanatics, even a peek from the street is worth the walk. Built by Gaudí in 1902, Casa Bellesguard is one of the architect's neo-Gothic designs. Fans of Gaudí's trademark colorful mosaic details need not despair, though, as he worked in some of those as well. Tall and compact with one sculpture-topped spire, Casa Bellesguard is adorned with metal grillwork, tiled benches resplendent with blue and red fish, and three Rapunzel-esque balconies. A stone staircase and landing to the left of the entrance gate provide a picturesque view of the building and the surrounding hills.

Parc d'Attracions

COL.LEGI DE LES TERESIANES

🚶 *C. Ganduxer 85-105. ☎ 93 212 33 54. FGC: Bonanova. Buses 14, 16, 72, 74. Call in advance to schedule a tour, offered Sept.-June Sa 11am-1pm. Free.*

Built from 1888 to 1889, the stately neo-gothic building now serves as a Catholic school dedicated to Saint Teresa. Gaudí designed the wing to the right, as you enter the gate, and while he was constrained by a low budget, he managed to pull together some innovative features. On the building's façade, a row of a repeating sym-

El Sagrat Cor

99

bols—JSH, for *Jesú Salvate Hombres* (Jesus Saves Men)—adorns the space between two rows of windows. The arcs of the lower windows are recall the shape of hands in prayer, while the pineapple shape which tops a tower on the left symbolizes strength. Though Gaudí was content to supervise most of the wing's construction, he fashioned the iron gate himself, repeating symbols of Saint Teresa. While these details can be appreciated from outside, it is the school's main internal hallways which are admired by architects worldwide for their perfect parabolic arches.

TIBIDABO

Tibidabo is named for the phrase the devil used to tempt Job: "Haec omnia tibidabo si cadens adoraveris me." ("All of this I will give to you if you worship me.") For many visitors today, "all of this" means the panoramic view from the top of the Sagrat Cor church—see below. The sights listed below are Tibidabo's main draws, but pay attention to the buildings on the hill as well. Particularly interesting are the colorful **La Rotonda** in Pl. JFK and **Casa Roviralta** (Av. Tibidabo 31, on the way up to Pl. Dr. Andreu), a stunning Modernist edifice and a National Historic and Artistic monument that now houses a restaurant. At the base of the Tibidabo mountain lies the distinctive silver-domed **Observatori Fabra,** built in 1904; piercing the skyline next to El Sagrat Cor is the highly-ornamented **Dos Rius** water tower, built in 1902 by Josep Amargós i Samaranch. Tibidabo is also home to several museums (see p. 121).

PARC D'ATTRACIONS

Pl. Tibidabo. ☎ 93 211 79 42. Open Jan.-Mar. Sa-Su noon-7pm; Apr. Sa, Su, and holidays noon-8pm; May F 10am-6pm, Sa, Su and holidays noon-8pm; June Th-F 10am-6pm, Sa, Su, and holidays noon-9pm; July M-F noon-10pm, Sa-Su noon-1am; Aug. M-Th and Su noon-10pm, F-Sa noon-1am; Sept. open 10am, closes 8-10pm, changing daily; Oct. Sa, Su, and holidays noon-8pm; Nov.-Dec. Sa, Su, and holidays noon-7pm; closed Dec. 25. 2500ptas/€15 for unlimited ride access; 1200ptas/€7,20 for the 6 most popular rides only; 2000ptas/€7 with a carnet joven; over 60 700ptas/€4; under 110cm tall 700ptas/€4; disabled visitors 700ptas/€4. Most attractions wheelchair accessible.

Opened in 1899, this colorful amusement park may be old-fashioned and on the small side, but the rides use the mountain itself to full advantage, some flinging the riders far out into the air. The park also has marionette and haunted house shows, miradors with pay-per-use binoculars (100ptas/€,50), the Museu de Autòmats (Robot museum; see p. 121), and 13 different restaurants and cafés.

EL SAGRAT COR

Pl. Tibidabo. ☎ 93 417 56 86. Lower stairs, which offer decent views, open 10am-7pm. Elevator to the top, for a better view, open daily 10am-2pm and 3-7pm. Elevator 200ptas/€1,20. Wheelchair accessible.

This neo-Gothic church of the Sacred Heart immediately recalls Paris' own Sacre Coeur in Montmartre. Founded in 1886 by St. John Bosco, the church has one of the best views in Catalunya.

TORRE DE COLLSEROLA

Bus #211 or a short walk from Vallvidrera or Tibidabo. ☎ 93 406 93 54. Open Nov.-Mar. M-F 11am-2:30pm and 3:30-6pm, Sa-Su 11am-6pm; Apr. 11am-2:30pm and 3:30pm-6pm, Sa-Su 11am-7pm; May 11am-2:30pm and 3:30-7pm, Sa-Su 11am-7pm; June M-F 11am-2:30pm and 3:30-7pm, Sa-Su 11am-8pm; July-Sept. M-F 11am-2:30pm and 3:30-8pm, Sa-Su 11am-8pm; Oct. M-F 11am-2:30pm and 3:30-7pm, Sa-Su 11am-7pm. Holidays have Sa-Su hours. 700ptas/€4, groups of 15+ 500ptas/€3 per person, under 7 free. MC/V. Not wheelchair accessible.

Over 288m above ground and 560m above sea level, Barcelona's main communications tower soars (quite controversially) into the skyline. Built to transmit TV and radio signals for the 1992 Olympics, the tower allows visitors up to the 10th platform in an external glass elevator (2min.), where captioned pictures of the city help explain the seemingly unending views.

PARC DE COLLSEROLA

Tourist office: Carretera de l'Església 92. ☎ 93 280 35 52. Tourist Office open daily 9:30am-3pm except Dec. 25-26 and Jan. 1 and 6.

Created in its present form by Barcelona's 1976 General Metropolitan Plan, the Parc de Collserola encompasses 16,000 acres of greenery within minutes of the city center. People come here to hike, bike, horseback ride, and drive on designated routes through the forest. There are more than two dozen restaurants, snack bars, and picnic places scattered throughout the hills. Before exploring the park, it is extremely useful to stop at the **Centre d'Informació**. Take the FGC train to the Baixador de Vallvidrera stop and follow the sandstone steps for 10min. There is a permanent exhibit in the center, on birds and the park itself, and the helpful staff sells numerous guides and maps. If this stuff is your gig, buy the hefty, trilingual Parc de Collserola Guide Book (3000ptas/€18) at the info center; it comes with color photos and a keyed map locating every single one of them (as well as which suggested hiking/biking route you can use to get there). The smaller, cheaper A Peu Per Collserola (1500ptas/€9) also has pictures and locator maps, but is only available in Catalan. The main map (available in English) is by far the most useful, as it plots every major road and service in the park. The center also has bathrooms, a snack bar, a public telephone, and a brief informational video about the park, on request.

Parc de Collserola is full of both natural and man-made sights worth tracking down. Most accessible of all is the **Museu-Casa Verdaguer** (see **Museums, p. 121**). Numerous lookout points in the park offer good views of the city and surrounding hills, especially the ■**Mirador de Vila Paula.** Take the FGC train from Pl. de Catalunya to the Peu del Funicular stop, walk up the hill from the station on Av. de Vallvidrera, follow it along the tight, immediate left turn, then a right turn, and then a few smaller twists and curves (about 10-15min.); it will be up the hill a bit on your right. If you've got a car, this is the place to bring your date for some romantic parking; if not, be very careful walking along the narrow, twisting highway, especially at dusk.

Also inside the park are more than 50 notable archaeological finds and ruins. The **Cova de l'Or,** the oldest cave dwelling in the park, dates back to the Neolithic period, 6000 BC (although it could not be visited at the time of publication). The terraced remains of a 4th-to-6th century BC **Laietana dwelling** can be seen on La Penya del Moro hillside. **Castellciuró,** a castle built in the 14th century over 12th-century remains, doubles as a particularly good lookout point. Interesting remains from the last century or two include the Modernist, turreted washing and disinfection pavilion **"El Castell,"** begun as a tuberculosis hospital on Tibidabo but never completed, and the remains of Dr. Salvador Andreu's **Arrabassada Casino.** Opened in 1911 with a proud exterior staircase reminiscent of the Paris Opera, it was closed down by municipal authorities in 1912 and is now in an advanced state of ruin. Legend has it that its closing was related to its popularity as a place to play roulette—Russian roulette and suicide room included.

Museums

Barcelona has always been on the cutting edge of defining what can be included in the category of "art;" if it can fit in a museum, you can bet a museum has been built in Barcelona to accommodate it. The city's museums range from Surrealist art and classical masterpieces to historical exhibits and one-of-a-kind curiosities, such as a shoe museum, an erotica museum, and even a hearse museum. It's impossible to rank these different institutions with respect to each other, so museums below are listed alphabetically by neighborhood, with a handy chart on p. 105 to search by type.

Serious culture vultures should consider investing in the **Articket** which gives half-price admission to six of Barcelona's premier art centers. It offers half-price admission to the Museu Nacional d'Art de Catalunya (MNAC; see p. 118), the Fundació Joan Miró (see p. 116), the Fundació Antoni Tàpies (see p. 112), the Centre de Cultura Contemporània de Barcelona (CCCB; see p. 111), the Centre Cultural Caixa Catalunya (in la Pedrera; see p. 77), and the Museu d'Art Contemporani de Barcelona (MACBA; see p. 111). The ticket, available at tourist offices (see **Service Directory**, p. 294) and the ticket offices of the museums, goes for 2496ptas/€15, and is valid for up to three months.

on the cheap

BY NEIGHBORHOOD

see map pp. 310-311

BARRI GÒTIC & LAS RAMBLAS

Free Time

Most museums in the city offer free entrance on certain days, so when you visit the following museums, try to get your timing just right.

Fundació Francisco Godia: Free tours Sa-Su at noon (see p. 113).

Museu d'Art Modern: Free first Th of month (see p. 110).

Museu de Geologia: Free first Su of month (see p. 110).

Museu de Zoologia: Free first Su of month (see p. 111).

Museu Etnològic: Free first Su of month (see p. 117).

Museu Frederic Marès: Free W 3-7 and first Su of month (see p. 106).

Museu Picasso: Free first Su of month (see p. 109).

Museu Tèxtil i d'Indumentària: free first Sa of month after 3pm (see p. 110).

For more cash-less culture, see **Free Time All the Time**, p. 106.

CENTRE D'ART DE SANTA MONICA

🔖 *Las Ramblas 7, on the right as you approach the port. M: Drassanes.* ☎ *93 316 27 27. Cultural center open M-F 9:30am-2pm and 3:30-7:30pm, Sa 10am-2pm. Gallery open M-F 11am–1:45pm, 5-7:45pm and Sa 11am-2:45pm. Call for info on exhibitions. Free.*

One can only imagine what the nuns of this former convent would have thought of shows such as Transsexual Express, a daring multimedia art exhibit presented here in summer of 2001. Today, the site houses a cultural information center, with info on museums and festivals throughout the city, and a museum of temporary contemporary art exhibits.

MUSEU DE CERA (WAX MUSEUM)

🔖 *Las Ramblas 4, on the left as you face the port. M: Drassanes.* ☎ *93 317 26 49. Open daily, 10am-10pm. 1100ptas/€6,60; children under 11 625ptas/€3,75.*

Close to 300 wax celebrities and legends will keep visitors guessing which figures are wax and which are just creepy-looking tourists. Themed rooms include a throne room, where Bill Clinton, Yasser Arafat, and Adolf Hitler stand just below King Juan Carlos and Queen Sofía, and an artist's studio, where Picasso, Miró, and Dalí work in close quarters. Catalunya buffs will appreciate historical figures such as Jaume I and the architectural tag-team of Güell and Gaudí. Everyone else will enjoy the horror room, filled with monsters, infamous villains, and gruesome scenes of death.

MUSEU D'HISTÒRIA DE LA CIUTAT

🔖 *In Pl. del Rei. M: Jaume I. Walk up C. Jaume I and take the first right. Enter on C. Verguer.* ☎ *93 315 11 11. Open June-Sept. Tu-Sa 10am-8pm, Su 10am-2pm; Oct.-May Tu-Sa 10am-2pm and 4-8pm, Su 10am-2pm. Closed Jan. 1, May 1, June 24, and Dec. 25-26. 600ptas/€3,60, students 300ptas/€1,80. Multimedia show 200ptas/€1,20. Your ticket can be used again if you ask them to issue you another access card on the way out. Most displays are in Spanish and Catalan, but the multimedia show and ruins pamphlet are available in English.*

There are two components to Barcelona's city history museum: the Palau Reial Major and the underground Roman archaeological excavations. Built on top of the fourth-century city walls, the **Palau Reial Major** served as the residence of the Catalan-Aragonese monarchs from the end of the tenth century through the 15th century. After the last Catalan king died in 1410, it began to deteriorate and was finally abandoned by royalty in the 16th century, when it was put to use as a seat for royal scribes and the Inquisition. In 1718, it was given to the Sisters of Santa Clara as a convent when Felipe's construction of the Ciutadella (see p. 42) forced them out of their original location. The nuns left at the start of the Spanish Civil War, and as restoration was begun on the building, the **Saló de Tinell** (Throne Room) was discovered wholly intact under a baroque chapel they had built. Finished in 1370, the huge Gothic space is believed to have been the place where Columbus was received by Fernando and Isabel after his journey to America. Today, it houses year-long temporary exhibitions; 2002 will explore the place of the bull in Mediterranean culture.

Next to the Saló de Tinell you will find the **Capella de Santa Agata** (Chapel of St. Agatha), begun in 1302 during the reign of Jaume II and now considered one of the most beautiful works of medieval architecture in Barcelona. Its star attraction is the *Epiphany* altarpiece done by Jaume Huguet in 1465; resplendent in gold, with highly realistic portrayals of the most important scenes in the life of Jesus, this *retablo* is in turn considered one of the best examples of Catalan Gothic painting in existence. From the chapel you can access the **Mirador del Rei Martí,** a watchtower built in 1557 but named for the last Catalan king; from here you can see the **Pl. del Rei,** the plaça formed by the Palau Reial Major, the Chapel of St. Agatha and the **Palau de Lloctinent,** a 16th-century modification of the royal palace which until 1994 housed the archives of the Crown of Aragó.

The second part of the museum lies underground, in an area discovered when space was being cleared for the Via Laietana. The largest underground excavation of any ancient city in Europe, this ▊archeological exhibit allows visitors to walk through incredibly intact remains of an entire corner of the Roman town of Barcino. You can see the original city boundary wall and walking paths, a dye-shop, and laundry shop which still has faintly visible soap residues, a fish product factory, and a fascinating wine production facility which has intact ceramic wine containers. You can also walk through a large portion of the sprawling Episcopal palace and see a mosaic floor from the home of a wealthy second-century Roman.

MUSEUMS BY TYPE

ART & ARCHITECTURE

Centre d'Art de St. Monica (p. 104)

Centre de Cultura Contemporània (p. 111)

Col.leció Thyssen Bornemisza (p. 118)

Fundació Antoni Tàpies (p. 112)

Fundació Francisco Godia (p. 113)

Fundació Joan Miró (p. 116)

Museu d'Art Modern (p. 110)

Museu Nacional d'Art de Catalunya (p. 118)

Museu Picasso (p. 109)

DECORATIVE ARTS

Museu de Ceràmica (p. 119)

Museu de les Arts Decoratives (p. 119)

Museu Tèxtil i d'Indumentària (p. 110)

HISTORY, CULTURE, & ARCHEOLOGY

Casa-Museu Gaudí (p. 118)

Casa-Museu Verdaguer (p. 121)

Museu Arqueològic de Catalunya (p. 117)

Museu Dioscesà (p. 107)

Museu Egipci (p. 114)

Museu Etnològic (p. 117)

Museu d'Història de Catalunya (p. 115)

Museu d'Història de la Ciutat (p. 104)

Museu Frederic Marès (p. 106)

Museu Marítim (p. 116)

(Continued on p. 107)

on the cheap

Free Time All The Time

Some museums in Barcelona offer the best deal of all: no admission ever. If you're looking for some low-budget culture, check out these spots anytime:

Centre d'Art de Santa Monica: see p. 104.

Museu-Casa Verdaguer: see p. 121.

Museu d'Autòmats: see p. 121.

Museu de Carrosses Fúnebres: see p. 115.

Museu de l'Esport: see p. 114.

Museu del Perfum: see p. 115.

MUSEU D'HOLOGRÀFIA

⚐ *C. Jaume I 1. ☎ 93 310 21 72; www.hello3d.com. 100ptas/€0,60. Open June-Sept. M-Sa 5-8pm. Oct.-May M-Sa 11:30am-1pm and 5-8pm.*

A small shop on the first floor sells various hologram trinkets and knickknacks; ask the store-owner to see the second-floor museum (only one room). Includes brief explanations in Catalan and Spanish on the history of the hologram and how holograms work, as well as a few impressive examples of this unusual art/science.

MUSEU DE L'ERÒTICA

⚐ *Las Ramblas 96, on the left as you walk toward the port. ☎ 93 318 98 65; www.eroticamuseum.com. Open daily 10am-10pm. 1200ptas/€7,20; students 1000ptas/€6.*

Barcelona's unique erotica museum examines the history of eroticism, from ancient Greece, Asia, and Africa to modern times. Of particular interest is the anthropological and sociological insights which can be gleaned from a careful examination of these societies' erotica. Um, yeah, okay. Just show us the fly honeys! Exhibits include vintage porn flicks from the 1930s and saucy international sculptures and sketches, depicting more sexual acrobatics than thought humanly possible. Wince at the rather medieval-looking "pleasure chair" (yikes) and giggle at the sex phones, which allow visitors to eavesdrop (in English, Spanish, French, or German) to "hot," "naughty" talk. The giant wooden phallus overlooking the Boqueria market (see p. 61) is an irresistible photo op. The museum also displays current erotic works for sale.

MUSEU FREDERIC MARÈS

⚐ *Pl. Sant Lu 5-6, in the Palau Reial. ☎ 93 310 58 00. From M: Jaume I, walk down C. Llibreteria and turn right on C. Freneria, which will lead you to the museum. Open Tu and Th 10am-5pm, W and F 10am-7pm, Su and holidays 10am-3pm. (Museum café only open April 1-Sept. 30 10am-10pm.) 500ptas/€3, students under 25 250ptas/€1,50, under 16 free. Free guided tours in Catalan and Spanish every Sunday at 11:30am; for private tours or tours in English, call ahead. The free floorplan pamphlet and one-page descriptions located in each major room are available in English. Free W 3-7pm and first Su of the month. Cash only. Wheelchair accessible.*

Frederic Marès (1893-1991) was one of Spain's better-known sculptors and an avid collector... of just about everything. In 1946, in a classic example of the individualized bourgeois patronage of the arts so common in Catalunya, he founded this museum and donated his entire private collection, as well as some of his own sculptures. The building itself was originally part of the Palau Reial Major, home to the monarchs of the Catalan-Aragonese dynasty (see p. 40) from the end of the tenth century through the 15th century. The Renaissance-style entrance door to the museum still has the original 16th-century royal sign above it, and the entrance courtyard dates from the 13th century (ground floor) and 15th century (upper galleries).

Inside the museum, the lower floors house a huge collection of Spanish and Hispanic sculpture, from pre-Roman times (including tiny Iberian religious figurines) through the 20th century. The upper floors contain Marès' "Sentimental Museum," an overwhelming collection of middle-class daily life objects from the Romantic era, from fans, jewelry, hair combs, and purses to watches, canes, pipes, and eyeglasses. In addition to Marès's collection, the entrance floor has a small temporary exhibition space to the left of the reception. Until February 2002, this will host a recreation of Marès's own 1926 exhibition in Madrid; his maternity pieces are particularly touching.

MUSEU DIOCESÀ

⚐ *Av. de la Catedral 4, right next to the cathedral.* ☎ *93 315 22 13. Open Tu-Sa 10am-2pm and 5-8pm, Su 10am-2pm. 300ptas/€1,80. Descriptions and free pamphlet guide are in Catalan, but the staff is extremely friendly and speaks Spanish whether you have questions or not. Wheelchair accessible.*

This small museum tends to be overshadowed by the cathedral next door, both literally and figuratively, but it is nothing short of a must-see for Roman wall aficionados, for it contains the city's only intact octagonal defense tower from Roman Barcino. As you walk up the floors of the museum, you can see the additions from each era of the tower's life: the round base at the bottom from the first century AD, the octagonal base on top of that from the fourth century, the next section from medieval times (look for uniform windows), and the fourth from the Gothic period (14th and 15th centuries; look for the higher, more delicate row of windows). From the top floor gallery, you can even see blackened stones from fires started by invading Muslim armies in the Middle Ages. The entrance to the museum galleries leads through the original wall and into a Gothic building that was originally (around 1000) the city's oldest homeless shelter/soup kitchen, the **Pia Almoina.** During the 18th century, under the dreaded Felipe V, the building was converted into a prison—you can see wall etchings by prisoners at the top of the stairs leading to the top floor. Most believe that the old-school graffiti includes a camping/outdoors scene and a long line of tally marks counting the passing days.

The museum's collection of religious artifacts covers two main periods, the Romanesque (12th and 13th centuries), and the Gothic (14th and 15th centuries). Highlights include an almost entirely intact church fresco from 1122, varied wood and marble Virgin sculptures, and a beau-

MORE MUSEUMS BY TYPE

(Continued from p. 105)

GET smart

What's in a Name?

Spanish speakers may wonder how Picasso, a native Spaniard, ended up with such a bizarre name; the double "s" in his last name does not exist in the Spanish language. The answer to Picasso's name lies in Barcelona. When the young Pablo Picasso arrived in Barcelona to study art, he underwent an important but little-known change. As opposed to his native Málaga where the Castillian accent pronounced his given name—Pablo Picazo—as *Picatho*, the Catalans spoke his name as *Picasso*. Feeling himself at home in the Catalan culture and with his friends and mentors at Els Quatre Gats café, the artistic genius took this regional change in stride and began to sign his name with the infamous and oh-so-un-Spanish mark of *Picasso*.

tifully handwritten Latin document by Felipe II. The museum's crown jewel, though, is the stunning, gold, diamond-adorned **Custodià del Pi**, made in 1587 and originally used in the nearby Santa Maria del Pi church. In the Catholic religion, the *custodià* is used to store the Host, or holy bread, before and after the rite of communion. Still in perfect condition today, it drips with ornate detail and delicate religious symbolism. Equally breathtaking is the view of the cathedral from the museum's top-floor gallery.

MUSEU DEL CALÇAT (SHOE MUSEUM)

🏛 *Pl. Sant Felip Neri 5. ☎ 93 301 45 33. M: Jaume I. Open Tu-Su 11am-2pm. 300ptas/€1,20. Only 1½ rooms, but you can call for guided tours. Pamphlet on the history of the museum 200ptas/€1,20.*

This bizarre but intriguing collection of footwear throughout history is a tribute to the ancient guilds of Barcelona, tracing the existence of master shoemakers to an official document in 1203 signed by the Bishop of Barcelona (even today a few faithful members tend to the guild's chapel in the Cathedral de la Sant Creu; see **Godfather Part Zero**, p. 66). The exhibit includes everything from early Roman sandals and 3rd-century monkswear to track spikes from the 1940s and the boots which Carles Vallés wore to the top of Mt. Everest to plant the Catalan flag. Modern-day men can leave their 20th-century machismo at the door and admire the pointed-toe, high-heeled men's boots of years past while women say their thanks that pricey, silver-plated dress shoes aren't quite the rage they once were. Most entertaining of all, perhaps, is the gargantuan shoe designed to fit the Columbus of the Monument a Colom (see p. 63).

LA RIBERA

MUSEU BARBIER-MUELLER

🏛 *C. Montcada 12-14. ☎ 93 310 45 16. M: Jaume I. Open Tu-Sa 10am-6pm and Su 10am-3pm. Combined admission with Museu Tèxtil i d'Indumentària next door; see below. 500ptas/€3, students and seniors 250ptas/€1,50. Free 1st Su of the month. Wheelchair accessible.*

This museum is chock-full of carefully arranged and displayed relics from the world of pre-Columbian America. Tapestries, carvings, ornaments, vases, sculptures, and countless other artifacts date from 200 BC and are taken from the sites of the Olmecs, Mayas, Aztecs, Coclé, Mochicas, and Incas. There are informational placards (available in English) scattered throughout the museum that explain the significance and cultural history of the many artifacts that are on display.

◼ MUSEU PICASSO

When I was a child, my mother said to me, "If you become a soldier, you'll be a general. If you become a monk, you'll end up as the Pope." Instead, I became a painter and wound up as Picasso.
 —Pablo Picasso

◗ *C. Montcada 15-19.* ☎ *93 319 63 10. M: Jaume I. Walk down C. Princesa from the Metro, and turn right on C. Montcada. Open Tu-Sa 10am-8pm, Su 10am-3pm. 800ptas/€4,80; students and seniors 400ptas/€2,40; under 16 free. Free first Su of each month. Wheelchair accessible.*

This incredible museum traces the development of Picasso as an artist, with a chronologically organized collection of his early works that weaves through five connected mansions once occupied by Barcelona's nobility. Although the museum offers little from Picasso's more well-known middle years, it boasts the world's best collection of work from his formative period in Barcelona. The museum showcases each of Picasso's re-inventions of himself, from his deeply personal, tormented Blue Period, to his form-fascinated Rose Period, to his reign as master of Cubism. Like the Fundació Miró (see p. 116), the museum is practically an autobiography of the artist's life, depicting his many (many) lovers, his emotional ups and downs, his obsessions with the bull and the taurine, his family, and the politics around him. The collection was started in 1963 with a donation from Picasso's friend Jaume Sabartés; it was later expanded by Picasso himself and by relatives after his death.

The museum boasts rare lithographs, ceramics, and even pencil sketches by an 11-year-old Picasso, beginning with some of Picasso's first paintings ever, including *The First Communion* (1896), and *Science and Charity* (1897). The evolution from this first realistic painting to Picasso's subsequent works is astounding. Following the suicide of his close friend Casagemas (whose lover Picasso had wooed away), Picasso entered his **Blue Period** (1901-1904), with paintings influenced by his own intense depression. These paintings are marked by blue tones, indicative of sadness, and sordid or marginalized subject matter: the homeless, the blind, the sick, and even the dead. *Desamparados* (1903) and *El Loco* (1904) are two of the museum's examples of this period.

After recovering from his depression, Picasso gradually moved into a new period, the **Rose Period** (1904-5). This period is characterized by pinkish tones and more optimistic subject matter. With an intense interest in form and anatomy, Picasso often visited the circus during these years, and circus strongmen, harlequins, and contortionists were frequently subjects of his Rose Period works; *El Retrato de la Señora Canals* (1905) is one of the works on display from this time period.

Most impressive of all the work in the museum is the display of the artist's 58 Cubist interpretations of Velázquez's *Las Meninas* (translated to *Ladies in Waiting*, which hangs in the Museu del Prado in Madrid). The original *Las Meninas* is a breathtaking, 7ft. masterpiece: a group painting of a familiar royal scene. Rather than the typical posed painting, Velázquez captured an instantaneous moment on canvas. Generally agreed to be the finest Spanish—if not international—painting, Spanish painters have created their own interpretations of *Las Meninas*, a sort of rite of passage into greatness. Francisco Goya considered himself the inheritor of Velázquez's position as the best Spanish painter, and hence etched the master's famous painting.

This pattern continued with Picasso, who considered himself the next in line for this title. What is most remarkable about Picasso is that instead of recreating the painting in its original grandeur, as Goya did, he chose to apply his own, unique styles as a way of interpreting Velázquez's mysterious work. He shows all of the main characters from the original painting, but rearranges them to emphasize different parts. *Las Meninas* is exalted for its rigid linearity and the mystery behind what Velázquez (who painted himself into the original) is painting on the canvas he is working on within the painting itself. Because of the linear construction and multiple focal points in the original, the subject of his painting within the painting is a mystery. However, this mystery is lost in Picasso's focused, cubist recreations, as Velázquez's unique usage of space is eliminated and the trick that Velázquez is playing on the spectator is lost. Picasso reinvents the many vantage points of the original in his Cubist reinterpretation of multiple angles and lines of vision, along his own terms. The reinterpretation of *La Meninas* was a very controversial move for Picasso, as he destroyed the magic of a painting in which Spaniards take national pride.

Easily Barcelona's most popular museum, lines at the Museu Picasso often snake a good way down C. Montcada. The best times to avoid the museum-going masses are mornings and early evenings when the crowd thins out.

MUSEU TÉXTIL I D'INDUMENTÀRIA

C. Montcada 12. ☎ 93 310 45 16. M: Jaume I. Open Tu-Sa 10am-6pm, Su 10am-3pm. Combined admission with Museu Barbier-Mueller, buy tickets there (see above). One ticket gets you into this museum, the Museu de les Arts Decoratives (see p. 119), and the Museu de Ceràmica (see p. 119) up to one month after purchase. 500ptas/€3, students and seniors 250ptas/€1,50. Free 1st Sa of the month after 3pm. Wheelchair accessible.

Showcases textiles and costumes beginning with Egyptian fabric remnants from the 3rd century and moving on to the glittering gowns and accessories of the Italian Renaissance. Imagine yourself in 16th-century armor, elaborate 18th-century Rococo bustles, or a swinging 60s tunic made entirely of coin-sized plastic circles. On the way out, don't miss the fashionable gift shop and the lovely outdoor café.

MUSEU DE LA XOCOLATA

Pl. Pons i Clerch, corner of C. Comerç. ☎ 93 268 78 78. M: Jaume I. Follow C. Princesa and turn left on C. Comerç. Open M and W-Sa 10am-7pm, Su 10am-3pm. 500ptas/€3, students and seniors 425ptas/€2,50. Workshops 1000ptas/€6. Wheelchair accessible.

Everything you ever wanted to know about chocolate and then some. This museum presents the history of chocolate from its origins and use in the Americas to its arrival in Europe to the present day, as well as chocolate's medicinal properties and (lack of) nutritional value. Naturally, there is a small café and shop where you can buy your own chocolate treats after the museum whets your appetite. Workshops on cake baking, the history of chocolate, and chocolate tasting are occasionally held during the week; call for information.

see map
p. 322

PARC DE LA CIUTADELLA

The following museums are all located in the Parc de la Ciutadella (see **Sights,** p. 72).

MUSEU D'ART MODERN

In Pl. D'Armes. M: Arc de Triomf. Follow Pg. Til.les to the statue of General Prim at the roundabout and turn left toward Pl. D'Armes; signs point the way to the museum. ☎ 93 319 57 28. 500ptas/€3, students and children 350ptas/€2. Free entrance first Thu of every month. Open Tu-Sa 10am-7pm, Su 10am-2:30pm. Wheelchair accessible.

This museum, a part of MNAC (see p. 118), is located in what used to be the citadel's arsenal. The museum houses a diverse collection of paintings, sculptures, and interior designs, all by 19th-century Catalan artists. Noteworthy works include Ramon Casas's *Plein Air*, Josep Llimona's *Desconsol*, Isidre Nonell's paintings of Gypsy women, and an entire room devoted to Josep Clará's *Noucentiste* sculptures. The museum also displays furniture designed by Antoni Gaudí for Casa Battló (see **Sights,** p. 81), as well as several of Puig i Cadalfach's Casa Amatller (see **Sights,** p. 80) fixtures. Also of note are two of Salvador Dalí's early portraits, his only paintings on display in Barcelona proper.

MUSEU DE GEOLOGIA

On Pg. Picasso, 2 buildings behind the Museu Zoologia. M: Arc de Triomf. ☎ 93 319 68 95. Entrance faces inside of park. Open Tu-Su 10am-2pm and Th 10am-6:30pm. 400ptas/€2,40; students and seniors 200ptas/€1,20; free first Su of each month. Wheelchair accessible.

Another park structure designed by Fontseré (with the help of Antoni Rovira i Trias), the Museu de Geologia opened in 1882 as the first public museum in the city. It boasts an extensive collection of rocks and minerals, many of them collected locally. The Paleontology room is equally well-endowed.

MUSEU DE ZOOLOGIA (CASTELL DELS TRES DRAGONS)

🚹 *Entrances on Pg. Pujades/Pg. de Lluís Companys and Pg. Picasso/C. Princesa. At the corner of Pg. Picasso and Pg. Pujades. M: Arc de Triomf.* ☎ *93 319 69 12. Open Tu-Su 10am-2pm and Th 10am-6:30pm. 500ptas/€3, students and seniors 250ptas/€1,50. Entrance to the Museu de Geologia included for an additional 100ptas/€0,60. Free first Su of every month. Wheelchair accessible.*

Designed as a restaurant for Expo '88, Montaner's Castell dels Tres Dragons (Castle of Three Dragons) was later used by the architect as a Modernist workshop. It takes its nickname from a contemporary poem by Frederic Soler. The splendor of the building's blue and white tile work and brick turrets can be best appreciated from outside, but should you choose to visit the museum, the stained glass and marble staircases will not disappoint. The museum displays an impressively large whale skeleton on the first floor, and an otherwise unremarkable collection of taxidermy and fauna samples. Most informational placards are in English.

The Pope at the Wax Museum

EL RAVAL

see map pp. 316-317

Both museums in el Raval are covered by the **Articket**, a worthwhile investment for those planning to hit a lot of the city's museums; see p. 103 for details.

CENTRE DE CULTURA CONTEMPORÀNIA DE BARCELONA (CCCB)

🚹 *Casa de Caritat, C. Montalegre 5. M: Catalunya or Universitat, next to the MACBA (see above).* ☎ *93 306 41 00. Open Tu-Sa 11am-8pm, Su 11am-3pm. 600ptas/€3,80, students 400ptas/€2,20, children under 16 free.*

At first glance, the center stands out for its jarring mixture of architectural styles, consisting of an early 20th century theater, an unassuming yellow and white creation, and its 1994 addition, an enormous and very sleek wing constructed of black glass. The institution itself stands out as well, with a wonderful variety of temporary photo and art exhibits, film screenings, and music and dance performances. Events in 2001 included a flamenco dance festival and an exposition of art and photography from present-day Africa. Check the *Guía del Ocio* for scheduled events.

Erotic Museum

🖼 MUSEU D'ART CONTEMPORANI (MACBA)

🚹 *Pl. dels Angels 1. M: Universitat or Catalunya.* ☎ *93 412 08 10; www.macba.es. From Pl. de Catalunya, take a right onto C. Elisabets and follow it to Pl. dels Angels.*

Gallery in La Ribera

111

kids
IN THE CITY

Don't Worry, Your Kids Will Eat It

If you're looking for a place to bring the kids for an afternoon, try out some of the following museums:

Fundació Miró. Sometimes kids understand this stuff better than adults; see p. 116.

Museu d'Autòmats. An interactive robot museum in and ever kid-friendly amusement park; see p. 121.

Museu de Cera. A gorey wax museum that will entertain older children; see p. 104.

Museu Egipci. Kids love mummies; see **p. 114**.

Museu FCB. More oriented towards sports-crazed little boys and their sports-crazed dads; see p. 119.

Museu de Zoologia. Animals from everywhere, stuffed and startling; see p. 111.

Open July-Sept. M, W, F 11am-8pm; Th 11am-9:30pm; Sa 10am-8pm, Su 10am-3pm. Oct.-June M-F 11am-7:30pm, Sa 10am-8pm, Su 10am-3pm. Closed Tu. 800ptas/ €4,81, students 550ptas/€3,30, 16 and under free.

Inaugurated in 1995, the construction of the gleaming white MACBA, designed by American architect Richard Meier, was the final product of a collaboration between Barcelona's mayor and the Catalan government to improve the lives of the residents of El Raval by restoring the neighborhood by turning it into an artistic and cultural focal point. Its brightness and scale are a startling contrast with the narrow alleys of the neighborhood where it sits. The building's sparse decor was designed to allow the art to speak for itself, which it has—the MACBA has received worldwide acclaim for its focus on avant-garde art between the two world wars. Eclectic and often interactive exhibits focus on three-dimensional art, photography, video, and graphic work from the past 40 years. The MACBA also has excellent rotating exhibits.

L'EIXAMPLE

see map pp. 314-315

FUNDACIÓ ANTONI TÀPIES

🛈 C. Aragó 255. ☎ 93 487 03 15; museu@ftapies.com. Around the corner from the Manzana de la Discòrdia, and between Pg. de Gràcia and La Rambla de Catalunya. M: Pg. de Gràcia. Library upstairs open by appointment only, Tu-F 11am-8pm. Museum open Tu-Su 10am-8pm. 700ptas/€4,20, students and seniors 350ptas/€2,10. Wheelchair accessible

Tàpies's bizarre wire sculpture (*Cloud with Chair*) atop Domènech i Montaner's red brick building announces this collection of contemporary, abstract art by Antoni Tàpies and many other contemporary artists from around the world. The top floor of the foundation is dedicated to famous Catalan artists, including Tàpies, while the other two floors feature special exhibits of other modern artists.

Tàpies is one of Catalunya's best-known artists; his art often defies definition, springing out of the traditions of Surrealism and Magicism and drawing inspiration from Picasso and Miró. His works are often a mixture of painting and sculpture, generally referred to as collage, although he is the creator of a number of abstract sculptures as well. Most of his paintings include a "T" in some form, a symbol that has been variously interpreted and misinterpreted as a religious cross, as sexual penetration, and as the artist's own signature.

Tàpies' use of unorthodox materials—objects found in the trash—and his dark, dirty colors are often interpreted as a protest against the dictatorship he grew up under and the subsequent urban alienation he felt pervading Spain's cities.

Tàpies' works use everyday materials, like sand, glue, wood, marble powder, dirt, and wire, to show the eloquence inherent in simplicity. His works have been compared to graffiti on city walls: silent, sometimes hideous expressions of protest that are somehow also an expression of art by the way they reflect the closed state of Spain during the time they were created.

The Fundació Tàpies is known for showcasing avant garde contemporary art, from kinetic sculptures to performance art and from globally famous masters to relative unknowns. The line-up for 2001-2002 includes exhibitions of the German photographer Hans Peter Feldmann (Nov. 22-Jan. 27), Danish painter Asger Jorn (Feb. 12-Apr. 21), a collection of contemporary Arab works (May 2-July 14), and the designs of Isidoro Valcárcel Medina (Oct. 2002). The library, reflecting Tàpies' own interests in Asia, is stocked with books on non-Western art and artifacts.

Museum of Contemporary Art

FUNDACIÓ FRANCISCO GODIA

🏛 C. València 284. ☎ 93 272 31 80; www.fundacionfgodia.org. Open W-M 10am-8pm. Free guided tours Sa-Su at noon (no English); otherwise call ahead for a guided tour (1000ptas/€6 per person). Wall descriptions and printed guides in English, Spanish, and Catalan. 700ptas/€4,50; students, over 65, and disabled 350ptas/€1,80. Joint ticket with the Museu Egipci (see above) 1400ptas/€7,80; students, over 65, and disabled 1000ptas/€6. MC/V. Wheelchair accessible.

The Fundació Francisco Godia was created in 1998 by the namesake's daughter in order to open his private art collection for public viewing. Francisco Godia (1921-1990) was a bizarre mix of astute businessman, Spain's best Formula One racecar driver, and passionate supporter of the arts. His collection, which fills 10 small rooms, runs from the 12th to the 20th century, with a heavy emphasis on medieval sculpture and painting, Spanish ceramics of the last 500 years, and modern paintings by Spanish artists like Ramon Casas, Isidre Nonell, and José Gutiérrez Solana. Highlights include Solana's bold, dark-lined *Bullfight at Ronda* (1927), Isidre Nonell's dark *Gypsy Woman* (1905), Francesc Gimeno's life-like *Mother and Daughter* (1898), and the popular piece *At the Racecourse* (1905) by Ramon Casas.

Museu del Perfum

MUSEU DE CLAVEGUERAM (SEWER MUSEUM)

🏛 Pg de St. Joan 98. M: Verdaguer. ☎ 93 457 65 50. Open Tu-Su 9am-2pm. 200ptas/€1,20.

The Teenage Mutant Ninja Turtles would have approved of Barcelona's openness to quirky museum collections: this one, a documentary on the development of Barcelona's sewers, was inspired by the major infrastructure renovations

History of Catalunya Museum

113

GET sm**art**

International Men of Mystery

Barcelona has always been at the center of the Spanish comics industry; it not only publishes 80% of the country's comics (some call the book-loving city the Boston of Spain), but was also the birthplace of Spain's best-known humor artist, Francisco Ibáñez (1936). Ibáñez's most beloved creation is *Mortadelo y Filemón,* a Spanish parody of Sherlock Holmes and Dr. Watson, with some mockery of the CIA thrown in for good measure. The goofy pair have been bumbling their way through challenging assignments for more than 40 years and are now read in more than a dozen European countries.

Ibáñez's most notable talent is his ability to stay afloat throughout major cultural change. Under Franco, he had to avoid anything in the slightest erotic; he was even forced to remove a picture of a dog eating a bone because censors were certain that the object was more erect than edible. More recently, Ibáñez has been questioned about the relationship between the two chummy male characters. His response: "No, they are not gay. They've had numerous relationships with women that have ended badly. How else could they have possibly turned out?"

required for the 1992 Olympics (see p. 46). With a proliferation of pictures and little-known historical information, it traces the city's waste plumbing from Roman times to modern. Unfortunately for curious tourists who have spent thousands of *pesetas* on water to accompany their restaurant meals, it does not explain Barceloneses' refusal to serve the city's tap water. Kowabunga, dude!

MUSEU DEL CÒMIC I DE LA IL.LUSTRACIÓ

🚇 C. Santa Carolina 25, between Trav. de Gràcia and M: Alfons X. ☎ 93 348 15 13; www.interars.com. Open M-Sa 10am-2pm and 5-8pm. 500ptas/€3, under 14 and over 65 350ptas/€2,10.

Comic strip artists in Spain have not had an easy time, between the Civil War, the economic difficulties of the postwar years, Franco's censorship, and—since the 1980s—the overwhelming growth of Japanese animation. This small private collection was carefully put together to serve as a representative sampling of some of the best comics done in Spain between 1915 and the 1970s. It includes a few original sketches and the only existing copy of some strips, as well as a temporary exhibition (changes every 3-4 months), usually on a well-known individual artist. For the politically minded, the Franco propaganda aimed directly at children is particularly interesting to see; look for the January 30, 1938 and July 18, 1939 editions of *Flecha,* the "*semanario nacional infantil*" of the time. For more info on comics in Barcelona, see **International Men of Mystery,** p. 114.

MUSEU DE L'ESPORT

🚇 C. Buenos Aires 56-8. ☎ 93 419 22 32. M: Hospital Clinic. Open M-F 10am-2pm and 4-8pm. Free.

For those looking for information on sports and recreation other than soccer, this museum is the place to be. Today, Puig i Cadafalch's Casa Company houses the Museu de l'Esport Dr. Melcior Colet, a collection focused on Catalan sports. The museum is named for the former owner of the house.

MUSEU EGIPCI

🚇 C. València 284, just to the left off Pg. de Gràcia when facing Pl. de Catalunya. M: Pg. de Gràcia. ☎ 93 488 01 88; www.fundclos.com. Open M-Sa 10am-8pm, Su 10am-2pm. Closed Dec. 25-26 and Jan. 1. Descriptions in Spanish and Catalan. 900ptas/€5,20; students, over 65 and disabled 700ptas/€4,50. Joint admission with the Fundació Godia (next door; see below) 1400ptas/€8,50; students, over 65 and handicapped 1000ptas/€6. Free tours in Spanish and Catalan Sa 11am and 5pm; call ahead to hire an English guide (1400ptas/€8,50). Library open Tu-Sa 4pm-8pm. MC/V. Wheelchair accessible.

In 1993, wealthy Barcelonese Jordi Clos decided to turn a private passion into Spain's only museum dedicated entirely to Pharaonic Egypt. It just recently moved to its current location on C. València and now has space for more than 500 Egyptian artifacts, including jewelry, pottery, and several displays focused on tombs, mummies, and the beliefs surrounding death in ancient Egypt. On Friday nights the museum hosts dramatic reenactments of Egyptian legends, complete with a tour of the museum and a free cup of *cava*, a Catalan champagne (Friday night visits 9:30-11pm. 1900ptas/€11,50, students 1700ptas/€10. Reservations required).

MUSEU DEL PERFUM

🚩 *Pg. de Gràcia 39. ☎ 93 216 01 46; www.perfum-museum.com. M: Pg. de Gràcia. Open M-F 10:30am-2pm and 4:30-8pm, Sa 10:30am-2pm. Free.*

The Museu del Perfum is easy to miss, located at the back of a perfectly ordinary-looking perfume store in an inconspicuous building between some of the city's most admired houses. The collection inside, however, is anything but missable, with nearly 1000 quirky, varied perfume containers, from 2nd-century BC Roman vials to 14th-century Arab pieces to miniatures from Pre-Columbian Ecuador. Some of the more original designs include a mouse, a lightbulb, the Eiffel Tower, and a suicidal bottle with a knife-shaped throat applicator. Even Salvador Dalí took a crack at this little-known art form, with a huge bottle titled "The Sun King."

MUSEU TAURÍ

🚩 *Gran Via de les Corts Catalanes 749, near M: Monumental. ☎ 93 245 58 04. Open M-Sa 10:30am-2pm and 4-7pm, Su 10:30am. Admission includes entrance to the museum, the bull-ring, and the bullpens. Museum descriptions in English, Spanish, German, and Italian. 450ptas/ €2,70; children 300ptas/€1,80.*

This dense, two-room collection proudly commemorates the tradition of bullfighting, with pictures of major fights and fighters, old posters and stamps, a colorful exhibit on the evolution of the bullfighter's costume throughout time, and a good handful of stuffed bulls' heads on the walls (minus, of course, however many ears their human opponents earned in completing the kill). You can also see a picture display on one much luckier beast, the first bull to be spared in the Plaza Monumental by unanimous public request (a remarkable feat, after more than 50 years of fights in the ring). Even he lost his ears, though, to reward the efforts of *matador* Andrés Hernando. For tickets to a bullfight (which is a less common form of entertainment in Barcelona than it is in the rest of Spain), see **Entertainment,** p. 171; for some perspective on the sport, see **No Bull,** p. 170.

POBLE NOU & PORT OLÍMPIC

see map p. 321

MUSEU DE CARROSSES FÚNEBRES (HEARSE MUSEUM)

🚩 *C. Sancho de Ávila 2. ☎ 93 484 17 00. M: Marina. From the metro, follow Av. Meridiana away from C. Marina until its intersection with C. Sancho de Ávila. Open M-F 10am-1pm and 4-6pm. Free. Not wheelchair accessible.*

Enter the gray office building right on the corner (there is no sign for the museum outside, and no apparent street number) and ask at the information desk inside for a tour of the Museu de Carrosses. This small collection of plush 17th- and 18th-century horse-drawn hearses may be morbid, but it is also surprisingly intriguing. Only virgins could ride to their grave in the white carriages, and only the richest families could afford brocades.

BARCELONETA

see map p. 322

MUSEU D'HISTÒRIA DE CATALUNYA

🚩 *Palau de Mar, Pl. Pau Vila 3, on the waterfront. ☎ 93 225 47 00. www.cultura.gencat.es/museus/mhc. 500ptas/€3; students, seniors, and children 350ptas/€2. Mandatory bag check 100ptas/€0,60. Open Tu-Sa 10am-7pm, W 10am-8pm, Su and holidays 10am-2:30pm.*

GET sm**art**

Miró's Obsessions

Like Dalí, Joan Miró had a repertoire of symbols he employed in his paintings and sculptures to convey certain themes. Calling them his "obsessions," Miró developed this language during WWII when he was living in Normandy. Miró's aimed "to express precisely all the golden sparks of our soul." He most frequently painted women and birds. Other obsessions include a **net** (the earth), **stars** (the unattainable heavens), and birds (connecting the two). His symbols are not all so lofty; don't confuse the stars with Miró's infamous **asterisk,** a symbol for the anus.

The colors and images Miró uses in his paintings also serve as a measure of his emotional state and the politics of the time. Paintings with dark backgrounds and brown tones that depict creatures with teeth are generally from the Civil War and dictatorship period (see p. 44), when Miró went into a self-induced exile and subsequent depression; tormented, nightmarish paintings from this time are his form of silent protest. Works with white backgrounds and bright primary colors, were created as the dictatorship relaxed and democracy began. The visual optimism of these works reflects Miró's own greatly improved emotional health and hopes for Spain.

This museum sits in the recently renovated Palau de Mar (Palace of the Sea) building. Although originally constructed in 1900 as a decidedly un-palatial port warehouse, the edifice is now a key contributor to the beauty of the Port Vell waterfront area. The four floors of the museum take you on an interactive journey through Catalan history, from its prehistoric roots to the 20th century. Unfortunately, in a display of regional pride, the majority of the secondary displays are written entirely in Catalan; major displays have Spanish and English explanations. The museum showcases unique interactive exhibits, which include a fake medieval horse and a full suit of armor to try on and check out in a mirror. Ask at the front desk to borrow an English or Spanish guide.

PORT VELL

see map p. 322

MUSEU MARÍTIM

Av. Drassanes, off the rotary around the Monument a Colom, the street to Columbus' back. M: Drassanes. ☎*93 342 99 20. Open M-Sa 10am-7pm. 900ptas/€5,40; under 16, students, and seniors 450ptas/€2,70. Wheelchair accessible.*

The *Drassanes Reiales de Barcelona* (Royal Shipyards of Barcelona) began constructing ships for the Catalan-Aragonese empire in the 13th century. Still amazingly well preserved today, the shipyards are considered the world's greatest standing example of Civil (i.e., non-religious) Gothic architecture. The complex consists of a series of huge indoor bays with slender pillars, where entire ships could be constructed at a time, and stored over the winter. Since 1941, the building has housed the Maritime Museum, which traces the evolution of shipbuilding and life on the high seas. Surprisingly high-tech and modern, the museum provides detailed and sleekly produced audio guides to the exhibits (in English, Spanish, German, and French). Model ships, medieval maps, and detailed dioramas illuminate the maritime history of man. The visits ends with The Great Adventure of the Sea, a Disney-like journey through life-size maritime reconstructions. In the galley of an actual 16th-century warship one can watch virtual slaves rowing, or later, under the stars, feel the strong breeze on the deck of a passenger steamship.

MONTJUÏC

see map p. 320

FUNDACIÓ JOAN MIRÓ

Av. Miramar 71-75. ☎*93 443 94 70; www.bcn.fjmiro.es. A funicular runs from inside the M: Paral.lel station at Av. Paral.lel and Nou de la Rambla.*

Turn left out of the funicular station; the museum is a 5min. walk up on the right. Open July-Sept. Tu-W and F-Sa 10am-8pm, Th 10am-9:30pm, Su 10am-2:30pm; Oct.-June Tu-W and F-Sa 10am-7pm, Th 10am-9:30pm, Su 10am-2:30pm. 1200ptas/€7,20; students and seniors 650ptas/€3,90. Wheelchair accessible.

One of Catalunya's great Surrealist artists, Joan Miró's works represent an alternative perspective of the world around him; where Dalí represented the world of dreams, Miró's works portray the perspective of childhood. Miró's work is often incorrectly referred to as "abstract" by confused tourists who do not know how to read his paintings; be sure to pick up a brochure to guide you through Miró's symbolism and artistic innovation (see **Miró's Obsessions,** opposite). Miró's works always refer to concrete images, and deciphering his imaginative interpretations of the world around him is remarkably satisfying.

Miró's works are a personal and poignant tour through Spanish 20th-century history; his fundamental optimism and his generosity have made him one of Spain's— not just Catalunya's—most beloved artists. Long unappreciated and oppressed in his homeland, when Miró finally had the means to create this institution, he symbolically named it the Miró Foundation, not the Miró Museum; while Miró's own works are always showcased at the museum, the museum is not meant to glorify the works of one man so much as it is meant to encourage appreciation of art in general and showcase young artists.

More than a museum, the Fundació Miró is a rotating collection of 10,000 of the artist's works, pieces by other artists inspired by Miró's unique style, and a foundation to support contemporary art and young Catalan artists. Designed by Miró's friend Josep Luís Sert, the Fundació links interior and exterior spaces with massive windows and outdoor patios. Skylights illuminate an extensive collection of statues, paintings, and *sobreteixims* (multimedia tapestries) from Miró's career, including the stunning *Barcelona Series*, which depicts Miró's personal reaction to the Spanish Civil War. It also includes several paintings from Miró's *Las Constelaciones* series, a reaction to Nazi invasion during WWII. His best-known pieces in the museum include *El Carnival de Arlequin, La Masia,* and *l'Or de l'azuz.* The museum also highlights Miró's close friend Alexander Calder's *Mercury Fountain,* commemorating the Civil War-torn town of Almáden and created for the 1937 World's Fair. Room 13 displays experimental work by young artists. The Fundació also sponsors music recitals in the summer months on Thursdays at 9pm (800ptas/€4,80), and occasionally hosts film festivals (check web site for listings).

MUSEU ARQUEOLÒGIC DE CATALUNYA

◪ Pg. Santa Madrona 39-41. ☎ 93 423 21 49; www.mac.es. From M: Espanya, take bus #55 up the hill to the Palau Nacional. When facing the Palau Nacional, the museum is to the left. Open Tu-Sa 9:30am-7pm and Su 10am-2:30pm. 400ptas/€2,40; students and seniors 300ptas/€1,80. Wheelchair accessible.

The exhibits here display artifacts from prehistoric times up to the constitution of Catalunya. Several rooms feature a collection of Carthaginian art from Ibiza and excavated relics from the Greco-Roman city of Empúries (see **Daytrips,** p. 201).

MUSEU ETNOLÒGIC

◪ Pg. Santa Madrona, uphill from Museu Arqueològic (see above). ☎93 424 68 07; www.museuetnologic.bcn.es. Open W and F-Su 10am-2pm, Tu and Th 10am-7pm. 500ptas/€3; students and seniors 250ptas/€1,50. Free 1st Su of every month.

This museum features a small but carefully selected display of documentary photographs, clothing, crafts, and artifacts from Japan, Australia, Latin America, and Africa. Special exhibits focus on individual countries and cultures.

▧ MUSEU MILITAR

◪ Inside the Castell de Montjuïc (see **Sights,** p. 89). ☎ 93 329 86 13. Open Mar. 15-Nov. 15 Tu-Su 9:30am-8pm, Nov. 16-Mar. 14 Tu-Su 9:30am-5pm. From M: Paral.lel, take the funicular to Av. Miramar and then the Teleféric de Montjuïc cable car, which runs up to the castle via the site of the former Parc d'Attracions. Funicular runs from inside the M: Paral.lel station at Av. Paral.lel and Nou de la Rambla. Teleféric open M-Sa 11:15am-9pm. One-way 500ptas/€3; round-trip 700ptas/€4,20. Or, walk up the steep slope on C. Foc, next to the funicular station. Museum entrance 400ptas/€2,40.

Inside the Castell de Montjuïc, the Museu Militar displays armaments and other Montjuïc relics—a particularly fascinating collection due to the castle's rich and sordid history. Keep an eye out for the 11th-century tombstones excavated from Montjuïc's Jewish cemetery, Barcelona's only remaining statue of Franco, and the second largest sword collection in Spain.

MUSEU NACIONAL D'ART DE CATALUNYA (PALAU NACIONAL)

🚹 *From M: Espanya, walk up Av. Reina María Cristina, away from the twin brick towers, and take the escalators. ☎ 93 622 03 60; www.mnac.es. Open Tu-Sa 10am-7pm, Su 10am-2:30pm. 800ptas/ €4,80; 1000ptas/€6 with temporary exhibits; students and seniors 550ptas/€3,40; 700ptas/ €4,22 with temporary exhibits. Museum entrance free first Th of every month. Wheelchair accessible.*

Designed by Enric Catá, Pedro Cendoya, and Pere Domènech for the 1929 International Exposition (see **Life & Times,** p. 44), the Palau Nacional has housed the Museu Nacional d'Art de Catalunya since 1934. The view from the Palau is one of the best in all of Barcelona. Its main hall is often used for public events, while the wings are home to the world's finest collection of Catalan Romanesque art, and a wide variety of Gothic pieces. The Romanesque frescoes, now integrated as murals into dummy chapels, were salvaged from their original, less protected locations in northern Catalunya's churches in the 1920s by Barcelona's city government. The resulting ambience is a surprisingly spiritual tour through some of Catalunya's medieval masterpieces. The museum's Gothic art corridor displays murals from stately homes and religious buildings in Mallorca; the paintings give a political history of the time. The Gothic corridor features painters Jaume Huguet and Bartolomé Bermejo.

In the midst of these displays, the MNAC is constructing and renovating separate areas of the building to house the Museu d'Art Modern collection, which will be displayed here beginning in 2003, allowing the museum to display an even broader collection of Catalan art. The museum also hosts temporary exhibits; 2001 showcased an exquisite Ramon Casas display, and planned events include a special photography exhibit of the Spanish Civil War (Oct. 2001-Jan. 2002).

ZONA ALTA

GRÀCIA

see maps p. 318 & 319

CASA-MUSEU GAUDÍ

🚹 *Inside the Park Güell (see **Sights**, p. 92). Located to the right of the Hall of One Hundred Columns, when facing away from the sea. Closest direct park entrance is Carretera del Carmel. ☎ 93 219 38 11. 400ptas/€2,40. Open daily Nov.-Feb. 10am-6pm, Mar.-Apr. and Oct 10am-7pm, May-Sept. 10am-8pm. Last entrance is 15min. before closing.*

Designed by Gaudí's friend and colleague, Fransesc Berenguer, the Casa-Museu Gaudí was the celebrated architect's home from 1906 to 1926 until he moved into the Sagrada Família several months before his death. Gaudí's leftover fence work from other projects was used to create the garden of metallic plant sculptures in front of the museum. The three-story house showcases some of Gaudí's anatomical furniture designs from the Casa Battló, paintings of several of his works by notable artists, and the master's own austere bedroom complete with his death mask. Several of Gaudí's architectural models and plans are also on view. The third floor displays several intriguing pieces by the sculptor Carlos Mani, who collaborated with Gaudí on La Sagrada Família.

PEDRALBES & LES CORTS

COL.LECIÓ THYSSEN-BORNEMISZA

🚹 *Baixada del Monestir 9. ☎ 93 481 10 41; www.museothyssen.org. FCG: Reina Elisenda, in the Monestir de Pedralbes (see p. 98). Same hours as the monastery. 500ptas/€3; students and over 65 300ptas/€1,80; under 16 free. Combined ticket with monastery 800ptas/€4,80; students 500ptas/€3; children free.*

The former dormitory of the St. Clare nuns now houses this small but formidable collection of medieval, Renaissance, and Baroque art, almost entirely religious paintings from the larger collection housed in Madrid. Highlights include works by Velázquez, Rubens, and Fra Angelico.

MUSEU DE CERÀMICA

🚩 *Av. Diagonal 686. ☎ 93 280 16 21. M: Palau Reial, 2nd and 3rd floors of the Palau Reial. One ticket gets you into both this museum and the Museu de les Arts Decoratives; (see below). Keep your receipt for entrance into La Ribera's Museu Tèxtil i d'Indumentària (see p. 110), the third of Catalunya's "Museums of Applied Arts," up to one month after purchase. Open Tu-Sa 10am-6pm, Su and holidays 10am-3pm. 800ptas/€4, students under 25 400ptas/€2,20, under 16 free.*

Spain's tradition of ceramics is on display in the Museum of Ceramics, which traces the evolution of Spanish sculpture from the 11th century to the present. The displays show off skillfully crafted plates, tiles, jars, and bowls gathered from all regions of Spain. The true highlight is found upstairs in the more abstract 20th century collection, which contains a small collection of ceramic works by Picasso and Miró. It's worth the visit just to imagine drinking *sangría* out of a pitcher designed by the master of Cubism. One of Barcelona's three museums of "applied arts" (the other two are Museu de les Arts Decoratives, below, and the Museu Tèxtil i d'Indumentària on p. 110).

Fundació Miró

MUSEU DE LES ARTS DECORATIVES

🚩 *Av. Diagonal 686. ☎ 93 280 50 24. M: Palau Reial, on the second floor of the Palau Reial (see p. 98). Same ticket at Museu de Cerámica; see above.*

Recognizing the artistic value of items often taken for granted in daily life, the Museum of Decorative Arts is one of Barcelona's three museums of "applied arts," (the other two are the Museu de Ceràmica below and Museu Tèxtil on p. 110) displaying home furnishings from as far back as the Middle Ages. A large collection of 19th-century furniture shows how the Catalan bourgeoisie lived. The eclectic collection also contains such items as a mop and bucket from the 1950s and an extensive display of industrial furniture from the 20th century.

At the Fundació Miró

🏛 MUSEU DEL FÚTBOL CLUB BARCELONA

🚩 *C. Aristides Maillol, next to the stadium. ☎ 93 496 36 08. M: Collblanc. Enter through access gates 7 or 9. Museum entrance 575ptas/€3,46; with 45min. stadium tour 1300ptas/€7,81; children under 13 425ptas/€3,50; with stadium tour 700ptas/€4,21. Tours begin at 10:30am, 11:30am, 12:30, 3, 4, and 5pm. Open M-Sa 10am-6:30pm, Su 10am-2pm.*

Busloads of tour groups from all over the world pour into this museum, making it a close second to the Picasso Museum as Barcelona's most visited. The museum merits all the attention it gets, as it has created a fitting homage to one of soccer's greatest clubs. Any sports fan will appreci-

View from National Museum of Catalan Art

ate the storied history of the team, which celebrated its centennial in 1999. Recent greats on the team include Maradona, Ronaldo, Luis Figo, and current stars Kluivert and Rivaldo. Room after room displays countless cups the team has won, including the coveted European Cup won in 1992. Other areas exhibit art related to the sport of soccer and photos of past teams; check out some of the funky uniform variations on the familiar blue and burgundy team colors. The high point, especially if you can't get to an actual match, is the chance to enter the stadium itself, sit down on the second level, and take in the enormity of Camp Nou (see **Entertainment,** p. 170). In the same complex, the gift shop sells all varieties of official FCB merchandise, and stands outside offer hamburgers, hot dogs (550ptas/€3,30 each), and drinks (300ptas/€1,80).

TIBIDABO

MUSEU-CASA VERDAGUER

Carretera de les Planes. ☎93 204 78 05. Call 93 315 11 11 for a guided tour. Take the FCG train to Baixador de Vallvidrera. Open W 10am-3pm and Sa-Su 11am-3pm. Free.

Jacint Verdaguer, the most important poet of the Catalan literary Renaissance, lived 24 days in this 16th-century house before dying on June 10, 1902. The rooms have been preserved as they were before his death, and detailed explanations of the artist's life and works fill the house; unfortunately for many visitors, all the explanations are presented in Catalan.

MUSEU D'AUTÒMATS

Located inside the Parc d'Attracions. Same hours as the park (see p. 100). Free.

A remarkably entertaining collection of 19th- and 20th-century automated displays, from models of ski hills and the park itself to full-fledged jazz bands, dancers in ballrooms, and a winking gypsy. Press the green buttons and watch 'em go.

MUSEU DE LA CIÈNCIA

C. Teodor Roviralta 55. ☎93 212 60 50.

Located at the halfway stop on the bus or tram from Pl. JFK to Pl. Dr. Andreu, the science museum offers extremely well-organized, hands-on exhibits great for kids. Unfortunately, it is closed for 2002 and much of 2003 for renovations.

GALLERIES

One of the capitals of cutting-edge art, Barcelona showcases many of the latest artistic trends. Many private showings display the works of both budding artists and renowned masters. Most of Barcelona's galleries are located in **La Ribera** around C. Montcada. The following galleries all welcome visitors and carry museum-quality works.

Art 52, C. Torrijos 52 (☎93 219 96 61). M: Fontana, in **Gràcia.** Gallery displays art from local as well as international artists. Friendly owners welcome browsers and window-shoppers. Open M 5-9pm, Tu-Su 10am-2pm and 5-9pm.

Galería Maeght, C. Montcada 25 (☎93 310 42 45; www.maeght.com). M: Jaume I, in **La Ribera.** 2 floors of display including pieces from Miró, Tàpies, Calder, and Giacometti. Adjacent shop carries a wide selection of art books, prints, posters, and postcards. Open Tu-Sa 10am-2pm and 4pm-8pm. AmEx/D/MC/V.

Galería Surrealista, C. Montcada 19 (☎93 310 33 11; fax 93 310 68 15). M: Jaume I, in **La Ribera.** Next to the Museu Picasso, and just as well-stocked. Specializes entirely in the work of Dalí, Miró, and Picasso, featuring limited editions, lithographs, and ceramics. Picasso's *Guernica* sketches are a steal at a mere 150,000ptas/€901,50 each. Open M-Sa 10am-8pm. AmEx/Mc/V.

Galería Montcada, C. Montcada 20 (☎93 268 00 14; fax 93 415 46 94). M: Jaume I, in **La Ribera.** Small gallery in the historic Palau Dalmases. Rotating, month-long exhibits generally spotlight Catalan artists. Open Tu-Sa 10am-2pm and 4-8pm. AmEx/MC/V.

Círculo del Arte, C. Princesa 52 (☎93 268 88 20; fax 93 319 26 51), in **La Ribera.** Spacious modern gallery with seasonal exhibits. Showcases mainly Spanish artists, with a sprinkling of Germans and Americans. Regular offerings of Miró, Calder, Keith Haring, and Claes Oldenburg. Open M-Sa 11am-8pm, Su 11am-2pm. MC/V.

Food & Drink

You can't turn a corner in Barcelona without encountering a restaurant, café, *cafetería*, or sidewalk food vendor. Food in Barcelona is delicious, of course, and more diverse than you'll find in the rest of Spain. Almost everywhere that sells food also sells alcohol, even McDonald's. Below is are listings of restaurants ranked by neighborhood; for a table of food by type, see p. 124. For a Spanish-language menu reader, see p. 131; for a brief synopsis of some Catalan specialties, see p. 138.

FOOD BY NEIGHBORHOOD

BARRI GÒTIC & LAS RAMBLAS

see map pp. 310-311

The Barri Gòtic is a gold mine of eclectic restaurants, from typical Catalan to Indian, Basque, vegetarian, Middle-Eastern, and more. Most food spots are unpretentious and intimate by default (not much space to go around in these old, old buildings). Between meals, the best places for coffee, drinks, and just hanging out are the Pl. Reial and the plaças surrounding the Església Santa Maria del Pi. For late-night munchies or to keep to a super-tight budget, head to the popular falafel and shawarma stands; the best options in price and taste are **Maoz Falafel** (C. Ferran 13; falafel 450ptas/€2,70; open Su-Th 11am-2am, F-Sa 11am-3am), and **Buen Bocado** (C. Escudellers 31; falafel 350ptas/€2,10; open Su-Th 1pm-2am, F-Sa 1pm-2:30am).

LAS RAMBLAS

Food on Las Ramblas is everywhere, decent, and generally unremarkable; people eat here more for the experience and convenience than the delicacies.

FOOD BY TYPE

FOOD BY TYPE

PAKISTANI
El Gallo Kiriko (127) — BG

PAN-ASIAN
Mandalay Café (135) — EIX
Mandongo (140) — PV

PASTA
Pasta Fiore (145)
Pla dels Angels (131) — ER

PERUVIAN
El Criollo (137) — EIX
Peimong (127) — BG

SANDWICH SHOPS
Bocatta (145)
Fresh & Ready (145)
La Baguetina Catalana (145) — BG
Mauri (134) — EIX
Pans & Co. (144)
Sandwich & Friends (129) — LR
Venus Delicatessen (127) — BG

SEAFOOD
Agua (138) — PO
La Mar Salada (139) — BA
La Muscleria (135) — EIX
La Oca Mar (138) — PO
La Oficina (139) — BA
Marina Moncho's (130) — PO
Merendero de la Mari (139) — PV
Restaurante Rias do Miño (139) — BAR

SPANISH
Bar Ra (131) — ER
Bar Restautante Los Toreros (132) — ER
Café de l'Opera (125) — Rmbl
Campechano (136) — EIX
L'Antic Bocoi del Gòtic (126) — BG
La Bodequeta (136) — EIX
Mi Burrito y Yo (130) — BG

TAPAS BARS
A'Roqueira (143) — SAR
ba-ba-reeba (133) — EIX
Barcelónia (130) — LR
Cal Pep (129) — LR
Euskal Etxea (129) — LR
Irati (125) — BG
La Flauta (137) — EIX
TapasBar (144) — PV
Txapela (133) — EIX
Txirimiri (130) — LR
Va de Vi (129) — LR
Xampanyet (129) — LR

THAI
Thai Gardens (134) — EIX

VEGETARIAN/VEGAN
Comme-Bio (135) — EIX
Govinda (128) — BG
Juicy Jones (126) — BG
La Bautequilla (135) — EIX
La Buena Tierra (140) — GR
L'Hortet (132) — ER
Restaurante Illa de Gràcia (141) — GR
Restaurante Self Naturista (129) — BG

BAR Barceloneta **BG** Barri Gòtic **EIX** Eixample **ER** El Raval **GR** Gràcia **HO** Horts **LC** Les Corts **LR** La Ribera **MJ** Montjuïc **PN** Poble Nou **PO** Port Olímpic **PV** Port Vell **Rmbl** Las Ramblas **SAR** Sarrià **ST** Sants **TI** Tibidabo

---

Café d l'Opera, Las Ramblas 74 (☎93 317 75 85). M: Liceu. A drink at this Barcelona institution was once a post-opera tradition for bourgeois Barcelonese. Today, the café caters to a mostly middle-aged crowd of all types. Outdoor seating available. Hot chocolate 265ptas/€2,80, *churros* 190ptas/€1,15. *Tapas* 250-400ptas/€3,30-2,40. Coffee and tea 300-500ptas/€1,80-3. Open M-Sa 9am-2:30am and Su 9am-3pm.

Italiano's, Las Ramblas 78. Nothing goes better with an ice cream on a hot summer day than ½L of beer, right? Find an outdoor table and test it out for yourself at this popular *heladería/cervecería*. Single scoop 225ptas/€1,25, triple 425ptas/€2,50. Beers 200-1000ptas/€1,20-€6. Coffee, tea, or *horchata* 375ptas/€2,25. Open daily 10am-2am.

LOWER BARRI GÒTIC

☙ **Les Quinze Nits,** Pl. Reial 6 (☎ 93 317 30 75). M: Liceu, in the back left corner of the plaza coming from Las Ramblas on C. Colom Pl. Reial. Without a doubt, one of the most popular restaurants in Barcelona, with nightly lines of up to 50 people waiting to get in (don't be afraid—they move quickly). Stylish white-linen decor with minimalist, ambient lighting and Catalan entrees at unbelievable prices (500-1200ptas/€3-7). No reservations. Open daily 1-3:45pm and 8:30-11:30pm. MC/V.

☙ **Irati,** C. Cardenal Casañas 17 (☎93 302 30 84). M: Liceu. An excellent Basque restaurant that attracts droves of hungry *tapas*-seekers. Ask for a plate, fill it with creative nibblers from the long bar covered in serving platters, and they'll count the toothpicks at the end to figure out your bill (160ptas apiece). Bartenders also pour Basque *sidra* (cider) behind their

TAPAS 101

Hopping from one *tapas* bar to another is a fun and cheap way to pass the evening. Don't wait to be seated and don't look for a waiter to serve you; most *tapas* bars are self-serve and standing room only. Take a plate and help yourself to the toothpick-skewered goodies that line the bars. Keep your toothpicks—they'll be tallied up on your way out to determine your bill. If you're tired of standing at the bar, most places offer more expensive sit-down menus as well. Barcelona's many *tapas* (sometimes called *pintxos*) bars, concentrated in La Ribera and Gràcia, often serve *montaditos*, thick slices of bread topped with all sorts of delectables from sausage to tortillas to anchovies. Vegetarian *tapas* are rare—be forewarned, for example, that slender white strands on some *montaditos* are actually eels masquerading as noodles. Generally served around lunchtime and dinnertime, *montaditos* are presented on platters at the bar. *Montaditos* go well with a glass of *cava*, bubbly Spanish champagne, or even a cup of *sidra*, a sour alcoholic cider generally poured from several feet above your glass.

backs—with the bottle high above your glass (150ptas/€0,90 for a taster). Starters 1500ptas/€9. Entrees 2500-3000ptas/€15-18. Open Tu-Sa noon-midnight, Su noon-4:30pm. *Tapas* served noon-3pm and 7-11pm. AmEx/MC/V.

🦞 **Los Caracoles,** C. Escudellers 14 (☎93 301 20 41). M: Drassanes. What started as a snail shop in 1835 is now a presumably more lucrative Catalan restaurant with mouth-watering decor: chickens roasting over open flames, walls and ceilings covered with oversized veggies and utensils, and your food sizzling in front of you in the walk-through kitchen. Dishes taste as good as they look; specialties include, of course, the *caracoles* (snails; 1900ptas/€11,50), suckled pig (2900ptas/€17,50) and chicken (1900ptas/€11,50). Expect a wait for dinner. Open daily 1pm-midnight. AmEx/MC/V.

Restaurante Bidasoa, C. Serra 21 (☎93 318 10 63). M: Drassanes. From the Metro, follow C. Clavé and take the 3rd left. For nearly 60 years, this small family restaurant has filled the stomachs and warmed the hearts of dozens of regular patrons. The simple Catalan food, made fresh while you wait, is good, cheap, and plentiful; come with an appetite and make it worth their while to give you a coveted table. Most dishes under 500ptas/€3. Open Tu-Su 1:30-4pm and 8pm-midnight. Closed Aug. Cash only.

Juicy Jones, Cardenal Casañas 7 (☎93 302 43 30; group dinner reservations ☎606 20 49 06). M. Liceu. A touch of psychedelic flower-power in Barcelona, with wildly decorated walls and a long bar spilling over with fresh fruit. The creative vegan *menú del día* (1175ptas/€7) features rice, veggies, soups, and salad (after 1pm only). Plethora of fresh juices 300-500ptas/€2-3. Very limited seating, with dining room in the back; Open daily Oct.-April 10am-11:15pm, May-Sept. 8am-11:15pm. Cash only.

L'Antic Bocoi del Gòtic, Baixada de Viladecols 3 (☎93 310 50 67). M: Jaume I, at the end of the street that starts as C. Dagueria, a left off C. Jaume I coming from Pl. del Angel (it changes names 3 times en route). For the most part, the only tourists who come to this small, intimate bodega-restaurant are those invited in part by local friends; formed in part by a 1st-century Roman wall, it's precisely the kind of tiny, romantic, and hard-to-find place one imagines stumbling upon in the "Gothic Quarter." Salads, patés, and sausages around 1000ptas/€6, artisan cheeses 1500-2000ptas/€9-12. Wine 1500-3000ptas/€9-18 per bottle. Open M-Sa 8:30pm-midnight. AmEx/MC/V.

Il Mercante Di Venezia, C. Jose Anselmo Clavé 11 (☎93 317 18 28). M: Drassanes. Gold drapes, dim lighting, and a lengthy menu of Italian food make this perfect for a romantic meal. Pasta 1000ptas/€6; pizza 1200ptas/€7; meat and fish dishes 1200-1800ptas/€7-11. Reservations recommended. Open Tu-Su 1:30-3:30pm and 8:30pm-midnight. MC/V. Just a few minutes further along C. Clavé, in Pl. Duc de Medinaceli, sister restaurant **Le Tre Venezie** (☎93 342 42 52) serves similar food in a sharper, cooler atmosphere, better for larger parties. Open W-Sa 1:30-4pm and 8:30pm-midnight, Su 1:30-3:30pm.

Venus Delicatessen, C. Avinyó 25 (☎93 301 15 85). M: Liceu, a right off C. Ferran coming from Las Ramblas. With a black-and-white tiled floor and monthly local art shows on the stucco walls, this Mediterranean café looks and feels like it belongs in New York City rather than Barcelona. Have lasagna, hummus, or an omelette with a glass of wine while you watch the street that inspired Picasso's *Mademoiselles d'Avignon.* Coffee, wine, pastries, and a large selection of vegetarian dishes (around 1000ptas/€6). Salads 750ptas/€5. *Menú del día* 1200ptas/€7. Open M-Sa noon-midnight. Cash only.

El Salón, C. l'Hostal d'en Sol 6-8 (☎93 315 21 59). M: Jaume I. Follow Via Laietana toward the water, turn right on C. Gignàs, and then right on tiny l'Hostal d'en Sol. This mellow bar-bistro is the perfect place to unwind after a day spent jostling fellow tourists. The terrace, nestled against a large section of 1st-century Roman wall, offers a taste of relaxing plaça life in one of the least touristed parts of the Barri Gòtic. Plates of bruschetta, gnocchi, chicken, or fish 1000-2000ptas/€6-12. Wine 200ptas/€1,20; beer 250-350ptas/€1,50-2. Restaurant open M-Sa 2-5pm and 8:30pm-midnight. Bar open daily 2pm-2:30am. AmEx/MC/V.

Oolong, C. Gignàs 25 (☎93 315 12 59). M: Jaume I, a right off Via Laietana coming from the Metro. A small but hip hole-in-the-wall that serves self-described "*comida mundial divertida*" (fun international food). The menu includes everything from duck breast, tortellini, and chicken fajitas to veggies with mango sauce and Caribbean salad. Salads 700-900ptas/€4-5,50. Hot dishes 1000-1200ptas/€6-7. Open M-Sa 8pm-2am, Su 8pm-1am. Cash only.

Kamasawa, C. Escudellers 39 (☎658 33 30 30). M: Liceu or Drassanes. An alternative experience in every sense of the word, with dim lighting, decor like a wedding (including twisting faux-marble columns and draped white veils) and exotic, romantic twists on health food, using everything from fruit and veggies to rice, noodles, and tofu. Salads 1000ptas. Set *menú* 1950ptas/€12. Meal for 2 with wine 5000ptas/€30. Open daily 6pm-1am. Cash only.

Peimong, C. Templers 6-10 (☎93 318 28 73). M: Liceu. From Las Ramblas, take C. Ferran. At Pl. Sant Jaume, veer right onto C. Ciutat and take the 2nd right on C. Templers. Generous portions of hen, goat, veal, duck, and fish cooked Peruvian style with rice (700-1000ptas/€4-6). Open Tu-Su 1-4:30pm and 8-11:30pm. MC/V.

El Gallo Kiriko, C. Avinyó 19 (☎93 412 48 38). M: Liceu. The 4th right off C. Ferran coming from Las Ramblas. Pakistani rice, Tandoori dishes, couscous, and fruit shakes. Lots of veggie options, and a nice chunk of 4th-century Roman wall to snuggle up against during dinner. If you're really lucky, they might even play some Pakistani MTV for you. Most dishes 600-800ptas/€3,60-4,80. Open daily noon-2am. MC/V.

Café d l'Opera

Les Quinze Nits

Pouring Sidra at Irati

Thiossan, C. del Vidre 3 (☎93 3317 10 31). M: Liceu, just off Pl. Reial, in the left corner toward the waterfront. A small funky Senegalese restaurant/bar/chill-out room, with good reggae music, great wall hangings, and a limited but unique menu: to drink, beer, ginger or *bissap* (both 300ptas/€1,80) and to eat, the daily African plate (800ptas/€4,80). Open Su and Tu-Th 8:30pm-2am, F-Sa 8:30pm-3am. Cash only.

The Grill Room, C. Escudellers 8 (☎93 302 40 10). M: Liceu. A very Catalan, very Barcelonese restaurant—and it seems that all of the tourists know it, too. Modernist decor and architecture, including ceramics-adorned walls and large still-life paintings, on the walls. The international and Catalan food is relatively affordable and the well-designed atmosphere merits coming to at least once if you'll be in town for a while. *Paella* 1600ptas/€9,60. Meat dishes 900-2000ptas/€5,40-12, fish plates slightly more. Open F-Tu 1-3:30pm and 8-11pm.AMEx/MC/V.

Can Cuilleretes, C. Quintana 3 (☎93 317 30 22). M: Liceu, just to the right off C. Boqueria coming from Las Ramblas. Founded in 1786, Can Cuilleretes actually won a Guinness World Record for being the second-oldest restaurant in Spain. The dining area is slightly cold, with white-tiled walls and dark wood seats, but it's worth trying their traditional local fare, if only to be a participant in an endeavour almost older than the USA. Fish tasting platter for 2 3300ptas/€19,80. Midday *menú* 1600ptas/€9,60 or 2100ptas/€12,60. Open Tu-F 1:30-4pm and 9-11pm. MC/V.

UPPER BARRI GÒTIC

Els Quatre Gats, C. Montsió 3 (☎93 302 41 40). M: Catalunya; take the 2nd left off Av. Portal de l'Angel. Usually translated as "the four cats," *Els Quatre Gats* is actually a figurative Catalan expression meaning "just a few guys," an ironically diminutive name considering the café's prestigious clientele. An old Modernist hangout of Picasso's with lots of Bohemian character; he loved it so much he designed a personalized menu (on display at Museu Picasso; see p. 109). Ramon Casas left his artistic mark as well, in the form of a self portrait of himself and a fellow artist on a bicycle built for two (on display in the Museu d'Art Modern; see p. 110). Reproductions of these works and more adorn the walls. Food is expensive here (entrees around 2000ptas/€12), making *tapas* the best way to go (200-600ptas/€1,50-3,60). Coffee is also cheap (150ptas/€1) and good. Live piano and violin 9pm-1am. Open M-Sa 9am-2am, Su 5pm-2am. Closed Aug. AmEx/MC/V.

Betawi, C. Montsió 6 (☎93 412 62 64). M: Catalunya, the 2nd left off Portal de l'Angel coming from the Metro. A peaceful, delicately decorated Indonesian restaurant with small tapestry-covered tables and woven place mats. The food verges on gourmet, both in taste and size. *Menú del día* 1275ptas/€7,70. Most entrees 1200-1500ptas/€7-9. Open for lunch M-Sa 1-4pm, for dinner Tu-Th 8-11pm and F-Sa 8-11:30pm. AmEx/MC/V.

Govinda, Pl. Vila de Madrid 4 (☎93 318 77 29). M: Catalunya, just to the right off Las Ramblas on C. Canuda. A true child of globalization: vegetarian Indian food served a few feet from a row of Roman tombs nearly 2000 years old, in one of the world's most pork-crazed countries. *Thali* (traditional Indian "sampler" meals with a variety of dishes on one platter; 2500-3000ptas/€15-18), as well as spring rolls, crepes, rice, Indian bread, fruit *lassis*, and more. International salad bar 700-1000ptas/€4-6. M-F *menú del día* 1300ptas/€7,80. Most entrees around 1200ptas/€7. Open for lunch daily 1-4pm, for dinner Tu-Th 8-11pm and F-Sa 8-11:45pm. AmEx/MC/V.

La Colmena, Pl. de l'Angel 12 (☎93 315 13 56). M: Jaume I. After more than 120 years in the Pl. de l'Angel, this absolutely divine pastry and candy shop has more than earned its prime location. Don't walk in unless you're prepared to buy, because you *will*—no one's strong enough to resist. Open daily 9am-9pm. AmEx/MC/V.

The Bagel Shop, C. Canuda 25 (☎93 302 41 61). M: Catalunya. From the Metro, walk down Las Ramblas and take the 1st left onto C. Canuda. Barcelona meets New York City. Diverse bagel selection (100ptas/€0,60 each), bagel sandwiches, and varied spreads, from cream cheese and peanut butter to caramel and chocolate (all 350-600ptas/€2-€3,50). Sept.-June they serve a Su pancake and eggs brunch 11am-4pm (800ptas/€4,80). Open M-Sa 9:30am-9:30pm. Cash only.

Terrablava, Via Laietana 55 (☎93 322 15 85). Cafeteria ease but much better taste. An all-you-can-eat buffet of fresh salads, veggies, pasta, pizza, meat dishes, fruit, and coffee. Lunchtime brings a circus of famished locals. Food also available a la carte to go. Buffet M-F

12:30-6pm 1095ptas/€6,50, 6pm-1am and Sa-Su 1395ptas/€8,50 (includes a drink). Open daily 12:30pm-1am. Cash only.

Restaurante Self Naturista, C. Santa Anna 11-17 (☎93 318 26 84). M: Catalunya, right off Las Ramblas. A self-service vegetarian cafeteria with enormous selection and enough dessert options to fill a bakery. Entrees under 500ptas/€3. Lunch *menú* 1025ptas/€6. Open M-Sa 11:30am-10pm. Cash only.

LA RIBERA

see map pp. 310-311

East of Via Laietana, La Ribera is home to numerous bars and small restaurants. Once a fisherman's enclave, the neighborhood is still far from touristed, but the few tourists who walk the several blocks over are well rewarded.

RESTAURANTS

La Habana Vieja, Carrer dels Banys Vells 2 (☎93 268 25 04). M: Jaume I. C. Banys Vells is parallel to C. Montcada. Pulsing Cuban music sets the mood in this friendly, family-style place. Large portions are perfect for sharing among friends. Cuban rice 600-900ptas/€3,60-5,42; meat dishes 1600-2000ptas/€9,62-12. Open daily 10am-4:30pm and 8:30pm-1am. AmEx/D/MC/V.

La Cocotte, Pg. del Born 16 (☎93 319 17 34). M: Jaume I. Eclectic international menu offers mostly vegetarian food in a cozy, red-tabled interior. Choose from regional cuisine as far-flung as moussaka (1100ptas/€6,60), vegetarian burritos (950ptas/€5,80), and chicken curry (975ptas/€5,90). Eat in or take out. Entrees 750-1100ptas/€4,05-6,60. Open Tu-Su 9pm-midnight.

Ikkiu, C. Princesa 11 (☎93 319 28 26). M: Jaume I. Cheap Japanese food, and lots of it. Daily 5-course lunch *menú* (with tempura or sushi) weekdays 975ptas/€5,80; weekends 1300-1500ptas/€7,80-9. Dinner entrees 600-1500ptas/€3,61-9. Tu-Sa 12:30-4pm and 9pm-midnight, Su 12:30-4pm. AmEx/D/MC/V.

Sandwich & Friends, Pg. del Born 27 (☎93 310 07 86). From M: Jaume I, follow C. Princesa and turn right on C. Comerç and right again on Pg. del Born. Sleek and super-trendy sandwich bar serves veggie or meat-filled goodies (535-925ptas/€3,22-5,56) and salads (625-725ptas/€3,76-4,36), all bearing proper names. Try the *Bim*—eggplant, gouda, zucchini, tomato, and onion on a baguette—for 705ptas/€4,24, or the *Elena*—white rice, corn, pears, lettuce, and a soy dressing—for 625ptas/€3,76. Open Su-W noon-12:30am and Th-Sa noon-1am.

TAPAS BARS

Xampanyet, C. Montcado 22 (☎93 319 70 03). M: Jaume I. From the Metro, cross Via Laietana, walk down C. Princesa, and turn right on C. Montcado. Xampanyet is on the right after the Museu Picasso. Juan Carlos, the 3rd-generation proprietor, treats everyone like family. The house special—*cava* (choose from 17 varieties)—is served with anchovies at the colorful bar. Glasses 120ptas/€0,72 and up. Bottles 900ptas/€5,40 and up. Open Tu-Sa noon-4pm and 7-11:30pm, Su 7-11:30pm. Closed in Aug. MC/V.

Va de Vi, C. Banys Vells 16 (☎93 319 29 00). From M: Jaume I, walk down C. Princesa, turn right on C. Montcada, right again on C. Barra de Ferro, and finally left on C. Banys Vells. Cavernous wine bar in 16th-century stone building, warmly lit by candles. Choose from over 170 varieties of wine (glasses from 275-675ptas/€1,60-4), a wide selection of cheeses (500-1200ptas/€3-7,20), and *tapas* (450-900ptas/€2,70-5,40). Open daily June-Sept. 7pm-2am, Sept.-June noon-3pm and 7pm-2am.

Cal Pep, Pl. de les Olles 8 (☎93 310 79 61). From M: Barceloneta, follow Pg. Joan de Borbó and turn right on Av. Marqués de l'Argentera and left on C. Palau. During peak hours it can be difficult to even find standing room in the small bar, but the fresh, unusual *tapas*—like sauteed spinach with garbanzo beans and smoked ham (650ptas/€4)—make it all worthwhile. Country-style sit-down restaurant in rear (entrees 685-1500ptas/€4,10-9). Beer 200ptas/€1,20. Drinks 500-1000ptas/€3-6. Open Tu-Sa 1-4:30pm and 8-11:45pm. Closed in Aug. D/MC/V.

Euskal Etxea, Placeta Montcada 1-3 (☎93 310 21 85). M: Jaume I, at the end of C. Montcada by Pg. del Born. Locals cram into the standing-room only bar to greet the endless

the BIG $plurge

Welcome to the Jungle

Whether you're looking to blow your cash on a big fish or a little donkey, Barcelona is the place for you.

Marina Moncho's, C. Marina 19-21, right next to the copper fish, in the **Port Olímpic.** Moncho's is more of an institution than a mere restaurant, with 10 locations in Barcelona, 5 of them on the beach. Each Moncho's offers a different dining experience; ask for the map brochure. This one serves up hearty, delicious Galician and Catalan fare with outdoor seating under Gehry's fish (p. 166). Entrees 1700-3000ptas/€10,22-18,03; 3-course meals 4000-5000ptas/€24,04-30,05. Open daily noon-2am. AmEx/MC/V. Wheelchair accessible.

Mi Burrito y Yo, Paso de la Enseñanza 2 (☎93 318 27 42). M: Jaume I, in the **Barri Gòtic,** to the left off C. Ferran immediately after Pl. St. Jaume. Not a touristy Mexican joint (*burrito* here means "little donkey"), but one of the most inviting, lively grill-restaurant/*bodegas* in the city. The basement room is warm, with red plaid decor and nightly live music (starting at 9:30pm). Specialties include the grilled meat (*carne a la brasa*) and *paella* (1950ptas/€12 per person). Starters around 1000ptas. Most entrees 1500-2500ptas/€9-15. Open M-Sa 1-4pm and 8pm-midnight, Su 1-4pm. AmEx/MC/V.

trays of delectable *tapas* that are brought out 12:30-2:30pm and 7:30-10pm. Sit-down restaurant in back serves Basque cuisine (entrees 1200-2850ptas/€7,20-18). *Tapas* 180ptas/€1; beer 235ptas/€1,40; drinks 175-375ptas/€1-2. Open Tu-Sa 12:30-11:30pm and Su 1-3:30pm.

Barcelónia, Pl. Comercial 11 (☎93 268 70 21). From M: Jaume I, follow C. Princesa almost to its end and turn right on C. Comerç; the plaça is ahead on the right. Neighborhood trendoids gather to feast on a traditional selection of *tapas* (140ptas/€0,90) in this blue-walled bar. Innovative sit-down menu includes dishes like *bacalao* (cod) with honey, pine nuts, and feta (1700ptas/€10,30). 3-course lunch *menú* 1200ptas/€7,20. Beer and wine from 175ptas/€1. Open Su-Th 1pm-midnight and F-Sa 1pm-1am.

Txirimiri, C. Princesa 11 (☎93 310 18 05). Enough *tapas* to feed a small village (150ptas/€0,90 each). Sit at the long wooden bar and try *la gula,* a seafood and veggie specialty from the Basque region. *Tapas* outshine the small lunch and dinner menu (entrees 695-895ptas/€4,22-5,40). Beer 250ptas/€1,50; *cava* and wine 300ptas/€1,80. Open Tu-Su noon-12:30am. MC/V.

CAFÉS

🔲 **Tèxtil Café,** C. Montcada 12 (☎93 268 25 98). M: Jaume I. Set in the picturesque courtyard of the Museu Tèxtil i d'Indumentària (see **Museums,** p. 110), in one of C. Montcada's Gothic masterpieces. Locals and tourists alike swarm around the café for a post-museum coffee or to relax over a full meal. Weekday lunch *menú* 1400ptas/€8,40. Wine and *cava* 250-350ptas/€1,50-2,10 per glass. Hot and cold sandwiches 360-1250ptas/€2,16-7,51. Open Tu-Su 10am-midnight. Wheelchair accessible.

Café-Bar Vincent Van Gogh, C. Princesa 23. M: Jaume I. An international joint for a young, pool-playing crowd. Works from the red-bearded master stand out against dark walls. Beer 325ptas/€2. Cocktails 800-900ptas/€4,80-5,40. Open Su-Th noon-3am, F-Sa noon-4am.

Suborn, C. de la Ribera (☎93 310 11 10). M: Barceloneta; entrance on Pg. Picasso across from Parc de la Ciutadella. Eclectic restaurant with plenty of vegetarian options by day, popular, bass-thumping bar by night. Entrees from salmon teriyaki to pasta with mascarpone, ricotta, lemon, and pesto (750-2300ptas/€4,50-13). Lunch *menú* 1300ptas/€7,80. Beer 300ptas/€1,80. Drinks 800ptas/€4,80. Open Tu-Th, Su 12:30-4:30pm and 9pm-2:30am, F-Sa 12:30-4:30pm and 9pm-3am.

Café del Born, C. Comerç 10 (☎93 268 32 72). M: Jaume I. Bistro-style café with more leg room than its neighbors. Vegetarian selections including hummus with pita, as well as traditional meat-filled Catalan dishes (entrees 625-1500ptas/€3,80-9). Tasty lunch *menú* 1200ptas/€7,20. Open Su-Th 9am-1am, F-Sa 9am-3am. V. Wheelchair accessible.

EL RAVAL

see map pp. 316-317

Students and blue-collar workers congregate in typical Catalan joints west of Las Ramblas. Restaurants line the streets and are fairly inexpensive. Most have simple decor, basic food, and lots of noise. Tiny local places reflect the ethnic diversity of the neighborhood. As the government continues its efforts to clean up and revitalize El Raval, trendier gourmet places have started to move into the area as well.

Bar Ra, Pl. de la Garduña (☎93 301 41 63). M: Liceu, just behind Las Ramblas' Boqueria market. Everything about Ra exudes cool, from its erotic Hindu mural, bursting with color, to the individually painted tablecloths at each table—to the waiters themselves. The artfully prepared international offerings, a mixture of traditional Spanish and trendy California, seldom disappoint. *Menú* 1300ptas/€7,80. Open M-Sa 1:30-4:pm, 9:30-2am. Dinner by reservation only.

Buenas Migas, Pl. Bonsuccés 6 (☎93 412 16 86). M: Catalunya, off Las Ramblas. This *focacceria* on the Pl. Bonsuccés offers the neighborhood's most pleasant outdoor dining. Enjoy coffee or tea (120-160ptas/€0,72-0,96) at one of the shaded tables across the street, or stay indoors with your *focaccia* (thick Italian bread; 300-500ptas/€1,80-3), in the rustic-feeling interior. The rich cakes (350ptas/€2,10) are definitely worth a try. Open Su-W 10am-10pm, Th-Sa 10am-midnight.

Colibri, C. Riera Alta (☎93 443 23 06). M: Liceu. Take C. Carme of Las Ramblas and make your 6th right onto Riera Alta; Colibri is 2 blocks up on the left. Colibri's market cuisine brings freshness, flair, and service to eating out in Barcelona. Impeccable wine selection and soft-jazz atmosphere. Dishes 1700-4000ptas/€10,20-24. Open M-F 1:30-6:30, 8:30-11:30pm. MC/V.

Restaurante Can Lluís, C. Cera 49 (☎93 441 11 87). M: Sant Antoni. From the Metro, head down Ronda S. Pau and take the 2nd left on C. Cera. For over 100 years, Can Lluís has been a defining force in Catalan cuisine. The menu overflows with hard-to-pronounce delicacies you've never tried before but should, among them *cabrit* (goat) and *conill* (rabbit). Daily *menú* (with good wine selection), 1600ptas/€9,60. Entrees 1350-2500ptas/€8-€15,10. Open M-Sa 1:30-4pm and 8:30-11:30pm. V.

Pla dels Angels, C. de Ferlandina 23 (☎93 329 40 47). Directly in front of the MACBA (see **Museums,** p. 111). The funky decor of this colorful eatery is fitting for its proximity to Barcelona's contemporary art museum. Sit outside and check out the museum, relax in the armchairs indoors, or get a table downstairs in the cool, crypt-like basement. Pastas 500ptas/€3, entrees 800-900ptas/€4,90-5,60. Open M 1:30-4pm; Tu-Th 1:30-4pm, 9-11pm; F-Sa 9pm-midnight.

MENU READER

Before traveling to Barcelona, you will want to consider any specific dietary needs you require to make sure they can be met during your visit. Below is a quick summary (in Spanish) of food you will encounter during your stay. *¡Buen provecho!*

aceitunas: olives.

aceite y vinagre: oil (olive) and vinegar; typically used as a salad dressing.

agua: water.

arroz: rice.

batido: milk shake.

bocadillo: a baguette sandwich.

calamares: calamari (squid).

chorizo: Spanish-style sausage; can be eaten in a sandwich with *pan* or as an appetizer.

churros: a rich, donut-like pastry eaten for breakfast with coffee or *chocolate,* a thick hot chocolate.

cerveza: beer.

cocido: stew. Varieties include *cocido madrileño* and *cocido gallego.* Both are meat and bean heavy.

cordero asado: roasted lamb with garlic.

ensalada: salad.

fideua: like *paella,* but uses noodles instead of rice.

fruta: fruit; generally eaten for breakfast or dessert.

galletas: cookies.

gambas: shrimp.

gazpacho: cold tomato soup.

granizado: flavored slush.

infusión: herbal tea.

jamón serrano: serrano ham; can be eaten in a sandwich with *pan* or as an appetizer.

lomo: cured ham; can be eaten in a sandwich with *pan* or as an appetizer.

(Continued on p. 133.)

the BIG $plurge

Zona Alta

Botafumeiro, C. Gran de Gràcia 81 (☎93 218 42 30). M: Fontana, in **Gràcia.** Upscale and highly reputed Galician seafood restaurant serves large portions (entrees 1800-4400ptas/€11-26) and offers a gargantuan *menú del día* (9000ptas/€45) complete with 3 courses, dessert, coffee, and wine—a good deal for a big splurge. Open daily 1pm-1am. Closed first three weeks of Aug. Reservations recommended. AmEx/D/MC. Wheelchair accessible.

☒ El Vell Sarrià, C. Major de Sarrià 93 (☎93 204 57 10). M: Sarrià, in **Sarrià.** The exposed ceiling beams and lace curtains of this 17th-century building make for a comfortable, slightly upscale dining experience. A covered patio overlooking the neighboring Pl. del Consell de la Vila offers slightly more informal seating. House speciality rice, *arroz Vell Sarrià,* serves two (1725-1990ptas/€10,37-11,42 depending on how it is topped). Entrees 900-2350ptas/€5,40-14. Reservations recommended. Open M-Sa 1:30-3:30pm and 9-11:30pm, Su 1:30-3:30pm. AmEx/D/MC/V.

mamacafé, C. Joaquim Costa (☎93 301 29 40), a right off C. Hospital. A great place to find healthy, fresh vegetarian and meat options with an exotic twist. The ambience manages to be casual without being divey, artsy without being pretentious. Options include ravioli stuffed with brie (1275ptas/€7,65), chicken drumsticks with curry raclette (1525ptas/€9,15), and salmon in lemon-rosemary oil. *Menú* 1175ptas/€7,20. Open Tu-Sa 1pm-1am, M 1pm-5pm.

Silenus, C. dels Angels 8 (☎93 302 26 80). From M: Catalunya, a right off C. Carme. Almost as much art gallery as restaurant, softly elegant Silenus is the place for good meals and quiet conversation. Art expositions on the walls, featuring local artists, change every couple of months. Fish and meat entrees include salmon and cod (1775ptas/€10,90) and the exotic *filete de kangoo*: yep, kangaroo (2400ptas/€15). Open M-Sa 1-5pm, 9pm-1am. MC/V.

L'Hortet, C. del Pintor Fortuny 32 (☎93 317 61 89). M: Catalunya, off Las Ramblas. The meat market oil paintings of gorgeous super models and actresses first catch your attention, but the solid vegetarian options keep it. *Menú* 1200ptas/€7,20. Light entrees, featuring pastas and couscous, 1200ptas/€7,20 and up.

Restaurante Riera, C. Joaquim Costa 30 (☎93 443 32 93). M: Liceu or Universitat. Off C. Carme coming from Liceu; off Ronda de Sant Antoni from Universitat, one block from the MACBA. The Riera family provides a feast fit for a very hungry king, complete with dessert (825ptas/€4,95). Open daily 1-4pm and 8-11pm.

Restaurante Biocenter, C. del Pintor Fortuny 25 (☎93 301 45 83). M: Catalunya, off Las Ramblas. Your ears will ring with Brazilian music and environmentalist propaganda, but the enormous buffet will keep you silently content. *Menú* with unlimited soup and salad, vegetarian entree (lots of tofus and pastas), and dessert for 1200ptas/€7,60. Open M-Sa 1-5pm.

Bar Restaurante Los Toreros, C. Xuclá 3-5 (☎93 318 23 25). M: Catalunya, on a narrow alley between C. Fortuny and C. Carme, both off Las Ramblas. Specializes in group meals—come with friends and order from one of the many *menús para grupos,* which feed at least 8 people (2100-3500ptas/€12,60-21 per person). The solo lunch *menú* is cheap, too (1000ptas/€6), and the nighttime *tapas* menu is extremely popular (2100ptas/€12,60). Open Tu-Sa 9am-1am, Su 9am-1pm. Main *menú* available 1-4pm.

Bar Restaurante Romesco, C. Sant Pau 28 (☎93 318 93 81). M: Liceu. From the Metro, walk up Las Ramblas and turn left onto C. Sant Pau. Take the 1st right; Romesco is immediately on the left. This small diner serves simple, dirt-cheap food. *Frijoles* (beans) and *crema catalana* are their specialties; their fries are among the best in Barcelona. Fish, chicken, and meat dishes 400-700ptas/€2,20-4,60. Open M-Sa 1pm-2am.

L'EIXAMPLE

see map pp. 314-315

Far from the hustle-and-bustle of the tourist-packed old city, l'Eixample is not a place to wander until you find somewhere to eat. These upper neighborhoods are full of good places to spend a long, enjoyable dinner (especially the left side), but they are spread out widely and interspersed with plenty of nondescript corner bars serving the endless apartment buildings in the area. If you want to sample one of l'Eixample's trendy, high-quality restaurants, you are best off picking one ahead of time and heading straight there. Expect to make reservations on weekends, and with some exceptions, be prepared to pay well for the food and atmosphere.

AROUND PG. DE GRÀCIA

Pg de Gràcia is lined with nearly as many tapas bars and cafés as shops and modernist architecture. Most are tourist-oriented, have sidewalk tables, and are on the expensive side, especially to eat outside (many charge up to 15% extra). On Friday and Saturday almost all of them stay open until 2am (during the week until 1 or 1:30am), so they are a good place for late-night food.

Txapela (Euskal Taberna), Pg. de Gràcia 8-10 (☎93 412 0289). M: Catalunya. This Basque restaurant is a godsend for the *tapas*-clueless traveler who wants to learn: the place mats have pictures with the name and description of each *tapa*, and you can order by number. About half the size of most normal *tapas*, each costs only 150ptas/€1. Open M-Th 8am-1:30am, F-Su 10am-2am. MC/V. Wheelchair accessible.

ba-ba-reeba, Pg. de Gràcia 28 (☎93 301 43 02). M: Pg. de Gràcia. One of the most obvious spots on the Passeig, the *tapas* here—bigger and glossier than usual—have definitely been Americanized, but if that's what you want, they taste good, especially the *pa amb tomaquet*. Entrees 800-1800ptas/€5-11. Most *tapas* 400-500ptas/€3, some 1000-1500ptas/€6-9. Sidewalk seating 15% extra. Take-out available. Open M-Th 7:30am-1:30am, F 7:30am-2am, Sa 8am-2am, Su 8am-1:30am. AmEx/MC/V. Wheelchair accessible.

Giorgio, C. Aragó 277 (☎93 487 42 31). M: Pg. de Gràcia, to the right off Pg. de Gràcia, coming from Pl. de Catalunya. Known for its rich *risotto*, Giorgio serves affordable Italian food in a blue-and-yellow dining room that looks much more expensive than it is. The wines are all Italian and equally easy on the wallet. Pizzas and pastas 1000-1200ptas/€6-7. Weekday *menú del día* 1720ptas/€10,50. Take-out available. Open daily 1-4pm and 8pm-midnight. AmEx/MC/V. Wheelchair accessible.

Madrid-Barcelona (Pa Amb Tomàquet), C. Aragó 282 (☎93 215 70 26). M: Pg. de Gràcia, on the corner with Pg. de Gràcia. Named for the railroad line

MENU READER

(continued from p. 131)

magdalena: muffin.

mantequilla: butter.

mazapán: marzipan.

menú del día: A daily set menu, served at lunchtime. Generally two courses, bread, dessert, a drink, and a very good deal.

orchata: tiger-nut milk; tastes like almond.

paella: a family-size rice dish typically filled with seafood or meat.

pan: bread; Spaniards typically eat the baguette kind. *Pan integral* is wheat bread; *pan de molde* is sliced bread.

pasteles: pastries.

patatas: potatoes. *Patatas bravas* are a popular *tapa* of potatoes in a spicy sauce.

pavo: turkey

pescado: fish. Varieties include *salmon* (salmon), *trucha* (trout), *bacalao* (cod), *atún* (tuna), *ángilas* (eel), and more.

pollo: chicken

polvorones: a holiday sweet made from crushed almonds and sugar

postre: dessert.

puerco: pork.

queso: cheese; some varieties include *Manchego* and *fresco*.

Raciones: larger portions of *tapas*.

sopa: soup.

tarta: cake.

tortilla española: a potato omelette

turrón: a chocolate-like holiday treat that can include goodies such as almonds and coconut.

zumo de naranja: orange juice.

What a Drag

Café Miranda, C. Casanova 30 (☎93 453 52 49). M: Universitat, in **l'Eixample.** Lavishly decked out in faux leopard fur and palm trees, this gay restaurant features male and female drag performers who serenade diners at regular half-hour intervals after 10:30pm. Seasonal menu includes Mediterranean delicacies like marinated calamari salad in black vinegar and spring rolls stuffed with goat cheese and spinach. The friendly waitstaff and mixed crowd make it a very popular place; reservations are recommended. Don't leave without taking a peek at the hot pink and electric blue (gender designated) bathrooms. Three-course *menú* 3300ptas/€19,83. Wine from 975ptas/€5,86 per bottle. Open daily 9pm-1am. MC/V.

that used to run here, this classy but cheap lunchtime hotspot attracts hordes of native businessmen and shoppers. Waiters ladle your soups and rice at your table, straight from the stove. Most entrees 800-900ptas/€5. Open M-Sa 1-4pm and 8:30-midnight. MC/V. Wheelchair accessible.

Hostal de Rita, C. Aragó 279 (☎93 487 23 76). M: Pg. de Gràcia, to the right off Pg. de Gràcia, coming from Pl. de Catalunya. Lines of up to 20 locals waiting to eat lunch here are not uncommon; the food is just as tasty and elegant as it is cheap. A fish- and chicken-based menu section is dedicated to low-calorie dishes. Weekday lunch *menú del día* 1100ptas/€6,80, IVA included. Entrees 800-1200ptas/€5-7. Open daily 1-3:45pm and 8:30-11:30pm. AmEx/MC/V. Wheelchair accessible.

Thai Gardens, C. Diputació 273 (☎93 487 98 98). M: Catalunya. The only Thai restaurant in Barcelona. Extravagant decor, complete with a wooden bridge entrance, lush greenery, and colorful pillows, make Thai Gardens a great place for a memorable date. Call ahead to reserve one of the traditional *kantok* tables (cushions on the ground, with space underneath for your feet). Lots of fish and chicken options, and food-to-go. Weekday lunch *menú* 1850ptas/€10,80; regular menú 3900ptas/€21. Pad thai 1000ptas/€6. Fish, meat, and curry entrees 1000-2000ptas/€6-12. Open Su-Th 1:30-4pm and 8:30pm-midnight, F-Sa 1:30-4pm and 8:30pm-1am. AmEx/MC/V. Wheelchair accessible.

Café Torino, Pg. de Gràcia 59 (☎93 487 75 11). M: Pg. de Gràcia. 2002 marks the 100th birthday of this café, originally designed by the likes of Gaudí, Puig i Cadafalch, and Falqués as a spot for sampling vermouth, at that time a drink novelty. The outdoor tables are blissfully cool and shaded in the morning. Coffee 150-200ptas/€1. Irish coffee 650ptas/€. Hot cocoa 300ptas/€1,80. Open Su-Th 8am-11:30pm, F-Sa 9am-1am. Cash only. Wheelchair accessible.

Chicago Pizza Pie Factory, C. Provença 300 (☎93 215 94 15). M: Diagonal, near the corner with C. Pau Claris, within sight of La Pedrera. These guys have done everything possible to be Uno's Chicago Pizzeria, short of stealing the name. Starters (onion rings, nachos, chicken caesar) 600-800ptas/€3,50-5. Individual deep-dish or thin-crust pizzas 1325ptas/€8. Take-out available. Open M-F 1-4pm and 8pm-midnight, Sa-Su 1-4pm and 8pm-1:30am. MC/V. Not wheelchair accessible.

Mauri, Rambla de Catalunya 102 (☎93 215 10 20). M: Diagonal. This *pastisseria* has been turning out delicate sweets, mouth-watering bonbons, and gourmet sandwiches since 1929. Come to buy delectable gifts, to have tea, coffee, or lunch in the restaurant, or simply to admire the cake decorations. A second location across the street, at no.103, specializes in candy and gift baskets (☎93 215 81 46). Open M-F 8am-9pm, Sa 9am-9pm, Su and holidays 9am-3pm. MC/V. Not wheelchair accessible.

L'EIXAMPLE DRETA

■ **Comme-Bio,** C. Gran Via 603 (☎93 301 03 76). M: Catalunya or Universitat, on the corner of Gran Via and Rambla de Catalunya. If you've started to wonder if vegetable harvests actually make it to Spain, come here for fresh salad, hummus, tofu, yogurt, or juice. While you're at it, read up on local yoga lessons and try on organic makeup. Restaurant, food-to-go, and small grocery store all in one. Pasta, rice, and veggie pizzas around 1000ptas/€6. Salads 800-1000ptas/€5-6. Open daily 9am-11:30pm. MC/V. Not wheelchair accessible. Another **branch** a few blocks away (Via Laietana 28; ☎93 319 89 68).

Juicy Jones

■ **Mandalay Café,** C. Provença 330 (☎93 458 60 17), between C. Roger de Llúria and C. Bruc. M: Verdaguer. Exotic international cuisine (mostly pan-Asian), including gourmet *dim-sum*, sushi, curry, and salads, served in a room so draped in color and sultanesque luxury it's been featured in coffee-table books on interior decorating. F-Sa night trapeze artist around 11pm. Daily *menú* 1200ptas/€7,20. Sushi plate 2000ptas/€12. Entrees 1500-2000ptas/€9-12. Open Tu-Sa 1-4pm and 9-11pm. MC/V.

■ **Laie Llibreria Café,** C. Pau Claris 85 (☎93 318 17 39; www.laie.es). M: Urquinaona. An ultra-cool lunch-spot for more than just bookworms (see p. 180). Indulge in the cheap, fresh all-you-can-eat buffet lunch (1250ptas/€8) in the open, bamboo-draped lunch room, then grab a coffee or drink at the bar on the way out. Vegetarian dinner *menú* 2250ptas/€14. Open M-F 9am-1am, Sa 10am-1am. AmEX/MC/V. Not wheelchair accessible.

Els Quatre Gats

La Batuequilla, C. Girona 88 (☎93 265 86 60). M: Girona, near the corner with C. Aragó, one block from the Metro. A small, neighborhood veggie restaurant, decorated almost exclusively in shades of green. A huge offering of fresh juices and fruit shakes and a M-F *menú del día* (1150ptas/€7). Veggie pizzas 900ptas/€5,50. Most entrees (including some meat and fish for carnivorous friends) 800-1400ptas/€5-€8.50. Open M-F 8am-8pm and Sa 9am-5pm, but they will cook dinner later for groups of 10 or more if you call ☎93 265 04 60. MC/V. Not wheelchair accessible.

Wok & Bol, C. Diputació 294 (☎ 93 302 76 75), between C. Roger de Llúria and C. Bruc. M: Girona. An elegant, stand-out Chinese restaurant, serving *dim-sum* (500-850ptas/€3-5 per small dish), whole Peking ducks (2400ptas/€14,50 per person), and Chinese fondue (2600ptas/€15,50), in addition to more common dishes like chow mein and veggie stir fries (700ptas/€4,20). Make reservations and then ponder the slightly eerie Chinese mannequins having tea in the window. Open M-Sa 1:30-3:30pm and 9:15-11:30pm. AmEx/MC/V.

Sushi at Ikkiu

La Muscleria, C. Mallorca 290 (☎93 458 98 44), on the corner with C. Bruc. M: Verdaguer. Mussels of every size, shape, and flavor, culled from Catalunya, France, Galicia, and the Netherlands served in a bustling basement. Main plates (a huge bowl of mussels

HOLY SHIT!
PART I

Christmastime in Barcelona is, with no disrespect intended, a pretty crappy way to celebrate the holiday. This isn't to say you should avoid the city during December—but if you do come, don't be startled by what appears to be feces in the windows of pastry shops and in the hands of young children. These marzipan cakes, called **tifas**, are a popular Christmas treat, disgustingly realistic, but by all reports pretty tasty.

The Catalan have a disturbing affinity for the scatological, which the Christmas season seems to bring to the forefront. On Christmas Eve, some Catalan families place under their tree a delightful little treat called the *Caga Tío*—the "Shit Log": a box filled with candies and goodies, covered by a blanket. The children then beat the shit out of it (pardon the pun) with sticks, chanting in Catalan: "Shit, log, shit, candies and nougat, and if you don't shit well, I'll bash you with my stick!" The log bursts open, rewarding the delighted children for their brutal attack on the defenseless log. For more on the Catalan affinity for Christmastime caga, see Holy Shit! Part II, p. 192).

for 1300ptas/€7,80) come with French fries. Lots of salads (800ptas/€4,80) and *cocas* (like pizza; 800-1000ptas/€4,80-6). Make reservations W-Sa. Open M-Th 1-4pm and 8:30pm-midnight, F-Sa 1-4pm and 8:30pm-1am. No Sa lunch July-Aug. MC/V.

Can Cargol, C. València 324 (☎93 458 96 381), on the corner with C. Bruc. M: Girona. Extremely popular Catalan restaurant with make-your-own *pan con tomate* and lots of snail options. Snails 1200ptas/€7. Fish and meat dishes 700-900ptas/€4-5,50, some 1500-2000ptas/€9-12. Make reservations on weekends. Open 1:30-4pm and 8:30pm-midnight. AmEx/MC/V.

El Rodizio Grill, C. Consell de Cent 403 (☎93 265 51 12), right next to M: Girona. All-you-can-eat Brazilian and Mediterranean buffet, featuring 10 grilled *shishkebab*-style meats plus chicken, salmon, and cod. Cold dishes include sushi, pasta, and salads. Lunch 1190ptas/€7,20. Dinner 1690ptas/€10,20. Desserts 390ptas/€2,40 extra. Open M-Th 1-4pm and 8:30pm-midnight, F-Sa 1-4pm and 8:30pm-1am, Su 1-4pm. MC/V.

Cullera de Boix, C. Ronda de St. Pere 24 (☎93 268 13 36), between C. Bruc and Pl. Urquinaona. M: Urquinaona. With metal chairs, light wood tables, and sleek hanging lamps, this upscale café/restaurant could easily be in Manhattan. Specializes in rice (1300-1500ptas/€7,80-€9) and salads (800ptas/€4,80). Midday *arroz del día* 745ptas/€4,50; *plato del día* 795ptas/€4,80. Reservations wise for weekend dinners. Open daily 1-4pm and 8pm-midnight. AmEx/MC/V.

A-Tipic, C. Bruc 79 (☎93 215 51 06) between C. Aragó and C. Consell de Cent. A lunchtime gem for vegetarians. A simple buffet (1200ptas/€7,20) that tastes more like home than a cafeteria, served in a relaxing blue-and-yellow dining room. Several salads, rice, pasta, veggie calzones, and sometimes chicken. Open M-F 1-4:30pm. Closed Aug. Cash only.

La Bodegueta, Rambla de Catalunya 100 (☎93 215 48 94), near C. Provença. M: Diagonal. An informal and affordable spot for Spanish wine, big *tapas* platters (especially good Iberian meats), and pleasant terrace seats on the Rambla. A good place to unwind with a drink before starting the evening. *Menú del día* served M-F 1-4pm (1250ptas/€7,50). Open M-F 7am-1:50am, Sa 8am-1:50am, Su 7am-1:15am. Cash only.

Campechano, C. València 286 (☎93 215 62 33). M: Catalunya, just to the right of Pg. de Gràcia coming from Pl. de Catalunya. This restaurant has gone all out to recreate the atmosphere of a 1940s *merendero* (BBQ/picnic area) on the Barcelona mountainside, from a few live trees and a painted forest wall to train-stop signs marking your progress "toward the mountain." Choose your favorite meat or poultry from their huge list and they'll grill it; french fries, salad, and a few other dishes serve as sides. Starters 800ptas/€5. Grilled entrees 1000-2000ptas/€6-€12. Open daily 1:30-4pm and 8:30-midnight. MC/V.

L'EIXAMPLE ESQUERRA

El Racó d'en Baltá, C. Aribau 125 (☎93 453 10 44). M: Hospital Clinic. Eccentric, colorful restaurant serves mainly Mediterranean fare as well as some traditional Catalan dishes like *fideua* noodles with shrimp (1200ptas/€7,20). Fr-Sa nights, the funky top floor with hanging sculptures is opened up for your dining pleasure. Appetizers and salads 950-1200ptas/€5,60-7,20. Fish and meat entrees 1575-2300ptas/€9,50-14. Bottles of wine and *cava* 600-2600ptas/€3,61-16. Open M 9pm-11pm and Tu-Sa 1-4pm and 9-11pm. AmEx/D/MC/V.

El Criollo, C. Aribau 85 (☎93 454 23 28). M: Hospital Clinic. A Peruvian oasis in l'Eixample. Choose from hearty dishes like the house specialty *ají de gallina*—shredded chicken in a thick, spicy nut sauce. Weekday lunch *menú* 1500ptas/€9. Appetizers 600-900ptas/€3,61-5,40. Entrees 925-1300ptas/€5,50-7,80. AmEx/D/MC/V.

Lunch at Ra

Restaurante Terrani, C. Londres 89 (☎93 321 15 22). M: Diagonal or Hospital Clinic. The creative Catalan cuisine with Italian influences at Terrani has drawn great reviews since it opened last year. The daily lunch *menú* is a filling and reasonably priced option, 1800ptas/€11; it includes three courses and wine. Appetizers 975-1350ptas/€5,80-8. Entrees 1450-2100ptas/€8,50-12,50. Dinner reservations suggested. Open daily 1:30-4 and 9pm-midnight. AmEx/D/MC/V.

Ginza, C. Provença 205 (☎93 451 71 93). M: Diagonal or FGC: Provença. Sleek, bamboo and wood-filled restaurant serves affordable Japanese food. Eat in or take out. Sushi 800-1200ptas/€4,80-7,20. Weekday four-course lunch *menú* 1100ptas/€6,60. Daily *menús* 1500ptas/€9 M-F, 1800ptas/€11 Sa-Su. Open daily 1-4pm and 8pm-midnight. MC/V.

Sangría at ba-ba-reeba

La Provença, C. Provença 242 (☎93 323 23 67). M: Diagonal. Enter through a hall of lanterns to a quiet banquet room with chandeliers and pastel tablecloths. Dishes lean towards a Mediterranean influence. Specialties include carpaccio, fresh fish, and vegetables. Entrees 1300-1800ptas/€7,80-10,90. Dress well. Open daily 1:30pm-4 and 9pm-midnight. AmEx/D/MC/V.

El Raconet, C. Enrique Granados 95 (☎93 218 10 57). M: Diagonal. Family-run corner eatery with sidewalk tables. Plenty of Catalan mainstays, including a wide selection of *bacalao* (cod), as well as vegetarian options. Small offering of bagels topped with cheeses or meats (750ptas/€4,50). Meat and fish entrees 750-1750ptas/€4,50-10,50. Open Su-W 8:30am-9:30pm, Th-Sa 8:30am-2am. Kitchen open Su-W 1:30-4pm and Th-Sa 1:30-4pm and 9pm-midnight. AmEx/MC/V.

La Flauta, C. Aribau 23 (☎93 323 70 38). M: Pg. de Gràcia. The house specialties, reasonably enough, are hot or cold *flautas*—skinny, crusty bread sandwiches stuffed with veggies, cheeses, and meats (half 425-795ptas/€2,50-4,25; whole 525-1100ptas/€3,10-

Thai Garden

137

CATALAN CUISINE

pa amb tomaquet/pan con tomate: toasted bread served with tomato and garlic. Sometimes comes prepared, but more authentic places let you do it yourself. Cut the tomato in half and rub it generously over the toast. Then cut the garlic in half and rub it on the toast. Be a little more careful with the garlic, or you'll be reeking of it for days to come.

crema catalana: The definitive Catalan dessert, a light custard with a caramelized top, very similar to *crème brulée*. So popular that ice cream stores sell *crema catalana* ice cream and Dunkin' Donuts offers a new *crema catalana*-filled donut. Especially delicious is the *crema catalana* liqueur, with the consistency of Kahlua or Bailey's and an nutmeg flavor similar to egg nog.

Espinacs a la catalana: another regional specialty: spinach sautéed with pine nuts, raisins, and sometimes anchovies.

Romesco de peix: a seafood medley in a *romesco* sauce of tomatoes, garlic, peppers, and nuts.

Fideus: like a *paella*, but prepared with a small noodle instead of rice.

Esqueixada: a shredded cod, olive, vinegar, tomato, bean, and red pepper salad.

Mel i Mató: honey and curd cheese, a dessert.

6,60). Plenty of vegetarian options and a large selection of *tapas del día*. Weekday three course lunch *menú* 1350ptas/€8. Salads 490-890ptas/€2,90-5,30. Open M-F 7am-1:30am and Sa 8am-1:30am. MC/V. **Branch** at C. Balmes 164-166.

see map p. 321

POBLE NOU & PORT OLÍMPIC

POBLE NOU

If you happen to be in the area, cheap, local food is readily available in Poble Nou, although you'll stick out as a tourist if you eat in the neighborhood watering holes. The El Portal restaurant is an exception to the rule, drawing crowds of visitors and natives alike.

El Portal, C. Pallars 120 (☎93 300 55 03). From M: Bogatell. From the Metro station, turn your back to the hill and follow C. Pujades to C. Pamplona, then turn left and walk 1 block to the intersection with C. Pallars. Behind the doors of this 4-story gem await delicious roasting and baking smells, and a homey, almost farmhouse-style decor that includes an outdoor terrace with its own bar. Specializes in fresh Mediterranean dishes, especially char-grilled meats and fish, and offers over 30 desserts. Entrees range 1500-3000ptas/€9,02-18,03; 3-course meals 3000-5000ptas/€18,03-30,05. Open daily 1-4pm. Wheelchair accessible. MC/V.

PORT OLÍMPIC

Food in the Port Olímpic area is not cheap, even in the fast-food restaurants that are starting to move in. For a budget day at the beach or walking the Olympic parks, pack a picnic lunch from the **supermarkets** listed on p. 293 and bring it with you. If you want to eat in the port itself, there are more than 20 restaurants, mostly seafood-based, to choose from. In most of them, a full three-course dinner meal will cost 5000-8000ptas/€30,05-48,08. The following three listings are standouts among the waterfront restaurants, which are always best in good weather.

Agua, Pg. Marítim de la Barceloneta 30 (☎93 225 12 72), the farthest establishment to the right of the copper fish. The upscale, Art Deco interior and innovative New American/Mediterranean menu belie reasonable prices. Sauces, rice dishes, and seafood are the specialties. Entrees 1200-2000ptas/€7,12-12,02; 3-course meals 3000-4000ptas/€18,03-24,04. Open M-Th 1:30-4pm and 8:30-11pm, F 1:30-4pm and 8:30pm-1am, Sa 1:30-5pm and 8:30pm-1am, and Su 1:30-5pm and 8:30pm-midnight. Reservations highly recommended. AmEx/MC/V. Wheelchair accessible.

La Oca Mar, Platja Nova Marbella (☎93 225 01 00), a 20min. walk up the beach from the Port Olímpic, keeping the water on your right. This is a bit of a hike if you don't have a car, but might be unusual enough to be worth it: the entire restaurant is built like a large ship, with a long "bow"/terrace extending far into the ocean for sunset-gazing. Best for large groups; small parties are seated inside, away from the panoramic views of the water. Most entrees 1500-2500ptas/ €9,02-15,03. Open daily 1pm-1am. AmEx/MC/V. Wheelchair accessible.

BARCELONETA

As the historic home of sailors and fishermen, Barceloneta houses a number of good seafood restaurants, with the same quality fish for lower prices than the waterfront or Port Olímpic areas.

La Oficina, Pg. Joan de Borbo 30 (☎93 221 40 05). This tiny port-side restaurant has some of the freshest fish around, proudly displayed in all its gory raw glory at the bar. Pull up a table under the umbrellas out-side, or squeeze inside to grab some marine-oriented *tapas* at the bar. *Tapas* 500-1500ptas/€3,01-9,02; steak and fish entrees 1500-2000ptas/€9,02-12,02. *Menú* 1200ptas/€7,12. Open daily 1-4pm and 8:30-11:30pm. MC/V.

Gazpacho at La Provença

Restaurante Rias Do Miño, Almirante Cervera 39 (☎ 93 221 71 37), at the beginning of the Pg. Marítim. With a spot right across the street from Platje Barce-loneta, the covered terrace has a view of the sea unobstructed by the boats of the harbor. Beyond just a pretty view, Rias Do Miño distinguishes itself with its comprehensive menu and big portions. Fish dishes range from 1500-2800ptas/€9,02-16,00, with a *menú* for 1200ptas/€7,20. Open 12-4pm, 8pm-mid-night. MC/V.

La Mar Salada, Pg. Juan de Borbo 58 (☎93 221 21 27). Seating for large groups available upstairs. The friendly staff makes this bright and open restaurant all the more pleasant. Penny pinchers should try the mussels (750ptas/€4,52), while bigger spenders can opt for the huge 2-person shellfish platter, a crusta-cean overload with lobster, crab, shrimp, clams, and oysters for 6000ptas/€36,06. *Menú* 1150ptas/ €6,91. Open W-M 1-4pm and 8pm-midnight.

Bustling Waiter at La Provença

PORT VELL

see map p. 322

Restaurants tend to group around two central areas: in the vicinities of the Palau de Mar and Maremagnum. The Port Vell side of the "Palace of the Sea" (on Port Vell at the far end of Pg. Colom) houses several fancy harbor side res-taurants, where well-dressed waiters serve lunch to tourists in baseball caps and flip-flops. (Din-ners, however, are considerably more formal.) The elegant **Merendero de la Mari** has an extensive seafood menu, including fresh lobster (1940ptas/ €11,65), and perhaps the best *paella* in the city. Order it with rice (2500ptas/€15) or *fideos* (2750ptas/€16,50), a small, thin pasta—a Catalan specialty. (☎93 221 31 41. Open M-Sa 12:30-4pm, 8:30-11:30pm. and Su 12:30-4:30pm. MC/V.)

Horse Meat

139

BREAKFAST OF CHAMPIONS

Several brave establishments open their doors for the city that keeps going until the early morning. If you find yourself winding down after an evening out, or up at dawn on your way out of town, try these early-bird breakfast options.

Bar Estudiantil, at Pl. Universitat 12, serves regular café-bar fare and hardly ever closes. (☎93 302 31 25. Open M-F 6am-2am and Sa-Su 5am-3am.)

For pry-your-eyes-open coffee, try the delightful, family-run Sechi Caffé Italiano at the bottom of Gràcia on Trav. de Gràcia 34. (☎93 200 56 93. Open M-F 7am-8:30pm, closed Aug.)

Or, luxuriate in the classy, high-ceilinged **Cafeteria Estació de França** in the train station. (☎93 310 16 33; just inside the Estació de França. Open M-F 6:30am-9pm, Sa-Su 5am-9pm.)

If you need help ordering your morning caffeine fix, check **Would You Like Coffee With That?** (p. 144).

The other areas where restaurants congregate is **Maremagnum**. Barcelona's glitzy leisure center has a number of unsurprisingly seafood- and tourist-oriented restaurants, mostly chains. Fast food joints, ice cream shops and pricey *tapas* places are in abundant supply. One exceptional choice, though slightly indulgent, is **Mandongo**, on the second floor. The decor evokes a beach-side bungalow, and the cuisine is a fusion of Asian and Mediterranean. In addition to sushi (1410ptas/€8,50) and the outstanding salmon in banana leaf (1820/€11), dishes include mouth-watering steaks (1950-3300ptas/€12-20) and a specialty paella (890ptas/€11,40), prepared to be eaten without a knife. (☎93 225 81 43. Open daily 1pm-midnight. MC/V.)

MONTJUÏC

see map p. 320

Food options in Montjuïc are scant at best. The mountain is littered with a few overpriced café-bars like the popular Bar Miralmar on the Miramar vista. The Fundació Miró, MNAC, Castell de Montjuïc, and Teatre Grec all have pleasant cafés, but to eat at a full-scale restaurant on Montjuïc means entering the depths of Poble Espanyol (see **Sights,** p. 91), where *menús* run 1950ptas/€12. One good option is **La Font de Prades** (☎93 426 75 19) which is set back in a quiet, less trafficked area of the village and serves traditional Catalan cuisine. Poble Espanyol also offers dinner flamenco shows at **El Tablao de Carmen** (see **Entertainment,** p. 176). Some restaurants, bars, and grocery stores also line Av. Paral.lel in Poble Sec.

ZONA ALTA

see maps p. 318 & 319

GRÀCIA

Gràcia offers a wide variety of cuisine in the dozens of restaurants that pack its narrow blocks. Traditional markets dot the neighborhood (see **Sights,** p. 96). Catalan menus abound, but Gràcia is also the place to find varied and reasonably priced vegetarian cuisine. Lebanese restaurants and tapas bars dominate Pl. del Sol and Pl. Virreina, while other veggie finds dot some of the smaller side streets.

La Gavina, C. Ros de Olano 17 (☎93 415 74 50). Funky Italian pizzeria complete with life-size patron saint and confessional candles. Pizzas serving several hungry people go for 750-1450ptas/€4,50-8,50; try the *Catalana*—tomato, mozzarella, chorizo sausage, garlic, and artichokes. Open Tu-Su 2pm-1am, F-Sa 2pm-2am. Wheelchair accessible.

La Buena Tierra, C. Encarnació 56 (☎93 219 82 13). M: Joanic. Follow C. Escorial for 2 blocks and turn left on C. Encarnació. Vegetarian delicacies!

Choose from an eclectic range of entrees like *moussaka* or tortellini with roquefort (650-1050ptas/€4-6,50) and feast in the backyard terrace. Open M-Sa noon-4pm and 8pm-1am. D.

Ikastola, C. La Perla 22. M: Fontana, off C. Verdi. Ikastola (the Basque word for "nursery school") serves mostly vegetarian dishes (350-600ptas/€2-3,60) to Gràcia's fringe crowd during the day and transforms into a popular bar at night. Write or draw on the chalkboard-covered walls. Open M-F 11am-1am, Sa-Su 5pm-3am.

Restaurant Illa de Gràcia, C. Sant Domènic 19 (☎93 238 02 29). M: Diagonal. Follow Gran de Gràcia for 5 or 6 blocks and make a right onto C. Sant Domènic. Satisfying vegetarian food picked at by stylish young health-nuts. Excellent selection of fresh juices. *Menú del día* 875ptas/€5,26. Salads 485-600ptas/€3-4. Entrees around 1200ptas/€7,5. Open Tu-F 1-4pm and 9pm-midnight, Sa-Su 12-4pm and 9pm-midnight. Closed in August. D/MC/V.

El 19 De La Riera, C. Riera De Sant Miquel 19 (☎93 237 86 01). M: Diagonal. Turn left on Diagonal, and C. Riera de Sant Miquel is the 1st right. Serves only organic food, including a salad bar and plenty of vegetarian options. Lunch *menús* 1000ptas/€6 and 1600ptas/€9,50; dinner entrees 1650-1950ptas/€10,50-12. Open M-W noon-5pm, Th-Sa noon-5pm and 8-11pm. MC/V.

El Tastavins, C. Ramón y Cajal 12 (☎93 213 60 31). M: Joanic, near Pl. Sol. A small offering of satisfying Catalan mainstays. No English menu (or speakers), but waiters become masters of charades impersonating the dishes they wish to explain. Entrees around 1500ptas/€9. Open Tu-Sa 1:30-4pm and 8:30-11:30pm, Su 1:30-4pm.

Equinox Sol, Pl. de Sol 14 (☎ 93 415 79 76). FGC: Gràcia or M: Fontana. "The King of Shawarma & Falafel" boasts 3 family-run Lebanese restaurants; their Pl. del Sol branch is the busiest. Take out or eat in. Shawarma 400ptas/€2,40; tabbouleh or falafel 350-650ptas/€2,10-4,80. Open daily 1pm-2am.

Xavi Petit, C. Bonavista 2 (☎93 237 88 26). M: Diagonal, off Gran de Gràcia. Cheese, meat, and chocolate-filled *crêpes* can be a hearty meal or just dessert. *Crêpes* run 425-725ptas/€2,50-4,50. *Crêpe*-less afternoon *menú* 1175ptas/€7,50. Standard selection of *tapas* 350-550ptas/€2-3,50. Open M-Sa 7:30am-11:30pm. AmEx/V.

HORTA

Horta's best-known restaurants are Can Cortada and Can Travi Nou. Neither is particularly cheap; nestled in spacious medieval dwellings, both are favorites of large tour groups, for good reason. The **Can Cortada** was built in the 11th century as a feudal defense tower and was converted into a farmhouse in the 15th century. On the way to the downstairs dining room you can still see the old underground dungeon tunnels and the horse feeding corner. (Av. de l'Estatut de Catalunya, a

Churros con Chocolate

Sampling Tapas

Interesting Seafood

141

Bakery

Brains

Making Friends with the Waiters

20min. walk toward the Velodróm from M: Montbau; it is visible from Pg. de Vall d'Hebron. ☎ 93 427 23 15. Three-course meal 3000-4500ptas/€18-27. Open daily 1:30-4pm and 8:30pm-1am. Reservations recommended. AmEx/MC/V. Wheelchair accessible.) Five minutes down the street, 17th-century **Can Travi Nou** has a cozier, more residential atmosphere. (The end of C. Jorge Manrique, a right off Pg. de Vall d'Hebron heading toward the Velodróm from M: Montbau. ☎ 93 428 03 01. Three-course meal 4000-5000ptas/€24-30. Open M-Sa 1:30-4pm and 8:30-11pm, Su 1:30-4pm. Reservations recommended. AmEx/MC/V. Wheelchair accessible.)

LES CORTS

Dining in Les Corts doesn't get too fancy. The neighborhood's small bars and cafés feed hordes of soccer fans on game days, but the area is not known for its cuisine.

L'Ancora, Passatge Costa 2 (☎ 93 440 00 07). M: Collblanc, off C. de Collblanc, next to the Metro station. A convenient *cervecería* (beer café). Start a debate over the latest Barça controversy while munching on *bocadillos* (350-400ptas/€2,10-2,40) or Catalan entrees (675-1200ptas/€4-7). Open daily 7am-8pm.

El Cargolet Picant, Riera Blanca 7 (☎ 93 334 04 54). M: Collblanc, at the corner of Trav. de Les Corts and C. Aristides Maillol. Busy even on non-game days, "The Spicy Snail" specializes in 9 snail dishes, about 1500ptas/€9 each. Less adventurous can choose from a number of meat entrees (700-1300ptas/€4,20-7,80). *Menú* 1100ptas/€6,60. Open daily 7am-2am.

SANTS

Sants boasts at least one phenomenal restaurant and several places worth leaving the station for a pre- or post-train meal. For travelers shamelessly craving fast-food American sweets, there is a Dunkin' Donuts in Pl. Sants, out the back of the station.

📧 **La Parra,** C. Joanot Martorall 3 (☎ 93 332 51 34), a steep alley right of C. Sants, 2 blocks before M: Hostafrancs (from the station). This hidden gem has been serving fresh Mediterranean fare in the same house for 2 centuries; when C. Sants was the main road into Barcelona, travelers would rest their horses here and eat before entering the city. Huge appetizers 1500-2200ptas/€9-13. Most entrees 1200-2000ptas/€7-12. Open Tu-Th 6pm-12:30am, Sa noon-midnight, Su noon-4:30pm. MC/V. Wheelchair accessible only with difficulty.

Calero's Pizzeria, C. Galileo 1 (☎ 93 411 04 13), on the right side of Pl. Sants, coming from the back of the station. An Italian haven for lovers of pizza and pasta (800-900ptas/€5 each). Open M-Th 8:30pm-midnight, F-Su 1-4pm and 8:30pm-midnight. AmEx/MC/V. Wheelchair accessible.

SARRIÀ

Sarrià is an excellent area for no-frills Catalan fare; most restaurants are on or very near C. Major de Sarrià. Come armed with your Catalan dictionary or just a sense of culinary adventure—most menus and waiters do not provide English translation. M: Sarrià or Reina Elisenda.

Casa Joana, C. Major de Sarrià 59 (☎93 203 10 36). Traditional, tasty Catalan dishes are served in big portions at reasonable prices. *Menú del día* (1900ptas/€11,41) includes an appetizer, entree, drink, and dessert. Reservations accepted, but not necessary. Open daily 1-3:45pm and 9-11pm. D/MC/V.

Foix de Sarrià, C. Major de Sarrià 57. Elegant local pastry institution named for Catalan poet J.V. Foix. Peruse the selection of homemade tarts and cream-filled delights (around 350ptas/€2,10) served in the gilded interior. Also stocks *gelato* (325ptas/€1,95), wine, cheeses, chocolates, and meats. Open daily 8am-9pm.

Ice Cream and Outdoor Elevator

Restaurante Maravillas, C. Cornet i Mas 38. From C. Major de Sarrià, turn onto C. Rocaberti and walk 1 short block. Three tasteful and romantic rooms with soft lighting and pastel walls. Entrees 900-2500ptas/€5,41-15,03; vegetarian options. Special three-course lunch *menú del día* during the week 1700ptas/€10,22. M-Sa 1:30-4pm and 9-11:30pm. MC/V.

Via Veneto, C. Ganduxer 10-12. FGC: Bonanova or bus #67 or 68 from Pl. de Catalunya to Av. Diagonal just past Pl. Francesco Macia. C. Ganduxer begins at Av. Diagonal; the restaurant is one block up on the right. Surrounded by the upscale shops and modern high-rise apartment buildings of lower Sarrià, Via Veneto is right at home. Swanky and pricey (most entrees around 2000ptas/€12)—complete with a doorman—Via Veneto serves Spanish, Catalan, and French dishes. Open M-F 1:30-4pm and 8:45-11:30pm, Sa 8:45-11:30pm. MC/V.

Granizado

A'Rogueira, Pl. d'Artos 6. A popular bar and restaurant with plenty of outside tables on the busy Pl. d'Artos. More affordable than most options on C. Major de Sarrià, which climbs uphill from the Plaça d'Artos. *Tapas* 400-1100ptas/€2,40-6,61; sandwiches 300-890ptas/€1,80-5,35; entrees 950-1975ptas/€5,41-11,87. Open daily 7am-2am.

TIBIDABO

Tibidabo has several options for food, but most of them require stretching yout budget; thirty- and forty-something professionals dominate the crowds here. Partway up the hill, in the Casa Roviralta, **El Asador de Aranda** serves medieval-style Castillian fare in manor-like dining rooms. (☎93 417 01 15; www. asadoraranda.com. Three-course meal 2500-4000ptas/€15-24. Open M-Sa 1-4pm and 9pm-midnight, Su 1-4pm only. AmEx/MC/V.) In Pl. Dr. Andreu, next to the funicular station, **La Venta** serves good Catalan food on the

Café con Leche

WOULD YOU LIKE COFFEE WITH THAT?

Spanish coffee is known for being quite tasty and quite strong. Don't expect a water-downed version of a cup of joe, because you're about to get the real thing. Also don't expect to find coffees to go, as European custom demands drinking leisurely on the spot.

Azucar: sugar.

Café: coffee with hot milk and sugar on the side; the *camarero* (waiter) will ask you to be more specific.

Cortado: an espresso-like coffee served in a smaller mug; it is mostly coffee with a bit of milk; sugar is provided on the side.

Café con leche: half coffee and half milk with sugar on the side; you can request to have it in a mug or a glass; generally consumed only at breakfast.

Café americano: a shot of espresso lengthened with hot water; closely resembles American coffee.

Café sólo: black coffee (no milk or sugar).

Café con hielo: iced coffee served in a tall glass; sugar on the side

Leche: milk.

Other options: You can also request to have a **doble de café** which means that the *camarero* will double the amount of coffee in your drink (and add some milk) and serve it in a tall glass.

terrace and in an enticing tiled and latticed interior. (☎93 212 64 55. Three-course meal 5000-6000ptas/€30-36. Open M-Sa 1-3:15pm and 9-11:15pm. AmEx/MC/V.)

There are numerous spots places in the park, but the best one accessible by public transportation is **Font de Les Planes,** a short walk across the highway bridge from the Les Planes FGC train station (take the S1 or S2 line from Pl. de Catalunya). The area includes both a full-service restaurant and a *merendero*—an open-air space with picnic tables, barbecue grills, paella pans, charcoal, ice, and more for rent—as well as ice cream, coffee, and alcoholic drinks for sale. Most people bring their own meat, seasonings, and side dishes and cook on the spot. In a pinch, bread and salads can be purchased from the restaurant; foosball and a small playground keep children entertained while parents cook. (Tables 600ptas/€3.50 each. Grills 400ptas/€2,50, plus 1000ptas/€6 deposit. Bag of coal 600ptas/€3,50. Paella pans 500ptas/€3 for 6 people, 600ptas/€3,50 for 8 people, 700ptas/€4 for 10 people, and 800ptas/€5 for 12 people, plus 500ptas/€3 deposit. Open W-M 9am-7pm.)

The adjacent **Restaurant Font de Les Planes** serves up make-your-own *pan con tomate*, paella, and grilled meats in a fresh, breezy patio-room with cheerful checkered tablecloths. (Paella and meats 1000-1500ptas/€6-9. Reservations recommended on weekends. Open Sept.-June M-F 9am-10pm, Sa 9am-midnight and Su 9am-9pm; July-Aug. daily 9am-midnight. MC/V.) The tourist map from the information center provides more information on *merenderos* and restaurants farther into the park (see p. 101).

CHAINS

RESTAURANT CHAINS

Pans & Company. Perhaps the most visible franchise in Spain, this fast-food *bocadillo* chain started up in 1991 right here in Barcelona, as its Catalan name attests. Since then, it has spread like a tasty virus. Hot and cold *bocadillos* of ham, chicken, tuna, or other fillings come with fries and a drink for 725-925ptas/€4,50-€5,50. Pre-prepared vegetable and pasta salads are 405ptas/€2,40. Learn to love Pans—this chain is inescapable.

TapasBar (☎93 680 35 90). In spite of its tacky name, TapasBar is a card-carrying member of the elite club of Grade A restaurant chains; their bright yellow logo is a stamp of quality of atmosphere as well as of food. They have nearly 30 locations in Spain and Portugal (6 of them in Barcelona) and specialize in, you guessed it, *tapas!* (Two popular locations include the Moll d'Espanya and near the Hotel Arts on Av. Litoral Mar.) For adventurous diners, they offer 2-person meals of 8 *tapas* each (1800-2600ptas/€9,70-

12,40). Most *tapas* 500-800ptas/€3-4,30. Coffee, desserts, full meals available. Open M-Th 8am-1am, F-Sa 8am-3am, Su 11am-1am. AmEx/MC/V.

FresCo, Ronda Universitat 29 (☎93 301 68 37). M: Catalunya, off Pl. de Catalunya. A hugely popular all-you-can-eat buffet extravaganza. 3 l'Eixample locations attract everyone from tiny female Spaniards picking delicately at their salads to packs of ravenous twentysomethings gorging themselves on a good deal. Either way, the endlessly varied salad bar, selection of pasta and pizza, frozen yogurt, coffee, and fruit are the perfect escape from meat-heavy Catalan staples. Lunch buffet 1095ptas/€6,60, dinner buffet 1395ptas/€8,40; both with 1 drink. Also at Av. Diagonal 449 and C. València 263. Reservations necessary on weekends. Open daily 12:45pm-1am. MC/V.

Fresh & Ready. This 7-store chain has rapidly become a crutch for busy Catalan career-minded types. They serve coffee, juice, and pastries like any café, but also offer a huge array of refrigerated, prepackaged salads, sandwiches, and yogurts to-go, ranging from Thai chicken and smoked salmon to simple *tortilla española*. The food is indeed fresh, though a little pricey for the small portions. Sandwiches and salads 400-500ptas/€2,40-3. Open Su-Th 8am-11pm, F-Sa 8am-midnight. Cash only.

La Baguetina Catalana (☎93 539 52 08). With more than 30 stores in Barcelona, La Baguetina is almost as ubiquitous as Pans & Co. Its main offerings include *bocadillos, palmeras*, croissants, and *cocas* (bread pizzas), but is best known for its late hours in tourist-heavy areas like Las Ramblas, where stumbling revelers line up for bready snacks until 3am on weekends. *Bocadillos* 300-500ptas/€2,40-3. *Cocas* 800ptas/€4,80. Opening hours range from 6-8am, depending on location, and closing hours from midnight to 3am. Cash only.

Pastafiore. Owned by the same company as Pans & Co., Pastafiore serves up quick Italian food, including spaghetti, lasagna, ravioli, and tortellini. The salads are less than delectable by the end of the day, but the hot dishes aren't half bad, and the midday *menú* (1200ptas/€7,20) is a decent deal for pizza, salad, and a drink. Pasta dishes around 700ptas/€4,20. Salads 500ptas/€3. Personal pizzas 600ptas/€3,60. Open Su-Th 12:30pm-midnight, F-Sa 12:30pm-1am. Cash only.

Bocatta. Virtually indistinguishable from the yellow Pans & Co. with which it competes, save the green decor. Hot and cold *bocadillos*, heavy on the ham. Value meals 700-900ptas/€4,20-€5,40. Salad selection a bit more varied (300-500ptas/€1,80-€3).

Vips, Rambla de Catalunya 7-9 (☎93 317 48 05). M: Catalunya. Barcelona's only representative of an international franchise, perfect for homesick Americans. Spanish and American food served in the restaurant, including grilled chicken salads, grilled veggie sandwiches, quesadillas, and hamburgers (most around 1000ptas/€6). The store sells books, road maps, and magazines, as well CDs, videos, snacks, drinks, and gifts and cards. 4 computers for pricey Internet use (8am-4pm 300ptas/€1,80 per 30min., 4pm-3am 200ptas/€1,20 for 15min.). Open M-F 8am-3am, Sa-Su and holidays 9am-3am. AmEx/MC/V. Wheelchair accessible.

Hard Rock Café, Pl. de Catalunya 21 (☎93 270 23 05). M: Catalunya. For those that want to rock and roll all night and party every day, but need an occasional break to eat. The two-hour wait on many nights can be a major bummer. Good burgers (1015-1550/€6,10-€9,30, including veggie burgers) and "Really Big Sandwiches" (1250-1450/€7,50-€9,29) dominate the menu. Open daily 12:30pm-1am. For t-shirt seekers, the gift shop opens at 10am.

COFFEE CHAINS

The following coffeehouse chains are roughly similar in prices and design; all serve a range of coffees and a small selection of ice cream, pastries, teas, and *bocadillos*, and generally offer breakfast specials for 250-500ptas/€1,50-3. **Jamaica** and **Il Caffe di Roma** are nearly indistinguishable. **Aroma** is the classiest of the lot, with warmly-lit, dark wood interiors that almost conceal its chain status.

Nightlife

The nightlife in Barcelona needs no introduction: whether you're looking for psychedelic absinthe shots, a great place for grunge rock, a sunrise foam party, or just someplace quiet to sit back and enjoy a drink (surrounded by fake gnomes), this city has it all. Things don't get going until late (don't bother showing up before midnight or 1am at a club) and keep going for as long as you can handle it. Check the *Guia del Ocio*, available at newsstands, for even more up-to-date listings of nightime fun.

NIGHTLIFE BY NEIGHBORHOOD

see map pp. 310-311

BARRI GÒTIC & LAS RAMBLAS

Nightfall is the only thing that really distinguishes the upper from the lower Barri Gòtic. The area above C. Ferran, dominated by shops, restaurants and hostels, virtually shuts down by midnight, while C. Ferran and below starts to look like a human river, with tourists and locals alike weaving their way from bar to bar. There are a few clubs in and near Pl. Reial, and several of the most popular places are hybrid bar/clubs, but overall the Barri Gòtic offers more for drinking and chilling than for wild and crazed late-night dancing; head to the Port Vell or Montjuïc if you're looking for that. Also be advised that while the Pl. Reial has some great nightlife spots (the standouts are listed below) and is not particularly dangerous, it is also a tourist-ed area with a colorful reputation that includes drug dealing, pick-pocketing, and prostitution. Don't go to this area looking for that action; it's not as visible as rumors would have you believe, and it is generally well-policed. The Pl. Reial is a fun place to pass the night, but watch your wallet, the people around you, and travel with a buddy.

ADULT NIGHTLIFE (NOT XXX)

We here at *Let's Go* know all too well that some aspects of Catalan nightlife get really old really fast. For those looking for a more mature crowd, devoid of drunk American teenagers and twenty-somethings, check out the following listings.

Casablanca (p. 161)

El Gran Casino (p. 159)

La Filharmónica (**p. 155**)

La Paloma (p. 153)

Les Gens que J'aime (p. 154)

Tarantos (listed under **Jamboree**; p. 150)

Universal (p. 163)

Up and Down (p. 162)

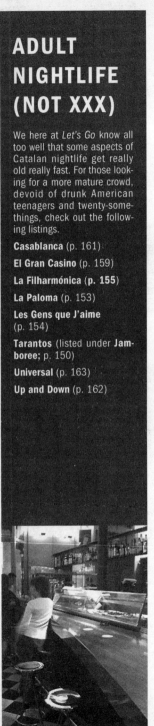

BARS

🎇 **El Bosq de les Fades** (☎93 317 26 49). M: Drassanes, down an alley just off Las Ramblas, near the water and next to the Museu de Cera. From the maniacal geniuses who brought you the wax museum, El Bosq de les Fades (the Forest of Fables) is a fairy tale world, complete with gnarly trees, waterfalls, gnomes, a small bridge, and plush side rooms. Overheard: "Dude, check out that fly honey hanging out at the corner table...oh damn, she's made of wax." Open M-Th until 1:30am, F-Sa until 2:30am.

Molly's Fair City, C. Ferran 7 (☎93 342 40 26). M: Liceu. With blaring music, fast-flowing imported beer, and a prime location next to the Pl. Reial, Molly's has become *the* meeting place for English-speaking backpackers in the Barri Gòtic, although plenty of Spaniards squeeze in as well. Guinness on tap 800ptas/€5. Bottled beer 500-600ptas/€3-3,50. Mixed drinks 1000ptas/€6. Open M-F 8pm-2:30am and Sa-Su 7pm-3am. Cash only.

Dot Light Club, C. Nou de Sant Francesc 7 (☎93 302 70 26). M: Drassanes, the second right off C. Escudellers coming from Las Ramblas. The chic atmosphere in this tiny 2-room bar/club is all about funky lighting and cutting edge DJ action every night. The bouncer outside is not actually looking to bounce; until it gets full, just nod hello and he'll open the door for you. Beer 400ptas/€2,50. Drinks 800ptas/€4,80. Th night indie film screenings 10:30pm-midnight. Open Th-Su 10:30pm-2:30am, F-Sa 10:30pm-3am. Cash only.

Schilling, C. Ferran 23 (☎93 317 67 87). M: Liceu. Though chandeliers, marble tables, and tinted windows cry out "exclusive," Schilling is surprisingly diverse and has a lot more breathing space than most bars in the Barri Gòtic. Mixed gay and straight crowd. Excellent *sangría* (pitcher 2000ptas/€12). Mixed drinks 700ptas/€4,20. Wine 250ptas/€1,50. Beer 300ptas/€1,50. Open M-F 9am-2am and Sa-Su 11am-2am. Cash only.

Margarita Blue, C. J. A. Clavé 6 (☎93 317 71 76). M: Drassanes, off Las Ramblas, 1 block from the port. With blue margaritas and retro 80s pop tunes, this Mexican-themed bar draws a flamboyant 20- and 30-something crowd of locals and tourists alike. Su night magic shows, Tu night drag queen performances (around 11:30pm/midnight). Creative Mexican food accompanies the tequila; most dishes run 800-1000ptas/€4,80-6. Blue margaritas 500ptas/€3. Beer 450ptas/€2,70. Tequila shots 300ptas/€1,80. Open Su-W 7pm-2am, Th 7pm-2:30am, F-Sa 7pm-3am (kitchen closes Su-Th at 1am, F-Sa at 1:30am). MC/V.

Fonfone, C. Escudellers 24 (☎93 317 14 24). M: Liceu or Drassanes. Atmospheric lighting and good sounds draw 1am crowds here, another bar/club mix with plenty of white leather couches and a small dance area. A different DJ every night, drawing from talent pools as far away as San Francisco, NYC, and London. Music includes lounge, house, free style, garage, and more. Beer 500ptas/€3. Drinks 1000ptas/€6. Open Su-Th 10pm-2:30am, F-Sa 10pm-3am. Cash only.

Café Royale, C. Nou de Zurbano 3 (☎93 412 14 33). M: Liceu, on the tiny street leading out of the corner of Pl. Reial occupied by Jamboree (go left out of the plaça if you're facing Las Ramblas). The self-proclaimed "only" place in the city to chill out to soul and funk, spun by DJ Fred Guzzo. Arrive by midnight if you want one of the velveteen or leather seats; after that, chances are you'll wait up to 1hr to get in. Mixed gay and straight crowd of 20- and 30-somethings. Beer 500ptas/€3. Drinks 800-1000ptas/€4,80-6. Open daily 6pm-3am. V; minimum charge 4000ptas/€24.

Glaciar Bar, Pl. Reial 3 (☎93 302 11 63). M: Liceu, in the near left corner coming from Las Ramblas. A hidden treasure in a sea of indistinguishable tourist bars. Laid-back atmosphere, lots of local patrons, plenty of outside tables, and free winter photo exhibits upstairs. Beer 325ptas/€2. Drinks 650ptas/€3,90. Jar of *sangría* 1600ptas/€9,60. Open M-Sa 4pm-2:30am and Su 8am-2:30am. Cash only.

Harlem Jazz Club, C. Comtesa de Sobradiel 8 (☎93 310 07 55). M: Liceu, between Pl. Reial and Via Laietana. Live music alternating between blues, jazz, reggae, flamenco, acoustic rock and more. Two sessions per night, Tu-Th and Su 11:00pm and 12:30am, F-Sa 11:30pm and 1am. The second session is always much more crowded, especially on weekends. Advance tickets/current play schedules available at tourist offices and www.atrapalo.com. F-Sa cover 750ptas/€4,50 (includes 1 drink); occasionally weekday shows charge cover as well. Open daily 10pm-4am. Cash only.

Barcelona Pipa Club, Pl. Reial 3 (☎93 302 47 32). M: Liceu, next to Glaciar Bar (see above). Decidedly unmarked; look for the small name plaque and ring the doorbell to be let in. This private smokers' club opens to the public daily from 11pm-5am. The decor is 100% Sherlock Holmes, the music jazz and fusion, the people a mix of local bartenders, artists, and tourists in the know. Occasional activities like tango classes and poetry readings. Gets crowded after 2am, no entrance allowed after 4am. Cocktails 800-1000ptas/€4,80-6. Beer 500ptas/€3. Cash only.

Paradís Reggae, C Paradís. M: Jaume I, right off Pl. St. Jaume. A mellow, underground feel and nightly reggae DJs. Sa nights, the sounds usually go live after midnight. Beer 400ptas/€2,40. Drinks 800ptas/€4,80. F-Sa cover 500ptas/€3 (includes 1 drink). Open Tu-Sa 11pm-3am. Cash only.

Hook Bar, C. Ample 35. M: Drassanes. Turn down C. J. A. Clavé off Las Ramblas, which will turn into C. Ample. The bar is near the end of the street, coming from Las Ramblas. If Peter Pan ever does grow up, this is where he'll come to drink; pirate gizmos and sailing paraphernalia deck the walls, and the cocktail menu includes drinks with names like the "Niños Perdidos" (Lost Boys). Mainstream tourist crowds tend

DRINKING LIKE A SPANIARD

Anís: anisette; a licorice flavored liquor.

Bosca: Vodka and a citrus carbonated beverage.

Calimocho: cheap red wine and Coke.

Cacique: rum with coke, lemon soda, or orange soda.

Cava: Catalunya's versions of champagne. Tasty and cheaper.

Cerveza: Beer! *Caña de cerveza* specifies draught beer. For more on beer, see p. 154.

Chupito: a shot, generally taken after dinner/at a club. different establishments have extensive and creative menus of these.

Creme Catalana: a sweet liquor, reminiscent of Bailey's.

Cuba Libre: Generally a rum and coke, although if you specify *con ginebra*, with gin it is.

mini: a liter of beer, usually in a large plastic cup.

mosto: sweet white wine.

Sangría: A changing recipe that depends on the taste of the maker. Generally, *sangría* is made up of very cheap wine, spiced up with hard liquor, fruit, fruit juice, and some form of citrus carbonated beverage. The wooden spoon is to keep the ice and the fruit OUT of your glass; don't dump it all in.

Sidra: Basque cider, poured from a height to aerate the cider.

Sol y Sombra: Cognac and anisette.

Ponché: Also known as the "silver bullet." A sweet liqueur.

Rioja: A region in Spain famous for its red wine.

Tinto: Red wine.

Don Simón: boxed wine; typically drunk with Casera.

LGB ▼
BARCELONA

LGB Nightlife

Barcelona (and the surrounding beach towns) have some of the best LGB nightlife around—everything from raging clubs to low-key bars. Check out these listings to find what suits your tastes. In particular, the part of the l'Eixample Esquerra between C. Urgell, C. Aragó, the Gran Via, and C. Aribau is a virtual mecca for gay partying.

not to make it this far from Las Ramblas, but it might be worth coming just to indulge in a little history: in 1809, Catalan revolutionaries plotting against the Bourbon monarchy were hanged here, and the hook is still visible in the ceiling. Beer 400-600ptas/ €2,50-3,50. Cocktails 800ptas/€5. *Tapas* 500-800ptas/€3-5. Open Tu-Th and Su 7:30pm-2am, F-Sa 7:30pm-3am. Cash only.

Casa El Agüelo, C. Avinyó 37 (☎93 310 23 25). M: Liceu, a right off C. Ferran, coming from Las Ramblas. A cozy medieval tavern of sorts, with brick walls, old fireplaces, long wooden tables, and a cavernous, dungeon-like basement. A good place for cheap beer with a big group of friends. Beer 250ptas/€1,50. Drinks 700-800ptas/€4-5. Open M-F 7pm-2:30am, Sa-Su 7pm-3am. Cash only.

PLAÇA "TRIPPY"

Officially named Plaça George Orwell, this is a popular hangout for Barcelona's alternative crowd. It is even rumored that the government removed all of the benches here to dissuade loitering and drug dealing; how successful they were is highly debatable. Two popular bar-restaurants in the plaça have outside seating. **La Verònica** serves pizzas, salads and drinks until 1am on weekends (12:30am during the week), while grungier, more casual **Bar Ovisos** also stays open until 1am, offering simple Catalan food and cheap beer (200ptas/€1,20 during the day, 300ptas/€1,80 at night).

CLUBS

🖺 **Jamboree,** Pl. Reial 17 (☎93 319 17 89). M: Liceu, in the corner immediately to your right coming from Las Ramblas. What was once a convent now serves as one of the city's most popular live music venues. Jazz or blues performances daily 11pm-1am (M-F 1000ptas/€6 with one drink, Sa-Su 1500ptas/ €9, some performances 2000ptas/€12; 200ptas/ €1,20 discount if you buy ahead of time at a ServiCaixa machine). At 1:30am, the brick basement area turns into a packed hip-hop dance club (open until 5am). Upstairs, the attached club **Tarantos** plays pop and salsa for an older, more sedate crowd. Jamboree cover Su-Th 1200ptas/€7 (includes one drink); F-Sa 2000ptas/€12. Cash only.

New York, C. Escudellers 5 (☎93 318 70 40). M: Drassanes, right off Las Ramblas. Once a strip joint, now the biggest club in the Barri Gòtic, with plenty of drink tables overlooking the red-and-black, strobe-lit dance floor. Crowds don't arrive until well after 3am; music includes reggae and British pop. Cover 11:30pm-2am 900ptas/€5,40 (includes 1 beer); 2-5am 1400ptas/€11,40, includes any drink. Open Th-Sa 11:30pm-5am. Cash only.

Karma, Pl. Reial 10. M: Liceu, in the back right corner coming from Las Ramblas. A basement-level dance club playing mostly rock and pop and filled with a

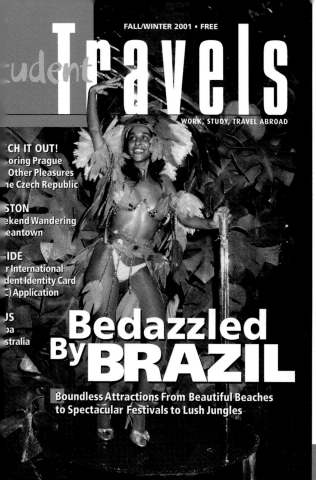

Got ISIC?

ISIC is your passport to the world

Accepted at over 17,000 locations worldwide.
Great benefits at home and abroad!

To apply for your International Student, Teacher or Youth Identity Card
CALL 1-800-2COUNCIL
CLICK www.counciltravel.com
VISIT your local Council Travel office

Bring this ad into your local Council Travel office and receive
a free Council Travel/ISIC t-shirt! *(while supplies last)*

bizarre mix of wild drag queens and calmer revelers, most in their late 20s or 30s. Beer 500ptas/€3. Drinks 900ptas/€5,50. Open Tu-Su midnight-5am. Cash only.

LA RIBERA

see map pp. 310-311

Plàstic Café, Pg. del Born 19 (☎93 310 25 96). M: Jaume I, follow C. Princesa and turn right on C. Comerç and right again on Pg. del Born. 'Café' is a misnomer for this jam-packed, hyper trendy bar, with an eclectic mix of international, house, and 80s pop spinning in the background. Friendly bartenders do fancy tricks with bottles. Beer 400-500ptas/€2,40-3. Mixed drinks 500ptas/€3 and up. Open Su-Th 10pm-2:30am, F-Sa 10pm-3am.

Palau Dalmases, C. Montcada 20 (☎93 310 06 73). A self-labeled 'Baroque space' in a 17th century palace fittingly decorated with lavish oil paintings, candelabras, and statues. Romantic candle-lit tables complete the atmosphere. Thursday is opera night with live performances at 11pm (3000ptas/€18, includes one drink). Mixed drinks 900-1500ptas/€5,40-9. Fresh juices 1200ptas/€7,20. MC/V.

Mudanzas, C. Vidreira 15 (☎93 319 11 37). M: Jaume I. Everything is black, even the suits. The only color comes from hundreds of illuminated bottles lining the wall behind the bar. A hip young professional crowd. Wide selection of rum, whiskey, and wines (200-800ptas/€1,20-4,80). Open Su- F 10am-2am, Sa 11am-2am.

Suborn, C. de la Ribera (☎93 310 11 10). M: Barceloneta, entrance on Pg. Picasso across from Parc de la Ciutadella. Eclectic restaurant with plenty of vegetarian options by day, popular bass-thumping bar by night. Entrees from salmon teriyaki to pasta with masterpiece, ricotti, lemon and pesto (750-2300ptas/€4,50-13). Lunch *menú* 1300ptas/€7,80. Beer 300ptas/€1,80. Drinks 800ptas/€4,80. Open Tu-Th, Su 12:30-4:30pm and 9pm-2:30am, F-Sa 12:30-4:30pm and 9–3am.

EL RAVAL

see map pp. 316-317

BARS

If glamorous clubs and all-night dancing are your scene, El Raval is not for you. El Raval is densely packed with a bar for every variety of bar-hopper: the Irish pubber, the American, the absinthe abuser, the social drinker, the lounge lizard, and the foosball maniac.

▧ **La Oveja Negra,** C. Sitges 5 (☎93 317 10 87). M: Catalunya. From Pl. de Catalunya, go down Las Ramblas and take the 1st right onto C. Tallers; C. Sitges is the 1st left. The most touristed tavern in town. Gossip (in English) about your European backpacking romp over foosball and huge pitchers of *sangría*. Pitchers of

Jamboree, Pl. Reial

Pool at La Oveja Negra

Beer at La Oveja Negra

ABSINTHE MINDED

Step inside the old-fashioned bars of El Raval and you are likely to find daredevils sipping *absenta*, the translucent golden firewater banned everywhere except Spain and the Czech Republic. This licorice-flavored alcohol comes from the ajenjo plant and is said to have hallucinogenic affects similar to peyote. Once France's national drink, 150-proof absinthe used to be all the rage among Impressionist painters and the Parisian bourgeoisie. Supposedly, the death of artist Paul Gauguin (and the discovery of more than 200 bottles of the stuff under his bed) prompted France to put an end to the party and call for absinthe abstinence.

Spain chose not to follow suit, however, and the drink is still available in a safer 100-proof. Served with a bottle of water, a sugar cube, and a small spoon, there is a certain method to the madness. First, soak the sugar cube in the flammable alcohol. Then, holding the cube in the spoon, light the sugar on fire, repeating as necessary, until the sugar has melted and can be stirred into the drink. The water serves either to dilute the strong-tasting drink, or as a chaser if you choose to take it straight up. Though hardly hallucinogenic, the drink can still do a number on the drinker, creating a detached, spaced-out feeling and causing memory loss. Sage bartenders warn that even two absinthes may end your night early, and that three or more can be, as our humble Let's Go researchers discovered, "bad news."

beer 1000ptas/€6, of *sangría* 1500ptas/€9. Open M-Th 9am-2:30am, F 9am-3:30am, Sa-Su 5pm-3am.

London Bar, C. Nou de la Rambla 34 (☎93 302 26 80). M: Liceu, off of Las Ramblas. Rub shoulders with unruly, fun-loving expats at this smoky Modernist tavern, around since 1910. Live music nightly, usually rock or blues. Beer 400ptas/€2,40; wine 300ptas/€1,80; absinthe 500ptas/€3. Open F-Sa 7pm-5am, Su, Tu-Th 7pm-3am. Closed M.

(El Café que pone) Muebles Navarro, Riera Alta 4-6 (☎907 18 80 96). Friends get friendlier as they snuggle on huge, comfy couches. Beer and wine 300ptas/€1,80. Mixed drinks 600-800ptas/€3,60-€4,80. Snacks 225-600ptas/€1,30-€3,60. Open Tu-Th 6pm-1am, F-Sa 6pm-2:30am.

Casa Almirall, C. Joaquim Costa, 33. A cavernous space with a decaying ceiling and weathered couches, the laid-back Casa Almirall is Barcelona's oldest bar. The staff will walk you through your first glass of *absenta* (absinthe; 500ptas/€3)—and cut you off after your second. (See **Absinthe Minded,** p. 152.) Beer 300ptas/€1,50, mixed drinks 600-800ptas/€3,80-4,90. Open daily 7pm-3am.

The Quiet Man, Marqués Barbera 11 (☎93 412 12 19). M: Liceu. Take C. Unió off Las Ramblas; after 2 blocks it becomes Marqués Barbera. As authentic an Irish pub as you'll find in Barcelona, with a homey decor, a good collection of Beleek (fine Irish china), and a warm Irish staff. Live music (traditional Irish or, surprisingly, jazz) F and Sa nights at midnight. Pints of imported drafts 650ptas/€3,90, bottles 550/€3,30; mixed drinks 850ptas/€5,10. Open daily 6pm-3am.

Moog, Arc del Teatre 3 (☎93 301 72 82). M: Drassanes, off of Las Ramblas, down the alley next to the Easy Everything internet center. One of the centers of the emerging BCN techno scene. Serious fans pack this small club for a late-night dose of hard electonica. Regular appearances by major International DJ's, especially on W nights. Cover and drink 2000ptas/€12, before 2am (with flyer given out on Las Ramblas) 1200ptas/€7,20. Beers 600ptas/€3,60, mixed drinks 1100ptas/€6,60. Open nightly, 12am-5am; most don't show up until 2 or 3. Upstairs, a lighter atmosphere, gay-straight mixed crowd, and 70's disco music distinguish **Villarosa,** open Tu-Su 1-5am.

Rita Blue, Pl. Sant Agustí 3, C. Hospital (☎93 342 40 86), off Las Ramblas. It's not clear why Rita is blue, considering the excellent live music at her restaurant/bar. Range of live music to suit many tastes at the downstairs level, plays W-Su nights (11pm). Lineup varies, but W is "World Music" night (tango, salsa, etc.), and Th nights are set aside for jazz. Other nights, expect DJs, poetry slams, and a few surprises. Beer 400ptas/€2,20, mixed drinks 700ptas/€4,10 and up. Open Th-Sa 6pm-3am; Su-W 6pm-2am.

La Confiteria, Sant Pau 128 (☎93 443 04 58). M: Universitat, at the corner of Rda. Sant Pau. At this former bakery, happily chatting customers have replaced the cookies and cakes on display in its large windows. Wood panels and soft frescoes decorate its classic, well-lit bar. Step into the back room for a decidedly more modern feel, with additional tables and rotating art and photography exhibits. Beer and wine 300ptas/€1,80, mixed drinks 700-800ptas/€4,20-4,80. *Tapas* 500-800ptas/€3-4,80.

Raval-Bar, C. Doctor Dou 19 (☎93 902 41 33). No matter how tired or stressed, locals come here to sit with friends, listen to music, and waste their night away on huge U-shaped couches. Beer 350ptas/€2,20, wine 250ptas/€1,50. Open Su-W 8pm-2:30am, F-Sa 8pm-3am.

Marsella Bar, C. Sant Pau 65 (☎93 442 72 63) M: Liceu. Follow C. Sant Pau off Las Ramblas to the corner of Sant Ramon. Enjoying a drink in a nineteenth-century tavern must have felt a lot like this. Religious figurines grace the dark wood-paneled walls of this weathered watering-hole; hopefully they're watching over the adventurous *absenta* drinkers (500ptas/€3). Beers 300ptas/€1,80, mixed drinks 700ptas/€4,20.

Acido Oxido, C. Joaquim Costa 61 (☎93 412 09 39). M: Universitat, first left off of Rda. Sant Antoni. Caters to a gay cliental. Order beers (1000ptas/€6, 1 drink minimum) from a briefs-clad bartender as you saddle up to the bar. Where some bars opt for sports or sitcoms on the bar TV, the Acido showcases hardcore gay porn videos, while patrons dance on the small dance floor in the back. Mixed drinks 1000-1200ptas/€6-7,60. Open Su-Th 6pm-9:30am, F-Sa 6pm-10:30am.

CLUBS

La Paloma, Tigre 27 (☎93 301 68 97). M: Universitat. With its elegant, theater-like interior, huge dance floor, and balcony seating, one would never guess that this dance hall was originally a factory (until its 1903 conversion to the Paloma of today). Live salsa and popular Spanish music keeps its more mature clientele dancing late into the night. Younger crowd on weekend, when the club turns into "Bongo Lounge," a raging dance scene. Dress well. Cover with drink 700ptas/€4,20. Drinks 700ptas/€4,20 each. DJ Th-F, live music Sa-Su. Open Th-Sa 6-9:30pm and 11:30pm-5:30am, Su 6-9:30pm.

L'EIXAMPLE

see map pp. 314-315

L'Eixample is a neighborhood known for acceptance of character, and there is a wide variety of nightlife options available here; from twentysomethings to gays (see p. 150), there is a place for everyone here. Most of the biggest and best *discotecas* are outside the tourist-heavy Ramblas area—these are where most natives do their dancing. Most of the places worth trekking to are located in the western l'Eixample Esquerra, although a few are scattered on the right side. The part of l'Eix-

El Café que pone Muebles Navarro

Casa Almirall

Raval Bar

153

BEER!

Barcelona beer-drinkers have been Dammed to an eternity of mediocre to sub-par beers, thanks to a near monopoly of the Damm brewing company. Barcelona's biggest brewery produces **Estrella Damm,** the default beer at nearly every bar in the city, often the only choice on tap. If you want to drink cheaply, get used to this somewhat bitter pilsner. Other less common variants include Voll-Damm, a 7.2% alcohol beast of a beer, and just plain Damm.

Of local beers, **San Miguel** is perhaps the best option, a bit smoother than its Damm counterparts. One can occasionally order southern Spanish beers such as **Cruzcampo,** which at least assure Barcelona drinkers that they're not missing much. **Heineken,** which has a brewery in Sevilla, is by far the most common import, with the Mexican **Corona** (here called *Coronita*) also a favorite. Perhaps spurred on by the uninspiring Spanish beer selection, the city has a surprising number of expat pubs, where one can always find a good pint of **Guinness.**

ample Esquerra (west of Pg. de Gràcia) between C. Urgell, C. Aragó, the Gran Via, and C. Aribau is dense with gay nightlife.

BARS

La Fira, C. Provença 171 (☎658 84 04 15). M: Hospital Clinic or FGC: Provença. A bar like no other, La Fira is a hodgepodge collection of fun house and circus castaways. Bartenders pour drinks under the big top for a hip crowd reclining in red pleather booths or dangling from carousel swings. Creepy fun house mirrors and laughing clowns complete the picture. DJs spin a mix of funk, disco, and oldies. Open M-Th 10pm-3am and F-Sa 10pm-4:30am.

Dietrich, C. Consell de Cent 255 (☎93 451 77 07). M: Pg. de Gràcia. A rather unflattering painting of Marlene Dietrich in the semi-nude greets a mostly gay crowd. Bartenders are scantily clad, and at 1am you can see even more flesh when the nightly drag/strip show begins. Trendy partiers crowd in to be part of the action. Beer 500ptas/€3. Drinks 800-1000ptas/ €4,80-6. Open Su-Th 10:30pm-2:30am and F-Sa 10:30pm-3:30am.

Fuse, C. Roger de Llúria 40 (☎93 301 74 99), between C. Gran Via and C. Diputació. M: Tetuán or Pg. de Gràcia. A cutting-edge Japanese-Mediterranean restaurant, cocktail bar, dance club, and Internet cafe all in one. Glass and metal tables and chairs, a long bar, and a techno and electronic dance floor with riser seating for people-watching. Mixed gay and straight crowd in their 20s. Beer 400ptas/€2,40. Restaurant open M-Sa 8:30pm-1am (3 courses with wine 4000-5000ptas/€24-30). Bar/club open Th-Sa 1-3am. Drinks 1000ptas/€6. MC/V.

The Michael Collins Irish Pub, Pl. Sagrada Família 4 (☎93 459 19 64). M: Sagrada Família, directly across the plaça from the church. Popular among locals in their late 20s and 30s. 100% Irish, from the waitstaff to the smoky, wooden decor. Pub food Sept.-June 1-8pm (sandwiches 500ptas/€3). American and European sports on the TV. Live music Th-Su after 11pm (Irish, local guitarists, covers of American rock). Pint of Guinness 600ptas/€3,60. Bottled beer 400ptas/€2,40. Drinks 800ptas/€4,80. Open daily 1pm-3am. Cash only.

Les Gens que J'Aime, C. València 286 (☎93 215 68 79), just off Pg. de Gràcia. M: Pg. de Gràcia. A dark, Modernist basement hangout dripping with chandeliers, mirrors, old paintings, plush corner sofas, and arm chairs. Background soul, funk, and jazz plays to a crowd of thirty-somethings. Beer 475ptas/€3. Drinks 800ptas/€4,80. Mini-bottles of wine 1350ptas/ €8,10. Open daily Su-Th 7pm-2:30am, F-Sa 7pm-3am. Cash only.

domèstic, C. Diputació 215 (☎93 453 16 61). M: Urgell. Multifaceted *bar-musical* with frequent poetry readings, art expositions, and live music. If all that seems too ambitious, it's also a fine place to just sit and have a drink. Artsy too-cool-for-capital-letters crowd takes in funk, acid jazz, and soul rhythms on domèstic's overstuffed red chairs. Small offering of eclectic Mediterranean food (dishes 500-1300ptas/ €3-7,80). Beer 350ptas/€2. Drinks 800ptas/€4,80. Open Tu-Th and Su 8pm-2:30am and F-Sa 8pm-3am.

berlin, C. Muntaner 240 (☎93 200 65 42). M: Diagonal. A slice of streamlined German style in Barcelona. Corner bar with marble accents and exposed light bulbs attracts area hipsters and hordes of l'Eixample yuppies. Beer 300-400ptas/€1,80-2,40. Drinks 600-800ptas/€3,61-4,80.

Topxi, C. València 358 (☎93 207 01 20), just off Pg. St. Joan. M: Verdaguer. A small, unpretentious bar/ club that just happens to put on some of the most flamboyant drag queen shows in the city—in close, intimate quarters. Daily shows at 2am, plus a sit-down show Su at 8pm. Mostly gay, but some women and straight couples as well. Cover 1000ptas/€6 for men, 1500ptas/€9 for women (includes 1 drink). Open Tu-Th 11pm-5am, F-Sa 11pm-6am, Su 7pm-5am. Cash only.

Beer at Pl. Pi

Caligula, C. Consell de Cent 257 (☎93 451 48 92). M: Pg. de Gràcia. Gay bar invokes a romantic, atmosphere with draped fabrics, tea lights, and massive floral arrangements. Chill crowd gathers around bar and sidewalk tables. Look out for a hot pink poodle! Beer 600-800ptas/€3,60-4,80. Drinks 1000ptas/ €6. Open daily 10pm-3am.

The Pop Bar, C. Aribau 103 (☎93 451 29 58). M: Hospital Clinic or FGC: Provença. Groovy baby, yeah! Join a hip crowd and travel back in time to the early 60s, when orange and brown was a cool color combination. DJs spin house and pop, as well as the requisite 60s tunes. Beer 500-600ptas/€3-3,60. Drinks 800ptas/€4,80. Open Tu-Sa 10pm-3:30am.

Aloha, C. Provença 159 (☎93 451 79 62). M: Hospital Clinic or FGC: Provença. Barcelona's Hawaiian paradise—complete with exotic caged birds, leis, and plenty of bamboo. Pool table and wide liquor selection. Try the *coco loco,* coconut milk and rum (1000ptas/€6). Second drinks are half price. Open Su-Th 6pm-3am and F-Sa 6pm-4am.

Cava at Xampanyet

La Filharmónica, C. Mallorca 204 (☎93 451 11 53). M: Hospital Clinic, FGC: Provença. English pub hosts live music (jazz, tango, blues, country) almost every night, and is a popular place for both young and old. Don't miss the country line dance classes Su and Tu nights. Daily *menú* 1300ptas/€7,80. Sunday's special is roast beef and potatoes. Pint of Guinness 600ptas/€3,61. Cocktails 800ptas/€4,80 and up. Live music cover 500-1000ptas/€3-6 (includes one drink). Open M-F 10am-3am, Sa-Su 11am-3am.

Let's Go, Av. Diagonal 337 (☎93 458 21 60), next to Pg. St. Joan. M: Verdaguer. They started out strong with the name choice, but seem to have lost their initial divine inspiration. Cheap beer is a draw (300ptas/€1,80). Foosball, pool, Spanish, and English pop music. Drinks 600-800ptas/€3,60-4,80. Open daily 6pm-3am. Cash only.

Absinthe

Beautiful Drag

Pl. del Sol

Van Gogh Bar

CLUBS

■ **Buenavista Salsoteca,** C. Rosselló 217 (☎93 237 65 28). FGC: Provença. Though the decorator is a bit heavy on the palm trees and neon, this over-the-top salsa club manages to attract a laid-back, mixed crowd. The music is irresistible and the dancers are not shy. Free salsa and merengue lessons W, and Th at 10:30pm. Free Su-Th; cover F-Sa 1500ptas/€9 (includes 1 drink). Open W-Th 11pm-4am, F-Sa 11pm-5:30am, Su 8pm-1am.

Salvation, Ronda de St. Pere 19-21, between C. Bruc and Pl. Urquinaona. M: Urquinaona. The place to come if you've sinned...and want to keep on sinning. A popular gay club with 2 huge dance floors and pounding house music. Su is a mixed crowd; F and Sa women have to have special passes, which they can request, midnight-3am at Dietrich (see p. 154) the night they want to go. Beer 700ptas/€4,20. Drinks 1200ptas/€7,20. Cover 1500ptas/€9 (includes 1 drink). Open F-Su midnight-6am.

La Boîte, Av. Diagonal 477 (☎93 419 59 50). M: Hospital Clinic, club is inside courtyard. More emphasis on dance than decor. Big names sometimes come to perform in this intimate disco setting. Live jazz, funk, and blues nightly midnight-2am. Drinks 700-1200ptas/€4,20-7,20. Music cover 1000-3500ptas/€6-21. Disco free entrance Su-Th after 2am, cover 1800ptas/€11 F-Sa after 2am (includes one drink). Open daily 11:30pm-5am.

Illusion, C. Lepanto 408 (☎93 247 36 00), right below M: Alfons X. A favorite destination of students and local kids in their 20s, this club is more happening in the winter than summer. Two dance rooms: house music in the main and salsa in the smaller. Go-go shows every 15min. or so, starting around 3am. Beer 600ptas/€3,60. Drinks 900ptas/€5,40. Must be 18+. Cover F 1000ptas/€6; Sa 1300ptas/€7,80; Su 1200ptas/€7,20. Open F midnight-5am, Sa 6-10pm (for 16+) and 12:30am-5:30am. Hosts a gay session ("T Dance") Su 7pm-midnight. Closed Aug. Cash only.

Satanassa, C. Aribau 27. M: Pg. de Gràcia. Dressed-down gay crowd dances up a storm in small *bar-musical* covered with candelabras and reliefs of naked men. All welcome. DJs spin funk, house, and pop. Drinks 500-800ptas/€3-4,80. Cover 1000ptas/€6 F-Sa only (includes 1 drink). Open Tu-Su midnight-3am.

Luz de Gas, C. Muntaner 246 (☎93 209 77 11). M: Diagonal. Chandeliers, gilded mirrors, and deep red walls set the mood in this hip, uptown club. Live music every night including the occasional big name jazz, blues, or soul performer like Branford Marsalis or Monica Green. After 1am, the chairs are folded up and the luxurious club becomes a high-class disco. Live music concerts from 2500ptas/€15; check the *Guía del Ocio* for listings. Beer 800ptas/€4,80. Drinks 800-1500ptas/€4,80-90. Open M-Sa 11pm-5am. Wheelchair accessible.

Aire (Sala Diana), C. València 236. M: Pg. de Gràcia. One of Barcelona's biggest and most popular lesbian clubs. Throngs of women crowd the multicolored dance floor, grooving to pop, house, and 80s classics. Women-only strip show from 7-10pm first Su of every month. Cover Su-F 500ptas/€3, Sa 1000ptas/€6 (includes one drink). Open Su-F 11pm-3am. Check out the Arena family's other gay discos: **Arena (Sala Classic)** at C. Diputació 233 plays 80s tunes; **Arena (Sala Dandy)** at Gran Via 593 pumps techno beats. The popular **Arena** at C. Balmes 32 is mostly for men, as is the more relaxed **Punto BCN** bar at C. Muntaner 63.

Sol, C. Villarroel 216 (☎93 237 86 58). M: Hospital Clinic or Diagonal. Party until the break of dawn with Barcelona's beautiful, uptown set. Downstairs disco plays pop and house, upstairs pool table and smaller, private disco. Drinks 800-1200ptas/€4,80-7,20. Cover 1500ptas/€9 (includes one drink). Open Th-Sa midnight-5:30am.

KGB, C. Alegre de Dalt 55 (☎93 210 59 06). M: Joanic. From the Metro, walk along C. Pi i Maragall and take the 1st left; to get a cab home, come back to Pi i Maragall. Loud rock and techno delivered to a mixed crowd of students and Soviet secret agents. Occasional live concerts 10pm-1am. Beer 500ptas/€3. Drinks 1000ptas/€6. Cover 1400ptas/€8,40 with 1 drink, 1800ptas/€10,80 with 2 drinks. Open F-Su 1-8am. Cash only.

Martin's, Pg. de Gràcia 130 (☎93 218 71 67), just before it turns into Gran de Gràcia. M: Diagonal. House and pop music in a dark, concrete dance room, with a pool table and a bar upstairs. Predominantly gay. Beer 650ptas/€3,90. Drinks 1000ptas/€6. Cover 1300ptas/€7,80 (includes 1 drink). Tu Bingo, Th Wheel of Fortune. Open daily midnight-5am. MC/V.

POBLE NOU

see map p. 321

If you want to party in Poble Nou, trade in your skimpy, clubbing outfit for something a little more grunge, brush up your foosball skills, and be prepared to indulge in some heavy metal with rebellious Spanish teens. This neighborhood is the place to be for alternative music and hard rock. Locals have put abandoned warehouses to good use in the blocks around M: Marina, and more than 20 bars and discos coexist within a few minutes of each other. The drinking here is remarkably cheap, and as the patrons are locals, not tourists, the crowd flow is the reverse of the rest of the city: packed during the school year and slower in the summer.

La Ovella Negra (Megataverna del Poble Nou), C. Zamora 78 (☎93 309 59 38). From M: Marina, walk 2 blocks along C. Almogàvers and turn right onto C. Zamora. This absolutely cavernous warehouse turned medieval tavern is the brother of La Oveja Negra in El Raval and is *the* place to come for the first few beers of the night, at a mere 300ptas/€1,80 per mug.

Fake Moustaches

Maremagnum at Night

Poble Espanyol at Night

RUTA DEL BACALAO

Spaniards pride themselves as the true party animals of Europe. Paris or London? Forget it; Spain puts them to shame in the nightlife department. Each Friday night teenage and twnetysomething Spaniards jump in their cars and drive off to the coast of Spain to begin La Ruta del Bacalao. Starting in such cities as Valencia or Gandia, people begin drinking, barhopping, and clubbing, gradually traveling up the coast and hitting the major coast cities. The partying continues all night long until they drop. But instead of heading home, these young partiers camp out on the beach and rest up during the day, so they can be well rested for another night of partying come sundown.

The all-weekend partying continues well through the weekend, until they hit the northernmost point of Spain, at which point they head home with a huge hangover. There is even a special drink associated with this tour of Spain: **agua de Valencia**, a mix of champagne, vodka, and lemon-flavored soda. You can check out the end of La Ruta at Tarragona (see p. 219).

Foosball games on the 2nd floor are nearly as intense as the real-life FCB/Real Madrid rivalry. Mixed drinks 550ptas/€3,31; filling *tapas* and *bocadillos* 300-500ptas/€1,80-3,01. Open Th-Su 5pm-3am, disco open Sept.-May, kitchen open until 12:30am. Wheelchair accessible. MC/V.

Razzmatazz, C. Pamplona 88 (☎93 320 82 00), 2½ blocks from M: Marina following C. Almogàvers. Another huge warehouse turned entertainment complex, with huge, strobe-lit dance floors and a few lounge areas. A 2-in-1 club: choose the front entrance for 3 rooms *or* the back entrance for 2; the entrances are not connected. Beer 400ptas/€2,40; drinks 800ptas/€4,81. Cover 1200ptas/€7,21, includes 1 drink. Open F, Sa, and holidays 1-5am. Not wheelchair accessible. MC/V.

DIXI 724, C. Pallars 97. Boasting cheap beer, a bizarre shark-turned-airplane hanging from the ceiling, and tons of space for college crowds. Open F-Su 6pm-3am.

Bar Coyote & Co., C. Pere IV 68. Offers a Western twist on the typical Spanish bar, complete with a poster of the Coyote Ugly girls. Open F-Su 6pm-3am.

Q3, C. Pere IV 49. A small heavy-metal haven, blasts Marilyn Manson. Open F-Sa 6pm-6am.

Boveda, C. Pallars 97. Boveda celebrates its impressive 10-year anniversary as a consistently popular club with loud, pounding dance beats. Open F-Sa 6pm-10pm and midnight-6am, Su 6pm-10pm.

Garatge Club, C. Pallars 195. You'll feel right at home when this club rolls up its graffiti-covered garage door to serve as a venue for hard rock concerts.

PORT OLÍMPIC

see map p. 321

Cinderella and the Port Olímpic have one thing in common: after midnight they become entirely different creatures. In contrast to the rest of Poble Nou, the Port Olímpic caters to tourists with money to burn. A long strip of single-room, side-by-side glitzy clubs fling open their doors in the port, and the once-peaceful walkway becomes a packed carnival of wild, skimpily dressed dance fiends and late-night eaters and drinkers (food options include McDonald's, Haägen-Daz, hotdog stands, and fish restaurants). Mixed drinks are expensive (1000-1200ptas/€6,01-7,21), but people seem to get enough to start table-dancing almost as soon as the doors open. **Pachito** is known for attracting exorbitantly dressed drag queens, while the **Kennedy Irish Sailing Club** (beer 700ptas/€4,21) is a popular haven for those who prefer pubbing to clubbing. There is no cover anywhere. If you don't like the music in one club, just shove your way outside and choose another; the range includes salsa, techno, hip-hop, and plenty of American pop. The entire complex is open 5pm-6am.

PASSEIG MARÍTIM

Just to the right of the port, facing the water, these establishments each have large buildings of their own and do charge cover.

Luna Mora, C. Ramón Trias Fargas, on the corner with Pg. Marítim. This lunar-themed, planetarium-like disco is by far the best place for late-night dancing on the beach. Two huge dance floors, one for salsa and one for house, and plenty of long couches. Beer 700-800ptas/€4,21-4,81, drinks 1000-1300ptas/€6,01-7,81. Th no cover, F-Sa 2000ptas/€12,02. "House couture session" F-Sa after 3:30am. Open Th-Sa 11:30pm-6am; the mostly local crowd doesn't arrive until 3am. Not wheelchair accessible.

Baja Beach Club, Pg. Marítim 34 (☎93 225 91 00). If Baywatch were a club, this would be it. When not platform-dancing, bikini-clad waitresses and shirtless muscle men serve drinks from coolers as patrons get their groove on amidst fake palm trees and a decorative speedboat. Indoor/outdoor restaurant and an ATM. Food served until 1am; entrees 1200-1700ptas/€7,21-10,22. Beers 300ptas/€1,80; drinks 600ptas/€3,61. Cover 2000ptas/€12,02; Su free for ladies, and free if you eat dinner. Open June-Sept. M-W 1pm-1am, Th and Su 1pm-5am, F-Sa 1pm-6am; Oct.-May M-W 1-5pm, Th-Sa 1pm-1am. Wheelchair accessible. MC/V.

Crazy Pianos, Pg. Marítim 32 (☎93 225 91 04). The Barcelona version of an international chain featuring live music on drums, keyboard, and fire-engine red grand pianos. Very tourist-oriented (mostly American music), but the song requests and sing-alongs can be a lot of fun. Also an indoor/outdoor restaurant with food daily 12:30pm-1am. Entrees 1500-3000ptas/€9,02-18,03. Beer 500-700ptas/€3,01-4,21. Cover 1200-3000ptas/€7,21-18,03, depending on the crowd, free with dinner. No sneakers. Live music M-Th 11:30pm-3am, F-Su 11:30pm-4am. Wheelchair accessible. MC/V.

El El, Pg. Marítim 36 (☎93 319 75 77). From the beach, hidden behind the Greek restaurant Dionisos; enter from above. Video screens, fog machines, colored strobe lights, and a lit-up raised dance floor. Beer 700ptas/€4,21. Drinks 800-1000ptas/€4,81-6,01. Cover 2500ptas/€15,03, includes 2 drinks; sometimes free if you eat dinner in Dionisos. Open July-Aug. daily midnight-6am, Sept.-June Th-Su midnight-6am. MC/V.

El Gran Casino, C. Marina 19 (☎93 225 78 78), under the fish. Minimum bets are quite low, despite the glam atmosphere. Entrance fee 750ptas/€4,51. Minimum bets for blackjack, American roulette, French roulette, craps, slots, and *punto banco* hover around 500ptas/€3,01. No sneakers. Passport ID required. An older crowd, mostly over 40. Open daily 1pm-5am. MC/V.

MAREMAGNUM

see map p. 322

Like Dr. Jekyll, Barcelona's biggest mall has more than one personality. By night, the waterfront shopping center transforms into an overwhelming tri-level maze of dance clubs, complete with escalators to cut down on navigating effort. Each club plays its own music, from pop to salsa to house, for crowds of international students, tourists, and the occasional Spaniard. Maremagnum is not the most "authentic" experience to be had in Barcelona, but it certainly is an experience. On those slower weekday nights or after bars close at 3am, this is the spot to hit. No one charges cover; clubs make their money off exorbitant drink prices. Catching a cab home can be a nightmare for bleary-eyed revelers. The Nitbus is one option (see p. 29); other adventurous souls get some coffee and croissants or *churros con chocolate* and wait for the Metro to re-open at 6am. All clubs are accessible by M: Drassanes and can be reached by walking to the ocean end of Las Ramblas and continuing over the ocean on La Rambla del Mar footbridge. What follows is just a taste of the salty nightlife that awaits.

Nayandei, top floor. Actually two clubs side by side: **Disco,** with scantily-clad go-go dancers and an open door policy, and **Boite,** slightly more exclusive, with a shoes/pants/decent shirt dress code. Whatever the outfit, both clubs play energetic dance-pop with a decidedly Latin flavor. Beer 800ptas/€4,80. Mixed drinks 1200ptas/€7,20. Open nightly 9pm-5am, Su 6pm-5am.

Star Winds, top floor. Pumping bass and non-stop house make this the choice of clubbers unable to stomach the cheesy pop or golden oldies playing elsewhere. Beer 800ptas/€4,80. Mixed drinks 1200ptas/€7,20. Open nightly 9pm-5am.

Mojito Bar (☎93 352 87 46), first floor. The windows of this *salsoteca* are often as crowded as the dance floor itself, as admirers gawk at the spectacular moves of dancers inside. All salsa and merengue attracts both truly excellent dancers and novices, who try valiantly to keep up. In the summer, salsa dance lessons M nights—call ahead for info and to sign up. Beer 700ptas/€4,20. Tropical drinks 1000ptas/€6. Open nightly 9pm-5am.

Irish Winds, top floor. Live Irish music entertains a mellow crowd, relaxing with their pints in this wood-paneled pub...is this really Maremagnum? A complete change of pace from the surrounding kooky club scene. Pints 600ptas/€3,60 and up. Live music F-Sa and M-W after midnight, Su after 8pm. Open M-Th 11pm-4am, F-Sa 11pm-5am, Su 8pm-4am.

Central Golf, top floor. The clubs upstairs surround this mini-golf course, a favorite drunken leisure activity. If you're seeing multiple holes, aim for the middle one. 800ptas/€5 per round. Open daily, 12pm-3am.

Fiesta, first floor. A mixed bag of hip-hop, pop, and oldies keep the full house dancing through the night. As crowded as it gets, which can be a blessing on early weeknights and a pain on weekends. Beer 900-1000ptas/€5,40-€6. Mixed drinks 1200ptas/€7,20 and up. Open M-Sa 9pm-5am, Su 6pm-5am.

MONTJUÏC

see map p. 320

BARS

🏿 **Tinta Roja,** C. Creu dels Molers 17 (☎93 443 32 43). M: Poble Sec. C. Creu dels Molers is 4 blocks down Av. Paral.lel, away from Montjuïc. An old factory that has been lovingly converted into a spectacle of Argentinian delights by owners and tango gurus Hugo and Carmen. Eclectically furnished with mirrors, deep red walls, and thrift-store leftovers, Tinta Roja is a multifaceted art space featuring tango dance and music shows (F-Sa 12:30am, 1800ptas/€10,90), tango lessons by Hugo himself (Tu 8:30-9:30pm, 3000ptas/€18 each), and a candle-lit bar offering *tapas* and Argentinian beer. Call ahead for show reservations. Open Tu-Th and Su 5pm-1am, F-Sa 5pm-3am.

🏿 **Mau Mau,** C. d'En Fontrodona 33 (☎60 686 06 17). M: Paral.lel. Follow C. d'En Fontrodona as it jogs right, past C. Blai. Look for a white door and ring the bell. Chill bar/lounge attracts a funky, young crowd who come to Mau Mau to talk, relax, and take in the jazz, hip hop, and funk beats. Mostly local crowd buys yearlong "membership" but out-of-towners need only sign in at the door. Drinks 500ptas/€3 and up. Open Th 11pm-2am, F-Sa 11:30pm-4:30am, Su 6-11:30pm.

Rouge, C. Poeta Cabanyes 21 (☎93 442 49 85). M: Paral.lel. Bathed in warm red light, Rouge is an über-hip bar/lounge with a clientele and a cocktail menu to match. Test out the Rouge Punch—rum, cane sugar, and lime (950ptas/€5,80) while the DJ/owner spins hip hop, electronica, jazz, and pop. Drinks 500-1000ptas/€3-6. Open Tu-Th 11pm-3am, F-Sa 11pm-5am.

CLUBS

🏿 **La Terrrazza/Discothèque,** Av. Marqués de Comillas (☎93 423 12 85). M: Espanya, in Poble Espanyol. Enter near the front gates of Poble Espanyol and shake it until the early morn in La Terrrazza's hip outdoor plaza. Barceloneses decked out in everything from Mango club wear to leather and chains groove to house beats and the occasional guest DJ. Same deal when the club heads inside (Oct.-May) and becomes *Discothèque*. Open Th-Su midnight-6am. Drinks 600-1200ptas/€3,60-7,20. Cover (includes 1 drink), Th 1800ptas/€10,90; F 2000ptas/€12 Sa 2500ptas/€15, 1500ptas/€9 Su.

🏿 **Torres de Ávila,** (☎93 424 93 09) next to the main entrance of Poble Espanyol. M: Espanya. A million-peseta construction that was at the height of club chic when it was built in the 80s. Still going strong as one of the city's hottest night spots—complete with glass elevators, 7 different bars, and a summertime rooftop terrace with gorgeous views of the city. DJs spin house and techno. Drinks 800-1400ptas/€4,80-8,40. Dress to impress. Cover (includes 1 drink) 2000ptas/€12. Open Th-Sa midnight-6:30 or 7am.

Club Apolo/Nitsaclub, C. Nou de la Rambla 113 (☎93 441 40 01). M: Paral.lel. Old 1950s dance hall hosts live music shows, usually reggae/rock/funk, and on F-Sa nights transforms into *Nitsaclub*, a hip hop/pop/soul extravaganza featuring a slew of international guest DJs.

Work it. Cover (includes 1 drink) 2000ptas/€12. Open midnight-6:30am.

Candela, C. Mexic 7-9. M: Espanya, parallel to Av. Reina María Cristina and close to Poble Espanyol. Brand new warehouse-style club is an un-touristed find featuring merengue and salsa rhythms. Occasionally has live music. Drinks 500-1500ptas/€3-9. Gets started late. No sneakers. Cover F-Sa 1000ptas/€6. Open F-Sa 11:30pm-5am, Su 8pm-late.

ZONA ALTA

GRÀCIA

see maps p. 318 & 319

After dark, local hipsters and alterna-kids are drawn to Gràcia like bees to honey. The scene is on the mellow side—groups and young couples converge on the area's many bars and crowd the plaças until well into the night, often accompanied by an amateur guitarist or two. Pl. Virreina and Pl. de Rius i Taulet have a variety of *tapas* bars and relaxed crowds. Pl. del Sol is the busiest place to party—try Sol Soler (☎ 93 217 44 40), Sol de Nit (☎ 93 237 39 37), and Cafe del Sol (☎ 93 415 56 63). All three are open daily until 2 or 3am.

BARS

■ **Gasterea,** C. Verdi 39.(☎ 93 237 23 43). M: Fontana. Follow C. Astúries for several blocks and make a right onto C. Verdi. Yellow walls cast a warm glow in this table-less bar. Grab a seat at one of the counters and dig in to Gasterea's selection of excellent, fresh *tapas* (150ptas/€1 each) like eggplant with herbed goat cheese. Su-Tu and Th 7:30pm-1am, F-Sa 7:30pm-2am.

Buda, C. Torrent de L'Olla 134 (☎ 65 884 48 64). M: Fontana. Follow C. Astúries and turn right on C. Torrent de L'Olla. Dungeon-esque bar with pool table and darts make Buda a chill spot to unwind. Beer 350ptas/€2, drinks 600ptas/€3,50. Open M-Th 9pm-2:30am, F-Sa 9pm-3am.

Flann O'Brien's, C. Casanova 264 (☎ 93 201 16 06). M: Diagonal. Authentic Irish pub with barrels for tables and rugby shirts hanging from the ceiling. Popular with Barcelona's English-speaking expats. Top off your evening with a Guinness or a mixed drink (400-850ptas/€2,50-5). Open daily 6pm-3am.

Casablanca, C. Bonavista 6 (☎ 93 237 63 99). M: Diagonal. Images of Rick and Ilsa beckon you to try one of Casablanca's *cava* (Catalan champagne) specialties, like the *Jalisco* with tequila and lemon juice (750ptas/€5)—in the plush, black marble and mirrored bar. Sophisticated crowd; dress accordingly. Open M-Th 6:45pm-2:30am, F-Sa 6:45pm-3:30am. MC/V.

Café de la Calle, C. Vic 11 (☎ 93 218 38 63) M: Fontana. Follow Gran de Gràcia downhill and turn right on

On the Rooftop at Torres de Ávila

Torres de Ávila

Mas i Mas

Trav. de Gràcia, then a left on the next block, C. Vic. A maze of rooms offers plenty of quiet places to converse at this gay- and lesbian-friendly bar. Rotating collection of art on the multicolored walls. Drinks 375-625ptas/€2,50-4. Open Su-Th 6pm-2am, F-Sa 6pm-3am.

Pirineus Bar, C. Bailen 244 (☎93 219 27 71). M: Joanic. A local bar with soul. Mixed crowd gathers here to watch Barça games or MTV on the big screen TV. *Tapas* 275-850ptas/€1,50-5; *menú del día* 1100ptas/€6,60. Open daily 7am-3am.

Blues Café, C. Perla 37 (☎93 416 09 65). M: Fontana. Follow C. Astúries to C. Verdi and turn right, walk 2 blocks to C. Perla, and turn left. Plastered with photos of blues legends. Plenty of cheap beer to go around (265ptas/€1,50). Open Su-Th 6:30pm-2am, F-Sa 6:30pm-3am.

Bahía, C. Seneca 12. M: Diagonal, walk uphill on Pg. de Gràcia and turn left on C. Seneca. Popular and funky lesbian-gay bar. Drinks 400-800ptas/€2,50-5; 500-1000ptas/€3-6 after 3:30am. All are welcome. Open Tu-Th 10pm-3am, F-Sa 10pm-9am.

CLUBS

Row, C. Roselló 208 (☎93 237 54 05). FGC: Provença. Trendy Spaniards and tourists alike converge on the multilevel, über-hip Row club, grinding to house and techno beats. The door policy leans toward snooty, so dress to impress. Cover 2000ptas/€12, drinks 500-800ptas/€3-5. Open W-Sa 11pm-5:30am.

Bamboleo, C. Topazi 24 (☎93 217 32 60) M: Fontana, above Pl. del Diamante. Cuban bar hosts salsa, techno, and rock DJs, and friendly, informal turns on the foosball table. Calimocho, mojitos, and piña coladas 600ptas/€3,50 each. Open M-Th 7pm-2:30am, F-Sa 7pm-3am.

LES CORTS

Up and Down, C. Numància 179, at Diagonal. M: Les Corts. This 2-in-1 club has something for the entire family. Thirtysomethings and above, dressed to the nines, live it up in the posh upstairs club. The kids head downstairs, where they get down to a mix of 80s and more recent pop. Beers at both 800ptas/€4,75; mixed drinks 1000ptas/€6. Jacket required. Hardly anyone goes downstairs before 3am. In the meantime, tons of young people wait it out across the street at **Green's Snack Cafeteria,** where they down 2-for-1 stiff drinks (600ptas/€6,60) until happy hour ends at 2:30am. Up: cover 2500ptas/€15, Open Tu-Sa 12am-6am. Down: cover 1500ptas/€9. Open Th-Sa 12am-6am.

SARRIÀ

A fairly tame neighborhood after dark, Sarrià lags behind its neighbors when it comes to nightlife. For low-key hangouts with just as much fun as downtown, try these spots on Major de Sarrià.

Caffe San Marco, C. Pedro de la Creu 15, on the corner of C. Major de Sarrià. Sarrià's version of an old-fashioned ice cream shop, complete with elaborate glass chandeliers and tasteful pale green curtains. *Gelato* 215ptas/€1,29 per cone; coffees and teas served as well. Open M-F 7:30am-9:30pm, Sa-Su 9:30am-8pm.

Antic Café, C. Major de Sarrià 97. Sparsely decorated bar/cafe caters to a hip, youngish crowd at night. Beer 200-300ptas/€1,20-1,80; mixed drinks 200-600ptas/€1,20-3,61. Open daily 10am-2am.

TIBIDABO

In the Pl. Dr. Andrey, **Mirablau** and **Mirabé** offer afternoon and nighttime drinks. Mirablau boasts a long bar with views of the city, a downstairs disco, and small *tapas* for the hungry. (☎93 418 58 79. Drinks 1000-1200ptas/€6-7. Open daily 11am-5am. AmEx/MC/V.) Next door up the hill, Mirabé has an elegant, romantic outdoor patio with a small illuminated pool. (☎93 418 56 67. Drinks 1000-1200ptas/€6-7. Open M-Sa 7pm-3am, Su 5pm-3am.) Dark, sultry **Meybeyé** opens for drinks and *tapas* from 11am to 7pm and from midnight to 3am. (☎93 417 92 79. Drinks 500-700ptas/€3-4 during the day, around 1000ptas/€6 at night.) On the way down the hill, **Partycular** draws a slightly younger crowd into an old mansion for dancing and drinks and **L'Atlantida,** a private club, hoards its views for members only.

CLUBS ELSEWHERE IN ZONA ALTA

The area around C. de Marià Cubí is always a safe bet for some fun nightlife, with its eclectic mix of late-night cafes, bars, and clubs, although they are all a substantial walk from FCG: Muntaner (hey, that's why taxis were invented). The following listings are some of this area's happenin' spots.

Otto Zutz, C. Lincoln 15 (☎93 238 07 22). FGC: Pl. Molina. Walk downhill on Via Augusta and take C. Lincoln when it splits off to the right. The place to see and be seen. Well-heeled Spaniards groove to house, hip hop, funk, and rap beats while Japanimation lights up the top floor. 9 bars. Occasionally has live music. 2500ptas/€15 cover includes 1 drink, but look for Otto Zutz cover discount cards at bars and upscale hotels all over the city. Open Tu-Sa midnight-6:30am.

Lizard, C. Plató 15 (☎93 414 00 32). FGC: Muntaner. Walk uphill on C. Muntaner 2 blocks and turn right on C. Plató. A spectacular iguana greets you from its glass cage at the entrance to Otto Zutz's sister club. One large red-lit dance floor bordered by 2 bars. DJs spin rap, hip-hop, and funk. No cover, drinks approx. 800ptas/€5. Open Th-Sa midnight-3:30am.

Bar Marcel, C. Santaló 42 (☎93 209 89 48), at C. de Marià Cubí. Before midnight, this enormously popular bar masquerades as a quiet, unassuming cafe. But when the clock strikes 12, locals *pack* the place in search of cheap drinks. Certainly not the fanciest bar in the neighborhood, but quite possibly the most loved. Coffee 200ptas/€1,20. *Tapas* 175-500ptas/€1,10-3. Beers 300ptas/€1,80, mixed drinks 400-500ptas/€2,40-3. Open Su-W 8am-2am, Th-Sa 8am-3am.

Mas i Mas, C. de Marià Cubí 199 (☎93 209 45 02), at C. Sagues. The friendly bartenders seem to enjoy working almost as much as the patrons love hanging out. This small, simply decorated bar gets cramped, but that just adds to the fun. DJ/bartender spins hip-hop and pop when not serving up beers (450ptas/€2,70) and mixed drinks (750ptas/€4,50). Open daily 7pm-2:30am.

Universal, C. Sagues 42, at C. de Marià Cubí. A slightly older crowd frequents Universal, where the steep drink prices make up for the lack of cover. The party begins at the bar downstairs, and continues above with plenty of dancing to English and Spanish language pop hits. Beers 800ptas/€4,75, mixed drinks 1000ptas/€6. No cover. Open M-Sa midnight-5am.

Entertainment

Barcelona offers a wide range of entertainment, from outdoor activities, sports, and bull-fights to shopping, cinema, festivals, and performances of all sorts. Consult the invaluable **Guía del Ocio,** 125ptas/€0,75 at newsstands, for info on movies (*Cine*), live concerts, (*Música*), nightlife (*Tarde/Noche*), and cultural events. While Barcelona proper has almost everything you could desire, those truly interested in outdoor activities should be sure to peruse our **Daytrips** chapter (see p. 187) for information on nearby beaches, mountain hikes, ski resorts, and other outdoor sports.

BEACHES

POBLE NOU

🔲 *Beach info* ☎ *93 481 00 53. Dogs, camping tents, motorcycles, soap, music, and restaurant food are not allowed on the beaches. Police, the Red Cross, and information are available on the promenade between Nova Icària and Bogatell, and at Nova Mar Bella, June 18-Sept.15, 10am-7pm. Only Mar Bella and Nova Mar Bella are fully wheelchair accessible.*

The beaches to the north of Port Olímpic (left, facing the water) include Platja Nova Icària, Platja del Bogatell, Platja Mar Bella, and Platja Nova Mar Bella (from the port to Nova Mar Bella is about a 20min. walk). Each of them has a lifeguard, shower stations, a restaurant on the walkway above the sand, and a refreshment stand on the beach. There is usually someone selling sunbathing chairs (500ptas/€3,01 per day) on Nova Icària, and people often bring volleyball nets and balls to the shore. Tops are very optional for female sunbathers, particularly at Mar Bella. The beaches are clean and safe for public use. Small coin-operated lockers are available at the Nova Mar Bella public bathrooms from 11am to 5pm (100ptas/€0,60).

WE'RE IN THE CHAM- PIONS, MY FRIENDS

Well, every great team needs an occasional dry spell, to make the successes seem all the more sweet. And at the moment, Barça is in the midst of a dry spell which has many of its fans choking on their *chorizo*. The team has struggled, winning no major cups in the past two seasons (2000 and 2001), and has had several coaching changes since the late 1990s. In 2001, Barça played poorly enough that the club nearly didn't qualify for the Champions' League, the league of the top clubs from all over Europe who play the following season for the European Cup. For *barceloni-stas*, devotees of the bur-gundy and blue, this would have been the ultimate embarrassment, signaling the disappearance of the team from the elite company of Europe's clubs. With one game left to qualify and a win needed in their last Spanish League game of 2001, the brilliant Brazilian star Rivaldo scored a hat trick against Valencia for a 3-2 win. His third goal of the match came in the 89th minute on a miraculous, seemingly impos-sible bicycle kick that saved an otherwise mediocre sea-son (a "miserable" 4th place finish out of 20 teams). With their inclusion into the 2002 Champion's League, hope remains in this football-mad city for Barça to return to the glory days of success long, long ago—as in 1992.

BARCELONETA

🚇 M: Barceloneta or any "Pgt Marítim" bus route. For daily information on the city's beaches, call 93 48 100 53. Police, Red Cross, and information services are all available in a booth behind the outdoor showers, open 10am-7pm.

Barceloneta's two main beaches, Platja San Sebastià and Platja Barceloneta, are the neigh-borhood's biggest draw, having been cleaned up and readied for public use during the Olympics. In the summer, natives and tourists alike flock to the area for a daily dose of sun and swim. One of the city's longest stretches of sand, San Sebastià is the beach at the end of Pg. Joan de Borbo, far-thest from the Port Vell area. On weekends in particular, the center area near the entrance is the most crowded of all. Venture farther afield for a less congested area. Open space does have its price—be prepared for some hardcore nudity. Toplessness is common on all the city beaches, but people begin to lose their bottoms as well toward the nether regions of San Sebastià. The exposed beach bums of San Sebastià prefer sunbathing over leisure sports, so bring your volleyball elsewhere.

The central beach on the Barceloneta penin-sula is Platja Barceloneta, which leads up to Port Olímpic and Frank Gehry's famous copper **Peix** (Fish) sculpture. Another public sculpture is **Homage to Barceloneta** by Rebecca Horn, which resembles a teetering stack of children's blocks. The proximity to the park and the recent con-struction of a pedestrian walkway along Pg. Marítim is sure to bring even more people to this already popular beach.

WATERFRONT ACTIVITIES

For those who would rather be active than lie in the sun, there are several options in the Vila Olímpica area, both on water and land. Boating and beach sports abound, and the coastal bike path runs about 4km in total length. Below is a list of beach clubs with different waterfront options, including plenty of nighttime beach-front fun.

BOAT TOURS

Las Golondrinas, Portal de la Pau (☎93 442 31 06). M: Drassanes, at the foot of the Monument a Colom, in the **Port Vell.** 2-decker ferries chug around the entire Port Vell, as far as Montjuïc and back. (35min.; July-Aug. daily every 35min. 11:30am-7:30pm, Sept.-June every hr. M-F noon-6pm and Sa-Su noon-7:30pm; 525ptas/€3,16, children 275ptas/€1,65.) A longer excursion includes a **tour of Port Olímpic.** (1½hr.; July-Aug. daily every 45min. 11:30am-

7:30pm, Sept.-June 3 per day 11am-4:30pm; round-trip 1325ptas/€7,90, seniors and students 950ptas/€5,70, kids ages 4-10 575ptas/€3,50.)

WATERSPORT RENTALS

Scenic, C. Marina 22 (☎93 221 66 66), on the right, facing away from the water, a short ways up C. Marina. Rents roller blades, scooters, and bicycles for 750ptas/€4,51 per hr., 2000ptas/€12,02 per half-day, or 2500ptas/€15,03 per day. (Students are usually given 2hr. for the price of 1.) Group tours every Tu and Th night, consisting of a bike ride through the Barri Gòtic and a catamaran ride with food and music (9pm-midnight; 2000ptas), as well as kayak trips once a month and other variable group tours. Call and ask what's coming up next. Open daily 10:30am-2pm and 4-9pm. AmEx/MC/V.

Beach near Olympic Port

Base Náutica de Mar Bella, Platja Mar Bella (☎93 221 04 32; www.basenautica.net). The Mar Bella nautical base offers classes in windsurfing (13,600ptas/€81,60 for 10hrs.), catamaran sailing (17,500ptas/€105,18 for 16hr.), sailboat sailing (23,200ptas/€139,43 for 16hr.), kayaking (8,500ptas/€51,09 for 10 hr.), diving and navigation (different prices for different categories). Membership brings a 30% discount for all courses and costs 22,500ptas/€135,23 per year. The base also rents kayaks, windsurfing boards, catamarans, and sail-boats by the hour and leads group kayaking, sailing, and catamaran trips; ask at the desk for details. Non-members 1000-4500ptas/€6,01-2705 per hr.; members 300-2700ptas/€1,80-16,23 per hr. Open M-F 10am-8pm.

Barceloneta Beach from Above

Centre Municipal de Vela, Moll de Gregal Port Olímpic (☎93 225 79 40, fax 93 224 39 06; www.vela-barcelona.com; cmv@fcv.es). In the left corner of the port as you walk toward the water, lower level. Like the nautical base, the municipal sailing center offers lessons in windsurfing, sailing, and navigation for children and adults, as well as member services including saunas and massages. A more expensive, elite option than the nautical base, with too many different offerings to list here; check the website or pick up an informational newsletter at the front desk. Open daily 10am-7pm.

OLYMPIC FACILITIES

For more facilities, see the list of gyms at the end of **Other Diversions** (p. 172)

HORTA & VALL D'HEBRON

Originally the Olympic cycling center, the **Velo-dróm** has since been converted into a community sports center. Annual membership is the only way to gain access; if you are interested, visit the

IMAX Port Vell

kids
IN THE CITY

Family Fun

Here are some more suggestions for activities that can
entertain families traveling
with children:

Biking: see **p. 169**.

Bowling: see **p. 171**.

Horseback riding:
see p. 170.

Movies: see p. 176.

Soccer Games:
see p. 168 for FCB or p. 172
for a cheaper option.

Swimming:
see p. 168 for pools and p.
168 for beaches.

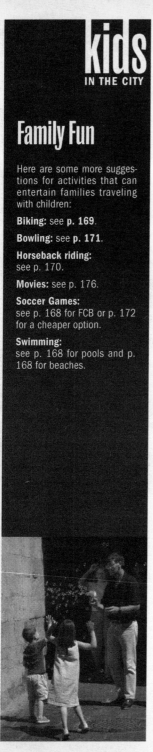

offices at entrance 16 (up and around to the right
of the building). Facilities include a space for
parties on the roof, soccer fields, basketball
courts, the cycling track, a snack bar, and organized tournaments. (Pg. Vall d'Hebron 185-201.
Face the Jardins Pedro Muñez Seco upon leaving
M: Montbau, turn left, cross the Ronda de Dalt at
the first opportunity and turn left; the Velodróm
will be ahead on your right. ☎93 427 91 42. Open
M 4-11pm, Tu-F 4-6pm and 8:30-11pm. Yearly
dues 6000ptas/€36. Not wheelchair accessible.)

Also left over from the 1992 Olympics are the
Centre Municipal de Tennis and **Centre Muncipal
d'Esports.** The tennis center offers playing
courts and a pool to members, and non-members can pay per visit to use the pool. (Pg. de
Vall d'Hebron 178. Same directions as Velodróm,
but the tennis center will be on the left. ☎93 427
55 00. Monthly membership 3670-6990ptas/€22-
42, plus 5500ptas/€33 joining fee. Pool 1000ptas/
€6 per day; under 12 600ptas/€3,50. Wheelchair
accessible.) The municipal sports center has a
variety of facilities, including a gym, pool, racquetball, yoga, and more. (Pg. Vall d'Hebron 166;
same directions as center. ☎93 428 39 52. Open
M-F 7am-11:30pm, Sa 9am-8pm, Su 9am-3pm.
Monthly dues 3100-4000ptas/€18-24. Single use
900ptas/€5,50; children and over 65 625ptas/
€3,50. Wheelchair accessible.)

MONTJUÏC

SOCCER GAMES

The **Estadi Olímpic de Montjuïc** hosts soccer
games for Barcelona's second beloved team,
R.C. Deportivo Espanyol, for **free;** see p. 172
for details on this economical alternative to the
Fútbol Club Barcelona.

SWIMMING

Piscines Bernat Picornell, Av. Estadi 30-40 (☎93
423 40 41; fax 93 426 78 18; www.bcn.es/picor-
nell), to the right when facing the stadium. Test your
swimming mettle in the Olympic pools—two gorgeous
facilities nestled in stadium seating. A favorite for
families and sunbathers. 700ptas/€4 for outdoor
pool, 1300ptas/€7,80 for workout facilities including
sauna, massage parlor, and gym. Outdoor pool open
M-Sa 9am-9pm and Su 9am-8pm. Workout facilities
open M-F 7am-midnight, Sa 7am-9pm and Su
7:30am-8pm.

THE GREAT
OUTDOORS

The Collserola mountains at Barcelona's back
door make for a great outdoors resource: hiking,
biking, picnicking, and horseback riding abound

in its moderate peaks. For other outdoor activities, such as skiing in the Pyrenees or hiking holy Montserrat, see **Daytrips,** p. 187.

PARC DE COLLSEROLA

The **Centro d'Informació,** (Carretera de l'Església 92; ☎ 93 280 35 52; open daily 9:30am-3pm except Dec. 25-26 and Jan. 1 and 6.) has all the information you'll need on activities in the park (see p. 101. The main map (available in English) plots major roads and services in the park; the staff can advise you on various facilities and options in the park.

HIKING

The information center provides numerous useful guides to hiking paths in the park. For those who want to stay close to home, there are five hikes, marked with red, yellow, orange, blue, and purple, which start and end at the center itself. One of these, the red path to the **Font de la Buderella** (Buderella Spring), is an easy hike to the Torre de Collserola, Tibidabo, or the town of Vallvidrera. (At the top of the hill after passing the spring, once the tower is in sight, stay to the right of the house and continue straight along the road; at the intersection with C. Alberes, turn right and head downhill to get to Vallvidrera or up the dirt hill to the left for the tower and Tibidabo.) The full walk from the information center to Vallvidrera or the tower takes a bit over an hour. To continue from the tower to Tibidabo will take another five to ten minutes; just walk uphill along the aptly named C. de Vallvidrera al Tibidabo. For more in-depth hiking in the park, the *Parc de Collserola Guide Book* lists five hikes which traverse large portions of the park and begin and end with public transportation. Separate guided tours for children, teens, and adults are also available for 13,000ptas/€78 per person, or you can arrange a unique itinerary with a guide and negotiate the price (some guides do speak English).

BIKING

Biking in the park is limited to the wider paths, but there are plenty of them. Ask at the information center for the Catalan only (but easy to understand) *Itineraris en Bicycleta* (500ptas/€3), a pamphlet with maps and descriptions of seven popular bike routes. There is no longer a bike rental shop near the park; you will have to rent one downtown and bring it up on an FGC train (see **Bike Rentals,** p. 290). Fortunately, most FGC stations are equipped with escalators and ramps along the stairwells. One of the most popular paths for biking and jogging in the area, though not very far into the park, is

Balancing an Egg on the Fountain

Dancing in the Dark

Picornell Olympic Pool

NO BULL

The average tourist leaves his first bullfight after only 2 of 6 bulls have been killed, but as fewer and fewer Spaniards attend *corridas* (bullfights), these inquisitive travelers are playing an increasingly important role in the economic survival of the sport. Anti-bullfighting sentiments among the native Spanish population are surprisingly strong. According to a 1992 survey by InterGallup S.A., 87% of Spaniards believe that it is wrong to make animals suffer for public entertainment or celebration, and 60% think that Spain has a bad reputation for its treatment of animals. Of those interviewed, 60% had not been to a single bullfight in the past decade, and more than 80% had not been even once in the past year. These numbers may be even higher in Catalunya, where there is no tradition of bullfighting and where the sport exists primarily to pacify tourists.

Formal anti-bullfighting groups could not form until Franco's anti-organization laws were lifted at his death, but the movement has since grown rapidly and is strongest in Barcelona. The international Anti-Bullfighting Campaign (ABC; www.adda-ong.org) organizes ringside protests at the first and last fight of the season in various cities, in addition to conducting ongoing political lobbies against the sport. It also circulates the *Bull Tribune* three times a year, in both English and Spanish.

the **Carretera de Aiges** (about 4km long). To get there, take the FGC from Pl. de Catalunya to the Peu del Funicular stop, catch the funicular, and press the request button to get out halfway up at C. de Aigües.

HORSEBACK RIDING

There are seven stables in the park, but most of them are far from public transportation access. One exception is the **Hípica Severino,** Pg. Calado 12, near the town of Sant Cugat. Guides here lead 1hr. trips every hour on the hour (10am-1pm and 4-7pm; ☎93 674 11 40. To get there, go to M: Lesseps and from there catch the A6 bus to Sant Cugat; get off at the Vasconcell stop, before reaching the Sant Cugat monastery. Call ahead to reserve a space. 1800ptas/€11.

SPECTATOR SPORTS

EL BARÇA

🚩 *The team plays at Camp Nou, on C. Aristides Maillol. ☎93 496 36 00; www.fcbarcelona.com. M: Collblanc. To get to the stadium from the Metro, head down C. Francese Layret and take the 2nd right onto Trav. de les Corts. A block later, a left will put you on C. Aristides Maillol, which leads to the ticket office and museum entrance (see **Museums,** p. 119). Tickets available for all club sport events. Ticket office open M-F (and the day before matches) 9:30am-1:30pm and 4:30-7:30pm.*

FÚTBOL CLUB BARCELONA

The term *Fútbol Club Barcelona*, FCB for short, refers to Barcelona's soccer team and their fervently devoted fan club (see **Life and Times,** p. 56). A visit to Camp Nou, home of FCB, can be compared to a religious experience for many fans. The team, commonly referred to as el Barça, has a motto of *"més que un club"* (more than a club), and it's easy to see why. El Barça is a symbol of Catalunya and its proud people, and the team carries the political agendas of the entire region (see **More than a Rivalry,** p. 56). The club has a devoted worldwide following, and boasts more than 100,000 members. Even the Pope, when visiting in 1982, signed the membership book and became an honorary member.

It's easy to forget that the FCB also has teams in several other sports, including basketball, rugby, and roller hockey, who play in other buildings in the Camp Nou complex, which includes a mini-stadium and the Palau Blaugrana (Blue-Burgundy Palace). The basketball team defeated Real Madrid for the 2001 championship of 2001, and its star, 7ft. tall Pau Gasol, is set to become both the first Catalan player in the NBA and the first Spaniard drafted in the top 10 picks of the NBA draft.

GETTING TICKETS

Inaugurated in 1957, Camp Nou stadium was expanded in 1982 to hold 120,000 for the World Cup, and today Camp Nou is Europe's largest football ground. However, getting tickets to a Barça match is not always easy; hardcore FCB fans already have tickets, leaving slim pickings for visitors. Matches usually take place on Sunday evenings at 9pm, and the bigger the match, the harder it is to get in. Tickets (*entradas*) are available at the ticket office and usually go on sale to the public the Thursday before the match. A number of scalpers also try to unload tickets in the days before the match, for copious amounts of cash. At the ticket office, expect to pay 5000-10,000ptas/€30-60, and bring your binoculars, as most available seats are on the third level. The seats may be in the nosebleed section, but even at that height, any Barça match is an incredible sports-spectating experience. The cheap seats offer a bird's eye view of the action and gorgeous views of the mountains of Tibidabo and Montjuïc. Even if you can't tell which player scored the goal, you'll have just as much fun celebrating it with 70,000+ newfound friends. For more on FCB, see **We're In the Champions, My Friends** (p. 166).

Football Stadium Camp Nou

BULLFIGHTING

Catalunya is not the stronghold of bullfighting in Spain; bullfights will typically not sell out and will be dominated with tourists.

Plaza de Toros Monumental, Gran Via de les Corts Catalans 743 (☎93 245 58 04). M: Monumental. Built in 1915 by Ignasi i Morell, the city bullring is one of very few prominent buildings in the city that draws overtly from Arabic architectural influences; it is rare touch of Andalucia in Catalunya. The *corrida* season runs Apr.-Sept., with fights every Su at 7pm. Tickets 2800-7500ptas/€17-45 in the sun, 3300-15,000ptas/€20-90 in the shade. Must be purchased at the bullring; ticket window open M-Sa 10:30am-2pm and 4-7pm, Su 10:30am-1pm. Cash only. For more on the sport, see also **Museu Taurí** (p. 115) and **No Bull! (**p. 170).

Barça Fans

OTHER DIVERSIONS

Both of these establishments are great for families, but they also draw decent crowds looking for an alternative to clubby nightlife.

BOWLING

Bowling Pedralbes, Av. Dr. Mariñón 11 (☎93 333 03 52). M: Collblanc. 14 lanes and a bar just a block from the Camp Nou stadium make for a welcome late-night change of pace. 10am-5pm 24ptas/€0,14 per frame; 5-11pm 40ptas/€0,24; 11pm-closing 58ptas/€0,35. Shoe rental 135ptas/€0,81. Open M-W 10am-2am, Th-Sa 10am-4am, Su 10am-midnight.

Plaza del Toros Monumental

on the cheap

Fútbol Fanatic

If your wallet can't handle the FCB's prices, but you still want the experience of a Spanish soccer game, try the Montjuïc facilities and Barcelona's other soccer stars.

Estadi Olímpic de Montjuïc, Pg. Olímpic 17-19 (☎93 426 20 89), on Av. Estadi. Constructed in 1929 and later used for the 1955 Mediterranean Games, the Olympic Stadium had to be seriously revamped to accommodate the 1992 Olympic crowds. At a capacity of 55,000 fans, it is now home to *R.C. Deportivo Espanyol*, a.k.a. *los periquitos* (parakeets), Barcelona's underdog soccer team. Stadium open daily 10am-8pm. Free. Obtain *R.C. Deportivo Espanyol* tickets from Banco Catalana or by phoning Tel- Entrada (24hr. ☎90 210 12 12).

ICE SKATING

Skating Pista de Gel, C. Roger de Flor 168 (☎93 245 28 00; www.skatingbcn.com), between C. Aragó and C. Consell de Cent, in **l'Eixample.** M: Pg. de Gràcia. One of only 2 ice-skating rinks in the city, and the only one open year-round and at night. 1750ptas/€10,50 for entrance, skates, and gloves; if you rent skates, you can bring 1 non-skate renter guest to the upstairs bar for free (beer 250ptas/€1,50). Day sessions Tu-F 10:30am-1:30pm, Sa-Su 10:30am-2pm. Night sessions Su-Th 5-10pm and F-Sa 5pm-midnight, with colored lights and music. The hours change frequently; call ahead. Cash only.

GYMS

Club Natació Atlètic-Barceloneta, Plaça del Mar, Pg. Joan de Borbo (☎93 221 00 10), across the street from the Torre San Sebastià cable car tower. This athletic club, on Platje San Sebastià, offers outdoor and indoor pools in addition to beach access, sauna, jacuzzi, and a full weightroom. Memberships start at 4055ptas/€24,37a month, but non-members can enter for 1075ptas/€6,46 a visit.

Nova-Icària Sports Club, Av. Icària 167 (☎93 221 55 80), on the corner of C. Arquitecte Sert. A full-service sports club, with weight lifting, aerobics, a pool, tennis courts, basketball courts, and more. Membership 5135ptas/€30,86 per month, but non-members can pay each time they visit and use anything in the club (1050ptas/€6,31). Open M-F 7am-11pm, Sa 8am-11pm, Su 8am-4pm, closed holidays.

Club Sant Jordi, C. París 114 (☎93 410 92 61). M: Sants. Passes available for other facilities, including sauna, weights, and stairmaster. Bring your passport. Pool 515ptas/€3,10 per hr. Open M-F 7am-10pm, Sa 8am-6pm, Su and holidays 9am-2pm. Closed Aug. 1-15.

Piscines Bernat Picornell, Av. Estadi 30-40 (☎93 423 40 41; fax 93 426 78 18; www.bcn.es/picornell), to the right when facing the stadium. Test your swimming mettle in the Olympic pools—two gorgeous facilities nestled in stadium seating. A favorite for families and sunbathers. 700ptas/€4 for outdoor pool, 1300ptas/€7,80 for workout facilities including sauna, massage parlor, and gym. Outdoor pool open M-Sa 9am-9pm and Su 9am-8pm. Workout facilities open M-F 7am-midnight, Sa 7am-9pm and Su 7:30am-8pm.

Velodróm, Pg. Vall d'Hebron 185-201 (☎93 427 91 42). M: Montbau. Face the Jardins Pedro Muñez Seco upon leaving M: Montbau, turn left, cross the Ronda de Dalt at the first opportunity and turn left; the Velodróm will be ahead on your right. Originally the Olympic cycling center, the Velodróm has since been converted into a community sports center. Annual membership is the only way to gain access; if you are interested, visit the offices at entrance 16 (up and around to the right of the building). Yearly dues 6000ptas/€36.Facilities include a space for parties on the roof, soccer fields, basketball courts, the cycling track, a snack bar, and organized tournaments. Open M 4-11pm, Tu-F 4-6pm and 8:30-11pm. Not wheelchair accessible.

Centre Muncipal d'Esports, Pg. Vall d'Hebron 166 (☎93 428 39 52). M: Montbau. Same directions as Velodróm, but the center will be on the left. The tennis center offers playing courts and a pool to members; non-members pay per visit to use the pool. Municipal sports center has a variety of facilities, including a gym, pool, racquetball, yoga, and more. Monthly dues 3100-4000ptas/€18-24. Single use 900ptas/€5,50; children and over 65 625ptas/€3,50. Open M-F 7am-11:30pm, Sa 9am-8pm, Su 9am-3pm. Wheelchair accessible.

THEATER, MUSIC, & DANCE

VENUES

Barcelona offers many options for theater aficionados, although most performances are in Catalan (*Guía del Ocio* lists the language of the performance). Reserve tickets through **Tel Entrada** (24hr. ☎90 210 12 12; www. telentrada.com) or any branch of **Caixa Catalunya** bank (open M-F 8am-2:30pm).

The **Grec-Barcelona** summer festival turns Barcelona into an international theater, music, and dance extravaganza from late June to mid-August (www.grec.bcn.com). For information about the festival, which takes place in venues across the city, ask at the tourist office or swing by the **Institut de Cultura de Barcelona (ICUB),** Palau de la Virreina, Ramblas 99. (☎93 301 77 75. Open for info year-round M-F 10am-2pm and 4-8pm. Grec ticket sales M-Sa 10am-9pm. Prices vary, but most performances cost 4000ptas/€24,10.)

Another resource for tickets is the Internet: www.travelhaven.com/activities/barcelona/barcelona.html provides 10% discounts for performances at: Palau de la Música Catalana, Gran teatre del Liceu, L'Auditorio, and Tablao Flamenco.

Palau de la Música Catalana, C. Sant Francesc de Paula 2 (☎93 295 72 00; www.palaumusica.org). M: Jaume I. Off Via Laietana near Pl. Urquinaona. Head up Via Laietana to the intersection of C. Ionqueres. Box office open M-Sa 10am-9pm, Su from 1hr. prior to the concert. No concerts in Aug.; check the Guía del Ocio for listings. Concert tickets 1300-26,000ptas/€7,80-125. MC/V.

Centre Artesá Tradicionarius, C. Trav. de Sant Antoni 6-8 (☎93 218 44 85; www.personal4.iddeo.es/tramcat), in **Gràcia.** M: Fontana. Catalan folk music con-

Grec Festival

Live Band at London Bar

Devil at the Pride Parade

173

SONIC BOOM

Those who prefer something a little more avant-garde to sugary pop and cookie-cutter rock should consider hitting Barcelona's summer mainstay, the International Festival of Advanced Music and Multimedia Arts—more commonly known as **Sónar**. Considered by many the best electronic music festival on the planet, Sónar brings hundreds of the world's best DJs to Barcelona for a 3-day nonstop party.

The festival aims to provide a forum for musical experimentation and innovation, and includes far more than just turntable techno. A technology showcase, conferences and debates, interactive exhibits, and film screenings all add to the continuous stream of performances. Sónar 2001 (featuring, among many others, Màsters at Work, Sonic Youth, and techno giant Jeff Mills) attracted more than 80,000 fans over 3 days and nights. By the time the dancing ended, at 10am of the festival's final night (morning?), exhausted fans were already eagerly anticipating Sónar 2002. Information and dates for Sónar 2002 were not available at the time of publication; for more information on Sónar, visit www.sonar.es.

certs Sept.-June F, 10pm. Tickets 1500ptas/€9. Classes in traditional Catalan music and dance (4000ptas/€24) offered each trimester; call for information. Building has a small cafe/bar and informational display on Catalan music. Open M-F 11am-2pm, 5pm-midnight. Closed Aug. Wheelchair accessible.

Gran Teatre del Liceu, Las Ramblas 51-59 (☎93 485 99 13; www.liceubarcelona.com. 24hr. ticket sales, ☎902 332 211), on **Las Ramblas.** M: Liceu. Founded in 1847, the Liceu was one of the world's leading opera stages until its interior was destroyed by a fire in 1994. It recently reopened after extensive repairs and has regained its status as the city's finest concert hall (see **Smooth-Opera-ater,** p. 64). Highlights for the 2002 season will include Monteverdi's *L'Orfeo* in February and Mozart's *Die Zauberflöte* (The Magic Flute) in July. Tickets begin at 1000ptas/€6 and rise fast, be sure to reserve tickets well in advance.

Teatre Lliure, C. Montseny 47 (☎93 218 92 51; www.teatrelliure.com), **in Gràcia.** M: Fontana. Showcases contemporary theater productions from summer festivals to Shakespeare. Call or check web site for information. Tickets may be purchased at the theater or by calling Tel Entrada. Shows May-Oct. Tu-Sa 9pm and Su 7pm, Nov.-Apr. Tu-Sa 9pm and Su 6pm. Closed in Aug. Tickets Tu-Th balcony 1700ptas/€10,50; orchestra 2000ptas/€12; F-Su balcony 2000ptas/€12, orchestra 2500ptas/€15. 20% discount for students and seniors. Wheelchair accessible.

Teatre Grec, Pg. Santa Madron 36, across from the Museu d'Arqueològia (Tel-Entrada ☎ 90 210 12 12; www.grec.bcn.es). From M: Espanya, take bus #55 to **Montjuic.** Located in the picturesque Jardins Amargós, the Teatre Grec was carved out of an old stone quarry in 1929 under the direction of Ramon Reventós. These days the open-air Grecian-style amphitheater is the namesake and occasional host of the Grec Barcelona Summer Theater Festival, which takes over Barcelona's major theaters from early June through July. Theater performances tend to be in Spanish or Catalan, but there are also plenty of music and dance shows to choose from. For information and tickets call Tel-Entrada or visit the Palau de la Virreina on Las Ramblas, 99. Outdoor cafe open July 8pm-3am.

Mercat de Les Flors, C. Lleida 59 (☎93 426 18 75; www.bcn.es/icub/mflorsteatre). From M: Espanya, take bus #55 to **Montjuic.** A converted flower market, now one of the city's major theater venues and a stage for the Grec festival. The Mercat de Les Flors and Teatre Grec will soon be incorporated into the *Ciutat del Teatre* (City of Theater)—a home for theater performance and training in Barcelona. Beginning in the late fall of 2001, the Mercat de les Flors will house the prestigious Teatre Lliure (see above). For tickets, call Tel Entrada or stop by the Palau de la Virreina at Las Ramblas 99.

Teatre Nacional de Catalunya, Pl. de les Arts 1 (☎93 306 57 00; info@tnc.es; www.tnc.es), near the intersection of Av. Diagonal and Av. Meridiana. M:

Monumental or Glòries, in **l'Eixample.** This national
theater hosts classical theater and ballet in its main
room (usually 1-2 months per show) and more varied
contemporary music, dance, circus, and textual performances in accompanying spaces. Tickets 2,600-
3,300ptas/€16-€20, Th 25% discount, for students
20% discount. Available over the phone, through ServiCaixa, or at ticket windows (open M noon-3pm and
4-9pm, Tu-Sa noon-9pm, Su noon-6pm). MC/V.

L'Auditori, C. Lepanto 150 (☎93 247 93 00;
www.auditori.es), between M: Marina and Glòries,
next to the Teatre Nacional, in **l'Eixample.** Soon to be
the new home of the city's Museu de la Música (currently closed to move), the Auditori is the dedicated
performance space of the city orchestra
(www.obc.es), although it occasionally hosts other
concerts as well. Symphony season from the end of
Sept. to mid-July, F at 7pm, Sa at 9pm, and Su at
11am. Tickets range from 1300-6950ptas/€7,80-
€41,80, depending on the day and seating zone (Su
is cheapest). Available by phone, at ticket windows,
or through ServiCaixa. MC/V.

Spanish Guitar

**L'Espai de Dansa i Música de la Generalitat de Cat-
alunya,** Trav. de Gràcia 62 (☎93 414 31 33;
espai@qrz.net; cultura.gencat.es/espai), just above
the intersection of Av. Diagonal and C. Aribau. M:
Diagonal or FCG Gràcia. Contemporary dance and
musical performances, many from Catalunya but
drawing from other provinces and countries as well.
Tickets usually 1500-2000ptas/€9-12. Available at
the ticket window or through ServiCaixa. M-Sa performances at 10pm and Su at 7pm. Ticket window open
M-Sa 6:30-9pm and Su 5-7pm. MC/V.

Palau d'Esports Sant Jordi (☎93 426 20 89) on
Montjuïc. For concert information, check
www.agendabcn.com or the *Guía del Ocio*, available at
any newsstand.

Palau de la Generalitat, Pl. Sant Jaume (☎93 402
46 16). M: Jaume I. The first Su of every month the
Palau hosts a free bell concert at noon.

Liceu Opera House

FLAMENCO

Although Catalunya does not have a tradition of
flamenco, a dance which originated with the
gypsies in Andalucia, a region in the south of
Spain, the tourist industry has fed the demand
for flamenco venues. Just because these venues
may be geared to tourists should in no way
reflect poorly on their quality; some of the best
flamenco musicians and dancers pass through
these establishments.

El Patio Andaluz, C. Aribau 242 (☎93 268 90 70; fax
93 268 90 62; www.gulliver.es/patio), in **Gràcia.** M:
Diagonal. From the Metro, take a left on Diagonal and
turn right on C. Aribau. Lively, Andalucian themed restaurant showcases traditional Spanish flamenco dancing. Show and 1 drink 4500ptas/€27,05; show and
menú del día from 7950ptas/€47,78. Daily shows at

Giant Figures at a Procession

LEISURE READING

Your first purchase in Barcelona should be the Spanish-language **Guía del Ocio** (Guide to Leisure), a weekly booklet that lists anything and everything happening in Barcelona in the coming week: concerts, restaurants, nightlife, galleries, games, free events, theater and dance performances, movie listings, and more. The guide comes out on Thursday or Friday, so be sure you're picking up the current guide. The guide is published in Spanish, but even those who don't speak Spanish will find the listings and advertisements easy enough to understand. The *Guía del Ocio* is available at newsstands all over the city for the very economical price of 125ptas/€0,75.

9:30pm and midnight. Call 9am-7pm for reservations. El Patio's red-paneled bar, Las Sevillanas del Patio, stays open until 3am for drinks and dancing.

El Tablao de Carmen, Av. Marqués de Comillas, inside Poble Espanyol (☎93 325 68 95; www.tablaodecarmen.com). M: Espanya, up the outdoor escalators, to the right when facing the Palau Nacional, in **Montjuïc.** Spacious, Andalucian-style restaurant and flamenco performance space with paper lanterns and Picasso-esque paintings was built on the site where the great Carmen Amaya danced for King Alfonso XIII at the opening of Poble Espanyol in 1929. Families and couples enjoy the sexy, energetic flamenco dancing and lyrical guitar rhythms. A tourist spot that will not disappoint. Open Tu-Su from 8pm; shows Su-Th 9:30pm and 11:30pm, F-Sa 9:30pm and midnight. Call ahead for reservations, which include entrance into Poble Espanyol (see **Sights**, p. 91). Dinner and show 8400ptas/€50; drink and show 4450ptas/€26,75. MC/V.

Guasch Teatre, C. Aragó 140 (☎93 323 39 50 or 93 451 34 62). M: Urgell, in **l'Eixample.** Often showcases flamenco; call for schedules.

CINEMA
MOVIE THEATERS

Movies in Spain come in two varieties and are marked accordingly in listings. The first is **vose** or **V.O.** *(versión original);* these descriptions indicate that the film will show in the original language in which it was produced, with Catalan or Spanish subtitles. The second variety are **doblado** (dubbed), with the original language lines dubbed over into Spanish or Catalan. Movies in Spain are generally not shown until 4 or 5pm and continue showing well after midnight. To find movie times and listings either check the *Guía del Ocio* (available at newsstands) or pass by the theater in question.

Icària-Yelmo Cineplex, C. Salvador Espriu 61 (☎93 221 75 85; tickets ☎90 212 41 34; www.yelmocineplex.es), in the **Vila Olímpica** mall. Boasts 15 screens and a wide range of Spanish and international films, both in the subtitled original version and the ever-entertaining dubbed version. Tu-Su 850ptas/€5,11; M, matinees, and students 600ptas/€3,11. Open 11am-11pm.

Verdi, C. Verdi 32 (☎93 238 79 90) M: Fontana, in **Gràcia.** Follow C. Astúries for several blocks and turn right on C. Verdi. Movie theater with plenty of V.O. English-language films. International selection leans toward recent artsy releases. Tickets Tu-F 825ptas/€5; Sa-Su 875ptas/€5,50; M 600ptas/€3,50. Students and senior tickets daily 4-7:30pm 600ptas/€3,50. Generally screens post-midnight shows F, Sa. Call Verdi directly or check the *Guía del Ocio* for times. Wheelchair accessible.

Cine Maremagnum, Moll d'Espanya (☎93 405 22 22.). M: Drassanes or Barceloneta, in the **Port Vell,** between the mall and the aquarium. 8 screens of dubbed Hollywood hits and a few Spanish-language originals. No English V.O. Tu and Th-Su 750ptas/€4,50, W 600ptas/€3,60.

IMAX Port Vell, Moll d'Espanya (☎93 225 11 11). M: Drassanes or Barceloneta, in the **Port Vell,** next to the aquarium and Maremagnum. 1 IMAX screen, an Omnimax 30m in diameter, and 3-D projection. Unfortunately for some, all features are in either Spanish or Catalan. Get tickets at the door, or through **ServiCaixa** automatic machines, or by phone. Tickets 1000-1500ptas/€6-9.

Filmoteca, Av. Sarrià 33 (☎93 410 75 90). M: Hospital Clinic, in **l'Eixample.** Screens classic, cult, and otherwise exceptional films. Program changes daily. 400ptas/€2,40 or 5000ptas/€30 for twenty films.

Méliès Cinemas, Villarroel 102 (☎93 451 00 51). M: Urgell, in **l'Eixample.** Two screens show classic films, generally spotlighting a particular director or actor. Tu-Su 600ptas/€3,61, M 400ptas/€2,40.

Casablanca, Pg. de Gràcia 115 (☎93 218 43 45) M: Diagonal, in **l'Eixample.** Features recently released indie films. Tu-F 800ptas/€4,80, Sa-Su 825ptas/€5, M 600ptas/€3,61.

Cine Malda, C. del Pi 5 (☎93 317 85 29). M: Liceu, in the **Barri Gòtic,** just inside the Malda Galería. This unusual theater is the only one in the city which lets you see two movies with one ticket. Two V.O. movies are screened in back-to-back pairs each week, including American and other international films; see the schedule flyers outside the ticket window. One ticket gains admittance to both shows. Tickets M 600ptas/€3,60, Tu-F 775ptas/€4,50, Sa-Su 825ptas/€5,90. Cash only.

Renoir-Les Corts, Eugeni d'Ors 12 (☎93 490 55 10). M: Les Corts, in **Les Corts** in the **Zona Alta.** From Trav. de Les Corts, take C. Les Corts, then the first left. Independent international films in V.O. 800ptas/€4,80; M, 600ptas/€3,60.

MOVIE RENTALS

Void, C. Santa Creu 1 (☎93 218 56 60; www.voidbcn.com). M: Fontana, above Pl. Virreina. If you're lucky enough to have access to a VCR in Barcelona, Void is the place to go for off-beat, interesting video rentals. If not, call ahead to reserve Void's big hot pink room and screen your favorite film on site (300ptas/€2 per person). Pick up a video catalogue or check the web site for Void's cinematic offerings from Scorsese to Rossellini. Open W-Sa 5-11pm, Su noon-3pm and 5-9pm. Wheelchair accessible.

Shopping

Barcelona is cosmopolitan, trendy, and trashy: shopping options reflect all these personalities. L'Eixample is full of designer stores, while other areas, like La Ribera and El Raval, have more unique, out-of-the-way shops. Our shopping chapter can only ever scratch the surface of the shopping options in Barcelona, but while we certainly can't list every second-hand store and designer boutique, we have tried to present a decent variety of shops. Below is an alphabetized list of categories of stores with listings beneath each category. If you're wondering what European clothing or shoe size your American size corresponds to, check the sizing chart in the **Appendix.**

ARTISANRY

Arlequí Máscares, C. Princesa 7 (☎93 268 27 52). M: Jaume I, in **La Ribera.** Masks, marionettes, and puppets of all kinds cram the walls and shelves of this 19th-century Modernist building. Most are made on the premises and prices start at 500ptas/€3 for a *papier mâché* finger puppet. Open M-Sa 10:30am-8:30pm and Su 10am-4pm. MC/V.

Art Escudellers, C. Escudellers 23-25 (☎93 412 68 01; export@escudellers-art.com; www.escudellers-art.com). M: Drassanes or Liceu, in the **Barri Gòtic.** C. Escudellers is a left off Las Ramblas between M: Liceu and Drassanes. Popular among the cruise ship crowd, this huge, well-stocked tourist store sells local craftsmanship from every part of Spain, from pottery and glassware to tea sets and handmade jewelry. The goods are sorted by region and labeled clearly with highlighted maps, and the basement level holds an art gallery/wine cellar. Open daily 11am-11pm. AmEx/MC/V.

2Bis, C. Bisbe 2 bis (☎93 315 09 54). M: Jaume I, just off Pl. St. Jaume, in the **Barri Gòtic.** This bright, colorful store is filled to the brim with arts and crafts from Catalan artists, including varied figurines, ceramics, glasses, jewelry and painted masks. Open M-Sa 10am-8:30pm. AmEx/MC/V.

GRÀCIA

While big name stores line the Gran de Gràcia, smaller eclectic boutiques are hidden in the streets on either side of the main thoroughfare. **Trav. de Gràcia** hosts specialty shops carrying everything from traditional Catalan pottery and lamps to kitchen wares and used books.

Locura Cotidiana, Pl. Rius i Taulet 12 (☎93 415 97 54). M: Fontana or Diagonal, FGC: Gràcia, in **Gràcia.** Reasonably priced, unusual jewelry and crafts. Many items are made in the store's rear workshop. Open M-Sa 10am-2pm and 4:30-8:30pm. MC/V.

do.bella, C. Astúries 43 (☎93 237 33 88). M: Fontana, in **Gràcia.** Stylish handmade beaded jewelry, bags, and silk scarves at affordable prices. All work done on the premises. Open M 5-8:30pm, Tu-Sa 11am–2pm and 5-8:30pm. AmEx/MC/V.

BOOKSTORES

Llibreria del Raval, C. Elisabets 6 (☎93 317 02 93). M: Catalunya, in **El Raval,** off Las Ramblas. Literature and nonfiction in four languages (Catalan, Spanish, English, and French) fill the shelves of this spacious bookstore, born in 1693 as the Gothic-style Church of la Misericòrdia. Pocket Catalan/Spanish and Catalan/English dictionaries (1100ptas/€6,60) prove useful for travelers. Open M-F 10am-8:30pm; Sa 10am-2:30pm and 5-8pm.

LAIE, Av. Pau Claris 85 (☎93 318 17 39; www.laie.es). M: Urquinaona, in the **La Ribera.** Small but adequate English book section with a selection of travel guides and a cafe upstairs. Bookstore open M-F 10am-9pm, Sa 10:30am-9pm. Cafe open M-F 9am-1am, Sa 10am-1am.

Bell Books, C. Sant Salvador 41 (☎93 237 95 19). M: Lesseps, in **Gràcia.** Follow Trav. del Dalt and make a right on C. Verdi and a left on Sant Salvador. Best used bookstore around, run by an eccentric British expat and her cat, Arnold Schwarzenegger. Trade-ins accepted. Open M-F 1-8pm and Sa 10am-8pm.

Come In, C. Provença 203 (☎93 453 12 04; casaidiomas@redestb.es). M: Diagonal or FGC: Provença, in **L'Eixample.** Barcelona's biggest English bookstore boasts an enormous, if slightly random, collection of literature, travel guides, and language books. Peruse the message boards outside for apartment listings and postings for English-Spanish classes and conversation partners. Open M-Sa 10am-2pm and 4:30-8pm.

Crisol Libros y Más, C. Consell de Cent 341 (☎93 215 31 21; www.crisol.es), just to the right of Pg. de Gràcia when facing Pl. de Catalunya. M: Pg. de Gràcia, in **l'Eixample.** This Madrid transplant stocks a wide range of music (lots of international titles), books (fiction, self-help, cooking, travel guides, road maps), VHS videos, DVDs, small gifts, and stationery. Also has a large children's section and some English novels and original version videos. Open M-Sa 8am-10pm. AmEx/MC/V.

Llibreria Francesa, Pg. de Gràcia 91 (☎93 215 14 17). M: Diagonal, in **l'Eixample.** Founded in 1896 on Las Ramblas, this bookstore has lost its original address but none of its popularity. In addition to novels and international press in English, Spanish, French, and Catalan, they carry travel guides, language dictionaries, grammar books, coffee table books, and more. They will also do orders in Spanish, English, or French. Open M-F 9:30am-2:30pm and 4-8:30pm, Sa 9:30am-2pm. AmEx/MC/V.

CLOTHING & ACCESSORIES

In **Barri Gòtic,** C. Portaferrissa and Av. Portal de l'Angel have lots of cheap, typical Spanish women's clothing stores. C. Boqueria is chock full of jewelry, accessories, and beads, C. Call with jewelry, jewelry, jewelry.

QKbcn, Trav. de Gràcia 176-78 (☎93 210 40 00). M: Joanic or FGC: Gràcia, in **Gràcia,** beneath Pl. Sol. Women's clothing boutique carries innovative and colorful designs from Basque and Catalan designers. Open M-Sa 10am-2pm and 5-9pm.

Zara, Pg. de Gràcia 16 (☎93 318 76 75). M: Pg de Gràcia, in **l'Eixample.** With 12 locations in Barcelona alone (grab a directory brochure at the counter), more than 200 stores in Spain, and almost that many abroad, Zara has hit paydirt: snazzy, very Spanish *à la mode* designer styles, but in much cheaper materials than you'll find on runways. The clothes you buy here may not last through next year, but you won't have spent too much, and by that time you'll want to come back for the newest look anyway. Expect to wait in line. Most skirts, pants, and shirts 2000-5000ptas/€12-30. AmEx/MC/V. Wheelchair accessible.

Mango, Pg. de Gràcia 8-10 (☎93 215 75 30). M: Pg. de Gràcia, in **l'Eixample.** Also boasts 12 other locations in the city; ask for a directory. The same idea as Zara, but done with a lot more flare: you'll find fewer staples and basic colors here and more funky dresses, sleek nighttime wear, and shiny accessories. It's also slightly more expensive than Zara. AmEx/MC/V. Wheelchair accessible.

Casa Ciutad, Av. Portal de l'Angel 14 (☎93 317 04 33). M: Catalunya, in the **Barri Gòtic.** Founded in 1892, this elegant, almost old-fashioned accessories store sells quality hair clips and barrettes, brushes, nylons, men's and women's underwear, toiletry kits, and nail care sets at reasonable prices. Open M-F 10am-8:30pm, Sa 10am-9pm. AmEx/MC/V.

Shopping on Pg. de Gràcia

0,925 Argenters, C. Montcada 25 (☎93 319 43 18). M: Jaume I, in **La Ribera.** Fashionable jewelry boutique nestled in one of C. Montcada's Gothic residences. Mainly silver designs, all by Spanish artists, start at 2000ptas/€12. Friendly staff welcomes window shoppers. Open M-F 10:30am-8:30pm, Sa 11am-8pm, Su 11:30am-3:30pm.

Rafa Teja Atelier, Santa Maria 18 (☎93 310 27 85), in **La Ribera,** across from the rear entrance of the church. M: Jaume I. Offers a wide selection of textiles, including lovely hand-painted scarves. Unusual clothing and jewelry. Open Tu-Th 10am-2pm and 4:30-8:30pm, F 10am-2pm and 5-9pm, Sa 1-9pm. AmEx/MC/V.

NAF NAF

Schindia, C. València 167 (☎93 451 28 16). M: Hospital Clinic, in **l'Eixample.** Hippie chic clothing and accessories imported from India and China. Open M-F 10:30am-9pm, Sa 11am-2pm and 5-8:30pm. Closed Sa in Aug. AmEx/MC/V.

DISCOUNT CLOTHING

There is not much concentrated discount shopping to be found inside the city proper; most is in the suburbs, accessible by car only, but here are a few establishments and areas.

Factory Store, Pg. de Gràcia 81 (☎ 93 215 03 80). M: Diagonal, in **l'Eixample.** A fabulous find for budget-traveling label whores: high-class Italian and American brands from last year at 20-50% discounts. Men's and women's suits, pants, skirts, dresses, and shirts from Versace, Polo Ralph Lauren, Dolce & Gabanna, Hugo Boss, Alberta Ferreti, Guess?, and more. Don't worry, in Spain everything from last year is still in style. Open M-Sa 10:30am-8:30pm. MC/V. Wheelchair accessible.

Taxi Moda, Pg. de Gràcia 26 (93 318 20 70). M: Pg. de Gràcia, in **l'Eixample,** down a small passageway off the main street. The same business model as **Fac-**

Trying on Shoes

tory Store, but a smaller selection and a few different brands. Open M-Sa 10:30am-2pm and 4:30-8:30pm. MC/V. Not wheelchair accessible.

Contribuciones, C. Riera San Miquel 30 (☎93 218 74 36). M: Diagonal, in **l'Eixample.** High-end Spanish and Italian labels are half-off at this designer discount store, though prices are still quite steep. Check out the top floor for better bargains. Open M-Sa 11am-2pm and 5-9pm. AmEx/D/MC/V.

H&M, C. Portaferrissa 16 (☎ 93 343 50 60). M: Catalunya, in the **Barri Gòtic.** A left off Las Ramblas. With its worldwide slogan of "fashion and quality at the best price," H&M is not unique to Barcelona and probably doesn't need an introduction; cheap and stylish, it is wildly popular in most of the 14 countries it has opened in. Shirts 1000-2000ptas/€6-12. Skirts and pants 3000-6000ptas/€18-36. Open M-Sa 10am-9pm. AmEx/MC/V.

La Tienda de los Milagros, C. Rera Palau 7 (☎93 319 67 30). Off Pl. de les Olles, in **La Ribera.** M: Jaume I. Praise the clothing gods for these funky, retro finds at decent prices. The "shop of miracles" stocks accessories and outfits from casual to club wear. Open M-F 10am-3pm and 4-9pm, Sa 10:30am-3pm and 4-9pm.

don bolso, C. València 247 (☎93 488 33 63), just to the right of Pg. de Gràcia when facing the Pl. de Catalunya. M: Pg. de Gràcia, in **l'Eixample.** If you're someone who must have lots of colorful bags and purses, but don't want to waste money Kate Spade-style, come here; all handbags are under 3000ptas/€18. No promise they'll last long, but they've got a colorful variety. Open daily 10am-noon and 4-8pm. MC/V.

CALLE GIRONA

One place to try for bargains is **Calle Girona,** between C. Casp and Gran Via, in **l'Eixample,** where you'll find a small line-up of discount shops offering girl's clothing, men's dress clothes, shoes, bags, and accessories (M: Tetuán. Walk two blocks down Gran Via and take a left on C. Girona).

Mango Outlet, C. Girona 37 (☎93 412 29 35). M: Girona or Tetuán, in **l'Eixample,** between C. Casp and Gran Via. Last season's Mango clothes and accessories at 20-30% discounts, during clearance sales up to 50%. A great place to buy random shirts and throw-away nightclub tanks, sometimes for as little as 500ptas/€3. Tax-free shopping. Open M-Sa 10:15am-9pm. MC/V. Wheelchair accessible.

Arrow, C. Girona 36 (☎93 245 18 08). M: Girona and Tetuán, in **l'Eixample,** between C. Casp and Gran Via. Overstocks and factory leftovers from the classic American men's shirtmaker, most at discounts around 25%. Tax-free shopping. Open Tu-Su 10:30am-2pm and 4:30-8:30pm, M 4:30-8:30pm. MC/V. Wheelchair accessible.

MERCAT ALTERNATIU

Another area to try for discounts is the **Mercat Alternatiu (Alternative Market)** on C. Riera Baixa in **El Raval** (M: Liceu. Take C. de l'Hospital—a right off Las Ramblas if you're facing the ocean—and follow it to C. Riera Baixa, the seventh right, shortly after the stone hospital building.) This street is crammed with second-hand and thrift stores covering everything from music to clothes.

Mies & Felj, C. Riera Baixa 5 (☎93 442 07 55). M: Liceu, in **El Raval.** This small store has a great selection of second-hand clothes, in good shape and at reasonable prices. The Adidas shirt and leather jacket collections are both worth a close look. Open M-Sa 11am-2pm and 5-9pm.

G.I. Joe Surplus, C. Hospital 82 (☎93 329 96 52). M: Liceu, off Las Ramblas, at the corner of Riera Baixa's Mercat Alternatiu, in **El Raval.** This well-known shop has a good variety of army/navy-type alternative clothing, at low prices. Now you know. And knowing is half the battle.

Discos Edison's, C. Riera Baixa 9 (☎93 441 96 74), in **El Raval.** All used, all the time. Buy or sell used CDs, records, or cassettes, most in the 500-1000ptas/€3-€6 range. This is the place to unload regrettable past purchases and pick up that Paula Abdul tape you've been wanting all these years.

Zeus, Riera Alta 20 (☎93 442 97 95). M: Sant Antoni, in **El Raval.** Specializes in gay videos (no lesbian action here), with an extensive collection in the front room. Venture into the back room for toys. Ask for the *plano gay,* a map of Barcelona and Sitges' main gay attractions. Open M-Sa 10am-9pm.

DEPARTMENT STORES & MALLS

Spain has a series of laws against franchises, to protect the economic prosperity of small businesses. The theory is that if franchises are allowed to be open all the time, small business, whose limited staff must take off Sundays and *siesta*, will have no way to compete. Americans will be shocked to see that these monstrous department stores are only open six days a week; commercial law prevents them from being open on Sundays, except for the first Sunday of each month.

El Corte Inglés, Pl. de Catalunya 14 (☎93 306 38 00). M: Catalunya, in **Pl. de Catalunya**. Behemoth department store. **Free map** of Barcelona available from the information desk. Also has English books,

El Corte Inglés

hair salon, rooftop cafeteria, supermarket, the *oportunidades* discount department, currency exchange, and telephones. Open M-Sa and first Su of every month 10am-10pm. M: Catalunya. Other branches: across the street from the tourist office, Portal de L'Angel 19-2 (M: Catalunya); Av. Diagonal 471-473 (M: Hospital Clinic); Av. Diagonal 617, (M: Maria Cristina).

Triangle, Pl. de Catalunya 4 (☎93 318 01 08; www.triangle.es). M: Catalunya, in **Pl. de Catalunya.** Since its opening in 1999, architecture buffs have bemoaned this shopping center's utter lack of imagination and style. Shopping buffs, however, are more enthusiastic about it, for its upper floor **FNAC** electronics store/bookstore and first floor of clothing and sunglass shops. **Saphora,** the world's biggest perfume store, is a warehouse-size olfactory paradise. Open M-Sa 10am-10pm. On the corner near the Ramblas sits the always-crowded **Café Zurich,** a recreation of the classic cafe that once occupied this site, torn down to accommodate the new mall.

Fancy Mannequins

Maremagnum, Moll d'Espanya (93 225 81 00; www.maremagnum.es). M: Drassanes, in the **Port Vell.** Small stores fill the first two floors of Maremagnum, the mall and all-around leisure superstop which dominates the skyline of the new waterfront. Stores open daily, most 11am-11pm. A must-see for *fútbol* (soccer) fans is the **Botiga del Barça,** a smaller version of the official F.C. Barcelona souvenir shop at the Camp Nou stadium (see p. 168), featuring posters, jerseys, and all varieties of memorabilia pertaining to the beloved Catalan team. Popular among kids, **Big Fun** is an arcade and game center on the second floor, open daily, past midnight on weekend nights. Air hockey (100ptas/€0,60), foosball (200ptas/€1,20), billiards, and mini-bowling (with bowling balls and pins half the normal size; 300ptas/€1,80) are just a few of the big, fun attractions. Also boasts a sizeable arcade and play area for small children.

Revolver Records

HOUSEWARES

The area around C. Banys Nou (M: Jaume I), in **La Ribera,** is a great place to look for antiques.

Vinçon, Pg. de Gràcia 96 (☎93 215 60 50; fax 93 215 50 37). M: Diagonal, in **l'Eixample.** More of an experience than a mere store, Vinçon has been setting the house decor standard in Barcelona since 1941. Cutting-edge bedroom sets decorate 100-year-old rooms, and rows of funky lamps and knick-knacks entertain wandering shoppers. Modernisme fans will want to see the original interior of the **Casa Casas** (see **Sights,** p. 82) on display here. Open M-Sa 10am-2pm and 4:30-8:30pm. AmEx/MC/V. Partially wheelchair accessible.

WAE, La Rambla de Catalunya 89 (☎93 487 14 13). M: Diagonal or Pg. de Gràcia, on the corner of C. Mallorca, in **l'Eixample.** Shop nearly bursts with brightly colored pillows, Eastern-influenced jewelry and housewares, and kitsch Mexican knick-knacks. Fun accessories and funny gifts. Open M-Sa 10am-8:30pm. AmEx/MC/V.

Next, C. Consell de Cent 248 (☎93 451 40 32). M: Pg. de Gràcia, in **l'Eixample.** Funky home and bath accessories and gifts with colorful, sleek designs. *The* place for lady-bug toilet seat covers, deluxe rubix cubes, or penis-shaped refrigerator magnets. Open M-Sa 10am-1:30pm and 4:30-8:30pm. MC/V.

MARKETS, FAIRS, & FLEA MARKETS

Barcelona has a number of good weekly outdoor markets, as well as some more seasonal fairs and sales. Local **painters** display their work in the **Plaça Oriole** (M: Jaume, in La Ribera) every Sa from 11am-7pm and Su 11am-2pm, while the **Plaça del Pi** (M: Liceu in Barri Gòtic) hosts a small **gastronomy** market on the first and third weekend of each month (F-Su 11am-2pm and 5-9pm). **Plaça Reial** (M: Liceu, in Barri Gòtic) is famous for its huge Sunday morning stamp and coin flea market (9am-2pm); its only real rival in size, perhaps, is the **Les Encants secondhand market** next to **Pl. Glòries** (M: Glòries, in L'Eixample; M, W, F, Sa 9am-7pm). **Antiques** are on sale every Thursday in front of the cathedral (9am-2pm. Christmastime brings a number of specialized fairs like the **Santa Llúcia market** in **Plaça Nova** (M: Liceu, in Barri Gòtic) and the **toy market** which takes place on the Gran Via. As always, particularly with the secondhand flea markets, watch your personal belongings in the shopping crowds.

Mercat de Sant Antoni, M: Sant Antoni, in **El Raval.** Barcelona's biggest flea market, with everything from antiques to anchovies. Visit M, W, F, or Sa for the best stuff. Book market Su mornings.

Farcells, C. Banys Vells 9 (☎93 310 56 35). M: Jaume I, in **La Ribera.** Second-hand bazaar has low prices for everything from dishes to furniture to record albums to clothing. Sift through the mountainous junk to find some real treasures. Open M-F 10am-8pm and Sa 10am

MUSIC

For music shopping in **El Raval,** the area around **C. Tallers** offers a good selection of new and used CDs and records.

Casa Beethoven, Las Ramblas 97 (☎93 301 48 26; www.casabeethoven.com; ludwigvb@casabeethoven.com). M: Catalunya, on **Las Ramblas.** At last, the secrets to performing Ricky Martin's greatest hits revealed! This unique music shop specializes not in recorded music, but in written. Books of sheet music fill the shelves, featuring greats such as Mozart, Clapton, Hendrix, and Martin. The impressive collection of scores to more traditional music ranges from tangos to string quartets, spanning centuries. Open daily 9:30am-5pm; winter 9am-1pm, 4-7:30pm.

FNAC, Pl. de Catalunya 4 (☎93 344 19 18). M: Catalunya, in **Pl. de Catalunya**. Branch at Av. Diagonal 549 (M: Maria Cristina). Multi-level one stop book and music shop. Well-stocked English books section, CDs and listening stations, videos, and a cafe. Credit card users beware: your transaction requires a passport as ID. Open M-Sa 10am-10pm.

Planet Music, C. Mallorca 214 (☎93 451 42 88; www.planetmusic.es). M: Diagonal, in **l'Eixample.** A huge selection of new music, including jazz, rock, pop, folk and classical. A bright, new-feeling, easy-shopping store with several locations in the city. Open M-Sa 10am-9pm (other locations 10:30am-2:15pm and 4:15-9pm). AmEx/MC/V.

Overstocks, C. Tallers 9 (☎93 412 72 85) in **El Raval.** Has the area's widest and most eclectic collection of CDs, from Spanish, English, and Catalan pop to trip-hop and jazz-funk. T-shirts, records, books, and music videos make this a one-stop music lover's dream. Ticket office for BBVA tickets to most major club shows. Open M-Sa 10am-8pm.

Revolver, C. Tallers 11 (☎93 412 73 58) in **El Raval.** Specializes in used CDs and vinyl. There is some pop, but the emphasis here is on punk and metal, with a nod to 60s psychedelica. Ticket office for BBVA tickets to most major club shows. Open M-F 10am-2pm and 4:30-9pm, Sa 10am-9pm.

SPORTS EQUIPMENT

Cap Problema Bicicletes, Pl. Traginers 3 (☎93 310 00 82; tienda@capproblema.com; www.capproblema.com). This bike shop offers a great deal for long-term visitors to Barcelona. For 42,000ptas/€253 you can buy a new bike with insurance and a padlock; after 1 month they'll buy it back for 50% of the price, after 2 months for 40%, and after 3 months for 35%. (700ptas/€4,20 per day for 1mo.; 420ptas/€2,50 per day for 2mo. ; 300ptas/€3 per day for 3mo.) Best of all, if you bring a cut padlock to prove the theft of your bike, they'll replace it for free. Open M-F 10am-2pm and 4:30-8:30pm, Sa 10am-2pm. MC/V.

Decathlon, C. Canuda, 20 (☎ 93 342 61 61). M: Catalunya, in **Barri Gòtic.** A left off Las Ramblas. This sports megastore takes "one-stop shopping" to a whole new level. Whatever you might need, from a tennis racket, basketball, or windbreaker to just a new pair of running socks, they'll most definitely have it. Open M-Sa 10am-9:30pm. AmEx/MC/V.

TATTOOS, ETC.

Tattoo Dolar, C. Boqueria 11 (☎93 268 08 29). M: Liceu, in the **Barri Gòtic.** A left off Las Ramblas. An extremely hygienic, sleek tattoo and piercing parlor. Tattoos 8000-24,000ptas/€48-240, depending on design. Piercing 7000-20,000ptas/€42-120, depending on location. Open M-Sa 10:30am-midnight and 4:30-8:30pm. AmEx/MC/V.

L'Embruix, C. Boqueria 18 (☎93 301 11 63). M: Liceu, in the **Barri Gòtic.** A left off Las Ramblas. Extremely popular among rebellious kids trying to sneak in a tongue ring while away from home; the waiting area is almost a self-contained social scene. Minimum for tattoos 6000ptas/€36; some designs go up to 40,000ptas/€240. Minimum for henna tattoos 2000ptas/€12. Normal piercing flat-rate 5500ptas/€33 plus pendant; genitalia 10,000ptas/€60 plus pendant. Walk-in piercing; reservations required for tattoos. Open M-F 9:30am-11:30pm, Sa 10am-9:30pm. MC/V.

Daytripping

COSTA BRAVA

Tracing the Mediterranean Sea from Barcelona to the French border, the Costa Brava's jagged cliffs and pristine beaches draw throngs of European visitors, especially in July and August. Early June and late September can be remarkably peaceful; the water is still warm but the beaches are much less crowded. In the winter Costa Brava lives up to its name, as fierce winds sweep the coast, leaving behind tranquil, boarded-up and almost empty beach towns. Unlike its counterparts, Costa Blanca and Costa del Sol, Costa Brava offers more than just high-rises and touristy beaches. The rocky shores have traditionally attracted romantics and artists, like Marc Chagall and Salvador Dalí, a Costa Brava native. Dalí's house in Cadaqués and his museum in Figueres display the largest collections of his work in Europe.

GETTING AROUND THE COSTA BRAVA

Transportation on the Costa Brava is seasonal, with frequent service during July and August, less service the rest of the tourist season (May-June and Sept.-Oct.), and little to no service in winter. **RENFE trains** (☎902 24 02 02; www.renfe.es) stop at Blanes, Figueres, and then farther north at Llançà and Portbou (near the French border). **Buses** are the preferred mode of transportation, often running along beautiful winding roads and connecting many major and less major towns with frequent and inexpensive service. **Sarfa** (☎93 265 65 08; www.sarfa.com), **Pujol i Pujol** (☎97 236 42 36), and **Teisa** (☎97 220 02 75) are Costa Brava's principal carriers.

Catalunya

FIGUERES (FIGUERAS)

In 1974, the mayor of Figueres (pop. 35,000) asked native Salvador Dalí to donate a painting to an art museum the town was planning. Dalí refused to donate a painting; he was so flattered by his hometown's recognition that he donated an entire museum. With the construction of the Teatre-Museu Dalí, Figueres was catapulted to international fame; ever since, a multilingual parade of Surrealism fans has been awed and entranced by Dalí's bizarre perspectives and erotic visions.

Though it is a beachless sprawl, Figueres hides other quality museums and some pleasant cafés. If you choose to extend your Figueres visit beyond Dalí's spectacle, the town's lovely Rambla is a good place to start for food, accommodations, and further sightseeing. It is also a convenient base for visiting the Costa Brava.

TRANSPORTATION

Trains: ☎ 90 224 02 02. To: **Barcelona** (1½hr., 21 per day 6:11am-8:58pm, 1200ptas/€7); **Girona** (30min., 21 per day 6:11am-8:58pm, 390ptas/€2,30); **Portbou** (30min., 12 per day 6:42am-11:16pm, 300ptas/€1,80).

Buses: All buses leave from the **Estació Autobuses** (☎ 97 267 33 54), in Pl. Estació. **Sarfa** (☎ 97 267 42 98; www.sarfa.com) runs to **Llançà** (25min.; July-Aug. 4 per day, Sept.-June 2 per day; 330ptas/€2) and **Cadaqués** (1¼hr.; July-Aug. 5 per day, Sept.-June 2-3 per day; 540ptas/€3,50). **Barcelona Bus** (☎ 97 250 50 29) drives to **Barcelona** (2¼hr., 4-6 per day, 1885ptas/€11) and **Girona** (1hr., 4-6 per day, 540ptas/€3,50).

Taxis: (☎ 97 250 00 08 or ☎ 97 250 50 43). Taxis line the Rambla and the train station.

Car Rental: Hertz, Pl. Estació 9 (☎ 90 240 24 05). Min. age 24. All-inclusive rental from 8900ptas/€54 per day. AmEx/D/MC/V.

ORIENTATION & PRACTICAL INFORMATION

Trains and buses arrive at **Plaça de Estació** on the edge of town. Cross the plaza and bear left on C. Sant Llàtzer, walk several blocks to Carrer Nou, and take a right to Figueres' tree-filled Rambla. To reach the **tourist office,** walk up the Rambla and continue on C. Lasauca straight out from the left corner. The blue, all-knowing **"i"** beckons across the rather treacherous intersection with Ronda Frial.

Tourist Office: Main office, Pl. Sol (☎97 250 31 55). Good map and free list of accommodations. Open July-Aug. M-Sa 9am-9pm and Su 9am-3pm; Apr.-June and Oct. M-Sa 9am-2pm, 4:30-8pm; Sept. and Nov.-Apr. M-F 9am-3pm. Two **branch offices** in summer, one at Pl. Estació (open mid-July to mid-Sept. M-Sa 9:30am-1:30pm and 4:30-7pm), and the other in a yellow mobile home in front of the Dalí museum (open July-Sept. 15 M-Sa 10am-2:30pm and 4-7pm).

Currency Exchange: Banco Central Hispano, Rambla 21. **ATM.** Open Apr.-Oct. M-F 8:30am-2pm; Nov.-Mar. M-F 8:30am-2pm, Sa 8:30am-1pm.

Luggage Storage: At the train station, large lockers 600ptas/€3,60. At the bus station 300ptas/€1,80. Bus station open daily 6am-10pm, train station open daily 6am-11pm.

Emergency: ☎ 112. **Police: Mossos d'Esquadra** (☎97 267 50 89), on C. Ter.

Internet Access: Pizza Fono, C. Sant Antoni 27 (☎97 261 00 55). 5 computers and takeout pizza. 30min. 300ptas/€1,80; 1hr. 500ptas/€3. Open Tu-Su 2-11pm.

Post Office: C. Santa Llogaia 60-62 (☎97 250 54 31). Open M-F 8:30am-2:30pm, Sa 9:30am-1pm. **Postal Code:** 17600.

ACCOMMODATIONS

Most visitors to Figueres make the journey a daytrip from Barcelona, but affordable accommodations in Figueres are quite reasonable. Most tend to be on the upper floors of small bars or restaurants. Some cluster on C. Jonquera, around the Dalí museum; others are located closer to La Rambla and C. Pep Ventura. The tourist office has an annually updated list of all pensions and hostels.

Hostal La Barretina, C. Lasauca 13 (☎97 267 64 12 or ☎97 267 64 12). From the train station, walk up the left side of La Rambla to its end and look for C. Lasauca directly ahead. A luxury experience—each room has TV, A/C, heat, and private bath. Reception is downstairs in the jointly owned restaurant. Reservations recommended. Singles 3500ptas/€21; doubles 6000ptas/€36. AmEx/MC/V.

Pensión Mallol, C. Pep Ventura 9 (☎97 250 22 83). Follow the Rambla toward the tourist office, turn right on Castell at its end, and take the 2nd left. Spacious, clean, and simply decorated rooms with shared bathrooms and firm mattresses; a very good value. Singles 2200ptas/€13; doubles 3700ptas/€22. Cash only.

Pensión San Mar, C. Rec Arnau 31 (☎97 250 98 13). Follow C. Girona off La Rambla and continue along as it turns into C. de la Jonquera; turn right on Travessera Rec Arnau and another right on C. Rec Arnau. Enter through the bar. Decorated with plants and no-frills furniture, Pensión San Mar offers one of the cheapest rooms in town. All rooms have bath. Singles 2000ptas/€12, doubles 4000ptas/€24. 30% deposit required for reservation. Cash only.

FOOD & NIGHTLIFE

After the sun goes down, a youngish crowd fills up the string of bars and outdoor tables on the Pl. del Sol. Occasionally there is live music, but even without it, Pl. Sol is where it's at. Restaurants near the Dalí museum serve overcooked *paella* to the masses; better choices surround the Rambla on small side streets. The **market** is at Pl. Gra and near Pl. de Catalunya (open Tu, Th, and Sa 5am-2pm with the widest selection on Th). Buy your own food at supermarket **MAXOR,** Pl. Sol 5. (☎97 251 00 19. Open July-Sept. M-Sa 9am-10pm; Oct.-June M-Sa 9am-9pm. MC/V.)

La Llesca, C. Mestre Falla 15 (☎97 267 58 26), just beyond Pl. Sol. Family-run restaurant specializes in *llesques*, toasted sandwiches topped with just about anything. *Menú* is a reasonable 1100ptas/€6,60; salads 450-675ptas/€2,8-4. Open M-Sa 7am-midnight, Su 6pm-midnight. AmEx/MC/V.

GET sm**art**

Decoding Dalí

Although Dalí's paintings can be confusing at first, aspects of their symbol-language are consistent enough to be translated. Here a few examples:

Look carefully at Dalí's **women.** Those portrayed in a cubist style are that way because they pose no threat to Dalí.

Most of Dalí's **landscapes** are of the rocky shores of Cadaqués.

A rotting **donkey** or **fish** is a symbol of the bourgeoisie.

The **crutches** propping up bits of soft flesh are symbols of masturbation.

The **grasshopper** is a symbol of terror, as Dalí had a great fear of the insect.

Staircases are a Freudian image, representing the fear of intercourse.

A **melting candle** is a symbol of impotence.

Lions represent animal aggression and **knives** are meant to be phallic symbols.

A **fish hook** (found in Dalí's head) is a symbol of his entrapment.

When asked about the famous **melting clocks,** Dalí replied, "the famous soft watches are nothing else than the tender, extravagant, solitary, paranoia-critical Camembert of time and space" (*Conquest of the Irrational,* 1969).

La Churraskita, C. Magre 5 (☎97 250 15 52). Hammocks and handweavings adorn the walls of this popular Argentinian restaurant. A romantic outdoor terrace hides out back. Wide selection of grilled meats (625-1550ptas/€3,60-9) as well as plenty of vegetarian options like pizza and salads (450-950ptas/€2,80-5,80). Open Tu-Su 1-4pm and 8pm-midnight. AmEx/MC/V.

Restaurante La Pansa, C. l'Empordá 8 (☎97 250 10 72). A comfortable, slightly more upscale restaurant serves meat and fish dishes and a popular 4-course *menú. Menú* 1200ptas/€7,20. Open M-Sa 1-4pm and 8-10pm, Su 1-4pm. AmEx/MC/V.

SIGHTS

⬛ TEATRE-MUSEU DALÍ

🄵 ☎97 267 75 00; fax 97 250 16 66; www.salvador-dali.org. From the Rambla, take C. Girona from the tourist office, which goes past Pl. Ajuntament and becomes C. de la Jonquera. Steps by a Dalí statue lead to the pink, egg-covered museum. Open daily Tu-Su Oct.-May 31 10:30am-5:45pm, June 10:30am-5:45pm, July-Sept. 9am-7:45pm. 1200ptas/€7; students and seniors 800ptas/€4,80.

Welcome to the enchanting world of the Surrealist master. This building was the municipal theater for the town of Figueres before it burned down in 1939—hence the name Teatre-Museu ("theater-museum") Dalí. When Dalí decided to donate a museum to Figueres, he insisted on using the ruins of the old theater, which was where he showed his first exposition as a teenager. The resulting homage to his first gallery is the reconstructed theater, covered in sculptures of eggs and full of Dalí's painting, sculptures, other creations, and his own tomb.

Despite his reputation as a fascist self-promoter, Dalí's personally designed mausoleum/museum/monument to himself should be approached as a multimedia experience, an electrifying tangle of sculpture, painting, music, and architecture. It's all here: Dalí's naughty cartoons, his dramatically low-key tomb, and many paintings of Gala, his wife and muse, one of which, when viewed through a telescope (10ptas/€0,01), transforms into a portrait of Abraham Lincoln. Careful when you look up at this work; if you're on the ground level, you're actually standing on Dalí's grave. The treasure trove of paintings includes, among others, the remarkable *Self Portrait with a Slice of Bacon, Poetry of America, Galarina,* and *Galatea of the Spheres.* Don't miss the spectacular *Sala de Mae West,* created by Dalí for the museum; when viewed from the lookout in the plastic camel, the furnished room resembles the face of actress Mae West. Other works include the surreal appearance of his own Cadillac in the middle of the museum. There is also a small offering of works by other artists selected by

Figueres

ACCOMMODATIONS
Hostal La Barretina, **6**
Pensión Mallol, **3**
Pensión San Mar, **1**

FOOD
La Churrasskita, **2**
La Llesca, **4**
Restaurante La Pansa, **5**

PLAÇA DEL PRESIDENT TARRADELLAS

C. Rubaudonadeu

Train Station

PLAÇA DE L'ESTACIÓ

(summer)

Estació Autobuses

C. Pompeu Fabra

Carrer Nord

Carrer de Colom

Carrer Sant Joan Baptista

Carrer Pi i Margall

Carrer Fossos

Calçada dels Monjos

Carrer Pella i Forgas

Carrer Mar

Avinguda de Vilallonga

Calçada Pou Artesia

Carrer Mendez Nuñez

Carrer Sant Llàtzer

Carrer Rentador

Carrer Sant Roc

C. de St.Francesc Paula

PLAÇA DEL GRA

PLAÇA DE L'ESCORRADOR

Carrer Concepció

C. Ntra. Sra. de Lourdes

Carrer Eres de la Vila

PLAÇA DE LA PALMERA

C. St. Cristòfer

Carrer Rutila

PLAÇA DE CATALUNYA

Carrer Castello

Carrer Bellaire

Pizzèrino

C. Maïca   Carrer St. J. Sol d'Isern

Carrer de Sant Antoni

Carrer Peralada

Carrer Sant Rafael

C. Blanc

Carrer Caamaño

PLAÇA ERNEST VILA

Carrer Nou

Carrer Ample

Carrer Muralla

C. Primfilat

C. de la Moratia

C. Joan Maragall

C. Forn Baix

Museu de l'Empordà

C. Pilar

C. St. Domènec

C. Tins

C. de Girona

Jardins Josep Puig Pujades

PLAÇA JOSEP PLÀ

TO (300m)

C. de la Barceloneta

PLAÇA DE L'AJUNTAMENT

Carrer Sant Pau

Carrer Sant Josep

Carrer Sant Vicenç

C. de Cadaqués

C. Isabel II

Carrer de la Jonquera

RAMBLA

Museu del Joguet

Banco Central Hispano

Carrer Vilafant

PL. GALA I SALVADOR DALI

(summer)

Teatre-Museu Dali

C. Cangó

C. Magre

Pujada del Castell

C. de Llers

C. Pep Ventura

C. Álvarez de Castro

Carrer Lasauca

Carrer de los Rodes

C. la Rosa

Carrer d'Olot

Torre Galatea

Sant Ferran

Verdaguer

Al Castell de

Ronda Cardenal Gomà

Ronda Mossèn Cinto

PLAÇA DEL SOL

Ronda Firal

TO CASTELL DE SAN FERRAN
TO CASTELL DE SAN FERRAN (500m)

Ronda del Rector Aroles

Parc Bosc

Passeig Nou

C. Mestre Falla

C. Poeta Marquina

Carrer Anglet de pagès

Carrer Empòrda

Maxor

N

200 yards
200 meters

191

HOLY SHIT! PART II

Visitors are often surprised by the infamous *caganer* (literally, "shitter"), a fixture of Catalan nativity scenes. The traditional nativity figures are all still there: the baby Jesus, Mary, Joseph, the kings, the shepherds...and there, hidden behind a bush or tree, is the *caganer*, a little ceramic guy with his pants around his knees, squatting down to do his business—and yes, there even is a ceramic business beneath him.

While this character may seem shocking, even offensive, to outsiders, Catalans swear the little dude has nothing but the best intentions. Catalans value regularity and regard the well-formed stool as the ultimate good, a sign of fertility and fortune. The *caganer* is, after all, fertilizing the earth and ensuring the health of the land. Some people collect these figures, which come in a variety of forms: Santa Claus, bride and groom, political figures such as Bill Clinton or José Maria Aznar, and even a man using the Internet as he squats, to name a few. So instead of cursing the next time you step in a mess left behind by a Catalan dog, stop and think how fortunate you are.

192

Dalí himself, including pieces by El Greco, Marcel Duchamp, and the architect Peres Piñero. While the museum is full of interesting art, not all the works are on the walls; look up as well.

MUSEU DEL JOGUET

🏠 *Hotel Paris, Rambla 10; enter on St. Pere.* ☎ *97 250 45 85; www.mjc-figueres.net. Open June-Sept. M-Sa 10am-1pm and 4-7pm, Su 11am-1:30pm and 5-7:30pm; Oct.-May Tu-Sa 10am-1pm and 4-7pm, Su 11am-1:30pm. 750ptas/€4,50; under 12 600ptas/€3,60.*

Delight in the wonders of your favorite childhood toys at the winner of Spain's 1999 National Prize of Popular Culture. A collection of antique dolls, blocks, board games, comics, rocking horses, toys for the blind, and more, as well as toys donated by famous Catalans such as Joan Miró and Salvador Dalí. Don't miss the impressive selection of Christmastime *caganers* (shitters), a Catalan favorite (see **Holy Shit!**, p. 192).

MUSEU EMPORDÁ

🏠 *Rambla 2.* ☎ *97 250 23 05. Open Tu-Sa 11am-7pm and Su 11am-2pm. 325ptas/€2, students and seniors 166ptas/€1. Free entrance with presentation of Teatre-Museu Dalí ticket (see above).*

A chronological presentation of the Alt Empordà region's art from Neolithic to Modern. On display are works by Casas, Tàpies, Dalí, and Miró, among others.

CASTELL DE SANT FERRAN

🏠 *Av. Castell de Sant Ferran; follow Pujada del Castell from the Teatre-Museu Dalí.* ☎ *97 250 60 94. Open daily July-Sept. 30 10:30am-7pm; Oct. 1-June 30 Tu-Su 10:30am-2pm. 350ptas/€2,10.*

A 10min. walk from the Museu Dalí, the massive 18th-century castle/fortress commands a spectacular view of the surrounding countryside and is the largest stone fortress in Europe at 12,000 sq. meters.

FESTIVALS

In September, classical and jazz music come to Figueres during the **Festival Internacional de Música de l'Empordà.** (Tickets available at Caixa de Catalunya. Call 97 210 12 12 or get a brochure at the tourist office.) From September 9th to 12th, the **Mostra del Vi de L'Alt Empordà,** a tribute to regional wines, brings a taste of the local vineyards to Figueres. Around May 3, the **Fires i Festes de la Santa Creu** sponsors cultural events, art and technology exhibitions, parties, and general merrymaking at the **Festa de Sant Pere,** held June 28-29, which honors the town's patron saint.

GIRONA (GERONA)

Girona (pop. 70,000) is a world-class city that the world has yet to notice. A Roman settlement and then an important medieval center, Girona was

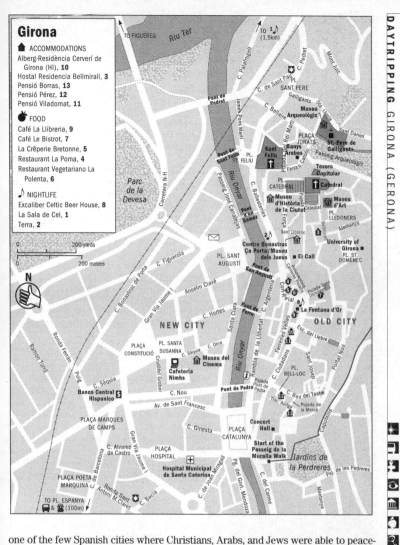

Girona

🏠 ACCOMMODATIONS
Alberg-Residència Cerverí de Girona (HI), **10**
Hostal Residencia Bellmirall, **3**
Pensió Borras, **13**
Pensió Pérez, **12**
Pensió Viladomat, **11**

🍴 FOOD
Café La Llíbreria, **9**
Café Le Bistrot, **7**
La Crêperie Bretonne, **5**
Restaurant La Poma, **4**
Restaurant Vegetariano La Polenta, **6**

🎵 NIGHTLIFE
Excaliber Celtic Beer House, **8**
La Sala de Cel, **1**
Terra, **2**

one of the few Spanish cities where Christians, Arabs, and Jews were able to peacefully coexist—for a time. Girona was the founding place of the renowned *cabalistas de Girona*, a group of 12th-century rabbis who created an oral tradition called the *Kabbala* based on numerological readings of the Torah (see **The Jewish Sepharad**, p. 194). The city is divided by the Riu Onyar, which separates the medieval alleys and Romanesque buildings of the old quarter from the Spanish dwellings of the new.

ORIENTATION & PRACTICAL INFORMATION

The **Riu Onyar** separates the new city from the old. The **Pont de Pedra** bridge connects the two banks and leads into the old quarter by way of C. Ciutadans, C. Peralta, and C. Força, which lead to the cathedral and **El Call**, the historic Jewish neighborhood. The **RENFE** and **bus terminals** are situated off C. de Barcelona, in the modern neighborhood. To get to the old city from the stations, head straight out through the parking lot, turning left on C. Barcelona. Follow C. Barcelona for two blocks until it forks at the traffic island. Take the right fork via C. Santa Eugenia to Gran Via de Jaume I, and continue across the Gran Via to C. Nou, which leads to the Pont de Pedra.

193

THE JEWISH SEPHARAD

Though Girona has a reputation for tolerance, the Jews of Girona were still victims of discrimination, ostracism, and eventual expulsion. Despite it all, they contributed ineradicably to the city's culture. The *aljama* (Jewish quarter) in Girona, once populated by 300 people, became a leading center for the study of the **Kabbala,** a mystical reading of the Torah in which number values are assigned to each Hebrew letter and numerical sums are interpreted to reveal spiritual meaning. Operating like a tiny, independent country within the city (inhabitants answered to their King, not the city government), El Call (see p. 196) was protected by the crown of Catalunya in exchange for financial tribute.

Until the 11th century, Christians and Jews coexisted peacefully, occasionally even intermarrying. Unfortunately, this did not last. Historical sources cite attacks and looting of the Jewish quarter in eight separate years, the first in 1276 and the last in 1418. Eventually, almost every entrance to El Call was blocked off. The reopening of the streets of El Call began only after Franco's death in 1975. In recent years, eight Spanish mayors have created a network called *Caminos de Sepharad*, an organization aimed at restoring Spain's Jewish quarters and fostering a broader understanding of the Sephardic legacy. for more on Jews in Catalunya, see **Catalan Jews,** p. 68.

Trains: RENFE (☎97 224 02 02 for info and reservations; www.renfe.es), in Pl. de Espanya. Info open daily 6:30am-10pm. To: **Barcelona** (1¼hr., 21 per day 6:12am-9:29pm, 930ptas/€5,60); **Figueres** (30-40min., 24 per day 6:15am-10:44pm, 390ptas/€2,30); **Madrid** (10½hr., 8:21pm, 6800ptas/€41); **Portbou** (50min.-1hr., 12 per day 6:15am-10:44pm 525ptas/€3,20); and **Paris** (11hr., 10:17pm, 17,700ptas-19,300ptas/€107-€116).

Buses: Station police ☎97 2 21 23 19. Station right next to the train station. **Sarfa** (☎97 220 17 96; window open M-F 6:45am-9:15pm, Sa 6:45am-1pm and 4:30-8pm, Su 6:45am-noon and 3:45-8pm; 10% discount for students; cash only) runs to **Palafrugell** (1¼hr., 17 per day, 590ptas/€3,50), for connections to Begur, Llafranc, Calella, and Tamariu and to **Tossa de Mar** (40min.; July-Aug. 2 per day, Sept.-June 1 per day; 580ptas/€3,50). **Teisa** (☎97 220 02 75; open M-F 9am-1pm and 3:30-7:15pm, Sa-Su 9am-1pm; cash only) drives to: **St. Feliu** (45min., 9-14 per day, 490ptas/€3); **Olot** (1¼hr., 9 per day, 720ptas/€4,30); **Ripoll** (2hr., 3 per day, 1240ptas/€7,50); **Lerida** (3½hr.; 2 per day; 2375ptas/€14,30, for students 2140ptas/€12,90). **Barcelona Bus** (☎97 220 24 32; M-F 7-10am, 11am-2pm, and 4:30-7pm; MC/V) express to **Barcelona** (1¼hr., 3-6 per day, 1345ptas/€8,10) and **Figueres** (50min., 2-6per day, 540ptas/€3,30).

Taxis: ☎97 222 23 23 or 972 22 10 20. Try Pl. Independència and Pont de Pedra.

Car Rental: Europcar is inside the train station, and other companies cluster around C. Barcelona, right outside. Must be 21+ (for most) and have had a license for at least 1-2 years. **Hertz,** C. Bailen 2 (☎97 241 00 68). Walk through the parking lot away from the train station and you will see C. Bailen leading off diagonally to your left. Min. age 25. Rentals start at 7000ptas/€42, plus 10ptas/€0,06 per km after the first 300km. Open M-F 8am-1pm and 4-8pm, Sa 8am-1pm. AmEx/MC/V; credit cards only.

Tourist Office: Rambla Llibertat 1 (☎97 222 65 75; fax 97 222 66 12), in a yellow building directly on the left as you cross Pont de Pedra from the new town. Tons of free info on the city and region. English spoken. Open M-F 8am-8pm, Sa 8am-2pm and 4-8pm, Su 9am-2pm. The **train station branch** (☎97 220 70 93) is to the right of the RENFE ticket counter. Open July-Sept. M-Sa 8am-1pm and 3-8pm.

Currency Exchange: Banco Central Hispano, one on the corner of C. Nou and Gran Via, another on Pujada Pont de Pedra (on the right after crossing the bridge into the old city). **ATMs.** Open Oct.-Mar. M-F 8:30am-2:30pm, Sa 8:30am-1pm; Apr.-Sept. 30 M-F 8:30am-2:30pm.

Luggage Storage: Lockers in train station (700ptas/€4,20 per 24hr.). Open M-F 6:30am-10pm.

Travel Bookstore: Ulysseus, C. Ballesteries 29 (☎/fax 97 221 17 73), on the left-hand side of the street as you walk up Ballesteries toward the Pl. Cathedral.

Very thorough offering of regional guides to Spain, as well as country guides for most of Europe; some in English (3000-4500ptas/€18-27). Open M-Sa 10am-2pm and 4:30-8:30pm. MC/V.

Supermarket: Hipercor: (☎97 218 84 00), on C. Barcelona; take a right out of the train station (15min.). El Corte Inglés' not-so-chic cousin. Groceries, clothing, telephones, currency exchange, English books, and cafeteria. Open M-Sa 10am-10pm.

Emergency: ☎112. **Police: Policía Municipal,** C. Bacià 4 (☎092). From Banco Central Hispano, turn right on the Gran Via, then right on Bacià.

Hospital: Hospital Municipal de Santa Caterina, Pl. Hospital 5 (☎97 218 26 00).

Internet Access: Corado Telephone, C. Barcelona 31 (☎97 222 28 75), across from the train station. 300ptas/€1,80 per hr. Open M-Sa 9am-2pm and 5-9pm. **Cafeteria Nimhs,** C. Sèquia 5 (☎97 222 03 86), next to Museu del Cinema. 200ptas/€1,20 for 15min., 500ptas/€3 per hr. Open M-F 8am-10pm.

Post Office: Av. Ramón Folch 2 (☎97 222 21 11), at the start of Gran Via de Jaume I. Turn right on Gran Via coming from the old city. **Second office,** Ronda Ferrán Puig 17 (☎97 222 34 75). **Lista de Correos** only. Both open M-F 8:30am-8:30pm and Sa 9:30am-2pm. **Postal Code:** 17070.

ACCOMMODATIONS

Rooms are only hard to find in July and August, when reservations are a good idea on weekends. Most budget accommodations are in the old quarter and are well-kept and reasonably priced.

Pensió Viladomat, C. Ciutadans 5 (☎97 220 31 76; fax 97 220 31 76), next door to the youth hostel. Light, open, well-furnished rooms and a dining/reading area with balcony. Rooms with bath have TVs, and guests get keys. Singles 2500ptas/€15; doubles 5000ptas/€30, with bath 7500ptas/€45; triples with bath 9500ptas/€57. Cash only.

Hostal Residencia Bellmirall, C. Bellmirall 3 (☎97 220 40 09). With the cathedral directly behind you, C. Bellmirall is straight ahead to the left; look for the blue hostel sign. Expensive but absolutely delightful rooms in a 14th-century stone house. Breakfast included and served in the cozy dining area or plant-filled garden patio. Make reservations. Closed Jan.6-Feb. 28. Singles 5300ptas/€32; doubles 8200ptas/€49, with bath 9200ptas/€55,50; triples 12,495ptas/€75,30; family room (for 4) 16,000ptas/€96,40 (IVA included). Cash only.

Albergue-Residència Cerverí de Girona (HI), C. Ciutadans 9 (☎97 221 80 03; fax 97 221 20 23). From the new city, cross Pont de Pedra, take a left on Ciutadans; it's about a block up on your left. The sterile, whitewashed walls and blue metal bunks in this college dorm building may cause flashbacks to sleep-away camp, but the price and location make it worthwhile. 8 beds available Oct.-June; 82 beds July-Sept.

Modernist Architecture in Figueres

Dalí Museum's Mae West Installation

Dalí Museum

Sleek sitting rooms with TV/VCR; rooms of 3 and 8 beds with lockers. Breakfast included; other meals 850ptas/€5,20. Sheets 350ptas/€2,10. Laundry 500ptas/€3. Internet 300ptas/€1,20 per hr. **Members only,** but HI cards for sale. Make reservations at the Barcelona office (☎93 483 83 63). Dorms 2000ptas/€12, over 25 2700ptas/€16,30. MC/V.

Pensió Pérez, Pl. Bell-lloc 4 and **Pensió Borras,** Trav. Auriga 6 (☎97 222 40 08). Continue straight after crossing Pont de Pedra into the old quarter onto C. Nou; Pl. Bell-lloc is on the right. To Pensió Borras from Pérez, take a right out the door and follow the street around the corner, making a left at its end. The Pérez is on the 2nd floor of the last building on your right. Both pensions, owned by the same woman, offer sparse rooms with good prices and location. Singles 2000ptas/€12; doubles 3500ptas/€21, with bath 4000ptas/€24; triples 4700ptas/€28. Cash only.

FOOD

Considered home to some of the best cuisine in Catalunya, Girona's specialties are its *botifarra dolça* (sweet sausage of pork with lemon, cinnamon, and sugar) and *xuixo* (sugar-sprinkled pastries filled with cream). Popular throughout Spain, *xuixo* originated in C. Argenteria, the continuation of La Rambla. By far the best place to find good, cheap food is on C. Cort Reial, at the top of C. Argenteria; La Rambla is home to rows of tourist cafés with ubiquitous terrace seating. In summer, an open **market** can is near the Polideportivo in Parc de la Deversa (open Tu and Sa 8am-3pm). Get your **groceries** at **Caprabo,** C. Sequia 10, a block from C. Nou off the Gran Via. (☎97 221 45 16. Open M-Sa 9am-9pm.)

La Crêperie Bretonne, C. Cort Reial 14 (☎97 221 81 20). Potent proof of Girona's proximity to France, this popular *crêpe* joint offers funky atmosphere in addition to good taste; old French posters decorate the stone walls, and your food is cooked inside a small bus bound for "Cerbère." *Menú* 1350ptas/€8,10. *Crêpes* 350-875ptas/€2,10-5,30. Unusual salads 850-925ptas/€5,10-5,60. Open M 1-4pm and Tu-Sa 1-4pm and 8pm-midnight. MC/V.

Restaurante La Poma, C. Cort Reial 16 (☎ 97 221 29 09). Internationally-influenced sandwiches, *crêpes*, pasta, pizza, and salads at unbelievable prices, in a friendly restaurant decked out in primary colors. Salads and pasta 650-750ptas/€3,90-4,50. Pizza 675ptas/€4. *Crêpes* 500-600ptas/€3-3,40. Open W-M 7:30pm-midnight. Cash only.

Café Le Bistrot, Pujada Sant Domènech 4 (☎97 221 88 03), a right off C. Ciutadans. Excellent food, an elegant, old-fashioned atmosphere, and a "quintessentially Girona" view. Fresh specialty pizzas 600-700ptas/€3,60-4,20. *Crêpes* 500-725ptas/€3-4,20. Lunchtime *menú* 1500ptas/€9, smaller version 1300ptas/€7,80. Terrace costs 10% extra. Open M-Th 1-4pm and 8pm-1am, F-Sa 1-4pm and 7pm-2am, Su 1-4pm and 8pm-midnight. MC/V.

Restaurant Vegetariano La Polenta, C. Cort Reial, 6 (☎97 220 93 74). Vegetarian *menú del día* with an international accent and innovative rice, tofu, and polenta dishes (1400ptas/€8,40; IVA included). This small restaurant fills up at lunchtime but maintains a quiet, pleasant atmosphere. Open M-F 1-4pm. MC/V.

SIGHTS

🔢 *At any one of the following museums, you can buy a combined ticket which gets you access to all 6 city museums for only 800ptas/€4,80 (good for a month).*

The narrow, winding streets of the medieval city, interspersed with steep stairways and low arches, are ideal for wanderers. Start your self-guided historical tour at the **Pont de Pedra** and turn left at the tourist office down tree-lined **Rambla de la Llibertat.** Continue on C. Argenteria, bearing right across C. Cort Reial. Up the flight of stairs, C. Força begins on the left.

EL CALL

🔢 *The entrance to the center is off C. Força, about halfway up the hill.* ☎*97 221 67 61. Center and museum open June-Oct. M-Sa 10am-8pm, Su 10am-2pm; Nov.-May M-Sa 10am-6pm, Su 10am-3pm. Museum costs 300ptas/€1,80, students and over 65 150ptas/€0,90, under 16 free. The tourist office also offers guided tours of El Call in July and Aug. for 1000ptas/€6 during the day and 2000ptas/€12 at night.*

The part of the old town around C. Força and C. Sant Llorenç was once the center of Girona's medieval Jewish community ("call" comes from *kahal*, "community" in

Hebrew.) The site of the last synagogue in Girona now serves as the **Centre Bonastruc Ca Porta,** named for Rabbi Moshe Ben-Nahman (Nahmanides), a scholar of Jewish mysticism and the oral tradition known as the *Kabbala* (see **The Jewish Sepharad,** p. 194). The center includes the **Museu d'Història dels Jueus Girona,** notable for its detailed wooden model of the original Call, as well as its collection of inscribed Hebrew tombstones.

CATHEDRAL COMPLEX

◪ *Tesoro* ☎ *97 221 44 26. Cathedral and Tesoro open July-Sept. Tu-Sa 10am-2pm and 4-7pm, Oct.-Mar. Tu-Sa 10am-2pm and 4-6pm, Mar.-June Tu-Sa 10am-2pm and 4-7pm; open year-round Su-M and holidays 10am-2pm. Tesoro and cloister 500ptas/€3.*

Farther uphill on C. Força and around the corner to the right, Girona's imposing Gothic **cathedral** rises a record-breaking 90 steps (its Baroque stairway is the largest in Europe) from the plaça. The **Torre de Charlemany** (bell tower) and **cloister** are the only structures left from the 11th and 12th centuries; the rest of the building dates from the 14th-17th centuries. The most unique feature of the cathedral is its interior, where the three customary naves have been compressed into one. It is the world's widest Gothic **nave** (22m) and is surpassed in sheer size only by St. Peter's in Rome. A door on the left leads to the trapezoidal cloister and the **Tesoro Capitular (treasury),** home to some of Girona's most precious possessions. The tesoro's (and possibly Girona's) most famous piece is the **Tapis de la Creació,** a 11th-century tapestry depicting the creation story.

MUSEUMS

MUSEU DEL CINEMA

◪ *C. Sèquia 1, one block north of C. Nou off C. Santa Clara.* ☎ *97 241 2 777. Open Oct.-Apr. M-F 10am-6pm, Sa 10am-8pm, Su 11am-3pm; May-Sept. daily 10am-8pm. In summer, 90min. guided tours in multiple languages Tu-Su at noon and 6pm; in winter, Sa 6pm and Su noon, in Spanish and Catalan only; 300ptas/€1,50. Private English tours 11,000ptas/€6,60 per guide. Museum entrance 500ptas/€3, for students and over 65 250ptas/€1,50, under 16 free. AmEx/MC/V.*

This unusual collection, the best of its kind in Europe, documents the rise of cinema from the mid-17th to the 20th century, with a few pieces from as early as the 11th century (Chinese shadow theater). It walks you through the chronological development of the camera obscura (9th-12th century), magic lantern (1659), panorama (1788), diorama (1822), Thomas Edison's kinetoscope (1891), and more, with several hands-on visual displays and a short film at the end. In summer, when they're cheaper, it's worth catching one of the guided visits in English.

Catalunya's Caganer

Teddybear at the Toy Museum

Devilish Puppet at the Toy Museum

CITY MUSEUMS

🛈 *At any one of the following museums, you can buy a combined ticket which gets you access to all 6 city museums for only 800ptas/€4,80 (good for a month).*

In addition to the Jewish Museum and the Cathedral *Tesoro*, Girona boasts four small city-related treasures, the Museu d'Història de la Ciutat, Banys Arabs, Museu Arqueològic, and the Museu d'Art, worth visiting in that order.

The remarkably well-done **Museu d'Història de la Ciutat** showcases 2000 years of Girona's history, from the first settlers in Catalunya to the present day; check out the festival giants and the room dedicated to Napoleonic War. (C. Força 27. ☎97 222 22 29. Open Tu-Sa 10am-2pm and 5-7pm, Su and holidays 10am-2pm. Some descriptions in English. 200ptas/€1,20, under 16 free.) To get to the **Banys Arabs** from the cathedral, with your back to the stairs, take a right on C. Ferran Catòlic. Inspired by Muslim bath houses, the graceful 12th-century structure once contained saunas and baths of varying temperatures; now they occasionally host art outdoor art exhibits. (☎97 221 32 62. Open Apr.-Sept. M-Sa 10am-7pm, Su 10am-2pm; Oct.-Mar. daily 10am-2pm. 250ptas/€1,50, students 100ptas/€0,60.) The **Museu Arqueològic** complements its archeological displays with detailed booklets on the history of the area (available in English), and the **Museu d'Art** holds medieval and modern art, including themed rooms on glass, ceramics, and liturgical art. The Museu Arqueològic is past the Banys Arabs through Pl. Jurants, on the right. (☎97 220 26 32. Open Tu-Sa 10:30am-1:30pm and 4-7pm, Su 10am-2pm. 300ptas/€1,80, for students 225ptas/€1,40, under 16 free.) The Museu d'Art is next to the cathedral. (☎97 220 38 34. Open Tu-Sa Mar.-Sept. 10am-7pm, Oct.-Feb. 10am-6pm; Su and holidays 10am-2pm. 300ptas/€1,80, for students and over 65 225ptas/€1,40.)

WALKS & TOURS

Girona's renowned 🏛**Passeig de la Muralla,** not for the faint of heart, begins at the bottom of La Rambla in Pl. de la Marvà. Take the steps up to the guard's rampart atop the old Roman defense walls and follow them around the entire eastern side of the old town. The walk ends behind the Cathedral, where the equally beautiful **Passeig Arqueològic** begins. Partly lined with cypresses and flower beds, this path skirts the northeastern medieval wall and also overlooks the city. (Passeig de la Muralla is open daily 8am-10pm.) For the less athletically inclined, a small trolley gives a 30min. guided tour of the main sights of the old town, including the town hall, Cathedral, St. Feliu church, El Call, and the walls. (In summer, leaves daily every 20-25min. from the Pont de Pedra, 10am-8pm or so. In winter, it runs less frequently, sometimes only weekends; check in the tourist office. Available in English. 500ptas/€3, for students 400ptas/€2,40.)

NIGHTLIFE & ENTERTAINMENT

La Rambla and **Pl. de Independència** are the places to see and be seen in Girona. Nightlife spots in the new city are scattered; the only concentrated locales are Pl. de Independència, the old quarter, and in summer, the expansive, impeccably designed **Parc de la Devesa,** which explodes with *carpas*, temporary outdoor bars. (Across the river from the old town, several blocks to the left. Open June-Sept. 15 Su-Th 10pm-3am and F-Sa 10pm-4:30am. Drinks 700-900ptas/€4,20-5,40. Cash only.) The bars and cafés in the old quarter are particularly mellow and relaxing, a good way to start the evening. In addition to the disco listed below, **Platea,** behind the post office on C. Fontclara, is a popular early morning dance spot on weekends.

Café la Llibreria, C. Ciutadans 15 (☎97 220 10 82). Behind the bookstore; enter on C. Ferreires Vellas, parallel to C. Ciutadans. Cocktails (600ptas/€3,60), beer (225ptas/€1,40), and *tapas* (350-450ptas/€2,10-2,70) served to chic intellectual types. Live music (usually guitar) W and F after 11pm. Internet 100ptas/€0,60 for 12min., 500ptas/€3 per hr. Open M-Sa 8:30am-1am, Su 8:30am-midnight. MC/V.

Excalibur Celtic Beer House, Pl. de l'Oli 1 (☎97 220 82 53), at the top of C. Ciutadans. The only authentic place in Girona to go for a pint of Guinness (600ptas/€3,60) and English-speaking expat company; it's a favorite of the university's English professors. Irish rock and American pop from the speakers, lots of European sports on the TV. Drinks 700ptas/€4,20. Open M-Th 6pm-12:30pm, F-Su 4pm-3am. MC/V.

It's Your World...

www.mci.com/worldphone

WorldPhone. Worldwide

MCI^{SM} gives you the freedom of worldwide communications whenever you're away from home. It's easy to call to and from over 70 countries with your MCI Calling Card:

1. Dial the WorldPhone® access number of the country you're calling from.
2. Dial or give the operator your MCI Calling Card number.
3. Dial or give the number you're calling.

- Barcelona   900-99-0014

Sign up today!
Ask your local operator to place a collect call
(reverse charge) to MCI in the U.S. at:

1-712-943-6839

For additional access codes or to sign up, visit us at www.mci.com/worldphone.

www.mci.com/worldphone

La Terra, C. Ballestries 23 (☎97 221 57 64), marked only by a small scrawled name on the concrete entrance step. Low marble tables, mismatched ceramics, and cozy nooks fill this understated student hangout. Try their fruit juices (400ptas/€1,80) or popular alcoholic juice concoctions (500ptas/€3). Open M-Th 5pm-1am, F-Su 5pm-2am. Cash only.

La Sala del Cel, C. Pedret 118 (☎97 221 46 64), a 15min. walk upriver from the Pont de St. Feliu, on the old town side. A complex more than a mere club, with 3 techno and house-blasting dance floors, a huge hangout area with black leather couches, a pool and slide, Play Station computers, a free massage room, and herbal party favors. Cover 2000ptas/€12 (includes 1 drink). Open F-Sa midnight-5:30am. MC/V.

Cinema Truffaut, C. Portal Nou 7 (☎97 222 50 44). From C. Nou, go right on C. Subida de la Merced, and then left right after the stairs. One foreign original version movie every week. 700ptas/€4,20, Th 550ptas/€3,30, for under 23 and over 65 300ptas/€1,80. Box office open daily 6pm-12:30am. Cash only.

FESTIVALS

During the second half of May, government-sponsored **flower exhibitions** spring up in the city; local monuments and pedestrian streets swim in blossoms, and the courtyards of Girona's fine old buildings open to the public. Summer evenings often inspire spontaneous *sardana* dancing in the city *plaças* (see **Gettin' Jiggy With it,** p. 52). Like the rest of Catalunya, Girona also lights up for the **Focs de Sant Joan** on June 24, an outdoor party featuring fireworks and campfires.

NEAR GIRONA: PÚBOL

🔁 *From Girona, take the train or bus to Flaça and pick up a taxi to Púbol, 3km away (approx. 1500ptas/€9).* **Sarfa** *(☎97 220 17 96 or 97 264 09 64) runs* **buses** *from Girona to Flaça; 30min.; M-F 7:45am-8:30pm (every 30min., Sa-Su 9am-8:30pm every hr.); 265ptas/€1,59).* **RENFE** *(☎902 24 02 02) trains connect Barcelona to Flaça (1hr. 40min; every 30min.-1hr. 6am-9:20pm, 960ptas/€5,80); and from Girona to Flaça (15min; several per hour; 6:15am-9:36pm; 180-210ptas/€1-1,40).*

In the late 1960s, the adoring Salvador Dalí bought a crumbling 14th-century castle in the tiny village of Púbol for his beloved wife and muse, Gala. The Surrealist master set about restoring the castle to its former glory, while insuring that it maintained a slightly time-worn appearance which he and his wife prized. Legend has it that when Gala moved into her Púbol mansion, Dalí declared he would never visit without her written request. Rumors further suggest that in Dalí's absence, Gala entertained a fair share of male visitors. The **Casa-Museu Castell Gala Dalí,** Púbol's major—and only—attraction, has been open to visitors since 1996. (☎97 248 86 55. Open Mar. 15-June 14 and Sept. 16-Nov. 1 Tu-Su 10:30am-6pm, Jun. 15-Sept. 15 daily 10:30am-8pm. Last entrance 45min. before closing. 700ptas/€4,25, students and seniors 500ptas/€3. Free guided tours at noon in Catalan and at 5pm in Castillian. Wheelchair accessible.) Besides Gala's tomb, tastefully sandwiched between the garage and gardens, the castle contains several of Dalí's works, including a colorful ceiling painting, a chess set made to resemble thumbs, and an elaborate gold and blue throne. The artist lived in the castle after Gala's death in 1982 and was almost killed when he accidently set fire to his bedroom two years later. One of his last works, a refined painting with strong, contrasting colors, sits on an easel in the castle's dining room. There is little else to see in tiny Púbol, but if you get hungry before or after visiting the castle, **Can Bosch,** on C. Fera Muralia, next door offers solid Catalan fare and is about the only option. (☎97 248 83 57. Open daily July 15-Aug. 31 9am-11pm, Sept.-June M-W 9:30am-6pm, Th-Su 9:30am-8pm. Daily *menú* 1100ptas/€6,50. MC/V.)

L'ESCALA & EMPÚRIES

L'Escala (pop. 5000, in summer 75,000) is a good launching point for the numerous coves and beaches in the area. Once a fishing village that made it big with anchovies, L'Escala's old quarter has pleasant pedestrian paths and tree-lined promenades, and the beaches and the Greek and Roman ruins of nearby **Empúries** make the town a very worthwhile trip from Palafrugell. Less cosmopolitan than some of its Costa Brava neighbors, L'Escala attracts mostly local tourists and day trippers.

ORIENTATION & PRACTICAL INFORMATION

For **Sarfa buses,** call 97 277 02 18. Tickets are available on the bus. Buses run to: Figueres (55min., 5 per day 7:10am-7:05pm, 485ptas/€2,90); Girona (1hr., 7:30am and 2:30pm, 555ptas/€3,40); and Palafrugell (35min., 5 per day 7:10am-6:55pm, 365ptas/€2,20). Buses stop in front of the tourist office. With your back to the tourist office, the ruins are to the left (walk down Rda. del Pedró) and the heart of the town is straight ahead (down Av. Ave Maria). L'Escala is a compact and very walkable town; its main thoroughfare, Av. Ave Maria runs from Pl. Escoles (tourist office) downhill to the water in a matter of several long blocks. The Alberg d'Empúries youth hostel arranges **mountain bike rental** if you contact them in advance, and **Empordá Bikes,** Av. Ave Maria 9, also rents bikes. (☎97 277 40 42. 500ptas/€3 per hr., 1900ptas/€11,42 per day; 10% discount when renting 2 or more bikes. Open June-Sept. daily 9am-1pm and 5-8pm; Oct.-June Tu-Sa 9am-1pm and 5-8pm.) The **tourist office,** Pl. Escoles 1, has a helpful map, tourist info, and **fax** service. (☎97 277 06 03; fax 97 277 33 85. Open June-Sept. M-Sa 9am-8:30pm, Su 10am-1pm; Oct.-May M-Sa 9am-1pm and 4-7pm and Su 10am-1pm.) The **Banco Central Hispano,** C. Maranges 16 has an **ATM** (open Apr.-Oct. M-F 8:30am-2:30pm; Oct.-Mar. M-F 8:30am-2:30pm and Sa 8:30am-1pm). Other resources include: **medical emergencies** (☎ 90 809 43 33); **municipal police,** C. Pintor Joan Massanet 24 (☎97 277 48 18); and the **post office,** next to the tourist office. (Open M-F 8:30am-2:30pm, Sa 9:30am-1pm.) The **postal code** is 17130.

ACCOMMODATIONS

Despite the abundance of options, finding a cheap room in L'Escala can be difficult, especially during the summer months.

Alberg de Empúries, Les Coves 41 (☎97 277 12 00). A 10min. walk from the Empúries ruins, in a grove of trees. Facing the tourist office, follow the road on the right toward the coast. When you get to the headless male statue, take a left down the small lane and into the wooded area; the hostel awaits about 5min. down the road. Across the road from some of L'Escala's loveliest beaches. Friendly owners, English books, and TV make it worth the walk. Breakfast included. **HI members** only; cards available. To guarantee reservations, call Barcelona's youth office 1 month in advance (☎93 483 83 63; www.tujuca.com). Reception hours 10am-1pm and 7-8:30pm. Mar.-June dorms 2000ptas/€12; over 25 2700ptas/€16,23; July-Sept. dorms 2350ptas/€14,12; over 25 3000ptas/€18; Oct.-Feb. dorms 1775ptas/€10,67; over 25 2400ptas/€14,42. Traveler's checks accepted. AmEx/MC/V.

Pensió Torrent, C. Riera 28 (☎97 277 02 78). From Pl. Escoles walk downhill 1 block on C. Pintor, turn left, and follow the street around the corner. Hostel has whitewashed rooms with clean bathrooms. Doubles 4500ptas/€27; off season 3000ptas/€18. Cash only.

Hostal Miryam, Rda. del Pedró 4 (☎97 277 02 87). Across the street from the tourist office. Rooms with TV, bath, and telephone. Doubles 7400ptas/€44. MC/V.

FOOD

From May to September, the town **market** is held daily 7am-2pm in **Pl. Víctor Català** (Oct.-Apr. Tu, Th, Sa-Su 7am-2pm). Alternatively, fill your basket at **MAXOR,** Pl. Escoles 2, across the street from the tourist office (open M-F 8am-2pm and 4:30-9pm, Sa 8:30am-9pm, Su 9am-2pm).

Restaurante-Bar Cal Galán, C. La Torre 18 (☎97 277 01 40). Enter around the corner on C. L'Usach. Cavernous and cool with exposed brick and stone ceiling, Cal Galán is good place to try local dishes in a former fishermen's hangout. Lunch *menú* 1175ptas/€7, dinner *menú* 1500ptas/€9. House speciality is pig's cheeks with fried egg and tomato. Entrees 525-850ptas/€3-5. Open daily Oct.-May M and W-Su 8:30am-midnight. Closed Nov. MC/V.

Pizzeria del Port, C. de Port 9 (☎97 277 03 34). Vegetarians will rejoice over the Italian-Mediterranean fare at this seaside establishment. Outdoor tables and fresh, delicious pizzas. *Menú* 1595ptas/€9,60; pastas 750-1100ptas/€4,50-6,60. Open daily May-Oct. 11am-4pm and 7pm-midnight; Nov.-Apr. Su-Tu, Th-Sa 11am-4pm and 7pm-midnight. MC/V.

La Flama, C. Enric Serra 15 (☎97 267 23 60). Sit indoors or out at this Mediterranean-themed restaurant with an extensive seafood menu. Daily *menús* from 1400ptas/€8,40 include wine. *Tapas* 300-875ptas/€1,80-5,20 and entrees 800-2300ptas/€4,80-13.

SIGHTS

EMPÚRIES

🚶 *To get to Empúries, walk 20-30min. north, following C. Mirador del Pedró to Camí Forestal (at the headless male statue), or take the little train, Carrilet (☎ 93 765 47 84), which stops across the street from the tourist office, to St. Martí d'Empúries and ask to get off at the ruins (June 15-Sept. 15 on the hr., every hr. 8am-9pm, 250ptas/€1,50).* **Ruins and museum** *(☎ 97 277 02 08; www.mac.es). Open daily June-Sept. 10am-8pm; Oct.-May 10am-6pm. 400ptas/€2,40; students and seniors 300ptas/€3,60. Audio-visual program screened every 30min. from 10:30am until closing; 300ptas/€3,60.* **Aquatic tour** *(☎ 609 136 00 04). Open 10am-7pm daily. 600ptas/€3,60 or 525ptas/€3,20 with ticket to ruins. Look for the CASC hut on the beach in front of the ruins; bring your swimsuit.*

Just 1km north of L'Escala are the ruins of Empúries. In the 7th century BC, Greek traders landed on a small island on the northeast Iberian coast. As the settlement grew, it moved to the mainland and became the prosperous colony of Emporion (meaning "marketplace"); four centuries later, it fell into Roman hands. Mostly knee-high remnants of both Greek and Roman cities, including some gorgeous mosaic floors and a Visigoth basilica, fill Empúries's 40 hectares of ruins. Excavation continues, backed by profits from the 1992 Olympic Games. (The Olympic torch first formally entered Spain through this ancient Greek port city, commemorated by the headless male statue.) A winding road at the entrance takes you through the remarkable ruins, from which the careful layout of the great ancient cities is visible. The small but wealthy **Museu Monogràfic d'Empúries** showcases a large collection of ceramics and Etruscan wares. Explanatory signs in a variety of languages throughout the ruins indicate the ancient urban plan amid the fountains, mosaics, and columns set against a backdrop of cypress trees and the breezy Mediterranean. If you can't get enough of Empúries, the **Centre d'Arqueològia Subaquática de Catalunya** (CASC) offers snorkeling tours of the remains of 2000 year old submerged ships off the city's shore.

OTHER SIGHTS

Half a kilometer north of the ruins is the entrance to the free **Parc Natural dels Aiguamolls de l'Empordà**, a protected habitat with miles of marshland and lakes, filled with plant and animal species. The park's information center (open daily 9:30am-2pm and 4:30pm-7pm) provides a free map and advice about different walks. For more details on the park, contact the information center, **El Cortalet** (☎ 97 245 42 22).

BEACHES

Playa del Barcos is the closest beach to the town's center, off C. del Port. The beaches near **Empúries**, a 30min. walk from the center of L'Escala, are more secluded and less trafficked. The **Playa de Les Muscleres** in front of the ruins and the **Playa de Portitxol** in the next cove, are both wonderful, family-oriented options with paddle boat rentals and shallow water.

NIGHTLIFE

The after-dark hot spots in L'Escala are the bars that line the beachfront around Playa de Barcos and shoot off the side streets in the older part of town. Most bars serve the town's specialty—*pan con tomate* topped with local anchovies.

CADAQUÉS & PORT LLIGAT

The whitewashed houses and small bay of Cadaqués (pop. 2000) have attracted artists, writers, and musicians ever since **Dalí** built his summer home in neighboring Port Lligat in the 1930s. Cadaqués is the bigger of the two towns (Port Lligat is basically just Dalí's house), which are so close to each other that they are virtually superimposed. To preserve the towns' authentic Mediterranean flavor, an affluent crowd of property owners and renters have kept at bay the commercial influx of sprawling condos, big hotels, and trains. Cadaqués has not been immune, however, to the trendy influence of the hordes of French tourists who flock there in the summer, and

GET sm**art**

Dalí or not Dalí?

When Spanish police busted into the Centre d'Art Perrot-Moore in Cadaqués in April 1999, they arrested Captain Peter Moore and his wife Catherine Perrot on charges of art forgery. Moore, a British Army captain, was a friend and assistant to Salvador Dalí for 20 years until the artist passed away in 1989. The private collection of Captain Moore was on display at the Centre d'Art Perrot-Moore, which was quietly shut down following the couple's arrest and subsequent release on bail. Police, aided by a team of art historians, are collaborating in their efforts to discover whether over 10,000 prints ready for sale at the Centre d'Art Perrot-Moore are fakes. Authorities believe that Moore pressured an ailing Dalí into signing thousands of blank pieces of paper which were then printed with "limited edition" lithographs and sold as Dalí originals. Dalí thus continues to be the scandal-monger of the art world, even in death.

droves of day trippers up from Barcelona to see Dalí's house; chic galleries and shops have cropped up to suit the cosmopolitan crowd. The rocky beaches and dreamy landscape attract their share of tourists, but Cadaqués preserves a pleasantly laid-back atmosphere. Be forewarned: if you're traveling to Cadaqués in between September and May, it's best to make it a daytrip only, as most food and entertainment options shut down in the off season.

TRANSPORTATION

Cadaqués has no train station, but Sarfa **buses** (☎97 225 87 13) run to: **Barcelona** (2½hr., 4-6 per day, 2365ptas/€14,20); **Figueres** (1hr., 5-7 per day, 540ptas/€3,30); and **Girona** (2hr., 1-2 per day, 1040ptas/€6,10).

Bike and Boat Rental: Escola de Vela Ones (☎93 753 25 12 or 93 232 18 90) sets up shop on the beach directly in front of the tourist office and rents kayaks, sailboats, and windsurfing gear. Choose from 3hr., 4hr., and 6hr. guided kayak excursions (4500-10,000ptas/€27-60), or head out on your own in a single kayak (1500ptas/€9 per hr., 4000ptas/€24 half day, 7000ptas/€42 full day), or a double kayak (2000ptas/€12 per hr., 6000ptas/€36 half day, 10,000ptas/€60 full day). Windsurfing gear (1500ptas/€9 per hr.) and sailboats (3000-5000ptas/€18-30) also available. Open daily July-Sept. 15 10am-8pm.

Animal Area Cadaqués (☎97 225 80 27) also has rentals, farther down the beach on Platja Es Poal. Kayaks 1200ptas/€7,20 per hr., 3000ptas/€18 per half day. Motorboats 8000ptas/€48 per half day, 15,000ptas/€90 per day. Scooters 4900ptas/€29 per half day, 6900ptas/€41 per day. Mountain bikes 700ptas/€4 per 2hrs., 1300ptas/€7,80 half day, 2000ptas/€12 full day.

ORIENTATION & PRACTICAL INFORMATION

The bus to Cadaqués halts at a small stone tower beneath a miniature Statue of Liberty. With your back to the Sarfa office, walk right and downhill on Av. Caritat Serinyana to the waterfront square, **Plaça Frederic Rahola,** where a signboard map with indexed services and accommodations will orient you.

Tourist Office, C. Cotxe 2 (☎97 225 83 15; fax 97 215 94 42), off Pl. Frederic Rahola, has a helpful map of Cadaqués and the surrounding beaches. Open July-Aug. M-Sa 9am-2pm and 4-9pm, Su 10:30am-1pm; Sept.-June M-Sa 9am-2pm and 4-7pm.

Currency Exchange: Banco Central Hispano, C. Caritat Serinyana 4 (☎97 225 83 62). Open Oct.-Mar. M-F 8:30am-2:30pm, Sa 8:30am-1pm; Apr.-Sept. M-F 8:30am-2:30pm.

Police: Pl. Frederic Rahola (☎97 215 93 43).

N

0 ___ 200 yards
0 ___ 200 meters

Cadaqués

ACCOMMODATIONS
Camping Cadaqués, 1
Hostal Cristina, 6
Hostal Marina, 5
Pensión Ranxo, 2

FOOD
Can Tito, 4
Restaurant Vehí, 3

NIGHTLIFE
Bar Melitón, 8
Casino, 7

C. C. Riba
C. del Duc
C. de ses Oliveres
C. de ses Pàres
C. des Puig
C. Peralles

C. de la Miranda
Animal Area
Cadaqués
C. d'es Pianc

Avinguda Rabola Victor

C. Hort d'en Sanés
C. de Sa Tortora
C. Amargura

C. Josep Pla

C. de Pablo Ruiz Picasso

C. de les Creus

C. de Sa Tortora

C. de Sant Antoni

C. Puig Vidal

C. Ses Flores

C. del Forn

C. del Palau

C. Palau

PL. DES PORTIXO

C. Rosset Miquel

On@

Passeig

C. de la Riba-Nemesi Llorens

Banco Central Hispano

PL DE FREDERIC RAHOLA

C. Coxe

Badia de Cadaqués

Riera de Sant Vicens

C. del Vigilant

Centre d'Art Perrot Moore

C. des Vigilant

C. DR. Bre TRÉMOLS

PL DR. TRÉMOLS

C. de la Riba-Nemesi Llorens

C. Silvi Randa

C. del Sol de l'Engirol

Avinguda de Caritat Serinyana

Sa Rierassa

C. Unió

C. de Santa Margarida

C. Font

C. Bellaire

C. del Calt

SA PLACA

C. Curos

C. E. Meifren

C. de Sa Figuera Morena

C. Narcís Monturiol

C. Quima Jaume

Museu de Cadaqués

C. de la Font Vella

C. de la Horta Vella

Riera de Sant Vicens

C. Tilla

C. Curro

C. St. Isidre

Portal d'Amunt

C. de l'Església

Santa Maria

C. Guillem Bruguera

C. Nou

C. Llampec

C. des Tro

C. Nou

C. de la Pruna

C. de Santa Bàrbara

C. Solitari

TO PORT LLIGAT & CASA-MUSEU
S. DALÍ (2km) &

Carretera a Roses i Figueres

Bus Station (SARFA)

Bus Office (SARFA)

203

Castell de Sant Feran

Arches at Castell de Sant Ferran

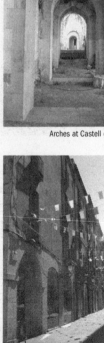
After the Festival

Medical Assistance: ☎ 97 225 88 07.

Internet Access: on@, C. Miquel Rosset 3 (☎ 97 225 10 42), just off Avda. Caritat Serinyana. 100ptas/€0,60 per 10min.; 400ptas/€2,40 per 30min.; 750ptas/€4,50 per hr. Open Su-Th 11am-2pm and 5-10pm, F-Sa 11am-2pm and 5pm-midnight or 1am.

Post Office, Av. Rierassa (☎ 97 225 87 98). Off C. Caritat Serinyana. Open M-F 9am-2pm, Sa 9:30am-1pm. **Postal code:** 17488.

ACCOMMODATIONS & CAMPING

As Cadaqués is a beach town, many accommodations are open only during the summer. Though prices for a room soar in these summer months, accommodations in Cadaqués can still be found for relatively reasonable prices.

Hostal Cristina, C. Riera (☎ 97 225 81 38). Right on the water, to the right of Avda. Caritat Serinyana. Bright, newly renovated rooms; rooftop terrace overlooks the water. Summer prices include breakfast. May-Sept. singles 4000ptas/€24; doubles 6000ptas/€36, with bath 8000ptas/€48, with TV 9000ptas/€54. Oct.-Apr. singles 3000ptas/€18; doubles 4000ptas/€24, with bath or terrace 6000ptas/€36, with TV 8000ptas/€48. MC/V.

Pensión Ranxo, Avda. Caritat Serinyana 13 (☎ 97 225 80 05), on the right as you walk down from the bus stop. Potted plants and whitewashed hallways lead to very clean and comfortable rooms. All rooms come with bath and include breakfast. Traveler's checks accepted. July-Sept. 15: singles 4000ptas/€24; doubles 8000ptas/€48. Sept. 15-June: singles 3000ptas/€18; doubles 6000-7000ptas/€36-42. MC/V.

Hostal Marina, C. Riera 3 (☎ 97 225 81 99), boasts clean rooms with modern furniture. Some rooms with balconies. Breakfast 550ptas/€3,30. Singles 3000ptas/€18, with bath 4000ptas/€24; doubles 5500ptas€33, with bath 8000ptas/€48. Open Apr.-Dec. MC/V.

Camping Cadaqués, Ctra. Portlligat 17 (☎ 97 225 81 26; fax 97 215 93 83), is 100m from the beach on the left on the way to Dalí's house; follow the signs for Hotel Port Lligat. Popular and crowded campsite; relatively clean. Amenities include pool, supermarket, and bungalows (from 3925-5370ptas/€23,58-32,27). 655ptas/€3,90 per person; 820ptas/€4,90 per tent; 655ptas/€3,90 per car; IVA not included. No dogs allowed. Open late Mar.- late Sept.

FOOD

Cadaqués harbors the usual slew of overpriced, unexciting tourist restaurants on the waterfront; wander into the back streets for more interesting options. **Groceries** can be purchased at **Super Auvi,** C. Riera. (☎ 97 225 86 33. Open July 15-Aug. M-Sa 8am-2pm and 4:30-9pm, Su 8am-2pm; Sept.-July 14 M-Sa 8:30am-1:30pm and 4:30-9pm.)

Can Tito, C. Vigilant 8 (☎97 225 90 70). An exceptional historic and culinary experience. The stone archway at the entrance to this elegant restaurant is 1 of 5 portals dating back to AD 1100 when Cadaqués was still a fortified village, at the mercy of roving pirates. 3-course lunchtime *menú* 1800ptas/ €10,90. Try the house specialty, *pastel de escalivada*, a *soufflé* of onions, peppers, eggplant, and pepperoni (950ptas/€5,80). Fish and meat entrees 800-2300ptas/€4,80-14. Open daily Mar.-Jan. 1-3pm and 8-10:30pm. MC/V.

Restaurant Vehí, C. de l'Església 6 (☎97 225 84 70). 2nd floor restaurant with panoramic windows offering lovely views. Serves up traditional Catalan fare with an emphasis on seafood. *Menús* (1400-1750ptas/€8,40-10,50) include wine. Entrees 950-2300ptas/€5,80-14. Open from Mar.-Oct.

SIGHTS & ENTERTAINMENT

The local church, **Església de Santa Maria,** is a 16th-century gothic building with a baroque altarpiece. Nearby, the **Museu de Cadaqués,** C. Narcis Monturiol 15, has changing exhibits, often with a Dalí theme. (☎97 225 88 77. Open daily mid-June to Sept. 10:30am-1:30pm and 3-8pm. 750ptas/€4,50; students 500ptas/€3.)

From the museum, take a pleasant walk (30min.) to ◙**Casa-Museu Salvador Dalí,** in Port Lligat, the home where Dalí and his wife Gala lived until her death in 1982. With your back to the Statue of Liberty, take the right fork and follow the signs to Port Lligat; eventually Casa de Dalí signs appear. At C. President Lluís Companys, where signs point to the house in two different directions, follow the one to the right—the other road is the auto route. Originally a modest fisherman's abode, the house was transformed to meet the aesthetic and eccentric lifestyle led by Dalí and his treasured wife. The egg-covered building flaunts Dalí's favorite lip-shaped sofa and more stuffed snakes and swans than you bargained for. Though only two (unfinished) Dalí originals remain in the house, the decorating style is a work in itself. (☎97 225 10 15. Open June 15-Sept. 15 daily 10:30am-9pm; Mar. 15-June 14 and Sept. 16-Nov. Tu-Su 10:30am-6pm. Make reservations for a tour 1-2 days in advance; tours are the only way to see the house. Multilingual tours every 10min. Ticket office closes 45min. before closing. 1300ptas/€7,80; students, seniors, and children 800ptas/€4,80.)

Those looking to go to more museums will be disappointed; the former Cadaqués crowd-pleaser, the Centre d'Art Perrot-Moore, has closed (see **Dalí or not Dalí?,** opposite). If you can't get enough Dalí, **boat rides** in Dalí's boat *Gala* leave in front of the house on the hour for a 55min. trip to Cap de Creus (☎617 46 57 57. Open 10am-7pm. 1500ptas/€9). Outdoor activi-

Catalan Flag

Matador

Seafood

ties in Cadaqués are popular, and in addition to **water sports** and **biking,** a map of various 2-8km **hikes** is available at the tourist office; see **orientation & practical information** for rental info.

NIGHTLIFE

When the sun sets, head to one of Cadaqués' beachfront bars for drinks and music. **Bar Melitón** (☎97 225 82 01), on the *passeig* has a popular terrace with plenty of tables. The oldest bar in the town, **Casino** (☎97 225 81 37), on Pl. Doctor Tremols, has high ceilings, big windows, and a stream of drink-sippers all day and into the night (pool table and coin-op Internet also available).

PALAFRUGELL

In the year 988, inhabitants of the beach town of Llafranc founded inland Palafrugell, seeking refuge from the constant plundering of Mediterranean pirates. Today, budget travelers come here to flee the wallet-plundering of seaside hotels and restaurants. Forty kilometers east of Girona, Palafrugell serves as a base for trips to nearby beach towns **Calella, Llafranc,** and **Tamariu,** which cater to wealthy Europeans whose idea of a budget accommodation is any hotel that doesn't leave mints on the pillow. To save some *pesetas*, stay in admittedly bland (and beachless) Palafrugell and daytrip to the beaches. The small beaches of the towns are connected by the **Camino de Ronda,** a series of stone footpaths allowing exploration of the rocky, wooded coast.

TRANSPORTATION

Buses: Sarfa, C. Torres Jonama 67-79 (☎97 230 06 23). Prices rise on weekends. To: **Barcelona** (2hr., 12 per day, 1750ptas/€10,50); **Calella** and **Llafranc** (12-24 per day, in winter 4-5 per day; 160ptas/€1); **Figueres** (1½hr., 3-4 per day, 800-950ptas/€4,80-5,70); and **Girona** (1hr., 15 per day, 515-600ptas/€3,60).

Taxis: Radio Taxi (☎97 261 00 00). 24hr. service throughout the area.

ORIENTATION & PRACTICAL INFORMATION

To get from the bus station to the center of town, turn right and walk down C. Torres Jonama to C. de Pi i Maragall. Then turn right and walk past the Guardia Civil and the market until you hit **Pl. Nova,** the main square of the town, off which are C. San Sebastià and C. Cavallers. On your way you'll pass the **Pl. l'Església** on the right. To get to the nearby beach towns of Calella, Llafranc, and Tamariu, take a bus (see **Transportation,** above), spin away on moped or mountain bike, or take a pleasant, if lengthy, walk through the countryside (about 1hr. to each town).

Tourist Office: Can Rosés, Pl. l'Església (☎97 261 18 20; fax 97 261 17 56). First right off C. Cavallers walking away from Pl. Nova. The *Guía Municipal* guide to the region is indispensable—ask for it. A **larger branch** is at C. Carrilet 2 (☎97 230 02 28; fax 97 261 12 61). From the bus station, go left on C. Torres Jonama, left again at the traffic circle, and walk about 200m. An inconvenient location, but loaded with info. Both open Apr.-Sept. M-Sa 10am-1pm and 5-8pm, Su 10am-1pm; Oct.-Mar. M-Sa 10am-1pm and 4-7pm, Su 10am-1pm; Carrilet branch also open July-Aug. M-Sa 9am-9pm and Su 10am-1pm.

Currency Exchange: Banco Central Hispano, the corner of C. Valls and C. Cavallers off Pl. Nova. **ATM.** Open M-F 8:30am-2:30pm; Oct.-Mar. also Sa 8:30am-1pm.

Emergency: ☎112. **Police:** ☎088. **Municipal police:** ☎97 261 31 01, Av. Josep Pla and C. Cervantes. Call them for **24hr. pharmacy** info.

Medical Services: Centro de Atención Primaria, C. d'Angel Guimerà 6 (☎97 261 06 07 Emergencies/ambulance: ☎97 260 00 03). Open 24hr.

Internet Access: Internet Papereria Palé, C. Cavallers 16 (☎97 230 12 48). 175ptas/€3 per 1st 15min., 550ptas/€3,30 per hr. Open Aug.-Sept. M 5-9pm, Tu-Sa 9am-1pm and 5-9pm, and Su 9am-1pm; Oct.-July Tu-Sa 9am-1pm and 5-9pm, Su 9am-1pm.

Post Office: C. Torres Jonama 14 (☎902 197 197). **Lista de Correos.** Open M-F 8:30am-2:30pm, Sa 9:30am-1pm. **Postal Code:** 17200.

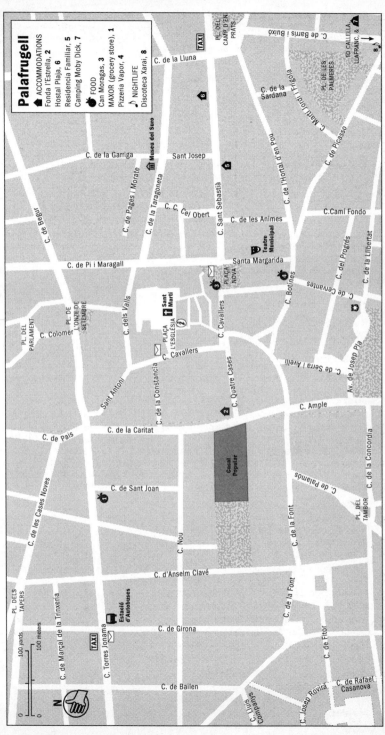

ACCOMMODATIONS & CAMPING

Though options are few, accommodation prices are reasonable and room quality high in Palafrugell. Be sure to call ahead on summer weekends.

Fonda l'Estrella, C. Quatre Cases 13-17 (☎97 230 00 05), at the corner of C. La Caritat, a right off C. Torres Jonama. High-ceilinged, well-lit rooms with sinks, off a Moorish courtyard bursting with plant life. Common baths, but even the bathrooms of this carefully preserved 1605 historic building are gorgeous. Breakfast 600ptas/€3,60. Singles 3000ptas/€18 (available only Apr.-May and Sept.-Oct.); doubles 6000ptas/€36,15.

Hostal Plaja, C. Sant Sebastià 34 (☎97 230 05 26), off of Pl. Nova. Grand, frescoed foyer gives way to a broad courtyard surrounded by spotless rooms, all with balconies, clotheslines, and new beds. For not much more, rooms with bathrooms are a significant jump in luxury over those without, with bottled water and TVs. Breakfast 1000ptas/€6. Singles 3000ptas/€18, with bath 4000ptas/€24; doubles with bath 8000ptas/€48.

Residencia Familiar, C. Sant Sebastià 29 (☎689 269 538), off Pl. Nova. Mattresses are on the saggy side but all rooms have sinks and some have high ceilings. No private baths. Singles 3000ptas/€18; doubles 6000ptas/€36; less for longer stays and for families.

Camping: Camping Moby Dick, C. Costa Verda 16-28 (☎97 261 43 07). Take the Sarfa bus to Calella and ask the driver to let you off. No white whale in sight, but it is close to the water. Nice showers. 600ptas/€3,60 per adult, 430ptas/€2,50 per child; 660ptas/€3,90 per tent; 600ptas/€3,60 per car. Open Apr. 10-Sept. 30.

FOOD

Restaurants near the beach are predictably expensive, making meals in Palafrugell proper a wiser option. Get **groceries** for daytrips at **MAXOR,** C. Torres Jonama 33. (Open M-Th 8:30am-2:30pm, 4:40-8:30pm; F-Sa 8:30am-8:30pm; Su 9am-2pm.) For some reason, the town has a disproportionately high number of pizzerias and Italian restaurants. Shrugs one local, "We just really like pizza." **L'Arcobaleno,** C. Mayor 3, brings a touch of Tuscany to Catalan classics. The delicious lunchtime *menú* has everything from lasagna to roast chicken (1200ptas/€7,20). (☎97 261 06 95. Open daily noon-4pm and 7pm-midnight. AmEx/MC/V.) Ice cream shops and restaurants with terraces dominate the Pl. Nova, including **Can Moragas,** a pizzeria and *crêpería.* Follow your individual pizza (1100ptas/€6,60) with one of many specialty *crêpes* with fruit and liqueur toppings (300-500ptas/€2,40.) (☎97 230 10 44. Open daily 8:30am-midnight. MC/V.) **Pizzeria Vapor,** C. de les Botines 12, is a popular restaurant with, in addition to the requisite pizza, (750-900ptas/€4,50-5,40), a fresh *menú* for 1600ptas/€9,60. (☎97 230 57 03. Pastas 1100ptas/€6,60. Regional entrees 950-1600ptas/€5,80-9,60. *Menú* F, Sa, and Su only. Open Tu-Su 1-5pm and 8pm-1am.)

SIGHTS & ENTERTAINMENT

In addition to nearby beaches, Palafrugell boasts one of the world's few cork museums. The **Museu del Suro,** C. Tarongeta 31, has everything you ever (never?) wanted to know about cork. From Plaça Nova, face C. Sant Sebastià, take a left onto C. Pi i Margall, and the second right onto C. Tarongeta; the museum is at the end of the block. (☎97 230 39 98. Open June 15-Sept. 15 daily 10am-2pm and 4-10m; Sept.16-June 14 Tu-Sa 5-8pm and Su 10:30am-1:30pm. 200ptas/€1,20, students and seniors 100ptas/€0,60. English explanations available.)

A Palafrugell Friday evening stroll ends up at the *plaça,* where young and old often dance the traditional Catalan *sardana* (see **Gettin' Jiggy With It,** p. 52) around 10:30pm in July and August. The tourist office prints a monthly bulletin of upcoming events; also check the *Guía Municipal.* The town's biggest party takes place July 19th to the 21st, when the dance-intensive **Festa Major** bursts into the streets. Calella honors **Sant Pere** on June 29 with lots of *sardana* dancing, and Tamariu celebrates on August 15, coinciding with the Assumption of the Blessed Mother. The **festivals of the hanaveres** (Spanish-Cuban sea songs) come to town every July.

BEACH TOWNS

🚍 *Take a Sarfa bus from Palafrugell to* **Calella** *(15min., 12-24 per day, 160ptas/€1,50). From Calella, follow the Camino de Ronda (see below) and walk 20min. or so to* **Llafranc.** *From Llafranc,* **Tamariu** *is a 2hr. walk farther along the path.* **Tourist Office** *at Tamariu, C. Riera.* ☎ 97 262 01 93. *Open June-Sept. M-Sa 10am-1pm and 5-8pm, Su 10am-1pm.*

CALELLA

Calella is the largest and liveliest of the three beach towns near Palafrugell, with lots of small restaurants and shops in the streets around the beach. The town is also a great starting point for a trip to Llafranc, since the beaches here are quite small, and not particularly special. The bus stops in the town, a short downhill walk to the beach at **Port Bo**. From there, take a left to get to the bigger **Canadell** beach, at the far end of which begins the Camino de Ronda path to Llafranc. Calella's **tourist office**, C. Voltes 6, provides maps of paths that criss-cross the area, including the **Camino de Ronda,** which climbs the coast from Calella to Llafranc. (☎ 97 261 44 75. Open daily July-Aug. 10am-1pm and 5-9pm; Apr-June and Sept. 10am-1pm and 5-8pm.)

The **Jardí Botànic de Cap Roig,** the botanical garden in front of Hotel Garbí, provides an excellent view of the coast. (☎ 97 261 53 45. Open daily June-Aug. 9am-8pm; Sept.-May 9am-6pm. 300ptas/€1,80.) Russian Colonel Nicolas Voevodsky built the garden's **seaside castle** after fleeing the Bolshevik Revolution. He and his wife planted and pruned the splendid maze of paths and flower beds with their own hands. To get to the garden, take a right at Port Bo and follow the road as far as Hotel St. Roc. There the Camino de Ronda starts up again—look for signs, and when in doubt, look for the small red and white stripes painted along the path as markers. The hike ends in a steep climb up a set of steps—45min. in all. The castle also hosts regular concerts and the **Festival de Jazz de la Costa Brava** in July and August. For tickets and info, contact any of the tourist offices or call 902 44 77 55.

LLAFRANC

The most popular of the beaches, Llafranc and its coarse sand are usually covered with French and German tourists. To get there from Calella, take a pleasant 15-20min. hike from Calella along the Camino de Ronda, which begins at the far end of Calella's beaches. There is a tourist office branch in Llafranc, C. Roger de Llúria. (☎ 97 230 50 08. Open daily July-Aug. 10am-1pm and 5-9pm; Apr.-June and Sept. M-Sa 10am-1pm and 5-8pm.) On the port side of the beach, **Barracuda Diving Center** (☎ 97 261 15 48) offers scuba diving courses (5 days, 50000ptas/€305) and rents equipment. Every two hours from 11am onward, they also have two-hour boat excursions to caves and inlets along the coast, with snorkeling and swimming (2000ptas/€12, children 1500ptas/€9). For an outdoor adventure, take a 40-minute walk from Llafranc to the ⛪**Ermita de San Sebastià.** Crowning the mountain of the same name (50m from the lighthouse), the hermitage offers views of the entire Palafrugell valley, beaches, and sea. From the far end of the Llafranc beach, hop onto the good old Camino and head up. At the paved road, wind up and up (and up), 40 minutes of climbing, to the lighthouse (unfortunately not open to visitors) and the lookout points. After the climb up and a nice rest at the peak, the remaining hour and fifteen minute hike to Tamariu will be a relative cinch.

TAMARIU

The beaches get quieter the farther you walk from Calella; Tamariu is the most peaceful, a reward for anyone who makes the challenging two-hour hike. From the far end of the Llafranc beach, take the Camino de Ronda and then the paved road up the mountain to the Ermita de San Sebastià. From there, the remaining 1 hour 15 minutes are easier, along the wooded Camino de Ronda to Tamariu. For all the tranquility but none of the blisters, take the **bus,** which loops to Tamariu and back 4 times a day (20min., 8:20am, 10am, 5:20pm, 7:45pm) from the town bus station.

NIGHTLIFE

Check out **Discoteca Xarai,** C. Barris i Buixo 42. Dance the night away; no athletic gear allowed. Take a right off C. Sant Sebastià onto C. Barris i Buixo and look for the lime-green and orange building. (Open weekend nights only.)

TOSSA DE MAR

Falling in love in (or in love with) Tossa de Mar is easy. In 1934, French artist Marc Chagall commenced a 40-year love affair with this seaside village, deeming it "Blue Paradise." When *The Flying Dutchman* was filmed here in 1951, Ava Gardner fell hard for Spanish bullfighter-turned-actor Mario Cabrera, much to the chagrin of Frank Sinatra, her husband at the time. (A statue of the actress in Tossa's old city commemorates her visit.) Like many coastal cities, Tossa (pop. 4000) suffers from the usual tourist industry blemishes: souvenir shops, inflated prices, and crowded beaches. That said, it resists a generic beach town ambiance, drawing from its historical legacy and cliff-studded landscape to preserve a unique small-town feel. Raised in the 12th century as a fortified medieval village, the sun-baked walls of Vila Vella continue to overlook Tossa's blue Mediterranean water.

TRANSPORTATION

Buses: Av. Pelegrí at Pl. de les Nacions Sense Estat. **Pujol i Pujol** (☎610 50 58 84) to **Lloret del Mar** (20min.; June-Aug. every 30min., Sept.-May every hr. 8am-9:15pm; 180ptas/€1). **Sarfa** (☎97 234 09 03) to **Barcelona** (1½hr.; 15 per day 7:40am-7:40pm, 1150ptas/€6,90) and **Girona** (1hr.; 2 per day, offseason 1 per day; 580ptas/€3,50).

Car Rental: Viajes Tramontana, Av. Costa Brava 23 (☎97 234 28 29; fax 97 234 13 20). **Avis** (☎90 213 55 31) and their affiliate, **Olimpia** (☎97 236 47 10), operate from the same storefront. Min. age 21. Expect to be asked for a major credit card, driver's license (international driver's license required for longer rentals), and passport. One-day rentals 6700-17,000ptas/€40,20-102. Open daily July-Aug. 9am-9pm, Apr.-June and Sept.-Nov. 9am-3pm and 4-8pm.

Mountain Bike and Moped Rentals: Jimbo Bikes, La Rambla Pau Casals 12 (☎97 234 30 44). Staff gives bike route information. Bring license for moped rental. Mountain bikes 500-700ptas/€3-4,22 per hr., 2500-3500ptas/€15-21 per day. Open M-Sa 9am-9pm and Su 9:30am-2pm and 4-8pm. AmEx/MC/V.

Boat rentals: Kayaks Nicolau, (☎97 234 26 46) on Mar Menuda, offers 1½hr. kayak excursions to Cala Bona (10am, noon, and 4pm; 1700ptas/€10,30). Kayak rental 800ptas/€4,80 per hr., paddle boats 1000ptas/€6. Open daily Apr.15-Oct.15 9am-6pm.

Taxis: ☎97 234 05 49. Wait outside the bus station.

ORIENTATION & PRACTICAL INFORMATION

Buses arrive at **Plaça de les Nacions Sense Estat** where **Avinguda del Pelegrí** and **Avinguda Ferrán Agulló** meet; the town slopes gently down from there to the waterfront. Walk away from the station down Av. Ferrán Agulló, turn right on Av. Costa Brava, and continue until your feet get wet (10min.). **Passeig del Mar,** at the end of Av. Costa Brava, curves along the **Platja Gran** (Tossa's main beach) to the old quarter.

Tourist Office: Av. Pelegrí 25 (☎97 234 01 08; fax 97 234 07 12; www.tossademar.com), in the bus terminal at Av. Ferrán Agulló and Av. Pelegrí. Grab a handy, thoroughly indexed map. English spoken. Open June 15-Sept. 15: M-Sa 9am-9pm, Su 10am-2pm and 4-8pm. Apr.-May and Oct.: M-Sa 10am-2pm and 4-8pm, Su 10:30am-1:30pm. Mar. and Nov.: M-Sa 10am-1pm and 4-7pm. Dec.-Feb. M-F 10am-1pm and 4-7pm, Sa 10am-1pm.

Currency Exchange: Bancos Central Hispano, C. Ferrán Agiló 2 (☎97 234 10 65). Open Apr.-Sept. M-F 8:30am-2:30pm; Oct.-Mar. M-F 8:30am-2:30pm and Sa 8:30am-1pm. **ATM.**

Police: Municipal police, Av. Pelegrí 14 (☎97 234 01 35), down the street from the tourist office. English spoken. They'll escort you to the **24hr. pharmacy.**

Medical Services: Casa del Mar (☎97 234 18 28 or 97 234 01 54), Av. Catalunya. Primary health services and immediate attention. The nearest hospital is in Blanes, about 30min. south.

Internet Access: Cyber-Café Bar La Playa, C. Socors 6 (☎97 234 09 22), off the main beach. 200ptas/€1,20 per 15min., 400ptas/€2,40 per 30min. Open daily May-Oct. 15 9:30am-midnight. **Scuba Libre,** Av. Sant Raimón de Penyafort 11 (☎97 234 20 26). Dive shop and café has several Internet terminals. 600ptas/€3,61 per hr. Open daily May-Oct. 8am-3am, Nov.-Apr. Sa-Su 8am-6pm.

Post Office: C. Maria Auxiliadora (☎97 234 04 57), down Av. Pelegrí from tourist office. Open M-F 8:30am-2:30pm, Sa 9:30am-1pm. **Postal Code: 17320.**

ACCOMMODATIONS

Tossa is a seasonal town, and therefore many hostels, restaurants, and bars are open only from May to October. During the summer and festivals, Tossa fills quickly. Make reservations in advance, as some establishments are booked solid in July and August. The **old quarter** hotels are the only ones really worth considering.

Fonda/Can Lluna, C. Roqueta 20 (☎97 234 03 65; fax 97 234 07 57). From Pg. del Mar; turn right onto C. Peixeteras, veer left onto C. Estalt, walk up the hill until the dead-end, go left, and then head straight. Delightful family offers immaculate single, double, and triple rooms, all with private baths. Breakfast included—eat on the rooftop terrace and enjoy a breathtaking view of the water. Washing machine 600ptas/€3,60. A popular choice with Spanish tourists, rooms are booked months in advance July-Aug., Oct.-Mar., and July-Aug. 2500ptas/€15 per person. Mar.-June and Sept. 2000ptas/€12. Cash only.

Pensión Carmen Pepi, C. Sant Miguel 10 (☎97 234 05 26). Turn left off Av. de Pelegrí onto Maria Auxiliadora and veer to your immediate right through the Pl. de l'Antic Hospital and onto C. Sant Miguel. This old, traditional house with its small courtyard has an authentic feel and good location. The high-ceilinged rooms, each with private bath, are somewhat beyond their prime. Breakfast 300ptas/€1,50. July-Aug. 31 singles 3000ptas/€18; doubles 6000ptas/€36. May-July 1 singles 2700ptas/€16; doubles 5300ptas/€32. Sept.-June singles 2200ptas/€13; doubles 4400ptas/€26. Cash only.

L'Hostalet de Tossa, Pl. de l'Església 3 (☎97 234 18 53; fax 97 234 29 69; hostalettossa@ctv.es), in front of the Sant Vicenç church. Clean and annually renovated with hotel-quality rooms. Many of L'Hostalet's 32 double rooms overlook its orange tree terrace and face the church. Rooms have baths and include breakfast. 2 common areas boast foosball, pool table, and TV. Apr.-May and Oct. 5800ptas/€34,86; June and Sept. 6800ptas/€140,87; *Setmana Santa* (Holy Week) and July-Aug. 8200ptas/€49,28. MC/V.

Pensión Moré, C. Sant Telmo 9 (☎97 234 03 39). Downstairs sits a dim, cozy sitting room with TV. Upstairs, large doubles and triples with views of the old quarter. July-Aug. 1800ptas/€11 per person; Sept.-June 1700ptas/€10 per person. Cash only.

Can Tort, C. Pescadors 1 (☎97 234 11 85 or 97 234 22 40). Friendly owner maintains 14 very clean double rooms in her pottery-filled restaurant-hostel. All rooms have bathrooms, homey furnishings, and views of Tossa's old quarter. Breakfast included. Apr.-June and Sept.-Oct. 5200ptas/€32; July 5800ptas/€35; Aug. 7400ptas/€45. Cash only.

Camping: Closest site is **Can Martí** (☎97 234 08 51; fax 97 234 24 61), at the end of La Rambla Pau Casals, off Av. Ferrán Agulló, 15min. from the bus station. Popular, tree-lined campsite. Hot-water showers, telephones, swimming pool, and restaurant. June 20-

Beachbums

Summertime Frolicking

Bikini-Watcher

LGB ▼

BARCELONA

A Night Out

Sitges shines especially bright in its gay nightlife scene, considered one of the best in Europe. The evening begins at **Parrot's Pub** on C. Primer de Maig, a place to relax with a drink outside before hitting the clubs. Ask here for a copy of the *plano gay*, the free map of gay establishments in Sitges and Barcelona. **Mediterráneo**, C. Sant Bonaventura 6, off C. Sant Francesc, shakes every summer night with two floors of drinking and dancing (open 10pm-3:30am). After hours, the crowds move to **Trailer**, C. Angel Vida 36, the hottest disco party in town, with DJs nightly and foam parties W and Su (opens at 2am).

-Aug. 31. 900ptas/€5,40 per person, 925ptas/€5,50 per tent, 525ptas/€3,20 per car; May 12-June 19 and Sept. 1-16 725ptas/€4,40 per person, 800ptas/€4,80 per tent, 425ptas/€2,60 per car. Traveler's checks or cash only.

FOOD

The old quarter has the best cuisine and ambiance in Tossa. Restaurants catering to tourists serve up *menús* at reasonable prices; most specialize in local seafood. If you need groceries, head to **Megatzems Palau,** C. Enric Granados 4. (☎97 234 08 58. Open daily June-Sept. 8am-9pm.)

Restaurant Marina, C. Tarull 6 (☎97 234 07 57). Faces the Església de Sant Vincenç and has outdoor seating for prime people-watching. A nice family restaurant. Multilingual menu features pizza, meat, and fish dishes, and lots of *paella*. Entrees 600-1600ptas/€3,61-9,60. *Menús* 1200ptas/€7,20 and 1500ptas/€9. Open daily *Setmana Santa* (Holy Week) to Oct. daily 11:30am-11:30pm. MC/V.

Pizzeria Anna, Pont Vell 19 (☎97 234 28 51). Turn right on Pont Vell from Pg. Mar; it's the small restaurant on the left-hand corner. Though homesick Italians might be a bit disappointed, the seafood-sick traveler will be in heaven. Seating inside and out. Pasta 700-900ptas/€4,22-5,40; pizza 850-1100ptas/€5-6,60. Open daily Apr.-Sept. noon-4pm and 7:30-11:30pm. AmEx/MC/V.

La Taberna de Tossa, C. Sant Telm 26 (☎97 234 14 47). In the heart of the old quarter, right off La Guardia. Serves up inexpensive house wine, traditional *tapas,* and provincial meat and fish specialities (entrees 725-1325ptas/€4,30-8). Set *menús* 1095-1295ptas/€6,60-7,80. Popular among Spanish tourists. Open daily Apr.-Sept. 1pm-4 and 7pm-1am, Oct.-Mar. F-Su 1pm-4 and 7pm-1am. V.

Restaurant Baserri, C. Codolar 18 (☎97 234 30 81). Near the Museu Municipal (see below). A more upscale experience, with a romantic dark wood and warm peach interior. Vegetarian-friendly, creative food with a Mediterranean flavor. Appetizers 800-1400ptas/€4,80-8,40. Entrees 1300-2000ptas/€7,80-12. Open daily July-Aug. 1-4pm and 8-11pm, Sept.-June Su-M and W-Sa 1-4pm and 8-11pm. MC/V.

SIGHTS

Inside the walled fortress of the Vila Vella, a spiral of medieval alleys leads to tiny Pl. Pintor J. Roig y Soler, where the ▨ **Museu Municipal** has a wonderfully displayed collection of 1920s and 1930s art, including—because the artist had a house here—one of the few Chagall paintings still in Spain. Tossa's Roman mosaics (dating from the fourth to the first century BC), and other artifacts from the nearby Vila Romana are displayed in the museum, originally a 12th-century palace. (☎97 234 30 81. Open June 1-15 M-F 11am-1pm and 3-5pm, Sa-Su 11am-6pm; June 16-

Sept. 15 10am-8pm; Sept. 16-30 M-F 11am-1pm and 3-5pm, Sa-Su 11am-6pm; Oct. M-F 11am-1pm and 3-5pm, Sa-Su 11am-5pm. 500ptas/€3, students and seniors 300ptas/€1,80.) From the museum, it is a short, picturesque walk uphill to the remains of the **Vila Vella** and gorgeous Mediterranean views.

BEACHES

Tossa's main beach, **La Platja Gran,** is surrounded by cliffs and draws the majority of beach-goers. To escape the crowds, visit some of the neighboring *calas* (small coves), accessible by foot. Hiking and mountain-biking paths also criss-cross the area and offer impressive views of the coastline. The tourist office pamphlet provides lots of information. Several companies, like **Fonda Cristal,** send glass-bottomed boats to nearby beaches and caves. Tickets are available at booths on the Platja Gran. (☎97 234 22 29. 1hr., 17 per day, 1100ptas/€6,60 per person.) **Club Aire Libre,** on the highway to Lloret, organizes various excursions and rents equipment for water sports. (☎97 234 12 77. Canoeing, kayaking 2200ptas/€13. Water skiing 4400ptas/€26 for 2 lessons. Scuba diving 44,000ptas/€264 for 5-day certification course. Sailing 1800ptas/€11 per hr. Windsurfing 1700ptas/€10,30 per hr.)

NIGHTLIFE

Bars line the streets of the old quarter and offer live music from time to time. **Bar El Pirata,** C. Portal 32, and its companion bar **Piratín** have outdoor tables overlooking the sea. (☎97 234 14 43. Open daily Apr.-Oct. 2pm-3am.) **Bar Trinquet,** C. Sant Josep 9, has a lovely tree-filled interior courtyard. DJs spin acid jazz and house on weekend nights. (☎659 61 39 30. Open daily Apr.-Oct. 7pm-3am.) For live music try **Don Pepe,** C. Estolt 6, a small, less-touristed bar which showcases a flamenco guitarist every night. (☎97 234 22 66. Open daily Apr.-Oct. 10pm-4:30am.)

MATARÓ

As far north of Barcelona as Sitges is south of Barcelona, the small town of Mataró has nearly comparable beaches to Sitges in a far more low-key setting. The biggest difference? Mataró is one of Barcelonans' best-kept secrets, long familiar to native day trippers but virtually untouched by outside tourism. Well, the secret's out now (sorry, Catalunya!), but don't expect this proud town to begin over-developing anytime soon; *mataronís* seem perfectly content to enjoy the expansive beaches and quiet downtown in relative peace. This wonderfully easy daytrip from Barcelona will have you out of the train station and onto the beach minutes after arrival.

TRANSPORTATION

Cercanías Trains (☎93 490 02 02) to Mataró run frequently from Barcelona-Sants and Pl. de Catalunya (Line 3; 40min., every 10-20min. 5:54am-11:29pm, 350ptas/€2,10). The last train from Mataró back to Barcelona is at 10:40pm.

ORIENTATION & PRACTICAL INFORMATION

The Renfe train station is considerately located right on the coast, just a few meters from the town beaches. Upon exiting the station, turn right, descend the ramp at the end of the block, and cross under the train tracks to get to the beach. To get to the town center, cross the street from the train station, turn right, and take the first left onto C. Lepanto. This street leads to La Rambla, the main street that circles around the commercial district centers. A right onto La Rambla cuts through Pl. Santa Anna to C. La Riera, the home of the **Ajuntament**—the town hall of Mataró. Come here for **tourist information,** La Riera 48 (open M-F 9am-7pm). The nearby cultural center, **Patronat Municipal de Cultura de Mataró,** C. Sant Josep, also has maps and information on upcoming events and festivals, usually in Catalan. (On the street off C. La Riera in front of the Ajuntament. ☎93 758 23 61. Open M-Sa 9am-2pm, 5-8pm.) Services include **Police:** ☎088. **Emergencies** (☎112). **Internet access** is available on two coin-fed machines at **Flin's Burger Restaurant,** La Rambla 22, in Pl. Santa Anna. (☎93 790 49 84. 100ptas/€0,60 per 10min. Open daily, 11am-midnight. The **postal code** is 08302.

IN THE CITY

Port Aventura!

☎ *902 240 202. Most easily accessible from Barcelona by the Port Aventura train (1½ hr.: 5 per day 1:56-10:55am, return 8 per day 4:48-10:07pm) that leaves from M: Pg. de Gràcia. Train ride plus admission 5300ptas/ €33; under 12 and over 60 3900ptas/€24.*

Just 8km outside of Tarragona is **Universal Studios'** Spanish theme park Port Aventura (Port Adventure), an easy trip from Tarragona and a great daytrip from Barcelona as well. Adults and kids alike will enjoy the park, with its thrilling rides, shops, games, and music and dance shows. The park's international-themed areas are each modeled after a different region of the world, including China, Polynesia, and the American West. The Templo del Fuego (Temple of Fire) roller coaster in "México" is the latest of Port Adventure's exciting attractions.

FOOD

Both on the beach and in town, quick-service cafés and *tapas* restaurants thrive by getting the beach crowd fed and back on the sand where they belong. **Racó d'en Margarit,** Pg. Callao 15, on the beach at the beginning of Platja del Callao, has a standard *tapas* selection (400-900ptas/ €2,40-€5,40) as well as a variety of *paellas* (1000-1300/€6-€7,80), with fast-food service and beachside seating. (☎ 93 790 66 78. Open 12pm-midnight.) **Restaurant Bar Iluro,** La Rambla 14, on Pl. Santa Anna, is a shady break from the sun near the center of town. If the breeze on the outdoor terrace isn't enough, the interior is air-conditioned. (☎ 93 790 32 08. Coffees or beers 200-400ptas/€1,20-€2,40. Seafood entrees 1500-2500ptas/€9-€15, meats 875-975ptas/€5,30-€5,95. Open daily 9am-2pm, 5-9pm.)

BEACHES

Mataró's beaches are the town's biggest draw, with soft sand, refreshing waves, and plenty of room to spread out, the beaches do tend to fill up on weekends and steamy afternoons. The first, **Platja del Varador,** is the widest, with enough room for three full beach-soccer fields behind its sunbathers. An outcropping of rocks, easily circumvented, separates it from the town's remaining two beaches, **Platja del Callao** and **Platja de St. Simó.** This long stretch extends more than a kilometer down the coast. Outdoors showers are everywhere, and Red Cross stations (Open 9am-6pm) are found on Varador and Callao beaches.

FESTIVALS

On the last weekend in July (26-29) Mataró pulls out all the stops in celebrating **Les Santes** (The Saints), its Festa Major in honor of patroness saints Juliana and Semproniana. Nearly a week of activities includes parades, concerts, fireworks, and all-night beach dance parties. The Friday afternoon parade is worth catching, with regal giants, spinning bulls with fireworks for horns, and the 400 year old "Aliga de Mataró" (the Mataró eagle), who performs a jig in front of the Ajuntament.

COSTA DORADA

SITGES

Forty kilometers south of Barcelona, the beach town of Sitges deserves its self-given title "jewel of the Mediterranean," with prime tanning grounds, lively cultural festivals, and a welcoming atmosphere of tolerance. A thriving gay community mingles with daytripping Span-

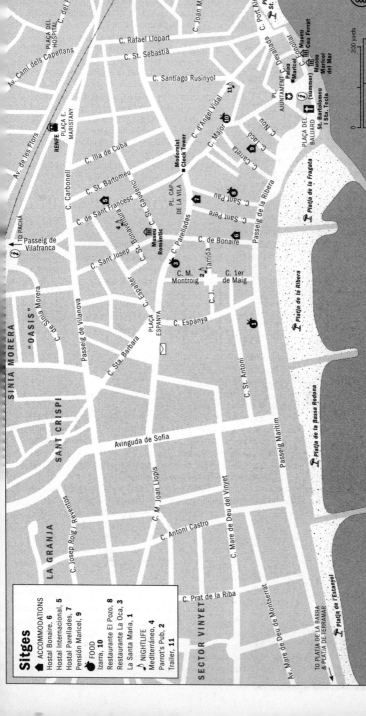

N

200 yards
200 metres

Sitges

ACCOMMODATIONS
Hostal Bonaire, 6
Hostal Internacional, 5
Hostal Parellades, 7
Pensión Maricel, 9

FOOD
Izarra, 10
Restaurante El Pozo, 8
Restaurante La Oca, 3
La Santa Maria, 1

NIGHTLIFE
Mediterráneo, 4
Parrot's Pub, 2
Trailer, 11

I'VE GOT THE TOWER

Imagine the difficulty you had the time you tried to lift a heavy-set friend on your shoulders. Now, imagine that person standing on your shoulders rather than sitting. And now just picture another guy on his shoulders...and another one on top of that. Shoulders hurt yet? With this in mind, consider in wonder Catalunya's *castellers*—the castle makers. The sport of creating *castells*—human towers (literally, "castles") is a popular competition in the province of Tarragona, usually performed at the most important town festivals in the main plaça of its towns.

Castell-making teams, called *colles*, wear a traditional costume called the *xiquet*, consisting of white pants, a shirt of the team color, and a cloth belt, which serves as a footholds for teammates. Hundreds of people crowd together to form the bottom layer, and the *colle* begins its grueling work. *Castells* vary in height, width, and degree of difficulty; the best teams can create up to nine stories of three to four people each, clinging tightly to each other's arms. The tower is topped off by a small girl or boy, called the *anxaneta* (weather vane), who fearlessly scrambles to the top and waves upon completion. Even trickier, the *castell* must then disassemble without collapsing into a jumble of tangled limbs. The *colles* are a source of great town pride, a symbol of trust and town unity. The huge crowds at the bottom layer catch the *castellers* should they fall, preventing injury.

iards, tourist families, and twentysomething partiers, all in search of lots of sun and a good time. The climate, with over 300 sunny days a year, sees to the former, while a vibrant night-life helps with the latter. Through it all, Sitges has not fallen into the commercial traps of a typical resort town; despite booming tourism, the old town somehow has kept traces of its fishing village past, with narrow cobblestoned streets and 19th century architecture. So close it's in the same area code as Barcelona, Sitges is the ideal daytrip for when the crowded city beaches just aren't cutting it, and is well worth a couple of days' stay.

TRANSPORTATION

Cercanías Trains (☎93 490 02 02) run from Estació Barcelona-Sants to Sitges (40min.; every 15-30min. 5:25am-11:00pm; 350ptas/€2,10) and continue on to **Vilanova** (7min.; every 15-30min. until 11:45pm; 160ptas/€1). The last train from Sitges back to Barcelona is at 10:25pm. To get to the beaches in between the two cities, rent a car in Barcelona (See **Service Directory,** p. 290) or in Sitges at **Car Office,** Oasis Local 14 (☎93 811 12 12), at the corner of C. Vilafranca and Vilanova, up C. Carbonell from the train station. For a **taxi,** call ☎93 894 13 29.

ORIENTATION & PRACTICAL INFORMATION

Most everyone coming into Sitges starts out at the RENFE train station, on Av. Carbonell, in the north of town. From here, the town center is a five minute walk, the beach about ten minutes. To get to both, take a right as you leave the station, and then your third left onto C. Sant Francesc. This will lead straight to the old town, and C. Parellades, the main path of stores and restaurants, which runs parallel to the ocean. Off of Parellades, any street will lead you to the waterfront. Pg. Ribera runs along the central and most crowded beaches.

For a good free map and info on accommodations, stop by the **tourist office,** Sínia Morera 1. From the station, turn right onto C. Carbonell and take the first big right, a block later. The office is across the street, a block to the left—look for the sign with the big "i." (☎ 93 894 50 04. Open in summer 9am-9pm; in winter W-M 9am-2pm, 4-6:30pm.) In summer, a smaller branch opens by the museums on C. Fonollar. (☎93 894 42 51. Open 10am-1:30pm, 5-9pm.) **Internet access** and **fax** service are available at **Sitges Internet Access,** C. Espanya 7 (☎93 811 40 03). 750ptas/€4,50/hr, 15min. 195ptas/€1,20. Open daily 11am-2am. Services include: **medical assistance** (☎93 894 64 26); **emergency** (☎93 894 39 49), way uptown on C. Samuel Barrachina; **Super Avui,** Carbonell 24, is a supermarket across from the train station. (Open M-Sa 9am-9pm, Su 10am-2pm.) The **post office,** in Pl. Espanya. (☎93 894 12 47. Open M-F 8:30am-2:30pm, Sa 9:30am-1pm. No packages Sa.) The **postal code** is 08870.

ACCOMMODATIONS

Accommodations are expensive and difficult to find on summer weekends, so consider daytripping to Sitges from Barcelona and reserve early if you plan to stay.

Hostal Parellades, C. Parellades 11 (☎93 894 08 01), 1 block from the beach. Offers standard rooms and an airy terrace that are dirt cheap for Sitges. Singles 3000ptas/€18; doubles 5000ptas/€30, with bath 6000ptas/€36; triples with bath 7200ptas/€43,50.

Hostal Casa-Bella, Av. Carbonell 12 (☎93 894 43 22), 1 block from the train station, take a right as you leave the station. Clean, modern rooms border on sterile. Singles with bath 5000ptas/€30; doubles with bath 8000ptas/€48.

Hostal Internacional, C. Sant Francesc 52 (☎93 894 26 90), off Carbonell. Provides bright rooms not far from the train station. Doubles 5500ptas/€33, with shower 6500ptas/€39.

Hostal Bonaire, C. Bonaire 31 (☎93 894 53 26), off Parellades, toward the beach. Though the 9 rooms are somewhat cramped, ceiling fans and TVs in every room make amends. Singles 4000ptas/€24,10, with bath 5000ptas/€30; doubles with bath 7000ptas/€42. MC/V.

Pensión Maricel, C. Tacó 13 (☎93 894 36 27), 1min. from the beach, nearest to the museums. Big double rooms all come with phones and fans, much needed on the occasional sticky summer night. Doubles with bath 7500ptas/€45. MC/V.

FOOD

Izarra, C. Mayor 24, behind the museum area. This Basque *tapas* bar provides just the right quick food fix before a hard night of club-hopping. Ask for a *plato* (plate) and grab whatever *tapas* look tastiest, from Basque fish *tapas* to more traditional Spanish *croquetas* to chicken wings (120ptas/€0,75 each). Big entrees (700ptas/€4,21 and up) and Basque *sidra* (cider, 300ptas/€1,80) also available. Open daily.

Restaurante La Oca, C. Parellades 41 (☎93 894 79 36). Chickens roasting on an open fire attract long lines of hungry tourists. Try the succulent *half-pollo al ast* (roasted chicken) for 795ptas/€4,80 or cover one with sauce for 895ptas/€5,40. The chicken *croquetas* (400ptas/€2,40) are outstanding. Open daily 1pm-midnight.

Restaurante El Pozo, C. Sant Pau 3 (☎93 894 11 04), off C. Parellades, is a throwback to the town's days as a quiet fishing village. Art on the walls of this tiny tavern depicts rustic scenes, and the food tastes as if it's fresh out of the water. Seafood-heavy menu,

Rolled Hay in the Countryside

Big Fishies, Little Fishies

Hiking in the Country

with wine or beer. Entrees 1100-2000ptas/€6,60-12 +IVA and include options like lobster soup, sole, shrimp, and squid. Open F-W 1-4pm and 7:30-11pm. MC/V.

La Santa Maria, Pg. Ribera 52 (☎93 894 09 99), near the waterfront, at the corner of C. Espanya. A leisurely lunch at Santa Maria's shaded terrace is well worth the lost hour of tanning time, with its casually elegant atmosphere, carefully prepared dishes, and views of the crowded beach. *Menú de la casa* 1500ptas/€9. Seafood dishes 1100-3150ptas/€6,60-€20, meats 1200-2300ptas/€7,20-€14. Open daily 1-5pm and 7-11:30pm. MC/V.

SIGHTS

The pedestrian walkway **Carrer Parellades,** with shopping, eating, and drinking galore, is the center of attention. Cultural activities may seem as undesirable as rain to some beachgoers, but Sitges has some can't-miss attractions, including Morell's whimsical **Modernist clock tower,** Pl. Cap de la Vila 2, above Optica at the intersection of Parellades and Sant Francesc. From the beach, the parish church on the waterfront is the city's most distinctive sight. Behind it, on C. Fonollar, the **Museu Cau Ferrat** hangs over the water's edge. Once home to Catalan modernist Santiago Rusinyol and a meeting point for young Catalan artists Picasso and Ramon Casas, the building is a shrine to Modernist iron, glass work, and painting (☎93 894 03 64). Next door, the **Museu Maricel del Mar** has a selective collection of Romanesque and Gothic painting and sculptures (☎93 894 03 64). Further into town, the **Museu Romàntic,** C. Sant Gaudenci 1, off C. Parellades, is a 19th-century bourgeois house filled with period pieces like music boxes and 17th- to 19th-century dolls. (☎93 894 29 69. All 3 museums open in summer Tu-Su 10am-2, 5-9pm; rest of the year Tu-F 10am-1:30, 3-6:30pm, Sa 10am-7pm, Su 10am-3pm. Combo entrance 900ptas/€5,40, students 500ptas/€3; otherwise 500ptas/€3 per museum, students and seniors 250ptas/€1,50.) Across the street from the museums, the stately **Palau Maricel,** on C. Fonollar, built in 1910 for American millionaire Charles Deering, wows visitors with its sumptuous halls and rich gardens. Guided tours are available on summer nights and include a glass of *cava* (8pm; 900ptas/€5,40); on Friday, Saturday, and Sunday nights, a piano and soprano concert complete the evening of luxury (1200ptas/€7,20 for tour, *cava*, and concert). Call ahead for reservations (☎93 811 33 11).

BEACHES

Plenty of soothing sand accommodates hordes of sun worshippers on hot summer days. At **Platja de la Fragata,** the beach farthest to the left as you face the sea, sand sculptors create new masterpieces every summer day. By midday, the beaches closest to downtown can become almost unbearably crowded. The best beaches, with calmer water and more open space, are a kilometer or two walk further down, at **Platja de la Barra** and **Platja de Terramar.** Rocks shield the beach here from waves, creating a shallow ocean swimming pool, ideal for children. Showers and Red Cross stations abound; in case of **emergencies,** call 93 811 76 25.

NIGHTLIFE

The place to be at sundown is **Carrer Primer de Maig,** which runs directly from the beach and Pg. Ribera, and its continuation, **Carrer Marquès Montroig,** which is off C. Parellades. Bars and clubs line both sides of the small street, blasting pop and house from 10pm until 3am. The clubs here are wide-open and accepting, with a mixed crowd of gay people, straight people, the occasional drag queen, and families. There's no cover anywhere, making for great bar/club-hopping. Beers at most places go for about 500ptas/€3, mixed drinks 1000ptas/€6.

Even crazier is the "disco-beach" **Atlàntida,** in Sector Terramar (☎93 894 26 77; foam parties Th and Su nights), and the legendary **Pachá,** on Pg. Sant Didac in nearby Vallpineda. Buses run all night on weekends to the two discos from C. Primer de Maig (☎93 894 22 98; Open Th-Su, midnight to 4am). Other popular nightspots can be found on C. Bonaire and C. Sant Pau, but most open only on weekends.

FESTIVALS

Sitges celebrates holidays with all-out style. During the **Festa de Corpus Christi** in June, townspeople collaborate to create intricate fresh-flower carpets. For *papier-*

mâché dragons, devils, and giants dancing in the streets, visit during the **Festa Major,** held August 22-27 in honor of the town's patron saint Bartolomé. Nothing compares to the **Carnaval,** on Sunday and Tuesday, in preparation for Catholic fasting during the first week of Lent (usually mid-February). Spaniards crash the town for a frenzy of dancing, outrageous costumes, and vats of alcohol. Tuesday night gets the wildest, as hundreds parade through the streets dressed in drag. On the first Sunday of March, a pistol shot starts the **Rally de Coches de Epoca,** an antique car race from Barcelona to Sitges. June brings the **International Theater Festival** (1500-3500ptas/€9-21 per show), and July and August the **International Jazz Festival** (1700ptas/€10,20 per concert). In mid-October, the one- to two-week **Festival Internacional de Cine Fantástico de Sitges** showcases the scarier side of film, with a varied menu of horror and gore flicks. From September 15 to 17, competitors trod on fresh grapes on the beach for the annual **Grape Harvest.**

DAYTRIP FROM SITGES: VILANOVA I LA GELTRÙ

🚆 *Cercanías trains run from Vilanova to Sitges (10min., every 15-30min., 160ptas/€1), continuing to Barcelona (50min., 350ptas/€2,10). Mon Bus (☎93 893 70 60) connects Vilanova to Sitges (200ptas/€1,20), Vilafranca (270ptas/€1,60), and Barcelona (480ptas/€2,90). The train station doubles as the bus station. Taxi from Vilanova to Sitges is about 1500-2000ptas/€9-€12.*

One of Catalunya's most important ports, **Vilanova i la Geltrù** are actually two cities in one: an industrial center and a well-groomed beach town. There is little in the dusty uptown area except for old churches and stone façades; most visitors spend the day on the beach (10min. from the train station). In the evening, Vilanovans generally forgo late-night madness for beach volleyball or soccer at Parc de Ribes.

To get to the **beaches,** exit the station, turn left on C. Forn de Vidre, take the third left onto the thoroughfare Rambla de la Pau, head under the overpass, and follow the *rambla* all the way to the port. The **tourist office,** with an excellent **map,** is about 50m to the right, in a small park called **Parc de Ribes Roges.** (☎93 815 45 17. Open July-Aug. M-Sa 10am-8pm, Su 10am-2pm; Sept.-June 10am-2pm and sometimes 4-7pm.) To the right, past the tourist office, is the wide **Platja de Ribes Roges;** to the left is the smaller **Platja del Far.** Expect fine sand, sun, and tons of company.

If you decide to stay in town, the popular **Can Gatell,** C. Puigcerdà 6-16, has clean rooms and full baths. With your back to the station, head down C. Victor Balaguer, the leftward of the two parallel streets; at the end, turn right onto La Rambla. Ventosa, and hang a quick left at the sign. (☎93 893 01 17. Doubles 7000ptas/€42,40; triples 9500ptas/€57,25.) The hostel's *menú* (1300ptas/€7,80; served M-F, includes wine) is popular with locals. A less expensive alternative is **Supermarket Orangutan,** Rambla de la Pau 36, on the way to the beach (open M-Sa 9am-1:30pm, 5-8:30pm).

TARRAGONA

Before Barcelona was even a twinkle in anyone's eye, Tarragona was an emerging city, key to Rome's colonization of Iberia (see **Life & Times,** p. 38). In 218 BC, the Carthaginian general **Hannibal** and his troops were tearing through Spain in a march toward Rome. The Romans, led by the super **Scipio brothers** Gnaeus and Publius, set out (successfully) to cut them off and turn them back to North Africa. They set up headquarters in a coastal port, then called Tarraco, and a provincial capital was born. Tarragona's strategic position made the city a thriving provincial power; today, an amphitheater and other ruins pay homage to the city's imperial glory days. These vestiges of Tarragona's Roman past are the city's most compelling attractions, but plenty of visitors are satisfied with lolling on the beaches in one of Catalunya's most important port cities.

TRANSPORTATION

Trains: ☎97 724 02 02, on Pl. Pedrera by the water. Info open daily 6am-9pm. The best transportation option. To: **Alicante** (3hr., 7 per day, 4500ptas/€27); **Barcelona** (1hr., 30-40 per day, 675ptas/€4); **Madrid** (7hr., 4 per day, 6000ptas/€36); **Sitges** (45min., 23 per day, 420ptas/€2,50); **Valencia** (2-3hr., 15 per day, 1860ptas/€11,40); **Zaragoza** (3hr., 8 per day, 2000ptas/€12).

Buses: ☎97 722 91 26, Pl. Imperial Tarraco. **Transportes Bacoma** (☎97 722 20 72) serves most destinations. To: **Barcelona** (1½hr., 8 per day, 1220ptas/€7,30) and **Valencia** (3½hr. 5 per day, 2500ptas/€15,10).

Public Transportation: EMT Buses (☎97 754 94 80) run all over Tarragona. Buses run daily 6am-11pm. 125ptas/€0,80, 10-ride *abono* ticket 700ptas/€4,20.

Taxi: Radio Taxi (☎97 722 14 14).

ORIENTATION & PRACTICAL INFORMATION

Most sights are clustered on a hill, surrounded by remnants of Roman walls. At the foot of the hill, **La Rambla Vella** and **La Rambla Nova** (parallel to one another and perpendicular to the sea) are the main thoroughfares of the new city. La Rambla Nova runs from **Passeig de les Palmeres** (which overlooks the sea) to **Plaça Imperial Tarraco,** the monstrous rotunda and home of the bus station. To reach the old quarter from the train station, turn right and walk 200m to the killer stairs parallel to the shore.

Tourist Office: C. Major 39 (☎97 724 52 03; fax 97 724 55 07), below the cathedral steps. Crucial **free map** and a guide to Tarragona's Roman ruins. Open June-Sept. M-F 9:30am-8:30pm, Sa 9:30am-2pm and 4-8:30pm, Su 10am-2pm; Oct.-May M-F 10am-2pm and 4:30-7pm, Sa-Su 10am-2pm.

Tourist Information booths: Pl. Imperial Tarraco, at the bottom of la Rambla Vella, just outside the bus station; another at the intersection of Av. Catalunya and Via de l'Impera Romi; a 3rd at the corner of Via Augusta and Pg. Sant Antoni. Open daily July-Oct. 10am-2pm and 4-8pm; Nov.-June Sa-Su 10am-2pm.

Luggage Storage: 24hr. at the train station. June-Aug. 400ptas/€2,40; Sept.-May 600ptas/€3,60.

Emergency: ☎112. **Police: Comisaria de Policía** (☎97 723 33 11), on Pl. Orleans. From Pl. Imperial Tarraco on the inland end of La Rambla Nova, walk down Av. Pres. Lluís Companys, and take the 3rd left to the station.

Medical Assistance: Hospital de Sant Pau i Santa Tecla, La Rambla Vella 14 (☎97 725 99 00). **Hospital Joan XXIII** (☎97 729 58 00), on C. Dr. Mallafré Guasch.

Internet Access: Futureland, C. Estanislao Figueras 19 (☎97 722 08 52), off the Imperial Tarraco rotunda. 500ptas/€3 per hr. Open M-F 10:30am-2:30pm and 4:30-10:30pm; Sa-Su 10am-2pm and 4:30-11pm. **Biblioteca Pública,** C. Fortuny 30 (☎97 724 05 44). Public library; free use of the computers with passport.

Post Office: Pl. Corsini 12 (☎97 724 01 49), below La Rambla Nova off C. Canyelles. Open M-F 8:30am-8:30pm, Sa 9am-2pm. **Postal Code:** 43001.

ACCOMMODATIONS & CAMPING

Tarragona is not known for its abundance of cheap beds, as most of the city's accommodations are two- to four-star hotels near the center. Shabby rooms can be found near Pl. Pedrera (by the train station) and better ones by Pl. Font, in the old quarter (parallel to La Rambla Vella), a much cleaner option.

Pensión Noria, Pl. de la Font 53 (☎97 723 87 17), in the heart of the historic town. Enter through the restaurant. Clean and bright rooms with pretty-in-pink bathrooms. Singles with bath 3400ptas/€21; doubles with bath 5900ptas/€36.

Hostal Forum, Pl. de la Font 37 (☎97 723 17 18), upstairs from the restaurant. Clean rooms and bathrooms don't leave space for spreading out, but a decent place to sleep for the night. Singles with bath 3000ptas/€18; doubles with bath 6000ptas/€36.

Camping: Several sites line the road toward Barcelona (Via Augusta or CN-340) along the northern beaches. Take bus #9 (every 20min., 105ptas/€0,60) from Pl. Imperial Tarraco. **Tarraco** (☎97 729 02 89) is closest, at Platja de l'Arrabassada. Well-kept facilities near the beach. 24hr. reception. 555ptas/€3,30 per person, per car, and per tent. Open Apr.-Sept.

FOOD

Pl. Font and Las Ramblas Nova and Vella are full of cheap *menús* (800-1200ptas/€4,80-7,20) and greasy *platos combinados*. Tarragona's indoor **Mercado Central** (market) takes place in Pl. Corsini next to the post office. (Open M-W and Sa 8am-2pm, Th-F 7am-2pm and 5:30-8:30pm. Flea market Tu and Th.) For **groceries,** head to

Camp de Mart

Auditori

Passeig de Torroja

200 meters

N

Passeig de Sant Antoni

Les Coques

Catedral

PL. DE S. ANTONI

Main Tourist Office

PL. DEL FORUM

C. Merceria

Museu Nacional Arqueològic

PL. DE SANTIAGO RUSIÑOL

PL. DEL REI

Museu de la Romanitat

Via Augusta

PL. ARCE OCHOTORENA

Baixada del Miracle

Platja del Miracle

TO PLATJA L'ARRABASSADA & PLATJÀ LLARGA

Passeig Marítim Rafael de Casanovas

Beach Access

Amfiteatre Romà

Info booth

Passeig Arqueològic

Entrance to Passeig Arqueològic

Info booth

Casa-Museu Castellarnau

Cavallers

Ferrers

Nau Destral

Major

Circus

Trinquet Nou

3

Ajuntament

PL. DE LA FONT

2

Av. de Catalunya

Av. Maria Cristina

Via de l'Imperi Romà

La Rambla Vella

C. Sant Agustí

C. Girona

C. Roger de Llúria

Baixada de Toro

C. Comte de Rius

Champlion

C. Sant Francesc

La Rambla Nova

Armanyà

C. Méndez Núñez

C. Pons d'Icart

4

C. Assalt

C. d'August

C. Orfuny

Regional Tourist Office

C. de la Unió

Av. Pau Casals

Rovira

Virgili

C. Estanislau Figueres

Monument to the Castellers

FONT DEL CENTENARI

Pau del Protectorat

General Contreras

PL. GENERAL PRIM

C. Reding

C. Cardenal Cervantes

C. Reding

C. Governador Gonzáles

PL. CORSINI

Canyelles

C. Soler

Mercat

Fòrum

Romà

C. Cardenal Cervantes

Gasòmetre

C. Apodaca

Rebolledo

C. dels Canvtixins

Sant Pau

TO 5 (500m)

TO 1 (50m)

Av. Ramón y Cajal

C. Cristóbal Colón

PL. PONENT

Mallorca

Sevilla

PL. DE BRAUS

Jaume I

Pere Martell

TO MUSEU I NECRÒPOLIS PALEOCRISTIANS (300m)

Info Booth

PL. IMPERIAL TARRACO

La Rambla Nova

Pare Palau

Av. Prat de la Riba

Tarragona

ACCOMMODATIONS
Hostal Fòrum, 2
Pensión Noria, 3

FOOD
Restaurante El Caserón, 4
La Teula, 1

NIGHTLIFE
Port Esportiu, 5

Champion, C. Augusta at Comte de Rius, between Las Ramblas Nova and Vella (Open M-Sa 9:15am-9:15pm.) **El Serrallo,** the fisherman's quarter right next to the harbor, has the best seafood. Try your food with Tarragona's typical *romesco* sauce, simmered from red peppers, toasted almonds, and hazelnuts.

La Teula, C. Mercería 16 (☎97 723 99 89), in the old city off Pl. Santiago Rusinyol, the plaça in front of the cathedral. Great for salads (500-750ptas/€3-€4,50) and toasted sandwiches with interesting veggie/meat combos (975-1100ptas/€5,90-€6,60). Lunch *menú* 1100ptas/€6,60. Open M-Sa 1-4pm and 8pm-midnight. MC/V.

Restaurant El Caserón, Trinquet Nou 4 (☎97 723 93 28), parallel to La Rambla Vella (off Pl. Font). Looks like a diner, serves home-style food. Entrees 800-1400ptas/€4,80-€8,40. Daily and nightly *menú* 1200ptas/€7,20. Open M-Sa 1-4pm and 8:30-11pm, Su 1-3:30pm.

SIGHTS

Tarragona's status as provincial capital transformed the small military enclosure into a glorious imperial port. Countless Roman ruins stand silently amid 20th-century hustle and bustle, all just minutes from the beach.

▓ ROMAN RUINS

🚩 *Nearly all monuments and museums open June-Sept. Tu-Su 9am-9pm; Oct.-May Tu-Su 10am-1:30pm and 4-6:30pm. Admission to each 300ptas/€1,80; students 100ptas/€0,60.*

Below Pg. Palmeres and set amid gardens above Platja del Miracle beach is the **Roman Amphitheater** (☎97 744 25 79), where gladiators once killed wild animals and each other; this barbaric but popular activity dates back to the founding of the city. In 259, the Christian bishop Fructuosus and his two deacons were burned alive here; in the sixth century, these martyrs were honored with a basilica built in the arena.

Above the amphitheater, across Pg. Sant Antoni, is the entrance to the excellent **Museu de la Romanitat** (☎97 724 19 52), which houses the **Praetorium Tower,** the former administrative center of the region, and the **Roman Circus,** the site of chariot races and other spectacles. Visitors descend into the long, dark tunnels which led fans to their seats, and see a model reconstruction of what the complex looked like. The Praetorium was the governor's palace in the first century BC. Rumor has it that the infamous hand-washer Pontius Pilate was born here.

The scattered **Fòrum Romà,** with its reconstructed Corinthian columns, lies near the post office on C. Lleida. Once the center of the town, its distance clearly demonstrates how far the walls of the ancient city had extended. To see what remains of the second-century BC walls, stroll through the **Passeig Arqueològic.** The walls originally stretched to the sea and fortified the entire city.

OTHER SIGHTS

The **Pont del Diable (Devil's Bridge),** a Roman aqueduct 10min. outside of the city, is visible on the way in and out of town by bus. Take municipal bus #5 (every 20min., 105ptas/€0,65) from the corner of C. Christòfer Colom and Av. Prat de la Riba or from Pl. Imperial Tarraco. Lit by octagonal rose windows flanking both arms of the cross is the Romanesque-Gothic **cathedral.** The interior contains the tomb of Joan d'Aragó. (C. Major near Pl. Seu. 300ptas/€1,80, students 100ptas/€0,80. Open June-Aug. M-Sa 10am-7pm; Sept.-May M-Sa 10am-12:30pm and 3-6pm.)

MUSEUMS

The **Museu Nacional Arqueològic,** across Pl. Rei from the Praetorium, displays ancient utensils, statues, and mosaics. (☎97 723 62 09. 400ptas/€2,40, students 200ptas/€1,20; includes admission to the Necropolis.) For a bit of the macabre, creep over to the **Museu i Necròpolis Paleocristians,** Av. Ramón y Cajal 78, at Pg. Independència on the western edge of town. The huge early Christian burial site has yielded a rich variety of urns, tombs, and sarcophagi, the best of which are in the museum. (☎97 721 11 75. 400ptas/€2,40, students 200ptas/€1,20; includes admission to Museu Arqueològic.) If you've had too much Roman roamin', descend the steps in front of the cathedral and take the third right onto C. Cavellares to visit the **Casa-Museu Castellarnau.** It housed the Viscounts of Castellarnau, 18th-century nobles. (☎97 724 22 20. 300ptas/€1,80.)

BEACHES

The hidden access to **Platja del Miracle,** the town's main beach, is along Baixada del Miracle, starting off Pl. Arce Ochotorena, beyond the Roman theater. Walk away from the theater until you reach the underpass, under the train tracks, to the beach. The beach is not on par with other Costa Dorada stops, nor even with the beaches of Barcelona—but it's not bad for a few hours of relaxation. A bit farther away are the larger beaches, **Platja l'Arrabassada,** with dirt-like sand, and the windy **Platja Llarga** (take bus #1 or 9 from Pl. Imperial Tarraco or any of the other stops).

NIGHTLIFE & ENTERTAINMENT

Weekend nightlife in Tarragona is on a much smaller scale than that of its northern neighbors Sitges and Barcelona. Between 5 and 9pm, Las Ramblas Nova and Vella (and the area in between) are packed with strolling families. After 9pm, the bars start to liven up; around 10pm on Saturdays in summer, fireworks brighten the skies. The most popular place to be is at **Port Esportiu,** a portside plaza full of restaurant-bars and mini-*discotecas.* Heading up La Rambla Nova away from the beach, take a left onto C. Unió; bear left at Pl. General Prim and follow C. Apodaca to its end. Cross the tracks; the fun will be to the left.

July and August usher in the **Fiesta de Tarragona** (☎97 7 24 47 95; 24hr. tickets ☎902 332 211). The **Auditori Camp de Mart** near the cathedral holds film screenings and rock, jazz, dance, and theater performances. A booth on Av. Catalunya at Portal del Roser sells tickets until 9pm for the 10:30pm performances (1000-2500ptas/€6-€15,10). Arrive at least one hour early.

ESSENTIAL INFORMATION

THE CATALAN PYRENEES... WITHOUT A CAR

For car-free itineraries through the Vall d'Aran and national park area, know that the towns listed as connected to Barcelona via **Alsina Graells bus** are also connected to each other. Connecting times for the 2 daily **year-round** buses in both directions are:

Barcelona 6:30am, Pont de Suert 11am, Vielha 11:45am

Barcelona 2:30pm, Pont de Suert 7pm, Vielha 7:45pm

Vielha 5:30am, Pont de Suert 6:30am, Barcelona 11:15am

Vielha 1:30pm, Pont de Suert 2:30pm, Barcelona 7:30pm

June through October, these daily connections are also available:

Barcelona 7:30am, La Terrassa crossing (right before Esterri d'Aneu on the official schedule) 12:40pm, Vielha 2:30pm

Vielha 11:44pm, La Terrassa crossing 1:50pm, Barcelona 7pm

On even-numbered years, the first Sunday in October brings the **Concurs de Castells,** an important regional competition featuring tall human towers, as high as seven to nine "stories," called *castells* (see **I've got the Tower,** p. 216). *Castells* also appear amid beasts and fireworks during the annual **Fiesta de Santa Tecla** (Sept. 23). If you're unable to catch the *castellers* in person, don't miss the monument to the *castellers* on La Rambla Nova, an impressive life-size *castell* of bronze Tarragonans.

INLAND

MONTSERRAT

With a saw of gold, the angels hewed twisting hills to make a palace for you.
      —Jacint Verdaguer, *Virolai*

With its 1235m peak protruding from the flat Río Llobregat Valley and its colorful interplay of limestone, quartz, and slate stone, Montserrat (Sawed Mountain) has long inspired poets, artists, and travelers alike. Over a thousand years ago, a mountaineer wandering the crags of Montserrat had a blinding vision of the Virgin Mary. His story spread, attracting pilgrims to the mountain in droves. In 1025 an opportunistic bishop-abbot named Oliba founded a monastery to worship the Virgin, who had become the spiritual patroness of Catalunya. Today, 80 Benedictine monks tend the building, most of which dates from the 19th century (although two wings of the old Gothic cloister survive). During the Catalan *Renaixença* of the early 20th century (see p. 43), politicians and artists like poets Joan Maragall and Jacint Verdaguer turned to Montserrat as a source of Catalan legend and tradition. In the Franco era (see p. 45), it became a center for Catalan resistance—Bibles were printed here in Catalan, and nationalist demonstrations were held on the mountain. Today, the site attracts devout worshipers and tourists who come to see the Virgin of Montserrat, her ornate basilica, the accompanying art museum, and perhaps most of all, the panoramic views of the mountain's awesome rock formations.

TRANSPORTATION

The R5 line of the **FGC trains** (☎ 93 205 15 15) connects to Montserrat from M: Espanya in Barcelona (1hr.; every hr. 8:36am-5:36pm; roundtrip including cable car 1875ptas/€11,30); be sure to get off at Aeri de Montserrat, not Olesa de Montserrat. From there, you'll need to catch the heartstopping **Aeri cable car** to get up to the monastery. (July-Aug. every 15min. daily 9:25am-1:45pm and 2:20-6:35pm; price included in train fares or 975ptas/€5,90 round-trip by itself. Cable car schedules change frequently; call 93 877 7701 to check the current one.) **Autocars Julià** runs a daily bus to the monastery, from right near the Estació Sants train station. (Leaves daily at 9am and returns at 5pm. Call 93 317 64 54 for reservations. 1500ptas/€9; you can pay with credit card over the phone. MC/V.) If you plan to use the funiculars at Montserrat to reach hiking paths, the **Tot Montserrat** is a good investment: available at tourist offices or in M: Espanya, it gets you roundtrip tickets for the FGC train, Aeri cable car, both mountaintop funiculars, entrance to the Museu de Montserrat and audiovisual display (see below), and a meal at the *cafetería*, all for 5400ptas/€33,20 (3250ptas/€20 if you buy it at Montserrat without the train fare included, which is cheaper than the individual fares combined.) At the end of the day, if you miss the last cable car or bus down the mountain, call 93 835 03 84 for a **taxi.**

PRACTICAL INFORMATION

Montserrat is not a town. It is a monastery with adjacent housing and food for pilgrims, both religious and of the camera-toting variety. Most visitor services are in Pl. Creu, the area straight ahead from the top of the steps from the Aeri cable car. The **info booth** in Pl. Creu provides free maps, schedules of daily religious services, and advice on mountain navigation. (☎ 93 877 72 01. Open daily July-Sept. 9am-7pm; Oct.-June M-F 10am-6pm, Sa-Su 9am-7pm.) For more detailed information, buy the *Official Guide to Montserrat* (900ptas/€5,20) or the official guide to the museum (1000ptas/€6). Other services in Pl. Creu include **currency exchange** with poor rates (open M-F 9:15am-2pm, Oct.-May Sa 9:15am-1:30pm.), **ATMs,** and a **post office** (open daily 10am-1pm). For an **ambulance** or the **mountain rescue team,** call 904 105 555.

ACCOMMODATIONS

For those who choose to spend the night at Montserrat, there are three options: camping, an apartment in one of two different buildings, or a room in the 3-star hotel. All but the campsite are wheelchair accessible, and all prices listed include the IVA. For reservations for the apartments or hotel, contact the **Central de Reserves i Informació** (☎ 93 877 77 01; fax 93 877 77 24; www.abadiamontserrat.net). The apartment administration office, **Administració de les Delles,** is located in the corner of the plaça. (Open daily 9am-1pm and 2-6pm; after 6pm they're at the Hotel Abat Cisneros reception. 2-day minimum stay, 7-day in July and August.)

Abat Marcet, the newer, nicer building, has rooms for 1-5 people, all with full bath, phone, TV, heat, a dining room, and a kitchen with microwave. (Singles 1750-4820ptas/€10,50-29; doubles 3500-6170ptas/€21-37.) **Abat Oliva,** which is much older than Marcet, has rooms for 2-7 people, but the kitchens have only hotplates for cooking, and there is no heat, so it closes in winter. (Doubles 3775-4100ptas/€22,50-24,50; quads 5925-6460ptas/€35,50-39). The **Hotel Abat Cisneros,** next to the basilica, has a restaurant and more comfortable bedrooms than the apartments. (Singles 3825-7000ptas/€23-42; doubles 6450-12,200ptas/€39-73,50. Breakfast included.) The **camp-**

site is a 5min. walk up the hill from the Sta. Cova funicular station. (☎93 835 02 51. Open Apr.-Oct. Office open daily 8am-9pm. 400ptas/€2,30 per person, under 12 300ptas/€1,50; 350ptas/€1,90 per tent. No fires allowed.)

FOOD

Food options on Montserrat are all marked clearly on the free map available from the info counters. If you want to take food hiking with you, you can get cookies and crackers at the 2-aisle **Queviures supermarket** in Pl. Creu, or meat and cheese at the **Pastisseria** (open daily 9am-7pm). For quick, informal food, try the **Bar de la Plaça,** next to the supermarket (*bocadillos* and hamburgers 400-450ptas/€2,30-2,70; open 9:30am-5pm), or the main **cafeteria** at the top of the steps from the cable car (open Apr.-Nov. daily 8:15am-8pm, Dec.-Mar. daily 8:15am-5pm; MC/V). The **self-service cafeteria** for *Tot Montserrat* card-holders is up the hill to the right from the cable car steps (open daily noon-4pm; closed Jan.), as is the scenic **Restaurant de Montserrat.** (*Menú del día* 1750ptas/€10,50, kids 725ptas/€4,30; IVA included. Open Mar. 15-Nov. 15 daily noon-4pm. MC/V. Wheelchair accessible.) The **Restaurant Hotel Abat Cisneros** offers the most expensive *menú* (3500ptas/€21) in the nicest setting. (Open daily 1-3:30pm and 8-9:45pm. AmEx/MC/V. Wheelchair accessible.)

SIGHTS

Above Pl. Creu, the entrance to the **basilica** looks out onto Pl. Santa Noría. To the right of the main chapel, a route through the side chapels leads to the 12th-century Romanesque **La Moreneta** (the black Virgin Mary), Montserrat's venerated icon of Mary. (Walkway open Nov.-June M-F 8-10:30am and noon-6:30pm, Sa-Su 8-10:30am, noon-6:30pm, and 7:30-8:30pm; July-Sept. daily 8-10:30am, noon-6:30pm, and 7:30-8:30pm.) Legend has it that St. Peter hid the figure, carved by St. Luke, in Montserrat's caves. Removed from Montserrat after the Napoleonic Wars and the Spanish Civil War (see p. 44), the solemn little figure found its way back and is now showcased in an elaborate silver case. For good luck, rub the orb in Mary's outstretched hand, and if you can, schedule your visit so that you can hear the renowned **Escalonia boys' choir** sing *Salve Regina* in the basilica. (Daily at 1pm, except July.)

Also in Pl. Santa María, the **Museo de Montserrat** exhibits a variety of art, ranging from a mummified Egyptian woman to Picasso, including his *Sardana of Peace*, painted just for Montserrat, and *Old Fisherman*. The museum's Impressionist paintings are its highlights; Ramon Casas' famous *Madeline Absinthe* is one of many evocative portraits. (Open Nov.-June M-F 10am-

Strolling in the Park

Fountain

Country Scene

SWM SEEKING...

Tall, dark, handsome, rich, famous, powerful, and searching for life partner. Enjoys water sports (competed on the Olympic sailing team). Educated at Georgetown. Looking for that special someone—attractive, charismatic, and preferably of noble lineage—to share interests and raise a family. His name is Felipe, the Prince of Asturias and heir to the Spanish throne. With his 30th birthday just behind him and his two elder sisters recently married, all eyes are on Felipe. Whom will he choose to be his queen when he takes over one of Europe's few powerful monarchies? The competition is fierce. Lovely ladies from wealthy families are stalking the streets of Madrid and the slopes of the Val d'Aran, but so far there are no front-runners. Cross your fingers and pack something nice—you could be the next queen of Spain.

6pm, Sa-Su 9:30am-6:30pm; July-Sept. M-F 10am-7pm, Sa-Su 9:30am-7pm. 600ptas/€3,50, students and over 65 400ptas/€2,50, under 10 free. Not wheelchair accessible.) The **Espai Audiovisual,** at the top of the steps by the cable car, offers a brief view, through CD-ROMs and video, of the life of a monk on Montserrat. (125ptas/€1. Open daily 9am-6pm.)

WALKS

A visit to Montserrat is not complete without a walk along the "mountain of a hundred peaks." Some of the most beautiful areas of the mountain are accessible only on foot. The **Santa Cova funicular** descends from Pl. Creu to paths which wind along the sides of the mountain to ancient hermitages. (Apr.-Oct. daily every 20min. 10am-6pm; Nov.-Mar. Sa-Su only, 10am-5pm. Roundtrip 400ptas/€2,40.) Take the **St. Joan funicular** up for more inspirational views of Montserrat. (July-Aug. daily every 20min. 10am-7pm; Sept.-Oct. and Apr.-June 10am-6pm; Nov.-Mar. M-F 11am-4:15pm, Sa-Su 10am-4:25pm. Roundtrip 975ptas/€6. Joint roundtrip ticket with the Sta. Cova funicular 1100ptas/€6,50.) The dilapidated **St. Joan monastery** and **shrine** are only a 20min. tromp from the highest station. The real prize is **Sant Jerónim** (the area's highest peak at 1235m), with its mystical views of Montserrat's rock formations. The enormous domes and serrated outcroppings resemble a variety of human forms, including "The Bewitched Friars" and "The Mummy." The hike is about 2½ hours from Pl. Creu or a one-hour trek from the terminus of the St. Joan funicular. The paths are long and winding but not all that difficult—after all, they were made for guys wearing long robes. En route, make sure you take a sharp left when, after about 45min., you come to the little old chapel—otherwise, you're headed straight for a helicopter pad. On a clear day the hike offers spectacular views of Barcelona and surrounding areas.

For **guided visits** and hikes, call 93 877 77 01 at least two weeks in advance. (Hiking tour in English 1000ptas/€6, museum tour 800ptas/€4,90, joint tour 1400ptas/€13,90. In Spanish, hiking and museum tour 600ptas/€3,80 each, joint tour 1100ptas/€6,80.) For rock-climbing and more athletic hiking in the area, call Marcel Millet at ☎93 835 02 51 or stop by his hiking/climbing office next to the Montserrat campsite.

CATALAN PYRENEES

RIPOLL

In the heart of Catalunya sits sleepy Ripoll (pop. 11,000), the region's strongest link to its proud early history. Ripoll houses the ninth-century monastery founded by Guifré el Pilós (Wilfred the Hairy; see p. 38), the founding father of Catalunya, as well as the tomb of the legend himself. The **Monasterio de Santa Maria** attracts visitors in search of Spain's Romanesque architectural legacy; its elaborately carved portal is one of the most famous in all of Spain. Ripoll also serves as a convenient base for excursions to the nearby town of Sant Joan de las Abadesses; its convent and Ripoll's monastery are the two great architectural relics of the age of Guifré.

PRACTICAL INFORMATION

RENFE, Pl. Mova 1 (☎97 270 06 44), runs **trains** to Puigcerdà (1hr., 7 per day 8:56am-8:54pm, 420ptas/€2,52) and Barcelona (1½hr., 5-12 per day 6:32am-8:04pm, 885ptas/€5,31). The bus station next door sends **Teisa buses** (☎97 220 48 68) to: Sant Joan de las Abadesses (15min., 5 per day, 175ptas/€1,05); Barcelona (4hr., 1 per day, 1800ptas/€10,80); Girona (2hr., 1 per day, 1100ptas/€6,60), via Olot. The **tourist office,** next to the monastery on Pl. Abat Oliba, gives out free maps. (☎97 270 23 51. Open daily 9:30am-1:30pm and 4-7pm.) Other services include: **emergency** (☎112); **police,** Pl. Ajuntament 3 (☎97 271 44 14); and the **post office,** C. d'Estació, facing the tree-lined park. (☎97 270 07 60. Open M-F 8:30am-2:30pm, Sa 9:30am-1pm.) The **postal code** is 17500. Connect to the **Internet** at **Xarxtel,** Pl. d'Espanya 10, a computer-electronics store that charges customers for use of their network connection. The **public library,** C. de les Vinyes 6, also offers free use of their computers. (Open M, Tu, Th, and F 4-8:30pm, W 9am-1:30pm, and Sa 10am-1:30pm.)

ACCOMMODATIONS

Ripoll is an ambitious daytrip; you can sleep at the luxurious **Fonda La Paula,** C. Berenguer 4, on Pl. Abat Oliba alongside the tourist office, which has cream-colored rooms with comfortable beds, TVs, and spacious, tiled bathrooms. (☎97 270 00 11. Singles 3320ptas/€20; doubles 5350ptas/€32; triples 7223ptas/€44. V.) The few other accommodations in town are pricey. **Hostal del Ripollès,** Pl. Nova 11, provides small-ish but well-furnished rooms, with TV, phone, and full bath. From the monastery's plaza, follow C. Sant Pere for two blocks. (☎97 270 02 15. Breakfast included. Singles 4500ptas/€27,10; doubles 6500ptas/€39,20; triples 7500/€45,20.) **La Trobada Hotel,** Pg. de Honorat 4, offers similar rooms at slightly higher prices, in a convenient location, on the right as your approach the Pont d'Olot, the bridge between the train/bus stations and the center of town. (☎97 270 23 53. Breakfast 500ptas/€3 per person. Singles 4500ptas/€27,10; doubles 8000ptas/€48,20; triples 9200ptas/€55,50.)

FOOD

Restaurants surround Pl. Gran. Follow C. Bisbe Morgades and take a right before the river on C. Mossen; the plaza is to the left. **Restaurante La Perla,** Pl. Gran 4, serves regional meat and fish entrees (600-1400ptas/€3,60-8,40. *Menús* 1100-2000ptas/€6,60-€12. ☎97 270 00 01. Open M-Sa 1-5pm and 8pm-midnight, Su 1-5pm. MC/V.) At **La Piazzetta,** Pl. Nova 11, the ambience and menu may Catalan, but the food is Italian. (Pizzas 875ptas/€5,25, most entrees 875-975ptas/€5,25-5,85. ☎97 270 02 15. Open M-Sa 1-3:15pm, 8-10:30pm, Su 8-10:30pm.) Stock up on **groceries** at the supermarket across from the bus station, **Champion,** C. Progress 33-37. (☎97 270 26 32. Open M-Th 8:30am-2pm and 4:30-9pm, F-Sa 8:30am-9:30pm, Su 10am-2pm. AmEx/MC/V.)

SIGHTS

Almost everyone who comes to Ripoll comes to see the incredibly intricate 11th-century portal of the ▧**Monasterio de Santa María.** To reach the monastery, take a left on C. Progrés from the train and bus stations, then follow it until it merges with C. Estació. Take the first left after the "metal dancers" (the colorful modern statues) onto Pont d'Olot, cross the river, and continue straight on C. Bisbe Morgades to the Pl. Ayuntament and Pl. Abat Oliba. (Church open daily 8am-1pm and 3-8pm. Free.)

Founded in AD 879 by Count Guifré el Pilós (Wilfred the Hairy), the Santa María monastery was once the most powerful in all of Catalunya. The arched doorway, nicknamed the "Stone Bible," is considered perhaps the finest piece of Romanesque architecture in all of Spain. It depicts scenes from the Old and New Testaments as well as a hierarchy of the cosmos and a 12-month calendar. Explanatory panels (in Catalan) attempt to decode the doorway. The panels directly around the door are representations of the twelve months, and the panels next to the arch depict the Exodus. After centuries of battering from the elements, the worn portal is now sheltered in a climate-controlled glass enclosure.

Inside you'll find the Romanesque basilica, very different from its original form due to extensive renovations. A number of tombs line the interior, the most famous of which lies to the left of the altar: that of Guifré el Pilós, the beloved Wilfred the Hairy (see p. 38). Killed in battle in AD 897, his bones were regathered and honored here in the early 1980s. The Catalan inscription basically reads "Here lies Wilfred the Hairy, Count of Barcelona...[and seven other regions], Founder of the National Catalan dynasty, and Rebuilder of Our Land."

Adjoining the church is a beautiful two-story Romanesque and Gothic **cloister,** with artifacts from the monastery dating back hundreds of years, surrounding a quiet courtyard. (Open 10am-1pm and 3-7pm. 100ptas/€0,80.)

Next door to Santa Maria is the **Museu Etnogràfic de Ripoll,** which houses a hodge-podge collection of artifacts from Ripoll's history, focusing on the industries of the town and its surrounding areas. (Open Tu-Sa 9:30am-1:30pm, 3:30pm-7pm.)

DAYTRIP FROM RIPOLL: ST. JOAN DE LAS ABADESSES

TEISA buses (☎97 274 02 95) connect Sant Joan to Ripoll (15min., 5-7 per day, 175ptas/€1,05), stopping next to the church. The helpful **tourist office,** Pl. l'Abadia 9 (☎97 272 05 99) is next door to the monastery alongside a 15th-century cloister. Office open M-F 10am-2pm and 4-7pm.

Wilfred the Hairy was nothing if not an equal-opportunity employer. After founding Ripoll's first monastery, he went on to endow a convent 10km away, to which he appointed his daughter Emma as the first abbess in 887. Sant Joan de las Abadesses (pop. 3700) developed around the nuns, but unfortunately some of The Hairy's successors were not so keen on female independence; their community was ousted in the 11th century and it took 100 years before anyone was allowed to move back. The Augustines who eventually took over turned the convent into a monastery. Today it contains a Romanesque **church** and adjoining **museum,** which proudly displays religious art and artifacts from throughout Catalunya. (☎97 272 23 53; museum and church 300ptas/€1,50; open daily July-Aug. 10am-7pm; Nov.-Feb. 10am-2pm; rest of the year 10am-2pm, 4pm-6pm.) The highlight of the candle-lit church may be the haunting **Santíssim Misteri,** a 13th-century wooden sculpture depicting Christ's removal from the cross. On Christ's forehead is a piece of the Host (the sacred bread of the Catholic Mass), that has been preserved for over 700 years.

PUIGCERDÀ

A challenging name for foreigners, Puigcerdà (pop.7000; Pwee-chair-DAH) has become a popular town by virtue of its stunning location in the mountainous Cerdanya region. Puigcerdà's view of the valley is beautiful, and the town serves as a cheap base for hiking, biking, or skiing the surrounding hillsides. Puigcerdà is perhaps best known for appearing in the 1993 *Guinness Book of World Records* for the world's longest *butifarra* (sausage), a Freudian nightmare measuring 5200m.

TRANSPORTATION

RENFE trains (☎97 288 01 65) run to: Barcelona (3hr., 6 per day, 1145ptas/€6,90); Núria (6 per day, round-trip train and *Cremallera* 2565ptas/€16); and Ripoll (1¼hr., 6 per day, 420ptas/€2,60). **Alsina Graells buses** (☎97 335 00 20) run to Barcelona (3¼hr., 2-4 per day, 2000ptas/€12) and La Seu d'Urgell (1hr., 7 per day, 670ptas/€4). From La Seu there is passage to **Andorra.** Buses depart in front of the train station and from Pl. Barcelona; purchase tickets on board. See the schedule in Bar Estació, to the right as soon as you walk into the train station. Taxis (☎97 288 00 11) wait on Pl. Cabrinetty. For **bike rental,** try **Sports Iris,** Av. de França 16. (☎97 288 23 98. Bikes 1500ptas/€9 half day, 2500ptas/€15 per day. MC/V.)

ORIENTATION & PRACTICAL INFORMATION

Puigcerdà's center is at the top of a hill. **Plaça Ajuntament,** located off the main plaça, is nicknamed *el balcón de Cerdanya* for its view of the valley and the less picturesque **train station** at the foot of the slope. Buses stop at the train station and the Pl. Barcelona, where it's best to get off. To reach Pl. Ajuntament from the inconvenient train station, walk past the stairs in the station's plaça until you reach the first real flight of stairs (between two buildings). Walk up and turn right at the top; then look for the next set of stairs on your left, just before a sign for C. Hostal del Sol. Climb these to the top and turn left on C. Raval de les Monges, where the final set of stairs winds up to the right. From the plaça, walk one block on C. Alfons I to **C. Major,** the principal commercial street. Turn left on C. Major to Pl. Santa Maria. From Pl. Santa Maria, with your back to the bell tower, walk diagonally to the left to Pl. Barcelona.

The **tourist office,** C. Querol 1, a right off Pl. Ajuntament with your back to the view, has an English-speaking staff that gives out maps and lodging listings. (☎ 97 288 05 42; info@puigcerda.com. Open July-Sept. 15 M-Tu 10am-1:30pm and 4:30-8pm, W-Sa 9am-2pm and 3-8pm, Su 9:30am-2pm; Sept. 16-June M 9am-1pm, Tu-F 10am-1pm and 4-7pm, Sa 10am-1:30pm and 4:30-8pm.) **Banco Central Hispano** is on Pl. Cabrinetty. (Oct.-Mar. M-F 8:30am-2:30pm, Sa 8:30am-1pm; Apr.-Sept. M-F 8:30am-2:30pm.) Other services include: **emergency** (☎091 or 092); **municipal police,** Pl. Ajuntament 1 (☎97 288 19 72); the **Centre Hospitalari** (☎97 288 01 50 or 97 288 01 54), in Pl. Santa Maria. Log on at **Punt com,** C. Espanya 10. (☎97 288 31 55. 200ptas/€1,20 per 30min. Open M-Sa 10am-1:30pm and 4-8:30pm, Su 10am-2pm.) The **post office,** Av. Coronel Molera 11, is off Pl. Barcelona on the left after a block and a half. (☎97 288 08 14. Open M-F 8:30am-2:30pm, Sa 9:30am-1pm.) The **postal code** is 17520.

ACCOMMODATIONS

Rooms in Puigcerdà come easily, if not cheaply. Most cheaper *pensiones* hole up off Pl. Santa Maria, in the old town. ▧ **Alfonso Habitaciones,** C. Espanya 5, offers decent, dimly lit rooms with TVs, bathrooms, and colorful bedspreads. Take a left off C. Alfons I when heading away from the church. (☎97 288 02 46. Singles 3000ptas/€18, with bath 6000ptas/€36; doubles with bath and breakfast 7000ptas/€42. Cash only). **Pensión Maria Victoria,** C. Querol 7, just past Pl. Ajuntament, has clean rooms with breakfast, full bathrooms, and a comfortable lounge with TV, foosball, and pool. Dining area has views of the mountains. (☎97 288 03 00. Singles 4000ptas/€24; doubles 7500ptas/€45. MC/V.) **Camping Stel,** 1km from Puigcerdà on the road to Llivia, offers full-service camping with the benefits of a chalet-style restaurant-bar and lounge. (☎97 288 23 61. Site with tent and car 2350ptas/€14, 710ptas/€4,30 per person, 220V electricity for 480ptas/€2,80. Restaurant *menú* 1500ptas/€9. Open weekends only June 1-Sept. 30 and Oct. 27-May 1.) If you're planning to ski in La Molina, try **Mare de Déu de les Neus (HI),** on Ctra. Font Canaleta, which has modern facilities and a beautiful location just 500m from the La Molina RENFE station and 4km from the slopes. In winter a bus goes up to the slopes every 30 minutes. (☎97 289 20 12, reservations ☎93 483 83 63. Breakfast included. Sheets 350ptas/€2. Reserve in high season. Doubles and triples available, same price per person. Jan.-Nov. dorms 2000ptas/€12, over 25 2700ptas/€16; Dec. dorms 2350ptas/€14, over 25 3000ptas/€18. MC/V.)

FOOD

The neighborhood off C. Alfons I is filled with markets and restaurants. For fresh produce, try the weekly **market,** Sundays 6am-5pm, at both P. 10 d'Abril and the Pl. Cabrinetty. Get **groceries** at **Bonpreu,** C. Colonel Molera 12, the small supermarket diagonally across from the post office. (Open M-Sa 9am-1:30pm and 5-9pm, Su 10am-2pm. MC/V.) Find vegetarian food at **El Pati de la Tieta,** C. dels Ferrers 20, which serves large portions of pasta and pizzas (1000-1600ptas/€6-9,60) and heavenly desserts in an ivy-covered outdoor patio. (☎97 288 01 56. Fish and meat entrees 1800-2800ptas/€11-17. Open daily 1-4pm and 8pm-midnight. MC/V.) At **Cantina Restaurant Mexicà,** Pl. Cabrinetty 9, you can kick back with a margarita (650ptas/€3,95) and take in some excellent tacos, fajitas, and quesadillas (975ptas/€5,85). Friendly staff keep the vibrant, colorful restaurant squeaky clean. (☎97 288 16 58. Entrees 725-1375ptas/€4,30-8. Open M 8:30pm-midnight, Tu-W and F-Su 2-4pm and 8:30pm-midnight. MC/V.) **El Galet,** Pl. Santa Maria 8, is a small brasserie with a meat-heavy menu and outdoor tables that face the church. (☎97 288 22 66. Entrees 875-2175ptas/€5,30-13. Open W-M 2pm-4:30 and 9-11:30pm. AmEx/MC/V.)

SIGHTS

Between ski runs and two-wheeled exploration, dash over to the **campanario,** the octagonal bell tower in Pl. Santa Maria. This 42m high 12th-century tower is all that remains of the Església de Santa Maria, and it is an eerie reminder of the destruction wreaked by the Civil War. Climb to the top for 360° views of Puigcerdà and the Pyrenees. (Open July-Aug. M-Tu noon-2pm and 5-8pm, W-Su 11am-2pm and 5-8pm. Free.) The 13th-century **Església de Sant Domènec,** on Pg. 10 d'Abril, contains several Gothic paintings considered to be among the best of their genre. (Open 9:30am-8pm. Free.) Puigcerdà's picturesque **Lake Estany,** a 5min. walk up C. Pons i Gasch from Pl. Barcelona, was created back in 1380 for irrigation purposes. It now serves the town well as a lovely place to rent a boat (300ptas/€1,80 per person per 30min.) or sit and have a drink at the adjacent café.

OUTDOOR ACTIVITIES

Puigcerdà calls itself the "capital of snow." **Ski** in your country of choice (Spain, France, or Andorra) at one of 19 ski areas within a 50km radius. The closest and cheapest one on the Spanish side is **La Molina** (☎97 289 20 31; www.lamolina.com). Nearby **Masella** (☎97 214 40 00; www.masella.com) offers the longest run in the Pyrenees at 7km. For cross-country skiing, the closest site is **Guils** (☎97 219 70 47). A little further out, try **Lles** (☎97 329 30 49) or **Aransa** (☎97 329 30 51). The Puigcerdà area is also popular for **biking;** the tourist office has a brochure with 17 potential routes mapped out. La Molina opens trails up for biking in the summer months, and provides rentals as well for 2925ptas/€12,62 per day. You can also navigate the trails on horseback for 2100ptas/€12 for an hour long excursion. For indoor sports, the **Club Poliesportiu Puigcerdà,** on Av. del Poliesportiu, has a pool, tennis, basketball courts, and a skating rink. (☎97 288 02 43. Open M-F 11am-10pm, Sa 11am-9:30pm, Su 11am-8pm. 675ptas/€3,8 per sports facility or 1000ptas/€6 per day.)

NIGHTLIFE & FESTIVALS

Cafés and bars crowd the plaças, particularly the adjacent Pl. Santa Maria and Pl. Herois. **Bar Miami** (☎97 288 00 13) and **Kennedy** (☎97 288 11 91) sit next to each other on Pl. Herois and have popular outdoor patios with good people-watching both day and night. **Central,** Pl. Santa Maria 6, is a hip bar with eclectic and cozy furniture.

Puigcerdà hosts several festivals throughout the year, including the popular **Festival de Música Clásica** during the last two weeks of July, the **Festa de L'Estany (Festival of the Lake)** with grand fireworks displays at the end of August, and at Easter, the **Antic Puigcerdà,** the town's biggest market and fair.

PARC NACIONAL D'AIGÜESTORTES

The full name of Catalunya's only national park is actually Parc Nacional d'Aigüestortes i Estany de Sant Maurici, a reference to the park's distinct halves. In the east lies the valley of the Riu Escrita, with the park's largest lake (*estany* in Catalan), the Estany de Sant Maurici; in the west, the wild tumbling of the Riu de Sant Nicolau through its own valley has earned the region the nickname *Aigües Tortes* ("Twisted Waters"). On a sunny spring day, the park's snowy peaks, flowered meadows, and glacial lakes (more than 100 of them) are a sight to behold. With over 10,000 hectacres to be explored, the park merits at least two days; if you rely on public transportation, it's hard to do it in fewer than three.

The best time to hike in the park is late spring to early summer. The mountains are deceptively placid from afar, as the unpredictable weather can be dangerous and some trails get cut off by streams during early spring melting and torrential late summer rains. Though the main trails are clearly marked, it is easy to get lost, and in winter, although the park is open for snowshoeing, trails are unmarked.

ORIENTATION

One particularly popular hike (and the one described below) is the east-west traverse through the park from the town of Espot (p. 231), the eastern gateway, to Boí (p. 232), the western gateway to the park. From **Espot** to the **Estany de Sant Maurici** is about 8km (2hr., shorter if by jeep), and from the lake a path climbs 3km (2hr.) to the **Portarró d'Espot,** the gateway between the park's two halves and a prime spot for viewing the scenery. From the pass it is 2km (1hr.) to the **Estany Llong** and the flat plains of the **Aigüestortes** themselves. Near the western tip of the Estany Llong lies the park's first *refugio*, also called **Estany Llong.** (Call the park info offices listed below for reservations. Open mid-June to mid-Oct. and winter weekends. 1975ptas/ €12 per person, with youth card 850ptas/€5.) From the **western park entrance** to the Estany Llong is 10km, and to **Boí** itself is another 4km along paved road (by taxi (600ptas/€3,60) or foot), a total of about three hours from the lake to town. The entire hike takes at least eight hours, shorter if you take jeeps and taxis en route.

PRACTICAL INFORMATION

For more detailed hiking information, contact the **park information offices** (in Espot ☎97 362 40 36; in Boí ☎97 369 61 89; general info ☎97 369 40 00). Don't rely on the free park maps from the park info office; it's worth the extra cash to buy the better, more detailed *Editorial Alpina* two-part map (925ptas/€5,60; available in area stores). The green *Editorial Alpina* guides, one each for Montardo, Vall de Boí, and Sant Maurici, are also a useful option (775ptas/€4,60). For those interested in details of flora and fauna, the official *Guía de Visita* costs 1500ptas/€9 in the park info office. The park's five **refugios** (the simple, dorm-style accommodations available in the park; 1500-2000ptas/€9-12 per person) and scattered open shepherd's huts are good accommodation options for those planning multi-day treks.

GATEWAYS TO THE PARK

ESPOT

The official gateway to the eastern half of the park, and the best way to enter if coming from the direction of Barcelona, is the quiet little town of Espot (pop. 350).

PRACTICAL INFORMATION

Unfortunately for those using public transportation, the **Alsina Graells bus** (☎93 265 65 08 or 97 327 14 70; see p. 223) only runs from Barcelona from June through October; even then, it only comes within 7km of Espot, on Highway C-147 at the La Torrassa crossing (5hr. 15min., 7:30am, 3660ptas/€22). From the La Torrassa gas station, you can call the park jeep service (☎97 362 41 05), take you to Espot (1000ptas/€6). The **park information office,** on Espot's main road (on the right as you enter town), provides good brochures and advice and can make park *refugio* reservations. (☎97 362 40 36. Open daily Apr.-Oct. 9am-1pm and 3:30-6:45pm, Nov.-Mar. M-Sa 9am-2pm and 3:30-6pm.) In a **medical emergency,** call 97 362 01 63.

ACCOMMODATIONS AND CAMPING

Many local residences take in travelers; inquire at the tourist office. **Casa Felip** provides rooms with lace curtains and private baths. Cross the main bridge, follow the road two blocks, and then turn left. (☎97 362 40 93. Breakfast 500ptas/€3. Sept.-June singles 3000ptas/€18; doubles 4000ptas/€24. July-Aug. singles 4000ptas/€24; doubles 5000ptas/€30. Cash only.) Another good option is the **Pensió Palmira,** which offers seven hotel-quality double rooms, as well as discounts for guests in its restaurant. (A sharp left right after crossing the main bridge; look for the P sign. ☎97 362 40 72. July 15-Sept. 30 and Nov.-Apr. 2700ptas/€16 per person, rest of the year 2200ptas/ €13. MC/V.) **Restaurant Palmira** is one of the most affordable in town even for non-guests, with a *menú* for 1600ptas/€9,60.

Càmping la Mola (☎97 362 40 24) and **Càmping Sol i Neu** (☎97 362 40 01), on the way to Espot, are grassy riverside sites with good facilities and pools. (Open June-Sept. and *Semana Santa*. 650ptas/€3,90 per person, per tent, and per car.)

GETTING TO THE PARK

Espot is 4.5km from the park entrance, but the walk to the park entrance is quite scenic. A jeep service runs from Espot to the **Estany Sant Maurici** (600ptas/€3,60) and to **Amitges** (1800ptas/€10,80, min. 6 people), a northern point in the park close to the best and biggest *refugio*. (☎93 325 00 07 or 97 325 01 09. In 2002 open Feb. 9-24, Mar. 23-31, and June 15-Sept. 29; call ahead to reserve a bed. Hot water, bathrooms, full meals and snacks. 1800ptas/€11, with dinner 3650ptas/€22. V.) From Estany de Sant Maurici to the Aigüestortes jeep-taxi stop is about 3½hr.).

VALL DE BOÍ

The village of Boí (pop. 150) is the best place from which to explore the western half of the park, although like Espot it is somewhat difficult to reach from Barcelona.

PRACTICAL INFORMATION

The **Alsina Graells** bus from Barcelona goes twice a day to **Pont de Suert** (4½hr., 6:30am and 2:30pm, 3350ptas/€20), where you can get a taxi to Boí for 2800ptas/€17. Boí's helpful **park information office** is in the main plaça near the town's striking Romanesque church. (☎97 369 61 89. Open daily Apr.-Oct. 9am-1pm and 3:30-6:45pm, Nov.-Mar. M-Sa 9am-2pm and 3:30-6pm.) The **Guardia Civil** can be reached at ☎97 369 08 15. In a **medical emergency** call 97 364 00 80.

ACCOMMODATIONS

Despite the nearby ski resort in Taüll, Boí retains a pastoral feel. Low arches and cobblestone streets surround several family-run accommodations, including **Casa Guasch,** which lets simple rooms (better inside than it appears from the street). With the church on your right, exit the main plaça through the stone arch, turn right through the next arch, then bear left and turn left again where the street ends; the entrance is on the left. (☎97 369 60 42. Doubles 3200ptas/€19. Open July-Aug. and Dec.-Mar. Cash only.) The park office also gives out a booklet listing every accommodation, restaurant, shop, and service in the town.

GETTING TO THE PARK

From Boí you can take a taxi (☎97 369 60 36; 600ptas/€3,60) up to the western park entrance, or all the way to the Aigüestortes jeep stop.

VAL D'ARAN

Some of the Catalan Pyrenees's most dazzling peaks cluster around green Val d'Aran, Catalunya's northernmost valley. The main river, Garona, flows into France, but it has been almost entirely cut off from Spain for most of its history, and until the middle of this century, consisted mostly of scattered farming and herding villages.

In 1924, a summer road pass and the area's first hydroelectric plant opened, and 1948 brought year-round access from Spain via the Túnel de Vielha. The biggest change of all, though, was the opening of the swank Baqueira-Beret ski resort in 1964. The best skiing in Spain has transformed the Val d'Aran; with only 7000 native residents, it now has beds for over 25,000 visitors, many at top-range prices. It has still managed to retain its removed, small-town charm, however, and there's more than just skiing to do here: the summertime outdoor activities are endless and the Romanesque churches are some of the best preserved in Spain.

TRANSPORTATION

The Val d'Aran curves like a fishhook, with the short end touching France to the north and the long straight portion touching Baqueira-Beret's peaks to the southeast's hook end. The main town of Vielha (see p. 233) lies near the center of the valley in the midst of a string of more than 25 villages, only about half of which are big enough to offer services to travelers. The most accommodating towns in the upper part of the valley are Vielha (see p. 233), expensive Baqueira (see p. 233), and the tiny hostel-filled town of Salardú (see p. 236) in between the two.

For the car-less, a local **Alsina Graells bus** travels through the valley daily, passing by each town approximately every hour during the morning and late afternoon/evening (more during the ski season). It runs all year, but get a schedule from the tourist office, as the exact times change by season (14min. from Vielha to Salardú, another 6min. to Baqueira-Beret; 135ptas/€0,90 per ride; 10 rides 1200ptas/€7,20). There is **no public transportation** in the valley at night, and taxis are rare (see p. 223).

BAQUEIRA-BERET

🛈 *Open year-round; ski season runs early Dec. to late Apr. Office in Barcelona: Pg. de Gràcia 2 (☎ 93 318 27 76). Office at the ski station: Apartado 60 (☎ 97 363 90 00. Prices for the 2001-2002 ski season will be set after the time of publication; the following prices are for the 2000-2001 season. One-day lift ticket 4600ptas/€27,60, children and half-day 2500ptas/€15. Weekend pass 8700ptas/€52,20, children 4700ptas/€28,20. 5 days (14hrs.) of ski lessons 13,000-13,800ptas/€78-83, for snowboarding 12,400ptas/€74,53. For more info, try www.baqueira.es.*

With 53 runs, 27 lifts, and an abundance of Atlantic snow, it is no wonder that Baqueira-Beret attracts the cream of Spanish society; girls, it's probably as good a place as any to have an encounter with eligible Prince Felipe (see **SWM Seeking,** p. 226). In addition to downhill skiing, the station has trails and equipment rental for cross-country skiing, snowshoeing, dogsledding, and snowboarding; it also offers guided excursions and has ski and snowboarding schools.

In the summer, the ⚑**Telesilla Mirador** (ski lift) keeps chugging up to 2500m elevation; ride it up alone or with a mountain bike for views of the valley. (Open early July to mid-Sept. 9am-6pm. Leaves from above the "Baqueira 1500" sign, up the steps as you enter Baqueira from Vielha. 1400ptas/€7,50, under 11 850ptas/€4,60.)

The **town** of Baqueira offers everything a skier could need, including a supermarket, ski store, ski repair, rental and storage, medical care, restaurants, and the one and only disco, **Pachá.** The village is stuffed to the brim with apartments and hotels, but cheap accommodations have disappeared entirely. Most visitors on a budget stay down the hill in **Salardú** (p. 236) or **Vielha** (see below); accommodation prices tend to drop the farther down the valley you go.

VIELHA

The biggest town in the Val d'Aran, Vielha (pop. 3500) combines the charm of its old quarter with the bustling activity of its main commercial thoroughfare. It offers every service the outdoorsy-type might desire, and the tourist office is equipped to help with questions or concerns regarding anything in the entire valley. Most visitors to the area stay here or in Salardú (p. 236), as accommodations are more affordable.

TRANSPORTATION

Buses: Alsina Graells (☎ 93 265 68 66; www.alsinagraells.es) goes twice daily from Barcelona to Vielha (5 hr. 15min., 6:30am and 7:30pm, 3725ptas/€22,50). June-Oct. they run an additional bus via a different route (7hr., 7:30am, 4410ptas/€26,50). See p. 223 for more information.

Taxis: ☎97 364 01 95 or ☎97 364 02 29.

ORIENTATION & PRACTICAL INFORMATION

The best orientation point in Vielha is the ironically named roundabout, a straight walk uphill from the main **bus stop** on **Av. Alcalde Calbetó Barra** (called **Carretera de Francia** until just before the stop). As you come upon the roundabout from the bus stop, Vielha's main commercial street **Av. Castièro** stems to the left. It shortly becomes **Av. Pas d'Arró** and then **Carretera a Baqueira** as it climbs to the ski resort. Both the **Riu Nere** and **Riu Garona** cut through Vielha, and the town centers around **Pl. Sant Antoni,** next to the main Riu Nere bridge.

Tourist Office: C. Sarriulèra 6 (☎97 364 01 10), a right off Av. Castièro just past Pl. Sant Antoni, coming from the roundabout. Tons of info on Romanesque churches, skiing, and other outdoor activities. Open June-July 9am-1pm and 4-8pm, Aug. 9am-9pm, Sept.-May 10am-1pm and 4:30-7:30pm.

Emergency: ☎088 or 97 364 00 80. Mossos d'Escuadra: ☎97 3640 972.

Internet Access: CCV Informática, C. Aneto 7 (☎97 364 12 88). From Av. Pas d'Arró, left on C. Deth Poi then right on C. Aneto. 700ptas/€4,20 per hr. Open M-F 9:30am-1:30pm and 4:30-8pm, Sa 9:30am-1:30pm.

Post Office: C. Sarriulèra 2 (☎97 364 09 12), right across from the tourist office. **Lista de Correos.** Open M-F 8:30am-2:30pm, Sa 9:30am-1pm. **Postal Code:** 25530.

ACCOMMODATIONS

Vielha is full of affordable hotels, most of them with hardwood floors and a rustic feel. If the following are full, the tourist office will help find you a place to stay.

Pensión Busquet, C. Major 11 (☎97 3640 238), a right off Av. Castièro from the round-about. Well-varnished wood floors, walls, and doors, woven bedspreads, and lace curtains; offers a snug ski lodge feel. July-Aug. and Dec.-Mar. singles 2500ptas/€15; doubles 5000ptas/€30. Rest of the year singles 2000ptas/€12; doubles 4500ptas/€27. Cash only.

Pensión Casa Vicenta, C. Reiau 3 (☎97 364 08 19), a right off Pg. Libertat, which intersects Av. Castièro at Pl. Sant Antoni. An upscale hostel with modern furnishings and private baths. Breakfast included. July to mid-Sept. and Dec.-May singles 3500ptas/€21; doubles 6300ptas/€38. Rest of the year singles 2700ptas/€16; doubles 5000ptas/€30. Cash only.

Hotel Ostau d'Oc, C. Castèth 13 (☎97 341 597). A left off C. Moncorbison, which is slightly to the right off the roundabout coming from the bus stop. The place to come during low season or if you want to splurge a little; the extremely nice rooms with heated tiled floors and TVs are worth the money. Comfy sitting room and a bar/breakfast/board game area. Breakfast 500ptas/€3. Aug., *Setmana Santa,* and Christmas week singles 5300ptas/€32; doubles 6600ptas/€40; quads 11,000ptas/€66. July-Sept. and Dec.-Mar. singles 3200ptas/€19; doubles 5200ptas/€31; quads 8,800ptas/€53. Rest of the year singles 2600ptas/€15,50; doubles 4400ptas/€26,50; quads 7,700ptas/€46. MC/V.

FOOD

Aranese cooking has been influenced strongly by neighboring France and by the valley's cold, snowy winters. Beef, lamb, and trout are often featured in main dishes, and *crêpes* (called *pasteres* or *pescajüs*) are popular here, as are thick meat and bean stews like *olla aranesa.* Vielha has a number of Catalan, Aranese, and international restaurants; none of them are exorbitantly expensive, but the ones listed below offer a particularly good bang for your buck. The **Supermercado Arnals,** C. Pas d'Arrò 3, stocks all the necessary basics for picnicking, hiking, or cooking. (☎97 364 00 64. Open M-Sa 9:30am-1:30pm and 4:30-8:30pm. MC/V.)

🔊 **Era Puma,** Av. Pas d'Arró 23 (☎97 364 24 49). A popular local place with tasty, traditional Spanish food and a light wood dining room/bar area. The dinner *menú* is an absolute steal: 2 plates, a basket of bread, a bottle of wine or water, and dessert, all for 1100ptas/ €6,60, IVA included. *Bocadillos* 400ptas/€2,40. Entrees 500-900ptas/€3-5,50. Salads 500ptas/€3. Open daily 1-4pm and 8-11pm. MC/V.

Pizzeria Papa, Av. Pas d'Arró 5 (☎97 364 16 32), inside the Galerias Giles. Good, cheap Italian food in a cheerful, bustling place. Pizzas 700-900ptas/€4,20-5,40. *Menú* 1100ptas/ €6,60 or 1600ptas/€9,60 (IVA included). Open F-W 1-3pm and 8-10:30pm. MC/V.

Restaurante Basteret, C. Mayor 6 (☎97 364 07 14), a right off Pl. St. Antoni coming from the roundabout. A good place to sample typical Aranese food, in an affordable local bar/restaurant on the bank of the Riu Nere. *Tapas* 175ptas/€1. Midday *menú* 1400ptas/€8,40. *Patês, tortillas,* cheeses, and meats 600-700ptas/€3,60-4,20. Open July-Aug. daily 1-4pm and 8pm-midnight. Closed M the rest of the year. Cash only.

SIGHTS & FESTIVALS

Romanesque churches and the relics of a long-isolated mountain culture draw almost as many visitors to the Val d'Aran as its beautiful natural surroundings. The small **Museu de Val d'Eran** charts the development of civilization in the valley, from its origins through Roman and modern times. (☎97 364 18 15. Open Tu-Sa 10am-1pm and 5-8pm, Su 10am-1pm. 200ptas/€1,20.) The **Església de San Miguel,** Vielha's simple 12th-century church, houses a large fragment of the *Christ de Mijaran,* a relic believed to have been destroyed in the 15th century. (Open daily 11am-8pm.) For those with a car or a serious penchant for the Romanasque, the tourist office offers a **Ruta de les Esglésies Araneses,** guided tours of the eight churches in the valley. (200ptas/€1,20, under 14 free. Inquire at the tourist office or museum.) For the truly lazy, a small tourist tram chugs its way from Pl. St. Antoni through town (every 30min. 11am-2pm and 5-9pm; 350ptas/€2,10, children 250ptas/€1,50).

The Aranese people's **popular festivals** and dances are where unique cultural traditions remain at their strongest. If possible, try to catch one of the valley towns during a *fiesta mayor* or *romería*. **Vielha** celebrates on May 22, Sept. 8, and Oct. 8, and **Salardú** on May 3 and Oct. 7. If you really want to pack in the carousing, from Aug. 15-16, seven different Aranese villages (including **Garòs, Gausac, Bossòt, Vilamòs, Vila, Bausen,** and **Mont**) celebrate their *fiestas mayores*.

OUTDOOR ACTIVITIES

Outdoor activities are the Val d'Aran's most popular attraction. In addition to skiing and snowboarding, offerings include rafting, kayaking, canyoning, mountain biking, 4 x 4 excursions, fishing, hunting, canoeing, and horseback riding. (Contact the **Escula de Equitación,** Ctra. Francia, for the latter. ☎97 364 22 44.) Several major companies, including **Horizontes** and **Deportur,** provide outdoor guides and equipment; the two based in town are listed below.

Alti-Sport, C. des Arroquetes 3 (☎97 364 27 93 or 639 31 29 32; www.aranweb.com/altisport), just across the bridge at the end of C. Reiau. Rafting 4400ptas/€33. Kayaking 7000ptas/€42. Canoeing 4000ptas/€24. Quads (2hrs.) 9000ptas/€54. Half-day and multi-day packages also available. 10% discount for groups on most activities. Open daily May-mid.Sept. 9am-1:30pm and 4:30-8:30pm. Cash only.

Camins del Pirineu, Av. Pas d'Arrò 5 (☎97 364 24 44; caminsguiaspirieno@retemail), inside the gallery. A more mountain-based company than Alti-Sport, with more guided tours and multi-day options. Bike rental 3200ptas/€19 per day. Guided day hike in the national park 6900ptas/€41.5. Intro mountain-climbing 15,000ptas/€90. Rafting 4500ptas/€27. Their office has a full list of offerings. Open daily 9am-1pm and 5-8pm. Cash only.

Palai de Gèu, Av. Garona 33 (☎97 364 28 64). Cross the Av. Deth Solan bridge at the end of Av. Pas d'Arró and go left onto Av. Garona. A double complex with pool-gym-sauna and an ice-skating rink. Pool-gym-sauna 775ptas/€4,60 per entry, children 575ptas/€3,50. Open M-F 8am-noon and 3-9:30pm, Sa-Su 11am-2pm and 4:30-9pm. Skating rink 875ptas/€5,30, children 675ptas/€4. Skate rental 500ptas/€3. Open M-F 5:30-8:30pm, Sa-Su noon-2pm and 4:30-9pm. 1-day access to everything in the complex (includes skate rental) 1800ptas/€10,80, kids 1400ptas/€8,60.

NIGHTLIFE

Nightlife in Val d'Aran depends on seasonal tourism; the only discos are in Baqueira and Vielha (one each). Most establishments that serve alcohol serve dinner as well.

Complejo Elurra, Ctra. a Baqueira, on the left just after the Av. Deth Solan bridge. Essentially the only place for young people in all of Vielha: 8-10 different bars fill an indoor complex, from chill guitar-themed hangouts to club-like rooms with pulsing music. Beer 300ptas/€1,50. Drinks 600ptas/€3,60. No cover. Open F-Sa approx. 11pm-4am. Cash only.

Discoteca Elurra, Ctra. a Baqueira (☎97 364 03 02), the star establishment and namesake of the Vielha nightlife complex. A flashy interior that plays off ski decor, with walls that look like chi-chi lockers and stool chairs with glacier-like backs. Spanish pop music, 3 bars, a DJ, several TV screens, and flashing lights. Also a smaller, more sedate "pub" attached for an older, more romance-inclined crowd. Beer 400ptas/€2,40. Drinks 900ptas/€5,40. Cover F-Sa 1000ptas/€6 (includes 1 drink). Open Su-Th 11pm-4:30am, F-Sa 11pm-5:30am. MC/V.

Eth-Clòt, in a tiny plaça immediately to the left off Pg. Libertat coming from Pl. St. Antoni. A self-consciously "authentic" Aranese bar, with stone walls, mountain print cushions, a metal stove, and even witches hanging above the bar. Mostly locals, but occasional tourists as well. Beer 300ptas/€1,80. Drinks 600ptas/€3,60. Open daily 10pm-3am. Cash only.

SALARDÚ

Just 3km down the road from Baqueira, Salardú (pop. 300) has the closest affordable housing to the Baqueira slopes. The enormous youth hostel **Albergue Era Garona (HI)** offers dorms of four and six beds, as well bike and ski rentals through the reception desk, a TV and rec room, self-serve cafeteria, library, and more. (The huge gray building right on the main road from Vielha. ☎97 364 52 71; reservations from Barcelona ☎93 483 83 63. Breakfast included, lunch and dinner plans available. Sheets 350ptas/€2,10. July-mid-Sept. and Jan.-Apr. dorms 2350ptas/€14,10, over 25 3000ptas/€18; Dec. 2000ptas, over 25 2700ptas/€16,20; rest of the year 1775ptas/€10,50, over 25 2400ptas/€14,40. IVA included. MC/V.)

Further off the main road, ▣**Refugi Rosta** occupies the oldest building in use in the village, with doubles and *refugio*-style dorm rooms (tight rows of single mattresses) for four to ten people. The cozy wood furniture and bright bedspreads and cushions feel like a Pyrenean home of 100 years ago might have, and the downstairs/restaurant serves meals (including vegetarian) in a romantic, slowly crumbling outdoor terrace; they will also pack picnics for guests. (Pl. Mayor, on the left at the end of C. Major, which starts straight ahead from the bus stop, just down the main road. ☎97 364 53 08; fax 97 364 58 14. Dorms 2500ptas/€15, 4500ptas/€27 with dinner. Doubles 3000ptas/€18 per person, 5000ptas/€30 with dinner. Breakfast included. MC/V.) For help finding other lodging in Salardú, call the town **info booth** at 97 364 57 26.

Planning Your Trip

DOCUMENTS & FORMALITIES

EMBASSIES & CONSULATES

For foreign consular services in Barcelona, check the **Service Directory** (p. 289).

SPANISH EMBASSIES & CONSULAR SERVICES ABROAD

Questions concerning visas and passports go to consulates, not embassies (which handle weightier matters).

Australia: Embassy: 15 Arkana St., **Yarralumla,** ACT 2600. Mailing address: P.O. Box 9076, Deakin, ACT 2600 (☎02 62 73 35 55; fax 62 73 39 18). **Consulates:** Level 24, St. Martins Tower, 31 Market St., **Sydney,** NSW 2000 (☎02 92 61 24 33 or 92 61 24 43; fax 92 83 16 95); 540 Elizabeth St., 4th fl., **Melbourne,** VIC 3000 (☎03 93 47 19 66; fax 93 47 73 30).

Canada: Embassy: 74 Stanley Ave., **Ottawa,** ON K1M 1P4 (☎613 747-2252; fax 744-1224). **Consulates:** 1 Westmount Sq., Suite 1456, **Montreal,** PQ H3Z 2P9 (☎514 935-5235; fax 935-4655); Simtoe Place, 200 Front St., Suite 2401, P.O. Box 15, **Toronto,** ON M5V 3K2 (☎416 977-1661; fax 593-4949).

Ireland: Consulate: 17A Merlyn Park, Ballsbridge, **Dublin** 4 (☎01 269 1640; fax 269 1854).

New Zealand: Refer to Embassy in Australia.

South Africa: Embassy: 169 Pine St., Arcadia, P.O. Box 1633, **Pretoria** 0001 (☎012 344 3875; fax 343 4891). **Consulate:** 37 Shortmarket St., **Cape Town** 8001 (☎021 222 415; fax 222 328).

UK: Embassy: 39 Chesham Pl., **London** SW1X 8SB (☎020 7235 5555; fax 7259 5392). **Consulates:** 20 Draycott Pl., **London** SW3 2RZ (☎020 7589 8989; fax 7581 7888); Suite 1A, Brook

ONE EUROPE

The idea of European unity has come a long way since 1958, when the European Economic Community (EEC) was created to promote solidarity and cooperation between its six founding states. Since then, the EEC has become the European Union (EU), with political, legal, and economic institutions spanning 15 member states: Austria, Belgium, Denmark, Finland, France, Germany, Greece, Ireland, Italy, Luxembourg, the Netherlands, Portugal, Spain, Sweden, and the UK.

In 1999 the EU established **freedom of movement** across 14 European countries—the entire EU minus Denmark, Ireland, and the UK, but plus Iceland and Norway. This means that border controls between participating countries have been abolished, and visa policies harmonized. While you're still required to carry a passport (or government-issued ID card for EU citizens) when crossing an internal border, once you've been admitted into one country, you're free to travel to all participating states. The only times you'll see a border guard within the EU are between the British Isles and the Continent and in and out of Denmark.

For more consequences of the EU for travelers, see **The Euro** (p. 244) and **EU customs regulations** (p. 242).

House, 70, Spring Gardens, **Manchester** M2 2BQ (☎016 1236 1233; fax 1228 7467); 63 N. Castle St., **Edinburgh** EH2 3LJ (☎013 1220 1843; fax 1226 4568); **others** in Liverpool and Belfast.

US: Embassy: 2375 Pennsylvania Ave. NW, **Washington, D.C.** 20037 (☎202 728-2330; fax 728-2308). **Consulates:** 150 E. 58th St., 30th fl., **New York,** NY 10155 (☎212 355-4080; fax 644-3751); **others** in Boston, Chicago, Houston, Los Angeles, Miami, New Orleans, Puerto Rico, and San Francisco. Also at www.spainemb.org.

TOURIST OFFICES

Spain's official tourist board operates an extensive website at www.tourspain.es. It also has offices in Canada, the US, and the UK.

Canada: Tourist Office of Spain, 2 Bloor St. W, Suite 3402, Toronto, ON M4W 3E2 (☎416 961-3131; fax 416 961-1992).

UK: Spanish National Tourist Office, 22-23 Manchester Sq., London W1U 3PX (☎207 486 8077; fax 207 486 8034; info.londres@tourspain.es).

US: Tourist Office of Spain, 666 Fifth Ave., 35th fl., New York, NY 10103 (☎212 265-8822; fax 212 265-8864). Additional offices in Chicago, IL (☎312 642-1992), Beverly Hills, CA (☎323 658-7188), and Miami, FL (☎305 358-1992).

PASSPORTS

REQUIREMENTS

Citizens of Australia, Canada, New Zealand, South Africa, and the US need valid passports to enter Spain and to re-enter their home countries. For citizens of some countries, Spain does not allow entrance if the holder's passport expires in under six months; check with the appropriate consulate to see if this applies to you. Returning home with an expired passport is illegal. European Union citizens need a National Identification Card.

PHOTOCOPIES

Be sure to photocopy the page of your passport with your photo, passport number, and other identifying information, as well as any visas, travel insurance policies, plane tickets, or traveler's check serial numbers. Carry one copy in a safe place, apart from the originals, and leave another at home. Consulates also recommend that you carry an expired passport or an official copy of your birth certificate in a part of your baggage separate from other documents.

LOST PASSPORTS

If you lose your passport, immediately notify the local police and the nearest embassy or consulate of your home government. To expedite its replacement, you will need to know all information previously recorded and show ID and proof of citizenship. In some cases, a replacement may take weeks to process, and it may be valid only for a limited time. Any visas stamped in your old passport will be irretrievably lost. In an emergency, ask for immediate temporary traveling papers that will permit you to re-enter your home country. Lost passports may be replaced in a matter of days, quicker with a copy of the passport. Your passport is a public document belonging to your nation's government. You may have to surrender it to a foreign government official, but if you don't get it back in a reasonable amount of time, inform the nearest mission of your home country.

NEW PASSPORTS

Citizens of Australia, Canada, Ireland, New Zealand, the United Kingdom, and the United States can apply for a passport at the nearest post office, passport office, or court of law. Citizens of South Africa can apply for a passport at the nearest Office of Foreign Affairs. Any new passport or renewal applications must be filed well in advance of the departure date, although most passport offices offer rush services for a very steep fee. Citizens living abroad who need a passport or renewal services should contact the nearest consular service of their home country.

VISAS & WORK PERMITS

VISAS

As of August 2000, citizens of South Africa need a visa—a stamp, sticker, or insert in your passport specifying the purpose of your travel and the permitted duration of your stay—in addition to a valid passport for entrance to Spain; citizens of the UK, the US, Canada, Republic of Ireland, Australia do not need visas for brief stays. Contact your local Spanish consulate for more information on what length of stay requires a visa and how to obtain one. US citizens can take advantage of the **Center for International Business and Travel** (**CIBT;** ☎ 800-925-2428), which secures visas for travel to almost all countries for a variable service charge.

Double-check on entrance requirements at the nearest embassy or consulate of Spain (listed under **Embassies & Consulates,** on p. 239) for up-to-date info before departure, or consult the webpage of your home country's State Department or Foreign Affairs Bureau.

WORK PERMITS

Admission as a visitor does not include the right to work, which is authorized only by a work permit. For more information, see **Working,** p. 283.

IDENTIFICATION

When you travel, always carry two or more forms of identification on your person, including at least one photo ID; a passport combined with a driver's license or birth certificate is usually adequate. Many establishments, especially banks, may require several IDs in order to cash traveler's checks; some stores in Spain require a passport if you want to use a credit card. Never carry all your forms of ID together; split them up in case of theft or loss. Keep a xerox of your passport in your suitcase and one at home.

For more information on all the forms of identification listed below, contact the organization that provides the service, the **International Student Travel Confederation** (**ISTC**), Herengracht 479, 1017 BS Amsterdam, Netherlands (☎ +31 20 421 2800; fax 421 2810; istcinfo@istc.org; www.istc.org).

TEACHER & STUDENT IDENTIFICATION

The **International Student Identity Card (ISIC),** the most widely accepted form of student ID, provides discounts on sights, accommodations, food, and transport; an ISIC card in Barcelona will cut admission to many museums and sights in half. The ISIC is preferable to an institution-specific card (such as a university ID) because it is recognized and honored abroad; other forms of student ID are generally not recognized

CUSTOMS IN THE EU

As well as freedom of movement of people within the EU (see p. 240), travelers in the countries that are members of the EU (Austria, Belgium, Denmark, Finland, France, Germany, Greece, Ireland, Italy, Luxembourg, the Netherlands, Portugal, Spain, Sweden, and the UK) can also take advantage of the freedom of movement of goods. This means that there are no customs controls at internal EU borders (i.e., you can take the blue customs channel at the airport), and travelers are free to transport whatever legal substances they like as long as it is for their own personal (non-commercial) use—up to 800 cigarettes, 10L of spirits, 90L of wine (60L of sparkling wine), and 110L of beer. You should also be aware that duty-free was abolished on June 30, 1999 for travel between EU member states; however, travelers between the EU and the rest of the world still get a duty-free allowance when passing through customs.

in Spain. All cardholders have access to a 24hr. emergency help line for medical, legal, and financial emergencies (in North America call 877-370-ISIC, UK collect +44 20 8762 8110, or France collect +33 155 633 144, elsewhere call US collect +1 715-345-0505), and cards issued in the US are also eligible for insurance benefits (see **Insurance**, p. 250). Many student travel agencies issue ISICs, including STA Travel in Australia and New Zealand; Travel CUTS in Canada; usit in the Republic of Ireland and Northern Ireland; SASTS in South Africa; Campus Travel and STA Travel in the UK; and Council Travel (www.counciltravel.com/idcards/default.asp) and STA Travel in the US (see p. 251).

The card is valid from September of one year to December of the following year and costs US$22. Applicants must be degree-seeking students of a secondary or post-secondary school and must be of at least 12 years of age. Because of the proliferation of fake ISICs, some services (particularly airlines) require additional proof of student identity, such as a school ID or a letter attesting to your student status, signed by your registrar and stamped with your school seal. The **International Teacher Identity Card (ITIC)** offers the same insurance coverage as well as similar but limited discounts. The fee is US$22.

YOUTH IDENTIFICATION

The International Student Travel Confederation also issues a discount card to travelers who are 26 years old or under, but are not students. This one-year **International Youth Travel Card** (**IYTC;** formerly the **GO 25** Card) offers many of the same benefits as the ISIC. Most organizations that sell the ISIC also sell the IYTC (US$22).

ISICONNECT SERVICE

If you are an ISIC card carrier and want to avoid buying individual calling cards or wish to consolidate all your means of communication during your trip, you can activate your ISIC's ISIConnect service, a powerful new integrated communications service (powered by eKit). With ISIConnect, one toll-free access number (☎ 900 931 951 in Spain) gives you access to several different methods of keeping in touch via the phone and Internet, including: a reduced-rate international calling plan that treats your ISIC card as a universal **calling card;** a personalized **voicemail** box accessible from pay phones anywhere in the world or for free over the Internet; **faxmail** service for sending and receiving faxes via email, fax machines, or pay phones; various **email** capabilities, including a service that reads your email to you over the phone; an online **"travel safe"** for storing (and faxing) important documents and numbers; and a 24hr. emergency **help line** (via phone or email at ISIConnect@ekit.com) offering assistance and medical and legal referrals. To activate your ISIConnect account, visit the service's comprehensive website (www.isiconnect.ekit.com) or call the customer service number of your home country (which is also your home country's access number): in **Australia** 800 114 478; in **Canada** 877-635-3575; in **Ireland** 800 555 180 or 800 577 980; in **New Zealand** 0800 114 478; in the **UK** 0800 376 2366 or 0800 169 8646; in the **US** 800-706-1333; and in **South Africa** 0800 992 921 or 0800 997 285.

CUSTOMS

Upon entering Spain, you must declare certain items from abroad and pay a duty on the value of those articles that exceeds the allowance established by Spain's customs service. Goods and gifts purchased at duty-free shops abroad are not exempt from duty or sales tax at your point of return and thus must be declared as well; "duty-free" merely means that you need not pay a tax in the country of purchase. Duty-free allowances were abolished for travel between EU member states on July 1, 1999 (see **Customs in the Eu,** p. 242), but still exist for those arriving from outside the EU. Upon returning home, you must similarly declare all articles acquired abroad and pay a duty on the value of articles in excess of your home country's allowance. In order to expedite your return, make a list of any valuables brought from home and register them with customs before traveling abroad. Also be sure to keep receipts for all goods acquired abroad.

MONEY

CURRENCY & EXCHANGE

The currency chart below is based on August 2001 exchange rates between local currency and Australian dollars (AUS$), Canadian dollars (CDN$), Irish pounds (IR£), New Zealand dollars (NZ$), South African Rand (ZAR), British pounds (UK£), US dollars (US$), and European Union euros (EUR€). Check the currency converter on the Let's Go Homepage (www.letsgo.com/thumb) or a large newspaper for the latest exchange rates.

PESETAS (PTAS)	
AUS$ = 99.7PTAS	100PTAS = 1AUS$
CDN$ = 123.79PTAS	100PTAS = 0.81CDN$
IR£ = 211.27PTAS	100PTAS = 0.45IR£
NZ$ = 79.15PTAS	100PTAS = 1.3NZ$
ZAR = 22.76PTAS	100PTAS = 4.4ZAR
US$ = 188.73PTAS	100PTAS = 0.53US$
UK£ = 267.98PTAS	100PTAS = 0.37UK£
EUR€ = 116.38PTAS	100PTAS = 0.6EUR€

As a general rule, it's cheaper to convert money in Spain than at home. However, you should bring enough foreign currency to last for the first 24 to 72 hours of a trip to avoid being penniless should you arrive after bank hours or on a holiday. Travelers from the US can get foreign currency from the comfort of home: **International Currency Express** (☎888-278-6628) deliver foreign currency or traveler's checks second-day (US$12) at competitive exchange rates.

When changing money, go to banks or *casas de cambio* that have at most a 5% margin between their buy and sell prices. You lose money with every transaction, so convert large sums (unless the currency is depreciating), but no more than you'll need.

If you use traveler's checks or bills, carry some in small denominations (the equivalent of US$50 or less) for times when you are forced to exchange money at disadvantageous rates, but bring a range of denominations since charges may be levied per check cashed. Store your money in a variety of forms; ideally, you will at any given time be carrying some cash, some traveler's checks, and an ATM and/or credit card.

THE EURO

Since January 2001, the official currency of 12 members of the European Union (to which Spain belongs) has been the euro. Actual euro bank notes and coins will be available beginning on January 1, 2002; but you shouldn't throw out your *pesetas* just yet. The national currencies remain legal tender through July 1, 2002, after which it's all euros all the time. *Let's Go: Barcelona* lists prices in both euros (€) and *pesetas*.

The currency has some important—and positive—consequences for travelers hitting another EU country after visiting Spain. For one thing, money-changers across the euro-zone are obliged to exchange money at the official, fixed rate (see below), and no commission (though they may still charge a small service fee). So now you can change your *pesetas* into *escudos* and your *escudos* into *lire* without losing fistfuls of money on every transaction. Second, euro-denominated traveler's cheques allow you to pay for goods and services across the euro-zone, again at the official rate and commission-free.

The exchange rate between euro-zone currencies is permanently fixed at 1 EUR = 40.3399 BEF (Belgian francs) = 1.95583 DEM (German marks) = 166.386 ESP (Spanish *pesetas*) = 6.55957 FRF (French francs) = 0.787564 IER (Irish pounds) = 1936.27 ITL (Italian *lire*) = 40.3399 LUF (Luxembourg francs) = 2.20371 NLG (Dutch guilders) = 13.7603 ATS (Austrian schillings) = 200.482 PTE (Portuguese *escudos*) = 5.94573 FIM (Finnish *markka*). For more info, see the webpage www.europa.eu.int.

MONEY FROM HOME

AMERICAN EXPRESS

Cardholders can withdraw cash from their checking accounts at the AmEx offices in Barcelona (up to US$1000 every 21 days; no service charge, no interest). AmEx "Express Cash" withdrawals from any AmEx ATM in Spain are automatically debited from the cardholder's checking account or line of credit. Green card holders may withdraw up to US$1000 in any seven-day period (2% transaction fee; minimum US$2.50, maximum US$20). To enroll in Express Cash, card members may call 800-227-4669 in the US. The AmEx national number in Spain is 900 994 426. The AmEx branches in Barcelona are listed in the **Service Directory** on p. 290.

WESTERN UNION

Travelers from the US, Canada, and the UK can wire money abroad through Western Union's international money transfer services. In the US, call 800-325-6000; in Canada, 800-235-0000; in the UK, 0800 83 38 33; in Spain, 900 633 633. To wire money within the US using a credit card (Visa, MasterCard, or Discover), call 800-225-5227. The rates for sending cash are generally US$10-11 cheaper than with a credit card, and the money is usually available at the place you're sending it to within an hour. There are Western Union representatives all over Barcelona, including one at **Admon Manuel Martín**, Las Ramblas 41 (open daily 9am-midnight). To locate the nearest Western Union location to you, consult www.westernunion.com.

US STATE DEPARTMENT

For US citizens only, and only in dire emergencies, the US State Department will forward money within hours to the nearest consular office, which will then disburse it according to instructions for a US$15 fee. If you wish to use this service, you must contact the Overseas Citizens Service division of the US State Department (☎ 202-647-5225; nights, Sundays, and holidays ☎ 202-647-4000).

TRAVELER'S CHECKS

Traveler's checks (American Express and Visa are the most recognized) are one of the safest and least troublesome means of carrying funds. Several agencies and banks sell them for a small commission. Each agency provides refunds if checks are lost or stolen, and many provide additional services, such as toll-free refund hotlines abroad, emergency message services, and stolen credit card assistance.

While traveling, keep check receipts and a record of which checks you've cashed separate from the checks themselves. Also leave a list of check numbers at home. Never countersign checks until you're ready to cash them, and always bring your passport with you to cash them. If your checks are lost or stolen, immediately contact a refund center (of the company that issued your checks) to be reimbursed; they may require a police report verifying the loss or theft. Ask about toll-free refund hotlines and the location of refund centers when purchasing checks, and always carry emergency cash.

American Express: Call 800 25 19 02 in Australia; in New Zealand 0800 441 068; in the UK 0800 521 313; in the US and Canada 800-221-7282; in Spain call 900 994 426. Elsewhere call US collect +1 801-964-6665; www.aexp.com. Traveler's checks are available at 1-4% commission at AmEx offices and banks, commission-free at AAA offices; while they are not accepted for payment at establishments, they are changed at local banks and therefore are a safe way to carry money. *Cheques for Two* can be signed by either of 2 people traveling together.

Thomas Cook MasterCard: In the US and Canada call 800-223-7373; in the UK call 0800 62 21 01; in Spain call 900 971 12 31; elsewhere call UK collect +44 1733 31 89 50. Checks available in 13 currencies at 2% commission. Thomas Cook offices cash checks commission-free; their office in Barcelona is at C. Diputació 300 in **l'Eixample.**

Visa Traveler's Cheques: In the US call 800-227-6811; in the UK call 0800 89 50 78; elsewhere call UK collect 44 20 7937 8091. To report lost or stolen checks in Spain, call 900 974 414. Call for the location of their nearest office.

CREDIT CARDS

Credit cards are widely accepted in Spain, and they often offer superior exchange rates—up to 5% better than the retail rate used by banks and other currency exchange establishments. Credit cards may also offer services such as insurance or emergency help. While credit cards are sometimes required to reserve hotel rooms or rental cars, cash is often required at budget establishments. **MasterCard** (a.k.a. EuroCard or Access in Europe) and **Visa** (a.k.a. Carte Bleue or Barclaycard) are the most welcomed; **American Express** cards work at some ATMs and at AmEx offices and major airports.

Credit cards are also useful for **cash advances,** which allow you to withdraw Spanish *pesetas* from associated banks and ATMs throughout Barcelona. However, transaction fees for all credit card advances (up to US$10 per advance, plus 2-3% extra on foreign transactions after conversion) tend to make credit cards a more costly way of accessing cash than ATM cards or traveler's checks. In an emergency, however, the transaction fee may prove worth the cost. To be eligible for an advance, you'll need to get a **Personal Identification Number (PIN)** from your credit card company (see **Cash Cards (ATM Cards),** p. 245). Be sure to check with your credit card company before you leave home, though; some companies have started to charge a foreign transaction fee.

Money From Home In Minutes.

If you're stuck for cash on your travels, don't panic. Millions of people trust Western Union to transfer money in minutes to over 185 countries and over 95,000 locations worldwide. Our record of safety and reliability is second to none. You can even send money by phone without leaving home by using a credit card. For more information, call Western Union: USA 1-800-325-6000, Canada 1-800-235-0000.
www.westernunion.com

WESTERN UNION | MONEY TRANSFER

The fastest way to send money worldwide.

CREDIT CARD COMPANIES

Visa (US ☎ 800-336-8472) and **MasterCard** (US ☎ 800-307-7309) are issued in cooperation with banks and other organizations. **American Express** (US ☎ 800-843-2273) has an annual fee of up to US$55. AmEx cardholders may cash personal checks at AmEx offices abroad, access an emergency medical and legal assistance hotline (24hr.; in North America call 800-554-2639, elsewhere call US collect +1 715-343-7977), and enjoy American Express Travel Service benefits (including plane, hotel, and car rental reservation changes; baggage loss and flight insurance; mailgram and international cable services; and held mail). The **Discover Card** (in US call 800-347-2683, elsewhere call US +1 801-902-3100) offers cashback bonuses on most purchases, but it is not widely accepted in Barcelona.

CASH CARDS (ATM CARDS)

Cash cards—popularly called ATM cards—are widespread in Spain and everywhere in Barcelona. Depending on the system that your home bank uses, you can most likely access your personal bank account from abroad. ATMs get the same wholesale exchange rate as credit cards, but there is often a limit on the amount of money you can withdraw daily (around US$500). There is typically also a surcharge of US$1-5 per withdrawal. Be sure to memorize your PIN code in numeric form; Spanish machines don't have letters on their keys. Also, if your PIN is longer than four digits, ask your bank whether you need a new number.

The two major international money networks are **Cirrus** (US ☎ 800-424-7787) and **PLUS** (US ☎ 800-843-7587). To locate ATMs in Barcelona, call the above numbers, or consult www.visa.com/pd/atm or www.mastercard.com/atm. Most ATMs charge a transaction fee that is paid to the bank that owns the ATM.

Visa TravelMoney is a system allowing you to access money from any ATM that accepts Visa cards. (For local customer assistance in Spain, call 900 951 125.) You deposit an amount before you travel (plus a small administration fee), and you can withdraw up to that sum. The cards, which give you the same favorable exchange rate for withdrawals as a regular Visa, are especially useful if you plan to travel through other countries after you visit Spain. Obtain a card by either visiting a nearby Thomas Cook or Citicorp office, by calling toll-free in the US 877-394-2247, or checking with your local bank or to see if it issues TravelMoney cards. **Road Cash** (US ☎ 877-762-3227; www.roadcash.com) issues cards in the US with a minimum US$300 deposit.

CURRENT & ADAPTERS

In Barcelona, electric current is 220 volts AC, enough to fry any 110V North American appliance. Americans and Canadians should buy an adapter (which changes the shape of the plug) and a converter (which changes the voltage; US$20). Don't make the mistake of using only an adapter (unless appliance instructions explicitly state otherwise). New Zealanders and South Africans (who both use 220V at home) as well as Australians (who use 240/250V) won't need a converter, but will need a set of adapters to use anything electrical.

COSTS

The cost of your trip will vary considerably, depending on where you go, how you travel, and where you stay. The single biggest cost of your trip will probably be your round-trip (return) **airfare** to Spain (see **Getting to Barcelona: By Plane,** p. 250). A **rail pass** (or **bus pass**) will be another potential expense (see **Getting to Barcelona: By Train,** p. 255). Before you go, calculate a reasonable per-day **budget** that will meet your needs.

STAYING ON A BUDGET

To give you a general idea, a bare-bones day in Barcelona (camping or sleeping in hostels/guesthouses, buying food at supermarkets) would cost about US$35; a slightly more comfortable day (sleeping in hostels/guesthouses and the occasional budget hotel, eating one meal a day at a restaurant, going out at night) would run US$50; and for a luxurious day, the sky's the limit. Don't underestimate the cost of partying in Barcelona; while some clubs may charge no cover, drink prices can get out of hand. Also, don't forget to factor in emergency reserve funds (at least US$200) when planning how much money you'll need.

TIPS FOR SAVING MONEY

Saving just a few dollars a day over the course of your trip might pay for days or weeks of additional travel. Take advantage of freebies: **museums** will typically be free once a week or once a month, and Barcelona often hosts free open-air **concerts** and/or **cultural events.** If possible, do your **laundry** in the sink; buy food in **supermarkets** instead of restaurants; split **accommodations** costs with trustworthy fellow travelers. With that said, don't go overboard with your budget obsession. Staying within your budget is important, but not at the expense of your sanity or health. For more tips on staying on a budget, check the **On the Cheap** sidebars scattered throughout this book.

TAXES

Spain has a 7% **Value Added Tax,** known as IVA, on all restaurants and accommodations. The prices listed in *Let's Go* (and on price tags) include IVA unless otherwise mentioned. Retail goods bear a much higher 16% IVA, although again, listed prices are usually inclusive. Non-EU citizens who have stayed in the EU fewer than 180 days can claim back the tax paid on purchases at the airport. Ask the shop where you have made the purchase to supply you with a tax return form.

HEALTH

Common sense is the simplest prescription for good health while you travel. Drink lots of fluids to prevent dehydration and constipation, wear sturdy, broken-in shoes and clean socks, and use talcum powder to keep your feet dry. For a basic **first-aid kit,** pack: bandages, pain reliever, antibiotic cream, moleskin, decongestant, motion-sickness remedy, diarrhea or upset-stomach medication (Pepto Bismol or Imodium), an antihistamine, and sunscreen.

In your **passport,** write the names of any people you wish to be contacted in case of a medical emergency, and also list any allergies or medical conditions a doctor would need to know about. Matching a prescription to a foreign equivalent is not always easy, safe, or possible. Carry up-to-date, legible prescriptions or a statement from your doctor stating the medication's trade name, manufacturer, chemical name, and dosage. While traveling, be sure to keep all medication with you in your carry-on luggage.

IMMUNIZATIONS & PRECAUTIONS

Travelers over two years old should be sure that the following vaccines are up to date: MMR (for measles, mumps, and rubella); DTaP or Td (for diptheria, tetanus, and pertussis), OPV (for polio), HbCV (for haemophilus influenza B), and HBV (for hepatitis B). For recommendations on immunizations and prophylaxis, consult the CDC (see below) in the US or the equivalent in your home country, and check with a doctor for guidance.

USEFUL ORGANIZATIONS & PUBLICATIONS

The US **Centers for Disease Control and Prevention (CDC;** ☎877-FYI-TRIP; www.cdc.gov/travel) is a source of information for travelers and maintains an international fax information service. The CDC's comprehensive booklet *Health Information for International Travel,* an annual rundown of disease, immunization, and general health advice, is free online or US$25 via the Public Health Foundation (☎877-252-1200). Consult the appropriate government agency of your home country for consular information sheets on health, entry requirements, and other issues for various countries. For quick information on health and other travel warnings, call the **Overseas Citizens Services** (☎202-647-5225; after-hours 202-647-4000), contact a passport agency or an embassy or consulate abroad. US citizens can send a self-addressed, stamped envelope to the Overseas Citizens Services, Bureau of Consular Affairs, #4811, US Department of State, Washington, D.C. 20520. For information on medical evacuation services and travel insurance firms, see the US government's website at http://travel.state.gov/medical.html or the **British Foreign and Commonwealth Office** (www.fco.gov.uk).

For detailed information on travel health, including a country-by-country overview of diseases and a list of travel clinics in the USA, try the **International Travel Health Guide,** Stuart Rose, MD (Travel Medicine, US$24.95; www.travmed.com). For general health info, contact the **American Red Cross** (☎800-564-1234).

MEDICAL ASSISTANCE ON THE ROAD

There are no particular health risks associated with traveling in Spain. The public health care system in Spain is very reliable; in an emergency, seek out the *urgencias* (emergency) section of the nearest hospital. For smaller concerns, it is probably best to go to a private clinic to avoid the frustration of long lines. Expect to pay cash up front (though most travel insurance will pick up the tab later), and bring your passport and other forms of identification. A single visit to a clinic in Spain can cost anywhere from US$40 to US$100, depending upon the service. Ask the tourist office, your consulate, or your accommodation for help finding a doctor or clinic.

Farmacias in Spain are also very helpful. A duty system has been set up so that at least one *farmacia* is open at all times in each town; look for a lit green cross. Spanish pharmacies are not the place to find your cheap summer flip-flops or greeting cards: they sell contraceptives, common medications, and many prescription drugs; and can answer simple medical questions and help you find a doctor.

If you are concerned about being able to access medical support while traveling, there are special support services you may employ. The *MedPass* from **GlobalCare, Inc.,** 2001 Westside Pkwy., #120, Alpharetta, GA 30004, USA (☎800-860-1111; fax 770-475-0058; www.globalems.com), provides 24hr. international medical assistance, support, and medical evacuation resources. The **International Association for Medical Assistance to Travelers (IAMAT;** US ☎716-754-4883, Canada ☎416-652-0137, New Zealand ☎03 352 20 53; www.sentex.net/~iamat) has free membership, lists English-speaking doctors worldwide, and offers detailed info on immunization requirements and sanitation. If your regular **insurance** policy does not cover travel abroad, you may wish to purchase additional coverage (see p. 250).

Those with medical conditions (diabetes, allergies to antibiotics, epilepsy, heart conditions) may want to obtain a stainless-steel **Medic Alert** ID tag (first year US$35, annually thereafter US$20), which identifies the condition and gives a 24hr. collect-call number. Contact the **Medic Alert Foundation,** 2323 Colorado Ave., Turlock, CA 95382, USA (☎888-633-4298; www.medicalert.org).

INSURANCE

Travel insurance generally covers four basic areas: medical/health problems, property loss, trip cancellation/interruption, and emergency evacuation. Although your regular insurance policies may extend to travel-related accidents, you may consider purchasing travel insurance if the cost of potential trip cancellation/interruption is greater than you can absorb. Prices for travel insurance purchased separately generally run about US$50 per week for full coverage, while trip cancellation/interruption may be purchased separately at a rate of about US$5.50 per US$100 of coverage.

Medical insurance often covers costs incurred abroad; check with your provider. **US Medicare** does not cover foreign travel. **Canadians** are protected by their home province's health insurance plan for 90 days abroad; check with the provincial Ministry of Health or Health Plan Headquarters for details. **Homeowners' insurance** often covers theft during travel and loss of travel documents (passport, plane ticket, rail pass, etc.) up to US$500.

ISIC and **ITIC** (see p. 241) provide basic insurance benefits, including US$100 per day of in-hospital sickness for up to 60 days, US$3000 of accident-related medical reimbursement, and US$25,000 for emergency medical transport. Cardholders have access to a toll-free 24hr. help line for medical, legal, and financial emergencies overseas (US and Canada ☎800-626-2427, elsewhere call US collect +1 713-267-2525). **American Express** (US ☎800-528-4800) grants most cardholders automatic car rental insurance (collision and theft, but not liability) and ground travel accident coverage of US$100,000 on flight purchases made with the card.

INSURANCE PROVIDERS

Council and **STA** (see p. 251) offer a range of plans that can supplement your basic coverage. Other private insurance providers in the US and Canada include: **Access America** (☎800-284-8300); **Berkely Group/Carefree Travel Insurance** (☎800-323-3149; www.berkely.com); **Globalcare Travel Insurance** (☎800-821-2488; www.globalcare-cocco.com); and **Travel Assistance International** (☎800-821-2828; www.worldwide-assistance.com). Providers in the **UK** include **Campus Travel** (☎01865 25 80 00) and **Columbus Travel Insurance** (☎020 7375 0011). In **Australia,** try **CIC Insurance** (☎9202 8000).

CONTACTING SPAIN

BY MAIL

Spain's postal service is good, although it may not be quite as fast as the country you are in. A letter should take about 4-5 working days to reach Spain from North America, 3-4 days from Europe, or 7 days from anywhere else with a decent postal system. Packages should hypothetically take the same amount of time, but are much more susceptible to enigmatic delays, and may take three weeks to get anywhere.

BY PHONE

Remember before you call that Barcelona is one hour ahead of Greenwich Mean Time, two hours ahead during Daylight Savings Time (GMT). To place an international call: first, dial the international dialing prefix of the country you are calling from (from Australia, dial 0011; Canada or the US, 011; the Republic of Ireland, New Zealand, or the UK, 00; South Africa, 09); second, dial the country code of the country you are calling to (to Spain, 34); third, dial the city code (for Barcelona, 93) and the local number. For more info on phones in Barcelona, see **Once In Barcelona,** p. 30.

GETTING TO BARCELONA

BY PLANE

When it comes to airfare, a little effort can save you a bundle. If your plans are flexible enough to deal with the restrictions, courier fares are the cheapest. Tickets ought from consolidators and standby seating re also good deals, but last-minute specials, air-are wars, and charter flights often beat these ares. The key is to hunt around, to be flexible, ind to ask persistently about discounts. Stu-lents, seniors, and those under 26 should never ay full price for a ticket.

AIRFARES

Airfares to Barcelona peak between June and August; major Catholic holidays are also expen-ive. The cheapest time to travel is during the winter, November to February. Midweek (M-Th norning) round-trip flights run US$40-50 cheaper than weekend flights, but they are less ikely to permit frequent-flier upgrades. Travel-ng with an "open return" ticket can be pricier han fixing a return date. Round-trip flights are y far the cheapest.

Fares for roundtrip flights to Barcelona from he US or Canadian east coast may cost US$700 or more in peak months, or US$350-500 in win-er months; from the US or Canadian west coast US$800 to well over $1000; from the UK, UK $100 to UK $450; from Australia AUS$1800 to AUS$2500.

BUDGET & STUDENT TRAVEL AGENCIES

While knowledgeable agents specializing in flights to Spain can make your life easy and help you save money, they may not spend the time to find you the lowest possible fare—they get paid on commission. Travelers holding **ISIC and IYTC cards** (see p. 241) qualify for big discounts from student travel agencies. Most flights from bud-get agencies are on major airlines, but in peak season some may sell seats on less reliable char-tered aircraft.

usit world (www.usitworld.com). Over 50 **usit campus** branches in the UK (www.usitcampus.co.uk), including 52 Grosvenor Gardens, **London** SW1W 0AG (☎0870 240 10 10); **Manchester** (☎0161 273 1880); and **Edinburgh** (☎0131 668 3303). Nearly 20 **usit NOW** offices in Ireland, including 19-21 Aston Quay, O'Connell Bridge, **Dublin** 2 (☎01 602 1600; www.usitnow.ie), and **Belfast** (☎02 890 327 111; www.usitnow.com). Offices all over the world, including a gateway office (offering full travel service) in Barcelona; see **Service Directory,** p. 294).

Council Travel (www.counciltravel.com). Countless US offices, including branches in Atlanta, Boston, Chicago, L.A., New York, San Francisco, Seattle, and Washington, D.C. Check the website or call 800-2-COUNCIL (226-8624) for the office nearest you.

CTS Travel, 44 Goodge St., **London** W1T 2AD (☎0207 636 0031; fax 0207 637 5328; ctsinfo@ctstravel.co.uk).

i **ESSENTIAL** INFORMATION

INTERNET FLIGHT PLANNING

The Internet is one of the best places to look for travel bargains— it's fast and convenient, and you can spend hours exploring options without driving your travel agent insane.

Many airline sites offer special last-minute deals on the Web:

www.travelpage.com
www.lastminute.com

Other sites do the legwork and **compile deals** for you:

www.bestfares.com
www.onetravel.com
www.lowestfare.com
www.travelzoo.com

For **student quotes,** try:

www.sta-travel.com
www.counciltravel.com
www.studentuniverse.com

Full travel services:

Expedia
(msn.expedia.com)

Travelocity
(www.travelocity.com)

Priceline
(www.priceline.com) allows you to specify a price, and obligates you to buy any ticket that meets or beats it; be prepared for antisocial hours and odd routes.

Skyauction
(www.skyauction.com) allows you to bid on both last-minute and advance-purchase tickets.

Just one last note—to protect yourself, make sure that the site you use has a secure server before handing over any credit card details. Happy hunting!

STA Travel, 7890 S. Hardy Dr., Ste. 110, Tempe AZ 85284 (24hr. reservations and info ☎800-777-0112; fax 480-592-0876; www.statravel.com). A student and youth travel organization with countless offices worldwide (check their website for a listing of all their offices), including US offices in Boston, Chicago, L.A., New York, San Francisco, Seattle, and Washington, D.C. Ticket booking, travel insurance, rail passes, and more. In the UK, walk-in office 11 Goodge St., **London** W1T 2PF or call 0870-160-6070. In New Zealand, 10 High St., **Auckland** (☎09 309 0458). In Australia, 366 Lygon St., **Melbourne** Vic 3053 (☎03 9349 4344).

StudentUniverse, 545 Fifth Ave., Suite 640, New York, NY 10017 (toll-free customer service ☎800-272-9676, outside the US 212-986-8420; help@studentuniverse.com; www.studentuniverse.com), is an online student travel service offering discount ticket booking, travel insurance, rail passes, destination guides, and much more. Customer service line open M-F 9am-8pm and Sa noon-5pm EST.

Travel CUTS (Canadian Universities Travel Services Limited), 187 College St., **Toronto,** ON M5T 1P7 (☎416-979-2406; fax 979-8167; www.travelcuts.com). 60 offices across Canada. Also in the UK, 295-A Regent St., **London** W1R 7YA (☎0207-255-1944).

Wasteels, Skoubogade 6, 1158 Copenhagen, (☎3314-4633 fax 7630-0865; www.wasteels.dk/uk). A huge chain with 165 locations across Europe. Sells Wasteels BIJ tickets discounted 30-45% off regular fare, 2nd-class international point-to-point train tickets with unlimited stopovers for those under 26 (sold only in Europe).

COMMERCIAL AIRLINES

The commercial airlines' lowest regular offer is the APEX (Advance Purchase Excursion) fare, which provides confirmed reservations and allows "open-jaw" tickets. Generally, reservations must be made seven to 21 days ahead of departure, with seven- to 14-day minimum-stay and up to 90-day maximum-stay restrictions. These fares carry hefty cancellation and change penalties (fees rise in summer). Book peak-season APEX fares early; by May you will have a hard time getting your desired departure date. Use Microsoft Expedia (msn.expedia.com) or Travelocity (www.travelocity.com) to get an idea of the lowest published fares, then use the resources outlined here to try and beat those fares. The Air Travel Advisory Bureau in London (☎020 7636 5000; www.atab.co.uk) provides referrals to travel agencies and consolidators that offer discounted airfares out of the UK. Low-season fares should be appreciably cheaper than the high-season (mid-June to Aug.) ones listed here. All major international airlines offer service to Barcelona, but the most popular carriers are listed here.

Cambios

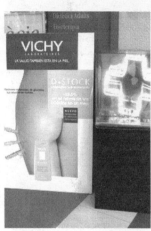
Farmacy

Information at Casa Robert

DISCOUNT AIRLINES

British Midland Airways: (UK ☎0870 607 05 55; US ☎800 788-0555; www.britishmid-land.com.) Departures from throughout the UK. London to Spain.

Air France: US ☎800 237-2747; www.airfrance.com. Connections to Barcelona from Paris.

British Airways: US ☎800 247 9297 UK ☎0845 77 999 77; www.british-airways.com. Flights through the UK throughout Europe.

Iberia: (in US and Canada ☎800 772-4642; in UK ☎(020) 7830 0011; in Spain ☎ 902 400 500; in South Africa ☎(11) 884 92 55; in Ireland ☎(1) 407 30 17; www.iberia.com) serves all domestic locations and all major international cities. **Aviaco,** a subsidiary of Iberia, covers only domestic routes. Ask about youth and other discounts—youth under 12 often get a 25% discount, and Iberia usually offers a range of ticket types with different restrictions and prices. Some fares purchased in the US require a 21-day minimum advance purchase. **Span-Air:** (in US ☎888 545-5757; in Spain ☎902 131 415; fax 971 492 553; www.spanair.com) also offers international and domestic flights.

AIR COURIER FLIGHTS

Those who travel light should consider courier flights. Couriers help transport cargo on international flights by using their checked luggage space for freight. Generally, couriers must travel with carry-ons only and must deal with complex flight restrictions. Most flights are round-trip only, with short fixed-length stays (usually one week) and a limit of one ticket per issue. Generally, you must be over 21 (in some cases 18). In summer, the most popular destinations usually require an advance reservation of about two weeks (you can usually book up to two months ahead). Super-discounted fares are common for "last-minute" flights (three to 14 days ahead). Not all courier services fly to Barcelona; flying into Madrid and taking a train to Barcelona is still an economical option(US$30 and up).

FROM NORTH AMERICA

Round-trip courier fares from the US to Western Europe run about US$200-500. Most flights leave from New York, Los Angeles, San Francisco, or Miami in the US; and from Montreal, Toronto, or Vancouver in Canada. The organizations below provide their members with lists of opportunities for an annual fee (typically US$ 50-60). Prices quoted below are round-trip.

Air Courier Association, 15000 W. 6th Ave. #203, Golden, CO 80401 (☎800-282-1202; elsewhere call US +1 303-215-9000; www.aircourier.org). Ten departure cities in the US and Canada to throughout western Europe (high-season US$150-360). One-year US$64.

International Association of Air Travel Couriers (IAATC), 220 South Dixie Highway #3, PO Box 1349, Lake Worth, FL 33460 (☎561-582-8320; fax 582-1581; www.courier.org). From 9 North American cities to Western European cities. One-year US$45-50.

FROM ELSEWHERE

Although the courier industry is most developed from North America, there are limited courier flights in other areas. The minimum age for couriers from the **UK** is usually 18. **Brave New World Enterprises,** P.O. Box 22212, London SE5 8WB (guideinfo@nry.co.uk; www.nry.co.uk/bnw), publishes a directory of all the companies offering courier flights in the UK (UK£10, in electronic form UK£8). **Global Courier Travel** (see above) also offers flights from London and Dublin to continental Europe. **British Airways Travel Shop** (☎0870 606 11 33; www.british-airways.com/travelqa/booking/travshop/travshop.shtml) arranges some flights from London to destinations in continental Europe (specials may be as low as UK£60; no registration fee).

TICKET CONSOLIDATORS

Ticket consolidators, or **"bucket shops,"** buy unsold tickets in bulk from commercial airlines and sell them at discounted rates. The best place to look is in the Sunday travel section of any major newspaper (such as the *New York Times*), where many bucket shops place tiny ads. Call quickly, as availability is typically extremely limited. Not all bucket shops are reliable, so insist on a receipt that gives full details of restrictions, refunds, and tickets, and pay by credit card (2-5% fee) so you can stop payment if you never receive tickets. For more, see www.travel-library.com/air-travel/consolidators.html.

Travel Avenue (☎800-333-3335; www.travelavenue.com) rebates commercial fares to or from the US (5% for over US$550) and will search for cheap flights from anywhere for a fee. **NOW Voyager,** 74 Varick St., Suite. 307, New York, NY 10013 (☎212-431-1616; fax 219-1793; www.nowvoyagertravel.com) arranges discounted flights, mostly from New York, to Barcelona. Other consolidators worth trying are **Airfare Busters** (☎800-232-8783; www.af.busters.com); **Interworld** (☎305-443-4929; fax 443-0351); **Pennsylvania Travel** (☎800-331-0947); **Rebel** (☎800-227-3235; travel@rebel-tours.com; www.rebeltours.com); **Cheap Tickets** (☎800-377-1000; www.cheaptickets.com); and **Travac** (☎800-872-8800; fax 212-714-9063; www.travac.com). Yet more consolidators on the web include the **Internet Travel Network** (www.itn.com); **Travel Information Services** (www.tiss.com); **TravelHUB** (www.travelhub.com); and **The Travel Site** (www.thetravelsite.com). Keep in mind that these are just suggestions to get you started in your research; *Let's Go* does not endorse any of these agencies. As always, be cautious, and research companies before you hand over your credit card number.

In London, the **Air Travel Advisory Bureau** (☎0207-636-5000; www.atab.co.uk) can provide names of reliable consolidators and discount flight specialists. From Australia and New Zealand, look for consolidator ads in the travel section of the *Sydney Morning Herald* and other papers.

CHARTER FLIGHTS

Charters are flights a tour operator contracts with an airline to fly extra loads of passengers during peak season. Charter flights fly less frequently than major airlines, make refunds particularly difficult, and are almost always fully booked. Schedules and itineraries may also change or be canceled at the last moment (as late as 48 hours before the trip, and without a full refund), and check-in, boarding, and baggage claim are often much slower. However, they can also be cheaper.

Discount clubs and **fare brokers** offer members savings on last-minute charter and tour deals. Study contracts closely; you don't want to end up with an unwanted overnight layover. **Travelers Advantage,** Trumbull, CT, USA (☎203-365-2000; www.travelersadvantage.com; US$60 annual fee includes discounts and cheap flight directories) specializes in European travel and tour packages.

BY TRAIN

Spanish trains are clean, relatively punctual, and reasonably priced. Spain's national railway is **RENFE** (☎902 24 02 02; international ☎93 490 11 22; www.renfe.es). *Tranvía, semidirecto,* and *correo* trains are very slow. RENFE offers extensive service in Spain and all of Europe, with a variety of trains. (Open daily 7am-10pm.) The Euromed has the fewest stops, while the Estrella, Talgo, Arco, Diurno and the Regional usually take much longer. The prices listed below are for the sitting *turista* class only (*preferente* and beds cost more.) Non-smokers (and non-chain-smokers) should consider buying a *no-fumador* (non-smoking) seat a few days in advance, as they are apt to sell out. (For more details on prices and routes, ask at an information window for an *horario*—schedule). Some of the most popular connections to and from Barcelona include: **Alicante** (4-5hr.; 8 per day, 6000-6700ptas/€36-41); **Bilbao** (8-9hr.; 3 per day, 5000-5200ptas/€30-32); **Granada** (11-12hr., 2 per day, 6300-7700ptas/€32-44); **Madrid** (7-8hr., 7 per day, 5100-6900ptas/€30-41); **Pamplona** (6-7hr.; 4 per day, 4300-4400ptas/€25,80-26,40); **Salamanca** (10-12hr.; 3 per day, 5800-6000ptas/€35-36); **San Sebastian** (8-9hr.; 3 per day, 5000ptas/€30); **Sevilla** (11-12hr.; 3 per day, 6400-10,200ptas/€39,20-61,20); **Valencia** (3-5hr.; 16 per day 7am-9pm, 3120-5200ptas/€20-33). International destination include **Milan** (through **Figueres** and **Nice**) and **Montpellier** with connections to **Geneva, Paris,** and various stops along the French Riviera. Discounts include: 20% discount with a youth card; 20% off for seniors over 65 Friday and Sunday and 40% off Monday, Tuesday, Wednesday, Thursday, Saturday; and 15% discount for round-trips.

There is absolutely no reason to buy a Eurail pass if you are planning on traveling just within Spain. Trains are cheap, so a pass saves little money, and may actually be more expensive than buying individual tickets. There are several passes that cover travel within Spain. Ages 4-11 are half-price; children under four are free. You must purchase rail passes at least 15 days before departure. Call 1-800-4-Eurail in the US or go to www.raileurope.com.

Spain Flexipass offers 3 days of unlimited travel in a 2-month period. 1st-class US$200; 2nd-class US$155. Each additional rail-day (up to 7) US$35 for 1st-class, US$30 for 2nd-class.

Iberic Railpass is good for 3 days of unlimited 1st-class travel in Spain and Portugal for US$205. Each additional rail-day (up to 7) US$45.

Spain Rail n' Drive Pass is good for 3 days of unlimited 1st-class train travel and 2 days of unlimited mileage in a rental car within a 2-month period. Prices US$255-365, depending on how many people are traveling and the type of car. Up to 2 additional rail-days and extra car days are also available, and a 3rd and 4th person can join in the car using only a Flexipass.

BY CAR

For more information on traveling by car once you get to Spain, check out **Once in Barcelona,** p. 29.

INTERNATIONAL DRIVING PERMIT (IDP). If you plan to drive a car while in Barcelona, you must be over 18. An International Driving Permit (IDP) is recommended, though Spain allows travelers to drive with a valid American or Canadian license for a limited number of months. It is a good idea to get one, in case you're in a situation (e.g. an accident or stranded in a small town) where the police do not know English; information on the IDP is printed in ten languages, including Spanish. AAA members and non-members alike can call US ☎800-AAA-HELP for info.

Your IDP, valid for one year, must be issued in your own country before you depart. An application for an IDP usually needs to include one or two photos, a current local license, an additional form of identification, and a fee.

CAR INSURANCE. Most credit cards cover standard insurance. If you rent, lease, or borrow a car, you will need a **green card,** or **International Insurance Certificate,** to certify that you have liability insurance and that it applies abroad. Green cards can be obtained at car rental agencies, car dealers (for those leasing cars), some travel agents, and some border crossings. Rental agencies may require you to purchase theft insurance in countries that they consider to have a high risk of auto theft.

SPECIFIC CONCERNS

WOMEN TRAVELERS

Women exploring on their own inevitably face some additional safety concerns, but it's easy to be adventurous without taking undue risks. If you are concerned, consider staying in hostels which offer single rooms that lock from the inside or in religious organizations with rooms for women only. Communal showers in some hostels are safer than others; check them before settling in. Stick to centrally located accommodations (like in the Barri Gòtic) and avoid solitary late-night treks or Metro rides.

Always carry extra money for a phone call, bus, or taxi. **Hitchhiking** is never safe for a lone woman, or even for two women traveling together. Choose train compartments occupied by women or couples. Look as if you know where you're going and approach older women or couples for directions if you're lost or uncomfortable.

Generally, the less you look like a tourist, the better off you'll be. Dress conservatively. Trying to fit in can be effective, but dressing to the style of an obviously different culture may cause you to be ill at ease and a conspicuous target. Wearing a conspicuous **wedding band** may prevent unwanted overtures; a mention of a husband waiting at the hotel may be enough to discount your potentially vulnerable, unattached appearance.

Your best answer to verbal harassment is no answer at all; feigning deafness, sitting motionless, and staring straight ahead at nothing in particular will do a world of good that reactions usually don't achieve. The extremely persistent can sometimes be dissuaded by a firm, loud, and very public *"Vete"*—"Go away" in Spanish. Don't hesitate to seek out a police officer or a passerby if you are being harassed. Memorize the relevant emergency numbers, and consider carrying a whistle on your keychain. A self-defense course will not only prepare you for a potential attack, but will also raise your level of awareness of your surroundings as well as your confidence. Also be sure you are aware of the health concerns that women face when traveling.

TRAVELING ALONE

There are many benefits to traveling alone, including independence and greater interaction with locals. On the other hand, any solo traveler is a more vulnerable target of harassment and street theft. Lone travelers need to be well-organized and look confident at all times. Try not to stand out as a tourist, and be especially careful in deserted or very crowded areas. If questioned, never admit that you are traveling alone. Maintain regular contact with someone at home who knows the number of your hostel and what you'll be doing from day to day. For more tips, pick up *Traveling Solo* by Eleanor Berman (Globe Pequot Press, US$17) or subscribe to **Connecting: Solo Travel Network,** 689 Park Road, Unit 6, Gibsons, BC V0N 1V7 (☎604-886-9099; www.cstn.org; membership US$ 28).

Alternatively, several services link solo travelers with companions who have similar travel habits and interests; contact the **Travel Companion Exchange,** P.O. Box 833, Amityville, NY 11701 (☎631-454-0880; www.whytravelalone.com; US$48).

OLDER TRAVELERS

Senior citizens are eligible for a wide range of discounts. If you don't see a senior citizen price listed, ask, and you may be delightfully surprised. The books *No Problem! Worldwise Tips for Mature Adventurers,* by Janice Kenyon (Orca Book Publishers; US$16) and *Unbelievably Good Deals and Great Adventures That You Absolutely Can't Get Unless You're Over 50,* by Joan Rattner Heilman (NTC/Contemporary Publishing; US$13) are both excellent resources. For more information, contact one of the following organizations:

Elderhostel, 11 Ave. de Lafayette, Boston, MA 02111 (☎877-426-8056; www.elderhostel.org). Organizes 1- to 4-week "educational adventures" in Barcelona on varied subjects for those 55+.

The Mature Traveler, P.O. Box 15791, Sacramento, CA 95852 (☎800-460-6676). Deals, discounts, and travel packages for the 50+ traveler. Subscription $30.

BISEXUAL, GAY, & LESBIAN TRAVELERS

As a predominantly Catholic country with a recent history of fascism, Spain leans towards the conservative side when it comes to recognizing the variety of the sexuality spectrum. However, Barcelona is perhaps the most accepting, most comfortable, and most exciting city in Spain for LGB travelers; it's proximity to gay-friendly **Sitges** is another plus (see **Daytripping,** p. 214). No special precautions should be necessary for gay travel in Barcelona.

For the inside scoop on all things gay and lesbian in Barcelona—from gay-friendly hostels to the best gay nightlife—check out the LGB Barcelona sidebars scattered throughout this guide. Listed below are contact organizations, mail-order bookstores, and publishers that offer materials addressing some specific concerns. **Out and About** (www.planetout.com) offers a bi-weekly newsletter addressing travel concerns and a comprehensive site addressing gay travel concerns.

RESOURCES

Gay's the Word, 66 Marchmont St., London WC1N 1AB (☎+44 20 7278 7654; www.gaystheword.co.uk). The largest gay and lesbian bookshop in the UK, with both fiction and nonfiction titles. Mail-order service available.

Giovanni's Room, 1145 Pine St., Philadelphia, PA 19107 (☎215-923-2960; www.queerbooks.com). An international lesbian/feminist and gay bookstore with mail-order service (carries many of the publications listed below).

International Lesbian and Gay Association (ILGA), 81 rue Marché-au-Charbon, B-1000 Brussels, Belgium (☎+32 2 502 2471; www.ilga.org). Provides political information, such as homosexuality laws of individual countries.

Gay in Spain: www.gayinspain.com. A webpage that offers comprehensive coverage of LGB resources and establishments in Spanish and English in Barcelona, Sitges, and Girona.

FURTHER READING

Spartacus International Gay Guide 2001-2002. Bruno Gmunder Verlag (US$33).

Ferrari Guides' Gay Travel A to Z, Ferrari Guides' Men's Travel in Your Pocket, and *Ferrari Guides' Inn Places.* Ferrari Publications (US$16-20). Purchase the guides online at www.ferrariguides.com.

The Gay Vacation Guide: The Best Trips and How to Plan Them, Mark Chesnut. Citadel Press (US$15).

TRAVELERS WITH DISABILITIES

Because sections of Barcelona are so old, it can be difficult to get around in certain neighborhoods, specifically, the Ciutat Vella, which includes the Barri Gòtic, La Ribera, and El Raval. Spain has made huge improvements over the last ten years, but wheelchair accessibility does not mean the same thing in Spain as in the US. Those with disabilities should inform airlines, hotels, and hostels of their disabilities when making reservations; some time may be needed to prepare the necessary arrangements. Call ahead to restaurants, museums, and other facilities to find out about the existence of ramps, the widths of doors, the dimensions of elevators, etc. Let's Go has investigated the accessibility of the sights and establishments we review; be advised, however, that when something is labeled "wheelchair accessible," that term may only denote an adequate width of doors and absence of steps, and not necessarily an accessible bathroom.

Guide dog owners will not need to quarantine their dogs, but they will need to provide a certificate of immunization, and those coming from the US must have their health certificate stamped by the USDA. The **rail** is probably the most convenient form of travel for disabled travelers in Europe: many (but not all) stations have ramps, and some trains have wheelchair lifts, special seating areas, and specially equipped toilets. For those who wish to rent cars, some major **car rental** agencies (Hertz, Avis, and National) offer hand-controlled vehicles.

For a progressive, modern city, Barcelona is severely lacking when it comes to wheelchair accessibility. Hostels, mostly in aging buildings, tend to have narrow doorways and only a few boast elevators. Restaurants and shops, particularly in the Barri Gòtic, La Ribera, and El Raval also tend to have unmanageable entrances. In this medieval area, the sidewalks are narrow and the streets marred with cobblestones. Most buses and trains are accessible, but may not function easily or properly. For wheelchair accessibility, major museums and sites tend to be the most reliable. For further information, consult the **Institut Municipal de Disminuits,** C. Llacuna 171, which provides specific information on accessibility (☎93 291 84 00). The Ajuntament information office has a map of wheelchair accessible routes, available at Pl. Sant Miquel or the TMB office in the Universitat Metro stop.

USEFUL ORGANIZATIONS

Mobility International USA (MIUSA), P.O. Box 10767, Eugene, OR 97440 (☎541–343-1284, voice and TDD; www.miusa.org). Sells *A World of Options: A Guide to International Educational Exchange, Community Service, and Travel for Persons with Disabilities* (US$35).

Society for the Advancement of Travel for the Handicapped (SATH), 347 Fifth Ave., #610, New York, NY 10016 (☎212-447-7284; www.sath.org). An advocacy group that publishes free online travel information and the travel magazine *OPEN WORLD* (US$18, free for members). Annual membership US$45, students and seniors US$30.

Directions Unlimited, 123 Green Ln., Bedford Hills, NY 10507 (☎800-533-5343). Books individual and group vacations for the physically disabled; not an info service.

MINORITY TRAVELERS

The Spanish suffer from little interaction with different ethnicities. Barcelona is perhaps the most international city in Spain, with a growing immigrant community and increasing diversity; however, it is only practical to note that a minority traveler may encounter a certain degree of curiosity with respect to their skin color, even in the city. In general, comments or reactions that minority travelers perceive as offensive are not meant to be hostile on the part of the offending party. This factor of intention does not excuse ignorance, which a minority traveler must unfortunately be prepared to encounter.

TRAVELERS WITH CHILDREN

Family vacations often require that you slow your pace, and always require that you plan ahead. When deciding where to stay, remember the special needs of young children; if you pick a hostel a small hotel, call ahead and make sure it's child-friendly. **Be sure that your child carries some sort of ID** in case of an emergency or in case he or she gets lost.

Museums and tourist attractions in Barcelona often offer discounts for children. Children under two generally fly for 10% of the adult airfare on international flights (this does not necessarily include a seat). International fares are usually discounted 25% for children from two to 11. Finding a private place for **breast feeding** is often a problem while traveling, so plan accordingly.

Barcelona is full of children and full of activities for families to do together; *Let's Go: Barcelona* features a special **Kids in the City** sidebar with suggestions for family- and kid-oriented activities. For more information, consult one of the following books: or check with a local library:

Backpacking with Babies and Small Children, Goldie Silverman. Wilderness Press (US$10).

Take Your Kids to Europe, Cynthia W. Harriman. Cardogan Books (US$18).

How to Take Great Trips with Your Kids, Sanford and Jane Portnoy. Harvard Common Press (US$10).

Have Kid, Will Travel: 101 Survival Strategies for Vacationing With Babies and Young Children, Claire and Lucille Tristram. Andrews McMeel Publishing (US$9).

Trouble Free Travel with Children, Vicki Lansky. Book Peddlers (US$9).

DIETARY CONCERNS

Spain can be a difficult place to visit as a strict vegetarian; meat or fish is featured in the vast majority of popular dishes. Most restaurants serve salads, and there are also many egg, rice, and bean based dishes that can be requested without meat. Be careful, though, as some servers may interpret a "vegetarian" order to mean "with tuna instead of ham." While you have to be careful to avoid miscommunications in non-vegetarian restaurants, Barcelona has a respectable number of vegetarian and vegan establishments to choose from—check the table of **Restaurants by Type,** p. 125.

The **North American Vegetarian Society,** P.O. Box 72, Dolgeville, NY 13329 (☎518-568-7970; www.navs-online.org), publishes information about vegetarian travel, including *Transformative Adventures, a Guide to Vacations and Retreats* (US$15).

For more information, visit your local bookstore, health food store, or library, and consult *The Vegetarian Traveler: Where to Stay if You're Vegetarian,* by Jed and Susan Civic (Larson Publications; US$16) and *Europe on 10 Salads a Day,* by Greg and Mary Jane Edwards (Mustang Publishing; US$10).

Travelers who keep **kosher** should contact synagogues in larger cities for information on kosher restaurants. If you are strict in your observance, you may have to prepare your own food on the road. A good resource is the *Jewish Travel Guide,* by Michael Zaidner (Vallentine Mitchell; US$17). For information on Jewish life in Barcelona, contact the *Communidad Israelita de Barcelona* at ☎93 200 85 13. This synagogue is located at 24 C. Porvenir and also houses a community center.

OTHER RESOURCES

Let's Go tries to cover all aspects of budget travel, but we can't put *everything* in our guides. Listed below are books and websites that can serve as jumping off points for your own research.

TRAVEL PUBLISHERS & BOOKSTORES

Hippocrene Books, Inc., 171 Madison Ave., New York, NY 10016 (☎212-685-4371; orders 718-454-2366; www.netcom.com/~hippocre). Free catalog. Publishes foreign language dictionaries and language learning guides.

Hunter Publishing, 130 Campus Dr., Edison, NJ 08818, USA (☎800-255-0343; www.hunterpublishing.com). Has an extensive catalog of travel guides and diving and adventure travel books.

Rand McNally, 150 S. Wacker Dr., Chicago, IL 60606, USA (☎800-234-0679 or 312-332-2009; www.randmcnally.com), publishes road atlases (each US$10).

Adventurous Traveler Bookstore, 245 S. Champlain St., Burlington, VT 05401, USA (☎800-282-3963 or 802-860-6776; www.adventuroustraveler.com).

Bon Voyage!, 2069 W. Bullard Ave., Fresno, CA 93711, USA (☎800-995-9716, from abroad 559-447-8441; www.bon-voyage-travel.com). Specializes in Europe. Free catalog.

Travel Books & Language Center, Inc., 4437 Wisconsin Ave. NW, Washington, D.C. 20016 (☎800-220-2665 or 202-237-1322; www.travelbks.com). Over 60,000 titles from around the world.

WORLD WIDE WEB

Almost every aspect of budget travel is accessible via the web. Within 10min. at the keyboard, you can make a reservation at a hostel, get advice on must-see Modernist sights from other travelers who have just returned from Barcelona, and get the latest soccer scores from the FCB website.

Listed here are some sites to start off your surfing; other relevant web sites are listed throughout the book. Because website turnover is high, use search engines (such as www.google.com or www.yahoo.com) to strike out on your own.

THE ART OF BUDGET TRAVEL

How to See the World: www.artoftravel.com. A compendium of great travel tips, from cheap flights to self defense to interacting with local culture.

Rec. Travel Library: www.travel-library.com. A fantastic set of links for general information and personal travelogues.

Backpacker's Ultimate Guide: www.bugeurope.com. Tips on packing, transportation, and where to go. Also tons of country-specific travel information.

Backpack Europe: www.backpackeurope.com. Helpful tips, a bulletin board, and links.

INFORMATION ON BARCELONA

The City of Barcelona Online: www.bcn.es/english/ihome.htm. The city's official webpage, covering everything from shopping and beaches to current events.

Barcelona: www.barcelona.com. A great resource for travelers, with information on car rentals and Internet cafés.

Tourist Office of Spain: www.okspain.org. The tourist office's official American webpage, full of links for everything from media to gastronomy.

Fútbol Club Barcelona: www.fcbarcelona.com. For those soccer enthusiasts among us, El Barça's official webpage is your guide to Catalunya's favorite team.

Barça Mania: www.barsamania.com is also a respectfully enthusiastic webpage.

Spanish Cheese: www.cheesefromspain.com. Complete with photos of some of Spain's most succulent dairy products. Lactose-intolerants beware.

Foreign Language for Travelers: www.travlang.com. Provides free online translating dictionaries and lists of phrases in both Spanish and Catalan.

PlanetRider: www.planetrider.com. A subjective list of links to the "best" websites covering the culture and tourist attractions of Spain. Please, no comments about the James Bond villainess name.

The Crapper: www.caganer.com. Get in touch with the Catalan celebration of regularity.

Floquet de Neu: www.zoobarcelona.com. The Barcelona Zoo's website, featuring a live feed of the world's only albino gorilla.

& OUR PERSONAL FAVORITE...

Let's Go: www.letsgo.com. Our constantly expanding website features photos and streaming video, online ordering of all our titles, info about our books, a travel forum buzzing with stories and tips, and links that will help you find everything you ever wanted to know about Barcelona.

Accommodations

While accommodations in Barcelona are easy to spot, finding a room in one can be more difficult. If you are traveling during busy times (mid-June until September, and the month of December), it's almost impossible to waltz into a Barri Gòtic hostel and find a vacancy. Those who want to stay in the touristy areas—Barri Gòtic or Las Ramblas—should make reservations weeks in advance. Consider staying outside the tourist hub of the Ciutat Vella; there are plenty of great hostels in the Zona Alta, like Gràcia (see p. 275), that will have more vacancies.

Hostels in Spain are generally not of the dorm variety, but rather a private, basic room, with or without a private bathroom. Because heat and electricity are expensive in Spain, travelers should not assume that rooms have A/C, TV, or phone in the rooms unless specified; also be aware that some establishments do not have heat in the winter. Many establishments demand credit cards over the phone, while others accept only cash; be sure you know the policy where you are staying so you can cover your bill. The IVA tax is not necessarily included in these quotes. The following accommodations are listed by neighborhood and ranked within neighborhood by decreasing value; for a list of accommodations by price, see p. 265.

see map pp. 310-311

BARRI GÒTIC & LAS RAMBLAS

The Barri Gòtic and Las Ramblas are the most sought-after destination for tourists; consequently, reservations are always recommended and usually necessary, weeks in advance. The neighborhood also has more dorm-style hostels than other areas.

the BIG
$plurge

Ciutat Vella

If your willing to spend a bit more for a central location, breakfast, and A/C, try one of the following:

Mare Nostrum, Las Ramblas 67 (☎93 318 53 40; fax 93 412 30 69). M: Liceu, on **Las Ramblas.** For those brought up with a silver spoon in their mouth (or those who wish they were). Mare Nostrum is like a modern resort. Chill in your A/C palace, gaze onto Las Ramblas from your balcony, lie under your new comforter, watch your satellite TV, and love your life. Doubles 7950ptas/€50, with bath 9500ptas/€57. Each additional person 2800ptas/ €17. Breakfast included, served 8am-11am. MC/V.

Hotel Principal, Junta de Comerç 8 (☎93 318 89 70; fax 93 412 08 19; www.hotel-principal.es). M: Liceu, in **El Raval.** From the Metro, head down C. Hospital and take a left onto Junta de Comerç. For a few extra euros, Hotel Principal offers far more comfort and amenities than most. 60 big rooms with A/C, telephone, satellite TV, and safes; ask for a balcony. Breakfast included. Singles 9820ptas/ €59; doubles 12,500ptas/ €75; 4000ptas/€24 per extra person. MC/V.

LAS RAMBLAS

▨ **Hotel Toledano/Hostal Residencia Capitol,** Las Ramblas 138 (☎93 301 08 72; fax 93 412 31 42; toledano@ibernet.com; www.hoteltoledano.com). M: Catalunya, just off Pl. de Catalunya. This family-owned, split-level hotel/hostel has been making tourists happy for almost 80 years. Rooms border on luxurious, with cable TV, phones, and some balconies. Hotel rooms include full bath, hostel rooms do not. English-speaking owner. 4th-floor Hotel Toledano: singles 4600ptas/€27,64; doubles 7900ptas/€47,50; triples 9900ptas/€59,50; quads 11000ptas/ €66,10. 5th-floor Hostel Residencia Capitol: singles 3400ptas/€20,43; doubles 5400ptas/€32,45, with shower 6200ptas/€37,25; triples 6900ptas/ €41,50, with shower 7700ptas/€46,30; quads 7900ptas/€47,50, with shower 8700ptas/€52,30. Reservations can be made over the website; book early. AmEx/MC/V. Wheelchair accessible.

▨ **Hostal Benidorm,** Las Ramblas 37 (☎93 302 20 54; www.barcelona-on-line.es/benidorm). M: Drassanes. With phones and complete baths in every neat room, balconies overlooking Las Ramblas, and excellent prices, this could be the best value on Las Ramblas. Singles 4000ptas/€24,10; doubles 5500ptas/ €33,10; triples 7000ptas/€42,20; quads 9000ptas/€54,25; quints10,500ptas/€63,25.

Hostal Parisien, Las Ramblas 114 (☎93 301 62 83). M: Liceu. Smack in the middle of the excitement (and noise) of Las Ramblas, 13 well-kept rooms keep its young guests happy. Balconies provide front-row seats to the street's daily pedestrian spectacle. Friendly owner speaks a bit of English, German, Dutch, and Italian. TV lounge; quiet hours after midnight. Singles 3500ptas/€21,10, with bath 4000ptas/€24,10; doubles 7500ptas/€45,20, with bath 8500ptas/€51,20.

Hotel Internacional, Las Ramblas 78 (☎93 302 25 66). M: Liceu, across from the Teatre Liceu. 60 surprisingly basic rooms, all with private bath, safe, and telephone, are not quite as nice as they should be for these prices, but the location couldn't be more central. Full breakfast included. Singles 9000ptas/€55; doubles 15,200ptas/€93; triples 20,000ptas/€121; Quads 23,800ptas/€144.

Hostal Marítima, Las Ramblas 4 (☎93 302 31 52). M: Drassanes, down a tiny alley off the port end of Las Ramblas. Follow the signs to Museu de Cera (See p. 104), which is next door. Nothing to write home about, but the location is convenient and rooms are comfortable. No reservations. Laundry 800ptas/ €4,80 (no dryer). Singles, doubles, and triples 3000ptas/€18,10 per person.

Pensión Noya, Las Ramblas 133 (☎93 301 48 31). M: Catalunya, above the noisy Núria restaurant. This 10-room hostel has time-warped back to the colors and styles of the 1950s. Bathrooms and hallways are cramped. No heat in winter. Hot water 8am-midnight. Singles 3000ptas/€18,10; doubles 5800ptas/€35; triples 7500ptas/€45,20.

ACCOMMODATIONS BY PRICE

UNDER €15 PER PERSON

Albergue Juvenil Palau (266)	BG
Albergue Mare de Déu (275)	GR
Casa-Huéspedes Mari-Luz (266)	BG
Hostal Avinyó (266)	BG
✠ Hostal Fernando (265)	BG
Hostal Marmo (266)	BG
Ideal Youth Hostel (271)	ER
Pensión Aris (267)	BG
Pensión Bienestar (266)	BG
Pensión Ciutadella (270)	LR
Pensión Ienesta (275)	MJ

UNDER €25 PER PERSON

Albergue de Juventud Kabul (266)	BG
Gothic Point Youth Hostel (270)	LR
Hostal Australia (271)	ER
Hostal Béjar (276)	SA
✠ Hostal Benidorm (264)	Rmbl
Hostal Bonavista (275)	GR
Hostal Campi (267)	BG
✠ Hostal de Ribagorza (269)	LR
Hostal Felipe II (273)	EIX
Hostal Fontanella (267)	BG
Hostal Girona (272)	EIX
Hostal Hill (273)	EIX
Hostal La Palmera (272)	ER
Hostal la Terrassa (271)	ER
Hostal Layetana (267)	BG
✠ Hostal Levante (266)	BG
Hostal Marítima (264)	Rmbl
Hostal Nuevo Colón (270)	LR
✠ Hostal Orleans (269)	LR
Hostal Paris (267)	BG
Hostal Parisien (264)	Rmbl
✠ Hostal-Residencia Barcelona (275)	MJ
✠ Hostal-Residencia Capitol (264)	Rmbl
Hostal-Residencia Neutral (273)	EIX
✠ Hostal-Residencia Oliva (272)	EIX
Hostal-Residencia Rembrandt (267)	BG
Hostal-Residencia Sants (276)	SA
Hostal-Residencia Windsor (272)	EIX
Hostal Rio de Castro (275)	MJ
Mare Nostrum (264)	Rmbl

Pensión 45 (271)	ER
Pensión Aribau (273)	EIX
Pensión Arosa (268)	BG
Pensión Diamante (272)	ER
Pensión Cliper (274)	EIX
✠ Pensión Fani (270)	EIX
Pensión Francia (274)	BAR
✠ Pensión l'Isard (271)	ER
Pensión Lourdes (270)	LR
Pensión Noya (264)	Rmbl
Pensión Puebla de Arenoso (274)	EIX
Pensión Regar (276)	SA
Pensión Rondas (270)	LR
Pensión San Medín (275)	GR
Pensión Santa Anna (268)	BG
Residencia Victoria (268) BG	

UNDER €40 PER PERSON

Hostal Cisneros (274)	EIX
✠ Hostal Eden (273)	EIX
✠ Hostal Lesseps (275)	GR
Hostal Opera (271)	ER
Hostal Palermo (269)	BG
Hostal Qué Tal (274)	EIX
Hostal-Residencia Europa (268)	BG
Hostal-Residensi Lausanne (269)	BG
Hostal San Remo (273)	EIX
Hostal Sofia (276)	SA
Hostal Valls (276)	GR
Hotel Call (269)	BG
Hotel Rey Don Jaume I (266)	BG
✠ Hotel Toledano (264)	Rmbl
Hotel Transit (276)	SA
Hotel Triumfo (270)	LR
Hotel Universal (273)	EIX
Pensión Dalí (268)	BG
Pensión Port-bou (270)	LR

OVER €40 PER PERSON

✠ Hostal Plaza (268)	BG
✠ Hostal Ciudad Condal (272)	EIX
Hostal de Mar (274)	BAR
Hotel California (268)	BG
Hotel Everest (273)	EIX
Hotel Internacional (264)	Rmbl
Hotel Joventut (272)	ER
Hotel Paseo de Gràcia (273)	EIX
Hotel Peninsular (272)	ER
Hotel Principal (264)	ER

BG Barri Gòtic **EIX** L'Eixample **ER** El Raval **GR** Gràcia **LR** La Ribera **Rmbl** Las Ramblas **MJ** Montjuïc **SA** Sants

LOWER BARRI GÒTIC

The following hostels are located in the lower part of the Barri Gòtic, between C. Ferran and the waterfront. Backpackers flock here to be close to the port and hip Las Ramblas; it is an ideal place to experience the old city's heady, fast-paced atmosphere. Again, Be careful with your wallet at night, especially in the Pl. Reial and below C. Escudellers.

✠ **Hostal Fernando,** C. Ferran 31 (☎/fax 93 301 79 93; www.barcelona-on-line.es/ fernando). M: Liceu. This hostel is so clean it shines, and so well located it fills almost entirely from walk-in requests. Dorm beds come with free lockers in the room; otherwise storage lock-

on the cheap

Youth Hostels in the Barri Gòtic

Albergue Juvenil Palau (HI), C. Palau 6 (☎93 412 50 80). M: Liceu. A tranquil refuge in the heart of the Barri Gòtic for the budget set. Kitchen (open 7-10pm), dining room, and 45 clean dorm rooms with lockers (3-8 people each). Breakfast included. Showers available 8am-noon and 4-10pm. Sheets 200ptas/€1,20. Reception 7am-3am. Curfew 3am. No reservations. Dorms 1900ptas/€11,50. Cash only.

Albergue de Juventud Kabul, Pl. Reial 17 (☎93 318 51 90; fax 93 301 40 34). M: Liceu. Head to the port on Las Ramblas, pass C. Ferran, and turn left onto C. Colon Pl. Reial; Kabul is on the near right corner of the plaça. This place is legendary among European backpackers; the cramped coed dormitory rooms can pack in up to 200 frat boys at a time. The tavern-like common area includes satellite TV, a small restaurant/snack bar, email kiosks (100ptas/€0,60 per 20min.), a pool table, blaring pop music, and even a few beer vending machines. Key deposit 1000ptas/€6. Be sure to lock up your valuables in the free in-room lockers. Sheets 300ptas/€1,80. Laundry 900ptas/€5,50. No reservations. June-Sept. dorms 2900ptas/€17,50, Oct.-May 1900ptas/€11,50. Cash only.

ers near the front desk are 200ptas/€1,20 per 24hr. Guests get keys. TV/dining room. Dorm beds 2500ptas/€15; doubles 5000-6000ptas/€30-36, with bath 7000-8000ptas/€42-48; triples 8500-9500ptas/€51-57. MC/V.

Hostal Levante, Baixada de San Miguel 2 (☎93 317 95 65; fax 93 317 05 26; reservas@hostallevante.com; www.hostallevante.com). M: Liceu. Walk down C. Ferran, turn right onto C. Avinyó, and take the 1st left onto Baixada de San Miguel. A hotel parading as a hostel: 50 large, tastefully decorated rooms with light wood interiors and balconies or fans, and a relaxing TV lounge. Ask for one of the newly renovated rooms. Singles 4000ptas/€24; doubles 6500ptas/€39, with bath 7500ptas/€45. Six apartments also available for 4-8 people each (kitchen, living room, laundry machines) 4000ptas/€24 per person per night. MC/V.

Casa de Huéspedes Mari-Luz, C. Palau 4 (☎/fax 93 317 34 63). M: Liceu. From Las Ramblas, follow C. Ferran, go right on C. Avinyó, left on C. Cervantes, and then right on tiny C. Palau. With 25 years under their belt, Mari-Luz and husband Fernando know how to make their hostel feel like a home. Narrow hallways flanked by ultra-clean dorm rooms for 4-6 people and a few comfortable doubles. Kitchen available June-Aug. (open only 8-10:30am).Guests get keys, and each dorm bed comes with a locker. Laundry 800ptas/€4,80. Reservations require a faxed photocopy of a credit card. Dorms 1900ptas/€11,50; doubles June 21-Aug. 15 6000ptas/€36, Aug.16-June 20 4800ptas/€29. MC/V.

Hostal Avinyó, C. Avinyó 42 (☎93 318 79 45; fax 93 318 68 93; reservas@hostalavinyo.com; www.hostalavinyo.com). M: Drassanes. With annual renovations, owners are on a mission to make Avinyó the most modern spot in the Barri Gòtic. 28 bedrooms with couches, high ceilings, fans, in-room safes, and stained glass windows. Singles 2500ptas/€15; doubles 4000-4600ptas/€12-14, with bath 5000-6000ptas/€15-18. Cash only.

Hostal Marmo, C. Gignàs 25 (☎93 310 59 70). M: Jaume I. A right off Via Laietana from the Metro. 17 rooms in an old house still bedecked with plenty of plants, lacy curtains, and tiled floors. All rooms have balconies. Reservations only accepted 2 days in advance. Singles 2200-2400ptas/€13,50-14,50, with bath 2500-2700ptas/€15-16,30; doubles 4200-4600ptas/€25,30-27,70, with bath 4500-4900ptas/€27-€30. Cash only.

Pensión Bienestar, C. Quintana 3 (☎93 318 72 83). M: Liceu, a left off C. Ferran, coming from Las Ramblas. The entrance looks utterly uninviting and brown is the dominant paint color inside, but many of the mattresses are new and the rooms are cheap for the location. Singles 2500ptas/€15; doubles 3500ptas/€21; triples 7000ptas/€42. Cash only.

Hotel Rey Don Jaume I, C. Jaume I 11 (☎/fax 93 310 62 08; r.d.jaume@atriumhotels.com). M: Jaume

I, a straight walk from the Metro. This building has seen much better days but still maintains a touch of regal opulence, with dark wood, marble stairs, and a tapestry-filled TV lounge. Stark, fluorescent-lit rooms all have balconies, phones, and bath. Safes available at main desk. Reservations recommended 1-2 months in advance (requires a credit card number). Singles 6000ptas/€36; doubles 9000ptas/€54; triples 12,000ptas/€72. AmEx/MC/V.

UPPER BARRI GÒTIC

This section of the Barri Gòtic encompasses the area south of Pl. de Catalunya, bounded by C. Fontanella to the north and C. Ferran to the south. **Portal de l'Angel,** the better-behaved little brother of Las Ramblas, is a broad pedestrian thoroughfare avenue running through the middle, southward from Pl. de Catalunya. Accommodations here are a bit pricier than those in the Lower Barri Gòtic, but tend to have a more serene ambiance and are much quieter at night. As with the lower Barri Gòtic, early reservations are essentially obligatory in June, July, and August. The nearest Metro stop is Catalunya, unless otherwise specified.

UNDER 4000PTAS/€24 FOR ONE PERSON

Hostal Campi, C. Canuda 4 (☎/fax 93 301 3545). The first left off Las Ramblas coming from M: Catalu-nya. A great bargain for the quality and location. The rooms are spacious, with light, comfortable furniture and lacy curtains. All with bath have TVs. Reservations accepted 9am-8pm. Singles 3000ptas/€18; doubles 6000ptas/€36, with bath 7000ptas/€42; triples 8000ptas/€48, with bath 9000ptas/€54. Cash only.

Hostal Fontanella, Via Laietana 71 (☎/fax 93 317 59 43). M: Urquinaona. Tastefully-decorated, with a floral waiting room and wood furniture in the rooms (fans, too). Reservations require a credit card number. Singles 3300ptas/€20, with bath 4300/€26; doubles 5500ptas/€23, with shower 6500ptas/€39, with bath 7500ptas/€45; triples 7700ptas/€46, with bath 9100ptas/€55; quads 9650ptas/€58, with bath 11,000ptas/€66. AmEx/MC/V.

Hostal-Residencia Rembrandt, C. Portaferrissa 23 (☎/fax 93 318 10 11). M: Liceu. The hallway common areas have a doll-house feel, and the pastel-colored rooms are all themed differently, ranging from "little kid" to "regal." Ask for one with a balcony. Fans 300ptas/€1,80 per night. Singles 4000ptas/€24, with bath 5500ptas/€33; doubles 6500ptas/€39, with bath 8800ptas/€53; triples 9000ptas/€54, with bath 10,000ptas/€60. One suite (12,000ptas/€72) with 2 balconies, a marble tub, and a sitting area. Cash only.

Pensión Aris, C. Fontanella 14 (☎93 318 10 17). Right off Pl. de Catalunya. 13 huge, clean, sparse rooms with fans and white-washed walls. Furniture could be sturdier, but the prices are impossible to beat for the location. Laundry 500-1000ptas/€3-6. Singles 2500ptas/€15; doubles 5000ptas/€30, with bath 6000ptas/€36. Cash only.

Hostal Layetana, Pl. Ramón Berenguer el Gran 2 (☎/fax 93 319 20 12). M: Jaume I, a short walk from the Metro going up Via Laietana toward the mountains. Look for the multinational flags on the third-floor balcony in the plaça. A sophisticated, peaceful hostel with extremely clean bathrooms and lots of space. Rooms with bath have fans; for others they are rentable at 200ptas/€1,20 per day. Singles 3400ptas/€20,50; doubles 5100ptas/€31, with bath 7350ptas/€44; triples 8000ptas/€48, with bath 10,200ptas/€61. MC/V.

Hostal Paris, Cardenal Casañas 4 (☎93 301 37 85; fax 93 412 70 96). M: Liceu. The bright yellow sign is visible from Las Ramblas, right across from the Metro. 42 well-kept rooms and a cafeteria-like common area overlooking the street. All rooms facing the inside patio have A/

ESSENTIAL INFORMATION

LAST MINUTE TRAVELERS

It takes balls to walk into Barcelona in July without a reservation, but we here at Let's Go know there are plenty of such adventure travelers out there. If you find yourself without a room, try one of the following options; none of these establishments take reservations, and therefore have a higher likelihood of vacancies in high season.

Albergue Juvenil Palau (p. 266)

Albergue de Juventud Kabul (p. 266)

Hostal Bonavista (p. 275)

Hostal Fernando (p. 265)

Hostal Marítima (p. 264)

Hostal Opera (p. 271)

Hostal Paris (p. 267)

LGB ▼
BARCELONA

She's Got a Lot of Pretty Boys...

You'll be bound to make some new friends at the **Hotel California,** C. Rauric 14 (☎93 317 77 66). M: Catalunya, a right off C. Ferran coming from Las Ramblas, in the Barri Gòtic. Such a lovely place. Caters to a gay clientele, ends up taking a mixed crowd into its sparkling clean, pleasant rooms, all with TV, phone, full bath and A/C. Take the price plunge, and you'll add comfort to the convenience of the Barri Gòtic. Breakfast included. Rent-me-a-room singles 7500ptas/ €45; doubles 12,000ptas/ €72; triples 15,000ptas/ €90. AmEx/MC/V.

C, all exterior ones have fans, and all with bath have TVs. Singles 3300ptas/€20, with bath 3700ptas/ €22; doubles 6000ptas/€36, with shower 7000ptas/€42, with bath 9000ptas/€54. No reservations. MC/V.

Residencia Victoria, C. Comtal 9 (☎93 317 45 97; victoria@atriumhotels.com). From Pl. de Catalunya, walk down Av. Portal de l'Angel and take a left on C. Comtal. Cafeteria-style lounge/dining room with outdoor terrace, kitchen, TV, and small library. Rooms are basic but more spacious than usual for this part of town. Laundry 400ptas/€2,40 (no dryer). Singles 3500-4000ptas/€21-24; doubles 5500-6000ptas/ €33-36; triples 8000ptas/€48. Cash only.

Pensión Santa Anna, C. Santa Anna 23 (☎/fax 93 301 22 46). Tight quarters, but the floors and bathrooms are spotless and the cheap, light bedroom furniture is easy on the eyes. All rooms have fans, and guests get keys. Singles 3000ptas/€18; doubles 6000ptas/€36, with bath 8000ptas/€48; triples 9000ptas/€54. Cash only. Not wheelchair accessible.

Hostal-Residencia Europa, C. Boqueria 18 (☎/fax 93 318 76 20). M: Liceu. The hallways and TV lounge here are cramped and gloomy, but the rooms inside have just enough light and air, and the location's unbeatable. Hot water 6:30am-noon and 6:30pm-midnight. Singles 3600ptas/€27; doubles 6400ptas/ €38,50, with bath 8200ptas/€49; triples 9000ptas/ €54, with bath 10,600ptas/€64; quads 11,600ptas/ €70, with bath 13,200ptas/€79,50. Cash only.

Pensión Arosa, Av. Portal de l'Angel 14 (☎93 317 36 87; fax 93 301 30 38), through a shared entrance with Andrew's Tie Shop. 7 airy rooms in a homey private flat, some of them overlooking Av. Portal de l'Angel. Guests get keys. Singles 3000ptas/ €18; doubles 5000ptas/€30, with shower 6000ptas/€36; triples (with shower) 7500ptas/ €45. AmEx/MC/V.

UNDER 7500PTAS/€45 FOR ONE PERSON

☒ Hostal Plaza, C. Fontanella 18 (☎/fax 93 301 01 39 or 93 317 91 08; www.plazahostal.com). Savvy, super-friendly Texan owners and quirky, brightly painted rooms with wicker furniture. The common room boasts black leather couches, a drink/coffee/ breakfast bar, a kitchen and tables, TV, phone, and Internet access with video-telephone. Laundry 1500ptas for 5kg. 24hr. reception, but they prefer to do all business 10am-10pm. Singles 7000ptas/€42, with bath 9000ptas/€54; doubles 9000ptas/€54, with bath 10,000ptas/€60; triples 12,000ptas/€72, with bath 13,000ptas/€78. 12% discount in Nov. and Feb. AmEx/MC/V.

Pensión Dalí, C. Boqueria 12 (☎93 318 55 90; fax 93 318 55 80; pensiondali@wanadoo.es). M: Liceu; C. Boqueria intersects with Las Ramblas right at the Metro. Designed as a religious house by Domènech i Montaner, the architect of the Palau de la Música Catalana, and originally run by a friend of Dalí's, Pensión Dalí still retains the stained glass and gaudy iron doors of its early years. Gold-and-brown hued rooms are a bit past their prime, but all have TVs and windows onto the street. Huge, couch-filled common room and Internet access (100ptas/€0,60 per 4min.). Singles 4400ptas/€26,50, with bath 6000ptas/€36; doubles 6500ptas/€39, with bath 7500ptas/€45; triples 10,200ptas/€61,50; quads 12,800ptas/€77. AmEx/MC/V.

Hostal-Residencia Lausanne, Av. Portal de l'Angel, 24 (☎ 93 302 11 39 or 93 302 16 30). M: Catalunya, wedged between two Zara display windows. A single-hallway hostel with a posh living room overlooking one of Barcelona's most popular pedestrian shopping streets. Singles 4500ptas/€27; doubles 6500ptas/€39, with shower 8000ptas/€48, with bath 12,000ptas/€72; triples 12,000ptas/€72; quads 16,000ptas/€96. Cash only.

Hostal Palermo, C. Boqueria 21 (☎/fax 93 302 40 02). M: Liceu. Large, party-conducive rooms with green plaid bedspreads. Small, plastic-chaired turquoise TV room and white-washed walls. Laundry 700ptas/€4,20, safe 200ptas/€1,20 per day. Singles 5500ptas/€33, with bath 7500ptas/€45; triples 13,500ptas/€81, with bath 18,000ptas/€108,50. Reservations require a credit card number. MC/V.

Hotel Call, Arco San Ramón del Call 4 (☎93 302 11 23; fax 93 301 34 86). M: Liceu. From Las Ramblas, take C. Boqueria to its end, then veer left onto C. Call; the hotel is on the first corner on the left. Quiet, pleasant rooms all have firm beds, phones, safes, A/C, and bath, although only some have windows. Singles 5350ptas/€32; doubles 7490ptas/€45; triples 9630ptas/€58; quads 10,275ptas/€62 (IVA included). MC/V.

LA RIBERA

see map pp. 310-311

Staircase at Hostal Rembrandt

🗺 **Hostal Orleans,** Av. Marqués de l'Argentera 13 (☎93 319 73 82). From M: Barceloneta, follow Pg. Joan de Borbó and turn right on Av. Marqués de l'Argentera. Spotless, newly renovated hostel with comfortable common area. All rooms have full bath and TV. Singles 3000-4500ptas/€18-27; doubles 8500ptas/€50, with A/C 9000ptas/€54; triples 9500-10000ptas/€56-60; quads 12000ptas/€72. AmEx/D/MC/V.

🗺 **Hostal de Ribagorza,** C. Trafalgar 39 (☎93 319 19 68; fax 93 319 12 47). M: Urquinaona. With your back to Pl. Urquinaona, walk down Ronda Sant Pere and turn right on C. Méndez Núñez. Hostel is 1 block down on the corner. 12-room hostel in ornate Modernist building complete with marble staircase and tile floors. Rooms have TVs, fans, and homey decorations. Doubles only. Oct.-Feb. 4000ptas/€24; with bath 6000ptas/€36; Mar.-Sept. 5500ptas/€33; with bath 7500ptas/€45. MC/V.

Checking Out the View

Pension Dalí

on the cheap

🐾 Pensión Fani

C. València 278 (☎93 215 36 45) M: Catalunya, just off Pg. de Gràcia on the left (facing Pl. de Catalunya). This long-term pension is dirt cheap and oozing with character and quirky charm, from colorful floor tiles and rows of hanging plants to a huge cage of birds in the sunroom. Rooms are generally rented by the month but can be used for a single night as well, if available. 3 shared bathrooms, full kitchen with refrigerator, pots, pans and utensils, dining room/TV room, laundry room (handwash and air-dry) with ironing board and iron, and pay phone. Bring your own towel. Singles 42,000ptas/€252 per month; doubles 80,000ptas/€480 per month; triples 120,000ptas/€720 per month. One-night stay 3000ptas/€18 per person. Payments due the 1st of each month. Cash only. Not wheelchair accessible.

Hostal Nuevo Colón, Av. Marqués de l'Argentera 19 (☎93 319 50 77). M: Barceloneta. Follow Pg. Joan de Borbó and turn right on Av. Marqués de l'Argentera. Newly renovated hostel with very clean, modern rooms and a large common area with TV. Singles 3900ptas/€24,40; doubles 5900ptas/€35, with bath 7900ptas/€47. 6-person apartments for rent (equipped with kitchens) 18,000ptas/€110. MC/V.

Pensión Ciutadella, C. Comerç 33 (☎93 319 62 03). M: Barceloneta, follow Pg. Joan de Borbó and turn right on Av. Marqués de l'Argentera and make the 6th left onto C. Comerç. Small hostel with 6 spacious rooms, each with fan, TV, and balcony. Doubles only. Oct.-May 5000ptas/€30,12; with bath 6000ptas/€36,15; June-Sept., 6000ptas/€36,15, 7500ptas/€45. Each additional person (up to 4), 1500ptas/€9. Cash only.

Pensión Lourdes, C. Princesa 14 (☎93 319 33 72). M: Jaume I. Cross Via Laietana and follow C. Princesa. Popular backpacker destination in the heart of La Ribera. 32 adequate, no-frills rooms with telephones. Common area with TV. Singles 3500ptas/€21; doubles 5000ptas/€30, with bath 6700ptas/€40. Cash only.

Pensión Rondas, C. Girona 4 (☎93 232 51 02; fax 93 232 12 25). M: Urquinaona. With your back to Pl. Urquinaona, walk down Ronda Sant Pere and turn left on C. Girona, hostel is on the right. Clean, basic rooms, some with balconies. English-speaking owner. Singles 3500ptas/€21; doubles 5500ptas/€33, with shower 6000ptas/€36, with full bath 6500ptas/€39. Cash only.

Pensión Port-bou, C. Comerç 29 (☎93 319 23 67). From M: Barceloneta, follow Pg. Joan de Borbó and turn right on Av. Marqués de l'Argentera and make the 6th left onto C. Comerç. Small hostel in 150-year-old building with high ceilings and balconies. Simple rooms with eclectic, mismatched furniture. Sept-June singles 4000-4500ptas/€24-27; doubles 5000-5500ptas/€30-33, with bath 7000-7500ptas/€42-4. July-Aug. singles 5000/€30; doubles 6000ptas/€36,15; with bath 8000ptas/€48. Extra person in double room 1000ptas/€6. Reservations suggested. Cash only.

Gothic Point Youth Hostel , C. Vigatans 5 (☎93 268 78 08; badia@intercom.es). M: Jaume I. Walk down C. de l'Argentera; C. Vigatans is the 1st street on your left. Large Modernist building with orange and black lobby area boasting picnic tables, free Internet access, and plants and art posters. A/C dorm-style rooms have individual curtained-off bed compartments, each with its own table and light. Rooftop terrace. Breakfast included. Sheet rental 300ptas/€1,80. Lockers 500ptas/€3. Beds 3424ptas/€21. MC/V.

Hotel Triunfo, Pg. Picasso 22 (☎93 315 08 60). M: Barceloneta. Walk up Pg. Joan de Borbó and turn right on Av. Marqués de l'Argentera and left on Pg. Picasso. Hotel is across from the Parc de la Ciutadella. Budget hotel with whitewashed walls and heavy floral curtains. All rooms have full bath, TV, and A/C. Singles 6800ptas/€40; doubles 10,800ptas/65€. MC/V.

EL RAVAL

see map pp. 316-317

Hostels in El Raval, the area west of Las Ramblas, are harder to come by and less-touristed; staying here will give you a better feel for the catalan lifestyle. Be careful in the area at night, particularly in the areas nearer to the port and farther from Las Ramblas.

☒ **Pensión L'Isard,** C. Tallers 82 (☎93 302 51 83; fax 93 302 01 17). M: Universitat. Take the C. Pelai Metro exit, turn left at the end of the block, and then left again at the pharmacy. Simple, elegant, and unbelievably clean—a great find. Bright rooms have enough closet space for even the worst over-packer. Ask for a room with a balcony. Singles 2800ptas/€16,80; doubles 4900ptas/€29,40, with bath 6500ptas/€39; triples 7300ptas/€43,80, with bath 8500ptas/€51.

Inside a Hotel Room

Hostal Australia, Ronda Universitat 11 (☎93 317 41 77). M: Universitat. Guests are family at this hostel, and the rooms make you feel that way; all rooms have embroidered sheets, curtains, balconies, artwork, and fans. Be prepared for the equally family-style quiet time, though, starting at 10pm. Curfew 4am. Singles 3300ptas/€19,80; doubles 5400ptas/€32,40, with bath 7000ptas/€42. MC/V.

Hostal La Terrassa, Junta de Comerç 11 (☎93 302 51 74; fax 93 301 21 88). M: Liceu. From the Metro, take C. Hospital and turn left after Teatre Romea. A hostel experience for the minimalist, with 50 small, basic, clean rooms. The social courtyard is a rarity among non-youth hostels. Singles 2700ptas/€16,20; doubles 4200ptas/€25,20, with bath 5200ptas/€31,20; triples 5700ptas/€34,20, with bath 6600ptas/€39,60. MC/V.

Hostal Nilo

Hostal Opera, C. Sant Pau 20 (☎93 318 82 01). M: Liceu, off Las Ramblas. Like the Liceu opera house next door, Hostal Opera has been recently renovated, making its sunny rooms feel like new. All rooms come with bath, telephone, and A/C. Singles 5000ptas/€30,10; doubles 8000ptas/€48,20; triples 10,000ptas/€60,30. No reservations. Handicapped accessible. MC/V.

Pensión 45, C. Tallers 45 (☎93 302 70 61). M: Catalunya. From Pl. de Catalunya, take the first right off Las Ramblas onto Tallers. What "45" lacks in name-choice originality, it makes up for in its simple charm. Old paintings and photographs decorate the walls of its eighteen small rooms. Singles 3100ptas/€19; doubles 5000ptas/€31, with bath 6000ptas/€40. Cash only.

Ideal Youth Hostel, C. Unió 12 (☎93 342 61 77; fax 93 412 38 48; ideal@idealhostel.com; www.idealhostel.com). M: Liceu, off of Las Ramblas, on the street next to the Gran Teatre Liceu. Concrete dorm-rooms and shared baths would make ideal air-raid shelters; hole up here for a good place to crash for a few nights. Bright and cheery staff make up for the some-

Balcony

271

what dim rooms. Lobby with cafeteria (breakfast 250ptas/€1,50) and two computers of free internet access. Laundry services, wash and dry 1000ptas/€6. Co-ed and single-sex rooms available. 2000ptas/€12 per person.

Hotel Peninsular, C. Sant Pau 34 (☎93 302 31 38). M: Liceu, off of Las Ramblas. This venerable building, now one of the fifty sights on the Ruta del Modernisme (see **Sights,** p. 59), served as the monastery for the Augustine order of priests in the mid-1800's. The rooms still have a certain austerity about them, although they are located off an inner patio with a bright skylight. The 80 rooms all come with telephones and A/C, and most have baths; breakfast included. Singles with bath 7000ptas/€42,20; doubles 7000ptas/€42,20, with bath 10000ptas/€60,30; triples 12000ptas/€72,30. MC/V.

Hotel Joventut, Junta de Comerç 12 (☎93 318 89 70; fax 93 412 08 19). Same owners, rates, and reservation info as Hotel Principal (see **The Big Splurge,** p. 264), but farther down the street. Same quality as its sister, with bigger rooms and no A/C. Breakfast included (served at Hotel Principal).

Hostal La Palmera, C. Jerusalén 30 (☎93 317 09 97; fax 93 342 41 36). M: Liceu. From Las Ramblas, just behind and to the right of the Boqueria market (see **Sights,** p. 63). Somewhat Spartan rooms feature new wood paneling and decent beds. Breakfast included (9-11am). Singles 4000ptas/€24,10; doubles 6000ptas/€36,20, with bath 7000ptas/€42,20; triples 9000ptas/€54,30.

Pensión Diamante, Carme 14 (☎93 317 63 11). M: Catalunya, off of Las Ramblas. Though the orange and yellow decor might make you think you're on the set of a 70s sitcom, you'll have good times in these dyn-o-mite rooms. A/C, TV, and refrigerators in its 15 rooms. 4000ptas/€24,10 per person, with bath 2000ptas/€12 extra.

see map pp. 314-315

L'EIXAMPLE

Barcelona's most beautiful accommodations lie along l'Eixample's wide, safe avenues—style is of the essence in this famously bourgeois neighborhood. Many hostels have colorfully tiled, carpeted interiors and Modernista elevators styled with wood and steel; most rooms have high ceilings and lots of light. L'Eixample is one of the more expensive places to stay in the city; as a newer neighborhood full of Modernist sights, classy restaurants, and fancy shops, it's a popular destination for tourists with a comfortable budget. L'Eixample is divided into left and right: *l'Eixample Esquerra* and *l'Eixample Dreta.*

AROUND PASSEIG DE GRÀCIA

Hostal Ciudad Condal, C. Mallorca 255 (☎93 215 10 40). M: Diagonal, just off Pg. de Gràcia, two blocks from La Pedrera. Prices reflect the generous amenities and prime location. All 11 rooms have full bath, heat, TVs, and phones; A/C soon to come. 24hr. reception. Must reserve with a credit card for late arrivals. Singles 8500ptas/€51; doubles 13,000-14,000ptas/€78-84. Prices often drop in winter. MC/V. Wheelchair accessible.

Hostal Residencia Oliva, Pg. de Gràcia 32 (☎93 488 01 62 or 93 488 17 89; fax 93 487 04 97). M: Pg. de Gràcia at the intersection with C. Diputació. Elegant wood-worked bureaus, mirrors, and a light marble floor give this hostel a classy ambiance. All 16 rooms have color TVs, and some overlook the Manzana de la Discòrdia. Reservations a must. Laundry 2000ptas/€12. Singles 3500ptas/€21; doubles 6500ptas/€39, with bath 7500ptas/€45; triple with bath 10,500ptas/€63. Cash only. Not wheelchair accessible.

Hostal Residencia Windsor, Rambla de Catalunya 84 (☎93 215 11 98). M: Pg. de Gràcia, on the corner with C. Mallorca. With carpeted hallways, gilded mirrors, and a plush TV room, this hostel lives up to its royal name. Rooms come equipped with comfy sleep sofas and heat in winter (no A/C). Singles 4500ptas/€27, with bath 5400ptas/€32,50; doubles 7200ptas/€43, with sink and shower 7800ptas/€47, with bath 8500ptas/€51; extra beds 1600ptas/€9,50 each. Cash only. Not wheelchair accessible.

Hostal Girona, C. Girona 24 (☎93 265 02 59; fax 93 265 85 32). M: Urquinaona, between C. Casp and C. d'Ausiàs Marc. A medieval twist on royal decor, with a cavernous stone entry foyer and dark carpeted and tiled hallways. Most of the 16 rooms have TVs, some have bath. Singles 3500ptas/€21; doubles 7000ptas/€42. MC/V. Not wheelchair accessible.

Hostal Residencia Neutral, Rambla de Catalunya 42 (☎93 487 63 90; fax 93 487 68 48). M: Pg. de Gràcia, on the corner of C. Consell de Cent. With Modernist mosaic floor tiles, a TV room just like home, and a classy breakfast dining area, this feels more like an old l'Eixample house than a hostel. All 28 rooms have fans, heating, and TVs. Laundry 2000ptas/€12. Continental breakfast 600ptas/€3,60. Snacks, soda, water, and beer available 24hr. for 200ptas/€1,20 each. Reservations a must, and they may ask for a credit card number. Singles 3800ptas/€23; doubles 5500ptas/€33, with bath 6500ptas/€39; triples 6800ptas/€41, with bath 7800ptas/€47. MC/V (but cash preferred). Not wheelchair accessible.

Hotel Universal, C. Aragó 281 (☎93 487 97 62). M: Pg. de Gràcia, 1 block to the left of Pg. de Gràcia when facing Pl. de Catalunya. This relaxing, tiny one-star hotel offers better bang for your buck than many hostels. All 18 rooms have full bath, heat, fans, TVs, phones, and free safes, and all but 4 have windows overlooking the street. For late-night munchies, the 24hr. reception sells water, soda, beer, cookies, and crackers for 200ptas/€1,20 each. Reservations require a credit card number and are highly recommended. Singles 5885ptas/€35,50; doubles 8025ptas/€48; triple 9415ptas/€56,60 (IVA included). MC/V. Wheelchair accessible.

Hotel Paseo de Gràcia, Pg. de Gràcia 102 (☎93 215 58 24; fax 93 215 37 24). M: Diagonal, on the corner with C. Rosselló. Double rooms here are a good deal for a 3-star hotel on the same block as La Pedrera. Beds could be softer, but the decor is definitely a step up from any hostel, especially the plush, old-fashioned waiting area. Try to get a room with a balcony on the Pg. de Gràcia. Breakfast 500ptas. Singles 8500ptas/€51; doubles 10,500ptas/€63 (IVA included). AmEx/MC/V. Wheelchair accessible.

L'EIXAMPLE DRETA

Hostal Hill, C. Provença 323 (☎93 457 88 14; hostalhill@apdo.com; www.kamimura.com), between C. Girona and C. Bailen. M: Verdaguer. A great deal for the price, with funky, Modern furniture and fans in the rooms. Guests get keys. Reservations with a credit card number. Singles 3900ptas/€23,50, with bath 4900ptas/€29,50; doubles 6000ptas/€36, with bath 7300ptas/€44. V.

Hostal San Remo, C. Bruc 20 (☎93 302 19 89; fax 93 301 07 74), on the corner with C. Ausiàs Marc. M: Urquinaona. This tiny hostel fills up quickly, with 7 rooms decked out with TVs, A/C, light blue curtains and bedspreads, spotless new furniture, and soundproof windows in the streetside rooms. Reserve at least a month ahead of time. Single 4500ptas/€27; doubles 7500ptas/€45, with bath 8500ptas/€51. Prices usually drop 1000ptas/€6 in off-season (Nov., Jan.-Feb.). MC/V.

Hostal Felipe II, C. Mallorca 329 (☎93 458 77 58), between C. Girona and C. Bailèn. M: Verdaguer. 11 well-kept rooms with lace curtains, new furniture, fans, TVs, and extremely clean bathrooms. Singles 3000ptas/€18; 5000ptas/€9 with bath; doubles 7000ptas/€42 (shower and sink only), with bath 8000ptas/€48. Cash only.

Hotel Everest, Trav. de Gràcia 441 (☎93 436 98 00), to the left of the main entrance to the Hospital de St. Pau. M: Hospital de St. Pau (see p. 82). This simple, recently redecorated hotel feels slightly more clinical than Domènech's lush Modernist creation next door, but the price isn't bad for the hotel amenities: TV, A/C, phones, heat, huge bathrooms, and even some balconies. Singles 7000ptas/€42; doubles 10,000ptas/€60; triples 13,000ptas/€78. Cash only.

L'EIXAMPLE ESQUERRA

Hostal Eden, C. Balmes 55 (☎93 452 66 20; fax 93 452 66 21; hostaleden@hotmail.com; www.eden.iberica.com). M: Pg. de Gràcia. From the Metro, walk down C. Aragó past Rambla de Catalunya to C. Balmes and turn left. Stained-glass and floral tiles mark the entrance hall of this luxurious hostel. Modern, well-kept rooms have TVs and most have big, brand-new bathrooms. Internet available in second floor lounge (100ptas/€0,60 for 5min.). May-Oct.: singles 4815ptas/€29, with bath 6420ptas/€38; doubles 5885ptas/€35, with bath 8560ptas/€50. Nov.-Apr.: singles 3815ptas/€23, with bath 5350ptas/€32; doubles 4815ptas/€29, with bath 7500ptas/€45. AmEx/MC/V.

Pensión Aribau, C. Aribau 37 (☎/fax 93 453 11 06). M: Pg. de Gràcia. From the Metro, walk down C. Aragó past Rambla de Catalunya to C. Aribau, and turn left. Basic, freshly painted

LGB ▼
BARCELONA

How *You* Doin'?

Hostal Qué Tal, C. Mallorca 290 (☎/fax 93 459 23 66; www.hotelsinbarcelona.net/ hostalquetal), near C. Bruc. M: Pg. de Gràcia or Verdaguer, in **l'Eixample Dreta.** This extremely high-quality gay and lesbian hostel has one of the best interiors of all the hostels in the city, with landscape painted walls in the coffee room, a chill, plant-filled inner patio for coffee or reading, and 14 carefully decorated rooms with their own distinctive colors and personality. Guests get keys. Morning tea and coffee included. Singles 5500ptas/ €33; doubles 8200ptas/ €49, with bath 10,500ptas/ €63; triples 11,000ptas/ €66. Cash only.

rooms have all the necessities: rather old sinks, TVs, and refrigerators. A few doubles even have A/C. Friendly owner speaks English. Singles 3500ptas/ €21; doubles with bath 7000ptas/€42; triples with bath 10,000ptas/€60. Cash only.

Hostal Cisneros, C. Aribau 54 (☎93 454 18 00). M: Pg. de Gràcia. From the Metro, walk down C. Aragó past La Rambla de Catalunya to C. Aribau. Large, bustling hostel with hotel-like standardized furniture and decorations. Aging rooms are kept very clean; all have telephones. Singles 6000ptas/€36, with bath 7000ptas/€42; doubles 8100ptas/€50, with bath 9200ptas/€56; triples with bath 15,100ptas/€90. MC/V.

Pensión Puebla de Arenoso, C. Aribau 29 (☎93 453 31 38). M: Pg. de Gràcia; walk down C. Aragó past La Rambla de Catalunya to C. Aribau and turn left. Small family-run *pensión* offers adequate rooms and clean, tiled bathrooms. Singles 3000ptas/€18; doubles 5000ptas/€30. Cash only.

Pensión Cliper, C. Rosselló 195 (☎93 218 21 88). M: Hospital Clinic; follow C. Rosselló for 4 blocks. *Pensión* in Modernist building offers large rooms with high ceilings that have seen better days. Bathrooms are functional, but not pretty. Singles 3000ptas/€18; doubles 6000ptas/€36, with bath 7000ptas/€42.

see map p. 322

BARCELONETA

Lodging is not Barceloneta's forte, and places to stay here are few and far between. A couple places can be found in the area around M: Barceloneta, but not in the neighborhood itself, which is purely residential.

Pensión Francia, C. Rera Palau 4 (☎93 319 03 76). M: Barceloneta. From Estació de França, turn left onto the main avenue (Av. Marqués de l'Argentera); C. Rera Palau is the 5th right. From the Metro, head toward town, cross Pl. Palau, and turn right onto Av. Marqués de l'Argentera; C. Rera Palau is the 2nd left. A young crowd fills the 14 rooms of this out-of-the-way gem, which features balconies and satellite TV in every room, gleaming furniture, and a friendly owner. Its location allows easy access to both the Barceloneta and La Ribera neighborhoods. Singles 3000ptas/ €18,03; doubles 4000ptas/€24,04, with bath 7500ptas/€45,08; triples with shower 8000ptas/ €48,08. MC/V.

Hostal de Mar, Plaza Palacio 19 (☎93 319 33 02; www.gargallo-hotels.com; reserve@gargallo-hotels.com), on the same street as the Museu d'Història de Catalunya, away from the port. M: Barceloneta. Private bathrooms for every room distinguish this busy hostel, which will cost you a little bit extra. Comfortable but not luxurious. Singles 7740ptas/ €46,52; doubles 9850ptas/€59,20; three people 35% extra.

see map p. 320

MONTJUÏC

The neighborhood of **Poble Sec,** at the foot of Montjuïc, is a diverse, working class community crammed with theaters and other night life options. Although this neighborhood does not have a particularly bad reputation, it is less touristed and may therefore require a little more confidence and awareness in terms of safety. The hostels listed here are close to the attractions on Las Ramblas and Montjuïc, but far enough away from the tourist hot spots to still be good deals.

◪ **Hostal-Residencia Barcelona,** C. Roser 40 (☎ 93 443 27 06; fax 93 442 50 75; hostalbarcelona@yahoo.es). M: Paral.lel, C. Roser is one block up Paral.lel in the direction of Pl. Espanya. Hostal is one block ahead on the right. Verging on hotel-like in quality and size, the Hostal Residencia has 63 rooms –all with TV and bath, most with A/C. Large, comfortable breakfast area with extensive buffet (550ptas/€3,50). Friendly, English-speaking staff. Singles 4000ptas/€24, doubles 7000ptas/€42, triples 9000ptas/€54, quadruples 11,500ptas/€70. Reservations suggested. AmEx/MC/V.

Pensión Iniesta, C. d'En Fontrodona 1 (☎93 329 10 15) M: Paral.lel, look for hostel sign across from metro on corner of Fontrodona and Paral.lel, enter on Fontrodona. Recently renovated hostel features TVs and fans in every room. Slightly cramped hallways give way to spacious rooms. July and August rates: singles 3000ptas/€18, doubles 6000ptas/€36, doubles with bath 8000ptas/€48. Off-season rates: singles 2500ptas/€15, doubles 5000ptas/€30, doubles with bath 7000ptas/€42. Each extra person in double 3000ptas/€18.

Hostal Rio de Castro, Av. Paral.lel 119 (☎93 441 30 46; hrcastro@teleline.es) Across from M: Poble Sec. Quiet, fifteen room hostel offers doubles only. All rooms have TVs, balconies, and sinks and are nicely furnished. Owner speaks English. Doubles 7000ptas/€42, doubles with bath 8560ptas/€50. MC/V.

ZONA ALTA

GRÀCIA

see maps p. 318 & 319

Locals outnumber travelers in Gràcia, a 5-10min. walk from M: Diagonal. Gràcia is Barcelona's deceptively quiet "undiscovered" quarter, but native 20-somethings have most definitely discovered Gràcia's lively weekend nightlife. The accommodations listed here are small and well kept. Last-minute arrivals might have better luck finding vacancies here during high season.

◪ **Hostal Lesseps,** C. Gran de Gràcia 239 (☎93 218 44 34; fax 93 217 11 80). M: Lesseps. Spacious, classy rooms sport red velvet wallpaper. All sixteen rooms have TV and bath, four have A/C (600ptas/€3,61 extra per day). Singles 5000ptas/€30; doubles 8000ptas/€48; triples 10,500ptas/€63; quads 12,500/€75. MC/V.

Pensión San Medín, C. Gran de Gràcia 125 (☎93 217 30 68; fax 93 415 44 10; www.sanmedin.com; info@sanmedin.com). M: Fontana. Embroidered curtains and ornate tiling adorn this family-run pension; twelve newly renovated rooms have nice furniture, sinks, and phones. Common room with TV. Owner speaks English. Singles 4000ptas/€24, with bath 5000ptas/€30; doubles 7000ptas/€42, with bath 8000ptas/€48. MC/V.

Hostal Bonavista, C. Bonavista 21 (☎93 237 37 57). M: Diagonal. Head toward the fountain at the end of Pg. de Gràcia and take the 1st right; the hostel is just off the traffic circle. Nine clean, well-kept rooms with sinks, decorated with grandmotherly knick-knacks. TV lounge. Showers 300ptas/€1,50. No reservations. Singles 2700ptas/€16; doubles 4100ptas/€24, with bath 5200ptas/€32. Cash only.

Albergue Mare de Déu de Montserrat (HI), Pg. Mare de Déu del Coll 41-51 (☎93 210 51 51; fax 93 210 07 98; www.tujuca.com), beyond Parc Güell (way out there). Bus #28 from Pl. de Catalunya and Nitbus N4 stop across the street from the hostel. Otherwise, from M: Vallcarca, walk up Av. República d'Argentina and cross the bridge at C. Viaducte de Vallcarca; signs point the way up the hill. This 180-bed government-sponsored hostel is complete with exquisite stained-glass windows and intricate tile work. Given the private woods, hilltop view of Barcelona, restaurant, Internet access, vending machines, and multiple common spaces, it is not surprising that travelers here are so friendly. **HI members only.** Breakfast included.

Sheets 350ptas/€1,80. Flexible 3-day max. stay. Reception 8am-3pm, 4:30pm-11:30pm. Lockout 10am-1:30pm. Midnight curfew, but doors open every 30min. midnight-3am. Reservations suggested. Dorms 2000ptas/€12; over 25 2700ptas/€16. AmEx/MC/V.

Hostal Valls, C. Laforja 82 (☎93 209 69 97). FGC: Muntaner. Walk downhill on C. Muntaner for 4 blocks and turn left on C. Laforja. Located in the wider streets of Gràcia, just above the L'Eixample border, Hostal Valls has several large common spaces with marble floors and modernista details. TV lounge. Singles 4400ptas/€27; doubles 7900ptas/€47, with bath 8900ptas/€53. Cash only.

Pensión Alberdi, C. Torrent de l'Olla 95 (☎93 217 30 25). M: Diagonal, walk up C. Gran de Gràcia, turn right on Trav. de Gràcia and left on C. Torrent de l'Olla, hostal is two blocks up on the left. 14 sparse rooms; very close to the Pl.del Sol. Singles 2500ptas/€15; doubles with bath 5000ptas/€30. Discounts for long stays. Cash only.

Aparthotel Silver, C. Bretón de los Herreros 26 (☎93 218 91 00; www.hotelsilver.com; silver@comfortable.com) M: Fontana, walk downhill on C. Gran de Gràcia for one block, turn right on C. Bretón de los Herreros, Aparthotel is on your right at the end of the block. Catering to short term tourists and longer term residents, Aparthotel Silver boasts 49 rooms, each with A/C, bath, TV, phone, and cleverly concealed mini-kitchens. Price range includes "inside" rooms (singles 9400ptas/€56,49; doubles 9900ptas/€59,50), standard rooms (singles 9900ptas/€59,50; doubles 10900ptas/€65,51; with terrace singles 10400ptas/€62,50; doubles 11400ptas/€68,5), and large rooms with terrace (singles 12500ptas/€75,12; doubles 13500ptas/€81,13). A third person can be added to the large rooms with terrace and the standard rooms for 2600ptas/€15,62 per day. AmEx/MC/V. Wheelchair accessible.

SANTS

The neighborhood around Sants-Estació is not Barcelona's most exciting, but there is plenty of safe lodging for late-night arrivals, and it is well connected by Metro to Pl. de Catalunya and Las Ramblas. If the following cheap beds are all taken, there are numerous three-star hotels in the area as well, for about double these prices. Try the **Hotel Roma,** Av. Roma 31, or **Hotel Onix,** C. Llanca 30.

Hostal Sofia, Av. Roma 1-3 (☎93 419 50 40; fax 93 430 69 43). Directly across from the front of the station; cross C. Numància on the left and look up for the blue sign. A sun-lit, breezy hostel with 18 rooms heated in winter. TVs and safes available. Closed Dec. 24-26 and July-Aug. Singles 5000ptas/€30, with bath 7000ptas/€42; doubles 8000ptas/€48, with bath 9000-10,000ptas/€54-60; triples 9000ptas/€54. Sept.-June singles 4000-5000ptas/€24-30, with bath 6000-7000ptas/€36-42; doubles 6000ptas/€36, with bath 7000-8000ptas/€42-48; triples 8000ptas/€48. MC/V. Wheelchair accessible.

Hostal Béjar, C. Béjar 36-38 (☎93 325 59 53). Exit the front of the station to the right, onto C. Rector Triado, go immediately left onto C. Mallorca, and then right on C. Béjar. Two private houses turned hostel; the annex boasts a cool, plant-lined interior stairwell. All 19 rooms have desks and heaters, most have fans, and some have balconies. Singles 3500ptas/€21; doubles 6000ptas/€36, with bath 7000ptas/€42; fold-out beds (to create triples or quads) 1500ptas/€9 each. MC/V. Wheelchair accessible.

Hostal Residencia Sants, C. Antoni de Campany 82 (☎93 331 37 00; fax 93 421 68 64). Leave the station from the back and follow C. Antoni through Pl. Sants, across C. Sants. A huge, somewhat sterile hostel with cramped hallways but a convenient location. All 75 rooms have heat but no A/C. Laundry service available. Singles 2900ptas/€17,5, with bath 3500ptas/€21; doubles 4600ptas/€27,5, with bath 5500ptas/€33. MC/V. Wheelchair accessible.

Pensió Regar, Av. Roma 5-7 (☎93 331 37 00), next to Hostal Sofia. A family home with 6 rented-out bedrooms and shared bathrooms. Space is tight and they only take reservations if you pay over the phone, but you can store luggage (500ptas/€3) and shower (1000ptas/€6) without a room. No heat or A/C. Laundry 1500ptas/€9. Single 4000ptas/€24; doubles 6000ptas/€36; triple 8000ptas/€48; quad 10,000ptas/€60. MC/V. Not wheelchair accessible.

Hotel Transit, C. Rector Triado 82 (☎93 424 60 13), the street immediately to the right out of the front of the station. 33 bare-bones, well-sanitized rooms with heat, bath, phones, and TVs. Doubles and triples have A/C. Cheapest hotel in area, but hostels offer better value. Singles 6420ptas/€38,50; doubles 9630ptas/€58; triples 11770ptas/€71. AmEx/MC/V. Wheelchair accessible.

CAMPING

Although there are no campsites within the city, intercity buses (200ptas/€1,20) run to all the following locations in 20-45 minutes. For more info, contact the **Associació de Càmpings de Barcelona,** Gran Vía de les Corts Catalanes 608 (☎93 412 59 55).

El Toro Bravo, Autovía de Castelldefells km 11(☎93 637 34 62; fax 93 637 21 15; info@eltorobravo.com; www.eltorobravo.com). Take bus L95 (210ptas) from Pl. de Catalunya to the campsite, 11km south. Beach access, laundry facilities, currency exchange, pool, 3 bars, and supermarket. Possibility for long-term stays. Reception 8am-7pm. Sept. 1-June 14 725ptas/€4,36 per person, 775ptas/€4,66 per site, 725ptas/€4,36 per car, 575ptas/€3,46 electricity charge. June 15-Aug. 31 760ptas/€4,57 per person, 810ptas/€4,87 per site, 760ptas/€4,57 per car, 575 ptas/€3,46 electricity charge. IVA tax not included. AmEx/MC/V.

Filipinas, Autovía de Castelldefells km 12 (☎93 65 828 95; fax 93 658 17 91), 1km down the road from El Toro Bravo, accessible by bus L95. Same prices and services as El Toro Bravo. AmEx/MC/V.

INSIDE

Living in Barcelona

Most people pass through Barcelona on vacation, but for people who want to stretch their stay out to a few months or more, there are plenty of options. Unfortunately, some concerns, like finding a job and an apartment, are easier done in Barcelona than from home. For an extensive listing of "off-the-beaten-track" and specialty travel opportunities, such as work or study, try the **Specialty Travel Index,** 305 San Anselmo Ave., #313, San Anselmo, CA 94960, USA (☎ 888-624-4030 or 415-455-1643; www.specialtytravel.com; US$6). Transitions Abroad (www.transabroad.com) publishes a bimonthly on-line newsletter for work, study, and specialized travel abroad.

LONG-TERM VISAS

Any stay of 90 days in Spain requires a visa; what you are doing with your time in Spain will dictate what sort of a visa you get. It is always better to get these papers in advance; making arrangements for a longer stay while you are already in Spain will entail alot of waiting in line and angry and intimidating visa personnel who will not be pleased you didn't do this from your home country. Spain has good border control, and if you are traveling back and forth from Spain in a period of over 90 days, you will not be permitted to re-enter the country if you do not have the appropriate visas. You will also get in serious trouble if a police officer ever asks to see your passport, which they have the right to do at any moment. Getting these visas is straight-forward, but is also usually a hassle. Call to make sure you have all the appropriate documents before going to the consulate, or you'll have to make several trips. The hardest times to get appointment are during the study-abroad crunch months of September and January; if you'll need a visa then, call for an appointment at least a month in advance.

Once you have your visa and have arrived in Spain, you will have to register at the *comisaria* (police station) immigration authority for an alien residency identification card. All persons staying in Spain more than 90 days must complete this process IN ADDITION TO having already obtained their visa. Your job/program/school will have to file papers with the *comisaria* regarding you, and will be able to direct you to the *comisaria* in question. Your experience there will entail giving fingerprints, a photo, and a signature; in return you will get an ID. Be prepared to wait in line.

STUDYING

Barcelona is a popular destination for study abroad because of its wealth of programs and its proximity to the rest of Europe. Depending on the needs and desires of a given student, many options are available.

For students with strong Spanish or Catalan skills, enrollment directly in a Spanish University in Barcelona may be the best option. The instructional language at public universities in Spain is a controversial point in regions like Catalunya and País Vasco, which have their own languages. Despite what they themselves might prefer, Catalan professors at public universities in Catalunya are required to offer classes in Spanish—not Catalan—if even one student in the class is uncomfortable with Catalan. Consequently, the choice between enrolling in a public or a private university may depend on whether a student wants to study Spanish or Catalan.

Study abroad programs, designed for foreign students, are another option for study in Barcelona, and are particularly popular for summer study. Some study abroad programs are affiliated with universities in Barcelona and allow students to take classes directly through the university; others are more self-contained programs for foreigners, with instruction in various combinations of English and Spanish, or only Spanish. These programs may be affiliated with an American university, but open to other students as well. While these programs have a reputation for creating self-contained social circles void of Spanish nationals, they often offer great benefits. They usually arrange housing, with a family or in a dorm, and excursions, both within the city and through Spain. Some also offer an internship placement program, for part-time work to complement class work. Barcelona is also a fantastic place to study art; most study-abroad programs will offer an art component, and students with a stronger interest can enroll directly in an art school.

Study abroad students will need to contact individual programs and universities to apply to them directly and find the requirements for their stay. Study for 90 days or more requires a student visa, procured at least two months in advance (see p. 281); the program in question should provide all the necessary and abundant paperwork.

STUDY VISAS

To obtain a study visa for Spain, you need to have arranged enrollment in a program. Most study abroad and language programs are accustomed to dealing with foreign students, and will send you everything you need for your visa automatically; if you are enrolling directly in a Spanish university, getting your visa may require a little more initiative on your part. At the very least, you should be prepared to present the comprehensive visa application form (best filled out in advance), your passport, passport photos, a medical letter, two letters from your institution verifying that you will be enrolled full-time there, and copious amounts of copies of these documents. In the interest of wasting as little time as possible, it is imperative that you discuss visa requirements both with your program and with your resident Spanish consulate. Be prepared that most consulates are only open in the morning and that some may require you to file for a visa in person, no matter how inconvenient that may be.

UNIVERSITIES

Most American undergraduates enroll in programs sponsored by US universities. Those fluent in Spanish may find it cheaper to enroll directly in the **University of Barcelona** (see below), though getting credit may be more difficult.

Other schools that offer study abroad programs to foreigners are listed below. Websites such as www.studyabroad.com are excellent resources, as are the following books, available at most libraries and many university career/study abroad offices: *Academic Year Abroad 2001-2002* (Institute of International Education Books; US$47); *Vacation Study Abroad 2001-2002* (Institute of International Education Books; US$43); and the encyclopedic *Peterson's Study Abroad* and *Summer Study Abroad 2002* (Peterson's; US$30 each).

Arcadia University for Education Abroad, 450 S. Easton Rd., Glenside, PA 19038, USA (☎866-927-2234; www.arcadia.edu/cea). Operates programs in Barcelona. Costs range from $2400 (summer) to $20,000 (full-year).

Central College Abroad, Office of International Education, 812 University, Pella, IA 50219, USA (☎800-

Art School, Pl. Veronica

A Bite to Eat in the Sun

Hanging Out on C. Portaferrisa

831-3629 or 641-628-5284; studyabroad.com/central). Offers semester- and year-long programs in Barcelona. US$25 application fee.

School for International Training, College Semester Abroad, Admissions, Kipling Rd., P.O. Box 676, Brattleboro, VT 05302, USA (☎800-336-1616 or 802-258-3267; www.sit.edu). Semester- and year-long programs in Barcelona run US$10,600-13,700. Also runs the **Experiment in International Living** (☎800-345-2929; fax 802-258-3428; eil@worldlearning.org), 3- to 5-week summer programs that offer high-school students cross-cultural homestays, community service, ecological adventure, and language training in Barcelona and cost US$1900-5000.

International Association for the Exchange of Students for Technical Experience (IAESTE), 10400 Little Patuxent Pkwy. #250, Columbia, MD 21044-3510, USA (☎410-997-2200; www.aipt.org). 8- to 12-week programs in Spain for college students who have completed 2 years of technical study. US$25 application fee.

International Studies Abroad, 901 W. 24th, Austin, TX 78705, USA (☎800-580-8826; www.studiesabroad.com). Semester programs at the University of Barcelona. Inquire for costs.

University of Barcelona (☎93 403 53 79; fax 93 403 53 87; ori-dir@pu.ges.ub.es). For academic exchange programs within the EU, contact ☎93 404 53 86; fax 93 403 53 87; becsoc@pu.ges.ub.es. For academic exchange programs outside of the EU, ☎93 403 53 81; fax 93 403 53 87; elo@pu.ges.ub.es. Foreign students looking for information about enrolling in the University of Barcelona and the procedure for obtaining a student visa, ☎93 403 55 62; fax 93 403 53 87; gema@pu.ges.ub.es.

LANGUAGE SCHOOLS

These programs are run by foreign universities, independent international or local organizations, and divisions of local universities. They generally cost anywhere from US$500 to US$15,000, depending on length and if they include lodging, food, and side trips.

Eurocentres, 101 N. Union St. #300, Alexandria, VA 22314, USA (☎703-684-1494; fax 684-1495; www.eurocentres.com) or in Europe, Head Office, Seestr. 247, CH-8038 Zurich, Switzerland (☎41 1 485 50 40; fax 481 61 24; info@eurocentres.com). Language programs for beginning to advanced students with homestays in Barcelona.

Language Immersion Institute, 75 South Manheim Blvd., SUNY-New Paltz, New Paltz, NY 12561, USA (☎914-257-3500; www.newpaltz.edu/lii). 2-week summer language courses and other programs in Barcelona in Spanish. Program fees are about US$295 for a weekend or US$750 per 2 weeks.

S.O.L. Barcelona, Entenza 320, ent. 1a, 08029 Barcelona, Spain (☎93 405 12 00; www.solbarcelona.com/eng/home_eng.htm). Classes in business Spanish and preparation for the D.E.L.E. exam for Spanish proficiency. Program fee US$500.

Consorci per a la Normalització Lingüística, C. Mallorca 272, 8a planta, 08037 Barcelona, Spain (☎93 272 31 00; www.cpnl.org/presentacio/welcome-t.htm). Organizes programs for adults learning Catalan.

WORKING & VOLUNTEERING

Shopper with Cell Phone

WORK PERMITS

American, Canadian, South African, and Australian citizens need a work visa to work in Spain. Those desiring such a visa should contact the Spanish consulate in the country for the exact requirements, which include: a passport, valid for at least six months to come, a job offer in Spain filed at the Ministry of Labor in Spain, a letter of good conduct from the police department in the city of original residence, a letter from a physician affirming good health and freedom from addiction, four passport photos, and approximately US$45. This visas may take four months or more to process, although certain cases may be rushed; call the consulate as many times as you have to make sure you have the necessary paperwork or you will have to wait and wait and wait. European Union citizens can work in Spain, and if your parents were born in an EU country, you may be able to claim the right to a work permit.

Little Girl at Poble Espanyol

OPTIONS FOR WORK

Popular temporary jobs for foreigners include au pair, teaching English, or waiting tables. Irish pubs are almost always staffed with English-speaking expats, and the demands for English tutors is high. A good way to line up a more permanent job from home is to get a job with an international corporation with offices in Barcelona; large consulting and investment banking firms generally have offices abroad.

The fact of the matter is that it is much easier to line up a job in Spain when you are already there; invaluable resources like "help wanted" signs just aren't visible from other countries, and the Internet can only get you so far. Get your

Birdcage in Window

hands on a copy of Catalunya's leading newspaper, *La Vanguardia*, to look at jobs ads; other publications are *El Periódico* and the English-language *Barcelona Metropolitan*.

For US college students, recent graduates, and young adults, the simplest way to get legal work permission to work abroad is through **Council Exchanges Work Abroad Programs.** Fees are from US$300-425. Council Exchanges can help obtain a three- to six-month work permit/visa and also provides assistance finding jobs and housing.

AU PAIR

interExchange, 161 Sixth Ave., New York, NY 10013 (☎212-924-0446; fax 924-0575; info@interexchange.org, www.interexchange.org).

Childcare International, Ltd., Trafalgar House, Grenville Pl., London NW7 3SA (☎+44 20-8906-3116; fax 8906-3461; www.childint.co.uk). UK£100 application fee.

TEACHING ENGLISH

International Schools Services, Educational Staffing Program, P.O. Box 5910, Princeton, NJ 08543, USA (☎609-452-0990; www.iss.edu). Recruits teachers and administrators for American and English schools in Barcelona. US$150 program fee.

Office of Overseas Schools, US Department of State, Room H328, SA-1, Washington, D.C. 20522 (☎202-261-8200; fax 261-8224; www.state.gov/www/about_state/schools/). Keeps a comprehensive list of schools abroad and agencies that arrange placement for Americans to teach abroad.

Teach Abroad (www.teachabroad.com). Posts listings of available positions for English-speaking instructors.

INTERNSHIPS

International Internships (www.internabroad.com). A webpage that searches international internship postings and directs you to links.

ITC Barcelona, Mediterrani, Estudis Superiors de Turisme, Edifici Mediterrani, Rocafort 104, 08015 Barcelona, Spain (☎800 915 55 40;www.itc-training.com). Arranges internships in communications, English as a Second Language, tourism, and other fields. US$1500 tuition; paid positions with benefits.

VOLUNTEERING

Volunteer jobs are readily available, and many provide room and board in exchange for labor. You can sometimes avoid high application fees by contacting the individual work camps directly.

Service Civil International Voluntary Service (SCI-IVS), 814 NE 40th St., Seattle, WA 98105, USA (☎/fax 206-545-6585; www.sci-ivs.org). Arranges placement in work camps in Barcelona for those 18+. Registration fee US$65-150.

Volunteers for Peace, 1034 Tiffany Rd., Belmont, VT 05730, USA (☎802-259-2759; www.vfp.org). Arranges placement in work camps in Spain. Annual *International Work Camp Directory* US$20. Registration fee US$200. Free newsletter.

Volunteer Abroad (www.volunteerabroad.com). A webpage that posts and searches listings of volunteer opportunities worldwide. In Barcelona and Spain, these opportunities usually involve teaching English.

LONG-TERM ACCOMMODATIONS

Care to stay a while? With a little research, footwork, and phone-calling, a person can find a place in Barcelona without too much trouble. Securing a *piso* (apartment) from outside the city can be difficult, however, so better to book a hostel for the first week of hunting. The easiest route is to check the many **bulletin boards** to look for possible sublets, often with English-speaking expats. For those seeking a private apartment, the city's **accommodation agencies** are a big help, and can refer you to other sources of information. The city **newspapers** are another option; *La Vanguardia* has a large classified section. Depending on the location and the apartment, good prices range from 30,000ptas/€180 to 50,000ptas/€300 per person per month. There are plenty of short-term establishments that also cater to long-term guests. Check the Accommodations chapter for info on the following places: Aparthotel Silver (p. 276), El Toro Bravo (p. 277), Pensión Alberdi (p. 276), and Pensión Fani (p. 270).

Expect to pay, in addition, an agency fee (where applicable) and monthly utilities. For convenience to public transportation and services, reasonable rents, and neighborhood safety, ⬛l'Eixample is a good all-around choice.

BULLETIN BOARDS

International House, C. Trafalgar 14 (☎93 268 45 11, 93 268 02 39.), M: Urquinaona. On the 2nd floor. Open 9am-9pm.

Centre d'Informació Assesorament per a Joves (CIAJ), C. Ferrán 32 (☎93 402 78 00; www.bcn.es/ciaj), off Las Ramblas. M: Liceu. Open M-F 10am-2pm and 4-8pm.

Universitat de Barcelona, Pl. Universitat (☎93 402 11 00). M: Universitat. Open M-F 9am-10pm.

RENTAL AGENCIES

⬛ **Habit Servei,** C. Muntaner 200 (☎93 240 50 23, fax 93 414 54 25; www.habitservei.com; : habitservei@habitservei.com). M: Hospital Clinic. The helpful, patient staff speaks English, and understands if you know nothing about renting an apartment in Spain. Wide price ranges and lengths of stay (including homestays and shared apartments), according to the client's needs. Open M-Sa 9am-2pm and 3:30-7pm.

Barcelona Allotjament, C. Pelai 12 (☎93 268 43 57; www.barcelona-allotjament.com), off Pl. de Catalunya. M: Catalunya. Reasonably priced apartments throughout the city. Open M-F 10am-2pm.

Habitatge Jove, C. Calàbria 147 (☎93 483 83 92; www.habitatgejove.com). M: Rocafort. The multilingual web site can locate an apartment before you even visit the office, at an excellent price—often no more than 3000ptas/€18 a person per month. The catch? Minimum length of rental is one year. M-F Open 10am-1pm, 3:30-5pm.

HOME EXCHANGES & HOME RENTALS

Home exchange offers the traveler various types of homes (houses, apartments, condominiums, villas, even castles in some cases), plus the opportunity to live like a native and to cut down on accommodation fees. For more information, contact **HomeExchange.Com** (☎805-898-9660; www.homeexchange.com), **Intervac International Home Exchange** (93 453 31 71; www.inter-

Back Doors

Feeding Pigeons in Pl. Calalunya

View of the Street

vac.com), or **The Invented City: International Home Exchange** (US ☎ 800- 788-CITY, elsewhere US ☎+1 415-252-1141; www.invented-city.com). **Home rentals** are more expensive than exchanges, but they can be cheaper than comparably serviced hotels. Both home exchanges and rentals are ideal for families with children or travelers with special dietary needs; you often get your own kitchen, maid service, TV, and telephones.

MONEY MATTERS

The quintessential Catalan bank is Caixa Catalunya (www.laCaixa.es), better known simply as **la Caixa**—the Bank. Its distinctive logo, a blue star next to red and yellow dots, was designed by none other than Joan Miró, the late Catalan artist. The numbers on its ATM machines often (though not always) include the corresponding letters—a Spanish rarity which is a huge help to password-dependent American users. Special Caixa ATM machine/computers, called **ServiCaixa,** use ATM cards to sell tickets to a wide list of events. Buy tickets here to the opera, FCB matches, movies, and the zoo, just to name a few of the choices. Other, lower-profile banks found in the Barcelona area include **BancSabadell, Caixa Penedès,** and **Banesto.**

HEALTH & FITNESS

MEDICAL CARE

For a complete listing of hospitals in Barcelona, check the **Service Directory,** p. 291.

Should you require a house call for a condition not requiring hospitalization, contact the appropriate number from the list of emergency numbers listed in the **Service Directory,** p. 291. Any hospital should be able to refer you to a dentist, optometrist, or opthamologist. Request documentation (including diagnoses) and receipts to submit to your home insurance company for reimbursement.

EU citizens can get reciprocal health benefits, entitling them to a practitioner registered with the state system, by filling out a E111 or E112 form before departure; this is available at most major post offices. They will generally treat you whether or not you can pay in advance. EU citizens studying in Spain also qualify for long-term care. Other travelers should ensure they have adequate medical insurance before leaving; if your regular insurance policy does not cover travel abroad, you may wish to purchase additional coverage (see **Planning your trip,** p. 250). With the exception of Medicare, most health insurance plans cover members' medical emergencies during trips abroad; check with your insurance carrier to be sure.

If you need a **doctor** *(un metge/un médico)*, call the local hospital for a list of local practitioners. If you are receiving reciprocal health care, make sure you call a doctor who will be linked to the state health care system. Contact your health provider for information regarding charges that may be incurred. Note that the same medicines may have different names in Spain than in your home country; check with your doctor before you leave.

GYMS

Active people will also want to check out the other athletic options, such as biking and horseback riding listed in **Entertainment,** p. 165.

Club Natació Atlètic-Barceloneta, Plaça del Mar, Pg. Joan de Borbo (☎93 221 00 10), across the street from the Torre San Sebastià cable car tower. This athletic club, on Platje San Sebastià, offers outdoor and indoor pools in addition to beach access, sauna, jacuzzi, and a full weightroom. Memberships start at 4055ptas/€24,37a month, but non-members can enter for 1075ptas/€6,46 a visit.

Nova-Icària Sports Club, Av. Icària 167 (☎93 221 55 80), on the corner of C. Arquitecte Sert. A full-service sports club, with weight lifting, aerobics, a pool, tennis courts, basketball courts, and more. Membership 5135ptas/€30,86 per month, but non-members can pay each time they visit and use anything in the club (1050ptas/€6,31). Open M-F 7am-11pm, Sa 8am-11pm, Su 8am-4pm, closed holidays.

Club Sant Jordi, C. París 114 (☎93 410 92 61). M: Sants. Passes available for other facilities, including sauna, weights, and stairmaster. Bring your passport. Pool 515ptas/€3,10 per hr. Open M-F 7am-10pm, Sa 8am-6pm, Su and holidays 9am-2pm. Closed Aug. 1-15.

Piscines Bernat Picornell, Av. Estadi 30-40 (☎93 423 40 41; fax 93 426 78 18; www.bcn.es/picornell), to the right when facing the stadium. Test your swimming mettle in the Olympic pools—two gorgeous facilities nestled in stadium seating. A favorite for families and sunbathers. 700ptas/€4 for outdoor pool, 1300ptas/€7,80 for workout facilities including sauna, massage parlor, and gym. Outdoor pool open M-Sa 9am-9pm and Su 9am-8pm. Workout facilities open M-F 7am-midnight, Sa 7am-9pm and Su 7:30am-8pm.

Velodróm, Pg. Vall d'Hebron 185-201 (☎93 427 91 42). M: Montbau. Face the Jardins Pedro Muñez Seco upon leaving M: Montbau, turn left, cross the Ronda de Dalt at the first opportunity and turn left; the Velodróm will be ahead on your right. Originally the Olympic cycling center, the Velodróm has since been converted into a community sports center. Annual membership is the only way to gain access; if you are interested, visit the offices at entrance 16 (up and around to the right of the building). Yearly dues 6000ptas/€36.Facilities include a space for parties on the roof, soccer fields, basketball courts, the cycling track, a snack bar, and organized tournaments. Open M 4-11pm, Tu-F 4-6pm and 8:30-11pm. Not wheelchair accessible.

Centre Muncipal d'Esports, Pg. Vall d'Hebron 166 (☎93 428 39 52). M: Montbau. Same directions as Velodróm, but the center will be on the left. The tennis center offers playing courts and a pool to members; non-members pay per visit to use the pool. Municipal sports center has a variety of facilities, including a gym, pool, racquetball, yoga, and more. Monthly dues 3100-4000ptas/€18-24. Single use 900ptas/€5,50; children and over 65 625ptas/€3,50. Open M-F 7am-11:30pm, Sa 9am-8pm, Su 9am-3pm. Wheelchair accessible.

Service Directory

ACCOMMODATIONS

Rental Agencies: Barcelona Allotjament, C. Pelai 12 (☎93 268 43 57; www.barcelona-allotjament.com) M: Catalunya. Open M-F 10am-2pm.

▨ **Habit Servei,** C. Muntaner 200 (☎93 240 50 23, fax 93 414 54 25; www.habitservei.com; habitservei@habitservei.com). M: Hospital Clinic. Open M-Sa 9am-2pm, 3:30-7pm.

Habitatge Jove, C. Calàbria 147 (☎93 483 83 92; www.habitatgejove.com). M: Rocafort. Multi-lingual web site can locate cheap pads—often no more than 3000ptas/€18 a person per month. Minimum rental contract one year. M-F Open 10am-1pm, 3:30-5pm.

Bulletin Boards: Centre d'Informació Assesorament per a Joves (CIAJ), C. Ferrán 32 (☎93 402 78 00; www.bcn.es/ciaj), off Las Ramblas. M: Liceu. Open M-F 10am-2pm and 4-8pm.

International House, C. Trafalgar 14, 2nd floor (☎93 268 45 11 or 93 268 02 39), M: Urquinaona. Open 9am-9pm.

Universitat de Barcelona, Pl. Universitat (☎93 402 11 00). M: Universitat. Open M-F 9am-10pm.

Home Exchange: HomeExchange.Com (☎805-898-9660; www.homeexchange.com).

Intervac International Home Exchange (93 453 31 71; www.intervac.com).

The Invented City: International Home Exchange (US ☎800-788-CITY, elsewhere US ☎+1 415-252-1141; www.invented-city.com).

AIRLINES

see also **Transportation Services,** p. 294.

Air Europa, (24hr. reservation and info ☎902 40 15 01; www.air-europa.com).

British Airways, El Prat de Llobregat Airport (☎93 298 34 55, 24hr. reservation and info ☎02 11 13 33; open 6am-7pm).

Delta (24hr. reservation and info ☎901 116 946; www.delta-air.com).

Easy Jet (24hr. reservation and info ☎902 299 992; www.easyjet.com)

Iberia/Aviaco, Pg. de Gràcia 30 (☎93 401 32 82; 24hr. reservation and info ☎902 40 05 00). Student discounts.

Spanair, Pg. de Gràcia 57 (☎93 216 4626; 24hr. reservation and info ☎902 13 14 15) offers fares that are often cheaper than Iberia.

AMERICAN EXPRESS

American Express, Pg. de Gràcia 101 (24hr. traveler's checks info ☎900 994 426). M: Diagonal. Open M-F 9:30am-6pm, Sa 10am-noon. Another office is located on Las Ramblas 74 (☎93 301 11 66). Open daily 9am-8pm.

BANKS

Banco de Espanya, Pl. de Catalunya 17 (☎93 482 47 00) and the **American Express** office (see above) charge no commission on traveler's checks.

La Caixa, Av. del Marquès de Comilla 6-8 (☎902 223 040). Phone lines open M-F 10am-8pm; call for hours of specific branches .

BICYCLE AND MOPED RENTAL

Vanguard Rent a Car, C. Londres 31 (☎93 439 38 80). Mopeds start at Tu-Th 4760ptas/€28 per day, F-M 7280ptas/€49,50 per day. Two person motos start at 6200ptas/€37,20 per weekday. Insurance, helmet, and IVA included. Must be 19, with identification, to rent.

Over-Rent S. A., Av. Josep Terradellas 42 (☎93 405 26 60). Motorcycles for rent 2500ptas/€15 per day, or 8200ptas/€49,20 per day. Minimum age of 23 to rent; call ahead to reserve one.

BUSES

see also **Transportation Services,** p. 294.

Alsa, (☎902 422 242; www.alsa.es), a division of Enatcar.

Enatcar, Estació Nord (☎902 422 242; www.enatcar.es). Open daily 7am-1am.

Linebús, Estació Nord (☎93 265 07 00). Discounts for travelers under 26 and over 60. Open M-F 8am-2pm and 3-8pm, Sa 8:30am-1:30pm and 4:30-8pm.

Sarfa, Estació Nord (☎902 30 20 25; www.sarfa.com). Open daily 8am-8:30pm.

CAR RENTAL

Avis/Auto Europe, Casanova 209 (☎93 209 95 33). Will rent to ages 21-25 for an additional fee of about US$5 a day.

Budget, Av. Josep Tarradellas 35 (☎93 410 25 08). Will not rent to under 25. Branch in El Prat de Llobregat airport (see p. 294).

Docar, C. Montnegre 18 (24hr. ☎93 439 81 19). M: Les Corts. Free delivery and pickup. From 2300ptas/€13,80 per day with 1500ptas/€9 insurance, 25ptas/€0,15 per km. Open M-F 8:30am-2pm and 3:30-8pm, Sa 9am-2pm.

Hertz, C. Tuset 10 (☎93 217 8076). M: Diagonal or FCG: Gràcia. Branch in El Prat de Llobregat airport (☎93 298 3637; see p. 294).

Tot Car, C. Berlín 97 (☎93 430 01 98). Free delivery and pickup. From 4500ptas/€27 per day, 21ptas/€0,13 per km. Insurance included. Open M-F 8am-2pm and 3-8pm, Sa 9am-1pm.

CLINICS

see also **Hospitals,** p. 291.

Barcelona Centro Médico (BCM), Av. Diagonal 612, 2nd fl., #14 (☎93 414 06 43), M: Maria Cristina. Coordinates referrals, including for foreigners.

CRISIS AND HELP LINES

Crisis Lines: Oficina Permanente de Atención Social (24hr. toll-free ☎93 319 00 42).

DISABILITY RESOURCES

Ajuntament, Pl. Sant Miquel. Information office has a map of wheelchair accessible routes and establishments. (Also available at TMB office in the Universitat Metro.)

Institut Municipal de Disminuits, C. Llacuna 171 (☎ 93 291 84 00). Provides specific information on accessibility of sites, restaurants, etc.

Taxi: ☎93 420 80 88.

EMBASSIES AND CONSULATES

American Consulate, Pg. Reina Elisenda de Montcada 23 (☎93 280 22 27; fax 93 280 61 75; www.embusa.es). FCG: Reina Elisenda.

Australian Consulate, Gran Via Carlos III 98, 9a piso (☎93 330 94 96; fax 93 411

0494; www.embaustralia.es/hours.htm). M: Maria Cristina.

British Consulate, Edificio Torre de Barcelona, Av. Diagonal 477 (☎93 366 62 00; fax 93 366 62 21; www.fco.gov.uk/directory/posts.asp?SM). M: Hospital Clinic.

Canadian Consulate, Elisenda de Pinós 10 (☎93 204 27 00; fax 93 204 27 01; www.canada-es.org/english/embassy.html). FCG: Reina Elisenda.

Irish Consulate, Gran Via Carlos III 94 (☎93 451 90 21; fax 93 411 29 21; www.goireland.com/low/visitorsguide/irembassies.html). M: Maria Cristina.

New Zealand Consulate, Trav. de Gràcia 64 (☎93 209 03 99; fax 93 209 08 90).

South African Consulate, C. Teodora Lamadrid 7 (☎93 418 6445; fax 93 418 0538; ww.link2southafrica.com).

EMERGENCY SERVICES

see also **Clinics** (p. 290), **Crisis Lines** (p. 290), and **Hospitals** (p. 291).

Emergency: ☎112

Local Police: ☎092

National police: ☎091

Medical: ☎061.

Police: Las Ramblas, 43 (☎93 344 13 00), across from Pl. Reial and next to C. Nou de La Rambla. M: Liceu. Tourists in need of assistance should visit the department labeled "Tourist attention", where they will find helpful multilingual officers. Open 24hr., tourist assistance open 8am-2am. Local Barcelona police coordinate with national police in emergency situations. The police also have offices beneath the Plaza de Catalunya on the side facing the Banco Nacional, and at the Barcelona-Nord bus station.

GAY AND LESBIAN SERVICES

Cómplices, C. Cervantes 2 (☎93 412 72 83). M: Liceu. From C. Ferrán, take a left onto C. Avinyó and then the 2nd left. A gay and lesbian bookstore with publications in English and Spanish as well as a decent selection of gay and lesbian films. Also provides an **informative map** of Barcelona's gay and lesbian bars and discos. Open M-F 10:30am-8:30pm, Sa noon-8:30pm.

HEALTH AND FITNESS

Centre Muncipal d'Esports, Pg. Vall d'Hebron 166 (☎93 428 39 52). M: Montbau. Same directions as Velodróm, but the center will be on the left. Open M-F 7am-

11:30pm, Sa 9am-8pm, Su 9am-3pm. Monthly dues 3100-4000ptas/€18-24. Single use 900ptas/€5,50; children and over 65 625ptas/€3,50. Wheelchair accessible.

Centre Municipal de Tennis, Pg. de Vall d'Hebron 178 (☎93 427 55 00). Same directions as Velodróm, but the tennis center will be on the left. Monthly membership 3670-6990ptas/€22-42, plus 5500ptas/€33 joining fee. Pool 1000ptas/€6 per day; under 12 600ptas/€3,50.

Club Natació Atlètic-Barceloneta, Pl. del Mar, Pg. Joan de Borbo. (☎93 221 00 10), across the street from the Torre San Sebastià cable car tower. Memberships start at 4055ptas/€24,37 per month; non-members 1075ptas /€6,46 per visit.

Club Sant Jordi, C. París 114 (☎93 410 92 61). M: Sants. Open M-F 7am-10pm, Sa 8am-6pm, Su and holidays 9am-2pm. Pool 515ptas/€3,10 per hr., closed Aug. 1-15.

Nova-Icària Sports Club, Av. Icària 167 (☎93 221 55 80), on the corner of C. Arquitecte Sert. A full-service sports club, with weight lifting, aerobics, a pool, tennis courts, basketball courts, and more. Membership costs 5135ptas/€30,86 per month, but non-members can pay each time they visit and use anything in the club (1050ptas/€6,31). Open M-F 7am-11pm, Sa 8am-11pm, Su 8am-4pm, closed holidays.

Piscines Bernat Picornell, Av. Estadi 30-40 (☎93 423 40 41; fax 93 426 78 18; www.bcn.es/picornell), to the right when facing the stadium. Outdoor pool open M-Sa 9am-9pm and Su 9am-8pm. Workout facilities open M-F 7am-midnight, Sa 7am-9pm and Su 7:30am-8pm.

Velodróm, Pg. Vall d'Hebron 185-201 (☎93 427 91 42). M: Montbau. Face the Jardins Pedro Muñez Seco upon leaving M: Montbau, turn left, cross the Ronda de Dalt at the first opportunity and turn left; the Velodróm will be ahead on your right. Open M 4-11pm, Tu-F 4-6pm and 8:30-11pm. Yearly dues 6000ptas/€36. Not wheelchair accessible.

HOSPITALS

Hospital Clinic, Villarroel 170 (☎93 227 54 00). M: Hospital Clinic. Main entrance at the intersection of C. Roselló and C. Casanova.

Hospital de la Santa Creu i Sant Pau (☎93 291 90 00, emergency ☎93 291 91 91), at the intersection of C. Cartagena and C. Sant Antoni Moria Claret. M: Hospital de Sant Pau.

Hospital Vall d' Hebron (☎93 274 60 00) M: Vall d'Hebron.

INTERNET ACCESS

 bcnet (Internet Gallery Café), Barra de Ferro 3 (☎93 268 15 07), right down the street from the Picasso museum. M: Jaume I. 250ptas/€1,50 per 15min., 600ptas/€3,61 per hr.; 10hr. ticket available for 3000ptas/€18. Open daily 10am-1am.

Café Interlight, Av. Pau Claris 106 (☎93 301 11 80; interlight@bcn.servicom.es). M: Urquinaona. 100ptas/€0,60 per 15min., 250ptas/€1,50 per hr. 9am-3pm 300ptas/€1,80 gets 1hr. of Internet and a coffee.

CiberOpción, Gran Via 602, across from the Universitat building. M: Universitat. 100ptas/0,60 for every ½hr. Open M-Sa 9am-am, Su 11am-1am.

Conèctate, C. Aragó 283 (☎93 467 04 43). M: Pg. de Gràcia. One block to the right of the Metro, facing away from Pl. de Catalunya. No telnet. Internet midnight-9am 200ptas/€1,20 for 2hr., 6pm-9pm 200ptas/€1,20 for 45min., and the rest of the time 200ptas/€1,20 per hr. Open 24 hours. Wheelchair accessible.

Correu Nou Ciber Café, Pl. Traginers 3 (☎93 268 46 88). M: Jaume I. 100ptas/€0,60 for 12min., 250ptas/€1,50 for 30min., 500ptas/€3 per hr. Black-and-white printing 75ptas/€0,45 per page. Color printing 125ptas/€0,75 per page. Open M-F 11am-11pm, Sa-Su 5-11pm. Cash only.

Cybermundo Internet Centre, Bergara 3 and Balmes 8, (☎93 317 71 42). M: Catalunya. Just off of the Pl. de Catalunya, behind the Triangle shopping mall. ½hr. 300ptas/€1,80, 1hr. 490ptas/€2,95; students ½hr. 250ptas/€1,50, 1hr 350ptas/€2,10.

 Easy Everything, Las Ramblas 31 (www.easyeverything.com) M: Liceu. 200ptas/€1,20 for about 40min.–price fluctuates according to the number of computers in use. Open 24hr. Also on Ronda Universitat 35, right next to Pl. de Catalunya, at the same prices.

El Pati d'Internet, C. Astúries 78 (☎93 292 02 45) M: Fontana. Internet use 150ptas/€1 per 15min., 225pta/€1,40 per 30min., 400ptas/€2,50 per hr. 5hr. tickets cost 1375ptas/€8,50, 10hr goes for 2500ptas/€15. M-F 10am-2pm and 4-10pm, Su 4-10pm.

h@ppy world, C. Muntaner 122 (☎93 454 91 69). M: Hospital Clinic. 200ptas/1,2€ for 30min, 375ptas/€2,25 per hr. Open M-Sa 10am-10pm, Su 5pm-10pm. Closed Su in Aug.

Idea, Pl. Comercial 2 (☎93 268 87 87; www.ideaborn.com). M: Jaume I, follow C. Princesa almost to its end and turn right on C. Comerç; the plaça is ahead on the right. 30min. 175ptas/€1, hour 300ptas/€1,80. Deposit required up front (300ptas/€1,80). Open M-Th 10am-1am, F-Sa 10am-3am, Su 10am-11pm. Internet access until 10:30pm daily.

Intergame, Pl. Rius i Taulet 8 (☎93 416 01 71). M: Fontana. Internet use 200ptas/€1,30 per hr., peak time (4pm-9pm) 400ptas/€2,50 per hr. Open M-Th 10am-11pm, F-Sa 10am-2am, Su 10am-midnight.

Internet Access, Tallers 8. 6 computers. 10 min. 100ptas/€0,60. Adults: 200ptas/€1,20 for 30 min., 100ptas/€0,60 each additional 20min. Students: 200ptas/€1,20 for 50min., 100ptas/€0,60 each additional 25min.

Internet Exchange, Las Ramblas 130 (☎93 317 73 27). M: Catalunya. 10ptas/€0,06 per minute; 2000ptas/€12 for 5hr., 4500ptas/€27 for 20 hr.; students 2500ptas/€15 for 10hr., 5000ptas/€30 for 30hr.

Locutorio, Gran Via 820 (☎93 246 36 07), right near the Monumental bullring, en route to Pl. Glòries, in **l'Eixample.** M: Monumental. Internet 150ptas/€0,90 per 30min., 300ptas/€1,80 per hr. Black-and-white printing 100ptas/€0,60 per page. Color printing 175ptas/€1 per page. Cash only.

Music Center-Internet, C. Córsega 171. M: Hospital Clinic. 200ptas/€1,20 per 30min. Open M-Th 8am-10pm, F-Sa 8am-3am.

Travel Bar, C. Boqueria 27 (☎93 342 52 52; www.barcelonatravelbar.com.) M: Liceu, just off Las Ramblas. 300ptas/€1,80 per 30min., 500ptas/€1,50 per hr. Open daily 9am-2am.

Workcenter, Av. Diagonal 441 (☎902 11 50 11; www.workcenter.net) M: Hospital Clinic or Diagonal. Branch: C. Roger de Lluria 2, M: Urquinaona. 100ptas/€0,60 per 10min. Open 24hr.

LAUNDROMATS

Lavandería Roca, Joaquim Costa 14 (☎93 442 59 82). Full service 1300ptas/€8, available in 3-4hr. Open M-F 8am-7:30pm, Sa 8am-2pm.

Tintorería Ferran, C. Ferran 11. M: Liceu. Ferran runs off Las Ramblas, just below Liceu. Full service 1500ptas/€9. Open daily 8:30am-2pm and 4:30-7:30pm.

Tintorería San Pablo, C. San Pau 105 (☎93 329 42 49). M: Paral.lel. Wash, dry, and fold 1800ptas/€10,80; do-it-yourself 1400ptas/€8,40. Open M-F 9am-1:30pm and 4-8:30pm.

LIBRARIES

Biblioteca Sant Pau, Carrer de l'Hospital, 56 (☎ 93 302 07 97). M: Liceu. Take C. Hospital off Las Ramblas and walk a few blocks down to a castle on your right; enter the courtyard and walk to its far end; the library is on the left. Do not confuse it with the Catalan library you'll see first, which requires permission to enter. Open in summer M and Th 10am-2pm; M-F 3:30-8:30pm, Sa 10am-2pm. Closed for 3 weeks in Sept.

Institut d'Estudis Norteamericans, Via Augusta 123 (☎ 93 240 51 10). Open Sept.-July M-F 9am-2pm and 4-7pm.

LUGGAGE STORAGE

Estació Barcelona-Sants. M: Sants-Estació. Small lockers 500ptas, large lockers 700ptas. Open 5:30am-11pm.

Estació França. M: Barceloneta. Small lockers 400ptas, large lockers 600ptas. Open 6am-11pm.

Estació del Nord. M: Arc de Triomf. Lockers 300-600ptas. Open 24hr.

MEDICAL SERVICES

See also **Clinics** (p. 290), **Hospitals** (p. 291), and **Emergency Services** (p. 291).
Association Ciutadana Anti-SIDA de Catalunya, C. Junta de Comerç 23 (☎ 93 317 05 05). AIDS information. Open M-F 10am-2pm and 4-7pm.

MOTO RENTAL

See **Bike and Moped Rental,** p. 290.

PHARMACIES

Pharmacies open 24hr. on a rotating basis. Check pharmacy windows for current listings.

POST OFFICES

Lista de Correos, Pl. de Antoni López (☎902 197 197: general info on Barcelona post offices). At the corner of Pg. Colom, the street that runs along the port from the Columbus Monument, and Via Laietana. Across the street from the port M: Jaume I or Barceloneta. Fax and *lista de correos*. Open M-F 8:30am-9:30pm. A little shop in the

back of the post office building, across the street, wraps packages for mailing (about 300ptas/€1,80). Shop open M-Sa 9am-2pm and 5-8pm. **Postal Code:** 08003.

Lista de Correos, C. Aragó 282, across from the Amena cell phone store, near Gaudí's Casa Battló. M: Pg. de Gràcia. Fax and *lista de correos* services available. Open M-F 8:30am-8:30pm; Sa 8:30am-1pm. **Postal Code:** 08007

Lista de Correos, Ronda Universitat 23, off Pl. de Catalunya. M: Catalunya. Open M-F 8:30am-8:30pm. Sa 9:30am-1pm.

RELIGIOUS RESOURCES

Comunidad Israelita de Barcelona (Jewish services), C. Avenir 29 (☎93 200 61 48).

Comunidad Israelita de Barcelona Jewish services). C. Porvenir 24 (☎93 200 85 13).

Comunidad Musulmana (Muslim services), Mosque Toarek Ben Ziad, C. Hospital 91 (☎93 441 91 49). Services daily at prayer times.

Església Catedral de la Santa Creu, In Pl. Seu, up C. Bisbe from Pl. St. Jaume. M: Jaume I. Cathedral open daily 8am-1:30pm and 4-7:30pm. Cloister open 9am-1:15pm and 4-7pm.

Església Santa Maria del Mar, Pl. Santa Maria del Mar (☎93 310 23 90). M: Jaume I. Open M-Sa 9am-1:30pm and 4:30-8pm, Su 9am-2pm and 5-8:30pm.

Església Sant Pau de Camp, M: Paral.lel, at the intersection of C. Sant Pau and C. Carretes, 2 blocks off Av. Paral.lel. Open W-M 5-8pm, closed Tu.

SUPERMARKETS

Champion Supermarket, Las Ramblas 113 (☎93 302 48 24). M: Liceu. From Liceu, walk up Las Ramblas and look to the left. All the essentials, as well as an inexpensive menu of ready-to-eat foods (meats 800ptas/€5,80 per kg and up) and salad bar. Open M-Sa 9am-9pm.

Condis, Junta de Comerç 19, in **El Raval,** off of C. Hospital. Open M-Th 9am-2pm, 5pm-9pm; F-Sa 9am-9pm.

El Corte Inglés, Pl. de Catalunya. M: Catalunya. The Spanish superstore has at its basement level a sizable supermarket, with a more exotic variety of items than found in most local places.

TAXIS

RadioTaxi (☎ 93 225 00 00).

Servi Taxi (☎93 330 03 00; www.servi-taxi.com).

Taxi Barcelona (☎630 900 908; www.taxi-barcelona.com).

Taxigroc (☎93 490 22 22; www.taxigroc.com).

Taxi 033 (☎93 303 30 33; www.taxi033.com).

Disabled travelers should call ☎93 420 80 88.

TELEPHONE SERVICES

International access numbers: AT&T : ☎900 990 011.

British Telecom: ☎900 964 495.

Canada Direct: ☎ 900 990 015.

MCI: ☎900 990 014.

New Zealand Direct: ☎900 991 836.

Directory Assistance: ☎1003 for numbers within in Spain, ☎1008 for numbers within in Europe, ☎1005 for numbers outside Europe.

TICKETS

See also theater venues in **Entertainment,** p. 173.

Institut de Cultura de Barcelona (ICUB), Palau de la Virreina, Ramblas 99 (☎93 301 77 75). Open for info year-round M-F 10am-2pm and 4-8pm. Teatre Grec ticket sales M-Sa 10am-9pm. Prices vary, but most performances cost 4000ptas/€24,10.

Tel Entrada (☎ 902 10 12 12). Call for information, listings, and reservations to theatrical and musical performances.

TOURS

Barcelona Tourism Office: leads professional walking tours of the Barri Gòtic leaving from the information office in Pl. de Catalunya; buy tickets there or at the Ajuntament in Pl. St. Jaume.

Bus Turístic: The easiest place to hop on the Bus Turístic is Pl. de Catalunya, in front of El Corte Inglés. Buses run daily (except Dec. 25 and Jan. 1) every 10-30min., 9am-9:30pm. Purchase tickets on the bus, at the Pl. de Catalunya tourist office, or at Estació Barcelona-Sants. 1-day pass 2200ptas/€13,22, children aged 4-12 1300ptas/€7,81, 2-day pass 2800ptas/€16,83.

Ruta del Modernisme: Passes (600ptas/€3,80; students and over 65 400ptas/€2,20; groups over 10 people 500ptas/€3 per person) are good for a month and give

holders a 50% discount on entrance to Palau Güell, La Sagrada Familia, Casa Milà (La Pedrera), Palau de la Música Catalana, Casa-Museu Gaudí, Fundació Antoni Tàpies, the Museu d'Art Modern, and other attractions. Purchase passes at Casa Amatller, Pg. de Gràcia 41, (see p. 59) near the intersection with C. Consedel (☎93 488 01 39).

Walking Tours of the Barri Gòtic: For walking tours, call 906 301 282. Sa-Su at 10am in Catalan and noon in English and Spanish. Tour group size is limited; buy tickets in advance. 1100ptas/€6,60, children aged 4-12 500ptas/€3.

TOURIST OFFICES

Aeroport El Prat de Llobregat (☎93 478 05 65), in the international terminal. Open daily 9am to 9pm. English-speaking agents offer information on Catalunya and Barcelona, maps and hotel reservations.

Informació Turística Plaça Catalunya, Pl. Catalunya 17S, below Pl. de Catalunya. M: Catalunya.Open daily 9am-9pm.

Informació Turística Plaça Sant Jaume, Pl. Sant Jaume 1, off of C. Ciutat. M: Jaume I. Open M-Sa 10am-8pm, Su 10am-2pm.

Oficina de Turisme de Catalunya, Palau Robert, Pg. de Gràcia 107 (☎93 238 40 00; fax 93 292 12 70; www.gencat.es/probert). M: Diagonal. Open M-Sa 10am-7pm, Su 10am-2pm.

TRANSPORTATION SERVICES

See also **Airlines** (p. 289), **Bike and Moped Rental** (p. 290), **Buses** (p. 290), **Car Rental** (p. 290), and **Taxis** (p. 293).

Airport: El Prat de Llobregat airport (☎93 298 38 38; www.aena.es/ae/bcn/homepage), 12km (8 mi.) southwest of Barcelona; see **Once in Barcelona,** p. 25.

Buses: Barcelona Nord Estació d'Auto-buses, C. Ali-bei 80 (☎93 265 61 32). M: Arc de Triomf, exit to Nàpols. Info office open daily 7am-9pm; see Once in Barcelona, p. 27.

Trains: Estació Barcelona-Sants, in Pl. Països Catalans. M: Sants-Estació. Buses to the station include #30 from Pl. de Espanya 44 through L'Eixample (stops at La Sagrada Familia), and N2. Station open M-F 4:30am-midnight, Sa-Su 5am-midnight. See also **Once in Barcelona,** p. 26.

Estació França, Av. Marqués de l'Argentera (☎902 24 02 02). M: Barceloneta. Buses include #17 from Pl. de Catalunya and N6. Open daily 7am-10pm.

RENFE, 24hr. info ☎93 491 31 83; www.renfe.es.

TRAVEL AGENTS

usit UNLIMITED, Ronda Universitat 16 (☎93 412 01 04; fax 93 412 39 84; www.unlimted.es). Open M-F 10am-8:30pm and Sa 10am-1:30pm.

WESTERN UNION

Admon Manuel Martín, Las Ramblas 41. Open daily 9am-midnight.

YOUTH SERVICES

Centre d'Informació Assesorament per a Joves, C. Ferrán 32 (☎93 402 78 00; www.bcn.es/ciaj), M: Liceu. One block off Las Ramblas. More of a student assistance office than a travel agency. No tickets for sale, but plenty of free advice and a bulletin board with youth events and opportunities. Excellent library of travel guides for browsing. Open M-F 10am-2 and 4-8pm.

Appendix

SPANISH & CATALAN PHRASEBOOK

ENGLISH	CATALAN	SPANISH
THE BASICS		
Hello	Hola	Hola
Good morning	Bon dia	Buenos días
Good afternoon	Bona tarde	Buenas tardes
Good night	Bona nit	Buenas noches
Goodbye	Adéu	Adiós
Please	Si us plau	Por favor
Thanks	Gràcies	Gracias
You're welcome	De res	De nada
Excuse me	Perdoni	Perdón
I don't understand Catalan/Spanish	No entenc català/castellà	No entiendo catalán/castellaño
Do you speak English?	Parleu anglès?	¿Hablaís inglés?
DIRECTIONS		
Where is...?	On és...?	¿Dónde está...?
...the bathroom	...els lavabos	... los aseos/servicios
...train station	...estació de trenes	...estación de trenes
...the church	...l'església	...la iglesia
...the hostel	...l'hostal	... el hostal
...store	...magatzem	...tienda
...the museum	...el museu	...el museo
...the market	...el mercat	...el mercado
...the pharmacy	...la farmàcia	...la farmacia
...the hospital	...l'hospital	...el hospital
ACCOMMODATIONS & TRANSPORTATION		
Do you have...?	Té...?	Teneís...?
...a room	...una habitació	...una habitación
...for one person	...per una persona	...para una persona
...for two people	...per dues persones	...para dos personas
...with a double bed	...amb un llit per dues persones	...con una cama matrimonial
...with two bed	...amb dos llits	...con dos camas
...with a bath	...amb bany	...con baño
How much does it cost?	Quan és?	¿Cúanto cuesta?
I would like a train ticket.	Voldria un bitlet	Quisiera un billete
round-trip ticket	un bitlet d'anar i tornar	un billete de ida i vuelta
DAYS & MONTHS		
Monday	dilluns	lunes
Tuesday	dimarts	martes
Wednesday	dimecres	miercoles
Thursday	dijous	jueves

ENGLISH	CATALAN	SPANISH
Friday	divendres	viernes
Saturday	dissabte	sábado
Sunday	diumenge	domingo
January	gener	enero
February	febrer	febrero
March	març	marzo
April	abril	abril
May	maig	mayo
June	juny	junio
July	juliol	julio
August	agost	agosto
September	septembre	septembre
October	octobre	octubre
November	novembre	noviembre
December	desembre	diciembre

NUMBERS

1	un/una	uno
2	dos/dues	dos
3	tres	tres
4	quatre	quatro
5	cinc	cinco
6	sis	seis
7	set	siete
8	vuit	ocho
9	nou	nueve
10	deu	diez
11	onze	once
12	dotze	doce
13	tretze	trece
14	catorze	quatorce
15	quinze	quince
16	setze	dieciseis
17	disset	diecisiete
18	divuit	dieciocho
19	dinou	diecinueve
20	vint	veinte
30	trenta	treinta
40	quaranta	quarenta
50	cinquanta	cincuenta
60	siexanta	sesenta
70	setanta	setenta
80	vuitanta	ochenta
90	novanta	noventa
100	cent	cien

AVERAGE TEMPERATURES

AVG TEMP	JANUARY	APRIL	JULY	OCTOBER
F°	52-59	52-64	75-69	66-72
C°	11-15	15-18	24-26	19-22

APPENDIX

SIZE CONVERSIONS

WOMEN'S CLOTHING

US SIZE	4	6	8	10	12	14	16
UK SIZE	6	8	10	12	14	16	18
EUROPE SIZE	36	38	40	42	44	46	48

WOMEN'S SHOES

US SIZE	5	6	7	8	9	10	11
UK SIZE	3	4	5	6	7	8	10
EUROPE SIZE	36	37	38	39	40	41	42

MEN'S SUITS/JACKETS

US/UK SIZE	32	34	36	38	40	42	44
EUROPE SIZE	42	44	46	48	50	52	54

MEN'S SHIRTS

US/UK SIZE	14	14.5	15	15.5	16	16.5	17
EUROPE SIZE	36	37	38	39	40	41	42

MEN'S SHOES

US SIZE	6	7	8	9	10	11	12
UK SIZE	5.5	6.5	7.5	8.5	9.5	10.5	11.5
EUROPE SIZE	38.5	39.5	40.5	41.5	42.5	43.5	44

METRIC CONVERSIONS

1 foot (ft.) = 0.30 meter (m)	1m = 3.28 ft.
1 mile (mi.) = 1.61 kilometers (km)	1km = 0.62 mi.
1 pound (lb.) = 0.45 kilogram (kg)	1kg = 2.2 lb.
1 gallon (gal.) = 4 quarts (qt.) = 3.78 liters (L)	1 L = 1.06 qt.= 0.264 gal.

Index

Maps

INSIDE

✚ Hospital	✈ Airport	💻 Internet Cafe	⛰ Mountain
🚓 Police	🚌 Bus Station	🏛 Museum	Park
✉ Post Office	🚆 Train Station	🏨 Hotel/Hostel	
ⓘ Tourist Office	Ⓜ Metro Station	⛺ Camping	Beach
🅢 Bank	⚓ Ferry Landing	🍎 Food & Drink	
Embassy/Consulate	✝ Church	🛍 Shopping	Water
▪ Site or Point of Interest	✝ Monastery	♪ Arts & Entertainment	
☎ Telephone Office	Theater	Nightlife	N
Cable Car	Beach	Pedestrian Zone	The Let's Go thumb always points NORTH.

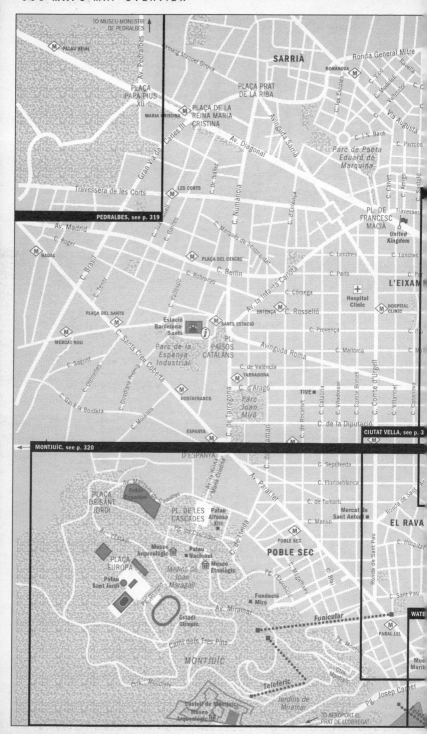

PEDRALBES, see p. 319

TO MUSEU-MONESTIR
DE PEDRALBES

PALAU REIAL

Av. Pedralbes

Passeig Manuel Girona

SARRIÀ

Ronda General Mitre

BONANOVA

C. Vilot

C. Madrilah

C. Valentor

Via Augusta

PLAÇA
PAPA PIUS
XII

MARIA CRISTINA

PLAÇA DE LA
REINA MARIA
CRISTINA

PLAÇA PRAT
DE LA RIBA

Av. les Escoles

C. J. S. Bach

C. Parroco

Gran Via de Carles III

Av. Diagonal

Avinguda Sarrià

Parc de Poeta
Eduard de
Marquina

C. d'Anet

C. Amigo

Travessera de les Corts

LES CORTS

C. Dr. Ibañez

PL. DE
FRANCESC
MACIÀ

Travesser

United
Kingdom

Av. Madrid

C. Roger

C. Numància

C. Marquès de Sentmenat

C. Londres

C. Londres

BADAL

C. Brasil

C. Galileo

PLAÇA DEL CENTRE

C. Berlín

C. Robrenyo

C. Paris

L'EIXAM

PLAÇA DEL SANTS

C. Terol

C. Vallespir

Av. la Infanta Carlota

C. Còrsega

Hospital
Clínic

HOSPITAL
CLÍNIC

ENTENÇA

C. Rosselló

MERCAT NOU

C. Sants Creu Coberta

Estació
Barcelona-
Sants

SANTS ESTACIÓ

C. Provença

C. Sagunt

C. Olzinelles

Parc de la
Espanya
Industrial

PL.
PAISOS
CATALANS

Avinguda Roma

C. Mallorca

C. Guadiana Prima

C. de València

C. Gaia la Bordeta

C. Moianès

HOSTAFRANCS

C. d'Aragó

TARRAGONA

Parc
Joan
Miró

C. de Rocafort

C. Calàbria

C. Viladomat

C. Comte Borrell

C. Villarroel

C. Comte d'Urgell

C. Casanova

TIVE

ESPANYA

C. de tarragona

ESPANYA

C. de la Diputació

CIUTAT VELLA, see p. 3

MONTJUÏC, see p. 320

D'ESPANYA

C. Sepúlveda

C. Floridablanca

Av. la Reina Maria Cristina

Av. Paral·lel

C. de Tamarit

Ronda de Sant An

PLAÇA
DE SANT
JORDI

Poble
Espanyol

Av. Marquès de Comillas

PL. DE LES
CASCADES

Palau
Alfonso
XIII

Pg. les Cascades

Mercat de
Sant Antoni

C. Manso

EL RAVA

PLAÇA
EUROPA

Av. l'Estadi

Museu
Arqueològic

Palau
Nacional

Museo
Etnològic

POBLE SEC

C. Lleida

POBLE SEC

C. de Blai

C. Magalhães

Ronda de Sant Pau

C. Hospital

Palau
Sant Jordi

Jardins de
Joan
Maragall

Pg. l'Exposició

C. Blai

C. Sant Pau

Pg. Olímpic

Fundació
Miró

Estadi
Olímpic

Av. Miramar

Funicular

WATE

PARAL·LEL

Camí dels Tres Pins

Pg. Montjuïc

MONTJUÏC

Ctra. Montjuïc

Mus
Marit

Gra. Miradels

Teleféric

Jardins de
Miramar

Castell de Montjuïc
Museu
Arqueològic

TO AEROPORT EL
PRAT DE LLOBREGAT

Pg. Josep Carner

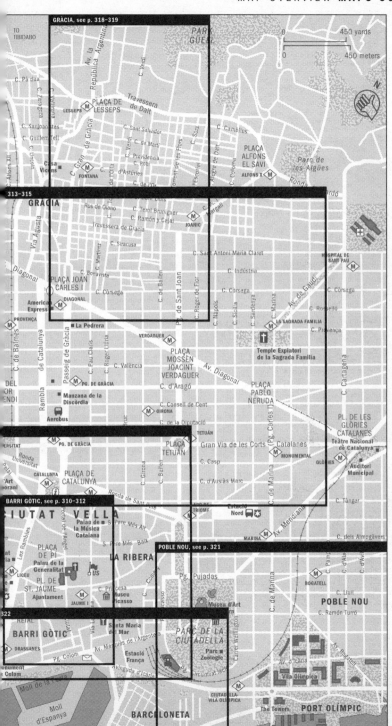

GRÀCIA, see p. 318–319

TO TIBIDABO

PARK GÜELL

0 ——————— 450 yards
0 ——————— 450 meters

N

C. Pa dua

Av. la República Argentina

C. Verdi

PLAÇA DE LESSEPS

LESSEPS M

Travessera de Dalt

C. Sanjoanistes

C. Guilem Tell

C. Sant Salvador

C. de Martí

C. Providencia

C. Gran de Gràcia

FONTANA M

C. d'Asturies

C. de l'Or

Casa Vicens

PLAÇA ALFONS EL SAVI

ALFONS X M

Parc de les Aigües

C. Camèlies

C. Coloma

Ronda

313–315

GRÀCIA

C. Sant Lluís

Ros de Olano

C. Terol Bruniguer

C. Ramón y Cajal

JOANIC M

Travessera de Gràcia

Via Augusta

Diagonal

C. Siracusa

C. Bonavista

C. Martinez

PLAÇA JOAN CARLES I

DIAGONAL M

American Express

C. Còrsega

C. de Bailén

Pg. de Sant Joan

Roger de Flor

C. Sant Antoni Maria Claret

C. Indústria

C. Còrsega

C. Nàpols

C. Sicília

C. Sardenya

C. Marina

Av. de Gaudí

HOSPITAL DE SANT PAU M

C. Còrsega

C. Rosselló

LA SAGRADA FAMÍLIA

C. Provença

PROVENÇA M

C. de Balmes

Passeig de Gràcia

C. Pau Claris

Roger de Llúria

La Pedrera

VERDAGUER M

C. València

PLAÇA MOSSÈN JOACINT VERDAGUER

Temple Expiatori de la Sagrada Família

DEL OR ENDI

Rambla de Catalunya

PG. DE GRÀCIA M

Manzana de la Discòrdia

Aerobus

C. d'Aragó

Av. Diagonal

GIRONA M

C. Consell de Cent

C. de la Diputació

PLAÇA PABLO NERUDA

(Pg. Carles I)

PL. DE LES GLÒRIES CATALANES

Teatre Nacional de Catalunya

ERSITAT

PG. DE GRÀCIA M

TETUÁN M

PLAÇA TETUÁN

Gran Via de les Corts Catalanes

C. Casp

C. d'Ausiàs Marc

C. de Marina

MONUMENTAL M

Auditori Municipal

GLÒRIES M

Ronda Universitat

'Art oral

CATALUNYA M

PLAÇA DE CATALUNYA

i

C. Girona

C. Balmes

Ronda de Sant

PG. DE

Estació Nord

BARRI GÒTIC, see p. 310–312

CIUTAT VELLA

Palau de la Música Catalana

S. Pere Més Alt

TRIOMF M

MARINA M

Av. Meridiana

C. dels Almogàvers

Les Ramblas

PLAÇA DE PÍ

Palau de la Generalitat

LICEU M

PL. DE ST. JAUME

Ajuntament

S. Pere Més Baix

LA RIBERA

JAUME I M

C. Princesa

Museu Picasso

POBLE NOU, see p. 321

Pg. Pujadas

Museu d'Art

C. de Marina

C. Pam

BOGATELL M

C. d'Ala

C. d'Av

C. Llull

POBLE NOU

C. Ramón Turró

322

BARRI GÒTIC

REIAL

DRASSANES M

Santa Maria del Mar

Av. Marquès de l'Argentera

Estació França

PK. Colom

PARC DE LA CIUTADELLA

Parc Zoològic

Carrer Wellington

Av. d'Icària

Vila Olímpica

onument Colom

Moll de la F

Moll d'Espanya

Avinguda d'Icària

Circumval·lació

CIUTADELLA VILA OLÍMPICA M

BARCELONETA

The Towers

PORT OLÍMPIC

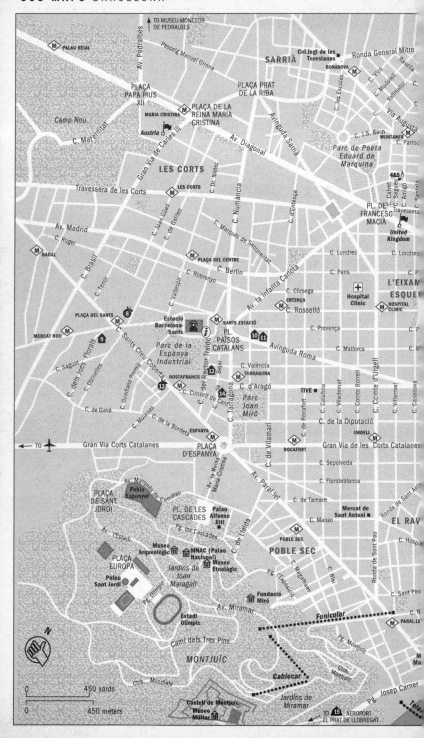

To Museu Monestir de Pedralbes

Av. Pedralbes

Passeig Manuel Girona

M PALAU REIAL

SARRIÀ

Col.legi de les Teresianes

Ronda General Mitre

BONANOVA M

C. Vico

C. Modolell

C. Valmador

Ravella

Via Augusta

PLAÇA PAPA PIUS XII

PLAÇA PRAT DE LA RIBA

MARIA CRISTINA M

Austria

PLAÇA DE LA REINA MARIA CRISTINA

Avinguda Sarrià

C. J.S. Bach

MUNTANER

C. Parro

Camp Nou

C. Maternitat

Gran Via de Carles III

Av. Diagonal

LES CORTS

Parc de Poeta Eduard de Marquina

4&5

C. Calvet

C. Sagües

C. Amigó

C. Sarrià

Travessera de les Corts

LES CORTS M

C. Dr. Ibáñez

C. Numància

C. d'Entença

PL. DE FRANCESC MACIÀ

C. Travessera

Av. Madrid

C. Roger

C. Joan Güell

C. de Galileu

C. Marquès de Sentmenat

United Kingdom

M BADAL

C. Brasil

C. Trator

PLAÇA DEL CENTRE M

C. Robrenyo

C. Berlin

Av. la Infanta Carlota

C. Londres

C. Londres

C. Paris

C. P

L'EIXAM ESQUE

PLAÇA DEL SANTS

8

C. Vallespir

C. Còrsega

C. Rosselló

ENTENÇA

Hospital Clínic

HOSPITAL CLÍNIC M

MERCAT NOU M

9

C. dels Jocs Florals

C. Sants Creu Coberta

Estació Barcelona-Sants

SANTS ESTACIÓ M

PL. PAÏSOS CATALANS

10 11

C. Provença

C. P

C. M

C. Sagunt

C. Olzinelles

Parc de la Espanya Industrial

i

Avinguda Roma

C. Mallorca

C. Guadiana

C. del Rector Triadó

C. de la Bordeta

Bejar

C. Molines

12

HOSTAFRANCS

13 M

C. Consell de Cent

C. València

TARRAGONA

C. d'Aragó

Parc Joan Miró

C. Tarragona

TIVE

C. de Rocafort

C. Calàbria

C. Vilamarí

C. Vilamarí

C. Comte Borrell

C. Comte d'Urgell

C. Villarroel

C. Casanova

C. de Gavà

C. de la Diputació

14

ESPANYA

M

URGELL M

ROCAFORT

Gran Via de les Corts Catalanes

To ✈

Gran Via Corts Catalanes

PLAÇA D'ESPANYA

Av. la Reina Maria Cristina

C. de Vilamarí

Av. Paral·lel

C. Sepúlveda

C. Floridablanca

PLAÇA DE SANT JORDI

Av. Marquès de Comillas

Poble Espanyol

PL. DE LES CASCADES

Pg. les Cascades

Palau Alfonso XIII

C. de Tamarit

C. Manso

Mercat de Sant Antoni

Ronda de Sant Ant

EL RAV

Av. l'Estadi

Museu Arqueològic

MNAC (Palau Nacional)

Museu Etnològic

POBLE SEC M

POBLE SEC

C. Hospi

PLAÇA EUROPA

Palau Sant Jordi

Jardins de Joan Maragall

Pg. l'Exposició

C. Blai

Pg. Olímpic

Fundació Miró

C. Magalhaes

C. Sant Pau

Ronda de Sant Pau

C. N

Estadi Olímpic

Av. Miramar

Funicular

PARAL·LE

C. N

M PARAL·LE

Camí dels Tres Pins

Pg. Montjuïc

Ctra. Mondials

MONTJUÏC

Cablecar

Ctra. Montjuïc

Pg. Josep Carner

N

0   450 yards
0   450 meters

Castell de Montjuïc

Museu Militar

Jardins de Miramar

To 15 AEROPORT EL PRAT DE LLOBREGAT

Tèle

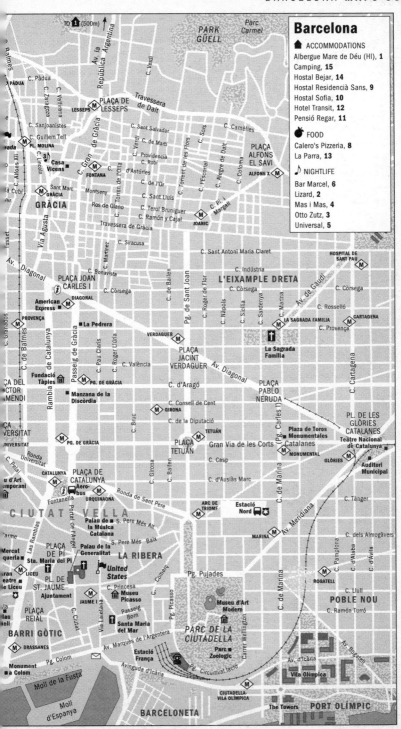

Barcelona

🏠 ACCOMMODATIONS

Albergue Mare de Déu (HI), **1**
Camping, **15**
Hostal Bejar, **14**
Hostal Residencià Sans, **9**
Hostal Sofia, **10**
Hotel Transit, **12**
Pensió Regar, **11**

🍎 FOOD

Calero's Pizzeria, **8**
La Parra, **13**

🎵 NIGHTLIFE

Bar Marcel, **6**
Lizard, **2**
Mas i Mas, **4**
Otto Zutz, **3**
Universal, **5**

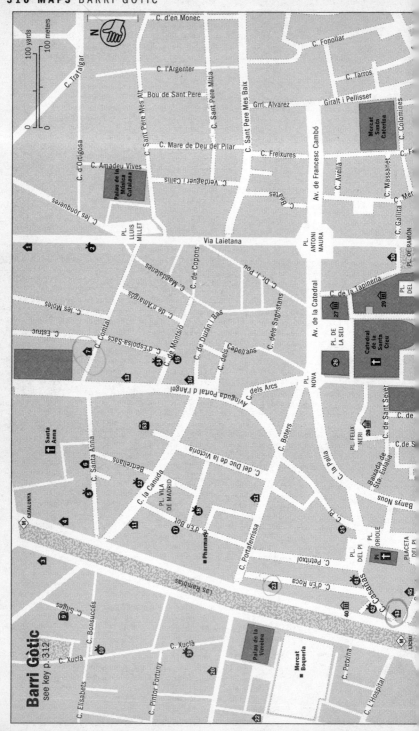

Barri Gòtic
see key p. 312

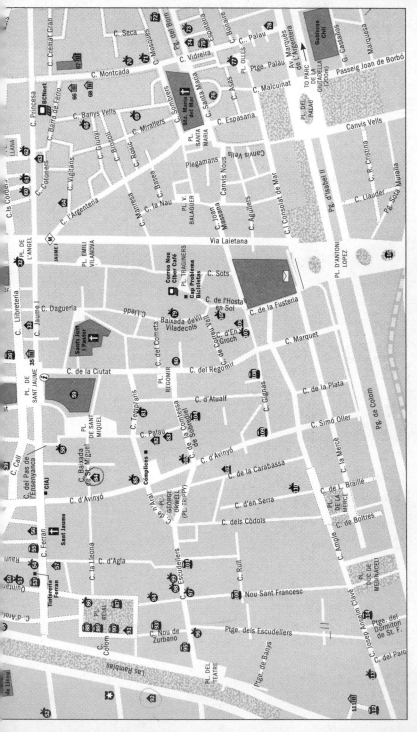

Barri Gòtic

see map pp. 310-311

♠ ACCOMMODATIONS

Albergue de Juventud
 Kabul, **91**
Albergue Juvenil Palau, **83**
Casa de Huéspedes
 Mari-Luz, **82**
Gothic Point Youth Hostel, **64**
Hostal Avinyó, **103**
Hostal Benidorm, **92**
Hostal Campi, **11**
Hostal Fernando, **56**
Hostal Fontanella, **1**
Hostal Internacional, **46**
Hostal La Palerma, **22**
Hostal Layetana, **30**
Hostal Levante, **84**
Hostal Marmo, **106**
Hostal Orleans, **78**
Hostal Palermo, **45**
Hostal Paris, **43**
Hostal Parisien, **23**
Hostal Residencia Europa, **48**
Hostal Residencia
 Lausanne, **13**
Hostal Residencia
 Rembrandt, **21**
Hotel California, **57**
Hotel Call, **39**
Hotel Rey Don Jaume I, **33**
Hotel Toledano/Hostal Residencia
 Capitol, **4**
Mare Nostrum, **44**
Pensión Arosa, **16**
Pensión Bienestar, **50**
Pensión Dalí, **47**
Pensión Diamante, **20**
Pensión Francia, **74**
Pensión Lourdes, **63**
Pensión Noya, **3**
Pensión Santa Anna, **6**
Residencia Victoria, **7**

♠ FOOD

L'Antic Bocoi del Gòtic, **79**
The Bagel Shop, **12**
Bar Ra, **52**
Bar Restaurant Los Tereros, **19**
Betawi, **15**
Buenas Migas, **10**
Buen Bocado, **98**
Cafe-Bar Vincent Van
 Gogh, **62**
Café de l'Opera, **49**
Cal Pep, **77**
Can Cuilleretes, **51**
Los Caracoles, **97**
La Cocotte, **73**
La Colmena, **32**
Euskal Extea, **71**
El Gallo Kiriko, **85**
Govinda, **18**
The Grill Room, **96**
La Habana Vieja, **65**
Ikkiu, **60**
Irati, **41**
Juicy Jones, **42**
Kamasawa, **99**
Maoz Falafel, **54**
Il Mercante Di Venezia, **113**
Mi Burrito y Yo, **58**
La Oficina, **116**
Oolong, **107**
Peimong, **81**
Els Quatre Gats, **14**
Les Quinze Nits, **86**
Restaurante Bidasoa, **110**
Restaurante Self
 Naturista, **5**
El Salón, **105**
Tapas Bar, **119**
Terrablava, **2**
Thiossan, **94**
Txirimira, **61**
Va de Vi, **69**
Venus Delicatessen, **102**
Xampanyet, **70**

♠ NIGHTLIFE

Barcelona Pipa Club, **88**
El Bosq de les Fades, **112**
Café Royale, **93**
Casa El Agüelo, **109**
Dot Light Club, **100**
Fonfone, **101**
Glacier Bar, **87**
Harlem Jazz Club, **104**
Hook Bar, **108**
Jamboree, **90**
Karma, **89**
Margarita Blue, **114**
Molly's Fair City, **53**
Mudanzas, **75**
New York, **95**
La Oveja Negra, **9**
Paradís Reggae, **36**
Plastic Café, **72**
Schilling, **55**

🏛 MUSEUMS

Museu Barbier-Mueller, **66**
Museu del Calçat, **28**
Museu de Cera, **111**
Museu de l'Eròtica, **40**
Museu d'Història de
 Catalunya, **118**
Museu d'Història de la
 Ciutat, **31**
Museu Diocesà, **27**
Museu d'Holografia, **35**
Museu Frederic Marès, **29**
Museu Picasso, **67**
Museu Tèxtil i
 d'Indumentària, **68**

○ SIGHTS

Ajuntament, **59**
Cap de Barcelona, **116**
Casa de l'Ardiaca, **26**
Centre Pati Llimona, **80**
Cine Malda, **25**
Fossar de les Moreres, **76**
Hebrew Plaque, **38**
Palau de la Generalitat, **37**
Roman Tombs, **17**
Temple of Augustus/Centre
Excursionista, **34**

L'Eixample

see map pp. 314-315

🏠 ACCOMMODATIONS

Hostal Bonavista, **10**
Hostal Cisneros, **42**
Hostal Ciudad Condal, **35**
Hostal Eden, **63**
Hostal Felipe II, **38**
Hostal Girona, **98**
Hostal Hill, **26**
Hostal Qué Tal, **36**
Hostal Residencia Neutral, **68**
Hostal Residencia Oliva, **78**
Hostal Residencia Windsor, **34**
Hostal San Remo, **97**
Hotel Everest, **3**
Hotel Paseo de Gràcia, **18**
Hotel Universal, **55**
Pensión Aribau, **59**
Pensión Cliper, **14**
Pensión Fani, **46**
Pensión Puebla de Arenoso, **60**

🍽 FOOD & DRINK

A-Tipic, **70**
ba-ba-reeba, **80**
La Batuequilla, **72**
La Bodegueta, **28**
Café Miranda, **85**
Café Torino, **45**
Campechano, **49**
Can Cargol, **56**
Chicago Pizza Pie Factory, **29**
Comme-Bio, **89**
El Criollo, **32**
La Flauta, **62**
Ginza, **24**
Giorgio, **53**
Hard Rock Café, **95**
Hostal de Rita, **54**
Laie Liberaria Café, **93**
Madrid-Barcleona, **69**
Mandalay Café, **30**
Mauri, **21**
La Muscleria, **37**
La Provença, **27**
El Racó d'en Baltá, **17**
El Raconet, **13**
Restaurante Terrani, **8**
El Rodizio Grill, **73**
Thai Gardens, **79**
Txapela, **92**
Wok & Bol, **82**
Vips, **91**

🍺 BARS

Aloha, **22**
berlin, **5**
Caligula, **61**
domèstic, **76**
La Filharmónica, **33**
La Fira, **23**
Les Gens que J'Aime, **50**
The Pop Bar, **31**

♪ CLUBS

Aire (Sala Diana), **43**
La Boîte, **7**
Buenavista Salsoteca, **15**
Fuse, **81**
Illusion, **2**
Let's Go, **39**
Luz de Gas, **4**
Martin's, **9**
The Michael Collins Irish Pub, **40**
Satanassa, **75**
Sol, **6**
Topxi, **57**

◯ SIGHTS

L'Auditori, **99**
Can Serra, **11**
Casa Amatller, **65**
Casa Batlló, **64**
Casa Calvet, **94**
Casa Comalet, **12**
Casa de las Punxes, **19**
Casa Golferichs, **86**
Casa Lactància, **87**
Casa Lleó Morera, **67**
Casa Milà (la Pedrera), **25**
Casa Olano, **52**
Casa Vidua Marfà, **51**
El Corte Inglés, **96**
Joieria Roca, **90**
Let's Go Bull (Meditation), **88**
The oldest house in L'Eixample, **71**
Palau del Baló de Quadras, **16**
Plaza de Toros Monumental, **84**
La Sagrada Família, **41**
Skating Pista de Gel, **74**
Teatre Nacional de Catalunya, **100**
Torre de les Aigües, **77**
Vinçon/Casa Casas, **20**

🏛 MUSEUMS & GALLERIES

Fundació Godia, **48**
Fundació Tàpies, **44**
Museu de Clavegueram, **58**
Museu del Perfum, **66**
Museu del Còmic i de la Il·lustració, **1**
Museu Egipci, **47**
Museu Taurí, **83**

L'Eixample
see key p. 313

Travessera de Gràcia

C. Maspons

C. Granada del Penedès

C. Lluís Atúnez

Gran de Gràcia

C. Penedès

C. Puigmartí

C. Goya

C. Difluvi

C. Siracusa

Via Augusta

C. St. Pere Màrtir

C. Mozart

C. de Tordera

Avinguda Diagonal

Casablanca

C. F. Giner

C. de Progrès

C. Londres

C. Sèneca

C. M. de la Rosa

C. Torres

C. del Torrent de l'Olla

C. de la Llibertat

C. París

C. Bonavista

C. del Perill

Music Center Internet

C. Còrsega

PL. JOAN CARLES I

C. Muntaner

C. d'Aribau

C. d'Enric Granados

C. Rosselló

DIAGONAL

Passeig de Gràcia

C. Balmes

C. Provença

Rambla de Catalunya

H@ppyworld

C. Mallorca

C. València

PL. DOCTOR LETAMENDI

PASSEIG DE GRÀCIA

Conèctate

C. de Bruc

C. Consell de Cent

C. de Roger de Llúria

C. de Pau Clars

C. Diputació

Universitat de Barcelona

Avinguda Gran Via de les Corts Catalanes

PASSEIG DE GRÀCIA

PL. DE LA UNIVERSITAT

UNIVERSITAT

Ronda Universitat

Ronda de Sant Antoni

PL. DE CASTELLA

C. Valldonzella

Bus Stop for Airport & Bus Turistic

PL. DE CATALUNYA

PL. URQUINAONA

C. Trafalgar

Ronda St. Pere

CATALUNYA

URQUINAONA

Barcelona Allotjament

CATALUNYA

C. Llorens i Barba

C. Santa Carolina

2♪

1 🏛

TO ✚ STA. CREU
I ST. PAU (150m) →

TO 3 (20m) →

✚

JOANIC

PL. D'EN
JOANIC

M

C. Romans

C. Pare Lainez

Travessera de Gràcia

món y Cajal

C. Oraror

C. H. Lazaro

C. de Sant Antoni Maria Claret

oles
lada
ol

C. de la Indústria

italia
odon

C. de Roger de Flor

Passeig de Sant Joan

C. Còrsega

C. Rosselló

C. de Marina

Avinguda de Gaudí

6

39♪

C. Provença

M VERDAGUER

PL. DE LA
SAGRADA
FAMÍLIA

40♪

41

M

PL. DE
GAUDÍ

C. Lepant

C. Padilla

PL. MOSSÈN
JACINT
VERDAGUER

C. Mallorca

LA SAGRADA FAMÍLIA

M

58 🏛

C. València

57♪

✝

C. Bailen

C. Aragó

PL. PABLO
NERUDA

PL.
HISPANITAT

3

Passeig de Sant Joan

74

C. Nàpols

C. Sicília

C. de Sardenya

Avinguda Diagonal

C. Diputació

MONUMENTAL

M

84

PL. DE
TETUÁN

M TETUÁN

83 🏛

sp

Passeig de Carles I

Locutorio 📱

as Marc

N

99

100

0   200 yards

0   200 meters

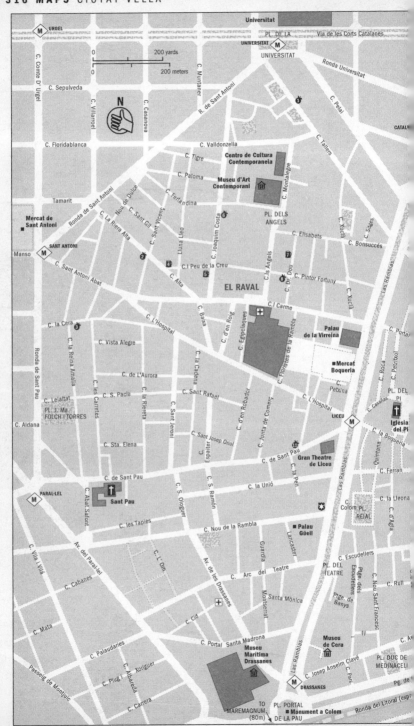

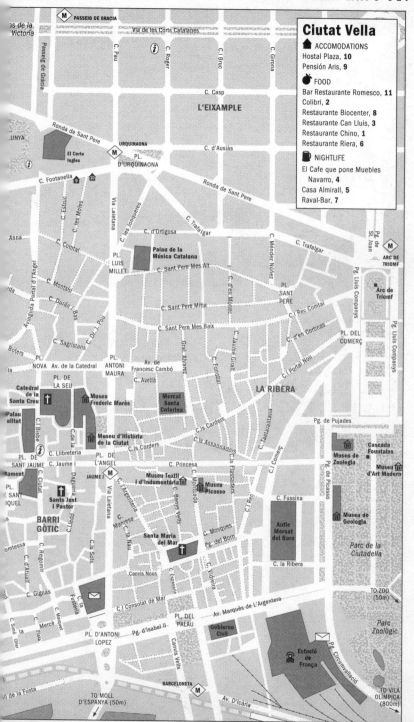

Ciutat Vella

🏠 ACCOMODATIONS
Hostal Plaza, **10**
Pensión Aris, **9**

🍎 FOOD
Bar Restaurante Romesco, **11**
Colibrí, **2**
Restaurante Biocenter, **8**
Restaurante Can Lluís, **3**
Restaurante Chino, **1**
Restaurante Riera, **6**

🍷 NIGHTLIFE
El Cafe que pone Muebles
 Navarro, **4**
Casa Almirall, **5**
Raval-Bar, **7**

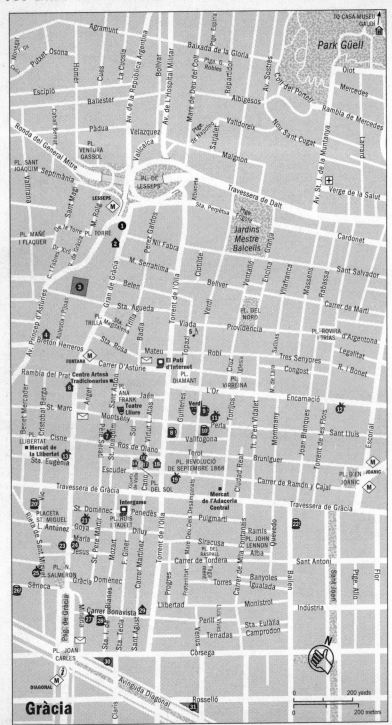

Gràcia

Gràcia

ACCOMMODATIONS
Aparthotel Silver, **4**
Hostal Bonavista, **29**
Hostal Lesseps, **2**
Pensión Alberdi, **18**
Pensión San Medín, **6**

FOOD
El 19 de la Riera, **25**
Botafumeiro, **13**
La Buena Tierra, **12**
Café del Sol, **15**
Equinox Sol, **16**
La Gavina, **7**
Ikastola, **11**

(CONT'D.)
Restaurant Illa de Gràcia, **21**
El Tastavins, **19**
Xavi Petit, **27**

PUBS
Bahía, **26**
Blues Café, **10**
Buda, **8**
Café de la Calle, **20**
Casablanca, **28**
Gasterea, **9**
Pirineus Bar, **22**
Sol de Nit, **17**
Sol Soler, **14**

CLUBS
Bamboleo, **5**

SIGHTS
Casa Cama, **23**
Casa Comalet, **30**
Casa de les Punxes, **31**
Casa Fuster, **24**
Casa Ramos, **1**
Casa Vicens, **3**

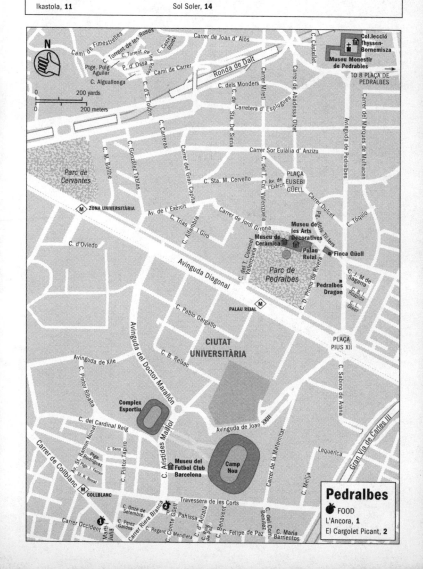

Pedralbes

FOOD
L'Ancora, **1**
El Cargolet Picant, **2**

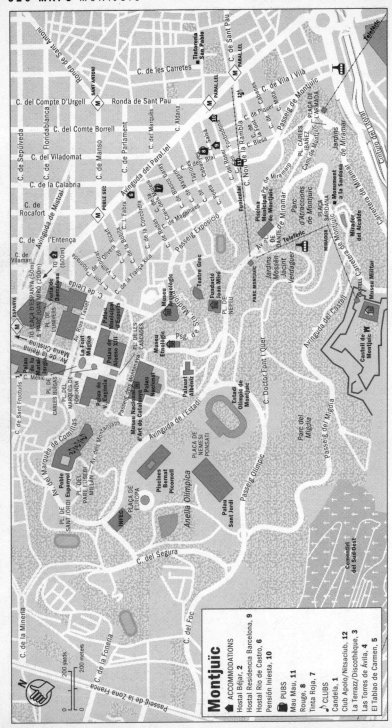

Montjuïc

♠ ACCOMMODATIONS
Hostal Béjar, **2**
Hostal Residencia Barcelona, **9**
Hostal Rio de Castro, **6**
Pensión Iniesta, **10**

♫ PUBS
Mau Mau, **11**
Rouge, **8**
Tinta Roja, **7**

♪ CLUBS
Candela, **1**
Club Apolo/Nitsaclub, **12**
La Terrazz/Discothèque, **3**
Las Torres de Ávila, **4**
El Tablao de Carmen, **5**

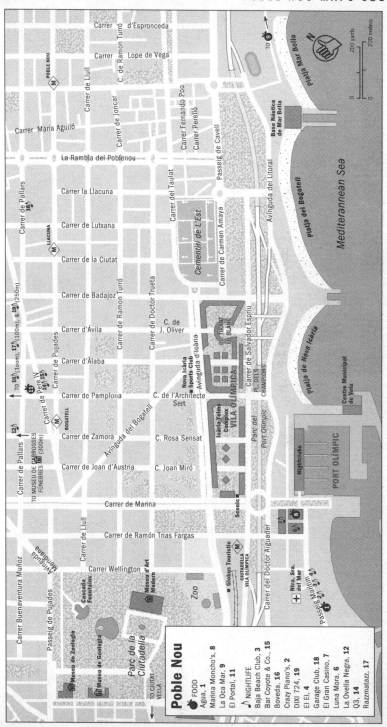

Carrer Turró d'Espronceda
Carrer Lope de Vega
C. de Ramon Turró
POBLE NOU M
Carrer de Llull
Carrer de Joncar
Carrer Maria Aguiló
Carrer Fernando Poo
Carrer Perelló
Passeig de Cavell
Base Nàutica
de Mar Bella
platja Mar Bella

La Rambla del Poblenou
Carrer del Taulat
Passeig del Litoral

Carrer la Llacuna
Carrer de Pallars 18
Cementiri de L'Est
Carrer de Carmen Anaya
platja del Bogatell

LLACUNA M
Carrer de Lutxana

Carrer de la Ciutat

Mediterranean Sea

Carrer de Badajoz
Carrer de Doctor Trueta
Carrer de Ramon Turró

TO 16 (100m), 17 (100m), & 19 (250m)
Carrer d'Àvila
C. de J. Oliver
Carrer de Salvador Espriu

Carrer de Pujades

Carrer d'Àlaba
Nova Icària Sports Club
Avinguda d'Icària
Carrer de Pere IV 14 15
platja de Nova Icària

Carrer de Pamplona
C. de l'Architecte Sert
VILA OLÍMPICA
PL. DELS CHAMPIONS

12
BOGATELL M
Carrer de Zamora
Icària Cinemi Complex
Parc del
Port Olímpic

Avinguda del Bogatell
C. Rosa Sensat
Centre Municipal de Vela

TO MUSEU DE CARROSSES
FÚNEBRES (300m)
Carrer de Joan d'Austria
C. Joan Miró

Carrer de Pallars

Carrer de Marina
Scenic
Nightclubs
PORT OLÍMPIC

Carrer de Llull
Carrer de Ramón Trias Fargas

7
6 8

Carrer Buenaventura Muñoz
Avinguda Meridiana
Carrer Wellington
M Globus Touristic
CAPELLA VILA OLÍMPICA
Carrer del Doctor Aiguader

Cascada Fountains
Museu d'Art Modern
Zoo
Ntra. Sra. del Mar

Passeig de Zoologia
Museu de Zoologia
Parc de la Ciutadella
Museu de Geologia

Passeig de Pujades
Passeig Marítim
2 3 1

TO CIUTAT VELLA

N
0   200 yards
0   200 metres

TO 9

Poble Nou

🍴 FOOD
Àgua, **1**
Marina Moncho's, **8**
La Oca Mar, **9**
El Portal, **11**

♪ NIGHTLIFE
Baja Beach Club, **3**
Bar Coyote & Co., **15**
Boveda, **16**
Crazy Piano's, **2**
DIXI 724, **19**
El El, **4**
Garage Club, **18**
El Gran Casino, **7**
Luna Mora, **6**
La Ovella Negra, **12**
Q3, **14**
Razzmatazz, **17**

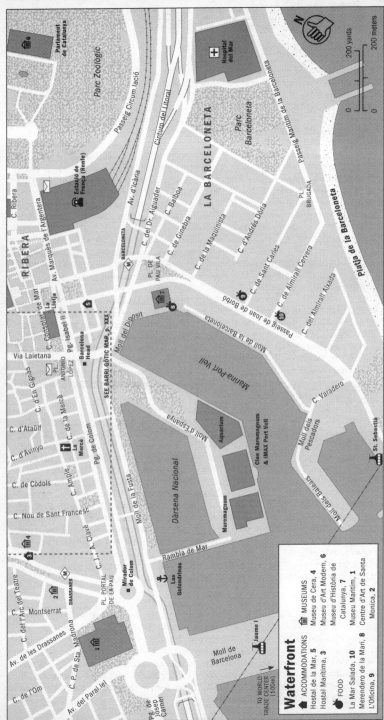

Waterfront

▲ ACCOMMODATIONS
Hostal de la Mar, **5**
Hostal Marítima, **3**

🍴 FOOD
La Mar Salada, **10**
Merendero de la Mari, **8**
L'Oficina, **9**

🏛 MUSEUMS
Museu de Cera, **4**
Museu d'Art Modern, **6**
Museu d'Història de
Catalunya, **7**
Museu Marítim, **1**
Centre d'Art de Santa
Monica, **2**

ABOUT LET'S GO

FORTY-TWO YEARS OF WISDOM

For over four decades, travelers crisscrossing the continents have relied on *Let's Go* for inside information on the hippest backstreet cafes, the most pristine secluded beaches, and the best routes from border to border. *Let's Go: Europe*, now in its 42nd edition and translated into seven languages, reigns as the world's bestselling international travel guide. In the last 20 years, our rugged researchers have stretched the frontiers of backpacking and expanded our coverage into the Americas, Australia, Asia, and Africa (including the new *Let's Go: Egypt* and the more comprehensive, multi-country jaunt through *Let's Go: South Africa & Southern Africa*). Our new-and-improved City Guide series continues to grow with new guides to perennial European favorites Amsterdam and Barcelona. This year we are also unveiling *Let's Go: Southwest USA*, the flagship of our new outdoor Adventure Guide series, which is complete with special roadtripping tips and itineraries, more coverage of adventure activities like hiking and mountain biking, and first-person accounts of life on the road.

It all started in 1960 when a handful of well-traveled students at Harvard University handed out a 20-page mimeographed pamphlet offering a collection of their tips on budget travel to passengers on student charter flights to Europe. The following year, in response to the instant popularity of the first volume, students traveling to Europe researched the first full-fledged edition of *Let's Go: Europe*. Throughout the 60s and 70s, our guides reflected the times—in 1969, for example, we taught you how to get from Paris to Prague on "no dollars a day" by singing in the street. In the 90s we focused in on the world's most exciting urban areas to produce in-depth, fold-out map guides, now with 20 titles (from Hong Kong to Chicago) and counting. Our new guides bring the total number of titles to 57, each infused with the spirit of adventure and voice of opinion that travelers around the world have come to count on. But some things never change: our guides are still researched, written, and produced entirely by students who know first-hand how to see the world on the cheap.

HOW WE DO IT

Each guide is completely revised and thoroughly updated every year by a well-traveled set of nearly 300 students. Every spring, we recruit over 200 researchers and 90 editors to overhaul every book. After several months of training, researcher-writers hit the road for seven weeks of exploration, from Anchorage to Adelaide, Estonia to El Salvador, Iceland to Indonesia. Hired for their rare combination of budget travel sense, writing ability, stamina, and courage, these adventurous travelers know that train strikes, stolen luggage, food poisoning, and marriage proposals are all part of a day's work. Back at our offices, editors work from spring to fall, massaging copy written on Himalayan bus rides into witty, informative prose. A student staff of typesetters, cartographers, publicists, and managers keeps our lively team together. In September, the collected efforts of the summer are delivered to our printer, who turns them into books in record time, so that you have the most up-to-date information available for your vacation. Even as you read this, work on next year's editions is well underway.

WHY WE DO IT

We don't think of budget travel as the last recourse of the destitute; we believe that it's the only way to travel. Our books will ease your anxieties and answer your questions about the basics—so you can get off the beaten track and explore. Once you learn the ropes, we encourage you to put *Let's Go* down and strike out on your own. You know as well as we that the best discoveries are often those you make yourself. When you find something worth sharing, please drop us a line. We're Let's Go Publications, 67 Mount Auburn St., Cambridge, MA 02138, USA (feedback@letsgo.com). For more info, visit our website, www.letsgo.com.

Will you have enough stories to tell your grandchildren?

Yahoo! Travel

Do You YAHOO!?

CHOOSE YOUR DESTINATION SWEEPSTAKES

No Purchase Necessary.

Explore the world with Let's Go® and StudentUniverse!
Enter for a chance to win a trip for two to a Let's Go destination!

Separate Drawings! May & October 2002.

GRAND PRIZES:

Roundtrip StudentUniverse Tickets

✓ Select one destination and mail your entry to:

☐ Costa Rica
☐ London
☐ Hong Kong
☐ San Francisco
☐ New York
☐ Amsterdam
☐ Prague
☐ Sydney

* Plus Additional Prizes!!

Choose Your Destination Sweepstakes
St. Martin's Press
Suite 1600, Department MF
175 Fifth Avenue
New York, NY 10010-7848

Restrictions apply; see offical rules for
details by visiting Let'sGo.com or sending SASE
(VT residents may omit return postage) to the address above.

Name: _____

Address: _____

City/State/Zip: _____

Phone: _____

Email: _____

Grand prizes provided by:

StudentUniverse.com   Real Travel Deals

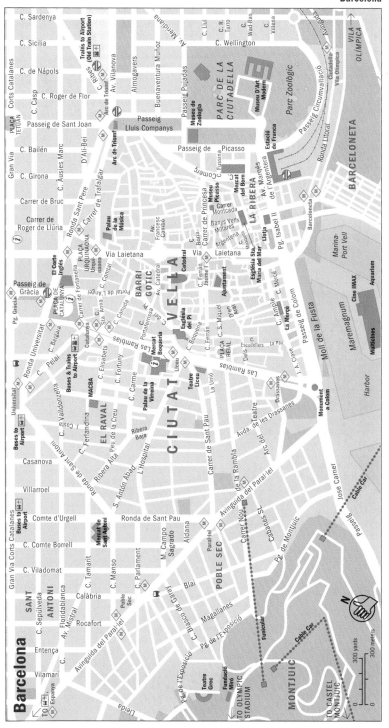

Barcelona

C. Sardenya
C. Sicilia
C. de Nápols
C. Roger de Flor
Passeig de Sant Joan
C. Bailén
C. Girona
Carrer de Bruc
Carrer de Roger de Llúria
Passeig de Gràcia
Ronda Universitat
Casanova
Villarroel
Comte d'Urgell
C. Comte Borrell
C. Viladomat
Entença
Vilamari

Corts Catalanes
PLAÇA TETUAN
Gran Via
C. Casp
C. Ausies Marc
D'Ali-Bei

Trains to Airport (Old Train Station)
Av. Vilanova
Almogavers
Buenaventura Muñoz
Passeig Pujadas

Av. Meridiana
C. Llull
C. R. Turro
C. Wad-Ras
Villena

VILA OLÍMPICA

C. Wellington

PARC DE LA CIUTADELLA
Museu de Zoologia
Museu D'Art Modern
Parc Zoològic

Arc de Triomf
Passeig Lluis Companys
Passeig de Picasso

Estació de França
Ronda Litoral
BARCELONETA

Passeig de Circumvallació
Av. Marquès de l'Argentera
Barceloneta
Marina-Port Vell

Palau de la Música
Via Laietana
El Corte Inglés
PLAÇA URQUINAONA
PLAÇA DE CATALUNYA
Catalunya

Museu Picasso
Mercat del Born
LA RIBERA
Carrer Montcada
Carrer de Princesa
Banys Vells
Millares
Argenteria
Llotja
Pg. Isabel II

BARRI GÒTIC
Catedral
Av. Catedral
Esglésa del Pi
Teatre Liceu
Palau de la Virreina
Mercat Boqueria
Las Ramblas

CIUTAT VELLA
Ajuntament
Església Sta. Maria del Mar

Maremàgnum
Cine IMAX
Aquarium
Multicines
Harbor

MACBA
EL RAVAL
Ribera Baja
L Hospital
Carrer de Sant Pau

Monument a Colom
Moll de la Fusta
Passeig de Colom

Mercat de Sant Antoni
Ronda de Sant Pau
M. Campo Sagrado
Aldana
Parallel

Avinguda del Paral·lel
Avda. del Teatre
Arc de les Drassanes

SANT ANTONI
C. Tamarit
C. Manso
C. Parlament
POBLE SEC
Blai
Magallanes

Carrer Nou
Cabanes S.L.
Pg. de Montjuïc

Cable Car
Jose Carner

N

MONTJUIC
Funicular
Cable Car

Teatre Greg
Fundació Miró
TO OLYMPIC STADIUM
TO CASTEL MONTJUIC

300 yards
300 meters

TO MUSEU-MONESTIR
DE PEDRALBES

Ⓜ PALAU REIAL

Av. Pedralbes

Passeig Manuel Girona

SARRIÀ

Col.legi de les
Teresianes ■

Ronda General Mit

BONANOVA
Ⓜ

C. Vico
C. Modolell
Vallmajor

C. les Escoles

Rave.

PLAÇA PRAT
DE LA RIBA

PLAÇA
PAPA PIUS
XII

PLAÇA DE LA
REINA MARIA
CRISTINA

MARIA CRISTINA

Austria 🏴

Camp Nou

C. Mazarnitat

Av. Diagonal

Avinguda Sarrià

C. J.S. Bach

Via Augu

MUNTANER
Ⓜ

C. Pa

Parc de Poeta
Eduard de
Marquina

Gran Via de Carles III

LES CORTS

Travessera de les Corts

LES CORTS
Ⓜ

C. Dr. Ibáñez

C. Numància

C. d'Entença

Calvet
Sagués
C. Amigó

PL. DE
FRANCESC
MACIÀ

Travess

United
Kingdom

Av. Madrid

C. Roger

Ⓜ BADAL

C. Brasil

C. Terror

C. Joan Güell

C. de Galileo

Ⓜ PLAÇA DEL CENTRE

C. Robrenyo

C. Berlin

C. Vallespir

C. Marquès de Sentmenat

Av. la Infanta Carlota

C. Londres

C. Paris

C. Córsega

ENTENÇA
Ⓜ C. Rosselló

Hospital
Clinic ✚

C. Lonc

L'EIXA
ESQU

HOSPITAL
CLÍNIC
Ⓜ

PLAÇA DEL SANTS
Ⓜ

Ⓜ C. Sants Creu Coberta

MERCAT NOU
Ⓜ

Estació
Barcelona-
Sants

Ⓜ SANTS ESTACIÓ
ℹ

PL.
PAÏSOS
CATALANS

C. Provença

C. Sagunt

C. dels Jocs Florals

C. Olzinelles

C. Guadiana Premià

Parc de la
Espanya
Industrial

C. del Rector Triadó

HOSTAFRANCS

Avinguda Roma

C. Mallorca

C. de Gavà

C. Molanès

C. de la Bordeta

C. Consell de Cent

C. Béjar

C. València

TARRAGONA
■

C. d'Aragó

Parc
Joan
Miró

C. Tarragona

TIVE ■

C. de Rocafort

C. Calàbria

C. Viladomat

C. Comte Borrell

C. d'Urgell

C. Villarroel

C. de la Diputació

URGELL

← TO ✈

Gran Via Corts Catalanes

ESPANYA
Ⓜ

PLAÇA
D'ESPANYA

ROCAFORT
Ⓜ

C. de Vilamarí

Gran Via de les Corts Catala

C. Sepúlveda

C. Floridablanca

Av. Paral·lel

Av. la Reina Maria Cristina

C. de Tamarit

Av. Marquès de Comillas

Poble
Espanyol

PLAÇA
DE SANT
JORDI

PL. DE LES
CASCADES

Palau
Alfonso
XIII

Pg. los Cascades

C. de Lleida

C. Manso

Mercat de
Sant Antoni ■

EL R

Ronda de Sant

Av. l'Estadi

Museo
Arqueológic 🏛

MNAC (Palau
Nacional) 🏛

Museo
Etnológic 🏛

POBLE SEC
Ⓜ

Pg. l'Exposició

C. Magalhaes

C. Blai

Ronda de Sant Pau

C. Ho

PLAÇA
EUROPA

Palau
Sant Jordi

Jardins de
Joan
Maragall

Pg. Olímpic

Fundació
Miró 🏛

C. Sant

Estadi
Olímpic

Av. Miramar

Funicular ●●●●●●●●●

Ⓜ PARA

Camí dels Tres Pins

Pg. Montjuïc

N 🧭

MONTJUÏC

Ctra. Mondials

Cablecar ●●●●●

Ctra.
Montjuic

Pg. Josep Carn

Jardíns de
Miramar

0 ___ 450 yards

0 ___ 450 meters

Castell de Montjuïc
Museo
Militar 🏛

TO AEROPORT
EL PRAT DE LLOBREGAT →

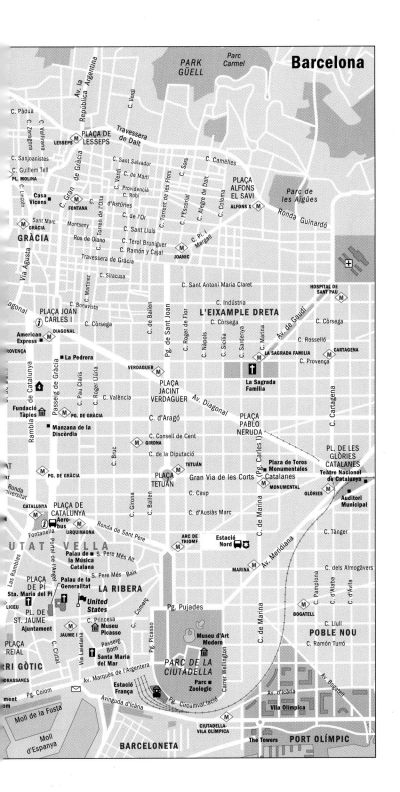

Barcelona Metro

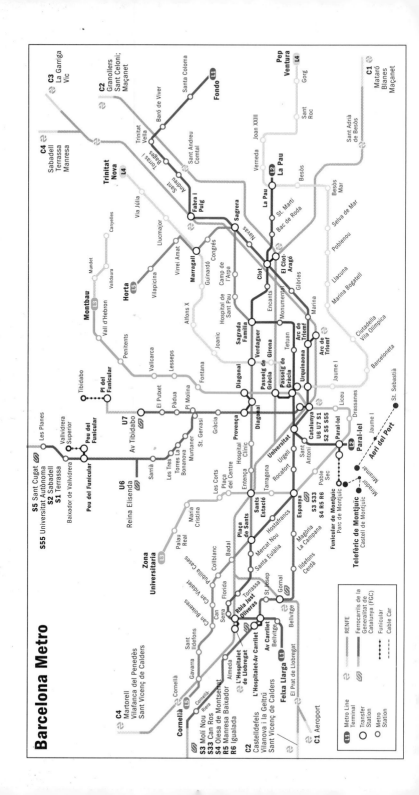